# China's Battle for Korea

TWENTIETH-CENTURY BATTLES

*Edited by Spencer C. Tucker*

# China's Battle for Korea
## The 1951 Spring Offensive

## Xiaobing Li

INDIANA UNIVERSITY PRESS    *Bloomington & Indianapolis*

*This book is a publication of*

INDIANA UNIVERSITY PRESS
Office of Scholarly Publishing
Herman B Wells Library 350
1320 East 10th Street
Bloomington, Indiana 47405 USA

iupress.indiana.edu

*Telephone orders*   800-842-6796
*Fax orders*   812-855-7931

*Manufactured in the
United States of America*

*Library of Congress
Cataloging-in-Publication Data*

Li, Xiaobing, [date]
  China's battle for Korea : the 1951 spring
offensive / Xiaobing Li.
    pages cm
    Includes bibliographical references and
index.
  ISBN 978-0-253-01157-2 (hardback)
  — ISBN 978-0-253-01163-3 (e-book) 1.
Korean War, 1950-1953—Participation,
Chinese. 2. Korean War, 1950-1953—
Campaigns. I. Title.
  DS919.5.L536 2014
  951.904'2351—dc23

                    2013037078

1  2  3  4  5   19  18  17  16  15  14

FOR MY PARENTS,
*Li Weiying and Zhang Xiaoyi*

# Contents

# Maps and Charts

CHARTS

# Acknowledgments

MANY PEOPLE AT THE UNIVERSITY OF CENTRAL OKLAHOMA (UCO), where I have been teaching since 1993, have contributed to this book and deserve recognition. First, I would like to thank Provost John F. Barthell, Vice Provost Patricia A. LaGrow, Dean of the College of Liberal Arts Gary Steward, and Dean of the Jackson College of Graduate Studies Richard Bernard. They have been very supportive of the project over the past twelve years. The faculty merit-credit program sponsored by the Office of Academic Affairs, a research grant from the Office of Research and Grants, and a research grant from the College of Liberal Arts at UCO provided funding for my research and student assistants.

I wish to thank my Chinese colleagues and collaborators at the China Academy of Military Science, China Academy of Social Sciences, Military Archives of the People's Liberation Army (PLA), Chinese National Defense University, Peking University, East China Normal University, China Society for Strategy and Management, China Foundation for International and Strategic Studies, Logistics College of the PLA, Nanjing Political Academy of the PLA, and provincial academies of social sciences and history museums in Heilongjiang, Jilin, and Liaoning. They made the many arrangements necessary for me to interview PLA officers and retired generals in 1999–2011. I am grateful to Chen Zhiya, Li Danhui, Niu Jun, Shen Zhihua, Wang Baocun, Wang Po, Yang Kuisong, Yang Shaojun, Zhang Baijia, Zhang Pengfei, and Zhang Tiejiang for their help and advice on my research in China. Thanks also to the staff of the China Reunification Alliance and the Veterans Affairs Commission of the Republic of China (ROC), in Taipei, Taiwan. They provided financial assistance and arranged many interviews for me with former prisoners of war during my several trips to Taiwan in 1996–2010.

Special thanks to Stanley J. Adamiak and Beverly Rorem, who proofread all of the chapters. Chen Jian, David M. Finkelstein, Walter Byung Jung, Steven I. Levine, Allan R. Millett, Richard Peters, David Shambaugh, Harold M. Tanner, Yafeng Xia, Shuguang Zhang, and Xiaoming Zhang made important comments on earlier versions of some chapters that were presented as conference papers. Pat Hoig proofread some of the chapters. Gregory Whitaker re-drew all the maps. Annamaria Martucci provided secretarial assistance. Several graduate students at UCO traveled with me to meet veterans, transcribed the interviews, and read parts of the manuscript. They are Colonel Ming-Hsien Chuang (ROC National Defense University, Chinese Nationalist Army, ret.), Major Phred Evans (U.S. Army, ret.), Technical Sergeant Charles D. Heaverin (U.S. Air Force, ret.), Captain Alex Zheng Xing (PLA, ret.), Haodu Li, Michael Molina, Senior Airman Oliver Pettry (U.S. Air Force), First Lieutenant Jimmy Xiangyao Xu (PLA, ret.), and Kevin Yang.

I also wish to thank Spencer C. Tucker, editor of the Twentieth-Century Battles book series for Indiana University Press, who offered many valuable suggestions and criticisms in the past four years. The press's anonymous readers also provided important suggestions. At the press, Robert J. Sloan, editorial director, patiently guided the production of the book. Any remaining errors of facts, language usage, and interpretation are my own.

During the research and writing over the past twelve years, my parents encouraged my interest in the Korean War and helped me with the contacts, interviews, and translations in China. I dedicate this book to them. My wife, Tran, and our two children, Kevin and Christina, got used to my working weekends and holidays and shared with me the burden of overseas travel. Their understanding and love made this book possible.

# Introduction: China's War against America

CHEN FULIANG (1931–2008) HAD DIED. I GOT THIS GRIEVOUS news when his wife called and canceled our interview. "You don't need to come," she said and hung up the phone. I made the trip to the village anyway, leaving the Australian film director and his Korean War documentary crew in Nanjing, the capital of southeastern Jiangsu (Kiangsu) Province.[1]

Simple and brief, Chen's funeral was held in Shangzhuang, a small village on Tongkeng Mountain, in Lishui County, Jiangsu. Chen had been born in that same village; he was a peasant, a family man, and a Korean War veteran. Not many villagers attended his funeral on that rainy spring day. No one mentioned his service in the People's Liberation Army (China's combined army, navy, air force, and strategic missile force commonly known as the PLA).[2] I was surprised by his tolerance of unfair treatment and humiliation: some villagers, in their eulogies, commented on how quiet Chen had remained when he was tortured and later mistreated as a "bad element" for more than twenty years after his repatriation. At that time China did not value its returned prisoners of war because it was the Chinese tradition to fight to the death, rather than be captured by the enemy. "He did nothing wrong," his daughter said, choked with tears, as she showed me photos of her father in uniform.[3]

In November 1950, at age of nineteen, Chen had gone to Korea as a "volunteer soldier" of the PLA. When the Chinese army lost the Spring Offensive Campaign (also known as their Fifth Phase Offensive) in 1951, tens of thousands of its soldiers became prisoners of war (POWs) in the hands of the United Nations Force (UNF). Chen was one of them.

China's Spring Offensive Campaign lasted from April 22 to June 10, 1951, and was the decisive battle of the Korean War. It changed the direction of the war and forever changed the lives of millions of people, including Chen and his family. After Chinese forces lost the campaign, Chinese leaders realized the limit of the country's military power and were willing to accept a settlement without victory. Truce negotiations began on July 10, 1951, and after the Korean Armistice was signed in 1953, Private Chen was repatriated back to China. However, his nightmare continued. POWs were treated as traitors and criminals in the age of Mao Zedong (Mao Tse-tung) (1893–1976), who had established the People's Republic of China (PRC) as a Communist state in 1949 and sent Chinese troops to Korea in 1950. Not until 1980, four years after Mao's death, did the Central Committee and Central Military Commission (CMC) of the Chinese Communist Party (CCP; or the Communist Party of China, CPC) issue No. 74 Document, which rehabilitated the 7,110 POWs of the Chinese People's Volunteer Force (CPVF) and recognized their services and sacrifices.[4] In October 1981 the Finance Bureau of the General Logistics Department (GLD) of the PLA announced that it would compensate the POWs. Beginning in 1983, each POW or his or her family received 10–16 yuan (about $3.30 to $5.30) a month.[5] It was too little and too late for Chen Fuliang, who had suffered for thirty years.

Today whether China and the United States will ever go to war is a perennial question in foreign policy circles, but many pundits forget that they already did so more than sixty years ago. In October 1950 China sent its army, in Mao's words, to "resist America, aid Korea, defend the homeland, and safeguard the country" ("Kangmei yuanchao, baojia weiguo")—giving rise to what became the war's common name in China, the War to Resist the United States and Aid Korea (WRUSAK; Kangmei yuanchao zhanzheng).[6] During the next three years, over 3.1 million Chinese troops fought the U.S.-led UNF. In reality the Korean War was a conflict between China and the United States, which provided 90 percent of the UNF troops. Facing vastly superior firepower, China suffered 1,027,146 casualties. Chen's province, Jiangsu, lost 8,444 men in the Korean War.[7] Although America's intent was to secure South Korea

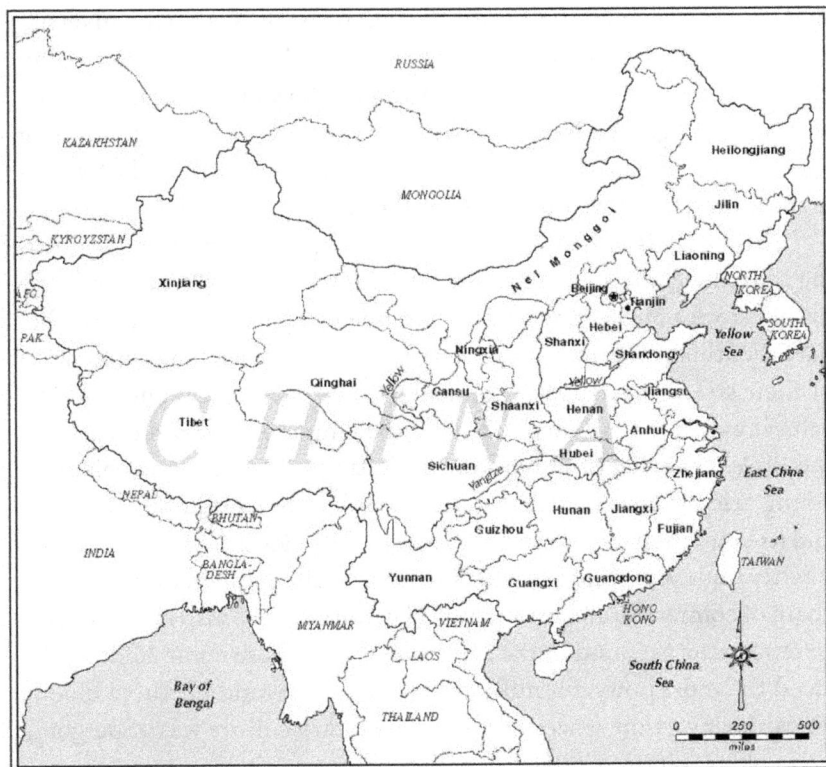

Map 0.1. East Asia

from an invasion by North Korea through a police action, North Korean tenacity and China's intervention created a bitter stalemate on the Korean Peninsula (map 0.1).

This book examines the Chinese 1951 Spring Offensive Campaign and seeks to explain its failure. What was the Chinese war strategy, and how did China's operational tactics affect the battle? How could a large force, holding the initiative, have been defeated so soundly? Did the Chinese make mistakes or simply encounter unforeseen problems? Why were the senior officers unable to view battle plans in advance and develop appropriate contingency plans? What lessons did China learn from the catastrophic defeat of its 1951 Spring Offensive? Students have asked these questions in my online graduate classes for Norwich University and my summer seminar at the U.S. Military Academy at West Point. In fact, whenever students of East Asian military history study China's military buildup, the North Korean nuclear crises, and the continuing U.S. commitment to the security of the Korean Peninsula in the twenty-first century, these are the questions they ask.

This study is aimed at answering these pivotal questions by looking into the relatively neglected study of the battle in PLA history. The untold stories of the rank and file provide unique insights into the behavior of those who fought against the UNF in Korea. The exploration of their strategic thoughts, combat conduct, and social and political values reveals the military culture of the Chinese army, which defined the PLA's characteristics both during and after the war. As a relatively young army in Asia, the PLA acted according to its traditional system and its consistent logic in military affairs. The views depicted here offer a better understanding of China's strategic culture, operational system, chain of command, and technological qualities. They also identify some general patterns found in the actions of the Chinese commanders who faced the most powerful military forces in the world for three bloody years, during a time when the Chinese military culture was undergoing a complex evolution.

Not all Chinese realize how drastically the Korean War changed their nation and its future, affecting their lives even today. Only with the passing of time has the war's impact become clear, and only with time have the Chinese people recognized the many unsolved problems of the war. A few still think that China's WRUSAK took place only in a specific time and under certain conditions, and thus that it belongs to the past. Xi Jinping (b. 1953) disagreed in 2010, as demonstrated in his speech as vice president of the PRC at the Sixtieth Anniversary Celebration of the CPVF's Participation in the WRUSAK. Xi believed that the tremendous impact and historical significance of the war "will never fade away with time."[8] In 2013 Xi became the president of the PRC and the commander in chief of the PLA. The war in Korea reshaped the Chinese military, turning it into a modern army with new technology, strategy, and tactics. Even if the war has been largely forgotten in America, it is by no means forgotten in China.

## THE DECISIVE BATTLE

On June 25, 1950, North Korea, or the Democratic People's Republic of Korea (DPRK), launched a surprise attack on South Korea, or the Republic of Korea (ROK), which signaled the beginning of the Korean War. U.S. President Harry S. Truman (1884–1972) quickly responded by sending in armed forces under a UN resolution, adopted on July 7, authorizing the use of all possible means to aid South Korea, and on August 4, the UNF repelled North Korea's invasion. On September 15, Gen. Douglas MacArthur (1880–1964) successfully landed American troops behind the North Korean forces at Inchon (Inch'ŏn), rapidly changing the military situation in Korea. The offensive of the North Korean People's Army (NKPA) quickly collapsed. On October 1, the UNF crossed the 38th Parallel into North Korea to liberate the country from the Communist regime of Kim Il-sung (1912–94); the UNF's advance was so rapid that by mid-October the troops would capture Pyongyang (P'yŏngyang), North Korea's capital. Kim wrote a letter to the Soviet leader Josef Stalin (1878–1953) on September 29, asking for direct military assistance from the Soviet Union. Kim also told Stalin in his letter that, if it was impossible for the Soviet Union to send troops to Korea, China should do so. After careful consideration, on October 5, Mao, who was then chairman of the CCP, and the members of the Politburo (Political Bureau) of the CCP Central Committee decided to send Chinese troops to Korea.

On October 8, Mao created the Chinese People's Volunteers Force, hoping by the use of the word "volunteers" to convince the world that the CPVF had not been organized by the Chinese government. By officially entering Korea, China risked full-blown war with the United States and the sixteen other countries that had joined the UNF and theoretically could invade China. In fact, the "volunteer" soldiers like Chen Fuliang were Chinese regular troops, commanded by Chinese officers. The first Chinese forces—three infantry armies and three artillery divisions, approximately 260,000 troops all told—entered North Korea on October 19, 1950. China kept its military intervention secret, and not until November would the PRC publicly acknowledge that Chinese forces had entered Korea to assist the North Koreans in repelling the American invasion. By late November, China had made a sizable commitment to Korea: thirty-three divisions, totaling more than 450,000 men.[9]

Beginning in October 1950, the CPVF launched the first of its Five Offensive Campaigns against the UNF in North and South Korea. This rapid and unexpected development surprised American generals. The CPVF's sheer numbers enabled the Chinese to overcome their inferiority in equipment and technology. In the First Offensive Campaign, from October 25 to November 7, the CPVF stopped the UNF's northward advance and stabilized the situation for North Korea for the first time since the Inchon landing. In the Second Offensive Campaign, from November 25 to December 24, the Chinese recaptured Pyongyang and pushed the battle line back to the 38th Parallel. During the Third and Fourth Offensive Campaigns, between January and March 1951, the CPVF crossed the 38th Parallel into South Korea; took Seoul, the capital of South Korea; and pushed the UNF south to the 37th Parallel. By mid-April, the Chinese had 950,000 troops in Korea, including forty-seven infantry divisions, eight artillery divisions, and four anti-aircraft artillery divisions.[10]

Of all these campaigns, the Chinese Fifth Offensive Campaign, or the Spring Offensive Campaign, proved the most decisive. Lasting from April 22 through June 2, 1951, it was the largest and longest Communist military operation of the war, as well as the largest battle since World War II (WWII). The CPVF-NKPA Joint Command deployed more than 700,000 men, including 600,000 CPVF troops, against 340,000 UNF troops. Marshal Peng Dehuai (P'eng Te-huai) (1898–1974),[11] commander in chief of both the CPVF and CPVF-NKPA Joint Command, predicted that "this is the battle [that] will determine the fate of the Korean War."[12] The CPVF Spring Offensive failed. The UNF put up a strong defense, driving the Communists north of the 38th Parallel again and inflicting 105,000 casualties. After the Chinese failure in this million-man battle, the war settled into a stalemate and a more conventional pattern of trench warfare along the 38th Parallel.

After their defeat in the Spring Offensive Campaign, the Communists never again came close to Seoul, nor did they mount another southward incursion of such magnitude. The loss forced Mao to reconsider both his political and military aims. Realizing the huge gap between Chinese capabilities and the ambitious aim of driving the UNF from the peninsula, the Chinese leaders became willing to accept a settlement without total victory. The Chinese Spring Offensive Campaign was the turning point that not only shaped the rest of the war but also led to truce negotiations in July 1951.

Although China's decision to intervene in the Korean War has been extensively documented in the West, much less is known about how the Chinese actually fought the U.S. military during the war.[13] Many previous historians have spent much time bemoaning China's decision to enter the war and fighting polemical battles against the country's political leaders, to the extent that the real operational story has almost been lost. One of the keys to understanding how the CPVF engaged the UNF can be found in the combat experience of the participants in the Chinese Spring Offensive Campaign.

Most Korean War histories cover the million-man battle in the spring of 1951 with an emphasis on UNF operations. Among these insightful assessments are works by Allan R. Millett, Billy Mossman, David Halberstam, and William Bowers, all of whom offer objective surveys and comprehensive interpretations by analyzing the military situation on the ground.[14] One of their main arguments is that the U.S. field commanders in Korea made a difference through their leadership style, operational experience, and command skills. Their combat success in April and May became a turning point in the Korean War for the UNF, which had switched from defensive to offensive operations since the Chinese intervened in October 1950. Lt. Gen. Matthew B. Ridgway (1895–1993), commander in chief of the UNF after MacArthur's dismissal, launched several offensives designed to destroy CPVF-NKPA personnel and supplies while also building confidence and fighting skills in the UNF during the early spring of 1951. Lt. Gen. James A. Van Fleet (1892–1992), commander of the U.S. Eighth Army, consolidated the supply line and emphasized training of the ROK divisions.[15] Through combat records, command reports, other government documents, and interviews with veterans, these authors have successfully provided a comprehensive operational history of U.S. ground forces during the Chinese Spring Offensive. There is an absence, however, of a perspective from the "other side of the hill." There is no solid operational history of the Chinese army in the Korean War, and no literature on their Spring Offensive.

Two important books on the Chinese leaders' decision making and strategic thinking in the Korean War do not give specific details of CPVF operations during the battle. In one of them, Chen Jian provides an excellent study of Communist China's Cold War experience from 1949 to 1972, when U.S. President Richard Nixon (1913–94) visited Beijing. Chen offers pathbreaking insights into the calculations, decisions, and divergent views of Mao and other Chinese leaders toward the world in general and the United States in particular. He argues that although the global Cold War was characterized by the confrontation between the United States and the Soviet Union, China's position was not peripheral but, in many key senses, central.[16] After the Chinese-American military confrontation in Korea, East Asia became a focal point of the global Cold War. The other significant book, by Shuguang Zhang, offers an extremely comprehensive treatment of the discussion of Mao's grand plans, explaining why China entered the Korean War in 1950 and why Mao opted to end the war in 1951 with a negotiated settlement. Zhang carefully constructs a framework to effectively present Chinese leaders' concerns that American historians might have overlooked. He puts individual leaders and commanders in the context of Chinese tradition and views their ideas about fighting the war through their historical experience, domestic politics, and military culture.[17] However, the scale and focus of these works do not allow either author to provide a day-to-day operational account of the Chinese Spring Offensive.

In China historians and scholars reopened the academic debate over this million-man battle in the late 1990s, departing from the official conclusion that the campaign was just another Chinese victory in the Korean War. Since the beginning of the twenty-first century, China has transformed itself from a third-world developing country to a global economic power, second only to the United States. While China has been rising, Russian power seems to have vanished almost overnight. Although the United States has been slowed down by its two wars in Asia and an economic recession, it remains the only superpower in the world. Also since the beginning of the twenty-first century, the Korean War has become one of the most discussed subjects in China.[18] Bin Yu states that "the Korean War is the only meaningful reference point for sustained PLA contingency operations beyond China's border. The Korean War is also the only real experience, no matter how outdated, that the PLA has had in operating against the U.S. ground forces."[19] Paying more attention to the lessons that can be learned, recent research by military historians in China focuses on the mistakes, miscalculations, and problems that led to the military disaster of the Spring Offensive. For political reasons, however, Chinese historians still have a long way to go before they can publish an objective account of the history of the campaign in their own country.

## CHINESE WARFARE

As the first book of its kind, this study provides readers with a balanced approach and fresh perspective on how the Spring Offensive was planned, conducted, and assessed by Chinese commanders, both in Beijing and on the Korean front. Told from the Chinese perspective, it begins with a quick examination of Chinese intentions, security considerations, and decisions related to why the Chinese entered Korea, as well as how their goals shifted. The analysis describes how Mao; Zhou Enlai (Chou En-lai, 1898–1976), premier and foreign minister of the PRC and chief of the PLA General Staff; Liu Shaoqi (Liu Shao-ch'i, 1898–1969), vice president of the PRC and vice chairman of the CMC; Marshal Zhu De (Zhu Teh, 1886–1976), commander in chief of the PLA; and other top leaders worked together in the Politburo, mobilizing the country for war through the movement to "resist America, aid Korea, defend the homeland, and safeguard the country."[20] Top CCP leaders decided how to prepare for and organize the war, as well as how to push for a quick victory, demonstrating the party's domination in Beijing and the close relationships between the party, the government, and the military from 1950 to 1953. A uniquely Chinese approach to fighting the war in pursuit of national objectives led to military cooperation as well as conflict between Beijing, Moscow, and Pyongyang.

The book also discusses how Mao applied his general military strategy to the Korean conflict. Maoist military strategy is rooted in the CCP's path to power through its twenty-two-year armed revolution: starting with guerrilla warfare and a survival strategy in 1928 against Jiang Jieshi (Chiang Kai-shek, 1887–1975); developing into popular people's warfare and a protracted war strategy in 1938 against Japanese invading forces; and concluding with successful mobile warfare, trench defense, and a final victory strategy in 1948 during the Chinese Civil War. Mao tried all of these strategies of revolutionary war in Korea against the UNF. Unfortunately for him, Korea was not China, and the UNF was very different from the Chinese Guomindang (Kuomintang; GMD) and Japanese troops he had fought before. The drawbacks of his strategy far outweighed its advantages. Mao had to shift his strategy and change the Chinese military command, structure, logistics, training, and technology. Although the changes he made were innovative and helped modernize the Chinese military in the long run, they did not happen quickly enough to deliver victory in Korea.

The book's main focus is on the Chinese operational experience. It examines the CPVF's battle plans and preparations, campaign organization and execution, tactical decisions, combat problem solving, application of technology, political indoctrination, and performance evaluation through the spring of 1951. It provides some insights into Chinese operations by illustrating the CPVF's chain of command at four different levels. The first level from the top down is the CPVF Commanding Headquarters (HQ), which designed and organized the Spring Offensive. The analysis explores the different personalities of CPVF top commanders such as Marshal Peng, Gen. Deng Hua (1910–80), Gen. Hong Xuezhi (1913–2006), and Maj. Gen. Xie Fang (1908–84), who shaped the campaign. Their observations show the progress and problems of Mao's war strategy.

The second level is the commanders of army groups and armies. The book discusses army group commanders such as Gen. Yang Dezhi (1911–94), Gen. Song Shilun (1907–91), and Lt. Gen. Wang Jinshan (1915–78); and army commanders like Lt. Gen. Zeng Shaoshan (1914–95), Lt. Gen. Wei Jie (1914–87), and Maj. Gen. Fu Chongbi (1916–2003), who executed the plans, deployed the troops, and conducted both offensive and defensive battles.[21] Their stories clearly reveal the experiences and outlook of those who carried out the high command's orders.

The third level is the commanders of divisions and regiments. The book discusses the command skills, communication channels, combat effectiveness, tactical flexibility, and problem solving of Gen. You Taizhong (1918–98), Gen. Xu Xin (1921–2005), Maj. Gen. Chen Xinzhong (1915–89), Senior Col. Zheng Qigui (1913–90), and Col. Zhao Zuorui (b. 1919).[22] Their remarkable experiences and the tremendous difficulties they faced provide new and penetrating insights into the Spring Offensive.

The fourth level is the battalion and company commanders who fought the battles and encountered the UNF troops, including Lt. Col. Guan Zhichao (b. 1925), Maj. Huo Zhenlu (1924–2007), Capt. Wang Xuedong (1928–2008), Capt. Zheng Yanman (b. 1927), and Capt. Zhou Baoshan (b. 1922).[23] The book recounts the various tactical problems they faced, from carrying out the massive attack (or human wave attack) to dealing with ammunition shortages. Because of the shortage of food, a problem they could not solve, the officers confronted disciplinary issues. Breakdowns in discipline ranged from soldiers' frequent refusals to follow orders to shooting officers from behind. The accounts of these commanders reveal the challenges the Chinese army faced and illustrate key differences between the Chinese army and U.S. armed forces.

The military operations and tactics of these commanders reflect the Chinese view of war. The security concerns, strategic decisions, and consistency throughout the war illustrate Chinese methods for conducting a war. Some of these methods were holistic, effective, flexible, and as successful as methods used in the West. Scholars in Europe and America have studied the 2,500-year history of Chinese warfare and military writings, including the classic *The Art of War* by Sunzi (Sun-tzu, 535–496 BC) and Mao's views on guerrilla warfare.[24] Mao's military theories, drawing heavily on ancient classics like Sunzi's book, remain a vital component of the Chinese military history and expertise. Mao's generals saw the traditional form or style of Chinese warfare—including deceptions and surprise attacks—as models to emulate.[25]

Comparing the Chinese and Western view of and approach to war is a popular topic of discussion among military experts and members of the general public.[26] Some historians draw a line between the Western and Chinese ways of waging war. Victor Hanson and Geoffrey Parker argue that there were variations in the Western way—particularly in the areas of military technology, discipline and training, continuity and flexibility, the goal of total defeat and annihilation of the enemy, and the organization for war.[27] John Keegan argues that China has followed an "'Oriental' style of warfare characterized by caution, delay, the avoidance of battle, and the use of elaborate ruses and stratagems."[28] This style of warfare is different from the Western way, which "stresses direct, face-to-face confrontation and the rapid resolution of military conflicts by main force."[29] Alastair Johnston and John Fairbank contrast the Chinese military doctrine with that of the West.[30] Fairbank focuses on three points about the Chinese way of war. First, a Chinese government dominated by Confucian ideology had a tendency to avoid war, neither using military force as an end unto itself nor glorifying military actions and martial heroism. Second, the Chinese army had a tradition of defensive land warfare, principally using geography to either wear down or pacify enemies instead of annihilating or attacking them. And third, China emphasized civilian control over the military and societal stability through a bond between the military and the bureaucracy, in contrast to the connection between military and commercial pursuits often seen in the West.[31]

In this ongoing discussion, some scholars have questioned others' views of the Chinese way of war as more Chinese military writings have become available. Among the dissenters are William Thompson, Kenneth Swope, Hans Van de Ven and Harold Tanner. For example, Thompson states that, although a comprehensive and holistic set of Chinese principles exist to deal with war, they do not describe a separate "way of war" that is distinct from that of the West.[32] These scholars contend that the Chinese invented or adopted many supposedly Western ways of warfare. David Graff and Robin Higham point out that Chinese military history has been considered too much through the lens of Confucian tradition. This sort of contrast between Western military history and Confucian tradition is the result of the "way of war" historians' failure to see similarities between Western armies and their Chinese counterparts.[33]

The findings in this book may suggest that the Chinese military experience in Korea has been too little studied. In comparison to the West experience in the Korean War, the Chinese experience offers a mixed picture. Nonetheless, countless parallels can be drawn between the CPVF and UNF in the war. For instance, the CPVF's discipline and constant strategic and tactical adaptation reflect both Chinese and

Western approaches to warfare. Both armies stressed the importance of rewards and punishments for soldiers, the selection of generals, and the manipulation of army morale. Strategies of annihilation and attrition were the norm in China as well as in the West. Both sides claimed to be aiding the Korean people, claims that justified the mobilization of forces. Both sides attempted to glorify their efforts in Korea, although China did not value returned Chinese POWs, since tradition said that soldiers should fight to death in order to honor their country rather than allow themselves to be captured.[34]

However, some of the findings in this book are diametrically opposed to the Western way of war. First, Chinese warfare is conducted by a political power center that can generate popular support for war. That power center could be a state government or a political party that can mobilize the entire country and concentrate its economic resources on war through highly centralized, well-organized, and very effective institutions. Since 1949 the central government of the PRC has had total control of the country's administration, policies, strategies, production, and distribution of goods and services at a level that no Western country could ever achieve.[35]

Second, the Chinese strategic culture traditionally does not consider protracted war as a favorable situation. Sunzi warned: "When employing them [soldiers] in battle, a victory that is long in coming will blunt their weapons and dampen their ardor. If you attack cities, their strength will be exhausted. If you expose the army to a prolonged campaign, the state's resources will be inadequate."[36] It is clear that he recognized the detrimental effects that incessant warfare had on the state.

Third, an important characteristic of the Chinese military is its emphasis on the human component in war. Mao firmly believed that a weak army could win a war against a strong enemy because he was convinced that a man could beat a weapon. "Weapons are an important factor in war, but not the decisive factor," Mao wrote. He also said explicitly that "it is people, not things, that are decisive." Mao's confidence in a human being's "subjective capability" to determine defeat or victory in war made sense to the Chinese officers and soldiers.[37] Shaped by a military culture and communist ideology, the Chinese belief in human superiority over technology suggests their contradictory attitude toward war and combat. The idea that a soldier or a warrior, because of his godliness and virtue, can vanquish stronger opponents has a long tradition. During the Korean War, the CPVF lacked the air force, tanks, and heavy artillery necessary for a successful campaign against more powerful and mechanized UNF troops. Rather than relying on superior technology to win, Chinese forces sought victory through a military advantage achieved by deception and application, and Chinese commanders and soldiers believed that their fighting spirit would lead them to victory.

In addition to basic rewards and punishments, Chinese generals employed a political spirit or mental energy flow (to use terms from communist ideology) to motivate the soldiers. The CPVF had soldiers take oaths to arouse their political consciousness and appealed to the righteousness of the cause. This was to instill a fighting spirit in the soldiers and make them feel their cause was worthwhile. This endeavor to understand energy flow may have given the Chinese a greater overall understanding, going even beyond the ancient Greeks—who believed the gods were the motivators of human behavior. Moreover, since China is rich in manpower, from time to time the Chinese army was not as averse to casualties as the UNF was. The CPVF's superior manpower enabled the Chinese to believe they might overcome their inferiority in equipment and technology. It seemed rational to the Chinese leaders that the large size of their force should be a decisive factor and lead them to victory.

In addition, the Chinese operational culture has a characteristic emphasis on secrecy, surprise, deception, and the organization of unorthodox troops, an emphasis that permeates the Chinese combat experience.[38] These very traditional strategies from the Chinese military classics helped leaders maneuver the CPVF units to a point where they could obtain the best advantage in the offensive campaigns. Although the Chinese were able to have armies of 300,000 troops appear unexpectedly, it was their ability to preserve their forces that may have been their greatest advantage. Like guerrillas in the Red Army in WWII, they could appear suddenly, attack, and then steal away to safety. The irregular or guerrilla warfare fought by the CPVF has become synonymous with a Chinese approach to war. Nevertheless, since WWII the Chinese military has constantly evolved. As the PLA won the Chinese Civil War and matured, the early guerrilla strategy and tactics were replaced, and the use of conventional mobile warfare rose to a point where the PLA did not want to return to its previous methods. One may have to wait to draw any broad conclusion concerning a Chinese way of war until all the Chinese documents and archives relating to the Korean War become available and historians are able to provide a thorough analysis of Chinese operations in that conflict.

## A NOTE ON SOURCES

Due to a lack of readily available sources for Western researchers, few areas in Chinese history pose more difficulties than the study of military history. The research in this volume is supported by primary and secondary Chinese sources that were made available only in recent years. Since the late 1990s there has been significant progress in the study of Chinese military history. The so-called reform and opening era in China has resulted in a more flexible political and academic environment compared to the time of Mao's reign, leading to a relaxation of the formerly rigid criteria for releasing party and military documents. Consequently, fresh and meaningful historical materials—including the papers of former leaders, party and governmental documents, and local archives—are now available. Certainly, the Chinese government still has a long way to go before free academic inquiry becomes a reality in China, but the value of opening documentary materials for the study of military history cannot be underestimated. China's renewed interest in the lessons of the Korean War has resulted in the availability of both in government documents and personal recollections, many of which were published in the 2000s.

The first group of sources used in this work is official Chinese records, including party documents, government archives, and military materials. The CMC documents in the PLA Archives (*jiefangjun danganguan*) under the General Staff Department (GSD) are still closed to scholars, although in the process of researching this book, I became a collaborator with military historians and archivists like Dr. Chu Feng of the PLA Archives, Col. Sun Lizhou of the GSD, Maj. Gen. Wang Baocun of the China Academy of Military Science (CAMS), Senior Col.

Yang Shaojun of the Logistics College of the PLA, and Lt. Col. Guan Zhichao of the Nanjing Political Academy of the PLA.[39] It is vital to note, however, that during most of the PLA's history, strategic and even tactical decisions were micromanaged by the Politburo of the CCP Central Committee. The primary sources used in this book include selected and reprinted party documents of the Central Committee, CMC, and CCP regional bureaus.[40] Some Chinese government documents have also been released in recent years. For example, in 2004 and 2009 the Ministry of Foreign Affairs declassified tens of thousands of diplomatic files from the early years of the PRC. A large number of these documents relate to China's involvement in the Korean War.[41]

The second group of sources is the writings, papers, and memoirs of Chinese Communist leaders, as well as interviews with them. Although Mao was the undisputed leader in terms of both theory and strategy throughout most of the PLA's history, the military leaders worked together and made the majority of important decisions within the CMC. Their papers, fundamental for any study of the PLA, include collected and selected military works, manuscripts, instructions, plans, and telegrams of Mao, Zhou, Zhu, Peng, Liu, Marshal Nie Rongzhen (Nieh Jung-ch'en, 1899–1992), Marshal Xu Xiangqian (Hsu Hsiang-ch'ian, 1901–90), and other top military leaders.[42] Among the most important are the three-volume *Jianguo yilai Mao Zedong junshi wengao, 1949–76* [Mao Zedong's military manuscripts since the founding of the PRC, 1949–76], the thirteen-volume *Jianguo yilai Mao Zedong wengao, 1949–76* [Mao Zedong's manuscripts since the founding of the state, 1949–76], and the four-volume *Jianguo yilai Liu Shaoqi wengao, 1949–52* [Liu Shaoqi's manuscripts since the founding of the state, 1949–52].[43] Maj. Gen. Xu Changyou, former deputy secretary general of the CMC, and Huang Zheng, senior fellow and department head of the CCP Central Archival and Manuscript Research Division, gave me considerable assistance in understanding the decision making of the CPVF Command. Senior Col. Wang Zhongchun of the Chinese National Defense University (NDU) and Dr. Liu Zhiqing of the CAMS also helped by sharing their archival collection and history research on the Spring Offensive Campaign.

In 1996–2010 I researched documents of the Chinese Nationalist Party (Guomindang, or GMD, in China; Kuomintang, or KMT, in Taiwan) during my four research trips to Taiwan. I have gone through the ROC Foreign Ministry documents at the Academia Sinica; the presidential papers of Jiang Jieshi, president of the ROC in 1927–49 and 1950–75, at the Academia Historica; and GMD party documents at the Party History Archives. I had opportunities to interview Gen. Jiang Weiguo (Chiang Wei-kuo, 1916–97), former secretary general of the ROC Council of National Security, son of Jiang Jieshi, and adoptive brother of Jiang Jingguo (Chiang Ching-kuo, 1910–88), president of the ROC in 1978–88. Among other GMD military leaders I interviewed in Taiwan were Chief Gen. Hao Baicun (Hau Pei-tsun, b. 1919), chief of the general staff in 1981–89, ROC defense minister in 1989–90, and prime minister in 1990–93; Gen. Fan Zeng, former vice defense minister; and Gen. Yin Jiwu, former deputy chief of the ROC Air Force. Their personal accounts of the wars with the Communist forces are valuable in examining the PLA from the other side.

The third group of sources is interviews, memoirs, and writings by Chinese generals and field commanders. From 1998 to 2010, my research focused on Chinese military officers of the 1950s. I collected their memoirs and interviewed retired PLA generals and officers such as Maj. Gen. Chai Chengwen (1915–2011), Senior Col. Guan Zhichao, Col. Zhao Zuorui, Maj. Huo Zhenlu, Capts. Wang Xuedong, Zheng Yanman, and Zhou Baoshan, as well as others in Beijing, Shanghai, Guangzhou, Nanjing, Wuhan, and Hangzhou.[44] The many details from their experiences made a remarkable contribution to this study by adding another perspective on the subject. No matter how politically indoctrinated they might have become, the generals are culturally bound to cherish the memory of the past. More important, they had only recently begun to feel comfortable in talking about their experiences and in allowing their recollections to be recorded, written, and even published. The 1990s brought a considerable number of military and war memoirs to Chinese readers as books and journal articles, in addition to printed reference studies for restricted circulation only.[45]

Since 2003 my research trips have focused on a fourth category of sources: the recollections of the PLA soldiers and junior officers in the Shenyang Military Regional Command, NDU, Logistics College of the PLA, Nanjing Political Academy of the PLA, and China's Academy of

Armed Police Force. I conducted more than two hundred interviews with these men. Their reminiscences offer an important source of information and opinion for those scholars and students of Chinese military history who do not read Chinese. Since I am a native speaker of Chinese, I conducted the interviews in that language. I translated some of them into English, and they contain new information on the Chinese role in the Korean War, previously unavailable in English. Each of the officers and soldiers provided a special, personal insight into a specific aspect of their experience, including the chain of command, combat planning, operations, logistics, political control, field communication, and, in some cases, POW experiences. I conducted more than two hundred interviews over fifteen provinces, from Heilongjiang in the north to Hainan in the south, collecting direct testimonies from Chinese soldiers.[46] I also had opportunities to interview several former CPVF POWs who had not returned to China but went to Taiwan after the Korean armistice was signed in July 1953. They are very critical of the Chinese operations in Korea and believe they made the right decision in coming to Taiwan rather than being repatriated to the mainland.

The individual recollections are a significant source of information and opinion for this work. Each interviewee paints a picture of a specific aspect of military experience. Oral history is a vital source for military historians in China. Recent exchanges between Chinese and American historians have included the relevance of oral history to studies of the chronology and major events of PLA history. These historians probably would agree that recently oral data has become more commonly used, not just for filling in factual gaps, but also for serving as the main source of information about both themes and frameworks of Chinese military history.

The last category of sources is secondary works in both Chinese and in English. The Chinese literature includes military publications, textbooks, and other educational materials about the PLA's history. I also interviewed generals and military historians who were still serving in the PLA, including Lt. Gen. Qin Chaoying, Maj. Gen. Wang Baochun, Dr. Liu Zhiqing, Senior Col. Wang Zhongchun, Col. Chen Zhiya, Col. Yang Shaojun, and Lt. Col. Wang Bo. These sources add a reliable Chinese perspective, which reinterprets a series of fundamental issues crucial to an understanding of the Chinese military. Covering many issues related to the Chinese military, recent published sources provide a useful research bibliography for students interested in the Chinese military as well as in the history of modern China. Having covered many issues on the Chinese military in published findings in recent years, these sources provide a useful research bibliography for students interested in the Chinese military as well as in the history of modern China. Given the overwhelming wealth of current literature on the Korean War, this work has filtered through the publications and attempted to create a clear analysis.

Unless otherwise indicated, all translations from the Chinese are my own.

This book presents the development of the Chinese 1951 Spring Offensive Campaign chronologically. Chapter 1 covers the top Chinese leaders' debates and decisions in the fall of 1950 concerning intervention in Korea. It discusses China's mobilization and other preparations for war as well as the Chinese battle formation through an examination of Chinese strategic culture. Chapter 2 examines the operational culture by studying the first four offensive campaigns of the CPVF, from November 1950 to April 1951, and identifies some advantages and disadvantages that Chinese troops had in Korea. Chapter 3 details the debates over the Fifth Offensive in late April 1951 and the political culture of the chain of command. Considerable disagreement arose among CPVF officers regarding the campaign, and most of the commanders disagreed with Peng, who favored the southward strike ordered by Mao, Kim, and Stalin. Despite their arguments, Peng was determined to launch his Fifth Offensive and retake Seoul. Chapter 4 reconstructs the first part of the Chinese offensive on the western front, from April 22 to 29, 1951. The CPVF launched a major attack across a forty-mile front, committing forty-four divisions, totaling 548,000 men, against the U.S. I and IX Corps. Chapter 5 explores the major reasons behind the failed Chinese attack in late April, including poor operational planning, heavy casualties, and a shortage of supplies. Chapter 6 deals with the second phase of the Chinese Spring Offensive on the eastern front, from May 16 to 21. The UNF were heavily concentrated in the west around Seoul, and the east was primarily defended by ROK troops. Sensing an opportunity in early May, Peng ordered 484,000 troops, including thirty-three Chinese divisions and three NKPA army corps, to attack the ROK forces and U.S. X Corps. This attack failed for the same reasons as the one before. Chapter 7 explains why no one in the CPVF anticipated that the UNF would make a sweeping counterattack on the morning of May 23, twelve hours before the scheduled Chinese withdrawal. This withdrawal, from May 23 to June 10, became the most disastrous operation in CPVF history. Chapter 8 analyzes how Chinese leaders changed their goal from total victory to a negotiated settlement. By that summer, however, the war had changed from a mobile war to a stalemate, a war in trenches. The CPVF continued fighting while negotiating for peace from July 10, 1951, until the Korean Truce Agreement was finally signed on July 27, 1953. The conclusion analyzes the CPVF's failure in battle, its command problems, inadequate communication, and limited Soviet support. The conclusion also examines some critical issues in modernizing the Chinese military, such as training, technology, and civil-military relations. China's intervention in the Korean War was the beginning of its military modernization.

The events of 1951 played an important role in the country's increase in international status. China reaped great benefits for the high price it paid in Korea. Having been founded only in October 1949, it rapidly proved its great power status in Asia as a new Communist state. Not only was China capable of fighting the world's most powerful country to a draw, but the war also proved that Chinese society was secure enough to withstand a terrible conflict. Those factors brought first the Soviet Union and later, after the Sino-Soviet split, the United States to seek Beijing's favor. Even now, the world's most powerful nations measure their standing in Asia by their relations with China. Although today most of the world only dimly remembers the Korean War and considers it to have been a relatively minor conflict, it was a formative moment in Chinese history. It gave Beijing immense political and military power. Mao used the war to declare an independent and powerful nation and to cement Communist control over the Chinese state and society in the following decades. By celebrating the war experience, the CCP promoted nationalistic pride and consciousness to mobilize popular support for its mass movements such as the Great Leap Forward (1958–60) and the Cultural Revolution

(1966–76). Combat experience bolstered China's military modernization along the Soviet model. The Chinese military culture that evolved from the Korean War created an interventionist attitude that led to the Taiwan Strait crises in 1954, 1955, and 1958; a border clash between China and India in 1962; participation in the Vietnam War from 1965 to 1970; and border conflicts with the Soviet Union in 1969–1973.[47] The Chinese army became a modern force under Mao's command, with a proclivity for active (or aggressive) defense in the Cold War.

# Note on Transliteration

FOR CHINESE TERMS AND NAMES OF PEOPLE AND PLACES, I HAVE used the Hanyu Pinyin romanization system. This is also used for the titles of Chinese publications. Chinese names are written in the Chinese way with the surname first, as in Mao Zedong. Some names of people in Hanyu Pinyin romanization are followed by the names in Wade-Giles romanization when they are first mentioned, as in Jiang Jieshi (Chiang Kai-shek). The same is true of some place names, as in Guangzhou (Canton).

The romanized names of most Korean people follow the traditional East Asian practice of putting the surname first, as in Kim Il-sung. Exceptions are made for a few people whose names are widely known in reverse order, such as Syngman Rhee. If a place name has different spellings in Korean and English literature, the English spelling appears in parentheses at the name's first appearance—for example, Hahwaokri (Hagaru-ri).

# Abbreviations

| | |
|---|---|
| AAA | anti-aircraft artillery |
| CAMS | China Academy of Military Science |
| CCP | Chinese Communist Party |
| CIA | Central Intelligence Agency (U.S.) |
| CMC | Central Military Commission (CCP) |
| CPPCC | Chinese People's Political Consultative Conference |
| CPVF | Chinese People's Volunteer Force |
| DPRK | Democratic People's Republic of Korea (North Korea) |
| ECRC | East China Regional Command |
| FAB | field artillery battalion |
| GLD | General Logistics Department (PLA) |
| GMD | Guomindang (or Kuomintang, KMT) |
| GSD | General Staff Department (PLA) |
| HQ | headquarters |
| KMT | Kuomintang (or Guomindang, GMD) |
| NEBDA | Northeast Border Defense Army (PLA) |
| NCO | noncommissioned officer |
| NDU | National Defense University (PLA) |
| NKPA | North Korean People's Army |
| PLA | People's Liberation Army |
| PLAN | PLA Navy |
| POW | prisoners of war |
| PRC | People's Republic of China |
| ROC | Republic of China (Taiwan) |

| | |
|---|---|
| ROK | Republic of Korea (South Korea) |
| UN | United Nations |
| UNF | United Nations Force |
| U.S. | United States |
| USSR | Union of Soviet Socialist Republics |
| WRUSAK | War to Resist the U.S. and Aid Korea |
| WWII | World War II |

# China's Battle for Korea

# ONE

# Beijing's Decision

MAO ZEDONG'S DECISION TO SEND CHINESE TROOPS INTO THE Korean War has been widely debated. Most Chinese military historians argue that Mao made a rational, correct, and necessary decision.[1] China's intervention secured its northeastern borders, strengthened Sino-Soviet relations, and saved the North Korean regime. China acted as a major military power for the first time since the First Opium War in 1839–42, against Great Britain. However, some historians in China, and many more in America, challenge this view and condemn Mao for gross misjudgments and an "idiosyncratic audacity" that cost the lives of hundreds of thousands of Chinese soldiers.[2] Still others take a middle position and argue that Mao had few political alternatives in his effort to achieve full acceptance in the Communist world and to assume leadership of Asian Communist movements in the early 1950s.[3] These scholarly efforts have laid a solid groundwork for a better understanding of the Chinese decision, yet the debate continues.

The examination of Beijing's decision to enter the Korean War reveals a new Chinese strategic culture that advocated active defense to help the North Koreans win the ongoing civil war and to protect the newly established Communist state from a possible U.S. invasion. By July 1950 the situation in Korea was beginning to worry Mao.[4] Between July 7 and July 22, Beijing mobilized forces in northeast China, or Manchuria, leading to an important strategic shift from defense toward intervention by early August. Military preparations accelerated through September, after Gen. Douglas MacArthur's Inchon (Inch'ŏn) landing and the collapse of the NKPA, leading to serious debates in early October and culminating on October 4 in a final decision to commit Chinese troops to help North Korea. By October 19 the vanguard units of the PLA, which were among its best forces, had crossed the Yalu River and entered North Korea. The roles of Mao and the Party Center—which included the Central Committee, Central Military Commission, and National Congress of the CCP—represented unprecedented activism in the Korean War: China was no longer playing the role of a passive spectator, or an adjunct, in global power politics. This newly vigorous internationalism revealed a profound change taking place in Communist China.

Although external Cold War factors may appear to be the only motive behind this change, the crucial strategic shift came about for significant internal reasons. Modern Chinese history has demonstrated that neither foreign invasion nor the support of an international power could create a strong, centralized national government. Instead, the government's power depended more on China's political stability and military strength than on its foreign relations. In this sense, by entering the Korean War, it is possible that Mao saw a chance to continue the Communist movement at home and to increase China's power abroad. Now that national security had been established by the Communists' winning the last battle of the Chinese Civil War (1946–49) against the GMD on Taiwan, Mao's strategic priorities were establishing the legitimacy the CCP needed as the ruling party, an economic recovery, and military modernization. His decision to enter the Korean War may also have been based on the PLA's superiority in manpower, which made Mao and his generals overconfident in their ability to drive the UNF out of the Korean Peninsula.

### "SOUTH HEAVY" AND AMPHIBIOUS PREPARATIONS

CCP leaders believed that Communist China had been founded, and could be maintained, by military power. By early 1950 China had the largest army in the world, totaling 5.4 million men. In contrast, U.S. armed forces had 1.5 million troops and the Soviet Union's forces numbered 2.8 million, although they had grown to 4.8 million by 1953. After

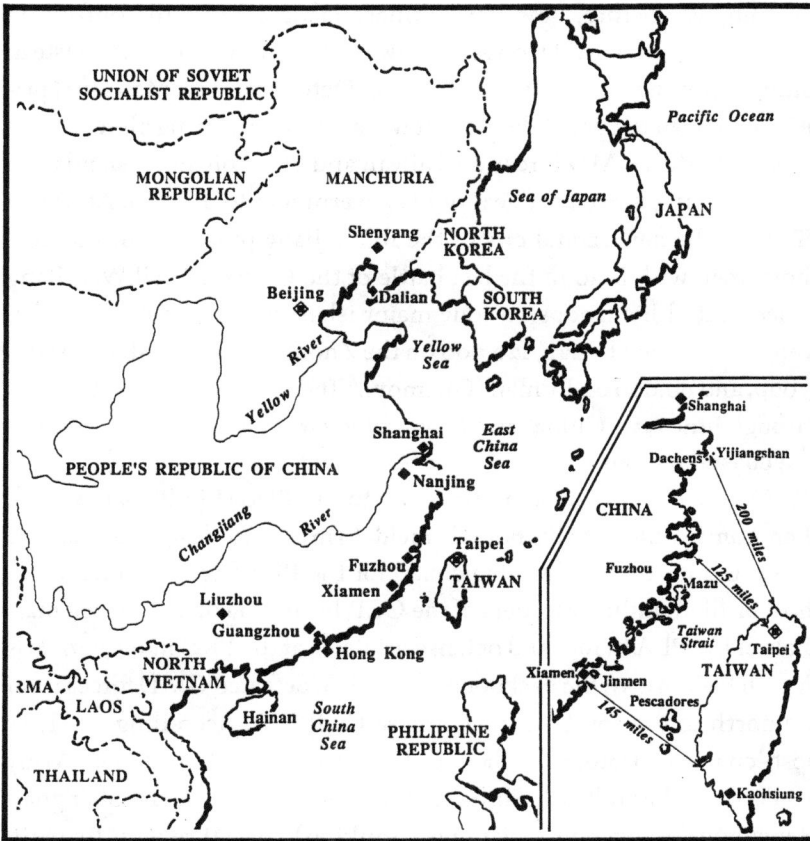

Map 1.1. China and Taiwan

the defeat of the GMD, the PLA transformed itself from a "liberation army" into a national force with two new goals: to repel foreign invasions and to defeat internal threats to the new regime. Similarly, the Chinese government's mission was to establish political order and national unity, to maintain domestic peace and tranquility, and to reorganize the military so as to be able to defend against foreign invasion. From this time forward, the PRC adopted an inward-looking governmental policy stressing national security and defensive military measures to consolidate and protect its territorial gains (map 1.1).

The year before, however, Chinese leaders had still confronted over one million GMD troops in Taiwan (Formosa) and southwestern China. After the founding of the PRC on October 1, 1949, Mao's first priority had been to consolidate the new state by eliminating all remnants of Jiang Jieshi's GMD forces on Taiwan and other offshore islands.[5] In late 1949 Jiang moved the seat of his government to Taiwan. At Taibei (Taipei), the new capital city of the ROC, Jiang prepared for the final showdown with Mao in the last battle of the Chinese Civil War. Jiang concentrated his troops on four major islands: 200,000 men on Taiwan, 100,000 on Hainan, 120,000 on the Zhoushan (Chou-shan) Island group, and 60,000 on Jinmen (Quemoy).[6] Therefore, from October 1949 through June 1950, China's military strategy was focused on its southern and coastal regions.

On October 31, 1949, in a telegram to Lin Biao (Lin Piao, 1906–71), then commander of the Fourth Field Army, Mao designed a "south heavy and north light" strategic plan for the PLA.[7] Lin was one of the most brilliant military leaders of the CCP, becoming one of the ten marshals of the PLA in 1955 and defense minister of the PRC in 1959–71. His Fourth Field Army, the backbone of the PLA, defeated GMD forces from the north to the south in the Chinese Civil War. According to Mao's post–civil war strategy for the four field armies, the "Third Field Army would defend Southeast China with a concentration in the Shanghai-Hangzhou (Hangchow)–Nanjing (Nanking) coastal region. Its main strength should prepare to take over Taiwan Island." The Fourth Field Army should "station five of its armies in Guangdong (Kwangtung) and Guangxi (Kwangsi) as the southern defense force centered on Guangzhou (Canton), and deploy three armies along the railways in Central China as strategic reserve forces available to move either south or north."[8] Following Mao's instructions, in late 1949 the Third Field Army, with one million troops in Southeast China, and the Fourth Field Army, with some 1.2 million troops in South China, were preparing for amphibious operations against the GMD-occupied islands to bring the Chinese Civil War to a close.[9]

In his "south heavy and north light" strategy of 1949, Mao considered Shanghai, Guangzhou, and Tianjin (Tientsin) as the three key points for national defense. Two of these points were in the south, where preparations for an amphibious attack on Taiwan were proceeding. In the meantime, Mao stationed three armies of the Fourth Field Army in central Henan (Honan) Province as strategic reserves. These armies would be transferred to the northeast in July–August 1950 and in October would become the first wave of Chinese forces to enter North Korea. In late 1949, however, Manchuria was not one of China's key defense points, having only one infantry army, the Forty-Second, of the PLA's fifty-seven infantry armies. Northeast China, which included the three provinces of Liaoning, Jilin (Kirin), and Heilongjiang (Heilungkiang) and shared borders with North Korea and the Soviet Union, had three artillery divisions, five local independent divisions, and one public security division, totaling 228,000 troops.[10]

In late 1949 the PLA high command followed Mao's strategy by concentrating on landing preparations against the GMD-held islands along China's southeastern coast. Mao, however, showed extra caution in this final battle in the Chinese Civil War against Jinmen and Taiwan because of a disastrous landing made by the Tenth Army Group of the Third Field Army on Jinmen, a small island group lying less than two miles off the mainland. The Twenty-Eighth Army of the Tenth Army Group had lost three infantry regiments, totaling 9,086 men, during an attempted landing on October 24 and 25, 1949.[11] Mao asked his coastal army commanders to "guard against arrogance, avoid underestimating the enemy, and be well prepared."[12] In the meantime, Su Yu (1907–84), deputy commander of the Third Field Army, warned the high command that it would be "extremely difficult to operate a large-scale cross-ocean amphibious landing operation without air and sea control."[13] Su, one of the most experienced commanders of the PLA after Lin, commanded the Third Field Army and defeated GMD forces in eastern China in 1948–49. In 1955 Su was made one of the ten grand generals and became chief of the PLA general staff.[14]

To better prepare a PLA amphibious campaign, in December the high command reorganized the headquarters (HQ) of the Twelfth Army Group, Fourth Field Army, into the HQ of the PLA Navy. Xiao Jinguang (Hsiao Kin-kuang, 1903–89), commander of the Twelfth, was appointed the first commander of the PLA's new navy.[15] Xiao became vice minister of defense in 1954 and was promoted to grand general in 1955. It is important to note that at this time the Chinese forces were numerically and technologically inferior to GMD air and naval forces.[16] That was partly why the Jinmen landing failed. Since the PLA had neither enough air power nor a modern navy, it would require Soviet aid.

## MAO, STALIN, AND THE TAIWAN LANDING PLAN

Mao arrived in the Soviet Union on December 16, 1949, for a state visit, hoping to get the military assistance China desperately needed through an alliance between the PRC and the Union of Soviet Socialist Republics (USSR). Stalin, however, was never an easy person for the Chinese to get along with, even though they were his Communist comrades. Frustrated after two fruitless meetings with Stalin in December, Mao was disturbed and annoyed that he was unable to meet with Stalin again for more than three weeks in January 1950.[17] Nevertheless, during the sixty-five days he spent in Moscow, Mao gained a better understanding of Stalin's intentions. Among other things, Stalin wanted to convince Mao that the Soviet Union had its own difficulties. There would be no free ride for China, which should share the responsibility for the worldwide Communist movement. Stalin made it clear that China should support Communist movements in other Asian countries.[18]

Preoccupied with European affairs, Stalin needed Chinese help with ongoing Asian Communist revolutions: the First Indochina War in Vietnam and North Korea's attempt at national unification. In addition, Stalin had no intention of challenging the Yalta agreement, which had been signed by the Soviet Union and the United States, that created a post-WWII international system and including the Soviet Union as one of the major powers. From 1946 to January 1950, Stalin was concerned that any change in the Yalta system might cause a direct conflict between the two superpowers. In his office, Stalin told Mao: "The victory of the Chinese revolution proved that China has become the center for the Asian revolution. We believe that it's better for China to take the major responsibility in supporting and helping [Asian countries]."[19]

Stalin engaged the PRC in the Cold War both ideologically and geographically. Whether it was the symbolic significance of the Communist group that ideologically bound China to show its duty, or simple nationalistic interest, China was required to make at least some commitment to support the Soviets in the Cold War. Even though Mao was unhappy with Stalin's demand, he understood the Soviet leader's intention and agreed to share "the international responsibility."[20] Chen Jian points out that "in an agreement on 'division of labor' between the Chinese and Soviet Communists for waging the world revolution, they decided that while the Soviet Union would remain the center of international proletarian revolution, China's primary duty would be the promotion of the 'Eastern revolution.'"[21]

In February 1950 Mao and Zhou Enlai signed the Sino-Soviet Treaty of Friendship, Alliance, and Mutual Assistance with Stalin in Moscow.[22] Zhou was political, diplomatic, and military leader of the PRC, serving as its premier in 1949–76 and foreign minister in 1949–58.[23] Zhou's most notable achievements were in the diplomatic realm. In his capacity as premier, he spent much of his time abroad, boosting the PRC's international standing. His diplomatic approach to the world, especially to the Communist bloc in the Cold War, was flexible and pragmatic. The Sino–Soviet Treaty ensured Soviet military assistance if China was invaded by an imperialist power—which the Communists probably thought was most likely to be the United States or Japan.

From the moment that Communist China came into being, Beijing's leaders regarded the United States as China's primary enemy and, at the same time, consistently declared that a fundamental aim of the Chinese revolution was to destroy the old world order dominated by American imperialists.[24] Through endless propaganda campaigns and constant indoctrination efforts, Beijing portrayed the United States as the bastion of all reactionary forces in the world.[25] From 1950 to 1971, the United States was thoroughly demonized by the PRC. As a result, in Mao's efforts to legitimize his "continuous revolution," the theme of "struggling against U.S. imperialism" occupied a central position. Chen Jian explains that the Maoist revolution's international aims served as a "constant source of domestic mobilization, helping to legitimate the revolution at home and to maintain its momentum."[26] The alliance between Beijing and Moscow was the cornerstone of the Communist international alliance in the 1950s.[27] The Sino-Soviet alliance also marked the beginning of a new stage of the Cold War in Asia. As part of the Sino-Soviet Treaty of

Friendship, Alliance, and Mutual Assistance, Mao and Zhou also signed a major naval pact with Stalin. The Soviet Union agreed to arm a new Chinese naval force with warships and equipment worth $150 million, half the total aid package granted through the treaty.[28]

Returning from Moscow in February 1950, Mao called a meeting of the PLA high command. During the discussions, Mao instructed Nie Rongzhen, acting chief of the general staff, and Su to plan attacks on Jinmen and Taiwan, with an emphasis on training airborne forces and preparing an additional four divisions for amphibious maneuvers.[29] As one of the top military commanders and Mao's senior aide in Beijing, Nie took part in high command decision making, planned major military operations, and shared responsibility for war mobilization. He ran the PLA general staff since Zhou Enlai, its chief, was preoccupied as the PRC's premier and foreign minister and because all the members of the staff had been on Nie's former Northern Military Region Staff—they were people who had worked with Mao in the Civil War and moved into Beijing with him. In 1955 Nie became one of the ten marshals in China.[30] On March 11, 1950, Su met Xiao Jinguang to discuss the first detailed plan to liberate Taiwan. According to the plan, the Third Field Army and the navy would deploy 500,000 troops to attack Taiwan.[31] The three armies in the Thirteenth Army Group of the Fourth Field Army would remain as a reserve for the attack, and the Nineteenth Army Group of the Fourth Field Army would deploy its three armies along the coast as a mobile force. In all, nearly 800,000 men would be involved in the invasion of Taiwan. In April the CMC approved the Su-Xiao plan. The Third Field Army began landing training in the late spring.[32]

In the meantime, Mao approved the Fourth Field Army's attack on Hainan Island. In April 1950, 100,000 men of the Fifteenth Army Group of the Fourth Field Army crossed the twenty-mile-wide Qiongzhou (Ch'iong-chou) Strait in the South China Sea and successfully landed on Hainan. The landing forces quickly overran the GMD garrison and captured the entire island. A month later the Seventh and Ninth Army Groups of the Third Field Army occupied the Zhoushan Islands in the East China Sea. In the late spring of 1950, the people on both sides of the Taiwan Strait expected an imminent PLA attack on Jinmen and Taiwan.[33] When the CCP held its Third Plenary Session of the Seventh Congress at Beijing on June 6–9, 1950, Mao urged the liberation of Taiwan and Tibet as the party's central tasks. Su reported on PLA preparations for invading Taiwan. The Party Center decided at the meeting that its first priority was to liberate Taiwan and Tibet, and its second was to eliminate the bandits and establish domestic stability and order.[34] In early June the East China Command landed forces on the GMD-occupied Dongshan and Wanshan Islands. But the Korean War broke out on June 25, altering Mao's plans.[35]

### BEIJING, PYONGYANG, AND THE NORTH KOREAN ATTACK

In Beijing on May 13, 1950, Mao Zedong was briefed by North Korean leader Kim Il-sung regarding a North Korean invasion of South Korea. Kim did not give Mao the attack's date, but Mao agreed with Kim's plan since it fit with Stalin's request that China promote Communist movements in Asia. The CCP leaders and PLA high command approved North Korea's bid for national reunification by force.[36] Even before October 1949, the CCP had enthusiastically supported Communist movements in neighboring countries, including Vietnam, Laos, Myanmar (Burma), and especially North Korea.

Before the founding of the PRC, in May 1949, Mao had met a delegation from the NKPA headed by Gen. Kim Ung, director of the NKPA Political Bureau. Kim asked the CCP leaders to allow Chinese soldiers of Korean origin to return to North Korea. During WWII and the Chinese Civil War, many young Koreans had joined the Chinese Communist forces, which allowed these men to enlist together as units, increasing and improving their combat effectiveness and local support. These ethnic units gave the PLA an advantage in winning the Civil War. Many Korean soldiers had joined the PLA in the belief that it would allow the establishment of a Korean autonomous region in Manchuria.[37] Mao accepted Kim's request and agreed that two Korean divisions (the 163rd and 164th) stationed in northeastern China could return to North Korea whenever the NKPA was ready for them. Another Korean division (the 165th) was still engaged in fighting in South China. Mao promised Kim that the division's return to North Korea would occur after it accomplished its mission in China. After the CCP's agreement, the 163rd and 164th Divisions of the PLA were transferred from northeastern China to North Korea in July 1949. They were reorganized into the NKPA's 5th and 6th Divisions. Seasoned Korean-Chinese soldiers, particularly those in artillery and engineering, gave the North Korean forces not only additional troops but also valuable technical support.[38]

In January 1950 Kim Il-sung sent another delegation to Beijing to request the return of the 165th Division. As Mao had promised, the CMC agreed with Kim Kwang Hyop, head of the North Korean delegation, to transfer the division from the PLA to the NKPA.[39] Then Kim asked Nie to arm and equip the soldiers before their transfer. After receiving approval from the CMC, Nie and his general staff transferred 14,000 Koreans, with weapons and equipment, to North Korea, where they were reorganized into the NKPA's 7th Division.[40] In the first half of 1950, the Fourth Field Army also transferred 23,000 Korean-Chinese soldiers from their infantry divisions, as well as engineering troops and railroad construction units, to North Korea. These Korean-Chinese soldiers played an important role in Kim Il-sung's initial invasion of South Korea.[41] The NKPA now had fifteen infantry divisions, totaling 150,000 men.

In the meantime, the PLA began sharing military intelligence with the NKPA. On January 7, 1950, China and North Korea signed an agreement to establish additional telegraph and telephone lines between them. The PLA high command also increased its military intelligence capabilities by sending observers into North Korea. Chai Chengwen, an expert on American military forces and a trusted member of the PLA's intelligence directorate, arrived in Pyongyang (P'yŏngyang) with more than a hundred Chinese operatives who were stationed in eight different places in the North Korean capital.[42] Later the same year, Zhou Enlai requested additional telephone lines between the two countries to better facilitate wartime communication.[43] Chai briefed Zhou on a regular basis.[44]

In April Kim Il-sung and Pak Il-u visited Stalin and discussed a possible national unification by force; as Kim put it, the idea was "to probe South Korea 'with the bayonet.'"[45] Although Stalin did not oppose the idea, the Soviet leader asked Kim to "make exact calculations about everything, and come back again with a specific plan."[46] In early May Kim went back to Moscow and "reported to Stalin that he was absolutely sure of the success of this venture." Stalin "expressed some doubt" but approved the North Korean's plan. Stalin also asked Kim to get Mao's approval.[47] On May 13 the North Korean delegation arrived in Beijing to brief Mao on Stalin's agreement with the Koreans. Even though the Chinese were concerned about possible foreign intervention, Mao agreed with Stalin's decision and supported Kim's military effort.[48] Kim and his delegation rushed back to Pyongyang, but they did not inform the Chinese of their operational details or of the planned date of attack.

On June 25, 1950, the NKPA launched a surprise attack on South Korea, commencing the Korean War. Mao was surprised, since neither the North Koreans nor the Russians had informed him of the attack schedule.[49] Taking a walk in the garden of his residence in Zhongnanhai[50] early that morning, Mao told his Russian translator Shi Zhe (1905–98) that "I have just heard the report from foreign broadcasting that a war has erupted in Korea."[51] Shi recalled: "Obviously, he [Mao] did not have prior knowledge of the outbreak of the Korean War on June 25." Three days later, Pyongyang sent a field-grade officer to Beijing, briefing the Chinese leaders on the situation in Korea. Mao told Shi that "they are our close neighbors. When they went to war, they did not consult with us. When they encounter troubles, they come to us."[52] Nevertheless, Beijing openly supported what the North Koreans called their national liberation. Unfortunately for Mao, two days after the Korean War broke out, the United States drastically changed its position on Taiwan.

## THE STRATEGIC SHIFT FROM TAIWAN TO KOREA

What really shocked Mao and the Chinese leaders was not the civil war in Korea, but the U.S. policy shift from a hands-off policy to a hands-on commitment to the safety of Taiwan.[53] On June 27, two days after the North Korean invasion of the South, and having reached a consensus with Congress and the Pentagon, President Harry S. Truman announced that the U.S. Seventh Fleet would be deployed in the Taiwan Strait to prevent a Chinese Communist attack on GMD-held Taiwan. However, David Finkelstein argues that Truman's order to the Seventh Fleet was not only to keep the Communists from invading Taiwan, but

also to keep the GMD from attacking the mainland, and thus widen-
ing the war beyond Korea. Finkelstein makes it clear that "Taiwan was
neutralized for purely military-strategic reasons. Washington could not
allow the island to be occupied by enemy forces while U.S. ground troops
were committed to a land war in Korea."[54] The Seventh Fleet's presence
in the Taiwan Strait marked a turning point in the cross-strait situation.
With Washington's direct involvement in the area, the PLA now faced
a serious challenge.[55]

The Chinese leaders considered the presence of the Seventh Fleet as
intervention into the Chinese Civil War as well as a direct threat to the
new republic. The Central Government held an emergency meeting in
Beijing at 5:00 PM on June 28, the day after Truman's order. Zhou Enlai
briefed the top officers and PLA high command. On the same day Zhou
denounced the move as "armed aggression against the territory of China
in total violation of the United Nations Charter." Zhou continued: "No
matter what obstructive action U.S. imperialists may take, the fact that
Taiwan is part of China will remain unchanged forever" and "all the
people of our country will certainly fight as one man and to the end to
liberate Taiwan."[56] Later the same day, at a government meeting, Mao
echoed this statement and denounced the U.S. action as an "open ex-
posure" of its "imperialist face."[57] On June 30 Zhou made it official that
the PLA would postpone its operations against Taiwan.[58] Beijing's point
of view can be best understood through one of Mao's speeches. Before
June 1950, liberating Taiwan was the PLA's primary task against GMD
forces. After June, Mao stated: "The American armed forces have occupied Taiwan, invaded Korea, and reached the boundary of northeast
China. Now we must fight against the American forces in both Korea
and Taiwan."[59]

Truman's order secured the ROC by preventing a well-planned PLA
landing on Taiwan by the end of June 1950, and on June 30 Zhou postponed the landing operation.[60] Later the CMC cabled Chen Yi (Ch'en
Yi, 1901–72), commander of the Third Field Army, that there would be
no attack on Taiwan until 1952 at the earliest. Chen also served as the
commander and political commissar of the East China Regional Command (ECRC) and had been preparing for the Taiwan landing. He was
appointed vice premier of the PRC and vice chairman of the CMC in

1954 and became one of the ten marshals in 1955 and foreign minister from 1958 to 1965.[61]

In November 1950, after Chinese troops had intervened in the Korean War, Mao ordered ECRC forces to put off all offshore offensive operations. To restrain the Tenth Army Group's desire to avenge its loss at Jinmen, the CMC issued another order to Ye Fei (1914–99), commander of the Tenth, that there would be no operations against Jinmen until the CPVF achieved a decisive victory in Korea.[62] These orders converted the coastal region from the front line of the Chinese Civil War to a rear area of the Korean War.

The U.S. president's order to the Seventh Fleet drew a line between the CCP and GMD forces in the Taiwan Strait. The U.S. policy transformed what had been part of the Chinese civil struggle into part of the global Cold War. The Truman legacy was keeping the military struggle "cold" in the Taiwan Strait and creating the foundation and opportunity for political, civil, and international competition in which both Chinese parties could find alternatives to the Civil War.[63] Nonetheless, Truman never intended to bring either Chinese party into the Korean conflict. Since late June, the NKPA had driven the ROK forces into a pocket around the southernmost city of Pusan. Here the UNF stopped the NKPA's offensive.

At that moment, the Chinese leaders had their own understanding of the Taiwan problem. Militarily, they believed that the Korean War caused the American military intervention in China. Even though Korea was apparently less important politically and emotionally to the Chinese than Taiwan, the war in Korea had brought the Seventh Fleet into the Taiwan Strait. The armed occupation of Taiwan appeared to be part of the U.S. war plan in Asia, a plan that aimed to destroy the one-year-old People's Republic in its cradle by attacking it from both the north and the south. The Chinese leaders thought that China must counter the coming invasion and defend itself, especially in the northeast, where it shared the border with Korea. Mao made it clear at the Politburo meeting on August 4, 1950, that "[we] will take back Taiwan, but now can't just sit by and watch Vietnam and Korea."[64]

Thus, in early July, Chinese leaders made a significant shift in strategy; instead of liberating Taiwan, they were now defending Manchuria.[65] An amphibious campaign against U.S. forces in the Taiwan Strait in the summer of 1950 could have been a military disaster for the PLA. MacArthur said that a Chinese Communist attack on Taiwan that summer would face "such a crushing defeat it would be one of the decisive battles of the world—a disaster so great it would rock Asia, and perhaps turn back Communism."[66] In late July, MacArthur led a high-level U.S. military delegation, including sixteen generals, on a visit to Taiwan in order to strengthen the island's defenses and bolster GMD morale. Subsequently, the United States organized a Military Advisory Assistant Group for Taiwan.[67] Before the end of August, the Truman administration had sent $140 million in military aid to Taiwan.[68] On September 18 the State Department approved the first military aid program to Taiwan, totaling $9.8 million and including weapons, ammunition, and equipment to guarantee the island's safety. Taiwan was now in a much better position to defend itself against a possible PLA attack. Even though MacArthur doubted that "the Red Chinese might commit themselves to such folly," he prayed "nightly—that they will."[69]

On July 1 and 2 Mao; Zhou; Liu Shaoqi, vice president of the PRC; Zhu De, commander in chief of the PLA; and other top leaders met and discussed the military situation in Korea. Zhu was one of the founders of the CCP armed forces in the 1927 and had been commander of the Red Army's Fourth Army in 1928 with Mao as his political commissar. After Zhu became commander in chief of the Chinese Red Army in 1930, he and Mao became so closely connected that to the Chinese peasant farmers they were known collectively as "Zhu-Mao." William Wei describes Zhu as "a brilliant military tactician who was known as the Chinese Napoleon."[70] After the founding of the PRC in 1949, Zhu continued to serve as commander in chief of PLA and vice chairman of the CMC. Probably because he never questioned Mao's leadership and decisions, Zhu became the first vice president of the PRC in 1954 and the first marshal of the PLA in 1955.[71]

After the second meeting of the CCP high command, Zhou briefed Russian Ambassador Nikolai Rochshin in Beijing the same evening. According to Rochshin's subsequent telegram to Moscow, Chinese leaders were not optimistic about Kim's advance in South Korea. They were worried about U.S. military intervention and a possible U.S. landing in the rear area of the NKPA.[72] They believed it necessary to bolster their forces in northeast China, along the Chinese–North Korean border. It was only after the Korean War broke out that China's military began to make significant strategic changes, shifting from a focus on attacking GMD-held islands to protecting the mainland. The concept of national defense against a possible Western invasion became the cornerstone of China's new strategic culture and its military modernization in the 1950s.

On July 7, when the United Nations adopted a resolution calling for all possible means to aid the ROK, the Truman administration announced it was sending in U.S. forces. The CMC, at Mao's suggestion, held the first national defense meeting in Beijing. Chaired by Zhou, the meeting was also attended by Zhu, Nie, Lin, Luo Ronghuan (Lo Junghuan, 1902–63), and chiefs of all the services and heads of all the general departments of the PLA. Luo had served as political commissar of the Fourth Field Army in the Chinese Civil War and became director of the General Political Department of the PLA after the founding of the PRC. The high command decided to establish the Northeast Border Defense Army (NEBDA) to forestall any emergency situation that might arise along the Chinese-Korean border.[73] The NEBDA would include the Thirty-Eighth, Thirty-Ninth, and Fortieth Armies, three strategic reserve armies in central China; and the Forty-Second Army, in the northeast. Zhou submitted the meeting minutes to Mao, including NEBDA commanding officer candidates, organizational structure, mobilization, deployment, logistics, and transportation. Mao approved the minutes and wrote on Zhou's report: "Agree; carry it out accordingly."[74]

On July 10, after Mao's approval, the CMC named Su Yu as the NEBDA commander and political commissar and made Xiao Jinguang, chief of the PLA Navy, its deputy commander, even though Mao's best generals were ready for an amphibious attack on Taiwan instead.[75] On July 13 the CMC issued the "Decision on Northeastern Border Defense" to all PLA general departments and army headquarters. The high command began transporting its best troops from central China to the northeast. By late July the Thirty-Eighth, Thirty-Ninth, Fortieth, and Forty-Second Armies and 1st, 2nd, and 8th Artillery Divisions, totaling 260,000 troops, had arrived in Manchuria under the NEBDA command.[76]

The high command, however, did not carry out its plan through the commanding structure of the NEBDA in July. In 1950 the PLA had not yet completed its transformation from a armed force rebelling against the state government of the GMD in 1946–49 to a national defense force for the new CCP state. Two interrelated problems arose: the level of the NEBDA command and the personalized chain of command within the command HQs. First of all, the NEBDA command was established at an army group level, lower than the high command had originally envisioned. In 1949–50, the PLA had a centralized chain of command with four levels. The CMC (level 1) was at the top of this military hierarchy, directly under Mao. The second level below the CMC were the four field armies under the command of marshals such as Peng Dehuai, Lin Biao, and Chen Yi, who in turn commanded the fifteen army groups. The third level was the army group commands: fifteen army groups commanded the fifty-seven infantry armies. The fourth level consisted of the armies, commanding more than two hundred divisions.[77]

In early July the CMC had considered a field army commanding structure, the second-level command, for the NEBDA—including army groups, many armies, and multiple services—directly under the CMC. That is why the CMC had appointed Su and Xiao, field-army level commanding officers, as commander and deputy commander of the NEBDA. But, for different reasons, neither reported to his position. Instead, Su was admitted to a hospital for a health problem, and Xiao was busy with the newly established PLA Navy (PLAN).[78] In 1950 the CPVF lacked a command-and-control doctrine to meet the requirements of modern warfare. The highest-ranking officer among the commanders who had reported was Deng Hua, commander of the Fifteenth Army Group, who had recently seized Hainan Island. Thus the NEBDA was downgraded to the army group level (level 3) under Gao Gang (Kao Kang, 1902–54), commander and political commissar of the PLA Northeast Military Region (level 2), rather than the CMC. Gao also served as vice president of the PRC and chairman of the CCP Northeast Bureau. On August 5 Mao ordered him to mobilize the NEBDA.[79]

Another problem was the last-minute switch of leading commanders for the NEBDA. The PLA command structure often favored personal relationships and political orthodoxy at the expense of ability and performance. A commander usually preferred to work with officers and staff that he knew. The sudden shift of strategy and the deployment of a large force from the south to the north put overwhelming pressure on Deng. As an army group commander, he rose to the challenges of increased responsibility and unexpected problems. However, he wanted to avoid the difficulty of working with an unfamiliar headquarters staff. In July, when the NEBDA was established, its Thirty-Eighth, Thirty-Ninth, and Fortieth Armies were under the command of the Thirteenth Army Group. The high command wanted to send its best officers to Korea, and for this reason they transferred Deng from the Fifteenth to the Thirteenth Army Group. Huang Yongsheng, commander of the Thirteenth Army Group, became commander of the Fifteenth Army Group, staying in Guangzhou, in southern Guangdong Province.[80] After accepting his new position, Deng asked the high command to switch HQs between the two army groups: his HQ of the Fifteenth would become the HQ of the Thirteenth. On July 15 the CMC approved Deng's request, and on July 25 the new Thirteenth Army Group HQ, now Deng's staff, moved to northeast China with him.[81] Throughout the summer, confusion and complaints occurred as a result of officer transfers, personnel replacement, headquarters relocations, and job changes.[82]

Mao later explained his strategic shift from the south to the north and, in his speech at the Chinese People's Political Consultative Conference (CPPCC) on October 23, 1951, justified fighting against the United States: "Chinese people would not have fought America if the U.S. forces had not occupied our territory of Taiwan, not invaded the DPRK, and not brought the war to our Northeastern border."[83] Historians in China agree that, until July 1950, none of these military preparations, including the subsequent organization of the CPVF, would have been construed as anything but strategically defensive. The Chinese defense strategy can be best understood in historical terms by focusing on three elements underlying Mao's intentions: the need for political legitimacy for the new regime, a global political context formed to a large extent by the United States and the Soviet Union in the Cold War, and the military resources available for the national defense at that moment.

## PREPARING TO INTERVENE IN KOREA

In July and August 1950, Kim's army stalled at the Pusan Perimeter. After stopping North Korea's offensive, the UNF were preparing a large-scale counteroffensive. Mao worried about whether the PLA's border defenses could stop the U.S. invasion of Manchuria that seemed likely to come. The Chinese army seemed no match for the U.S. armed forces, which formed 90 percent of the UNF and had air, naval, and ground firepower that were vastly superior to those of the Chinese. The PLA was an "anachronism," consisting of irregular "foot soldiers" without air and naval weaponry.[84] Its guerrilla command structure was "rudimentary," and its equipment was a "hodgepodge" and largely "obsolete."[85] Unlike the battles fought against GMD in the 1940s, in this war the PLA would have to stop the most powerful army in the world. Failing to defend the country's northeastern border would end the CCP's twenty-eight-year streak of military victories and might even cost the Communists control of China.

Mao had his own ideas about how to overcome the technology gap between the Chinese and the American forces. He favored taking the fight to the enemy rather than a reactive strategy. Instead of waiting for U.S. forces to invade Manchuria from North Korea, Mao decided to fight them in Korea and prevent an invasion of China. The new strategy meant defending China in Korea. This proactive form of defense would stop the enemy outside the Chinese borders and avoid a major confrontation on the mainland. It made sense to the Chinese generals: no matter what the outcome of their fighting in Korea was, they would not be in danger of losing their country.

On October 14, 1950, Mao explained the new strategy in a telegram to Zhou Enlai, who was meeting Stalin in Moscow. Omitted in the reprinted text of Mao's telegram are two important sentences: "We do it in such way to advance the national defense line from the Yalu River to the line of the Tokchon-Nyongwon and areas south of it. This is absolutely possible and beneficial [to us]."[86] Mao considered the UNF northward advance an immediate threat to China's national security, and Chinese intervention was necessary to prevent any UNF invasion of China. Thus the Chinese defense line was more than a hundred miles southeast of the

Yalu River in North Korea. Mao's plan changed the approach of China's national defense from fighting an enemy force along the Chinese border to fighting a potential invader in a neighboring country. However, Mao's proactive defense would become more offensive and aggressive in nature. The new strategy led to the Chinese intervention in the Korean War in 1950 and later interventions in the Vietnam War in the 1960s.

According to Mao's Cold War theory, there would be a clash between the China and the United States sooner or later. In the 1950s the United States intruded in Taiwan and threatened China's security in three areas: Korea, Vietnam, and the Taiwan Straits. Concerned with the geopolitical, regional economic, and transportation issues involved in these three conflicts, the Chinese Communists believed America's intervention in Korea was the most critical threat to their new regime. Mao described American involvement in the three areas as three knives threatening China: America in Korea was like a knife over her head, in Taiwan was another at her waist, and in Vietnam was third at her feet.[87] Thus Korea, instead of Taiwan, was considered the most immediate threat. Moreover, China was much more likely to win in Korea since it had a better chance of victory in a land war than with an amphibious landing on Taiwan. Later, Zhou explained this at a CPVF commanders meeting:

> It is inevitable for us to have a showdown with the American imperialists. The question is how to choose a place for this fight. Although it is certainly up to the imperialists, we do have a choice at the moment. When the imperialists choose Korea as the battleground, it favors us. So we decided to resist America and aid Korea. Let's think about these three possible battlegrounds. No matter which part of the war you're talking about, you can see the differences. If the fighting had taken place in Vietnam, to say nothing of a naval war over the offshore islands, it could have been much more difficult than our fighting here [in Korea].[88]

China began planning an intervention to "assist the Korean people."[89] On August 4, 1950, after the UNF had halted North Korea's invasion, Mao called a Politburo meeting to discuss preparations for China's possible involvement in the conflict. Mao told the top leaders that the American imperialists would be even more aggressive and threatening to China if they won the war; thus, China must aid Korea. The Chinese leaders could, of course, decide the timing of their intervention.[90] The troops in the four NEBDA armies would "change to volunteer uniform and use volunteer flags" to assist the Korean people and participate in the Korean War. The next day, Mao ordered the NEBDA troops "to get ready for fighting in early September" in Korea.[91] At a mid-August meeting, most of the NEBDA commanders said they believed that the best time for the Chinese to take action was after the UNF had crossed the 38th Parallel, but before they had "established a foothold" in North Korea.[92]

From that point on, China began mobilizing for an intervention in Korea, although the high command realized that four armies were not enough men. In August, following Mao's instructions, Zhou chaired several CMC meetings on how to transport more troops from the southeast to Manchuria. On September 6 the CMC transferred the Fiftieth Army from central Hubei (Hupei) Province to northeast China, giving the NEBDA a fifth army. In the meantime, the CMC established new units with modern technology for the NEBDA, including four air force regiments, three tank brigades, and eighteen antiaircraft artillery regiments.[93] According to CMC decisions, the Ninth Army Group, the main strength of the Third Field Army, which had been prepared for invading Taiwan, would serve as the second wave of the NEBDA. The army group, which included three infantry armies, was transferred in August from Fujian (Fukien) and Zhejiang (Chekiang) Provinces on China's southeastern coast to the Shandong (Shantung) Peninsula, where the forces could be quickly moved by sea to northeastern China. The Nineteenth Army Group of the First Field Army would move by rail from central China, to serve as the NEBDA's third wave (map 1.2).

All these movements reveal an important strategic shift on the part of the PLA high command, moving from a defensive position to an intervention. Mao had determined in early August to send troops to Korea. He had confidently explained his thinking on how to defeat U.S. forces in Korea to national leaders at the Ninth Plenary of the Central Government of the PRC on September 5: "You [the United States] fight in your way, while I fight in mine. You can use nuclear bombs, and I use my hand grenades. I will find your weakness and chase you all away. Eventually, I can defeat you."[94] Mao's optimistic attitude about a potential war against the United States had a contagious effect on Chinese political and military leaders during early stages of the Korean War.[95]

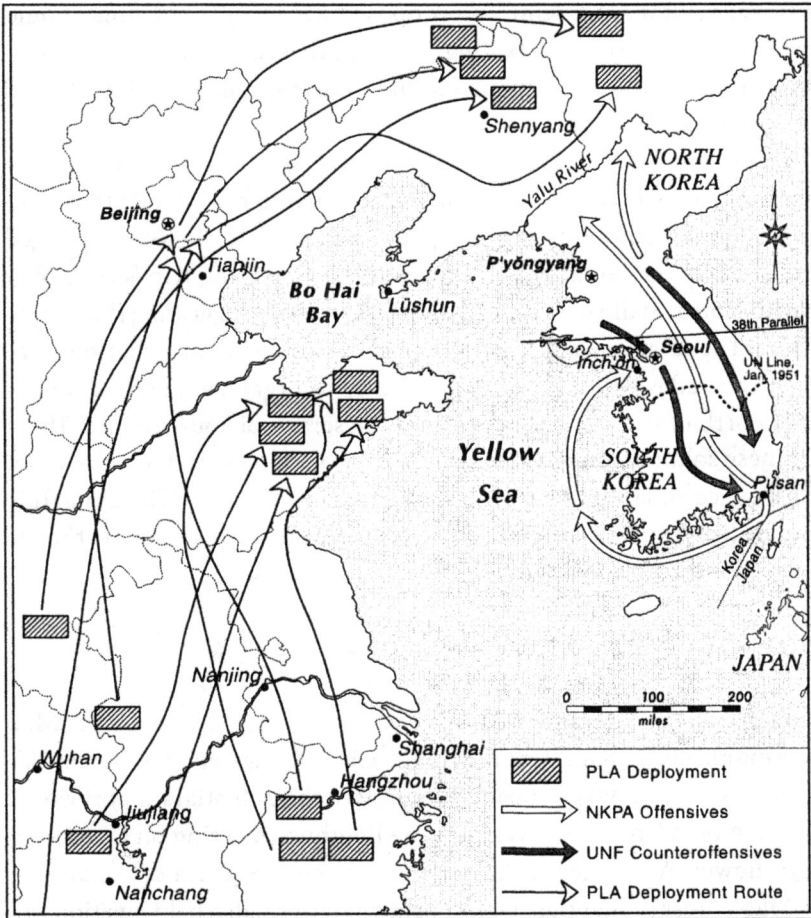

Map 1.2. PLA Deployment, June–October 1950

On September 15 MacArthur successfully landed troops in Inchon, which rapidly changed the military situation in Korea. Informed by periodic reports from his agents in Pyongyang, Mao watched these developments with growing dismay. After the UNF landed at Inchon, Kim's army did not respond quickly enough to prevent Seoul from being retaken in late September. Nor could Kim halt the collapse and retreat of the NKPA back across the 38th Parallel. Facing a military disaster, Kim quickly sent representatives to Moscow and Beijing asking for additional military aid. Kim also proposed to Stalin that China should send troops to Korea. In Beijing, among other matters, the North Koreans requested more equipment and ammunition, and Zhou agreed the same day.[96]

On October 1 the ROK 3rd Division crossed the 38th Parallel, the first unit of the UNF to enter North Korea in order to liberate the country from the Communist regime. The goal of the UNF in Korea changed from saving the South Korean government to ending Kim's control of North Korea. Stalin telegraphed Mao on October 1 suggesting that China "should send at once at least five to six divisions . . . so that our Korean comrades will have an opportunity to organize a defense of the area north of the 38th Parallel under the screen of your troops." These Chinese soldiers could be "considered as volunteers" and remain under Chinese command.[97] Mao's foresight in establishing the NEBDA in July and decision to concentrate five armies in Manchuria in August made such an intervention possible.

### THE FINAL DECISION

Chinese leaders began debating sending their troops to Korea. Mao communicated to Kim Il-sung through Chai Chengwen that this consideration was under way, probably hoping that the potential support would stiffen North Korea's resolve.[98] At the Politburo meeting on October 2, 1950, however, divergent views were expressed. The Politburo members, as Mao's most influential and important advisers, also held positions on the CMC. Most of the members expressed deep reservations about any military intervention in the Korean War. Gao opposed the idea, arguing that the CCP had just won the Civil War, and the newly founded republic could not afford another major war, this time against the United States. Nie agreed with Gao: "It would be better not to fight this war as long as it was not absolutely necessary."[99] Others at the meeting also worried about the poorly equipped PLA's ability to stop the superior U.S. forces in Korea. The military leaders knew that, even though they had won the Civil War, the PLA was merely a revolutionized peasant army—it was not yet a professional, modern force. Lin, vice chairman of the CMC, feared China's ground forces would suffer very heavy losses and suggested that instead they should "strengthen the border defense" and "assist the North Koreans in fighting a guerrilla war." Lin surprised all the other military leaders, including Mao, when he declined Mao's request to command all Chinese forces in Korea.[100]

China's final decision to enter the Korean War was not an easy and rapid process, particularly since Mao found it difficult to get other Chinese leaders on board. During those days in early October, as he pondered whether China should commit forces to Korea, Mao suffered from persistent insomnia and other symptoms. The chairman confessed to his comrades that dispatching Chinese troops to the Korean War was one of the most difficult decisions in his political life.[101] Mao believed that China had no alternative to military intervention. He recognized the UNF advance into North Korea as a direct, immediate threat, and he also took into account the Sino-Soviet relationship.[102] First of all, Mao worried about Stalin's distrust of the CCP. He also feared that the Soviet Union might intend to isolate China from the Socialist and Communist camp. Finally, Mao wanted to prevent the Soviet Union from sending Russian troops into northeast China.[103]

Since the Politburo did not reach any decision on military intervention on October 2, Mao called an expanded meeting of the group two days later to break the deadlock. Twenty-two political and military leaders attended the second meeting, which continued on October 5. To bring in more political supporters from outside Beijing, Mao sent an airplane to Xi'an (Si'an), in northwestern Shaanxi (Shensi) Province, to bring Peng Dehuai, the CMC vice chairman and commander of the PLA Northwest Military Region, to the enlarged meeting. Peng arrived at about 4:00 PM on October 4, when the participants were discussing the disadvantages of sending troops to Korea. Mao was not happy about the "reasonable and logical" discussions of the majority, and said: "When we, however, are standing on the side, just watching other people who are undergoing a national crisis, we feel terrible inside, no matter what we may pretend."[104] Peng expressed no opinions during the afternoon discussions.

With all these issues on the table, Peng could not sleep that night. As one of the PLA's most dedicated and experienced generals, he had worked closely with Mao since the Long March (1934–35). His revolutionary fervor and military aggressiveness had gained Mao's attention and favor during the Anti-Japanese War (1937–45). With Zhu, he was one of the PLA's most experienced marshals. At the age of fifty-one, Peng was facing the toughest decision in his military and political career, and he could not enjoy the soft bed in the Beijing Hotel; even after moving to the floor, he still could not fall asleep. Mao's words were reverberating through his mind, and he understood why Mao needed him at the meeting.[105] Early in the morning of October 5, Mao sent Deng Xiaoping, secretary general of the CCP Central Secretariat, to the Beijing Hotel, inviting Peng to discuss matters with Mao at Zhongnanhai.[106]

When the Politburo meeting continued its discussions in the afternoon of October 5, Peng strongly supported Mao's idea, arguing that "sending the troops to aid Korea is necessary. . . . If the American military places itself along the Yalu River and in Taiwan, it could find an excuse anytime it wants to launch an invasion."[107] Many participants at the meeting were impressed by Peng's firm stand.[108] His support convinced the majority to agree to send troops—which would be known as the CPVF—to aid North Korea and resist American aggression. By the end of the day, the Politburo had decided that China would send troops to Korea.[109]

On October 8 Mao issued orders reorganizing the NEBDA into the CPVF and appointing Peng as its commander in chief and political commissar.[110] According to these orders, the CPVF would include four infantry armies and three artillery divisions, nearly 260,000 men. At a meeting with Kim Il-sung in Beijing in October 1970, Mao recalled China's defense mobilization in July and told the North Korean leader that Chinese forces would have had a greater advantage "if we could have had seven armies rather than five armies."[111] It seemed to Mao that the more armies China sent to Korea, the better chance they had to win the war. Despite the name, the troops of the CPVF were simply the same Chinese troops that had been assigned to the Korean border. The CPVF command was actually the PLA's front command. Peng once joked about being a "volunteer" in the CPVF HQ on the Korean front. "Volunteers, indeed," he said. "I am not a volunteer . . . it is my chief who sent me here."[112]

## MOBILIZATION, TRAINING, AND
## LOGISTICS FOR INTERVENTION

Mao sent Zhou on an emergency trip to Moscow on October 8 to request air support for the Chinese troops in North Korea. Such operations might include attacks on American air bases in Korea, but not attacks on U.S. bases in Japan. The Chinese leaders were correct about identifying UNF air attacks as their most serious operational problem. The nature of Soviet air support dominated Zhou's negotiations with Stalin, and these unsuccessful talks, interpreted for Mao by Zhou in a series of messages to Beijing, almost brought Chinese military intervention in Korea to a halt. Stalin promised only to provide interceptors, a ground-based radar system, and several regiments of antiaircraft artillery for the defense of Manchuria, including the air space above the Yalu River. He refused to provide air cover for the Chinese divisions fighting in Korea.[113]

Nevertheless, Stalin promised to accelerate the creation of the PLA air force, and Chinese pilots were already being trained to fly Russian jet fighters, MiG-15s, and Soviet jet light bombers. Not only would the Russians provide aircraft, but they also would provide material support to establish Communist air bases in Korea. During their ten-day negotiations, Zhou also requested that Stalin modernize and standardize PLA weapons, from small arms to heavy artillery, and transfer thousands of trucks (and some trained Russian drivers) to the PLA for logistical operations on both sides of the Yalu River. Meanwhile, Mao conferred with his inner circle on October 12–13; on October 14 he issued orders that the CPVF preparations should continue.[114]

The PLA had no difficulty sending a large infantry force to Korea in late 1950. In May of that year, the PLA had a total of 5.5 million troops, including an infantry force of 5.4 million, 38,000 in the Navy, and 57,000 in the Air Force. It planned a postwar demobilization to ease the heavy financial burden on the new republic. On June 30 the CMC and State Council jointly issued the "Resolution on the Task of Demobilization," which called for retiring a million troops in 1950. The Central Committee of Demobilization opened up more than one thousand Veteran Administration (VA) offices across the country in July to arrange for the Civil War veterans' retirement. By mid-October, just before China dispatched the CPVF to Korea, the PLA had been reduced to 4.6 million troops.[115] However, planned operations in Korea soon suspended further demobilization. Many VA offices changed their signs from "Veteran Administration Office" to "New Recruitment Office," using the same staff at the same location.[116]

Some officers recall the mobilization for the Korean War as a much easier task than demobilizing after the Civil War.[117] Chinese historians believe that the military victory in 1949, and the new order in Chinese society, earned the PLA support for its Korean War mobilization in 1950.[118] Their writings show that this revolutionary enthusiasm produced more peasant volunteers than the recruitment officials could handle. In some cases, officials had to send thousands of would-be soldiers home.[119] Why did millions of young peasants volunteer to go to Korea and fight against America? Several economic and political factors played important roles in their motivation. Enlisting meant economic security and new opportunity under the Communist regime. After eight years of the Anti-Japanese War and three years of the Chinese Civil War, many rural youths had nothing left to lose and everything to gain in 1950 by joining the CPVF or PLA.[120]

Serving in the Communist forces thus became economically practical in both rural and urban areas after the Chinese Civil War. The PLA was the only social institution that had the resources and opportunity to rebuild, especially in cities. The army played a major role in establishing a new order in urban areas. From 1948 to 1953, the PLA established military administrations as a postwar system of urban control and management in all cities and sent tens of thousands of officers to cities in order to take over legislative, executive, and judicial systems, while generals and marshals served as mayors. Troops replaced city law enforcement and security forces; they also took over banks, utility companies, public transportation, and school districts, in addition to controlling cities' food, water, fuel, and other supplies. Serving in the CPVF and PLA could provide economic security and a valuable revolutionary identity.

Nevertheless, after a large number of new recruits joined the army, the high command faced a new task: to motivate the troops to fight a war in Korea. The NEBDA (and later CPVF) HQ prepared troops in three ways before they entered Korea. First, NEBDA or CPVF units were given political education. Since mid-August 1950, the NEBDA had been working on the "psychological condition of the soldiers who were preparing for the war."[121] After a two-month political education course, Du Ping (1908–99), director of the NEBDA Political Department, reported that approximately 50 percent of the soldiers were ready "with a positive attitude toward participating in the Korean War." Most of them were Civil War veterans and CCP members. They even "submitted written statements asking to fight the American troops and help the Korean people" before the CCP Politburo's decision to participate in the war. About 30 percent of the troops were what Du called "intermediate elements," who would fight as ordered and did not care if there was a war or not. The last 20 percent of the soldiers were "in an unsettled state of mind."[122] In Zhou's words, these soldiers were afraid of fighting the U.S. troops, naming the bridge over the Yalu River the "gate of hell" and complaining that "to resist America and aid Korea is like poking our nose into other people's business" and would only "draw fire against ourselves."[123]

The second part of the NEBDA's preparation for war was combat training and upgrading technical support. In September, for example, Wang Yang (b. 1920), commander of the 116th Division, Thirty-Ninth Army, organized an intensive training program with two phases. A new division commander at the age of thirty, Wang first focused on exercises in small-group combat tactics, including training in the use of small arms, antitank and anti-aircraft weapons, and demolition material.[124] The second phase dealt with operational tactics, an area new to many Civil War veterans. Wang recalled that two of his battalions participated in one of the group attack exercises on a small hill. The battalion commanders felt crowded when hundreds of soldiers charged the same point at once. The division HQ also brought in WWII veterans, who had fought alongside U.S. troops in Myanmar, to describe the training and characteristics of U.S. soldiers.[125] On October 15 Wang's division became part of the CPVF. After its reorganization, a rocket artillery battalion and an antitank battalion were added to the division. In addition, the 116th Division established an HQ security battalion, an antiaircraft artillery battalion, and a medical battalion. The Chinese operated ably with what they produced, and they saw no need for major institutional changes for a foreign war. Whatever new technologies became available or imported from the Soviet Union were readily integrated into existing structures, subject to the Chinese system in 1950–51.

The third part of the preparation effort was the development of an army logistics system. During the Civil War, local guerrilla commands had supplied the regular troops. On July 26 the CMC ordered the Northeast Military Region to establish a new logistics HQ to supply the NEBDA in Manchuria.[126] The newly established Northeast Logistics HQ began operating in early August, creating departments for weaponry and ammunition, finance, transportation, medical services, housing, and personnel in northeast China. On August 31 the Northeast Logistics HQ expanded into three separate HQs, totaling 7,800 officers and staff. By the end of September they had supplied the NEBDA with 1,600 tons of ammunition, 10,000 barrels of gasoline, 1,054 trucks, and 995 artillery pieces, and stocked up to twenty million rounds of ammunition, 840,000 artillery shells, and 300,000 hand grenades. By the end of October these HQs had also supplied 16,000 tons of grain, 400 tons of cooking oil, 920 tons of dry and canned food, 340,000 winter coats, and 360,000 winter boots to the CPVF troops.[127]

Another effort the NEBDA made was to standardize its weaponry to ease supply problems. Lacking enough Soviet weaponry for all its five armies, it standardized one weaponry system for each army. In mid-August, for example, its Thirty-Eighth Army began replacing all its rifles and guns with Japanese-made weapons, while the Fortieth Army used mostly American-made weapons captured from GMD troops.[128] Standardized weapons and integrated training programs raised the level of proficiency across the army. To offset a shortage of automatic weapons, soldiers learned to recover automatic firearms that might be dropped when their comrades were killed. The success of the CPVF's early offensive campaigns proved that the new standardized weapon system had increased the Chinese combat effectiveness on the battleground. Training and war preparations were crucial for the Chinese infantry to successfully engage their enemy in the Korean War.

On October 25, 1950, the Chinese government announced that it would send the CPVF to Korea to fight the WRUSAK.[129] In fact, CPVF troops had already crossed the Yalu River and entered North Korea on October 19. China surprised the UNF Command when its troops launched a massive offensive south of the Yalu in early November. At home, the CCP rallied the nationwide "Great Movement for Resisting America and Aiding Korea," to mobilize the entire country for the war effort. Ultimately, China would send more than three million troops to Korea. Its economy was converted into a war economy. During the war, the Chinese government transported into Korea a total of 5.6 million tons of goods and supplies. Between 1950 and 1953, China's military spending represented up to 38 percent of the country's annual budget.[130] The Korean War was the first time that Chinese armed forces engaged in large-scale military operations outside of China. Except for the thinly disguised title of "volunteers," the Chinese military fully mobilized for war against one of the best militaries in the world.

# TWO

# From the Yalu to Seoul

AT 6:00 PM ON OCTOBER 16, 1950, THE RECONNAISSANCE TEAM of the Forty-Second Army of the CPVF crossed the Ji'an (Chi-an) Bridge and advanced sixty miles into Korea before the following dawn. That night, the army's 370th Regiment of the 124th Division moved across the Yalu River at Ji'an-Manpu, marching about twenty miles. These were the first Chinese combat troops to enter North Korea.[1] However, the following afternoon they received a message: "Stop advance. Wait for order."[2] They halted until 9:00 PM the next day, when Mao Zedong ordered all four infantry armies and three artillery divisions of the CPVF to secretly begin crossing the Yalu on the evening of October 19, the day the Chinese army officially entered the Korean War. At 5:30 PM on the nineteenth, the advance guard of the CPVF Fortieth Army crossed the river by a train traveling over the Andong (Antung; today's Dandong)–Sinuiju Bridge and then marched south to meet forward elements of the U.S. I Corps on October 25.[3] All the CPVF troops had removed any Chinese army insignias from their uniforms in order to maintain their claim of being volunteers.

By the end of October, two more armies joined the CPVF's first wave, bringing the total to eighteen infantry divisions, three artillery divisions, and supporting troops—in all, approximately 300,000 men. All these troops were in Korea by early November.[4] By late November, Chinese forces in Korea totaled thirty-three divisions, or nearly 450,000 men, and this was only the beginning of the Chinese involvement. This rapid deployment was accomplished without alerting the UNF Command. The Chinese high command was hoping its greater numbers, coupled with the element of surprise, would offset its inferior equipment and technology. It seemed rational to the Chinese that a larger force would be a decisive factor, giving them victory.[5]

China had shocked the UNF Command when it launched the first of its massive offensive campaigns south of the Yalu in early November. MacArthur reported to Washington that the United States now faced "an entirely new war" in Korea.[6] In early December the CPVF's second offensive pushed the battle line back to the 38th Parallel and Communist forces recaptured Pyongyang (P'yŏngyang), North Korea's capital. By early January 1951, in a third campaign, the CPVF had crossed the 38th Parallel into South Korea; captured Seoul, South Korea's capital; and pushed the UNF down to the 37th Parallel.[7] Chinese strategy and tactics proved effective for the CPVF's first three offensives, during the first three months. Chinese morale soared, and at that point Chinese support for the war was at its strongest. When the CPVF launched its fourth offensive, in late January, many people in China expected that the CPVF would soon achieve its goal: driving the UNF out of the Korean Peninsula. By the end of the fourth offensive, in the spring of 1951, nearly 950,000 Chinese troops were serving in Korea, including forty-two infantry divisions, eight artillery divisions, four anti-aircraft artillery (AAA) divisions, and four tank regiments.[8]

These first four offensives, between November 1950 and April 1951, shaped the Fifth Offensive Campaign, also known as the Spring Offensive. This chapter examines the CPVF's plans and preparations, as well as campaigns' organization and execution, tactical decisions, communications, combat problem solving, and performance evaluation. The different personalities of CPVF top commanders such as Peng Dehuai, Deng Hua, and Hong Xuezhi played an important role both in Beijing and on the Korean front, and in CPVF General HQ and army group commands. This chapter also discusses tactics developed by the PLA in the Chinese Civil War that it was now applying to the Korean War. These tactics included massing its forces to outnumber the UNF whenever possible, encircling the UNF through flanking operations, and achieving surprise through night operations and close-range engagements to negate the usually superior UNF firepower.

## A DEFENSIVE LINE AND CHAIN OF COMMAND

Before the Chinese armies entered Korea, Mao had worked out a defensive plan to position the CPVF around the 40th Parallel between the Yalu River and Pyongyang, and to then wait for the UNF to advance. Mao asked Peng "to set up two or three defensive lines . . . in the areas north of the Pyongyang-Wonsan railroad and south of the Tokchon [Teokcheon]–Yongwon [Yeongwon or Nyongwon] highway." The chairman continued: "During the next six months, our troops will not initiate an attack on Pyongyang or Wonsan if the enemy remains in those two places and does not take the offensive."[9] This initial strategy would build a defensive line in the mountainous areas north of Pyongyang and Wonsan, more than 120 miles south of the Yalu, to stop any invading force. It would be necessary for the CPVF troops to travel between 120 and 180 miles southeast to reach these defensive positions. The deeper into Korea the CPVF reached, the better it was for China's security, in Mao's view. A superior number of Chinese troops could weaken the UNF and then, six months later, the Chinese might have a chance to strike back.

To carry out Mao's defensive strategy, Peng rushed from Beijing to Manchuria, meeting with army and division commanders in Shenyang on October 14. He made it clear that the CPVF's task was to protect North Korea by taking up positions in the north that had not been occupied by the UNF: "Korea is a narrow peninsula, and the enemy currently has some advantages. Therefore, [we should] combine positional warfare and mobile warfare. If the enemy moves, we should stop them and make sure they won't advance. If [we] find their weakness, attack immediately, cut through into their rear, and eliminate the enemy. Our task is to defend the land."[10] The CPVF chief laid out defensive tactics, reminiscent of trench warfare, at the meeting: "Our defense positions should be constructed in depth. Each squad will be divided into three or four groups and will dig several bunkers, spreading out in the shape of a plum blossom to form crossfires at a distance of twenty or thirty meters [roughly twenty or thirty yards] in order to support each other."[11] Peng believed that these efforts would reduce CPVF casualties during UNF air raids and artillery bombardments. At the meeting he also ordered each army to send reconnaissance teams to Korea on October 16, since the chief lacked reliable intelligence on the battleground. After the Shenyang meeting, all army commanders returned to their HQs immediately and made their operational and reconnaissance plans.[12]

On October 18 Mao decided that all CPVF troops should immediately "enter northern Korea for war operations." He instructed the CPVF commanders that "in order to maintain strict secrecy, the troops should start to cross the river after dusk every day and stop [crossing] at 4:00 the next morning; by 5:00 AM all troops should be completely under cover, which should be carefully checked."[13] On October 19 at Andong, Peng passed on Mao's order to the army commanders and finalized the armies' defensive positions in North Korea. Peng said: "To stabilize the war situation and to guarantee that the NKPA can collect and reassemble their troops, we must organize our defense in the favorable positions north of the indented part of the Korean peninsula." Peng ordered the commanders "to reach the positions on time, construct your defense works immediately, and send out reconnaissance teams to watch the enemy movements."[14] After the meeting, all the army commanders returned to their HQs and held divisional commander meetings to carry out Peng's orders. These were the last commander meetings before the troops left China for Korea.[15]

The CPVF chain of command took shape in October 1950 and continued throughout the Korean War, while Mao exercised operational control from Beijing (chart 2.1). At the center of operations, Mao made strategic decisions and campaign plans, using a stream of telegrams to the CPVF General HQ. Peng and his staff implemented Mao's plans by tailoring each operation, organizing forces, and executing battle plans, and they sent Mao daily reports from the front. Peng issued detailed orders to the army commanders; later, during the Fifth Offensive Campaign, a link was established between the CPVF HQ and the army commands. When army commanders later ordered their divisions to accomplish their missions, the new chain of command proved to be less institutional in nature, and more personality driven. On several occasions during the Fifth Offensive Campaign in the spring of 1951 an individual commander lost contact with his superior officer, and the chain of command was broken.

**Chinese People's Volunteer Force**
Commander & Political Commissar:
Peng Dehuai

**NE Military Region Logistics Office**
Chief: Zhang Mingyuan

**13th Army Group**
Commander: Deng Hua
Political Commissar: Lai Chuanzhu
Deputy Commanders: Hong Xuezhi/Han Xianchu
Chief of Staff: Xie Fang

**50th Army**
Com.: Zeng Zesheng
Pol. Com.: Xu Wenlie
Chief of Staff: Shu Xing

**66th Army**
Com.: Xaio Xinhuai
Pol. Com.: Wang Zifeng
Dep. Com.: Chen Fangren

**Artillery Command**
Commander: Kuang Yumin

**Engineer Command**
Commander: Chen Zhengfeng

148th Division

149th Division

150th Division

196th Division

197th Division

198th Division

**38th Army**
Commander: Liang Xingchu
Pol. Com.: Liu Xiyuan
Dep. Com.: Jiang Yonghui
Chief of Staff: Guan Songtao

**39th Army**
Commander: Wu Xinquan
Pol. Com.: Xu Binzhou
Dep. Com.: Tan Youlin
Chief of Staff: Sehn Qixian

**40th Army**
Commander: Wen Yucheng
Pol. Com.: Yuan Shengping
Dep. Com.: Cai Zhengguo
Chief of Staff: Ning Xianwen

**42nd Army**
Commander: Wu Ruilin
Pol. Com.: Zhou Biao
Dep. Com.: Hu Jicheng
Dep. Pol. Com.: Guo Chengzhu
Chief of Staff: Liao Zhongfu

112 Division
Com.: Yang Dayi

113 Division
Com.: Jiang Chao

114 Division
Com.: Zhai Zhongyu

115 Division
Com.: Wang Fuzhi

116 Division
Com.: Wang Yang

117 Division
Com.: Zhang Jiecheng

118 Division
Com.: Deng Yue

119 Division
Com.: Xue Guofu

120 Division
Com.: Luo Chunsheng

124 Division
Com.: Su Kezhi

125 Division
Com.: Wang Daoquan

126 Division
Com.: Huang Jingyao

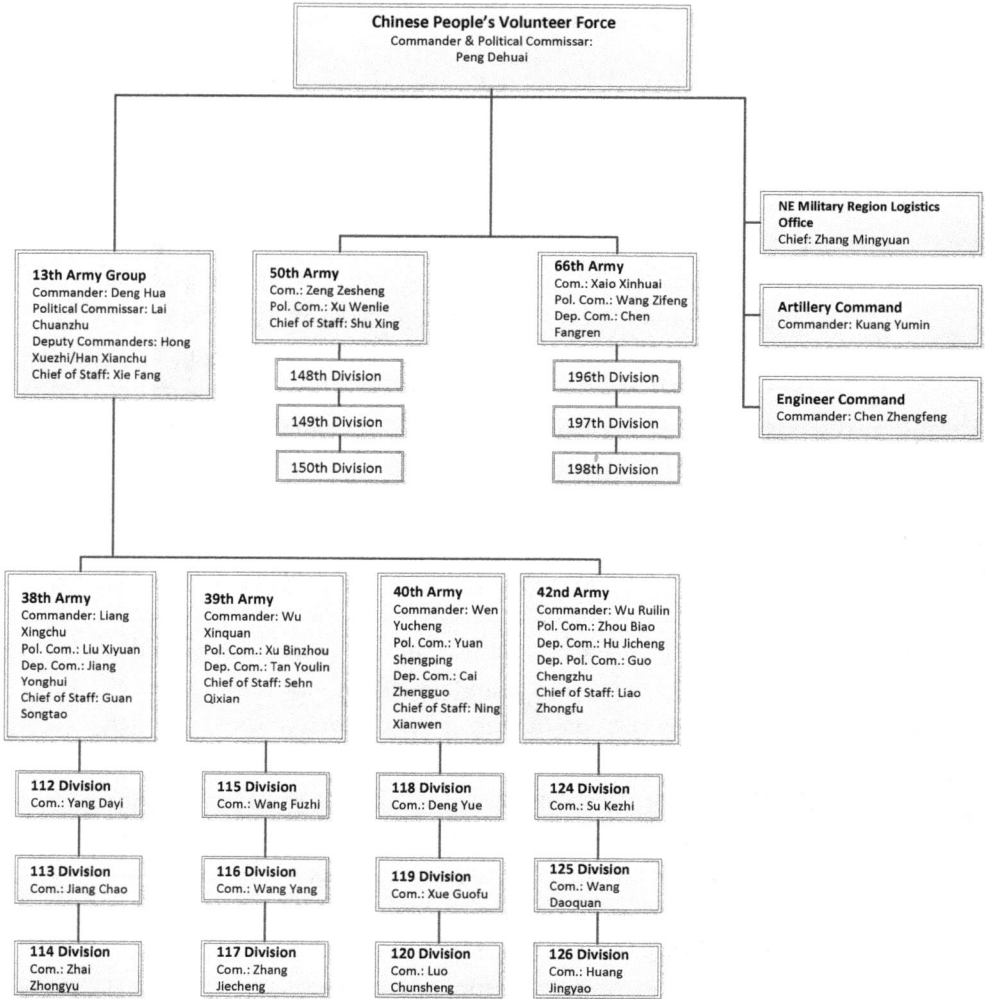

Chart 2.1. The CPVF Chain of Command, November 1950

Mao micromanaged CPVF operations from Beijing "at the expense of his commanders on the ground in Korea."[16] He was briefed daily by Nie Rongzhen, acting chief of the PLA General Staff, with intelligence, battle reports, and proposed plans. Nie's General Staff Department (GSD) divisions of operations, planning, intelligence, and communication carried out PLA staff and operational functions. Based on Nie's reports and proposals, Mao drafted his own telegrams and sent these instructions to Peng in Korea.[17] Even though Mao received Peng's reports and plans each day, he continuously, and often abruptly, changed or modified Peng's plans; in hindsight, "Peng's approach to the war was markedly cautious and conservative, and arguably more realistic compared to Mao's."[18] Putting political considerations over strategic realities, Mao pushed Peng to launch one offensive campaign after another against the UNF. Shuguang Zhang argues that "having long dominated military-strategic planning, Mao did not want to give up his commanding role. Now with his personality cult established, he was obsessed with his self-image as the CCP's ultimate commander-in-chief of military affairs."[19] Allan Millett points out that "the planning revealed Mao's way of war, micromanaging by 'war on the map.'" Even though "the chairman had more than twenty years' experience in planning campaigns, Mao's instructions to Peng Dehuai . . . allowed little independent initiative" for the CPVF command.[20]

Although Mao dominated the operational planning and took his role as commander in chief seriously, the PLA and the CPVF had not adopted a command-and-control doctrine that could meet the requirements of modern war. Among the Chinese officers, institutional relationships were much weaker than interpersonal ones. Within the CPVF, the personal ties among commanders mattered a great deal, and Peng became frustrated when attempting to implement Mao's unrealistic plans without the close control and personal support of the army group and army commanders. Peng had commanded the PLA's First Field Army from northwest China, but the majority of the CPVF armies in 1950–51 belonged to the Forth Field Army from northeast China, which had been under the command of Lin Biao since the Chinese Civil War, and the Third Field Army from Southeast China, under the command of Chen Yi and Su Yu.[21]

Moreover, Peng had no staff after being appointed CPVF commander and political commissar on October 8. During his ten-day stay in Beijing, he worked at the PLA GSD and gathered a dozen of his secretaries from the Northwest Military Region HQ in Xi'an. Peng complained to the CPVF commanders about the lack of a headquarters and staff: "[We are] now in the middle of war. Even though I am issuing orders as the

commander and political commissar of the CPVF, I don't have a commanding office. How can I command the CPVF to engage the battles?"[22]
Beijing had no time to establish a CPVF General HQ for Peng before
he entered Korea.

Despite an inadequate staff, on October 19 Peng crossed the Yalu
River with one secretary, one Korean interpreter, and several guards, all
traveling in one car and one midsize truck. Peng rode with Gen. Pak Il-u,
North Korea's minister of the interior; on the far side of the Yalu he was
received by Vice Prime Minister Pak Hon-yong, who accompanied Peng
to look for Kim Il-sung.[23] They could not find Kim until the morning of
October 21, when they discovered him at a small village near Taeyu-dong
(Taeyo-dong), about fifty miles southeast of the Chinese-Korean border.
During the previous three days Beijing had been unable to contact Peng,
and no one in the CPVF knew where in Korea its commander in chief
was. On his way to meet Kim, Peng's truck, carrying the radio and his
guards, was too slow and could not keep up with his car. Peng did not
want to wait for the truck, so he decided to go on ahead in his car. Thus
there was no radio or other communication between Peng and Beijing,
or between him and his CPVF, for three days. The truck driver and radio
crew finally located Peng at Taeyu-dong with Kim Il-sung.[24]

It soon became apparent that the commander needed an official
headquarters. On October 24 Peng was joined by the HQ of the CPVF
Thirteenth Army Group.[25] At Peng's suggestion, endorsed by the CMC,
Mao agreed to transfer the Thirteenth Army Group HQ to the CPVF
General HQ. On October 25 Mao telegraphed the Thirteenth Army
Group that "in order to accommodate the current needs of the great
task of struggles, the Commanding and Political Departments and other
departments of the Thirteenth Army Group should be immediately reorganized accordingly as the Commanding and Political Departments and
other departments of the People's Volunteers."[26] Peng announced the
order the same day, with Deng named as his first deputy commander and
vice political commissar. As one of the most experienced commanders
in the Fourth Field Army in the Chinese Civil War, Deng had been commander of the Fifteenth Army Group and the Thirteenth Army Group.
At the age of forty in 1950, he had also commanded the NEBDA before
it became the CPVF, and in 1950–51 he was Peng's most trusted com-

mander. In 1951–52 Deng was chief CPVF delegate at the truce talks, and he replaced Peng as commander in chief of the CPVF in 1953. Returning from Korea, Deng was made regional commander in 1954, general in 1955, and deputy chief of the PLA General Staff in 1956.[27]

On October 25, 1950, Peng also announced the appointments of Hong Xuezhi as second deputy commander, Han Xianchu (1913–86) as third deputy commander,[28] Xie Fang (1908–84) as chief of staff, and Du Ping as director of the Political Department.[29] To coordinate with the NKPA, Peng also appointed North Korean Gen. Pak Il-u as vice commissar of the CPVF. Pak was one of Kim's three most trusted generals in the NKPA; in addition, Pak had worked in China during WWII and spoke fluent Chinese.

The overnight upgrading of the army group headquarters to a general headquarters was a step toward committing Chinese troops as soon as possible, but it led to command and control issues between the General HQ and the army groups in the field. Peng's secretaries were in charge of each section in the General HQ, and the former directors of the officers in the Thirteenth Army Group became associate or assistant directors to Peng's secretaries in the General HQ.[30] There were seven sections and one office in the General HQ: the operations, intelligence, communication, internal affairs, telegraph encoding, headquarters attached units, and administration sections and the headquarters coordinating office. The head of the Operations Section was Ding Ganru, who had worked as deputy chief of the Operation Office in the Northeast Regional Command before he joined the CPVF. Cui Xingnong was in charge of the Intelligence Section, which was composed of only six officers. Cui had served as chief of the Intelligence Office of the Thirteenth Army Group Command and been the Chinese military attaché to North Korea before joining the CPVF. The director of the Political Task Department was Du Ping, who had served as director of the Political Task Department of the Thirteenth Army Group in 1950 and had been granted the rank of lieutenant general in 1955. His department consisted of five divisions: secretariat, organization, propaganda, security, and civilian mobilization.[31]

The Thirteenth Army Group commanded four infantry armies, three artillery divisions, and one AAA regiment. The 119th and 120th Divisions of the Fortieth Army were transported by train from Andong into North Korea. The 118th Division crossed the Yalu at Changdian (Changtien or Changtienhekow). The Forty-Second Army crossed the river from Ji'an and Linjiang (Linkiang) using pontoon bridges. The Thirty-Eighth Army followed the path of the Forty-Second Army. The first Koreans its soldiers saw were the security troops of the NKPA, stationed on the Korean side of the Yalu Bridge where they had lined up and cheered in broken Chinese: "Welcome the CPVF coming to Korea to fight!"[32] The Chinese were impressed by the NKPA's Soviet-made automatic rifles and brand-new heavy machine guns. The CPVF troops had a mix of bolt-action WWII Japanese rifles, old American rifles captured from the GMD army in the Chinese Civil War, and several trucks and tanks.

To conceal their movements, Chinese troops took to the mountains as they had been instructed. They moved almost entirely on foot and had little in the way of motor transport, armor, artillery, or air support. They moved mostly at night, avoiding main roads, advancing twenty to thirty miles before the next dawn, and hiding in camouflaged tents in the forest during the day. Peng's advance seemed to match what Sunzi says: "So veiled and subtle, to the point of having no form; so mysterious and miraculous, to the point of making no sound. Therefore he can be arbiter of the enemy's fate."[33] Unimpeded by heavy weapons, the Chinese relied on mobility, concealment, and nighttime surprise attacks, all of which proved to be extremely effective in their first encounter with the UNF on October 25. U.S. reconnaissance aircraft found it difficult to detect the Chinese troops. Gen. Matthew Ridgway explained why the UNF Command had missed the "clear meaning of the mounting evidence" by saying that "because the Chinese left no signs whatever of the presence of a moving army, there was some grounds for the skepticism of the High Command as to the presence of large enemy forces."[34]

## THE FIRST ENCOUNTER

From October 25 to November 7, 1950, the Chinese forces attacked the UNF in ambushes rather than in the defensive campaign planned by Mao and Peng. Mao's plan had been based on the assumption that the NKPA would defend Pyongyang and slow down the UNF northward offense. At that moment, the NKPA had a total of 250,000 men, including nine infantry divisions and one tank division in North Korea, nine divisions training in Manchuria, and the remnants of nine infantry divisions in South Korea. An effective defense in NKPA-controlled areas could conceivably allow the CPVF to gain a firm footing in North Korea and stop the northward offense of the UNF.[35] Attacking the enemy force or launching offensive campaigns was neither Mao's nor Peng's main objective.

At the meeting with Kim on October 21, Peng learned that Chinese intelligence was either not accurate or was outdated by two or three days, and he realized the impossibility of carrying out Mao's plan to defend the 40th Parallel.[36] The UNF had advanced deep into North Korea, and some UNF troops had already reached the 41st Parallel; Kim and the NKPA had lost control of more than 70 percent of the country. After the U.S. I Corps captured Pyongyang on October 19, MacArthur ordered the UNF to devise an immediate offensive covering the entirety of North Korea. Advancing with tanks and trucks, UNF units—especially the ROK divisions—quickly moved northward. Even though information on large-scale Chinese movement and deployment was available, U.S. intelligence officers failed to convince MacArthur that China was intervening in the Korean War.[37] On October 20 the ROK II Corps, including the 6th, 7th, and 8th Divisions, reached areas eighty miles from Mao and Peng's defense line in the west. The next day the Capital Division of the ROK I Corps took over Hongwon in the east, where the CPVF Thirty-eighth and Forty-second Armies were supposed to build their defenses. On October 21 some of the ROK divisions were only about twenty to forty miles from the Chinese armies, and some UNF vehicles had actually passed the place at Taeyu-dong where Peng and Kim met between October 21 and 23. Peng recalled that "the enemy troops have already advanced farther north of Taeyu-dong where we stayed. . . . I and Kim were lucky not to be captured."[38]

Kim told Peng that after the NKPA lost Pyongyang on October 19, North Korea's defense had collapsed. Kim could communicate with fewer than 50,000 of his troops. Peng agreed that, since the NKPA had failed and was dispersed, no Chinese army could reach its planned defense positions, approximately 120–180 miles south of the Yalu River. But

Peng also knew that the UNF Command had not detected the sudden influx of a large number of the Chinese troops. Peng reported to Mao that, by maneuvering at night and resting during the day, his first wave of 300,000 Chinese troops remained undetected in North Korea for two weeks in October.[39]

After receiving Peng's report, Mao immediately changed his war plans, moving from a positional defense to an ambush of ROK divisions. At 2:30 AM on October 21, he telegraphed Peng and other CPVF commanders, instructing them to attack and "eliminate three or more divisions of the puppet [South Korean] troops and thereby gain our first victory after entering Korea. Hope Peng and Deng work out the plan in detail and carry it out carefully." Mao calculated that "up to this moment, neither the Americans nor the puppets have foreseen that our Volunteers would enter the war; that is why they are bold enough to advance separately in the east and west."[40] One hour later, Mao emphasized the plan change from defense to a surprise attack in another telegram. At 3:30 AM he explained to Peng and other commanders: "The current issue is to gain the opportunity to win the campaign; the issue is to complete campaign deployment within a few days so that the campaign can be conducted several days later; it is not an option that we can have a period for deployment and defense construction before we talk about offensives."[41] At 4:00 AM, Mao sent another telegram to Peng and Deng Hua to control Myohyangsan (Mohyangsan), Sobaeksan (Sopaeksan), and other heights located at the junction of Pyongan-namdo, Pyongan-pukdo (Pyongan-bukdo), and Hamkyong-do (Hamgyong-do).[42] Obviously, Mao had abandoned his defense plan and was ready to launch an attack.

On October 21 Peng reestablished telegraph contact with Beijing. He telegraphed Mao at 4:00 PM and agreed with Mao's change of plan: "Currently, the American and puppet armies are advancing farther north without facing any effective resistance by the NKPA." Peng also saw the advantage of the CPVF's secret entry into Korea and the troops' concealed movement: "The enemy will continue their separate and rash advances before they discover our army's deployments. Thus, our army is obviously capable of eliminating the enemy in a mobile warfare campaign."[43] After discussing the matter with Kim, Peng proposed a new campaign plan in his telegram to Mao at 7:00 PM on October 22: "This campaign plan is to employ three armies to eliminate two puppet divisions through the battle opportunity, while using one army to pin down the remaining enemy troops. Thereafter, [we can] spread into the mountainous areas north of Pyongyang and Wonsan, stabilize the [war] situation in the North, and develop the guerrilla warfare in South Korea."[44] The reason for the guerrilla warfare was that the CPVF did not have air support. Peng stated in his telegram that it was better for the CPVF to maintain a defensive position in the mountainous areas north of Pyongyang and Wonsan for the next six months, waiting for the opportunity to launch a counteroffensive.

Since Mao had made up his mind to shift from a defensive to an offensive strategy, he was unhappy about Peng's conservative plan for his first campaign in Korea, and Mao questioned Peng's arguments of defense in his reply telegram on October 23: "The first one [question] is whether the currently disposed campaign will make use of surprise attacks, which will be completely beyond the enemy's anticipation." His "second question is to what extent the enemy air raids can actually inflict casualties on our troops and hinder them from carrying out war operations. . . . Third, if the United States ships five to ten more divisions to Korea before our troops are able to wipe out several American divisions and several puppet divisions in our mobile warfare and the operations aiming at those isolated posts, the situation will also become disadvantageous to us." Mao tried to convince Peng that "all these points will be tested by this campaign and [the campaigns] within the next several months. I am convinced that we must do all we can to gain a complete victory in this campaign, to keep up a high morale to fight effectively under the enemy's air raids, and to eliminate more units of the enemy's forces before the enemy transfers more troops to Korea from America or elsewhere, so that their reinforcements will never match up with their losses."[45] Mao also asked Peng to eliminate three to four ROK divisions rather than the two divisions outlined in Peng's plan.

During the morning of October 24, Peng and Pak moved their command post from Datong to an abandoned gold mine near Taeyu-dong.[46] Deng, Hong, Han, and the Thirteenth Army Group HQ arrived at Taeyu-dong at approximately noon. The following day, Peng read the CCP Central Committee's decision and reorganized the Thirteenth HQ into the CPVF General HQ.[47] At his first operational meeting, Peng decided to concentrate the Thirty-Eighth, Thirty-Ninth, and Fortieth Armies, as well as one division of the Forty-Second Army in the Unson (Unsan)–Huichon area along the western front, in order to initially eliminate the ROK 6th and 8th Divisions. The Forty-Second Army would build defense works in the Chosin (Changjin) area and pin down the eastern front's UNF. Each CPVF unit, according to Peng, "should look for your own opportunity during your movements in order to circulate and eliminate the enemy troops."[48] Although Peng was required to implement Mao's detailed operational plans, he still carried on the Chinese Communist military tradition of giving field commanders certain autonomy in their operations. During the Chinese Civil War, it had been common practice, not exceptional, for a field commander to make his own decisions on how to fight a battle as long as he could accomplish the mission assigned to him.

On October 25 the CPVF Fortieth Army, under the command of Wen Yucheng (1915–89), engaged in the first battle against the UNF since the Chinese forces entered Korea. As one of the Long March veterans, Wen had become division commander in the Anti-Japanese War and army commander in the Chinese Civil War.[49] On October 24 his 118th Division, comprised of 13,000 men, passed through Taeyu-dong and then moved southeast toward the western front, arriving at Ryangsu-dong. His 119th and 120th Divisions, totaling 25,000 troops, passed through Taechon and then moved northeast to Nytae-dong (map 2.1).

The 118th Division's commander, Deng Yue (1918–2000), learned about the UNF's pursuit of the fleeing NKPA remnants and civilian refugees. Deng radioed his vanguard 354th Regiment to halt its advance and wait for the enemy several miles north of the small crossroad village of Onjong (Onjeong). The regiment stopped at a hill occupied by the 2nd Regiment of the ROK 6th Division. At 10:00 the next morning, the 3rd Battalion of the ROK 2nd Regiment moved out of Onjong and into the Chinese trap. The CPVF 354th Regiment opened fire and destroyed the ROK battalion with the assistance of the 353rd Regiment, killing 325 and capturing 161 South Koreans within two hours.[50] That morning the CPVF 360th Regiment of the 120th Division encountered the 6th Medium Tank Battalion of the ROK 1st Division when their tanks ran into

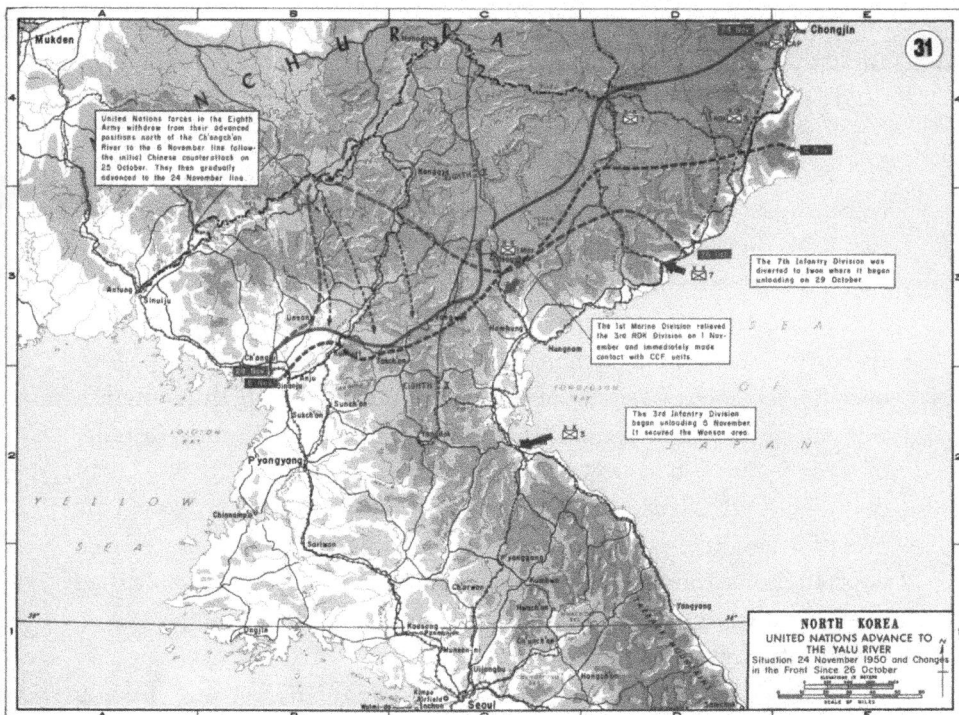

United Nations forces in the Eighth Army withdrew from their advanced positions north of the Ch'ongch'on River to the 6 November line following the initial Chinese counterattack on 25 October. They then gradually advanced to the 24 November line.

The 7th Infantry Division was diverted to Iwon where it began unloading on 29 October

The 1st Marine Division relieved the 3rd ROK Division on 1 November and immediately made contact with CCF units.

The 3rd Infantry Division began unloading 5 November. It secured the Wonsan area.

NORTH KOREA
UNITED NATIONS ADVANCE TO THE YALU RIVER
Situation 24 November 1950 and Changes in the Front Since 26 October

Map 2.1. The First CPVF Offensive Campaign

Chinese positions on their way toward Unson. The 360th Regiment commander made a decision to attack before receiving a divisional order.[51] The battle of Unson lasted for three days, and these two engagements became the first shots of the CPVF in the Korean War. October 25 is celebrated in China as the official anniversary of the CPVF's WRUSAK. Deng Yue was promoted to army commander in 1954 and major general in 1955.[52]

The CPVF's First Campaign, which lasted from October 25 to November 7, was not well planned given that the UNF moved much faster and farther north than the Chinese had expected. The CPVF commanders considered the campaign a meeting engagement or contact battle. The four Chinese armies had head-on engagements with the ROK 1st, 6th, and 8th Divisions as well as the U.S. 1st Cavalry Division. During the First Campaign, the CPVF Command concentrated 120,000 to 150,000 men in the area north of the Chongchon-gang River. Facing 50,000 UNF troops, the Chinese had a three to one numerical advantage. The CPVF used the combat tactics that the PLA had perfected during the Chinese Civil War, such as surprise attacks, roadblocks to separate enemy units, and night attacks to negate the enemy's usually superior firepower. Nevertheless, the CPVF did not reach its goal, which was to eliminate at least two ROK divisions in the campaign.

On October 27 the CPVF Command sent its Fortieth Army to attack the ROK 8th Division at Huichon, while the Thirty-Eighth Army rushed to the south of Huichon to block the ROK division's retreat. However, ROK troops pulled out of Huichon when the CPVF Thirty-Eighth was still thirty-five miles away.[53] Disappointed at this failure, Peng redeployed the Fortieth to Onjong in an effort to surround the 7th Regiment of the ROK 6th Division. On the evening of October 28, Peng issued the order for a night attack. By the next morning, the Fortieth reported that two battalions from the ROK 6th and another two from the ROK 8th had been eliminated. When the Fortieth launched another night attack on the twenty-ninth, the ROK 7th Regiment was destroyed.[54]

Peng also instructed the CPVF to engage the ROK troops first, in order to gain some experience before dealing with the more powerful U.S. units.[55] In fact, some Chinese troops tried to avoid U.S. troops, and the CPVF's first encounter with an American unit was accidental. The Thirty-Ninth Army had attacked Unson on the night of November 1, believing the town to be held by ROK units. Only after sighting enemy soldiers that were much taller and heavier than they expected did the Chinese soldiers realize that they were engaging the Americans; the U.S. 8th Regiment of the 1st Cavalry Division had taken over the defense of Unson from the ROK 15th Regiment. The Americans were caught completely off guard. Some even believed the approaching Chinese soldiers were South Korean soldiers and tried to shake hands with them. The 347th Regiment, 116th Division, Thirty-Ninth Army, opened fire at close range.[56] After fighting from November 1 to 4, the Thirty-Ninth reported that the U.S. 8th Cavalry Regiment and ROK 12th Regiment of the 1st Division had been decimated, with more than 2,000 casualties.[57] After the first encounter with Americans, many in the CPVF Command believed that the UNF reliance on technology might be to their own disadvantage.[58] Their mechanized units traveled along roads; their artillery troops required uninterrupted supplies; and their infantry troops typically operated during daytime, since they depended on air cover. The Chinese troops quickly gained battlefield experience, helped immensely by a nucleus of career officers and Civil War veterans.

On November 3 the U.S. Eighth Army Command ordered a retreat of all UNF from north of the Chongchon-gang River. Since the CPVF troops were unable to catch the motorized enemy by foot, the CPVF Command ordered all armies on the western front to cease the offensive completely. On November 7 in the east, the Forty-Second Army disengaged from the ROK Capital Division and U.S. 1st Marine Division at the Chosin Reservoir. During the First Campaign, the Chinese estimated 15,000 enemy casualties.[59] The CPVF stabilized the North Koreans' military situation for the first time since the Inchon (Inch'ōn) landing, providing valuable breathing space by pushing the front line south of the Chongchon River.[60] Geography favored the Chinese. The mountains and forest camouflaged their movements and diluted UN air attacks. The narrowness of the Korean Peninsula made it possible to fortify and defend a relatively short front. Although the CPVF had fought only limited engagements between October 25 and November 7, and despite 10,000 Chinese casualties, Peng believed that the First Campaign was a victory for the CPVF.[61] The commander in chief recalled that CPVF troops "had eliminated six or seven 'puppet' battalions and a small unit of the American army," forcing the UNF to retreat to the Chongchon-gang and Tokchon region.[62] Zhang points out that the First Campaign had convinced Chinese commanders that "they had accomplished a great deal: the troops had settled in North Korea and experienced their first combat."[63] They were ready for the next large-scale offensive campaign.

## THE SECOND OFFENSIVE CAMPAIGN:
### A TASTE OF VICTORY

From November 25 to December 24, 1950, the Chinese fought the Second Offensive Campaign. To prepare a large-scale offensive, the PLA high command in late October and early November sent reinforcements from China as the second wave of the CPVF. The Sixtieth Army moved into the area west of Kusong (Kuseong) on November 1, and that night the Fiftieth Army entered North Korea from Andong. On October 26 in Beijing, Mao met Song Shilun, commander of the Ninth Army Group, and discussed Song's new assignment in Korea. Then forty-three years old, Song commanded the Twentieth, Twenty-Sixth, and Twenty-Seventh Armies, totaling 150,000 men.[64] On November 1 his Twenty-Seventh Army—advance troops of the Ninth Army Group—started to cross the Yalu, followed by the Twentieth and Twenty-Sixth Armies. The Ninth Army Group, a major force, had prepared for the Taiwan campaign; it moved east undetected and was soon engaged in the Second Offensive Campaign. By late November China had dispatched thirty-three divisions, totaling 450,000 soldiers, to Korea. Thus, Peng had a total of 240,000 men on the western front facing 130,000 UN troops, and another 150,000 men on the eastern front facing 90,000 UN troops, a ratio of nearly two to one.[65] With superior manpower, both Mao and Peng expected a major, if not final, victory over the UNF in the second campaign. Therefore, in early December 1950, Chinese representatives to the United Nations refused to end the Korean conflict with a negotiated peace.[66]

Although the CPVF First Offensive Campaign surprised MacArthur, he continued to believe that the Chinese force was symbolic and was insufficient to halt his final campaign to unify Korea. His objective was to return to the offensive: drive the Chinese back to the Yalu and complete the reunification of Korea. In November MacArthur ordered the U.S. Eighth Army north along the western front and sent the X Corps eastward. Gen. Walter Bedell Smith, director of the Central Intelligence Agency (CIA), agreed with the general, estimating that "between 15,000 and 20,000 Chinese Communist troops organized in task force units are operating in North Korea while the parent units remain in Manchuria." Smith reported to President Truman on November 1 that China's "main motivation at present appears to be to establish a limited 'cordon sanitaire' south of the Yalu River."[67]

Peng suggested to Mao that the UNF be lured into preset traps as far north as possible, so that UNF divisions with extended supply lines might be more easily isolated and destroyed. Mao approved Peng's plan and said: "Our strategy is to lure the enemy in deep, and seek opportuni-

ties to annihilate the enemy one after another."[68] In another telegram on
the same day, Mao instructed Peng:

> Tokchon is very important. Our army must strive to open another front in the
> area north of the Wonsan-Sunchon [Suncheon] railroad. By wearing down
> the enemy's strength in that area, [you can] solve the problems in front of the
> Wonsan-Pyongyang line, and make the areas north and west of Tokchon, Kujang
> [Kurchang], and Yongbyon your rear base. This will be advantageous in pro-
> tracted warfare. At present, please consider this in relationship to the situation
> and decide whether [you] can accomplish this.[69]

On November 8 the UNF probed the CPVF positions north of the
Chongchon-gang River. In their reply to Mao, Peng and Deng reported
that they were planning to adopt a strategy of "inducing the enemy to
advance while allowing ourselves the time to have rest and make read-
justments."[70] Mao quickly agreed with the CPVF commanders, and emphasized the need to "strive to launch one or two campaigns respectively
on the eastern and western fronts from this month to early December.
Annihilate seven or eight regiments of the enemy in total, and push
the fronts forward to the area around the Pyongyang-Wonsan railroad
line. Thus, our army will basically win the war."[71] Thereafter, the CPVF
Command pulled its armies back into the mountainous areas of central
North Korea in order to lure the UNF into the North and prepare for
the next attack.

On November 13 the CPVF held its first expanded party committee meeting at Taeyu-dong to evaluate the First Campaign and plan
for the Second.[72] At that meeting the CPVF leaders decided that, since
their forces lacked adequate air, artillery, and armor support, they would
conduct mobile warfare: trading space for UNF casualties. The next
campaign would lure the UNF into a deep trap, where Chinese troops
could encircle and eliminate UNF units one by one. At the meeting, each
army was encouraged to devise plans to destroy at least one or two UNF
regiments in the Second Offensive Campaign.[73] To lure the UNF to advance, all the CPVF armies continued to withdraw between November
17 and November 20. Peng's mobile tactics, pretending that the Chinese
were weak, enticed the UNF to advance faster and farther.

The CPVF Command reduced radio communication and tightened
its control of information about troop movements from November 17

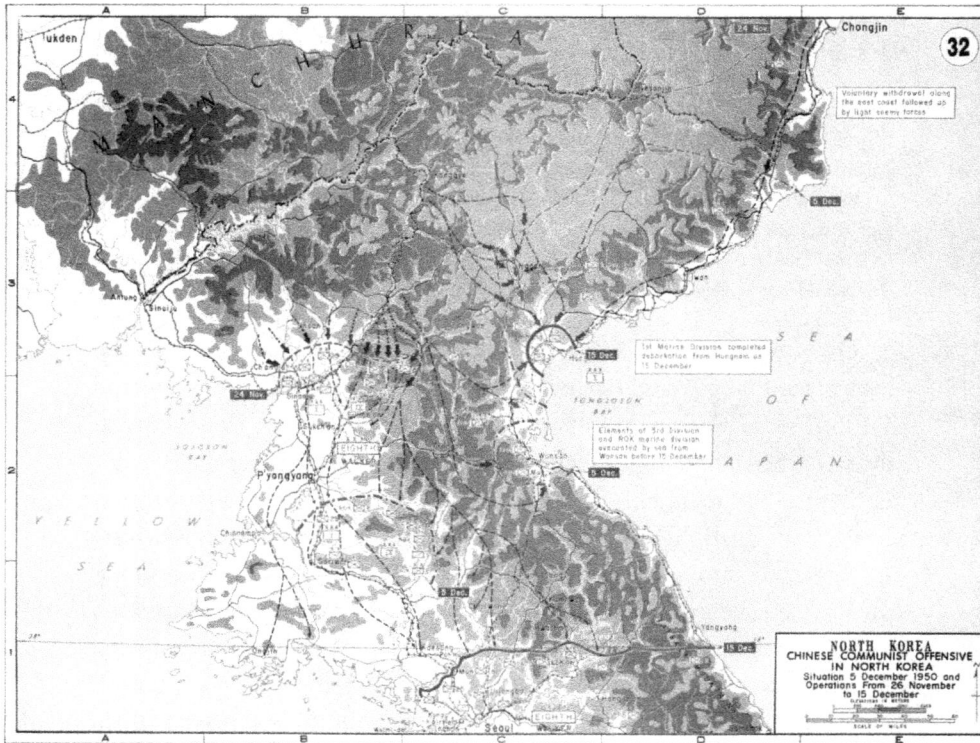

Map 2.2. The Second CPVF Offensive Campaign

to November 24. In addition, it released 103 UNF POWs (including 30 Americans) on November 18 with disinformation that the CPVF was running out of food and ammunition and was withdrawing to China.[74] By the twenty-first Peng had deployed the Thirty-Eighth, Thirty-Ninth, Fortieth, Forty-Second, Fiftieth, and Sixty-Sixth Armies in areas of favorable terrain in Puckchin on the western front.[75] On that day he ordered the Twentieth and Twenty-Seventh Armies to rush through the mountains to area around Chosin on the eastern front. The Second Offensive Campaign consisted of two prongs: the first was an advance along the Chongchon-gang River on the western front against the U.S. Eighth Army's I and IX Corps from November 25 to 30, and the other was an advance in the east against the U.S. X Corps of the Eighth Army at the Chosin Reservoir from November 27 to December 12 (map 2.2).

Peng's deception worked. The UNF advanced more rapidly. By November 21 the U.S. I Corps, including the U.S. 24th Division, British 29th Brigade, and ROK 1st Division, had reached the area between Yongwon and Paecheon (Paekchon, Paekcheon, or Pakchon), less than twenty miles from the Chinese armies on the west. On the eastern front, the U.S. X Corps, including the U.S. 1st Marine and 7th Infantry Divisions, approached the Chosin area. On November 24 MacArthur made one of several home-before-Christmas statements when he visited the Eighth Army HQ with Gen. Walton H. Walker (1889–1950), commander of the U.S. Eighth Army. After MacArthur learned that the UNF's northward advance faced little resistance on the western front, he told the commanders: "You can tell them [the troops] that when they get up to the Yalu, Jack, they can all come home. I want to make good my statement that they will get Christmas dinner at home."[76]

On the evening of November 25, two days after Thanksgiving, the CPVF launched the Second Offensive Campaign against MacArthur's "home-by-Christmas" offensive. Four Chinese armies, the Thirty-Ninth, Fortieth, Fiftieth, and Sixty-Sixth, conducted an all-out attack on the U.S. Eighth Army's I and IX Corps over a hundred-mile-wide front on the west. The U.S. I Corps organized strong defensive firepower, and its units stayed close together, having learned of the Chinese flanking and encircling tactics from previous engagements. The CPVF did not break through the front line of the U.S. I Corps that night. However, the Thirty-Eighth Army on the UNF's right broke the defense of the ROK 7th Division of the U.S. IX Corps at Tokchon on the twenty-sixth. The Thirty-Eighth reported that it had annihilated more than 5,000 ROK troops and occupied Tokchon by that evening.[77] In the meantime, the Forty-Second Army, also on the right, attacked the positions of the ROK 8th Division of the U.S. IX Corps at Yongwon. After the Thirty-Eighth and Forty-Second breached the right flank of the U.S. IX Corps, they were able to turn southwest and envelop the UNF at the Chongchongang River on November 27.[78]

Peng ordered the Thirty-Ninth, Fiftieth, and Sixty-Sixth Armies to attack the U.S. 2nd and 25th Divisions of the IX Corps. The CPVF armies blocked the 2nd Division's withdrawal, causing heavy U.S. casualties. During the morning of November 28, the CPVF Thirty-Eighth

Army rushed to Samso-ri, outflanking the entire U.S. IX Corps.[79] On the twenty-ninth the UNF Command began an overall retreat in the west to allow the Eighth Army to withdraw back into South Korea. On December 4 the UNF evacuated Pyongyang, which the CPVF Thirty-Ninth Army occupied on December 6.[80]

On the eastern front, the CPVF's attack on the U.S. X Corps in late November differed from its assaults against the U.S. I and IX Corps in the west. The Chinese Ninth Army Group, including the Twentieth, Twenty-Sixth, and Twenty-Seventh Armies, was ill prepared for the attack after coming from Southeastern China, where it had prepared to invade Taiwan, not Korea. The troops, dressed in light canvas shoes and quilted cotton uniforms, were not equipped for the bitter cold Korean winter. In addition, the men were hastily thrown into combat without proper training and supplies. Some officers complained that the suppliers failed to keep up with the troops. The cold winter hit the Ninth Army Group exceedingly hard. The commanding officers had no idea of the severity of winter weather in North Korea. Capt. Wang Xuedong, First Company, 172nd Regiment, 58th Division, Twentieth Army, told the author during an interview: "We came from Southeast China, where the average annual temperature is about 72 degrees Fahrenheit. When we left our homes in early November, the temperature was about 60 degrees. Two weeks later, when we entered Korea, the temperature there had dropped to below zero."[81] Many men became ill and could not keep up the pace of approximately 120 miles in seven days, through mountains and forests. In Wang's 58th Division, for example, 700 men died of severe frostbite during the first week in Korea.[82]

The planners at the CPVF HQ were not aware of all the Ninth Army Group's problems. On November 25 Peng ordered Song Shilun, commander of the Ninth, to launch his attack in the east as the CPVF began its second all-out offensive campaign. But Song asked for a two-day delay since his armies were not yet in position for an attack. His Twentieth Army had arrived at the Chosin Reservoir area, but the Twenty-Seventh was still on its way, while the Twenty-Sixth remained along the Chinese-Korean border, waiting new supplies of Russian weapons and equipment to replace the army group's obsolescent weaponry.[83]

The CPVF Command had to accept the delay in the Ninth Army Group's attack. Finally, on November 27, the Ninth issued an attack order centered on the Chosin Reservoir. The attacking force consisted of eight infantry divisions, including the 58th Division. Officers of the 58th believed that some of their tactics were very successful during the initial attack. First, they had the element of surprise, as their entry into North Korea and their movement to the eastern front had remained undetected by the UNF. Second, they had separated the U.S. 1st Marine and 7th Infantry Divisions into five pockets by the following morning. Third, the 100,000 men of the Ninth Army Group were able to surround and isolate these separate American units.[84]

Even though the Chinese trapped the 1st Marine Division at Hahwaok-ri (Hagaru-ri) and cut it into three sections, they could not destroy each section completely. Despite being divided and surrounded, the 1st Marines successfully formed defensive perimeters at three places. They also constructed a makeshift airstrip for resupplying them with ammunition and winter equipment, as well as for evacuating their wounded.[85] On November 29 the Marines counterattacked, in order to break the Chinese encirclement and to unite their scattered units. Wang recalled this engagement with the 1st Marines at the Chosin Reservoir as a battle that swayed back and forth, but in which the fighting was always intense. During the three days of fighting, his regiment suffered extremely heavy casualties. They also ran out of ammunition and were receiving less than half their daily ration of food, while the temperature had dropped to twenty degrees below zero.[86] The Ninth Army Group's poor preparation became a lesson in what to avoid that Mao and the PLA high command drummed into their other army group commanders.

On November 30 the Ninth was forced to change its plan. Instead of attacking the 1st Marine and 7th Divisions at the same time, it decided to concentrate its attack on the 7th Division at Sinhung-ri (Chinhung-ri). On November 30 the Ninth employed two infantry divisions and all its artillery to attack the 32nd Regiment of the U.S. 7th Division. On December 1 the attacking Chinese troops overran the 32nd. This is the only case in the Korean War in which the CPVF destroyed an entire U.S. regiment.[87]

On December 1 Marines broke through the Chinese encirclement and began their retreat to the south. Unable to stop them, the Twentieth Army received orders to pursue them and slow their retreat until the Twenty-Sixth Army, which was still over fifty miles away, could join the battle.[88] It never did. On December 12, having broken the Chinese roadblocks and staved off some attacks on its way south, the 1st Marines linked up with the U.S. 3rd Division at Hamhung (Hamheung). The Ninth Army Group alone could not eliminate the 1st Marine Division. On December 24 the Marines boarded ships at Hungnam Harbor and withdrew to Pusan, South Korea. Following this setback, the CPVF Command ordered the Ninth Army Group to disengage the U.S. X Corps on the eastern front. The Chinese Second Offensive Campaign was over by December 24.[89]

On the whole, the Second Offensive Campaign was a major victory for the CPVF. American air power forced the Chinese to take their operations to the countryside in the night, and most of the Chinese supplies traveled by foot. Although most Chinese soldiers had tremendous physical endurance, they suffered over 80,000 casualties during the Second Offensive Campaign.[90] The Chinese attacked from the surrounding hills and often established roadblocks, which not only forced American troops back but also threatened to cut them off. The U.S. 1st Marine Division's retreat has become a part of Marine lore, but it was still a retreat, not a victory. The fierce fighting, combined with the bitter cold, made Chosin one of the worst battles of the Korean War for both the Americans and the Chinese.[91] Amazingly, under such conditions, the Chinese troops even found ways of moving artillery to their frontline positions high in the mountains. In nine days the CPVF pushed the battle line back to the 38th Parallel and recaptured Pyongyang. The Second Offensive Campaign "represented the peak of CPVF performance in the Korean War."[92]

Mao and Peng were extremely pleased with the Second Offensive Campaign's outcome. According to Chinese statistics, the CPVF inflicted 36,000 UNF casualties, including 24,000 Americans.[93] Walker, commander of the U.S. Eighth Army, was killed in a traffic accident when a truck driven by a ROK soldier jumped lanes. Among the 80,000 Chinese casualties were 30,700 combat and 50,000 noncombat casualties. Mao Anying, one of Mao Zedong's sons, was killed on November 25 in a U.S. air raid against CPVF General HQ.[94] During its battle at the Chosin Reservoir, the Ninth Army Group lost 40,000 men in three weeks of fighting, liquidating three divisions.[95] Many casualties were related to the weather. Having lost half its troops, the badly depleted army group was recalled to China on December 17. China funneled as many troops into Korea as its transportation and supply system could handle. Mao's conviction that any battle could be conducted following the principles of mobile warfare dominated the Chinese military doctrine during the early offensive campaigns, from the fall of 1950 to the early spring of 1951.[96] These large-scale mobile tactics, like encirclement and annihilation, proved very effective in the first two offensive campaigns.

### THE THIRD OFFENSIVE CAMPAIGN: TO WIN THE WAR

From December 31, 1950, to January 8, 1951, the CPVF fought its Third Offensive Campaign against a strong UNF defense along the 38th Parallel. Peng had not scheduled the new offensive earlier because CPVF armies were exhausted after four weeks of constant movement and fighting during the Second Offensive Campaign. The CPVF also faced mounting problems, including food and ammunition shortages. The Chinese armies on the western front had fewer than 300 trucks for almost 300,000 troops, and the supply lines were now twice as long as they had been during the First Offensive Campaign. On the eastern front, the Ninth Army Group had more than 30,000 officers and men disabled by severe frostbite, and some 1,000 had died of frostbite.[97] The entire army group became a giant field hospital for three months as men recovered from frostbite. On December 8, before the end of the Second Offensive Campaign, Peng requested a pause until the following spring and to confine the forthcoming campaign to areas north of the 38th Parallel. The chief commander asked Mao to "let [the troops] stop in areas several miles north of the 38th Parallel, allowing the enemy to control the parallel, so that we will be able to destroy the enemy's main force the next year."[98]

Mao, encouraged by the CPVF's initial gains, rejected Peng's request. Instead, he changed the CPVF's strategic goal from defending North Korea to going on the offensive to drive the UNF out of the South. The new goal was far beyond the Chinese forces' capabilities. Mao told Kim Il-sung about this new plan during Kim's visit in Beijing on December 3: "It is better for us to take over not only Pyongyang, but also Seoul. [Our] main goal is to eliminate more enemy troops, first of all, to eliminate all of the ROK troops. It will effectively force the U.S. withdrawal [from Korea]."[99] Mao seemed confident of the CPVF's victory, which would not only save North Korea but also solve the problem of the entire Korean Peninsula. In the meantime, the Soviets also believed that China had an opportunity to resolve the Korean problem through a total victory of the CPVF. On December 4 Andrei Gromyko, the Soviet foreign minister, told Wang Jiaxiang (1906–74), the Chinese ambassador to Moscow, that "according to the current situation in Korea, it is perfectly proper [for us] to call for 'striking the iron when it is hot,' as the old Chinese saying goes."[100]

Mao declined Peng's request to pause until spring in his telegram of December 13, telling the chief: "At present, America, Britain, and other countries are asking our army to stop north of the 38th Parallel so they can reorganize their troops to continue the war. Thus, our army must cross the 38th Parallel. It will be most unfavorable in political terms if [our forces] reach the 38th Parallel and stop north of it." Obviously, Mao was putting his own political considerations over Peng's military calculations. The chairman instructed Peng to "continue your southward march, [and] look for opportunities to wipe out several enemy units, hopefully in the areas south or north of Kaesong, or the area not far from Seoul."[101] Beijing also rejected a peace proposal made by thirteen non-Western countries to the UN Security Council in December.[102]

Peng reluctantly agreed with Mao's next offensive plan. Mao was trying to convince the chief of the necessity of crossing the 38th Parallel. On December 21 Mao told Peng: "America and Britain are making use of people's old impressions about the 38th Parallel for their political propaganda. They are attempting to lure us into a ceasefire. Thus, it is essential right now for our armies to cross the 38th Parallel and engage in one more campaign. Then, they can rest and reorganize." Mao shared his further thoughts about the war's outcome: "Generally speaking, as long as all or most of the puppet forces are destroyed, the American forces will be isolated and will not be able to remain in Korea for a long period. If several more American divisions can be wiped out, the Korean problem will be solved more easily."[103] Mao connected the mission of the CPVF to the solution of the Korean conflict. He emphasized to Peng on December 26 that "we should understand that the Korean problem cannot be settled without experiencing a serious struggle, without eliminating all or at least most of the puppet forces, and without eliminating at least 40,000 or 50,000 more of the American and British forces."[104] In the same telegram, Mao also set out a new rule for the CPVF: "Not to go back to the motherland [China] until the enemy forces in Korea have been eliminated."[105] Mao wanted total victory.

Peng held a CPVF Command meeting on December 15 to shape the Third Offensive Campaign against the UNF defenses in South Korea. The UNF Command had established five defensive lines south of the 38th Parallel and designated them as Lines A, B, C, D, and E, respectively. Eight UNF divisions were deployed along the parallel on Line A. MacArthur gave Ridgway, who had taken command of the U.S. Eighth Army on December 26 after Walker's death, instructions not to risk the destruction of the Eighth Army. As a result, the Eighth established lines on which any withdrawing UNF elements would be able to coordinate movements. Line C passed along the south bank of the Han-gang River. At Yangpyong (Yangpyeong), the line extended across the Korean peninsula to the east coast. Forty miles south of this, Line D passed from the west coast at Pyongtaek northeast to the east coast at Woonpo-ri.[106]

At the CPVF Command meeting, the Chinese planned to cross the 38th Parallel to attack UNF Line A on the western front, concentrating five armies, including one NKPA army corps, to break through Line A. The plan included some of the tactics used in the previous campaigns to penetrate the enemy's line, separate the enemy forces, isolate and circulate some units, and then destroy those units. These five armies would then continue their attacks farther south toward Lines B and C and possibly seize Seoul. In the meantime, the CPVF would deploy four more armies, including two NKPA army corps, to carry out diversionary attacks on the UNF on the eastern front.[107] Mao approved the CPVF's plan for its Third Offensive Campaign. On December 24–27, the six CPVF armies—which were still poorly provisioned (food from home met only a quarter of the minimum needs)—and three NKPA army corps moved into their attack-staging sites. On the evening of the twenty-eighth, the NKPA I and V Corps crossed the 38th Parallel into South Korea.

On New Year's Eve the CPVF launched its Third Offensive Campaign across the 38th Parallel, in an operation very different from ear-

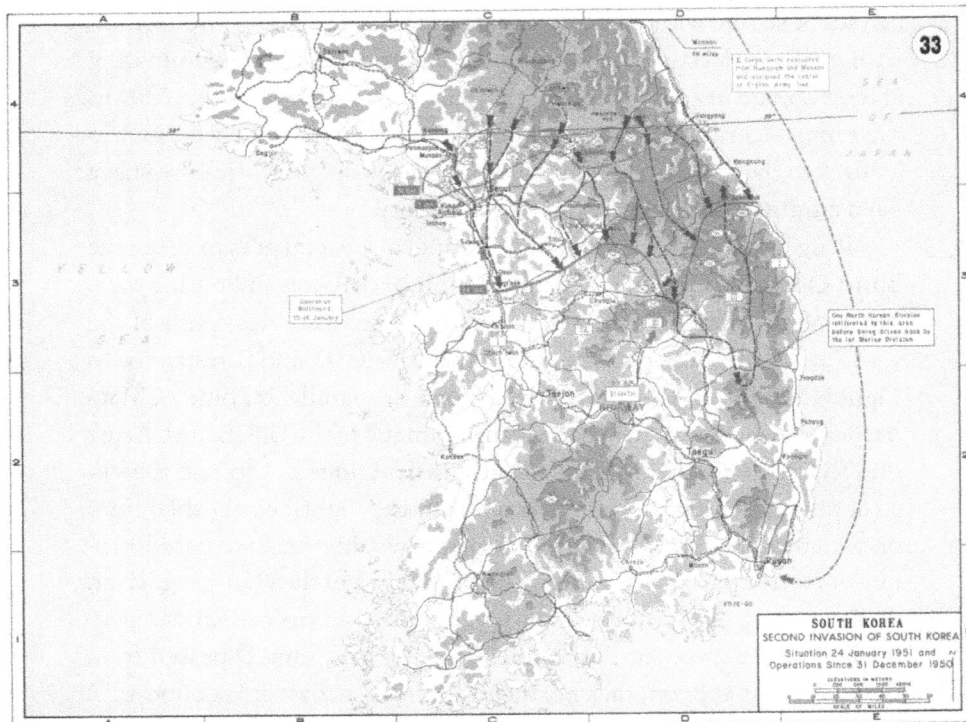

Map 2.3. The Third CPVF Offensive Campaign

lier engagements. At 5:00 PM, the CPVF attacks were preceded by an
artillery and mortar barrage on UNF Line A. After the artillery, the
troops of the Thirty-Eighth, Thirty-Ninth, Fortieth, and Forty-Second
Armies charged the defenses of the U.S. I and IX Corps directly north of
Seoul. By January 1, 1951, CPVF armies had driven a wedge between the
U.S. 24th and 25th Divisions and had broken through the ROK 1st and
5th Divisions that held the connecting area of Line A between the two
American divisions. On January 2 another Chinese division penetrated
the UNF east of Seoul and threatened to envelop the city. Ridgway
ordered the U.S. I and IX Corps to fall back into a bridgehead around
Seoul along Line B. U.S. I and IX Corps formed a new defense line with
ten infantry regiments, several hundred tanks, and fifteen artillery battalions of 105 mm, 155 mm, and 8-inch howitzers to support the infantry[108] (map 2.3).

In the meantime, on December 31, the CPVF Sixty-Sixth Army and NKPA II and V Corps attacked across the parallel in the east. Their successful thrust threatened to envelop the ROK II Corps, which struggled to hold back Chinese penetration in the center. On January 1 the Sixty-Sixth surrounded and eliminated two regiments of the ROK 2nd Division and one regiment of the ROK 5th Division.[109] On January 2 the ROK II Corps collapsed. The CPVF and NKPA armies pushed to the east of Seoul and outflanked the U.S. I and IX Corps. To avoid a disaster, Ridgway disregarded the desperate pleas of the ROK government to save the capital, and at 3:00 PM on January 3 he ordered a withdrawal from Seoul to Line C, along the south bank of the Han-gang River.[110]

In the afternoon of January 4, two divisions of the CPVF Thirty-Ninth and Fiftieth Armies and NKPA I Corps entered Seoul. The next day Peng ordered the Fiftieth Army and two divisions of the NKPA I Corps to cross the Han-gang.[111] On January 7 the Fiftieth took Kimpo (Keumpo), and on January 8 the NKPA I Corps occupied Inchon. In the meantime, the Forty-Second and Sixty-Sixth Armies continued their drives, shifting their thrust to central South Korea. Their moves threatened to envelop the U.S. I and IX Corps, which were defending Line C. To prevent the Chinese from cutting off U.S. troops, Ridgway again ordered withdrawal of all UNF troops, this time back to Line D.[112] Since the mechanized UNF withdrew faster than the Chinese could advance, Peng ended the CPVF Third Offensive Campaign on January 8.

In a matter of eight days, the CPVF had crossed the 38th Parallel, moved into South Korea, recaptured Seoul, and pushed the UNF down to the 37th Parallel.[113] The UNF was forced to retreat eighty miles south. According to Chinese reports, the CPVF and NKPA lost 8,500 men during the Third Offensive Campaign, including 5,800 CPVF and 2,700 NKPA casualties.[114] By this time the American and UN forces had brought to bear superior firepower on the ground and in the air, inflicting heavy casualties and serious damage to CPVF troop movements and lines of supply and communication. After the Third Offensive Campaign, the CPVF Command required a more cautious strategy.

Beijing, however, was overwhelmed by the victory of the campaign. After taking over Seoul, the Chinese government organized parades and parties in China, and even celebrated with fireworks. To many Chinese, the CPVF seemed to be winning the war in Korea. The CCP mouth-piece, *Renmin Ribao* (People's daily), published an editorial on January 5 that called for "driving the American invading forces into the seas."[115] Russian advisers in Beijing even asked the CPVF Command why the Chinese did not follow up their victory and pursue the UNF farther into South Korea. Pressure was mounting for another attack. Kim and Pak visited Peng at the CPVF General HQ and ordered the chief to continue the Chinese offensive without a break.

### THE FOURTH OFFENSIVE CAMPAIGN:
### BURDEN OF VICTORY

Under tremendous pressure from the political leaders of all three Communist countries (China, the Soviet Union, and North Korea) for a quick victory, the CPVF Command recognized the growing gap between political goals and strategic realities.[116] As the CPVF struck farther south, its tactics, such as surprise attacks, flanking operations, and encirclement and annihilation, began losing their effectiveness. In the meantime, the UNF had recovered from its early surprise and launched a counterattack on January 25, 1951. Hong, deputy chief of the CPVF, recalled: "We were compelled to fight the fourth campaign."[117]

From January 25 until April 21, the CPVF engaged in its Fourth Campaign. Instead of a mass offensive, it became a series of back-and-forth mobile battles. From January 25 to February 10, the CPVF rushed to defend the Han-gang River. The UNF's rapid shift from its defensive posture in early January to a large-scale offensive in less than two weeks surprised the CPVF Command.[118] Ridgway led four U.S. divisions, two British-led brigades (the 27th and 29th Commonwealth Brigades), one Turkish brigade, and two ROK divisions in a two-pronged offensive toward Seoul. The CPVF's Fiftieth Army and the 112th Division of the Thirty-Eighth Army took up defensive positions on the southern bank of the Han-gang to stop Ridgway's northern advance. The Fiftieth, formerly the GMD Sixtieth Army of Jiang Jieshi that had surrendered to the PLA in the Chinese Civil War, faced a perilous challenge and barely survived the first week. On February 4 the CPVF sent its Thirty-Eighth Army to reinforce the Fiftieth, but it was too late. U.S. forces broke

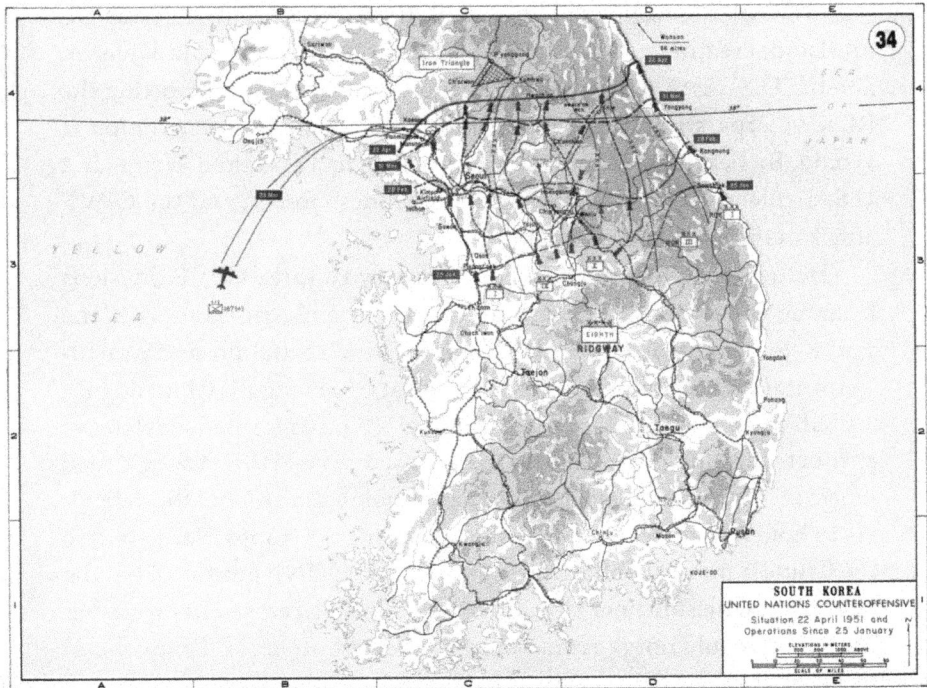

Map 2.4. The Fourth CPVF Offensive Campaign

through the Fiftieth Army on February 7 and drove the army north of the Han-gang.[119] From February 7 to 16, the Thirty-Eighth Army stood alone against the U.S. 24th and 1st Cavalry Divisions, suffering heavy casualties. The army's 112th Division lost two of its three regiments (the 334th and 336th) in less than ten days. By February 18 the Thirty-Eighth had also withdrawn to the area north of the Han-gang River[120] (map 2.4).

To alleviate the pressure on the Han-gang River in the west, the CPVF Command ordered six armies to attack the UNF in the east, specifically the ROK divisions, from February 11 to 15. On the night of February 11, the Fortieth and Forty-Second Armies, along with the 117th Division of the Thirty-Ninth Army of the CPVF, mounted a massive attack on the ROK 8th Division at Hoensong (Hoengsong or Hoeng-seong). The Sixty-Sixth Army of the CPVF attacked, with the goal of surrounding the enemy's rear, while the NKPA II and V Corps were sent to block the ROK 5th Division.[121] The ROK 8th Division was an-nihilated, creating a salient in the UNF front. The U.S. 2nd Division and the U.S. 187th Airborne's regimental combat team, supporting the ROK I Corps, struggled to block the CPVF and NKPA penetration at Wonju. By February 14 four CPVF divisions had assaulted Wonju, but U.S. artillery wreaked havoc on these Chinese forces, and the CPVF attack in the east came to a halt.[122]

In the next Chinese attack, on February 13, three CPVF divisions from the Thirty-Ninth, Fortieth, and Forty-Second Armies attacked the 23rd Regiment of the U.S. 2nd Division, a French battalion, and an artil-lery battalion, totaling 6,000 UNF troops, at Chipyong-ni (Chipyongni), a small town west of Hoensong. These UNF units formed a defensive perimeter around the town, and they refused to yield this strategic road junction. Ridgway believed this was a key point and ordered the defend-ers to hold it against an estimated 25,000 Chinese troops. For two days the Chinese mounted attack after attack against UNF positions, but the defenders, with sufficient air and artillery support, refused to surrender. The CPVF could not organize another effective attack on Chipyong-ni by February 15. Finally the encircled defenders were saved by the arrival of elements of the U.S. 1st Cavalry Division.[123] It was the end of the Chi-nese attacks in the Fourth Campaign.

The battle of Chipyong-ni was a serious setback for the Chinese. Some of the UNF officers considered it a turning point after the Chinese intervention, comparing it to the Inchon landing during the North Ko-rean offensive in 1950.[124] The failed attack exposed the CPVF's weakness in attacking fortified positions and convinced American policymakers that the UNF could stop Chinese offensives and stabilize the situation in Korea. The State Department agreed with the Joint Chiefs of Staff at a joint meeting in February that "generally speaking, military operations in Korea are now stabilized, although there will be a certain amount of give and take . . . [the current] positions are likely to remain approxi-mately as they are now."[125]

Unable to break through the U.S. Eighth Army line in central Korea while trying to hold back an Eighth Army drive west of the penetra-tion, on February 17 Peng determined that the CPVF would assume a defensive stance and withdraw to the 38th Parallel.[126] To make sure that

Mao understood the military difficulties, Peng rushed back to Beijing on February 21 and personally briefed him. Peng later recalled that he "reported to the chairman about the military situation in Korea and asked for his strategic guidance. I pointed out that the Korean War could not be a quick victory."[127] Mao agreed with Peng, saying: "Win a quick victory if you can; if you can't, win a slow one."[128] Peng was relieved of some political pressure as Mao became more strategically flexible on the Fourth Campaign.[129] Mao explained to Stalin on March 1 that "the current campaign on the Korean front clearly shows that the enemy will not withdraw from Korea until they lose their major forces. It will, however, take time [for us] to eliminate the enemy's major forces. Therefore, the Korean War may possibly become a prolonged war, and we should be prepared at least for two more years." Mao also warned Stalin that "within the next one and a half months, it may possibly happen that the enemy will return to or enter areas both south and north of the 38th Parallel since our new armies [from China] have not arrived and the armies [in Korea] have not yet been replenished."[130]

Thus, after February 1951 Mao's strategic goal in the war had changed from driving the UNF out of the peninsula, a quick victory, to eliminating several U.S. and ROK divisions a year while defeating any enemy landing behind the front line, a prolonged war. Mao believed that it would "take a several years to inflict casualties of hundreds of thousands of American troops to make them [the United States] beat a retreat in the face of difficulties."[131] The war's objective had shifted from a total Chinese victory to an American withdrawal from Korea.

The American forces, however, showed no sign at all of withdrawing; instead, they intensified their northward offensives. On March 7 the UNF launched another offensive in the west. The CPVF Command ordered a further withdrawal north of the 38th Parallel, while organizing some defenses on March 8. The UNF recaptured the battered capital of Seoul from the NKPA defense force, and a few days later UNF troops moved into Chuncheon (Chunchon). On March 23 the U.S. 187th Airborne dropped 4,000 troops in the area north of Seoul to block NKPA troops' withdrawal. On March 28 the U.S. Army employed helicopters to transfer thirty men to the rear area of the CPVF Twenty-Sixth Army and to occupy two positions. It was the first time helicopters were used in ground operations in military history. When the advance brought the UNF close to the 38th Parallel, Washington decided to make the cross-ing a tactical decision rather than a political one. Since in Ridgway's opinion the parallel was "neither defensible nor strategically important," he determined, with MacArthur's approval, to "continue the advance."[132] By early April UN troops had reached the Kansas Line, a few miles north of the 38th Parallel, close to the Iron Triangle.[133] For the UNF, however, attention shifted from battlefield to politics—the Truman-MacArthur controversy. The fundamental problem between the president and the general was that MacArthur wished to expand the war into China, block-ading the Chinese coast, using GMD troops from Taiwan, and bombing targets on the Chinese mainland—all of which contradicted Washing-ton's policy. On April 11, 1951, Truman relieved MacArthur of command.

On April 21 CPVF troops disengaged after the UNF stopped its northern advance along the 38th Parallel. The Chinese Fourth Cam-paign lasted eighty-seven days. The CPVF and NKPA suffered a total of 53,000 casualties, while the Chinese lost 42,000 men, including 4,379 missing in action.[134] In the spring of 1951, the PLA sent additional rein-forcements to Korea to offset losses and meet the new demands of rap-idly expanding military operations and unexpected manpower needs.[135] By mid-April the Chinese forces in Korea had increased to 950,000 troops, including forty-two infantry divisions, eight artillery divisions, four AAA divisions, and four tank regiments. All were ground forces; no air units had been formally committed to the war.[136] Supporting these combat forces were logistical troops consisting of six supply services headquarters, four railroad engineering divisions, eleven engineering regiments, and one public security division, for an additional 180,000 men. With over a million troops committed to the Korean conflict, the Chinese leaders would not realize that their goal of driving the UNF out of Korea was unattainable until after the CPVF's Fifth Offensive Campaign, from April 22 to June 10, 1951.

# THREE

# The Last Battle for Victory

AFTER FEBRUARY 1951 CHINA'S STRATEGIC GOAL SHIFTED FROM driving the UNF out of the Korean Peninsula for quick victory to fighting a protracted war. Mao explained to Stalin on March 1 that if the Chinese forces could inflict hundreds of thousands of casualties on American troops in the next few years, it would force a U.S. withdrawal,[1] and the CPVF would have to deliver a heavier blow in the next offensive. Based on these discussions, Mao and Peng Dehuai began planning the Fifth Offensive Campaign, or the Spring Offensive, in early 1951.

To ensure victory in their Fifth Offensive, Mao and the CMC committed to sending additional Chinese forces to Korea. In March Mao sent China's second wave, consisting of nine armies with twenty-seven infantry divisions.[2] The first wave of the CPVF had consisted of nine armies with thirty infantry divisions and three artillery divisions and had been engaged in Korea since October 1950.[3] The strongest units in the second wave were the Third Army Group from Southwest China, which had three armies with nine infantry divisions;[4] and the Nineteenth Army Group from North China, which had three armies with nine infantry divisions.[5] With the arrival of these forces, the CPVF in Korea had doubled, from 450,000 troops in January to 950,000 men in mid-April. These numbers included 770,000 combat troops in forty-two infantry divisions, eight artillery divisions, and four AAA divisions.[6] With the NKPA's 350,000 men in six army corps, the Communist forces had almost 1.3 million troops. In comparison, the UNF had some 340,000 men, including 150,000 U.S., 130,000 South Korean, and 60,000 troops from other countries.[7] On the eve of their next campaign,

Chinese forces alone had a three to one numerical superiority over the UNF.

After the second wave arrived in Korea, the CPVF Command began planning the Spring Offensive. On March 14 Peng made it clear to his generals that "the next campaign will be the decisive battle" of the Korean War.[8] The Chinese high command seemed confident of both eliminating a large number of UNF troops and moving its own forces south of the 38th Parallel. Mao, Peng, and most of the Chinese generals believed that the human factor would lead them to victory in the decisive battle. Their military perspective reflected China's massive population. It seemed rational to Chinese commanders that the CPVF's superior manpower would enable the Communist forces to overcome their inferiority in equipment and technology. The leaders centered their campaign on the people and their fighting spirit in night attacks and close combat, as opposed to the UNF's reliance on technology. The Chinese high command might have found inspiration from a principle of Sunzi: "Throw them [your soldiers] where there is no escape. And they will fight with the courage of the heroes."[9]

The Chinese launched the Spring Offensive on April 22, and it lasted until June 10, 1951. The battle became the largest campaign in the PLA's history, but despite its use of a million men, the offensive failed. The CPVF lost the decisive battle and suffered about 105,000 casualties, while the UNF had a total of 39,274 casualties.[10] More important, instead of the CPVF advancing southward, the UNF pushed further north. Why did the human factors fail to have the results that they had before? What had gone wrong with the Chinese calculation and planning? This chapter examines how the CPVF commanders ignored potential problems while they planned the campaign. As the CPVF doubled its troops on the front, it also doubled its needs, which contributed to shortages of food and ammunition as well as problems of transportation and communication. Moreover, as the war continued, the CPVF's previous tactics began to lose their effectiveness as the UNF became accustomed to them. By this time, the UNF had overwhelmingly superior firepower, both on the ground and in the air, and it could inflict heavy casualties as well as interrupt troop movements and cut supply lines. In the meantime, the newly arrived Chinese armies, unfamiliar with the terrain and lacking experience in foreign warfare, had a tendency to underestimate the UNF.[11] With poor intelligence and communication, the CPVF Command failed to pay sufficient attention to the battle readiness, cooperation between army groups, and the new tactics of the UNF. The additional failure to develop a contingency plan in case of a setback led to the disastrous conclusion of the Chinese Spring Offensive.

## MAO'S GOAL, REINFORCEMENT, AND RUSSIAN AIR SUPPORT

Mao's goal for the Chinese forces was to eliminate four UNF divisions and two brigades, or about 50,000 enemy troops, in the offensive. He told Stalin on March 1, 1951: "We are planning to eliminate tens of thousands of American and [South Korean President] Syngman Rhee's troops within two and a half months between April 15 and the end of June in the areas both south and north of the 38th Parallel. Then we will advance forward to the south of the Han River."[12] Stalin agreed with this plan on March 5, and on the 7th Mao issued orders to Peng to employ all troops along the front line and to attack the UNF before it could get a firm foothold north of the 38th Parallel.[13] In April Mao ordered Peng explicitly to strike hard and eliminate three U.S. divisions, one ROK division, and two British and Turkish brigades.[14]

Mao considered nothing more important than annihilating an entire enemy division or brigade. Shuguang Zhang states that Mao's goal "was to completely wipe out one enemy unit in each battle."[15] Mao explained the concept of annihilation in 1936, when he stated that "injuring all of a man's ten fingers is not as effective as chopping off one, and routing ten enemy divisions is not as effective as annihilating one of them."[16] Mao further added the war of annihilation to CCP military doctrine in the Chinese Civil War, when the Communist approach was transformed from traditional guerrilla warfare to conventional mobile warfare. In his 1946 directive, "Concentrate a Superior Force to Destroy the Enemy Forces One by One," Mao instructed the CCP that "only complete annihilation can deal the most telling blows to the enemy, for when we wipe out one regiment, he will have one regiment less, and when we wipe out

one brigade, he will have one brigade less." Mao noted: "Complete annihilation demoralizes the enemy's troops and depresses his followers; it
raises the morale of our troops and inspires our people."[17] Mao explained
this annihilation strategy to Stalin in 1951 when he observed that "set-
tling the issue of Korea may take us several years to deplete the hundreds
of thousands of American troops and to force the United States to quit
after having learned the difficulties."[18]

Mao continued to employ some of the strategies and tactics he had
successfully used in revolutionary war in 1948–49, such as outnumbering the enemy to wipe out entire enemy units (regiments and even divisions), engaging the enemy in mobile operations, and achieving surprise
whenever possible through night attacks and close-range engagements
to avoid superior enemy firepower. The Korean War, however, was not
the Chinese Civil War. And U.S. forces differed from the Japanese and
GMD forces that Mao had previously fought. Mao seemed to ignore
Sunzi's advice: "Know the enemy, know yourself; and victory is never
in doubt, not in a hundred battles."[19] Xu Yan points out that Mao's strategy and the tactics that he had developed in the past did not reflect
changes in Korea and failed to meet the demands of modern warfare.[20]
There was a huge gap between Mao's campaign goals and strategic reality
in the spring of 1951. The CPVF still lacked the air force, tanks, and heavy
artillery necessary for a successful campaign against the more powerful
and mechanized UNF troops. Mao's campaign goals of annihilating
six UNF divisions and brigades seemed beyond the CPVF's capability.

Mao's calculation was based on the increasing CPVF manpower. He
told Stalin that "after all of the nine armies of the second wave arrive, we
will launch a new and stronger campaign."[21] In February the Nineteenth
Army Group—the Sixty-Third, Sixty-Fourth, and Sixty-Fifth Armies,
110,000 strong—rushed to North Korea. The army group HQ and Yang
Dezhi, commander of the Nineteenth (chart 3.1), moved into Korea
with the Sixty-Fourth Army from Andong on February 16 and reached
the areas south of Chucheon-ri (Chuchon-ri) on March 12.[22] His Sixty-
Fourth Army entered Korea from Andong on February 16–17, marched
to Pyongyang (P'yōngyang) and Sunan (Suan) on February 27, and
reached the areas of Nancheon (Nanchon) and Pyeongsan (Pyongsan)
on March 18.[23] The Sixty-Third Army entered Korea from Changdian

```
                            ┌─────────────────┐
                            │ CPVF            │
                            │ Headquarters    │
                            │ Commander: Peng │
                            │ Dehuai          │
                            └─────────────────┘
```

| 19th Army Group | 3rd Army Group | 9th Army Group |
|---|---|---|
| Commander: Yang Dezhi | Commander & Pol. Com.: | Commander & Pol. Com.: |
| Pol. Com.: Li Zhimin | Chen Geng | Song Shilum |
| Dep. Commander & Chief | Dep. Commander: Wang | Dep. Commander: Tao |
| Of Staff: Zheng Weishan | Jinshan | Yong |
| Chief of Pol. Com.: Chen Xianrui | Dep. Pol. Com.: Du Yide | Chief of Staff: Qin Jian |

| 63rd Army | 12th Army | 20th Army |
|---|---|---|
| Commander: Fu Chongbi | Commander: Zeng Shaoshan | Commander: Zhang Yixiang |

| 187th Division | 31st Division | 58th Division |
|---|---|---|
| 188th Division | 34th Division | 59th Division |
| 189th Division | 35th Divison | 60th Division |

| 64th Army | 15th Army | 26th Army |
|---|---|---|
| Commander: Zeng Siyn | Commander: Qin Jiwei | Commander: Zhang Renchu |

| 190th Division | 29th Division | 76th Division |
|---|---|---|
| 191th Division | 44th Division | 77th Division |
| 192nd Division | 45th Division | 78th Division |

| 65th Army | 60th Army | 27th Army |
|---|---|---|
| Commander: Xiao Yingtang | Commander: Wei Jie | Commander: Peng Deqing |

| 193rd Division | 179th Division | 79th Division |
|---|---|---|
| 194th Division | 180th Division | 80th Division |
| 195th Division | 181st Division | 81st Division |

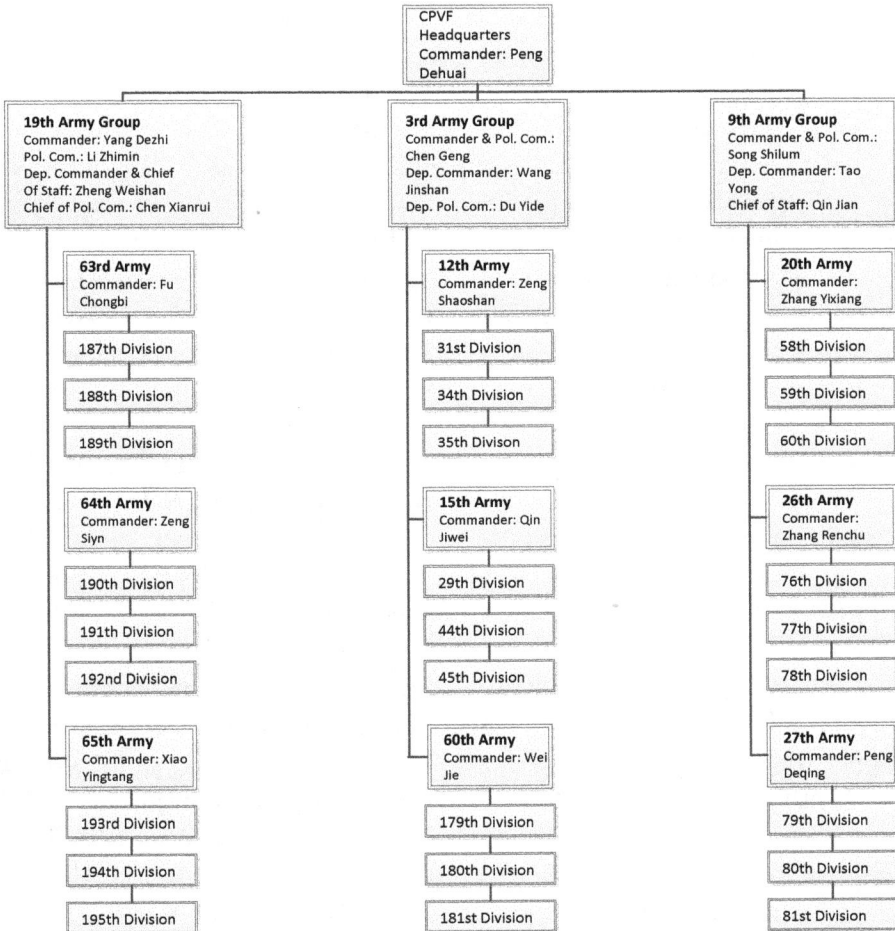

Chart 3.1. The CPVF Chain of Command, April 1951

and Jiuliancheng (Kiuliencheng) on February 18–20, marched to Seong-cheon (Songchon) on February 28, and reached the areas of Sapyeon-ri (Sapyon-ri) and Toksan (Tosan) on March 10.[24] The Sixty-Fifth Army entered Korea from Andong on February 21–22, marched to the north of Suncheon (Sunchon) on March 2, and reached the areas of Shingye (Singye) and Chucheon-ri on March 18.[25]

On March 16 the CMC established the Third Army Group in Beijing for the Korean War and appointed Chen Geng (1903–61) as its com-

mander and political commissar. His Twelfth Army came from the Third
Field Army in eastern China; his Fifteenth Army was from the Fourth
Field Army in the south; and his Sixtieth Army came from the Second Field Army in the southwest.[26] All of these armies, totaling 120,000
troops, entered Korea in March, although Chen did not go to Korea until
late June because of health problems. The Third Army Group HQ moved
into Korea under the command of Wang Jinshan (1915–78), deputy commander of the group who was in charge during Chen's absence.[27] For
more on Chen and Wang, see below. The group's Twelfth Army entered
Korea from Changdian on March 18 and reached Euicheon (Ichon)
and Munan-ri (Munanri) on April 10.[28] The Fifteenth Army entered
Korea from Andong on March 20 and reached the areas of Euicheon
and Shingye on April 12.[29] The Sixtieth Army entered Korea from Andong on March 23 and reached the areas of Euicheon and Shingye on
April 14.[30]

Mao's second wave also included the Forty-Seventh, Sixty-Seventh,
and Sixty-Eighth Armies, totaling another nine infantry divisions.[31] The
Forty-Seventh Army from central Hunan Province and consisting of the
139th, 140th, and 141st Divisions, or about 30,000 troops, entered Korea
on April 11.[32] The Forty-Seventh Army was ordered to construct airports
north of Pyongyang after entering Korea.[33] The Sixty-Seventh and Sixty-
Eighth Armies belonged to the Twentieth Army Group from northern China. The Sixty-Seventh Army consisted of the 199th, 200th, and
201st Divisions, while the Sixty-Eighth consisted of the 202nd, 203rd,
and 204th Divisions. The Twentieth Army Group reached Tianjin and
Tanggu (Tang-ku) in April. The CMC ordered these armies to get ready
to enter Korea in the spring.

To prepare for the Spring Offensive, Mao and the Chinese high command had accumulated four army groups: the Third, Ninth, Thirteenth,
and Nineteenth. The four army groups commanded fourteen armies—
the Twelfth, Fifteenth, Twentieth, Twenty-Sixth, Twenty-Seventh, Thirty-
Eighth, Thirty-Ninth, Fortieth, Forty-Second, Forty-Seventh, Sixtieth,
Sixty-Third, Sixty-Fourth, and Sixty-Fifth—with forty-two infantry divisions, eight artillery divisions, and four AAA divisions. The Thirty-
Eighth and Forty-Second Armies, after fighting nonstop throughout the
first four campaigns, were ordered to defend the coastal areas against a

possible UNF landing in North Korea. Thus the CPVF front-line ground combat forces totaled 548,000 troops. The total number of CPVF ground forces was 770,000 men.[34] The CPVF also had support troops totaling 180,000 men, in six supply services headquarters, four railroad engineering divisions, eleven engineering regiments, and one security division. By the middle of April 1951, the Chinese forces in Korea had increased to 950,000 men.[35]

The arrival of the CPVF's second wave made the already precarious supply situation worse. Peng sent several urgent telegrams to Mao and Zhou Enlai complaining about these difficulties in February and early March. On March 11, 1951, for example, he wrote Zhou: "Currently, no improvement appears in the transportation. Our troops often run out of food and fight without meals. It is impossible [for them] to find any food locally. The enemy has increased their air power, which will certainly not reduce our difficulty, but increase it, if our air force can't protect our transportation and logistics. This will affect the next decisive battle."[36] Mao knew the CPVF's problems, and he needed more Russian support. He telegraphed Stalin emphasizing the continuous U.S. bombing of CPVF supply lines: "Only about 60–70 percent of our army's logistical supplies reach the front, while 30–40 percent of them are destroyed by air raids and bombs during their shipment." Then Mao made a careful request: "Comrade Peng Dehuai eagerly hopes that the Soviet Air Force could provide air coverage over the Pyongyang-Wonsan line and areas north of the line, and that the Soviet Air Force could forward their air force bases currently operating [in China] into Korea."[37] Stalin received Mao's telegram on March 1 and approved the Chinese request on March 5. Stalin also transferred two more fighter divisions from China to North Korea on March 15, 1951.[38]

We know now that the Soviet Air Force participated in the Korean War. Following Stalin's orders, Maj. Gen. N. B. Belov, Soviet Union Air Force, arrived in northeastern China as early as August 1950 with one division.[39] Twelve Soviet Air Force divisions under Belov's command arrived in China within the next three months.[40] They included six MiG-9 fighter divisions, two MiG-15 fighter divisions, one La (Lavochkin)–9 fighter division, one Il (Ilyushin)–10 fighter division, and one Tu-2 bomber division. To protect these divisions were ten tank regiments and eleven AAA regiments of the 87th and 92nd AAA Divisions, which had 1,186 AAA cannons and 648 anti-aircraft machine guns.[41]

Their mission was to protect the bridges across the Yalu River and the power plants, railroads, and airports fifty miles south of the Chinese–North Korean border. The Russian pilots who flew into Korea had to take off from China.[42] They wore Chinese uniforms, were not allowed to communicate in Russian while they were in the air, swore never to tell of their Korean War service, and most important, could not be captured as prisoners of war. All Russian airplanes were repainted with Chinese or North Korean markings. On November 1, 1950, seven days after the Chinese engaged the UNF on the ground, Russian fighters began patrolling Korean air space. On that first day, six Yak-9 fighters engaged American fighters and bombers over the Anzhou area, with the Russians claiming to have shot down two B-29 bombers and one Mustang fighter while losing two Yak-9s.[43] Belov reported to Stalin that his pilots shot down twenty-three U.S. airplanes in the first half of November. Stalin was impressed and, as the result, sent 120 newly designed MiG-15 jet fighters to the Korean War.[44] In mid-November, the Soviet Air Force established the Sixty-Fourth Air Force Army under Belov, to command all the Soviet Air Force divisions and ground units along the Chinese–North Korean border.

In January 1951, when the three Chinese offensive campaigns had pushed the front southward to the 37th Parallel, the Russian air support seemed inadequate. On February 24, during a trip to Beijing, Peng and Nie Rongzhen, talked to Gen. S. E. Zakharov, the Soviet chief military representative to the PLA General Staff, and requested an extension of Soviet air coverage farther south to protect the CPVF transportation and communication lines. Zakharov declined their request. Peng complained to Mao and Zhou on February 26 and 28 and insisted that Mao send this request directly to Stalin.[45] After receiving Mao's telegram, Stalin ordered Belov to transfer two Russian fighter divisions, the 151st and 324th Divisions of the Sixty-Fourth Soviet Air Force, from China to North Korea on March 7. On March 15 Stalin telegraphed Mao, informing him that two fighter divisions would be transferred.[46] These two divisions boasted many WWII pilots and excellent training; they were among the strongest in the Soviet Air Force. Their arrival threatened the

UNF air operations north of the 38th Parallel and created an air space controlled by the Soviets, known as "MiG Alley."[47] In April Lt. Gen. T. A. Lobov replaced Belov as the commander of the Soviet Sixty-Fourth Air Force.

By the summer of 1951, the Sixty-Fourth had deployed 190 MiG-15s and two AAA divisions to North Korea. Still, to hide Russian involvement, Russian airplanes could not fly over UNF-controlled areas or south of the 39th Parallel. The CPVF Command complained about these restrictions since they meant the Russian fighters could not support the Chinese ground operations.[48] Chinese forces also suffered casualties caused by friendly fire from the Russian fighters, including two Chinese airplanes that were mistakenly shot down by the Russians. Stalin, however, had his own considerations: the Soviet Union did not want a war with America in Korea, or anywhere else in East Asia.[49] Nevertheless, Shen Zhihua concludes that Soviet air support played an important role in helping the Chinese intervention in the Korean War.[50]

Stalin also increased the number of the Soviet military advisers in China. Most of the 80,000 Soviets sent to China in the early 1950s were military advisers.[51] The Soviet Military Advisory Group General HQ in Beijing assigned its advisers to all the PLA headquarters in the capital and sent many others to the PLA regional, army, and divisional commands.[52] Unlike civilian advisers, who were under the supervision and management of the Soviet embassy in Beijing, the military advisers were directly under the Soviet high command in Moscow. Gen. S. E. Zakharov, deputy chief of the Soviet General Staff, served as head of the military advisory group to China in 1950–51. In 1951–53 he was followed by Gen. Mikhail Kalasovski.[53] With Russian support and Chinese reinforcements, Mao decided to launch the Spring Offensive. He had faith in the CPVF and in Peng's absolute loyalty and strong generalship. Personal relations were a very important factor in the Chinese chain of command.

## PENG'S DECISION: INTELLIGENCE AND DEBATE

Although Mao was the undisputed decision maker in Beijing and retained control over the planning and implementation of the various phases of the war, the chairman trusted Peng to put his plans into action.[54] Peng was a legendary CCP commander, one of the three most respected commanders of the PLA. Born into a poor peasant family, Peng lost his mother when he was eight and begged on the streets for food for his two younger brothers. At seventeen, he enlisted in a warlord army in central Hunan Province. Then he served as a GMD officer and became a brigade commander before joining the CCP in 1928. He subsequently commanded the Fifth Army of the Chinese Red Army. As one of the PLA's most dedicated generals, Peng had worked closely with Mao, serving during the Long March and as deputy commander of the Eighth Route Army in 1937–45. He had been deputy commander in chief of the PLA since 1949. After the Korean War, Peng became China's first defense minister in 1954 and one of the ten PLA marshals in 1955.[55] Outspoken, stubborn, and willful, Peng was well known for his strong personality and short temper, often yelling at his subordinates. Peng had executed Mao's orders without any problem through the first four campaigns in the Korean War.[56]

In the spring of 1951, while Mao was certain of victory, Peng tried to plan an immediate attack on the UNF with a possibility of retaking Seoul. The sooner the campaign could be launched, the better the chance of victory. Peng feared an imminent U.S. amphibious landing behind Chinese lines. While the CPVF was planning the Spring Offensive in early March, its Command's Operation and Intelligence Departments proposed a campaign plan to Xie Fang, the chief of staff of the CPVF. Chinese intelligence warned the CPVF Command of a planned U.S. landing along the coast of North Korea in conjunction with continuing UNF attacks.[57] Trained in the Japanese Infantry School in the 1920s and at a Russian university in Moscow in the 1940s, Xie was an experienced CCP intelligence officer and skilled PLA operational planner. In 1941 he had worked as division head in the Intelligence Department of the CMC at Yan'an, the CCP's wartime capital, where Mao changed his given name from Peiran to Fang (meaning "liberation").[58] Xie served as chief of staff of the Fourth Field Army's Thirteenth Army Group in 1950. After he received the information about the probable U.S. landing, Xie believed that, like MacArthur's Inchon (Inch'ŏn) landing the previous September, it could threaten the rear and flanks of the CPVF and NKPA.[59]

Xie immediately reported the potential landing to Peng.[60] The CMC confirmed the information on American landing preparations in April. In a telegram to Peng in that month, the CMC warned the CPVF: "Regarding the enemy movements, we learned that U.S. 40th and 45th Divisions have arrived on Hokkaido, Japan. The friendly intelligence reported that the United States has sent two divisions to Japan, and two more divisions are on their way to Japan. It is unclear if the United States has sent four or six divisions to Japan."[61]

Both Beijing and the CPVF Command were misinformed about the U.S. landing. The Chinese did not have their own intelligence sources, and North Korea failed to provide accurate information. The CMC in Beijing depended almost totally on public news from Japan and Taiwan to determine UNF deployments and reinforcements. In the same telegram, the CMC told Peng: "Tokyo [April] 25th news reported that four U.S. divisions have arrived in Japan. [We] have ordered the [CMC] Operation Department, Intelligence Department, and New China News Agency to concentrate their staff on listening to four radio broadcastings and news releases of Japan, America, Jiang [Jiang Jieshi], and Rhee [Syngman Rhee]. We will pass on any information to you as soon as it becomes available."[62] In fact, the UNF did not plan a landing in North Korea in April 1951. The Joint Chiefs instructed Lt. Gen. Ridgway on May 1 as follows:

> All United States forces currently deployed in FECOM [Far East Command] except 40th and 45th Inf Divs. These divs will not be employed outside Japanese Islands without authority from JCS [the Joint Chiefs of Staff], and the integrity of personnel and units in these divs will be preserved. For planning purposes you may assume that in event implementation of Jt [Joint] Outline Emerg[ency] War Plan is directed while UN forces are in conflict with Communist forces in Far East, all SAC [Strategic Air Command] units operating in Far East Theater will be redeployed as required to support strategic air offensive.[63]

The Joint Chiefs seemed to want these two infantry divisions to be reserves for the UNF in case of Russian intervention in the Far East. The 45th Division was responsible for the security of Hokkaido, the northernmost island of Japan, through the rest of the year. In December 1951 the division deployed to Korea.[64]

However, in March the Chinese high command was convinced that Ridgway would conduct an amphibious landing in the Chinese-Korean rear areas so as to cut the CPVF and NKPA's transportation and communication lines, forcing them to fight on two fronts at once. The lack of reliable sources and limited experience with foreign wars seriously impaired the Chinese ability to have an accurate picture of UNF intentions. The top Chinese leaders' individual interpretations became critical, as they assimilated incoming information into their personal experience and political agendas. The U.S. landing at Inchon in September 1950, which had crushed the NKPA, stood out in the minds of both Peng and Xie; neither wished to repeat Kim Il-sung's mistake. This distorted analysis contributed to a mistaken and costly fear. The misinformation made it impossible for Peng to have a comprehensive understanding of U.S. intentions and to explore some of Ridgway's disadvantages, in contrast to how the Chinese had handled MacArthur's miscalculations and ignorance a few months before.

Chinese intelligence failures led Peng to miscalculate the situation and rush into a new offensive campaign before his forces were fully ready. In early March he considered making an immediate southward strike before the U.S. could carry out an amphibious landing. As Sunzi said, "it is the nature of the army to stress speed; to take advantage of the enemy's absence; to travel unanticipated roads; and to attack when they are not alert."[65] At a CPVF Command meeting on March 11, Peng proposed having the CPVF forces strike the advancing U.S. I and IX Corps, pushing them back south of the 38th Parallel and retaking Seoul if possible. He set mid-April as the starting time for the Spring Offensive, when the main strength of the second wave would reach the front.[66]

However, considerable disagreement arose among CPVF commanders regarding how and where to conduct the Spring Offensive. Most of the commanders disagreed with Peng, preferring a defensive operation that would lure the UNF north of the 38th Parallel and then strike. Since all of the CPVF commanders except Peng had come from the Fourth Field Army's Thirteenth Army Group, which composed the main strength of the CPVF, they had similar military experiences and were able to easily share their ideas and support each other.

At the meeting, Hong Xuezhi, the thirty-eight-year-old deputy commander of the CPVF, suggested letting the UNF advance further north into the CPVF-controlled Keumhwa (Kumhwa or Kimhwa)–Cheorwon (Chorwon) area, where the CPVF could launch an attack. With only six years of elementary education, Hong had joined the CCP armed forces when he was sixteen. He had become an experienced commander of the Heilongjiang Provincial Command, the Sixth Army of the Northeastern Field Army, and Forty-third Army of the Fourth Field Army in the Chinese Civil War. In 1949–50 he had served as the chief of staff of the Fifteenth Army Group and deputy commander of the Thirteenth Army Group. Hong was the only Chinese commander who was promoted to general twice, in 1955 and in 1988.[67] In charge of CPVF operation, logistics, and security, Hong had successfully protected the CPVF HQ and had personally saved Peng's life twice during UNF air raids, when Peng refused to leave his office for a shelter in the cave.[68] At the meeting, Hong argued: "If we attack the enemy south of the area, the enemy will fall back quickly, making it difficult for us to annihilate an entire enemy unit."[69] Peng disagreed: "We can't fall back any further. There are too many disadvantages to letting the enemy advance into these areas. Cheorwon is an open plain, terrible terrain for coping with enemy tanks. Besides, what are we going to do about our war ammunition and food stored at Mukae-ri [Mukyeok-ri]? No, by no means should we allow the enemy into these areas! We must fight against them south of Keumhwa and Cheorwon!"[70] Nevertheless, Hong continued to argue for a different strategy.

Deng Hua, first deputy commander and deputy political commissar under Peng, sided with Hong. Deng had been closely associated with Peng since at least 1928 and was one of the most experienced army commanders of the PLA.[71] At the CPVF commanders' meeting, however, Deng said: "I still agree with Hong Xuezhi as his suggestions have merits. The enemy should be lured in deep before we strike hard. Currently, the Third and Nineteenth Army Groups have just entered Korea, and the Ninth Army Group is just moving out toward the front. None of these forces are familiar with the terrain in this area, and they are marching south in a hurry." He continued: "Allowing the enemy into our controlled areas would let us wait at our ease for the exhausted enemy, and have more time to be better prepared and get familiar with the local conditions."[72] Xie and Du Ping, director of the CPVF Political Department, expressed their support for Hong's suggestion.[73]

Feeling isolated at the meeting, Peng became upset and demanded: "Do you want to fight this battle or not?" Faced with Peng's stubbornness, his subordinates conceded. Xie backed down first, modifying his opinion and adding: "I just think twice, and believe that Chief Peng's proposal has some good reasons, and is very thoughtful." Hong said: "Chief, we are all your staff, and our job is to make suggestions for your reference and consideration. You are the commander in chief, and you will make the final decision."[74]

The CPVF commanders could rarely ignore or refuse the often unattainable goals set up by Stalin, Mao, or even their own chief, Peng. They always argued for tactical flexibility so that realistic objectives could be pursued and lower expectations met. However, the Chinese generals feared and respected Peng. They served him loyally and did not intend to challenge his authority. The commander in chief had to have absolute authority over all aspects of the operation and be in total control of the CPVF, so that he could make changes depending on the situation at any moment without having to seek consensus from his deputies. This fact prevented any of his subordinates from undermining his authority.

Despite their arguments, Peng was determined to launch his southward offensive and retake Seoul. Bin Yu points out that Peng made his decision because he attempted to "seize the initiative after months of being pressed by the UN forces."[75] The perceived threat of a U.S. landing also rushed Peng into scheduling the campaign early, and visions of enemy tanks careening across the open plains toward his supply depots gave him reason to dismiss ambushing the UNF in Keumhwa and Cheorwon. Allan Millett points out that "Peng believed the only justification for the attack was that it prevented United Nations Command from undertaking a second amphibious landing and overland drive toward Wonsan."[76]

## OBJECTIVES, OPERATION PLANS, AND REPLACEMENTS

In March 1951 the UNF Command discovered that the CPVF and NKPA were assembling strategic forces at the front and assumed that they would conduct offensive operations in late April or early May. However, encouraged by several successful UNF drives, Ridgway, commander of the U.S. Eighth Army, had decided to continue the UNF assault.[77] He promised MacArthur that he would be cautious in conducting the new offensive, would restrict field operations to areas with full logistical support, and would not outrun his supply lines. On March 27 Ridgway called an operational meeting that was attended by all army and division commanders from the Eighth Army. At the meeting, he formally issued orders to begin Operation Rugged, a new offensive that would permit the UNF to move north of the 38th Parallel and occupy Line Kansas.[78] Running just north of the 38th Parallel, Line Kansas started where the Han and Imjin Rivers met in the west and extended eastward to the Hwacheon (Hwachon) Reservoir, ending at Yangyang on Korea's eastern coast. Beginning on April 2 the U.S. Eighth Army crossed the 38th Parallel as part of Operation Rugged. On April 9 the U.S. I and IX Corps and ROK I Corps reached Line Kansas.[79]

On April 6 Peng chaired a Spring Offensive commanders' conference at Keumhwa, including all the commanders and political commissars at the army, army group, and HQ levels. The chief told his generals that "the best time for our counterattacks is now. The enemy troops are exhausted and not at full strength. They have not supplied their ranks to compensate for their casualties, and have no reinforcements in sight." He added: "According to the information, MacArthur and Ridgway visited the eastern front in the past few days. The enemy seems to be planning a new offensive in the east, and a landing along the eastern coast in the Tongcheon [Tongchon]–Wonsan areas. They want to push all the way to the north of the 39th Parallel."[80]

Peng then outlined the objectives for the Spring Offensive. First, this campaign would prevent the enemy from landing in North Korea. The chief pointed out that "this campaign is extremely important . . . [because] we must smash the enemy's plan. . . ."[81] Peng's first campaign objective was a practical one: it was strategically important for Mao to accept, and it was not too hard for the CPVF to achieve. As Sunzi wrote, "thus, the highest realization of warfare is to attack the enemy's plans."[82] Since the first objective of the offensive campaign was to derail a UNF plan, Peng remained flexible, and the CPVF would be able to respond to the UNF advance's speed and locations. Peng reasoned:

Considering that our second group has not been fully assembled, we will allow the enemy forces to move to Keumhwa, Munteng-ri [Mundung-ni], and Kaeseong before conducting our counterattacks. Should the enemy move faster than we anticipate, we will launch counterattacks around April 20; should the enemy move slower than we anticipate, we will begin our attacks in early May. If we wait until the enemy has already made its landings and been strengthened with reinforcements, our difficulties will multiply considerably.[83]

The second objective was to exceed Mao's expectations by destroying three U.S. divisions, three ROK divisions (Mao had asked for only one), and three British and Turkish brigades (Mao had asked for two). Peng asserted: "We must eliminate several enemy divisions and smash the enemy's war plans."[84] The main targets were the U.S. 3rd, 24th, and 25th Divisions; ROK 1st, 2nd, and 6th Divisions; British 27th and 29th Brigades; and the Turkish Brigade under the U.S. I and IX Corps. All of these enemy forces were on the western front between Munsan and Chuncheon (Chunchon). Peng ordered the newly arrived Third and Nineteenth Army Groups to concentrate their six armies on the western front, stage primary attacks, and wipe out these six enemy divisions and three brigades. Some of Peng's lieutenants and staff members at HQ wondered about this objective since even during the First and Second Campaigns, when the UNF had been caught by total surprise, the forces of the first wave had never destroyed an enemy division or a brigade. They had destroyed only one U.S. regiment in a single battle during the previous campaigns. Since the CPVF had been unable to wipe out one enemy division in the past six months, how could they be successful now? But no one dared to ask any more questions at the conference.[85]

Peng's last campaign objective was to "regain the initiative."[86] He explained that "the enemy forces continue to push forward and will continue their attacks northward after occupying the 38th Parallel." He estimated that the UNF would increase its forces, fortify its line, and bring its superior firepower to bear. In such a case, it could be very difficult for the CPVF to break through UNF defenses.[87] The chief called on all CPVF commanders to do everything in their power to make the offensive successful before the UNF consolidated its positions. "This campaign is of enormous significance," Peng emphasized. "It is the key to whether we will gain the initiative in this war or not, and it is the key to whether the Korean War can be shortened or will be prolonged. If we can annihilate a substantial number of enemy forces, we can not only take back the initiative from the enemy on the Korean battleground, but also deepen the discord within the enemy camps." Peng also warned: "If this campaign is not successful, we will not only lose the initiative in the war, but also will ensure that the war will be a prolonged fight with many more difficulties in the future. We must strive to make this war as short a conflict as possible."[88] All of the commanders at the conference reflected Peng's enthusiasm and optimism. At the conference Peng also asked that all the armies conduct political mobilization and tactical training to better prepare their troops. They should invite officers from the troops of the first wave to pass on operational experience and combat lessons. Furthermore, all army and division commands needed to organize operational and tactical reconnaissance in their operational areas.[89]

On April 10 Peng and the CPVF Command made the final decision to block the continuing UNF advance at the Keumcheon (Kumchon)–Munhyeo-ri (Munhye-ri or Munhyeri) line, where the CPVF prepared to attack. Peng telegraphed his campaign plan to Mao that evening. According to this plan, two armies of the Ninth Army Group would smash open the gap by attacking Kapyeong (Kapyong) at the center and would separate the UNF forces in the west from those in the east in the mountainous Hwacheon-Chuncheon (Chunchon) area. Three armies of the Ninth Army Group would then launch flanking attacks on the right side of the western UNF forces, while three armies of the Nineteenth Army Group would attack the left flank of the UNF and complete the campaign's encirclements. The Third Army Group would launch frontal attacks to cut the enemy into pieces and eventually eliminate the several UNF divisions along the 38th Parallel.[90] Mao fully agreed with Peng's campaign plan. In his reply, however, Mao still worried about a possible UNF landing at Wonsan. He instructed Peng that "the main strength of the Forty-Second Army should be deployed inside the city and surrounding areas so as to safely secure Wonsan."[91]

On April 11 the CPVF Command issued new combat instructions titled "Directives on Guiding Principles and Tactical Guidelines for the Campaign." The directives emphasized the principle of "assembling superior forces and wiping out the enemy forces one by one."[92] Under this guideline, the CPVF Command instructed all its armies to use ample force to cut an attacked enemy unit into several pieces on an operational level and then cut each piece into smaller pieces on a tactical scale and annihilate the entire unit. In addition, the directives asked commanders at all levels, especially those who were newly arrived, to make detailed plans for their maneuvers and to maintain constant, direct command over their units. Since many of the newly arrived commanders lacked experience in foreign warfare, the CPVF Command gave specific instructions on how to coordinate infantry, artillery, and tank forces; how to attack tanks; and how to remove mines. On April 15 all participating CPVF forces began moving to assemble at the attack line.[93] Three days later Peng ordered that all CPVF forces were to complete their battle preparations by April 20 and launch the offensive before night fell on either April 21 or 22.[94] This followed Sunzi: "War is such that the supreme consideration is speed."[95]

The CPVF Command worked out a detailed operational plan for the Spring Offensive. At the center of the front line, Kapyeong was where the UNF eastern and western forces met. The Fortieth Army of the Ninth Army Group would move out from Keumhwa and attack the ROK 6th Division on its front. Then the Fortieth would move south and smash open the gap by attacking Kapyeong, which was defended by the British 27th Brigade.[96] In the meantime, the Ninth's Thirty-Ninth Army would break through the U.S. 1st Marine Division at Hwacheon and move south to attack Chuncheon, which was defended by the U.S. 1st Cavalry Division. The Thirty-Ninth would then set up a defense line from north to south along the Hwacheon-Chuncheon line to protect Kapyeong and the Fortieth Army and separate the western front from the eastern front, preventing the enemy from moving reinforcements from one to the other.[97]

On the UNF right, in the meantime, the rest of the Ninth Army Group would engage in flanking attacks and operational encirclements. Its Twentieth, Twenty-Sixth, and Twenty-Seventh Armies would quickly move out from Keumhwa heading south, bypassing Kapyeong and reaching Chenpeongcheon (Chenpongchon), east of Seoul, and cutting off the U.S. 24th and 25th Divisions, completing their encirclement and destruction.[98]

On the UNF left, the Nineteenth Army Group would engage in flanking attacks and encirclement along the western coast. Its Sixty-Third, Sixty-Fourth, and Sixty-Fifth Armies would attack the ROK 1st Division in its front and destroy it, then drive all the way to the north of Seoul, cutting off and encircling the U.S. 3rd Division, British 29th Brigade, and Turkish Brigade.[99]

In the center of the western front, the Third Army Group would launch the main frontal attacks to destroy the UNF divisions and brigades. Its Twelfth and Fifteenth Armies would first attack and destroy the U.S. 3rd Division (two regiments), while the Sixtieth Army would eliminate the Turkish Brigade. These armies would then unite in order to wipe out the U.S. 24th and 25th Divisions.[100]

To prepare the CPVF for a UNF landing, the Spring Offensive's operational plan deployed the Thirty-Eighth, Forty-Second, and Forty-Seventh Armies at Wonsan, Angteok (Yangdok), Seocheon (Songchon), and Pyongyang to protect the CPVF's rear from amphibious landings and airborne attacks. The NKPA's II and VI Corps were also deployed in the Hoeyang, Hwacheon-ri (Hwachon-ni), Sanison (Sariwon), and Jaeyeong (Chaeryong) areas to repel these anticipated attacks.[101] The NKPA I Corps was to wipe out the enemy forces at Kaesong and Jangtam (Chongdan), leaving one division to defend the coast at Yeonan (Yonan) and Paecheon (Paekcheon, Paekchon, or Pakchon). Meanwhile, the main forces of the corps were to cross the Imjin River and wipe out the enemy units at Munsan before conducting an offensive advance toward Seoul, via Koyang. The corps would also be responsible for garrison duties in Seoul after securing the city.

The problem with Peng's plan was that most of the CPVF attacking forces were newly arrived armies that had no actual experience in a foreign war. Peng intended to rotate to the rear the exhausted veteran armies, which had been engaged in the previous campaigns and had suffered more than 100,000 casualties during the previous four months.[102] To get the recuperation they needed in the rear, the veterans would be replaced by newly arrived armies, the main attacking forces in the Spring Offensive. Korea became a laboratory for combat training of Chinese officers and soldiers. Later the PLA developed this into a regular rotation system, a legacy of its Korean War experience.[103]

Peng intended to strengthen the attacking force and limit Chinese casualties through rotation. Though sound in theory, his plan proved damaging. Early experiences gained from fighting the UNF were key components of any Chinese victory. Without veteran commanders and soldiers, it proved impossible to meet the Chinese campaign objectives: inexperienced troops could not win their battles.[104] In fact, it took about three months for a Chinese officer to learn the rudiments of combat leadership. Chinese veterans often commented during the interviews about "getting hard," the process of being able to deal with the horror and terror of battle.[105] They all agreed that it took about two months before a soldier could perform effectively in combat.

### OPTIMISTIC BUT INEXPERIENCED COMMANDERS

The immediate engagement of a million-man force put overwhelming pressure on the Chinese officer corps. Army group commanders and officers rose to the challenges of increased responsibility and unexpected problems. Four army groups (the Thirteenth, Ninth, Third, and Nineteenth, which entered Korea in that order) were engaged in the Spring Offensive, including sixteen armies with forty-eight infantry divisions. The Third and Nineteenth Army Groups, the campaign's strike force, had only arrived in Korea in February and March.

The Third Army Group was newly established and was not ready for action. To mobilize more troops for Korea, the CMC had decided to found the group on February 18, 1951, assigning to it the Twelfth Army from the PLA's Third Field Army in eastern China, the Fifteenth Army from the Fourth Field Army in southern China, and the Sixtieth Army from southwestern China.[106] In March, when the CMC appointed Chen army group commander and political commissar, he was still in Vietnam, serving as a Chinese military adviser to Ho Chi Minh (1890–1969) in the First Indochina War (1946–54) against the French forces. Chen was one of the most experienced and dedicated generals of the PLA. During the Chinese Civil War, he had been commander and political commissar of the Fourth Army Group. In June 1950 Liu Shaoqi, vice chairman of the CCP and vice president of the PRC, appointed Chen the CCP Central Committee's representative in Vietnam in charge of the Chinese military advisers to Ho.[107] After receiving his appointment to Korea in March 1951, Chen's health problems became so serious that he could not walk and had to stay in Beijing for treatment. Chen would command the Third Army Group in Korea until late June 1951.[108] Without its commander, the army group moved to the Chinese-Korean border in March and entered North Korea in April.

Wang Jinshan, the Third Army Group's deputy commander, was in charge during the commander's absence, with Du Yide (1912–2009) as his deputy political commissar and Wang Yunrui (1910–89) his chief of staff.[109] In 1936, at the age of twenty-one, Wang Jinshan had been appointed commander of the 93rd Division of the Thirty-First Army. During WWII, Mao bragged that the Red Army had a "Madman Wang," who was fighting invading Japanese troops like crazy.[110] He served as first deputy commander of the Third Army Group in 1949–50 and was appointed lieutenant general in 1955.Wang and other commanders entered Korea with the Third Army Group HQ from Andong in late March and attended the CPVF conference on April 6.

After Peng Dehuai's speech at the Spring Offensive commanders' conference on that date, the rest of the CPVF Command, including Deng, Hong, Xie, and Du Ping, briefed the commanders of the two newly arrived army groups. They cautioned commanders like Wang that American forces were very different from the Japanese and GMD forces they had fought before and were not to be taken lightly. Then the officers who had participated in the previous four CPVF campaigns and had firsthand experience fighting the technologically superior UNF also briefed the conference about the difficulties they had experienced. The newly arrived commanders, however, did not pay a great deal of attention to their advice. The newcomers were still influenced by the many victories they had won against millions of GMD forces. Wang even told his staff during a break in the conference that all the enemy forces present in Korea added together did not match the 550,000 GMD troops the PLA had wiped out in just sixty days in its successful Huaihai Campaign (1948–49).[111]

The Third Army Group commanders were confident of their victory in the next campaign. They believed that since the CPVF had launched four successful offensives with only six or seven armies in the past months, the CPVF should have a bigger victory during their Spring Offensive with fourteen armies. The CPVF had also increased its artillery from four to eleven divisions and its combat engineers from three to nine regiments, and for the first time four tank regiments would participate. Wang and other commanders predicted they would annihilate several American divisions. No such feat had been accomplished by the first wave of the CPVF armies, even during the First and Second Campaigns, when U.S. forces had been caught by surprise. Wang even boasted to Peng, after his briefing, that "Chief Peng, there is no problem for our one army group to eliminate one U.S. division. I guarantee you that our Third Army Group will capture at least 5,000 American soldiers as prisoners."[112]

Peng was carried away by his new force commanders' enthusiasm and optimism. And the newly arrived commanders agreed with Peng's aggressive plan and did not question its unrealistic objectives. Peng's deputies, including Deng, Hong, and Xie, were of equal rank with Wang Jinshan and Yang and could warn the newly arrived, inexperienced commanders no further; they failed to emphasize the importance of not taking the enemy too lightly. Deng even asked to step down in order to let the newly arrived army group commanders to serve as first and second deputy commanders.[113] After Peng rejected his request, Deng sent a telegram to the CMC asking for the new commanders to be included in the CPVF Command. On June 1, 1951, the CMC notified Peng that Chen, commander of the Third Army Group, would serve as the second deputy commander of the CPVF Command (though Chen could not arrive in Korea until August 22),; and that Song Shilun, commander of the Ninth Army Group, would serve as third deputy commander.[114] Deng remained as first deputy commander after Peng. Later the CMC also appointed Yang, commander of the Nineteenth Army Group, as deputy commander of the CPVF.[115]

Yang was the commander of the other newly arrived force, the Nineteenth Army Group; Li Zhimin (1906–87) was his political commissar and Zheng Weishan (1915–2000) his deputy commander and chief of staff. [116] At age forty, Yang led his Nineteenth Army Group from northwestern China to the Chinese-Korean border in early February, and they entered Korea later that month. Yang reported to the commanders' conference on April 6 that his army group was in good spirits, had high morale, and was ready to fight. Both officers and soldiers were very confident that they would defeat UNF troops, and they were eager to engage the Americans.[117] Deng tactfully warned the newly arrived commanders that "according to our experience in the past four campaigns, the American forces were definitely different from the GMD troops. The Americans have absolute superiority in air and naval support, and their artillery and tank forces are much stronger than those of the GMD. Even though the CPVF won the first four campaigns, our six armies in the west and the Ninth Army Group in the east had very tough fights."[118] However, his advice was ignored. Yang promised Peng that his army group was ready, and that as soon as Peng could issue him the order, his armies would win the Spring Offensive.[119]

After the CPVF conference, Yang held his army group planning meeting at Chwachung-dong, on April 9. All commanders and officers from the divisional level above attended the meeting. Yang passed on the CPVF campaign decisions and discussed the army group operational plans. His commanders and officers were as enthusiastic and optimistic as Yang himself about the "long awaited" fight.[120] In fact, the Nineteenth Army Group had not waited long, and it was not well prepared for the Spring Offensive. Nevertheless, all the officers promised Yang they would score a victory in the first battle. After the meeting, the Nineteenth Army Group Command issued an order to all armies "to be triumphant in the first battle."[121]

The Ninth Army Group was the only army group at the conference that had been part of the first wave and had engaged the UNF during the CPVF's Second Offensive in November–December 1950. Song Shilun was the commander and political commissar of the Ninth Army Group, with Tao Yong (1913–67) as his deputy commander and Qin Jian (1911–59) the chief of staff.[122] During the Korean War, Song became the third deputy commander of the CPVF.[123] His Ninth Army Group included three armies, the Twentieth, Twenty-Sixth, and Twenty-Seventh Armies, with nine infantry divisions, totaling 150,000 troops. The Ninth Army Group had entered Korea in early November. It had engaged the U.S. 1st Marine and 7th Infantry Divisions at the Chosin Reservoir on the eastern front from November 27 to December 12, 1950, as discussed in chapter 2.[124] The Ninth Army Group failed to destroy the U.S. 1st Marine

Division, losing 50,000 men—nearly three infantry divisions—in three weeks of fighting.[125]

However, at the April 6 conference Song explained that his failure at the Chosin Reservoir had resulted from lack of food, winter clothing, and ammunition. He shared the optimism and confidence of the newly arrived commanders and believed that the Ninth Army Group would definitely achieve a victory in the Spring Offensive.[126] Although Song did not mention it, the commanders knew that he desperately wanted to take revenge against the Americans and regain his reputation. Thus, all three army groups, encouraged by Peng and supported by the CPVF Command, seemed ready to fight the offensive. Peng telegraphed Mao on April 10 that the Third, Ninth, and Nineteenth Army Groups were to concentrate on the western front, attacking the U.S. I and IX Corps. The Ninth and Nineteenth Army Groups would flank the U.S. forces from both sides, while the Third would launch a frontal attack to cut the enemy forces into several pieces. Then the three army groups would conduct all-out attacks to win a complete victory and eliminate several enemy divisions along the 38th Parallel. After their success, the army groups would move farther south, deep into enemy territory.[127] Mao approved Peng's plan on April 13.[128]

## CPVF LOGISTICS AND RUSSIAN AID

The UNF Command's strategy became clear by the spring of 1951. After seizing and consolidating their new positions, they launched quick attacks so that the Chinese troops did not have enough time to resupply or reinforce their weary troops. The UNF used this strategy with the specific goal of depleting the CPVF of its soldiers and supplies. It worked. Although the CPVF campaign planners based their operations on the assumption that they would have significant reinforcements in Korea, the issue of maintaining combat effectiveness and adequate supplies became top priorities for the CPVF Command.

In the spring of 1951 the Chinese–North Korean forces nearly tripled in number compared to the troops in the previous four campaigns. Providing adequate support for these troops now became an even more daunting challenge. At the commanders' conference on April 6, the

CPVF Command listed specific preparations for the Spring Offensive, ordering the logistical units to speed up their stockpiling of ammunition and food. Since most Koreans had fled the areas between the 38th and 37th Parallels, there would not be any local food supply. Peng pointed out to his commanders that "it becomes our major problem now: how to overcome difficulties in this 300-*li* [about ninety-mile] no-grain area south of the 38th Parallel."[129] To deal with the supply problem, the CPVF Command required all operational forces to carry five days' of rations. Logistics branches, moving closely behind the front, would provide an additional five days' supply of food.

To meet the operational requirements of the newly arrived combat forces, four supply lines were formed, along with a network for supporting divisions and regiments. All the logistics forces were assigned transportation responsibility by section, which significantly increased the efficiency of the transportation and distribution of supplies.

By early April the CPVF had stockpiled 15,000 tons of food and three to five basic units of ammunition in storage. The PLA high command assigns a basic number or unit for ammunition for each weapon used by its troops. The basic unit varies from time to time: during the Korean War a basic unit for a hand gun, for example, was twenty-four bullets. Despite all these changes, the CPVF's logistics efforts did not fundamentally improve, and the forces were capable of providing supplies to meet the soldiers' minimum requirements for only a short period. There was still no guarantee that they could meet operational demands.[130]

The high command continued to improve the CPVF logistics and transportation by establishing its own logistics department in Korea during the Spring Offensive. Before May 1951, supplying the CPVF was under the command of the PLA's Northeast Regional Command's Logistics Department. On April 16 the CMC decided to "organize the Logistic Department of the CPVF General Headquarters between Andong [in China] and the site of the CPVF Headquarters [in North Korea]."[131] In late April Hong was summoned to Beijing, and he briefed Zhou Enlai about the CPVF's logistical situation. Hong emphasized three logistic problems: long supply lines, delays in getting much-needed food and ammunition, and weak defenses against UNF air attacks.[132] Hong believed that managing CPVF's logistics in Korea, rather than relying on the PLA's Northeast Regional Command in China, would improve the front's logistic supply and services. Zhou told Hong that "the CMC will discuss your request and make its plans as soon as possible."[133] On May 1 Mao Zedong and Zhu De, commander in chief of the PLA, met Hong at the Tiananmen tower during the Labor Day celebration in Beijing. Mao asked Hong and the CPVF commanders "to carefully learn [from] the experience of each battle."[134]

After his return, Hong drafted the "CPVF Directives on the Logistical Supplies Problem" on May 3, which systematically summarized the experience of the CPVF and the lessons it had learned. On May 14 Peng chaired the CPVF commanders' meeting at Kongsudong (Kongseodong) to discuss how to organize its logistics department. The meeting nominated Hong as the CPVF logistics commander and reported its decision to the CMC for approval.[135] On May 19 the CMC issued its "Decision on Strengthening the Volunteer Forces' Logistics Tasks" and ordered that "the Logistics Department of the CPVF should be established immediately. It will command and manage all the Chinese logistics units and facilities within Korea. The CPVF Logistics Department is under the direct command of the CPVF leading commanders.... The Logistics Department from now on will take charge of all the CPVF's logistics forces, including supporting troops and rear supply units (such as the engineering corps, artillery units, public security, radio communication, highway transportation, railroad engineering, construction forces, and hospitals)."[136] The CMC appointed Hong as commander of the CPVF Logistics Department, with Zhou Chunquan (1905–85) as the political commissar, Zhang Mingyuan (b. 1909) as the deputy commander, and Du Zheheng (b. 1913) as the vice political commissar.[137]

Under Hong the CPVF Logistics Department set up a new system that better fit the CPVF's needs during the Spring Offensive: supplying front locations, rather than specific army units.[138] Before May 1951 the PLA system had first delivered food and munitions from China through the PLA's Northeast Regional Command's Logistics Department to each CPVF army. The army then distributed the supplies to its divisions, each division delivered them to its own regiments, and so on. Food and ammunition shipments always lagged behind the operations.[139] During the first two campaigns, the CPVF met only one-quarter of the food needs of its front-line troops. In the third campaign, front-line troops received 30–40 percent of their minimum needs. These shortfalls seriously constrained CPVF operations. Hong's new logistics system established supply depots along the front lines, supplying all troops stationed within that area. Even though units shifted, the area supply depot remained and could be used by both Chinese and North Korean troops.[140] The new system improved the CPVF logistics capacity at the regiment and battalion levels and increased the front-line troops' combat effectiveness. The Chinese military's performance in Korea, like its solutions to battlefield problems as a rule, was not elegant, but it was effective. Although the Chinese had a steep learning curve, they very often achieved their battlefield objectives.[141]

To strengthen logistics support for the Spring Offensive, the newly established CPVF Logistics Department had grown to six branches, including two Chinese-Korean border offices, thirty-one major logistics stations, eleven truck transportation regiments, seventeen heavy equipment transportation regiments, eight manpower transportation regiments, eight traffic garrison regiments, seven garrison battalions, and eleven stretcher regiments—for a total logistics force of 180,000 men. The department ordered its thirty-nine field hospitals to prepare to receive 40,000–50,000 wounded soldiers during the campaign. It also ordered its engineering force to begin repairing highways from Seocheon to Angteok via Teokhyion-ri, Yeongwon, and Munsan, in case enemy amphibious landings cut off traditional routes.[142]

The CPVF forces badly needed large numbers of automatic weapons and munitions in this modern war. Mao telegraphed Stalin on November 8, 1950, asking the Soviets to provide 140,000 automatic rifles with fifty-eight million rounds of ammunition, 26,000 submachine guns with eighty million rounds, 7,000 light machine guns with thirty-seven million rounds, 2,000 heavy machine guns with twenty million rounds, and other weapons and munitions.[143] After its second wave entered Korea, the CPVF demanded more Russian military aid to support its offensive campaign against the UNF. Soviet military aid was indispensable for the CPVF's large-scale operations on the Korean front. During the first quarter of 1951, for example, the CPVF needed 14,100 tons of ammunition. China's own defense industry produced a mere 1,500 tons, and the Soviet Union supplied another 12,000 tons between January and March.[144] On May 22, 1951, Stalin telegraphed Mao: "We are providing you with 372 MiG-15 jet fighters with no charge. [You] only pay their shipment from Russia to China." The Soviet leader gave more details on the fighters' delivery and added: "We have made a transportation plan to ship these 372 airplanes to China. The first shipment of 72 warplanes will arrive in China before June 20. The other shipments will arrive thereafter shortly. [We] guarantee that you will receive all of the 372 warplanes by early August."[145] But they were too late for the Spring Offensive.[146]

In May 1951 Mao and the CMC sent Xu Xiangqian (Hsu Hsiang-ch'ian, 1901–90) to the Soviet Union to purchase more arms from the Russians. Xu had joined the CCP in 1927 and became one of its military leaders after the party established its own armed forces. During the Chinese Civil War, he served as deputy commander of the Northern Military Region and commander and political commissar of the First Army Group. After the founding of the PRC, Xu was appointed chief of the PLA General Staff in 1949, vice chairman of the CMC in 1954, vice premier in 1965, and defense minister in 1978–81. He became one of the ten Chinese marshals in 1955.[147] Xu led a Chinese military delegation to Moscow to talk with the Soviet government in the spring of 1951 and to purchase Soviet-made weapons and equipment to arm sixty Chinese infantry divisions.[148] According to the Sino-Soviet agreement, China received a $1.34 billion loan from the Soviet Union in 1951–53 as military aid. The Soviets also transferred machinery technology for production of rifles, machine guns, and artillery pieces.[149] Additionally, Chinese and North Korean armies received aid from Eastern European countries such as Poland, Romania, and Czechoslovakia.[150] Romania provided forty-one railroad cars full of war materials for the North Korean and Chinese troops in April 1951, including hospital equipment (in two rail cars) and medicine (in ten rail cars) for a hundred-bed hospital. Romania sent twenty-two medical personnel, who arrived in China on April 8.[151]

Nevertheless, very few CPVF armies received the Russian weapons before the Spring Offensive. Hong complained that since the Soviet Union did not have sufficient transportation to deliver the arms immediately, the CPVF received Russian arms for only sixteen out of sixty infantry divisions in 1951.[152] The Twentieth Army Group's two armies, the Sixty-Seventh and Sixty-Eighth, replaced all of their weaponry and equipment with newly arrived Russian arms when they reached Tianjin (Tientsin) and Tanggu, preparing to enter Korea.[153] They were the first Chinese armies, including six infantry divisions, to be rearmed with Soviet weapons during the Korean War. These Chinese divisions were equipped according to Soviet standards. Each infantry division, totaling 14,963 men and officers, included three infantry regiments, one artillery regiment, one tank or mobile artillery regiment, one AAA battalion, and one antitank artillery battalion. In total, each Russian-armed division had 13,938 infantry weapons, 303 artillery pieces, 261 trucks, and 84 armored vehicles.[154] Rearmed by Russian weapons and equipment through the Korean War, Chinese weaponry became standardized.

But however skilled the Chinese became at conducting warfare with grenades and developing survival skills, in the Korean War they did not have the use of automatic weapons and tanks, advanced forms of artillery pieces, or a modern command and control system. To make armed soldiers effective in a unit structure required a quality training program with Russian-made weapons. The CPVF did not establish a centralized training program in China or Korea for the integration of new weapon systems. The lack of a standardized weapons instruction and mandatory training on all infantry weapons limited the level of proficiency across the CPVF armies. When the Twentieth Army Group's two armies, the Sixty-Seventh and Sixty-Eighth, replaced all their weaponry and equipment with newly arrived Russian arms, the Army Group Command conducted prewar training for all its commanders at the army, division, and regimental levels to address issues regarding fighting the U.S.-led UNF in a modern war. The command invited commanders from the CPVF's first wave to share their experiences. The Twentieth Army Group entered Korea in June 1951, better prepared than the army groups that were rushed into Korea in October 1950 and February 1951.

UNF divisions had, for the most part, moved into the CPVF attacking zone, especially a salient at the Cheorwon front, and appeared to be moving farther north. Therefore, Peng and the other commanders of the CPVF-NKPA Joint Command made a decision to launch the Spring Offensive at dusk on April 22, 1951. Still concerned that the United States might make amphibious landings on the eastern and western coasts in the CPVF's rear, Peng decided to begin the offensive ahead of schedule. As a result, most of the Chinese attacking troops had not completed their preparations. Despite the superior manpower and the use of tactics that had been effective in the previous campaigns, the CPVF fell short in the Spring Offensive. Peng had made some irretrievable strategic mistakes before the campaign even started.

First, the second wave of the CPVF forces had not been able to get a sufficient amount of rest after making the long journey from China into Korea. Some of the army commands had not even finished surveying the local terrain before being called on to launch their attacks. Peng's rush to launch the offensive doomed the Chinese forces. Whatever advantage they might have held was lost in poor battle planning. Second, the mistakes were made not only by Peng, but also by the high command in Beijing, and they trickled down through the chain of command to the field generals. The strategic outlook, doctrinal tenets, and emphasis on manpower were partly to blame. Some of the Chinese commanders realized that the human factor was no longer a decisive issue on the battleground. They continued to bring new weapons and more technology to their forces, but it was too little and too late for them to win the Spring Offensive. Third, because of the sudden increase of Chinese forces in Korea—a two- or threefold increase since the Fourth Offensive—their logistical forces were stretched far too thin to guarantee that troops at the front would receive even the minimum amount of food and ammunition. The CPVF forces had been hastily thrown into the largest attack since the outbreak of the war. Fourth, the CPVF lacked an intelligence network, a cohort of professional staff officers, and an effective communication system for allowing units to collaborate. In other words, the Chinese army had not yet become modernized. Its transition from a guerrilla army in WWII to a modern army began in the Chinese Civil War, and it was not completed until the end of the Korean War, after its humiliating defeat in the 1951 Spring Offensive.

Figure 1. Zhou Enlai signs the Sino-Soviet Treaty of Friendship, Alliance, and Mutual Assistance in Moscow, February 1950.

Figure 2. Mao Zedong (*right*) and Peng Dehuai in Beijing in 1951.

Figure 3. Peng Dehuai (*front row, second from right*), Kim Il-sung (*front row, center*), and other commanders of the CPVF-NKPA Joint Command at Taeyudong, North Korea, April 1951.

Figure 4. Yang Dezhi (*pointing at the map*) and his army group commanders at the front, May 1951.

Figure 5. Zhu De (*center*) and Zhou Enlai (*behind and to his right*) meet CPVF logistics representatives in Beijing, winter 1951.

Figure 6. CPVF troops charging through the wreckage of a U.S. Army convoy along the Han-gang River, North Korea, April 1951.

Figure 7. CPVF logistics troops unloading supplies
from railroad cars near the Iron Triangle, June 1951.

Figure 8. Chinese casualties in the Spring Offensive,
April 22–26, 1951. *National Archives*

Figure 9. A CPVF logistic unit repairs a road in Korea, May 1951.

Figure 10. CPVF casualties during the withdrawal, May 1951.

Figure 11. The 134th Regiment, 45th Division, CPVF Fifteenth Army, uses tunnels to defend their positions on Hill 597.9, October 1952.

Figure 12. Peng signs the Korean Armistice agreement at Kaesong, July 1953.

# FOUR

# The First Step: Three Problems

ON APRIL 22, 1951, CHINESE FORCES LAUNCHED THEIR LARGEST attack on the U.S. Eighth Army, across the 38th Parallel along a forty-mile front. Three CPVF army groups on the western front—including eleven armies and totaling 548,000 men from thirty-three infantry divisions, four field artillery divisions, two long-range artillery divisions, four anti-aircraft divisions, and one rocket division—would open the Spring Offensive.[1] Peng Dehuai believed the 1951 Spring Offensive would be "the decisive battle" of the Korean War.[2] The Chinese Spring Offensive became the largest offensive in PLA history. Eighteen newly arrived CPVF infantry divisions, at full strength and newly equipped with Soviet weapons, saw action for the first time. Two thousand artillery pieces were gathered on the western front, about six times as many as China had had in October 1950 when she entered the war.[3] In addition, three NKPA corps, totaling 150,000 troops, also participated, and the joint CPVF-NKPA forces consisted of nearly 700,000 men battling against 340,000 UNF troops.[4]

The Chinese Spring Offensive sought to "annihilate several enemy divisions, stop their [landing] plan, and regain the initiative."[5] If possible, the CPVF would retake Seoul, the capital of South Korea, and move south of the 38th Parallel. The CPVF had not been able to destroy any UNF divisions during the four previous offensives, between October 1950 and early April 1951. Moreover, UNF counterattacks had pushed Chinese forces farther north, forcing them to withdraw from Seoul. Chinese leaders had high hopes that the Spring Offensive in late April would turn the tide on the Korean battleground. As a battle of annihilation, Mao Zedong expected to wipe out 50,000 UNF troops. Mao asked Peng on April 28 to "concentrate on striking hard the puppet [ROK] 1st Division, U.S. 3rd, 24th, and 25th Divisions, Turkish Brigade, and British 28th Brigade, and annihilate [them] as much as possible in the current campaign."[6] If these four divisions and two brigades of the U.S. I Corps were destroyed, that would open the CPVF's road to the south and Seoul. If the Chinese won this decisive battle, Communist forces would end the war with a total victory within a year. Mao hoped the CPVF would "win [a] quick victory if possible; or at least win some advantage instead."[7] Mao's unrealistic expectation of eliminating a large number of UNF troops set up an ambitious strategy of annihilation for the CPVF's Spring Offensive.

This strategy soon exhausted the CPVF's resources, exposed many Chinese weaknesses, and permitted the UNF to defeat the CPVF in the offensive. When Peng received Mao's telegram of April 28, the main strength of the CPVF on the western front had crossed the 38th Parallel and been engaged in six days of fierce fighting. Nevertheless, the CPVF had not encircled the U.S. I Corps as planned, nor had it destroyed a regiment, let alone an entire UNF division, as Mao had requested. The first step in the Spring Offensive had failed to achieve the campaign's objective of annihilating UNF divisions and brigades. Instead, Chinese forces suffered heavy losses, and Peng called off the attacks on April 29.

Several major reasons accounted for the early Chinese setbacks of April 22–29. UN and U.S. forces had overwhelmingly superior firepower both on the ground and in the air. The UNF inflicted heavy casualties and serious damage on the CPVF troops, transportation, and supplies. In retrospect, the CPVF Command had miscalculated and made three major strategic mistakes. First, Peng and his commanders had rushed troops into the offensive before they were combat ready. Second, Peng had used the same strategy of "divide, encircle, and annihilate" in the four campaigns from November 1950 to April 1951 and had failed to develop new strategies and tactics. Third, the CPVF Command did not improve transportation methods for maintaining supplies. Limited food and ammunition supplies prevented sustained operations from succeeding.

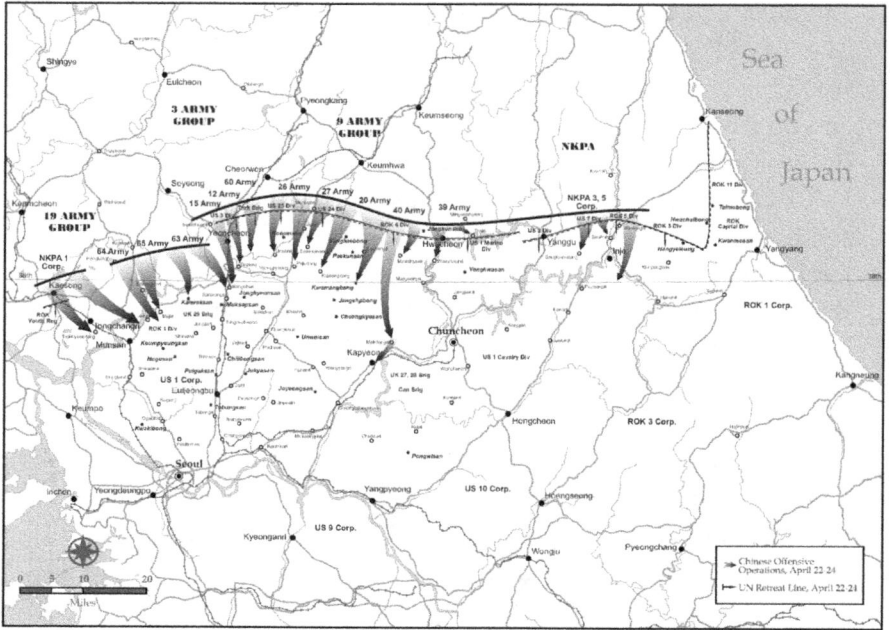

Map 4.1. Initial attacks of the first step, Spring Offensive, April 22–24, 1951

## CHANGE IN PLANS: RUSH TO THE ATTACK

In the spring of 1951 the U.S. Eighth Army deployed its I Corps in the west, its IX Corps in the center, and its X Corps in the eastern section of the Korean Peninsula. As the U.S. I and IX Corps moved north of the 38th Parallel into what the Chinese had designated the annihilation zone (especially the U.S. 24th and 25th Divisions, bulging out at the Cheorwon [Chorwon] front), Peng decided to launch all-out counterattacks on the western front at dusk on April 22[8] (map 4.1).

At 5:00 PM, the CPVF Ninth Army Group, totaling 250,000 men, attacked the U.S. IX Corps in the center. The Chinese Spring Offensive had begun. The five armies of the Ninth Army Group struck a sixteen-mile UNF defensive line held by the ROK 6th and U.S. 24th, 25th, and 1st Marine Divisions. The Chinese Thirty-Ninth and Fortieth Armies broke through the line held by the ROK 6th Division and penetrated into the central mountainous areas, separating the ROK 6th Division from the

U.S. 1st Marine Division and dividing the western UNF divisions from those on the eastern front.[9]

At 7:00 PM on April 22, the CPVF Third and Nineteenth Army Groups, totaling 270,000 men, launched attacks against the U.S. I Corps in the west. These CPVF armies, however, were not ready for such a large-scale offensive and failed to break through the defenses of the ROK 1st Division and the British 29th Brigade. When Peng issued his order to attack, many men of the Third Army Group were still some distance from their starting positions and had to run for thirty to sixty minutes to reach their staging areas. Their late arrival meant they missed the scheduled artillery barrage, which had temporarily neutralized the first line of UNF defense for their advance.[10] Even when the CPVF artillery fire extended into the second line of the UNF defense positions, some of the attacking forces had still not reached their staging positions. The main strength of the Nineteenth Army Group did not penetrate deeply enough into the rear of the U.S. I Corps, nor did it reach Euijeongbu (Uijongbu) and encircle the U.S. 3rd, 24th, and 25th Divisions.[11] This failure made it impossible for Peng to achieve his goal of annihilation.

The uneven combat performance of the Chinese armies in the first week of the Spring Offensive resulted from differences in combat readiness. The five armies of the Ninth Army Group were better prepared for the new offensive and performed better than the six armies in the Third and Nineteenth Army Groups. The Ninth Army Group entered Korea in 1950 as part of the first wave of the CPVF.[12] Its Thirty-Ninth and Fortieth Armies arrived in October and served in the first four offensives, gaining combat experience in six months of fighting.[13] Both armies had been fighting continuously in the Fourth Offensive from January to April.[14] Its Twentieth, Twenty-Sixth, and Twenty-Seventh Armies arrived in November and had participated in the three previous campaigns.[15] Song Shilun, commander of the Ninth Army Group, had fought the tough battle at Chosin Reservoir against the U.S. 1st Marine and 7th Infantry Divisions that winter. Even though his Twentieth and Twenty-Seventh Armies lost 40,000 men and liquidated three infantry divisions at Chosin Reservoir during the Second Offensive, from November 27 through December 12, 1950, Song had learned valuable skills, and he and his group wanted revenge against the Americans.[16]

The Ninth Army Group suffered heavy casualties through the winter of 1950, and the CMC reinforced Song with 18,000 seasoned veterans and 30,000 new recruits in February 1951. These 48,000 men received newly arrived Russian-made weapons in Shenyang before leaving China for Korea.[17] Moreover, in March, Hong Xuezhi, deputy commander of the CPVF in charge of weaponry and logistics, provided the Ninth Army Group with additional artillery, transportation, and medical troops.[18] Its Twentieth Army was reinforced with two artillery regiments, its Twenty-Sixth Army with one field artillery regiment and three antitank companies, and its Twenty-Seventh Army with two field artillery regiments and three antitank companies.[19] Hong also sent forty-four new trucks and three surgical teams to the Fortieth Army.[20] The CPVF Command anticipated between fifty and sixty thousand wounded in the Spring Offensive.[21]

It was imperative that before the Ninth Army Group launched its attacks on April 22, all five of its armies be deployed at their offensive staging positions. Its Twentieth, Twenty-Sixth, and Twenty-Seventh Armies were already at their positions at the Cheorwon and Keumhwa area near the "Iron Triangle" (map 2.4). The Thirty-Ninth and Fortieth were also in position, with the first in the Sanyang-ri (Sanyangri) area and the second at Pokjosan and Yutan-ri (Yutanri), southeast of Keumhwa. All fifteen divisions of the five armies were well prepared before the new offensive campaign, and they attacked with organized, forceful, and quick actions throughout the first week of the Spring Offensive, April 22–29.[22]

In contrast, the six armies of the Third and Nineteenth Army Groups had just arrived in the spring as part of the second wave of the Chinese forces.[23] The Third Army Group—made up of the Twelfth, Fifteenth, and Sixtieth Armies, totaling 150,000 troops—was from southwestern Sichuan (Szechwan) and southeastern Guangdong Provinces. The men traveled more than 1,500 miles from southwest China to northeast Manchuria in early 1951. The three armies were deployed to Korea in late March and arrived in the Euicheon (Ichon) area in mid-April, about thirty miles from the front line.[24] The Twelfth Army entered Korea from Changdian on March 18, marched south, and arrived at Euicheon and Munan-ri (Munanri) on April 10. The Fifteenth Army entered Korea from Andong on March 20, reaching the areas of Euicheon and Shingye on April 12. The Sixtieth Army crossed into Korea on March 23, marching south to the areas of Euicheon and Shingye on April 14.[25]

The Third Army Group expected to replace the armies of the first wave and take over their positions on the front in April and May. Chen Geng, commander and political commissar of the group, was absent because he had been hospitalized in Beijing since March (see chapter 3). Wang Jinshan, deputy commander of the Third, was in charge during the Spring Offensive. Wang received orders that his armies had one month after their arrival to prepare for combat, and that he should organize extensive in-country training to familiarize them with the battleground from mid-April to mid-May. In the meantime, they would receive new equipment and adequate ammunition and food. The newly arrived armies received some artillery reinforcements: the 28th, 29th, 30th Regiments (minus the 1st Battalion) and the 403rd Antitank Regiment, from the 2nd Artillery Division. But they did not receive the promised rest time and the planned training period. On his arrival in Korea, Wang received Peng's new order that his armies were to immediately rush to the offensive staging areas between Soyeong and Cheorwon. Most of the divisions had fewer than five days, rather than a full month, to prepare for combat.[26]

Peng had moved up the starting time by approximately three weeks, from mid-May to April 22. When the CPVF Command planned the Spring Offensive in late March, the intended starting date had been mid-May.[27] According to Peng's original plan, the Third Army Group would have a month to prepare its troops for the key task—frontal attacks on the U.S. I Corps to be conducted while the Ninth and Nineteenth Army Groups flanked the corps from both right and left to completely encircle it and annihilate the U.S. 3rd, 24th, and 25th Divisions, ROK 1st Division, British 29th Brigade, and Turkish Brigade under the command of the U.S. I Corps.[28] However, Peng worried that the United States might be planning to make amphibious landings on the east and west coasts behind Chinese positions (see chapter 3), and he believed such a UNF landing in North Korea "will cut our throat."[29] Peng explained his serious concerns in a telegram to Mao in late April:

> According to the information disclosed by various sources, four American Na-
> tional Guard divisions (with 18,000 soldiers per division) have been dispatched
> to Japan. Our spies tell us the United States has also dispatched two regular
> divisions of 50,000 soldiers to Japan. Three divisions of the 36,000 troops of the
> Rhee's puppet [ROK] forces are now being trained in Japan, and are to be sent to
> South Korea. If the above enemy force numbers are correct, there will be about
> 150,000 new troops entering Korea. We assume it is possible that the enemy
> will conduct amphibious landings at our rear while using part of its forces to
> strengthen its forces at the front.[30]

The unverified intelligence about possible UNF amphibious landings had become Peng's worst nightmare and his first priority in decision
making.[31] Peng seemed to have been more concerned about losing the
war than winning it.

Peng convinced Mao of the need for an earlier start of the Spring Offensive: "We had originally planned to start this offensive in early May.
However, for the purposes of delaying enemy's amphibious attacks and
avoiding fighting on two fronts simultaneously," the CPVF should start
the offensive earlier, on April 22.[32] Brian Catchpole points out that "as
Peng feared a possible amphibious landing in his rear, time was of the
essence."[33] The CPVF's weapons and firepower were vastly inferior to
those of the U.S. armed forces, the most powerful military in the world.
Each CPVF army had a total of 45,000–50,000 troops, equipped with
198 artillery pieces (mostly 75 mm guns), 120 trucks, and no tank. Each
American army had about 1,428 artillery pieces (mostly 105 and 155 mm
guns), 7,000 trucks, and 430 tanks.[34] With the same number of troops,
the American infantry had far greater firepower than the CPVF infantry.
And in the first half of 1951, the CPVF still operated without air cover or
support, which meant that UNF air forces constantly hindered CPVF
movements.

Moreover, in the spring of 1951, the UNF had recovered from its
earlier surprise in the war and adopted a cautious strategy under Ridgway, who became UNF commander after President Truman dismissed
MacArthur on April 11.[35] On April 14 Ridgway turned over command
of the U.S. Eighth Army to Lt. Gen. James A. Van Fleet. In mid-April,
the new Eighth Army Command, learning the force of the CPVF strategic reserves, slowed the northward offense of U.S. I Corps under the
command of Gen. Frank W. "Shrimp" Milburn and IX Corps under the

command of Maj. Gen. William Hoge. The Eighth Army braced for a new Chinese offensive.

Peng's decision to start the offensive a month earlier was also partially based on his calculation of the perceived battleground situation. To lure the U.S. IX Corps further into North Korea and facilitate Chinese counterattacks, Peng ordered the front-line troops to fall back and lure the enemy to advance farther north. On April 15 Peng ordered the Twenty-Sixth, Thirty-Ninth, and Fortieth Armies to withdraw to new positions farther north of the 38th Parallel.[36] After April 17 the UNF met fewer Chinese forces above Line Kansas. After visiting the front from east to west, on April 21 Van Fleet suggested to Ridgway that Van Fleet's troops take advantage of the Chinese withdrawal and move farther north; Ridgway agreed. The U.S. IX Corps moved farther north into Peng's trap but covered only two to three miles on April 21.[37]

Running out of patience, Peng advanced the starting time of the CPVF Spring Offensive Campaign to April 22. Based on the military analysis and instructions from the CMC, the commanders of the Sino-Korean Joint Forces reached the consensus that the CPVF and NKPA forces should not move too far north of the 38th Parallel, in case the enemy made amphibious landings in the north. Hong recalled that, even though there were different opinions, the commanders all agreed that the Sino-Korean forces should do everything they could to inflict maximum casualties on the UNF in order to deplete its strength, pin down its main forces in the south, and thus avoid facing two battle fronts simultaneously.[38]

Peng sent his change of plans to Mao, knowing that the chairman preferred a short war. During their meetings in Beijing in February, Mao had given Peng very clear instructions: "Win [a] quick victory if possible; or at least win some advantage instead."[39] In April Mao approved Peng's new plan.[40] Having ignored the lack of accurate information, necessary training, command communication, and much needed supplies, Peng and the CPVF Command ordered the assault troops to enter their attack-staging areas. All Chinese forces had to be combat ready for the new offensive campaign by midnight on April 21.[41]

Peng's sudden change, moving the offensive's starting date up by almost a month, threw all the forces of the second wave, including the

Third and Nineteenth Army Groups, into action without necessary preparations. Most of the divisions were not combat ready, and some had not
received much-needed food and ammunition.

The Nineteenth Army Group was assigned to conduct flank attacks
on the left side of the U.S. I Corps. Its three armies—the Sixty-Third,
Sixty-Fourth, and Sixty-Fifth—were to break through the defense line
of ROK 1st Division and British 29th Brigade and penetrate deep into the
rear of the U.S. I Corps, cutting off any retreat. But most of the group's attacking forces had not yet reached their staging areas when they received
orders to attack on the evening of April 22.[42]

Zeng Siyu (b. 1911), then commander of the Sixty-Fourth Army and
later deputy commander and chief of staff of the Nineteenth Army Group,
recalled that his army was not prepared when he received the order to
launch the attack on April 22.[43] Some of his troops had not yet arrived
at their staging areas, and his artillery pieces were still on their way into
position. He called Yang Dezhi, commander of the Nineteenth, asking
for one more day to get his army ready for combat. Yang hung up the
phone—meaning "no," according to Zeng.[44]

Having served in the PLA under Peng for a long time, Yang never
questioned Peng's decisions and always followed orders. His loyalty and
toughness had made him the commander of the Nineteenth Army Group
at the age of forty-one. His three armies, totaling 150,000 men, moved
into Korea and reached the areas south of Chucheon-ri in March.[45] He
knew that some of his newly arrived armies had reached the front lines
just days before the offensive started, and some had not even reached
their staging areas when they were ordered to attack.[46] There was no
time for their in-country orientation or training with their new Soviet
weapons. But Yang carried out Peng's order without hesitation.

The Sixty-Fourth Army under the command of Zeng was assigned
to conduct operational flanking maneuvers, to crush the ROK 1st Division's defenses north of the Imjin-gang River, and to cross the river with
four regiments of the 191st and 192nd Divisions.[47] However, the regiment
commanders were not familiar with the daily tides of the Imjin River.
When the 572nd Regiment was crossing the river at midnight, the tide
suddenly came in and the river rose from three to five feet to more than
twenty feet. Several hundred men of the 572nd were drowned in the river

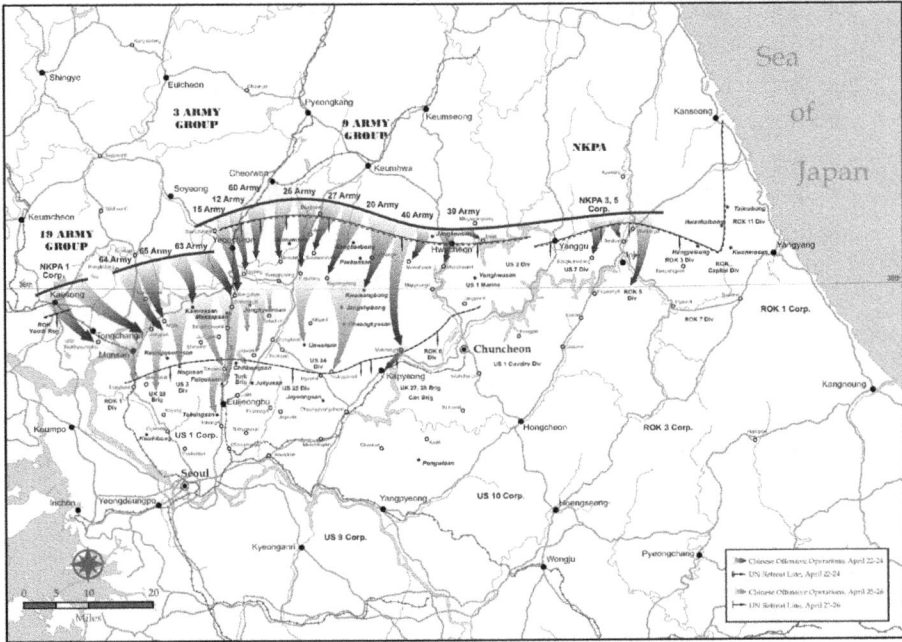

Map 4.2. Continuing attacks of the first step, Spring Offensive, April 22–26

between 1:00 and 2:00 A M.[48] Other regiments had similar losses when they crossed the river.

The 191st and 192nd Divisions conducted their attacks too late after the artillery barrage.[49] After running to reach their staging positions, the exhausted attacking forces had been unable to attack the ROK 1st Division with sufficient strength. After reaching positions at Jangpa-ri (Jangpari) and Kosakdong (Kosadong), the two divisions were held in check on the south bank of Imjin-gang, north of Mitunsa, and found themselves unable to break through the ROK 1st Division's defense line from April 23 to the 26th[50] (map 4.2).

Obviously, the second wave of the CPVF, including both Third and Nineteenth Army Groups, was not ready for such a major offensive campaign. Some divisions did not receive sufficient rest after making the long journey from China to the border, as well as another 200–400 mile march into the middle of Korea. Catchpole points out that "strong troops were often exhausted by the style of their advance—a jogtrot of 10–15 miles before an attack."[51] Army and divisional commands had not even finished a survey of the local terrain. The three army group commands had not yet established communications among themselves, and each army group command had to go through Peng's General HQ to locate other units. Peng and his staff did not have time to meet any of the striking force commanders at division level even once. Later intelligence on UNF operational plans and the development of the war provided clear evidence that Peng's rush to change plans was a fatal mistake. The million-man CPVF-NKPA offensive caused few losses and minimal damage to the UNF, but it led to unusually high casualties for the Chinese forces, especially among the Third and Nineteenth Army Groups. Peng admitted later that the change of plans was one of four major strategic mistakes he made during his military career.[52] After the collapse of the Spring Offensive, Mao blamed the CPVF's failure on "too much haste, too large scale, and too far into the [enemy's] territory."[53]

## INFLEXIBLE STRATEGY: ENCIRCLEMENT
## AND ANNIHILATION

Mao was right about the two problems the CPVF faced in late April—launching such a major offensive without necessary preparation or sufficient supplies—but he was wrong about its being "too far into the [enemy's] territory" since no CPVF force advanced more than fifty miles into UNF-held territory. In fact, it was because of their slow movement and lack of deep penetration that the Chinese armies failed to encircle and annihilate the U.S. I Corps. Mao dismissed his rigid campaign strategy as another important reason for the Chinese setback on April 22–29. In retrospect, however, that strategy of divide, encircle, and annihilate was excessively inflexible as well as out of date, leading to the disastrous results of the CPVF offensive. To annihilate four UNF divisions and two brigades, according to Mao, the Chinese Ninth Army Group should separate the U.S. I Corps from the IX Corps in the center. The Nineteenth Army Group should encircle the I Corps from the west and block its retreat at Euijeongbu, and then the Third Army Group should annihilate the divisions and brigades of the I Corps.

This Chinese strategy employed numerical superiority to divide and "encircle the enemy forces completely, strive to wipe them out thoroughly and do not let any escape from the net."[54] It was a typical campaign strategy for the Chinese Communist military, a way for a weak army to defeat a stronger opponent in battle. It had evolved in the domestic revolutionary wars (1927–37), the Anti-Japanese War (1937–45), and Chinese Civil War (1946–49), and it had become a traditional strategy that the PLA used to win battles.

However, in Korea, the Chinese Communist forces faced the U.S. Army, a vastly different opponent than the GMD in the Civil War. In the spring of 1951, Mao and Peng continued to use the traditional campaign strategy and rigid combat tactics. Sunzi warned about inflexibility, saying that "an army does not have fixed strategic advantages (*shih*) or an invariable position (*hsing*). To be able to take the victory by varying ones' position according to (*yin*) the enemy's is called being inscrutable (*shen*)."[55] Nevertheless, the encirclement and annihilation strategy proved effective in the first two CPVF campaigns, from October to December 1950. The Chinese forces launched surprise attacks and then flanked and encircled a UNF unit, cutting off its connections, and set up road blocks to stop it from withdrawing. During the Second Offensive, in November–December, the Ninth Army Group scored the CPVF's only major encirclement-annihilation success during the three-year war in Korea when it wiped out an entire U.S. regiment (the Thirty-Second) of the U.S. 7th Infantry Division.[56]

Soon, however, the UNF recovered from such early surprises and, by studying the CPVF's unchanging pattern of encirclement and annihilation, learned how to defend against and defeat the Chinese strategy. During the Third Offensive, in January, the encirclement strategy began to lose its effectiveness, and the CPVF was unable to completely destroy any U.S. unit. When a UNF unit discovered Chinese troops on both flanks or behind, it immediately withdrew to keep from being encircled. To fight back during the CPVF Fourth Offensive, in February–April, the UNF adapted a number of effective countermeasures to prevent annihilation after the completion of an encirclement, using it as an opportunity to inflict more casualties on the attacking Chinese troops. Instead of retreating quickly, the UNF units reorganized their troops into a stronghold protected by tanks and self-propelling artillery and awaited reinforcements. Thomas Fleming points out that "Ridgway ordered that no unit be abandoned if cut off. It was to be 'fought for' and rescued unless a 'major commander' after 'personal appraisal' Ridgway-style—from the front lines—decided its relief would cost as many or more men."[57] Jongnam Na states: "Gen. Ridgway focused on eliminating the CPVF's advantage in manpower."[58] When UNF units were under attack, they called in air raids and artillery firepower to support their defense. The UNF firepower inflicted such heavy casualties on the attacking Chinese troops that they had to give up and withdraw after a few assaults. The UNF battles of attrition under Ridgway's command were very different from MacArthur's technique of rapidly advancing for a quick victory.[59]

The UNF was not only technologically superior to the CPVF, but it was also able to develop new and effective tactics to win battles against Communist forces. These countermeasures were widely employed by the UNF commands against the Chinese Spring Offensive. Moreover, the UNF had discovered the CPVF preparations and immediately made force adjustments and strengthened defensive lines in response.[60] In April Van Fleet cautiously deployed the main UNF forces along three defensive lines. The first line ran from Yeoncheon (Yonchon) through Tongducheon-ri (Tongduchon-ri) and Hwacheon to Jichon-ri; the second was from Euijeongbu to Chuncheon (Chunchon); and the third was from Suwon to Wonju.[61] Each defense line relied on overwhelming firepower on the ground from artillery and tanks to inflict as many casualties as possible on the attacking Chinese troops in order to stop their encirclement.

By the spring of 1951, American commanders had adapted to the encirclement strategy. Moreover, April 1951 became a turning point from defense to offense for the UNF. Van Fleet launched several limited offensives to destroy CPVF personnel and supplies and increase the confidence and fighting skills of the U.S. Eighth Army. The U.S. commanders had made a difference in the war due to their operational experience and commanding skills. The UNF's new strategy was clear: "namely, that the objective of combat operations was to inflict high losses on the enemy while keeping UN losses to a minimum, and that substantial reinforcements should not be expected."[62] After seizing and consolidating its new positions, the UNF would launch rapid attacks so that the CPVF would not have time to rest or reinforce its weary forces, a strategy of exhaustion. Allan Millett concludes that "the United Nations Command divisions that awaited the Fifth Offensive had put defeat behind them. Withdrawals, yes; tactical errors, yes; and some operational difficulties, yes; but defeat, no."[63]

Thus, in the spring of 1951, the CPVF Command faced a war in which the UNF Command had adopted a cautious strategy, slowly advancing northward in order to inflict more casualties on the CPVF-NKPA forces. However, the Chinese commanders refused to study the modified UNF war strategy, ignoring one of Sunzi's classic principles: "Know the other, know yourself, and the victory will not be at risk."[64] They continued to follow their rigid strategy without any alteration, using the same tactics of "divide, encircle, and destroy."[65] They followed what Mao had said at the PRC's Ninth Central Government Plenary on September 5, 1950: "You fight your [way], I fight mine; you use atomic bombs, I use hand grenades. I will find your weak point and track you down; I can defeat you in the end."[66]

The Chinese high command failed to respond to the novel tactics of the UNF forces on the Korean battleground. The Chinese Spring Offensive was conducted with a stupefying lack of flexibility and creativity, from the most senior marshal down to regimental levels. Over 105,000 Chinese were killed, wounded, or captured by the UNF during the offensive. Shuguang Zhang states that "Mao and the other CCP leaders truly believed in the importance of flexibility in war, but they did not employ the principle as a safeguard against risky actions."[67] Zhang points out four reasons behind Mao's inflexibility in early 1951: he underestimated the UNF's military strength, he was hopelessly impatient for a quick victory, he was overconfident in the "favorable momentum" that the second wave of the CPVF appeared to create after entering Korea, and he believed that "human power would eventually overcome objective difficulties."[68]

Even though repeated CPVF attempts to trap significant portions of UNF troops had failed in the Third and Fourth Campaigns, in January–March 1951, Mao and Peng again employed the same encirclement-annihilation plan as a strategy for the Spring Offensive. In April the CPVF Command issued two sets of instructions, "Directives on Campaign Principles and Tactics Guidelines" and "Directives on Guiding Principles and Tactical Guidelines for the Campaign," to all army and divisional commands. First, the command emphasized its timeworn principle of "assembling superior forces to encircle one enemy unit at a time and annihilate it."[69] The directives also called on all CPVF and NKPA commanders to break each UNF unit into several parts on an operational level, and then to further divide each section into smaller pieces on a tactical scale, in order to annihilate them.[70] On April 13 the Political Department of the CPVF General HQ issued "Instructions on the Political Tasks for the Fifth Campaign." It specified that while the army groups were to eliminate the UNF divisions, "each army must annihilate one or two enemy regiments during the offensive campaign."[71] On April 18 Peng ordered all three army groups to be combat ready by the 20th and to start the attacks on either April 21 or 22.

Following his plan, Peng ordered Song's Ninth Army Group to engage in flanking attacks and operational encirclements on the UNF right. The Ninth would move out from Keumhwa and head south to Chenpeongcheon, where it would cut off the U.S. 24th and 25th Divisions from other UNF units.[72] Its Twentieth Army was to move west to cut off the rear of the British 27th Brigade and then eradicate the brigade. After that, the Twentieth Army would move into Paekcheon (Paecheon) to separate the U.S. 24th Division from the other UNF units.[73] The Twenty-Sixth Army's mission was to stop, by any means, the UNF's northern advance toward the CPVF's positions at Kalmalmyeon, Naeka, Oeka, and Keumhaksan. After the attacks had begun, the Twenty-Sixth would move from Kalmalmyeon to Munhyeo-ri (Munhye-ri or Munhyeri) and stop the U.S. 24th and 25th Divisions from moving further north or northeast, so as to protect the Twenty-Seventh Army's right flank. Eventually, the Twenty-Sixth Army would help the Twentieth and Twenty-Seventh Armies wipe out the U.S. 24th Division.[74] In addition, the Thirty-Ninth and Fortieth Armies would move into areas west and southwest of Sanyang-ri after the attacks began and drive through the middle of the UNF line, separating UNF troops on the eastern and western fronts.[75]

According to Peng's plan, the Nineteenth Army Group would flank any U.S. I Corps left along the western coast in order to complete its encirclement.[76] The group's Sixty-Third Army was to cross the Imjin-gang River from Seokho and Oteung-ri and then advance into Kamraksan to cut off connections between the British 29th Brigade and the U.S. 3rd Division. The Sixty-Fourth Army, after crossing the Imjin-gang, would thrust directly into Euijeongbu, cutting off the UNF retreat and blocking the arrival of its reinforcements. If successful, the Sixty-Fourth would then move toward Seoul and attempt to recapture that city.[77] The Sixty-Fifth Army was to cross the Imjin River from Shindaeso and destroy UNF units south of the river.[78]

Peng's plan called for the Third Army Group was to attack the U.S. I Corps at its center during the first phase of the Spring Offensive.[79] After breaking through the U.S. I Corps' defense, the Twelfth Army would first wipe out the Turkish Brigade and then join the Fifteenth Army in annihilating the U.S. 3rd Division.[80] The Fifteenth would move directly to Yeoncheon along the Imjin-gang River to destroy first the 65th Regiment of the U.S. 3rd Division, then the division's headquarters, and later one more U.S. regiment.[81] The Sixtieth Army would strike toward Pugok-ri and Jung-ri, between the U.S. 25th Division and the Turkish Brigade. The Sixtieth would also prevent the U.S. 24th Division from moving west and acting as reinforcements. The NKPA I Corps was to first destroy the UNF troops at Kaeseong and Munsan, then move toward Koyang and Seoul. Once Seoul was taken, the NKPA I Corps was to assume garrison duties for the South Korean capital.[82]

But the CPVF-NKPA attacking forces never reached Seoul, and Peng's encirclement and annihilation plan also failed. None of the CPVF army groups were able to destroy a single UNF division, brigade, or regiment during the first vital step of the Spring Offensive. Peng later recounted:

> We, however, were unable to eliminate even one regiment of American forces. Our troops had destroyed whole [American] battalions in six or seven locations and wiped out only one entire puppet division [the ROK 6th Division]. The rest of the enemy troops we had eliminated were merely parts of their units. It would take us two days to annihilate an entire American regiment if we could surround it. The problems were that our army's technology and equipment were so backward and that enemy air and mechanized forces tried so hard to save

their troops.... In many cases, if we surrounded enemy troops but could not
annihilate them the same night, they would be rescued one way or another the
next day.[83]

During the first week of the offensive, April 22–29, the CPVF armies encircled more than a dozen UNF units, including U.S. regiments,
British battalions, and the Turkish Brigade. But none of the Chinese
armies could destroy any of them, with one exception: the CPVF Sixty-
Third Army managed to destroy the 1st Battalion of the Gloucester Regiment, British 29th Brigade, on April 22–25.[84] Peng spoke to Mao of the
unsuccessful annihilation campaign as early as April 26, but Mao did not
understand why one CPVF army was unable to annihilate one U.S. regiment.[85] Mao questioned Chen and Xie Fang about this failure to achieve
the goal of the Spring Offensive on May 27, when he met them in Beijing.
And Mao asked the same question when he met six field commanders from the Thirty-Eighth, Thirty-Ninth, Fortieth, and Forty-Second
Armies on May 30 and 31.[86]

The CPVF field generals eventually convinced Mao that their recent
battlefield experience demonstrated that the encirclement and annihilation strategy no longer worked. A CPVF nighttime attack could not
destroy any American unit larger than a company in a single night, and
U.S. battalions and regiments easily broke through CPVF roadblocks
with their superior firepower and air support during the daytime.[87] Mao
shifted the Chinese strategic goals from annihilation to attrition warfare
in June 1951.

Mao telegraphed Peng in June and instructed him that "our mouths
should not open too wide when fighting the American forces. We must
adopt the tactic of 'eating sticky candy'—bit by bit."[88] Thus, the CPVF
Command was able to shift its operation from large-scale mobile offensives in the spring to small-scale piecemeal attacks in the summer. Mao
telegraphed Peng on June 11 that he had "talked to Comrade Kim Il-sung.
We agreed not to launch any large-scale counteroffensive campaign for
the next two months."[89] However, it was too late for Peng to save the
Spring Offensive. Nor could any new Chinese strategy and tactics be
implemented before the humiliating defeat of the CPVF in the spring
of 1951.

## THE OFFENSIVE WITH LIMITED SUPPLIES

Peng had planned a two-week offensive to meet Mao's objective of annihilating six UNF divisions and brigades (Peng wanted seven) on the
western front from April 22 to early May. However, because of the shortage of food and ammunition, he was forced to cut his offensive one week
short, and he ended the first phase on April 29 without the destruction
of a single UNF division or brigade. The Chinese inability to supply a
large force engaged in mobile warfare was the third problem the CPVF
faced in the spring of 1951.

Peng and the CPVF Command knew the problems in Chinese logistics and supply in Korea before they launched the Spring Offensive.
Among the major problems were broken supply lines, heavy losses of
much-needed food and ammunition during shipments, and the lack of
protection from UNF air raids.[90] Inadequate supplies seriously constrained CPVF operations, and by the spring of 1951 the Chinese high
command had not improved the CPVF logistics and transportation.
During the first step of the Spring Offensive, the CPVF met only 44–50
percent of its daily needs of 550 tons of food and ammunition. Chinese
logistics and transportation could keep up with only half of the troops'
daily needs for seven to ten days, in spite of Peng's encouragement to the
logistics units. He even promised them that, if the CPVF won a victory
in the Spring Offensive, half of the resulting awards would go to the
logistics units.[91]

In retrospect, when the Spring Offensive began, the CPVF's efforts
to improve logistics had not succeeded. Because of the sudden two- to
threefold increase in CPVF forces since March, supplies in April and
May were stretched far too thin to guarantee that even the forces at the
front would receive their minimum daily requirements. The Chinese
striking forces on the western front were also not adequately supplied,
especially with food and ammunition. In addition, UNF air raids also
caused serious damage to CPVF logistics and transportation. During
one UNF air bombing of a train station in April, for example, the Chinese lost 1,440 tons of cooked food and grain, 45,000 gallons of cooking
oil, 408,000 sets of uniforms and jackets, 190,000 pairs of shoes, and

large amounts of other supplies.[92] Hong complained to Zhou in Beijing
that, with intensive UNF air raids, less than 60 percent of the Chinese
supplies were able to reach the front. Among the losses, 30 percent were
"destroyed by air raids and bombings during transportation between
the rear and the front" in Korea.[93] During the Spring Offensive, UNF
air raids successfully cut the CPVF transportation lines, thereby forcing
Peng to end the offensive campaign one week early.

The Ninth Army Group was better prepared than the other two
groups, but the Ninth's five armies had run out of food and ammunitions by the fifth day of the Spring Offensive. Song was aware of the
transportation problems that would affect his supplies, so the Ninth
Command required all attacking army personnel to carry enough food
and ammunition for themselves for a five-day period.[94] The infantry also
transported artillery shells. Each soldier carried an average of 60–70
pounds of supplies when launching an attack.[95]

In the evening of April 22, Song's Thirty-Ninth and Fortieth Armies
broke through the UNF line that ran through the central mountainous
areas of the Korean Peninsula. Their penetration separated the ROK
6th Division from the U.S. 1st Marine Division and split the western
UNF divisions from those on the eastern front. Forces from the Thirty-
Ninth Army, under the command of Wu Xinquan (1912–92), occupied
Hwacheon and linked up with the Fortieth Army.[96]

Wen Yucheng, appointed commander of the Fortieth Army at the
age of thirty-six, sent his 118th Division to break the UNF line through
the ROK 6th Division's positions. The 118th broke through the ROK 6th's
defenses at Hakshina-ri (Hakashinari), Sachang-ri (Sachangri), and Ke-
onyacheon (Keonyachon).[97] The 118th quickly cut sixteen to eighteen
miles into UNF territory, reaching Hwaeumdong the next day.

On April 23 the 3rd Battalion of the 354th Regiment in the 118th Division reached its designated target—Mukdong-ri (Mukdongri), northeast of Kapyeong—by marching five miles per hour, climbing 3,000-
foot heights at Hyounhyeon (Hyounhyon), and crushing the UNF defense lines.[98] To guard the left flanks of the Ninth Army Group, Wen
dispatched his 119th Division to Sachang-ri to protect the highway
between Jichon-ri (Jichonri) and Sachang-ri from the U.S. 1st Marine
Division at Hwacheon. Wen also ordered his 120th Division to move

toward Jiuam-ri (Jiuamri) and Kunyangdae and to occupy Turyusan and Jangkunsan.[99]

On April 24 the 120th Division reached Mapyeong-ri, its designated target, and joined forces with the Thirty-Ninth Army to prevent the U.S. 1st Marine Division east of Pukhan-gang River from moving west.[100] The 120th intercepted one battalion from the U.S. 1st Marine Division. However, it was unable to wipe out the U.S. force even after an all-night attack, due to a lack of artillery and antitank guns. The 120th then marched twelve miles deeper into the ROK 6th Division's rear, disrupting the South Koreans' force deployment. The Thirty-Ninth and Fortieth Armies had managed to split the UN forces down the middle within the first two days of the campaign, facilitating their encirclement of the ROK 6th Division.[101] The army commanders hoped they could capture some UNF supplies after destroying the enemy units, as they had often managed to do during the Chinese Civil War. Unfortunately, that did not happen.

In the meantime, the Twentieth, Twenty-Sixth, and Twenty-Seventh Armies of the Ninth Army Group flanked the western UNF from the right. Zhang Yixiang (1914–90), commander of the Twentieth Army, ordered his 60th Division to attack the ROK 6th Division.[102] On April 24 the 60th Division's 179th Regiment broke through the ROK 6th's lines, and the ROK defense collapsed.[103] When the 6th Division fled south under the heavy Chinese attacks, it abandoned 29 American howitzers, 41 mortars, and 160 vehicles.[104] But the Chinese could not remove the vehicles or artillery pieces since none of the soldiers knew how to drive. They secured 27 trucks and destroyed all the remaining vehicles and equipment at the site.[105]

By April 24, the Ninth Army Group had accomplished its first-stage task of splitting the UNF down the middle and flanking the U.S. IX Corps on the right.[106] Its armies moved forward ten to eighteen miles, occupying the areas of Yonghwadong, Oeyasadong, and Paekunsan. The Twenty-Sixth Army, under the command of Zhang Renchu (1909–69), occupied positions northwest of Jipo-ri (Jipori) and began to strike toward Yeongpyeon (Yeongpyon).[107] The 80th and 81st Divisions of the Twenty-Seventh Army broke through the middle of the U.S. 24th Division's defenses and occupied Jaoeuibong and Yonghwadong by April 24.[108] Song adjusted his force deployments, ordering all five armies to "seize the opportunity to cut off the enemy's southern retreat, advancing with courage and a strong will to split them into groups for annihilation." He also instructed all armies to make "bold decisions in accordance with the enemy's situation" and to act "rapidly and decisively to make sure no opportunities are lost."[109] On April 25 the Ninth Army Group began an attempt to destroy the U.S. 24th Division, which had been cut off and encircled by the Twentieth and Twenty-Seventh Armies in five places southeast of Paecheon and south of Seopo.[110] However, the Chinese armies were unable to destroy any of the 24th's regiments or even a U.S. battalion.

There were several reasons for this failure. First, UNF forces, under the pressure of CPVF massive attacks, had already made a systematic withdrawal. On April 23 Gen. James Van Fleet ordered Gen. Frank Milburn, commander of U.S. I Corps, and Gen. William Hodge, commander of U.S. IX Corps, to pull back their forces and establish new defensive positions along Line Kansas.[111] Van Fleet had studied and understood the CPVF's attack pattern, giving him an advantage in saving his forces from a Chinese onslaught. He ordered his forces to withdraw approximately twelve to twenty miles per night, which was the distance that the undersupplied CPVF forces were expected to be able to advance. The U.S. troops soon were far enough to keep them out of striking range of the Chinese forces, but close enough to maintain contact with the CPVF attacking forces. With accurate information about the Chinese positions and movements, Van Fleet was able to call air, artillery, and tank strikes against the CPVF forces during the daytime, inflicting huge casualties on the helpless Chinese ground forces.[112] This weakened the attacking CPVF forces enough to significantly reduce the power of their previously terrifying night assaults.

The superior UNF ground firepower and air cover doomed the Chinese attempt to block the withdrawal of the U.S. 24th Division to failure. Zhang Yixiang, the commander of the Twentieth Army, sent his 59th Division to Jangmyeong-ri (Jangmyongri) to cut off the U.S. 24th Division's retreat. However, because of the strong defensive firepower, the 59th could not reach that point and complete the encirclement before the U.S. troops withdrew to the south.[113] On April 27, the Twenty-Seventh

Army began its attacks on the U.S. 24th Division.[114] The Ninth Army Group Command also ordered the Fortieth Army to extend its forces south of Kapyeong to block reinforcements heading toward the U.S. 24th Division's flank.[115]

Intensified UNF air raids targeted CPVF logistic depots and transportation lines. Marc Bernstein describes this in detail: "On April 23, the Far East Air Forces flew more than 1,100 sorties. . . . During April 24–26, the pilots continued to fly more than 1,000 sorties a day."[116] According to UNF official statistics, more than 30 percent of these missions were air attacks on railways, bridges, roads, and warehouses in North Korea and on CPVF-NKPA logistic troops.[117] The Chinese logistics could not keep up with the armies' movements and operations due to fierce UNF air raids and artillery bombardment. At this point, the CPVF attacking armies were running short of supplies.

On April 27 the fifth day of the Spring Offensive, the Twentieth and Twenty-Seventh Armies ran out of food and ammunition. Without ammunition and artillery shells, the armies were unable to destroy one American battalion or even a company of the U.S. 24th Division within the next two days.[118] Nie Rongzhen recalled that the troops of the Twenty-seventh Army "broke through the UNF defensive line in the Hyon-ri area" and cut off the U.S. 24th Division's retreat. But "they had to call a halt to their attacks [on the U.S. 24th from behind] for three days to wait for supplies of munitions and food, consequently losing a good battle opportunity." Nie pointed out that the UNF had "found out the pattern of the CPVF operations." He continued: "They [the Americans] knew that our forward offensive depended entirely on the food and munitions carried by the attacking troops themselves. Usually, the troops' food and munitions could support only a one-week-long operation; indeed, the American army called our charges 'one-week attacks.'"[119]

To cut off the U.S. 24th Division's retreat, the Fortieth Army sent its divisions to attack the British 27th Brigade at Kapyeong. But the Chinese troops faced a strong defense by the Third Royal Australian Regiment of the British 27th Brigade.[120] Millett points out that "the Battle of Kapyeong bought time for the U.S. 24th Infantry Division to withdraw in good order for one day, then turn and engage the CPVF Twenty-Seventh and Twentieth Armies in an all-day battle that stopped the Chinese."[121] The Chinese divisions, still waiting for food and ammunition, were unable to prevent the U.S. 24th from breaking through roadblocks and retreating south. On April 29, after the U.S. 24th had withdrawn, the Chinese divisions occupied Jipo-ri (Jipori or Jinpeol-ri), Joyeongsan (Jonghyeonsan), Cheongpyeongcheon, Kapyeong, and Chuncheon, without annihilating a single American unit.[122] In the meantime, Van Fleet dispatched the British 28th Brigade, two battalions of the Canadian 25th Brigade, and the U.S. 7th Regiment, 1st Cavalry Division, to the Kapyeong area, strengthening the UNF defensive line there and filling the gap opened by the attacks from the CPVF Fortieth Army. He also dispatched the U.S. 1st Cavalry Division (minus its 7th Regiment) to strengthen Seoul's defenses, the ROK 7th Division to defend Inje's, and the ROK 9th Division to defend Hyeon-ri (Hyonri or Hyeongri).[123]

The failure to annihilate the U.S. 24th Division resulted from the lack of supplies for the attacking forces of the Ninth Army Group. The force of 548,000 men had been hastily thrown into the largest-scale attack of the Korean War to date. Its supplies were stretched far too thin to guarantee that its armies could receive even a basic daily minimum of food and ammunition. To deal with the supply problem, the Ninth Army Group Command had required all operational armies to carry five days' worth of food when the Spring Offensive started, on April 22, but by April 27–28 the attacking forces were running out of food and ammunition.[124]

On April 29 the Ninth Army Group pulled back its Twenty-Sixth Army from north of Pyeongkang (Pyeongchang) and resupplied it.[125] The Ninth's main forces remained in the areas south of Keumhwa (Kumhwa), Cheorwon (Chorwon), and Makim-ri (Makimri), with one division deployed at Kapyeong, Cheongpyeongcheon, and Motong-ri (Motongri) to monitor UNF activities. Those CPVF forces (including the Thirty-Ninth and Fortieth Armies) that had successfully split and penetrated the UNF troops in the center had been unable to sustain their assault without continuous logistical support. The Thirty-Ninth was deployed at Chuncheon and Hwacheon for resupplying while it remained prepared to protect the CPVF main forces. Two days later, the Fortieth Army moved back to Sawon-ri (Sawonri) for resupplying.[126]

After one week of offensive moves, Peng called off all attacks along the western front due to the lack of supplies. He explained to Mao on April 26 that "we were not adequately prepared, especially on food and ammunitions, and out transportation has not been improved." Peng suggested that "we must build up highways from Seocheon to Yangteok as soon as possible and make it our future primary transportation and supply line in the front center without any delays caused by two-way traffics. This had caught our attention when we first entered Korea but it has not been completed today due to the lack of efforts."[127] On April 28 Mao and the CMC approved Peng's request that the CPVF end its southward offensive on the western front.[128] On April 29 the first step of the CPVF Spring Offensive ended, having achieved few of the expected results but having incurred heavy Chinese casualties.

# FIVE

# The Costly Offensive in the West

BETWEEN APRIL 22 AND APRIL 29, 1951, THE FIRST STEP OF THE Chinese Spring Offensive began sparking what Allan Millett has described as the "most widespread and intense fighting of the Korean War."[1] The CPVF launched its greatest offensive against the U.S. I Corps, along the western portion of the 38th Parallel. Peng Dehuai and his CPVF-NKPA Joint Command sent more than 700,000 men into battle in an attempt to cross the 38th Parallel, annihilate five divisions and two brigades of the U.S. I Corps, and retake Seoul. After eight days of fierce fighting, all three CPVF army groups had broken through defense lines of the UNF and either reached or crossed the 38th Parallel.

Although the CPVF's Ninth Army Group achieved some of its operational goals by opening a gap near Kapyeong and separating the U.S. I Corps in the west from the U.S. Eighth Army's IX Corps in the center and X Corps in the east, overall the offensive failed. The main CPVF armies were unable to penetrate deeply enough into UNF lines to encircle and destroy even a single division or brigade. The CPVF Third Army Group, fighting against the center of the U.S. I Corps, and the Nineteenth Army Group on the left of the I Corps, faced serious operational problems due to lack of preparedness and supplies and, worst of all, heavy casualties during the first week of the Spring Offensive.

The devastating number of casualties forced Peng to halt his offensive. From April 22 to the 29th, Chinese forces suffered between 35,000 and 60,000 casualties, losing more than 5,000–8,000 men every day, compared to only 4,000 UNF casualties during the week.[2] The estimated casualty ratio between the CPVF and UNF was about 10–15 to 1 (about 3 to 1, according to Chinese official statistics), much higher than Peng's expectation of 1 to 1 or even 1 to 2.[3] Specifically, the Sixty-Third, Sixty-Fourth, and Sixty-Fifth Armies of the Nineteenth Army Group lost roughly a third to a half of their combat troops in the first week of the campaign.[4] These heavy casualties slowed down the Nineteenth Army Group's drive and made the encirclement of the I Corps impossible. And the losses made Peng's campaign goal of annihilating any division or brigade, or even a regiment of the UNF, virtually unattainable. With Mao's approval in Beijing on April 28,[5] Peng called off the Chinese offensive on April 29 and ended the costly, unsuccessful campaign on the Korean western front.

Two major factors behind the severe Chinese losses were the new tactics employed by UN and U.S. forces and their overwhelmingly superior firepower on the ground and in the air. In retrospect, the strategic and tactical issues and unsolved operational and supply problems from the CPVF Command down to the divisional commands also contributed to unusually heavy casualties of the CPVF troops during the first week of the Chinese Spring Offensive.

In addition to other factors, first, Mao's strategy of annihilation locked the CPVF into attacking large UNF units like divisions and brigades, which eventually exhausted Chinese resources and energy, giving the UNF opportunities to inflict heavy casualties on the CPVF forces. Second, the CPVF Command had overestimated the combat effectiveness of the Chinese forces, basing their assessment on the earlier successful offensive campaigns against the UNF in the winter of 1950. Its leaders believed that once they had doubled the Chinese forces in the spring of 1951, the CPVF's increased numerical superiority would win a bigger victory. Third, the CPVF Command ignored indications that the UNF had changed its strategy and improved its defenses by April 1951. Peng rushed a half-million men to the front without air cover, training, or essential supplies. Fourth, at the army group and army command levels, the commanders did not have enough needed resources, except their human resources, to solve many battleground problems such as inferior firepower, poorly organized encirclements, and lack of transportation and communication. Peng, who had access to the resources, underestimated the UNF's defensive firepower. High Chinese casualties resulted from the army commanders' unfamiliarity with the Korean terrain and current UNF tactics, unrealistic plans to encircle and annihilate entire UNF divisions or brigades, and the Chinese inability to coordinate artillery support with infantry assaults. Finally, divisional and regimental commanders could not sustain their assault without tanks and experienced continuing shortages of supplies and medical assistance. Under pressure from the army commands, they organized massive assaults to attack UNF defensive positions. The massed frontal attacks caused severe losses during the first step of the Spring Offensive.

### MASSED ATTACKS

During that first step, the Chinese launched massive attacks one after another whenever sufficient troops were available. The ROK official military history notes that "the Chinese April offensive was based on the 'human wave tactics,' employing 305,000 soldiers (270,000 Chinese and 35,000 North Koreans) as the main weapon."[6] In fact, before the offensive campaign started, Peng and his command cautioned the Chinese generals to be "careful" in their attacks to reduce casualties.[7] The massed attack was not one of the offensive tactics mentioned in the CPVF's operational instruction on April 11. Mao also emphasized "self-preservation" as one of the objects of revolutionary war.[8]

Nevertheless, Mao also believed that the "destruction of the enemy" is more important than "the preservation of oneself." "It should be pointed out," Mao says, "that destruction of the enemy is the primary object of war and self-preservation the secondary, because only by destroying the enemy in large numbers can one effectively preserve oneself." He continues: "China, though weak, has a vast territory, a large population and plenty of soldiers." Thus, he suggested that CCP commanders "make use of our two advantages, namely, our vast territory and large forces" in the Anti-Japanese War by "employing several divisions against one enemy division, several tens of thousands of our men against ten thousand of his."[9] The CPVF Command followed Mao's strategy of revolutionary war in the Spring Offensive by "concentrating a big force" since "this is the way to deal with one or indeed with any advancing enemy column."[10]

For example, on April 18, the CPVF Command issued another set of instructions, "Directives on Guiding Principles and Tactical Guidelines for the Campaign," which set up the principle of "assembling superior forces and wiping out the enemy forces one by one."[11] Peng's April 18 instruction to all the CPVF armies also said: "All the commands must stick to the principle of concentrating superior forces and firepower to destroy the enemy by tactical separation and operational encirclement."[12] The new order put Chinese commanders under tremendous pressure to exploit their manpower. Under those guidelines, all CPVF armies were required to use ample forces to divide UNF units into several pieces on an operational scale, in an attempt to annihilate each piece. To attack the UNF with massive forces was also included in the CPVF's political mobilization instruction on April 19.[13]

Peng and his commanders believed the CPVF's superior numbers would offset its inferior equipment and technology and would be a decisive factor in winning the battle. Both officers and soldiers believed their "fighting spirit" would lead them to victory.[14] However, when the CPFV confronted a more modern army with superior firepower and air support, the death toll among the Chinese was horrendous. In the cases of the Third and Nineteenth Army Groups, the army and division commanders had also deemed it necessary to sacrifice small units to save larger forces and accomplish their missions. They had an advantage in numbers of troops and were guaranteed reinforcements and replenishment during and after the Spring Offensive, but unfortunately, James Van Fleet, the new commander of the U.S. Eighth Army, was prepared for that tactic. In Stanley Sandler's words, Van Fleet "even welcomed the next Chinese offensive," since the UNF Command had changed its strategy to attrition warfare and had been looking for the opportunity to destroy more Communist forces.[15]

After dark on April 22, the CPVF Nineteenth Army Group—the Sixty-Third, Sixty-Fourth, and Sixty-Fifth Armies, totaling 110,000 troops—launched attacks on the left flank of the U.S. I Corps. The American corps consisted of the U.S. 3rd, 24th, and 25th Divisions; the British 29th Brigade; the Turkish Brigade; and the ROK 1st Division. After the initial Chinese night attacks, at noon on April 23, Van Fleet ordered the two UNF corps to pull back their forces to establish a new defense

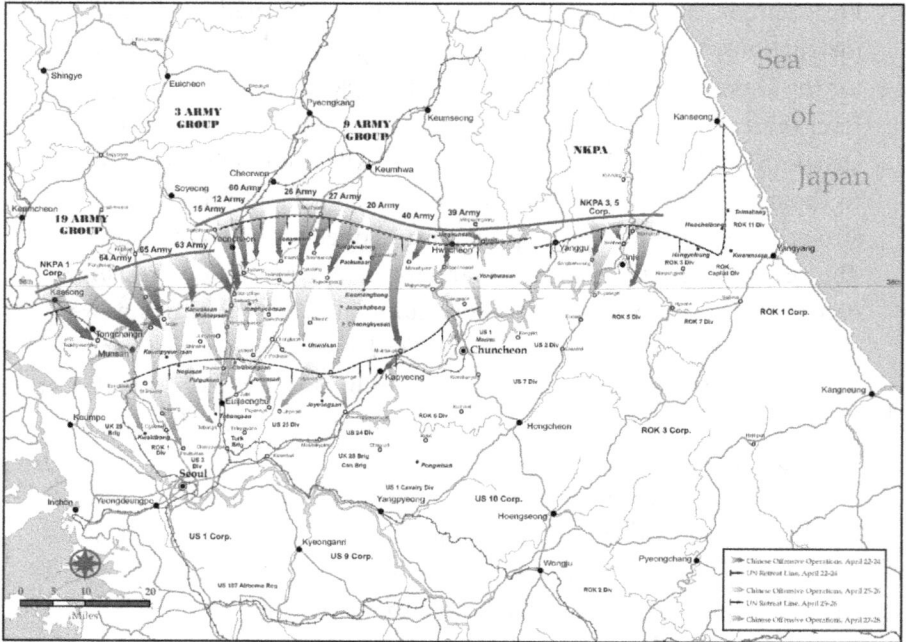

Map 5.1. CPVF attacks through the first step, Spring Offensive, April 22–28

along Line Kansas. Then Milburn ordered the ROK 1st Division and British 29th Brigade to firmly defend positions at Munsan-ri (Munsanri or Munsan-ni), Mitunsa, and Shinam-ri (Shinamri or Shinam-ni), an area between the Imjin-gang River and Route 33, the main road to Seoul through Euijeongbu.[16] Holding these positions would delay the CPVF's attacks, protect the left wing of the U.S. Eighth Army's main forces, and facilitate the efforts of the U.S. I and IX Corps to withdraw and build up a new defense line "to inflict high losses on the enemy while keeping UN losses to a minimum"[17] (map 5.1).

The Chinese Sixty-Fourth Army—the 190th, 191st, and 192nd Divisions, totaling 28,000 men—was ordered to break through the ROK 1st Division—the 11th, 12th, and 13th Regiments, totaling 8,000 troops— and drive into Euijeongbu, the rear of the U.S. I Corps, and to cut off its retreat. Most attacking forces of the Sixty-Fourth Army had not yet reached their staging areas when orders to attack arrived.[18] After running to reach their staging areas, the two attacking divisions of the Sixty-Fourth were unable to attack the ROK 1st Division with sufficient strength due to extreme exhaustion. The stubborn defense of the ROK troops held the Chinese 191st and 192nd Divisions on the south bank of the Imjin-gang at Mitunsa.[19] Since the Sixty-Fourth was stopped at the Imjin-gang River, the entire Nineteenth Army Group made no progress on April 24. At 1:00 PM on April 25, the CPVF-NKPA Joint Command telegraphed the Nineteenth Army Group Command that the Nineteenth must overcome all difficulties and fight harder to break through the UNF defense line and head south to Euijeongbu. The CPVF Command warned that the Nineteenth Army Group's failure would jeopardize the entire offensive.[20]

The Nineteenth Army Group Command was outraged with the failure of the Sixty-Fourth Army to progress after it crossed the Imjin-gang. If the Sixty-Fourth failed to break through the ROK defense, the army group would not be able to flank the U.S. I Corps and complete the encirclement. This meant that the CPVF Spring Offensive would not succeed in annihilating several UNF units of the U.S. I Corps. Yang Dezhi, commander of the Nineteenth Army Group, sent two telegrams at 3:00 PM on April 23 to Zeng Siyu, commander of the Sixty-Fourth. In the first he warned: "You must overcome all the difficulties and accomplish your task at all cost. Penetrate into Euijeongbu and occupy the designated targets by tonight."[21] The second telegram warned Zeng harshly that "any unsuccessful attack means death. If the divisions of the Sixty-Fourth Army fail to reach their assigned points or fail to accomplish the campaign goals, [the commanders are] subject to severe punishment by our revolutionary disciplines."[22] To carry out the army group's order and avoid any punishment, the Sixty-Fourth Army committed its reserves, the 190th Division.[23]

To ensure the 190th Division's success, Zeng rushed to the division HQ on the afternoon of April 23. Zeng told Chen Xinzhong, commander of the 190th Division, that "the army command can't expect too much from the 191st and 192nd Divisions, which have been deadlocked in their attacks over a ten-mile front. Your division has to take over the Tobung-san Mountain before 10:00 AM tomorrow."[24] Chen, then thirty-six, felt pressured because the Sixty-Fourth Army's breakthrough of the ROK defensive line, and perhaps the entire Nineteenth Army Group's success, would depend on his attack. He promised Zeng that the 190th Division, totaling 12,000 men, would accomplish the mission at all cost. The division crossed the Imjin-gang at 6:00 PM that evening.[25]

At 4:40 AM on April 24, Chen sent four battalions, estimated at 3,600 men, from the 190th Division's 568th and 570th Regiments to a hilly area between Masan-ri (Masanri) and Tongmun-ri (Tongmunri), two ROK positions. Chen hoped to break through between the two ROK regiments, but his battalions failed.[26] Chen rushed to the forward command post and ordered Wang Zhongqiu, commander of the 3rd Battalion, 568th Regiment, to "send your entire battalion to Hill 276 at once! Take it, be awarded; fail, be punished! Understood?"[27] Chen felt that he had to sacrifice one or more of his battalions if necessary, since Mao had justified "the encouragement of heroic sacrifice in war." War, Mao said, "exacts a price, sometimes an extremely high price. Partial and temporary sacrifice [nonpreservation] is incurred for the sake of general and permanent preservation."[28] Wang promised his superior officer that the 3rd Battalion would take the hill.

Wang did not have tank or artillery support, since the artillery troops had been delayed by a U.S. air raid on the north bank of the Imjin-gang. His battalion faced a position that was well defended by the Fourth Company, 15th Regiment, ROK 1st Division. The ROK infantry company was supported by a tank company and under UNF air and artillery cover. Like other Chinese commanders, Wang had full confidence in his men. Brave and politically motivated, these 830 young men were experienced and had high morale, even though they were armed only with light weapons and were poorly supplied. Hoping to increase his chances of success, Wang organized his attacking force by sending his entire battalion at once against the ROK position on top of the hill (Hill 276). In the massed formation of his frontal attack, his Ninth Company was in the center, Seventh Company on the left, and Eighth Company on the right.[29] Wang led the assault himself with the Eighth Company. While the attacking Chinese troops blew bugles and whistles, their officers shouted commands, and more than 600 men followed. The ROK officers from the Fourth Company recalled that the "Chinese launched two human-wave assaults against the hill."[30]

Some Western historians view the massed Chinese assaults as, in the words of Jeff Kinard, "human wave" attacks carried out "in an effort to overwhelm their better-armed opponents and capture their weapons."[31] Edward O'Dowd claims that "American infantrymen dubbed these massed groups of Chinese soldiers 'hordes,' and the attacks became known as 'human waves' [in Chinese, *renhai zhanshi*]."[32] Brian Steed states that "the Korean War is a demonstration of human wave tactics used against UN forces at the tactical level of strategy."[33] He further argues that "as the terrain became less restricted, they [the Chinese forces] turned to the use of human wave assaults as the basic strategy from the operational level and below."[34] Bruce Elleman describes the Chinese "human wave" attacks during the CPVF First Offensive, in October–November 1950: "Simultaneously, they attacked from the north, northwest, and west, utilizing frontal assaults composed of waves of infantry variously described as a 'human sea' or a 'swarm of locusts.'"[35]

The early Chinese offensives proved that the massed attacks were effective from October 1950 until February 1951. During that time, CPVF attacks at the company or battalion level usually surprised UNF troops, especially the nighttime attacks and those in close combat.[36] Some early successes of large-scale assaults were due to the "element of surprise and the Communist forces' ability to exploit the weakness of the coalition troops," especially ROK forces.[37] O'Dowd points out that "expensive or not, the shock of a human wave attack often forced the defenders to break ranks to escape from the attacking mob, upon which the position would be lost."[38] By early 1951, however, a Chinese large-scale attack lacked the element of surprise and merely exhausted the Chinese soldiers. When the CPVF attacked and troops were exposed, the UNF Command hit them with "everything in the U.S. Eighth Army arsenal, plus whatever the navy and the air force could deliver."[39]

By April 1951 the U.S. Army had enormously increased its logistical support to the South Korean Army, so the ROK Fourth Company had effective defensive firepower at Hill 276.[40] Marc Bernstein describes the CPVF massive attack, about which one UNF officer told a *Time* correspondent in April 1951 that "they attack and we shoot them down. Then we pull back, and they have to do it all over again. They're spending people the way we spend ammunition."[41] Theodore White, an infantryman in the U.S. 24th Regiment, recalled: "When they charged they'd be so close together you couldn't miss. But they had so many men. During the daytime you could see hundreds of bodies lying out there on the hillside, and you'd think, how could they take any more of that? But the next night they'd do it again."[42] White described how his unit dealt with the Chinese "human wave" attacks in April: "We'd take up a position and hold it for a while, until it seemed like we'd be overrun. But at the last minute we'd always get the word to pull back. Now what I understand is, that business was General Ridgway's idea. He was still out to kill as many Chinese as possible, and the longer a unit held on to a position, the longer the artillery could stay forward and blow the hell out of the Chinese."[43]

Eventually, the Chinese 3rd Battalion, 568th Regiment, 190th Division, overran the ROK position and took Hill 276, having 31 ROK soldiers killed, 42 wounded, and 25 captured. However, the 3rd Battalion lost nearly three-quarters of its men in the massive attack: 237 dead and 115 wounded.[44] The battalion could not advance further, nor could it put up any effective defense because of its severe casualties at Hill 276 on April 24. The following day, the ROK 1st Division launched a counterattack with one tank company and two battalions of the 15th Regiment under air support and artillery cover. The ROK battalions regained control of Hill 276 and closed a nearby breach in this sector, created by the Chinese 190th Division, Sixty-Fourth Army.[45]

Everywhere else along the Sixty-Fourth Army's front line, the Chinese attacking force commanders had the same understanding of their mission as Chen, the 190th Division commander; all used the same tactics of massed formation attacks. The Chinese offensives during the first week of the Spring Offensive proved that the massed attacks had lost their effectiveness, even in nighttime and close combat. During a night attack, the Chinese assaults could not annihilate the UNF unit overnight. During daytime close combat, the Chinese massed attacks were stopped by a barrage of UNF fire, and Chinese troops could not move close to UNF positions. Following Van Fleet's orders, each UNF defense line had overwhelming firepower superiority on the ground with artillery and tanks.

All divisions of the Sixty-Fourth Army suffered heavy losses, totaling 10,000 casualties from April 23 through April 28. This made it impossible for the Sixty-Fourth to penetrate deeply into the rear of the U.S. I Corps after its divisions broke through ROK 1st Division's defensive line.[46] Only one battalion, the 3rd Battalion of the 569th Regiment, along with an army reconnaissance team, made it deep into UNF territory, striking toward Tobung-san near Euijeongbu, about twenty miles north of Seoul, the campaign objective for the Sixty-Fourth Army.[47] The Sixty-Fourth failed to accomplish Peng's encirclement plan for the Spring Offensive. The commanders and political commissars of its 191st and 192nd Divisions were immediately dismissed from their positions by the CPVF Command and were punished later, not for troop casualties, but for failed missions.[48] Chen, however, was promoted for his successful massed attack on Hill 267.[49]

Even though the Chinese soldiers were politically motivated and able "to advance straight at the enemy," according to O'Dowd, "human wave attacks rarely are the tactical choice of a combatant" who faces an opponent with greater firepower.[50] Nevertheless, it seemed necessary for division commanders like Chen to send entire battalions to charge a hill to break through the ROK lines. The 190th Division's massed attacks were a critical component of the Sixty-Fourth Army's mission of breaching the ROK defenses; and the Sixty-Fourth's success could guarantee that the Nineteenth Army Group would be able to penetrate and encircle the U.S. I Corps. The only problem the Chinese faced was the UNF's overwhelming firepower. The Chinese armies continued attacking until their losses from that firepower were too high to launch another attack. Shuang Shi, a former officer in the PLA, acknowledges that the Chinese suffered such unexpected casualties because their "human wave" attacks faced the UNF "fire wave" defense strategy.[51]

Peng was forced to end the first step of the Spring Offensive earlier than he planned. He explained this to Mao and the CMC on April 26:

The enemy forces are pressed closely together without any gaps for us to exploit. With its absolutely superior technical equipment and weapons, the enemy has chosen to move from one point to the next in conducting a solid, tactical offense, and has conducted phased resistance when it retreats. We have been unable to break open gaps for penetration deep into the enemy rear without engaging in bloody, costly battles. These are the reasons why we were unable to conduct flanking and encirclement maneuvers at Euijeongbu after fighting for three nights.[52]

## CASUALTIES OF UNF FIREPOWER

Having solved the problem of Chinese night attacks, Lt. Gen. Van Fleet ordered his forces to withdraw only a short distance per night, the distance that the short-supplied CPVF troops could travel overnight, in order to maintain close contact with Chinese attacking forces throughout the following day. Staying in contact allowed the UNF to employ its superior air, artillery, and tank firepower and inflict as much damage as possible on the CPVF attacking forces during daylight. The intensive UNF air raids and artillery bombardment inflicted heavy casualties on the Nineteenth Army Group during the first week of the Spring Offensive. Ridgway recalled that "from April 21 to 29, UN fliers had flown 7,420 missions and the incessant pounding of our big guns had pockmarked the whole face of the countryside."[53]

After April 22 UNF air forces intensified their strikes and raids on Chinese targets. Their planes also engaged in close support operations against the attacking Chinese forces: "The Fifth Air Force alone flew some three hundred forty close support sorties on the 23rd . . . and the 1st Marine Air Wing flew over a hundred fifty missions."[54] Sandler points out that "massive and precise bombing by formations of USAF [U.S. Air Force] B-29s also broke up impending major Communist attacks, a welcome change from the earlier obliteration of empty landscapes along the Pusan Perimeter."[55] Since the Chinese armies had no air cover, the CPVF Command had limited time to prepare and launch attacks. All troops were prohibited from day-time cooking, lighting fires, or shooting at American airplanes with light weapons, lest they give away their position.[56] Despite extra anti-air efforts and the improvement of their air defenses, the CPVF attacking forces suffered heavy casualties from UNF air strikes and widespread bombing from April 22 to the 29th.

When the Sixty-Fourth Army of the Nineteenth Army Group crossed the Imjin-gang early in the morning of April 23, UNF air observers reported the Chinese crossing operation at three points near Korangpo-ri (Korangpori). The UNF began intensive air strikes and artillery bombardments, stopping the crossing operation by 11:00 AM. UNF air raids split the Sixty-Fourth Army along the river.

To help the Sixty-Fourth with its crossing, the Nineteenth Army Group Command sent the Sixty-Fifth Army as reinforcements that afternoon.[57] The group commanders believed that the additional troops and the determined attempts by these two armies could overcome UNF fire along the river and overwhelm the UNF defenses.[58] The Sixty-Fifth Army—the 193rd, 194th, and 195th Divisions, totaling 29,000 men—sent two of its divisions to cross the Imjin-gang in an attempt to join the Sixty-Fourth in attacking the British 29th Brigade. However, because the Sixty-Fourth was still stalled in front of them, the two divisions were unable to advance toward their operational targets.[59] As a result, five CPVF divisions, numbering more than 60,000 men, found themselves sitting ducks crowded along a narrow, ten-mile strip of land south of the Imjin-gang and north of Changpa-ri (Changpari), Kosadong, and Maji-ri (Majiri). For two days they suffered extremely high losses from repeated waves of concentrated UNF artillery, tank, and air attacks.[60] The Sixty-Fourth and Sixty-Fifth Armies had lost so many troops that they could not advance far enough to flank the U.S. I Corps and reach Euijeongbu.[61]

The effectiveness of the UNF air forces led Peng and others in the CPVF Command to change their air defense policy. No longer did they prohibit their troops from firing at American airplanes with light weapons; instead, they now encouraged the men to fire back on the UNF warplanes with whatever means available. Xu Yan has concluded that heavy casualties at the Imjin-gang River illustrated one of the greatest lessons learned by the CPVF in the Korean War: it was no longer practical or effective for the Chinese to concentrate large numbers of forces for massed attacks.[62]

The CPVF Third Army Group faced difficulties to those encountered by the Nineteenth when it attacked the U.S. I Corps on April 22. The Third Army Group—the Twelfth, Fifteenth, and Sixtieth Armies, totaling 150,000 troops—was ordered to conduct breakthrough attacks on a narrow front in the center, less than ten miles wide. At the time the order to attack was issued on April 22, all the group's armies had not yet reached their staging areas. They had been forced to run for thirty to sixty minutes before they reached the front lines, which meant that the attacking infantry forces were unable to use pre-assault barrages against the

UNF defense.[63] Even after artillery fire had extended into the UNF positions, the infantry forces still had not reached their staging areas. When engaging the U.S. I Corps, the army group met stubborn resistance from the U.S. 3rd Division and the Turkish Brigade, backed by UNF air and artillery support. The Turkish artillery battalion fired 2,554 shells on April 22–23. And each UNF FAB fired more than 1,000 shells during the first day. There were twenty-six UNF FABs on the western front.[64]

According to Peng's plan, the Fifteenth Army of the Third Army Group—the 29th, 44th, and 45th Divisions, totaling 32,000 men— would advance to Keumko-ri via Kamsubong in order to encircle the U.S. 3rd Division—the 7th, 15th, 30th, and the 65th Infantry Regiments, along with four FABs, totaling 10,000 troops.[65] On April 22 the Fifteenth Army ordered its 29th and 44th Divisions to penetrate the U.S. defensive line and surround the U.S. 65th Regiment (the Puerto Rican Regiment) of the 3rd Division from both sides. By 1:00 AM on April 23, the two Chinese divisions had occupied Manadong, Oyeubong, and Tapgkeo-ri, encircling the U.S. 65th Regiment and cutting off its retreat.[66]

However, the U.S. 3rd Division did not retreat immediately under Chinese attacks. Its men followed Van Fleet's order and defended their positions with well-organized air and ground fire support.[67] The 3rd Division ordered its 65th Regiment to hold on as long as possible, so it could inflict the maximum number of casualties on the Chinese attacking forces. The U.S. 65th Regiment firmly defended its lines against massive attacks by the 29th and 44th Divisions. UNF air strikes and artillery bombardment caused heavy Chinese casualties during the first day of attacks. The Fifteenth Army had only 30 AAA pieces and 111 anti-aircraft machine guns, not enough to provide an effective defense against the UNF air strikes.[68] The 86th Regiment of the 29th Division, for example, lost more than 40 percent of its combat strength. In the Fourth Company of its 2nd Battalion, only 13 of 145 men survived; all the officers of the Fifth Company—its captain, lieutenants, and sergeants— were killed in action.[69] These severe losses in the two key divisions significantly reduced the strength of the Chinese forces after the first day, requiring immediate reinforcement and regrouping.

Nevertheless, the 44th Division attacked again the next morning, but it failed to break through the lines of the 65th Regiment, which had built up a strong defense supported by tanks, air cover, and artillery fire. Subsequently, the U.S. regiment broke through the Chinese encirclement and that afternoon began withdrawing south. In the afternoon of April 23, the Third Army Group Command adjusted its plans following the retreat of the U.S. 65th Regiment. The command ordered the Sixtieth Army to send one more division to reinforce the 29th and 44th Divisions by reaching the areas of Hwabongchon, Tandong, and Pankeo-ri (Pankori) on April 24. The newly arrived Chinese division set up another block at Tandong and Yuoyok.[70] However, the Chinese division failed again to stop the U.S. 65th Regiment, which broke through the Third Army Group's encirclement on April 26, aided by substantial UNF air, artillery, and tank support.

According to Peng's order, the Twelfth Army of the Third Army Group—the 31st, 34th, and 35th Divisions, almost 30,000 troops—attacked the Turkish Brigade, whose three infantry battalions totaled 5,000 men. Zeng Shaoshan (1914–95), commander of the Twelfth Army, ordered his 34th and 35th Divisions to simultaneously attack the Turkish Brigade on its left and right.[71] The Chinese divisions, however, met a strong Turkish defense at Chomok and Puheungdong (Puhingdong), and Zeng realized the difficulty in breaking through the Turkish line because of superior UNF fire support.[72] He added his reserve force of the 30th Division, another 13,000 men, to the attacks.

At 7:00 PM on April 22, the 34th Division began its precharge barrage with only a few artillery pieces, since the 28th Artillery Regiment had been unable to reach its position due to air attacks. Although Chinese infantrymen marched eighteen miles per night on mountain paths, the motorized artillery troops were able to travel only about twelve miles per night since they could not easily navigate the narrow paths of the mountains. The horse-drawn artillery traveled only five miles per night.[73] The staff of the division asked You Taizhong (1918–98), commander of the 34th Division, to postpone the attack and wait for the artillery's arrival.[74] You replied: "We can't delay our attack because of the lack of the artillery support. Send the first wave of two regiments to attack at once! I don't believe we can't defeat these enemy troops just with our bayonet and grenades!"[75] The 34th Division Command sent two of its three regiments, totaling 3,200 troops, on a massed frontal attack against the

Turkish positions at Hill 477.3 and Hill 500. Even though the Chinese took the hills and forced the Turks to withdraw, the two regiments suffered severe casualties.

To complete the encirclement of the Turkish Brigade, the Third Army Group ordered its Sixtieth Army to block the Turks' retreat by moving through Kotaesan and Hwainbong and then occupying Jijangdong to prevent any possible UNF rescue. The Sixtieth Army—the 179th, 180th, and 181st Divisions, totaling 31,000 troops—rushed ten miles into the Turkish rear and occupied Kacheok-ri (Kachokri). By 4:00 AM on April 23, the 181st Division of the Sixtieth had occupied Pugok-ri (Pugokri) and separated the Turkish Brigade from the U.S. 25th Division.[76] Wang Chenghan (1917–2009), commander of the 181st Division, sent his 541st Regiment to flank the Turkish Brigade on its right side.[77] The 541st Regiment under the command of Wang Zibo (b. 1922) broke though the Turkish defenses that morning.[78] The Turkish Brigade's position collapsed, and the brigade began its retreat. Due to the lack of artillery support that morning, the Chinese 34th, 35th, and 181st Divisions were unable to halt its withdrawal. Wang Zibo, the 541st Regiment's commander, complained that the three divisions came from two different armies, the Twelfth and the Sixtieth, and there was no communication between the Chinese divisions and regiments before the offensive and no cooperation during the attacks. Wang did not know what the nearby CPVF regiments were doing. He did not get his instructions ahead of time, and he had to stop after completing each assignment to await further orders. Because of this delay, his regiment lost an opportunity to block the Turkish retreat after the Chinese broke through the Turkish defensive line that night. The new order, which arrived the following morning, instructed Wang to block the Turks—who had already retreated.[79]

On the afternoon of April 23, the Third Army Group Command adjusted its encirclement plan following the Turkish Brigade's retreat. The command ordered its Twelfth and Sixtieth Armies to set up roadblocks to stop the Turkish withdrawal. Zeng, the Twelfth Army commander, assumed that the Turkish Brigade had not completed its withdrawal from Paecheon and ordered his 34th, 35th, and 36th Divisions to attack Paecheon. The 34th Division occupied Paecheon on April 24, cutting the highway between Paecheon and Euijeongbu.[80]

On April 26 the U.S. 23rd Infantry Regiment of the 2nd Division traveled along the Soyang River. The Chinese 34th and 35th Divisions ordered their regiments to attack the U.S. 2nd Division convoy and to block three hundred trucks loaded with American infantrymen. The Chinese regiments launched an immediate assault on the U.S. 23rd Regiment from hills along the road. The 34th and 35th Divisions, with the assistance of the 181st Division, fought for two days against the U.S. troops. The Chinese regiments soon ran out of ammunition and food and had to disengage on April 27. The 23rd Regiment of the U.S. 2nd Division "suffered 72 troopers killed, 158 wounded and 190 missing" and abandoned more than 150 vehicles. But in return, it had inflicted "an estimated 2,200 deaths and 1,400 wounded on the Chinese 34th, 35th, and 181st Divisions."[81] With the American rescue, the Turkish Brigade managed to withdraw through Paecheon to safety. In their defense and withdrawal from April 23 to 27, the Turks lost 300 men, while the Chinese Twelfth Army suffered over 2,000 casualties, including Wu Yansheng (1918–51), commander of the 105th Regiment, 35th Division, who was killed by a UNF air strike.[82] This was yet another example of the failed Chinese strategy of encirclement and blocking.

From April 23 to 25, the 120th Division, Fortieth Army, Ninth Army Group, attacked the U.S. 92nd Armored Field Artillery Battalion, which had self-propelled 155 mm howitzers under the command of Lt. Col. Leon Lavoie, along the Chichon-ri road. The battalion used its twelve tracked gun carriages and four attached 8-inch towed howitzers to hold its position by direct fire. The Chinese lost 2,000 men, while the 92nd had only four dead and eleven wounded.[83] The Chinese division was unable to annihilate the U.S. FAB, even though it captured some of its guns and equipment.

During the battle of Kapyeong, the Third Australian Regiment received tank support from Company A under the command of Lt. Kenneth Koch of the U.S. 72nd Tank Battalion.[84] Koch had fifteen Sherman tanks that provided significant support to the Australians' defense and inflicted heavy casualties on the Chinese attacking forces on April 23–25. On the night of the twenty-fourth, Koch's tanks fired "162 rounds of 76 mm main armament ammunition, 32,000 rounds of .30 caliber machine-gun and over 11,000 rounds of .50 caliber. . . . Between 2:00 A M and first light, the tanks had been fighting at ranges from 15 feet to 75 yards and at times the crews were obliged to repel Chinese attacks by hurling grenades from their turrets and using their 'grease guns'—a type of submachine-gun—on their assailants."[85] Koch estimated that his tanks had killed between 100 and 150 Chinese attacking troops that night.

It became impossible for the Chinese to annihilate a UNF division or a regiment that had superior firepower in the air and on the ground. Sandler mentions the captured Chinese soldiers who "began to deprecate their army doctrine of 'man over weapons,' conceding that such theories worked only when their enemy's technological superiority was not too great."[86]

### HIGH-COST BLOCKS

After completing any encirclement, Chinese forces had to block the UNF's retreat and potential rescue before any annihilation could take place. These forces suffered heavy casualties during the first phase of the Spring Offensive. The CPVF Sixty-Third Army's annihilation of the British Gloucestershire Battalion (hereafter, the Glosters) at Solma-ri (Solmari) on April 24–25 is a case in point.

Although the British 29th Brigade held its ground according to Van Fleet's order, the Chinese Sixty-Third Army of the Nineteenth Army Group—the 187th, 188th, and 189th Divisions, totaling 29,000 troops—was able to encircle the Gloster Battalion of the 29th Brigade on April 24. Then the Sixty-Third had to stop rescue attempts from three different directions on April 24–25. Eventually the Chinese 187th Division annihilated the British battalion, killing 250 British troops and capturing 570. However, the 188th and 189th Divisions of the Sixty-Third Army lost 10,000 lives in the process of supporting the 187th's attacks.[87] These huge losses resulted from Chinese blocking engagements devoid of sophisticated defense work and necessary artillery support to effectively separate the British Gloster Battalion from its relief forces.

The Sixty-Third Army under the command of Fu Chongbi had been the first force from the Nineteenth Army Group to cross the Imjin-gang on April 22.[88] After the crossing, Fu ordered his three divisions to simultaneously attack the four battalions of the British 29th Brigade between

Muksapsan and Shinam-ri.[89] The 187th Division, under the command of thirty-year-old Xu Xin, reached Solma-ri and attacked the British Gloster Battalion on April 23.[90] Xu ordered his 561st Regiment to occupy Sakimok from Kamraksan, circle behind the Gloster Battalion, and cut off its retreat.[91] His 559th Regiment broke though the British defenses from west of Kamraksan and severed the connections between the Gloster Battalion and other British units. Xu then deployed his reserve forces, the 560th Regiment, to conduct frontal assaults on the four Gloster companies commanded by Lt. Col. James P. Carne, who was forced to give up several defensive positions.[92] By 4:00 AM on April 24, the 187th Division, totaling 12,000 troops, had completed its encirclement of the British Gloster Battalion, approximately 1,000 men, on Hill 235, where Carne's battalion HQ was located.[93]

Nevertheless, Fu knew that Xu's encirclement of the British battalion did not guarantee its successful annihilation. The British Gloster Battalion was one of Britain's most honored elite forces, and Fu and Xu correctly assumed that the UNF Command would try everything possible to rescue the Glosters. After receiving reports of the British situation, Lt. Gen. Ridgway flew from Tokyo to the front in order to direct the rescue effort of the British battalion himself. At the U.S. 3rd Division airstrip around noon on April 24, Ridgway met with Van Fleet, Milburn, and Gen. Robert H. "Shorty" Soule, commander of the 3rd Division.[94] These four leaders agreed that a suitable strategy would be to send three rescue forces to Solma-ri from different directions. First, the 3rd Division would send two battalions of the 65th Regiment from the east, reinforced by the 64th Tank Battalion and the 10th FAB, with orders to attack the Chinese encirclement of the Glosters. Second, the battalions from the 12th Regiments of the ROK 1st Division would launch attacks on the CPVF from the west. Third, the British 29th Brigade would send its own rescue forces, together with the Philippine 10th Battalion, to attack Kamak-ri (Kamakri) with the support of twenty tanks. The American generals agreed that these three rescue forces should be able to allow the Gloster Battalion to escape from the Chinese encirclement.[95]

The CPVF Sixty-Third Army paid a heavy price on April 24–25 for blocking the relief attempts at Tokyojang, Shinam-ri, and Kamak-ri.[96] The CPVF's 561st Regiment of the 187th Division and 564th Regiment of the 188th Division occupied two hills abutting the road, including the "no-man hill," in order to block the Philippine 10th Battalion, attached to the British 29th Brigade at Shinam-ri. The Philippine 10th Battalion Combat Team launched an attack on the hills held by the Chinese 561st Regiment at 3:30 PM on April 24. The Filipino attacking force continued to charge the position of the 561st Regiment's 3rd Battalion at the no-man hill, with UNF close-combat air support throughout the remainder of the day.[97] Having no artillery support or antitank guns, the 3rd Battalion troops used hand grenades and explosives against the UNF tanks. By the end of the seventh Filipino assault, the Chinese 3rd Battalion had lost more than half of its men. At the no-man hill, only a few men of the Fifth and Sixth Companies of the 3rd Battalion survived the Filipino charges and UNF firepower.[98] Only one man of the Seventh Company of the 564th Regiment, 188th Division, at the other hill, survived the blocking battle on the twenty-fourth.

On the same day, in its attempt to rescue the Glosters, the U.S. 65th Regiment began its attacks with the 1st and 3rd Battalions against the Chinese 565th Regiment of the 189th Division. Rather than waiting for U.S. tanks to enter their lines, Chinese regimental commanders sent out small teams with grenades and explosives in an effort to stop them. "Fearing they would be cut off when they sighted Chinese moving on their flanks," the U.S. tanks withdrew.[99] In the meantime, the CPVF's 559th Regiment of the 187th Division stopped a rescue attempt by the 12th Regiment from the ROK 1st Division at Shinam-ri.

While the Sixty-Third Army prevented the U.S., ROK, and Filipino forces from reaching the encircled British at Solma-ri, the 187th Division intensified its attacks on the besieged Gloster Battalion. By 8:00 AM on April 25, the 560th Regiment of the 187th occupied the key height, Hill 235. At 10:00 AM, Xu launched his final attacks on the Glosters.[100] By noon Xu's troops finally overran the British battalion, and the Chinese claimed to have killed 1,000 Glosters and captured twenty-six artillery pieces, eighteen tanks, and forty-eight trucks.[101] However, the Sixty-Third Army had suffered thousands of casualties in order to guarantee Xu's victory over a British battalion.[102]

Ridgway recalled: "The 1st Battalion of the Gloucestershire Regiment was cut off and overrun by the enemy in spite of repeated I Corps efforts to relieve it. Lt. Col. James P. Carnes (who had been with that regiment for twenty-six years) and his men courageously and grimly held on to their position for several days, until their ammunition was exhausted. Only a few of the battalion's soldiers made their way back to UN lines."[103] Milburn reported: "It appears that every effort was made to reach the Gloster battalion when conditions over the remainder of the front are considered."[104] Van Fleet attributed the U.S. Eighth Army's failed relief efforts to "the strength and determination of the Chinese attacks, the Chinese capability to exploit early penetrations by infiltration and enveloping actions."[105] The CPVF's Sixty-Third Army appeared not to have been casualty adverse, and the Chinese had been determined to annihilate the British Gloster Battalion at any cost.

The Sixty-Third Army, like all the CPVF armies in the first step of the Spring Offensive, carried on Peng's encirclement and annihilation strategy and tactics but suffered heavy casualties in blocking battles. To give another example, on the night of April 26, the Sixty-Third Army occupied Kwakibong (Kwajaebong), Ogeum-ri (Ogeumri), and Paekuntae and intercepted one American regiment and large numbers of tanks and trucks at Teokye-ri and Haejeong-ri (Haejeongri).[106] The Sixty-Third's commander ordered his 189th Division to set up a roadblock to prevent the U.S. regiment from retreating. The division did not have sufficient time to build effective defense works against the U.S. tanks, and under fierce air and artillery supporting fire, the 189th Division suffered heavy casualties.[107] The following day, the Chinese division was unable to stop the U.S. regiment's retreat to the south.[108]

### THE BATTLE FOR SEOUL:
### THE END OF THE FIRST STEP

On April 28, the main forces of the CPVF on the Korean western front had all reached or crossed the 38th Parallel. The Ninth Army Group had occupied Jipo-ri, Joyeongsan, Cheongpyeongcheon, Kapyeong, and Chuncheon on the U.S. I Corps' left. The three armies of the Third Army Group had attacked the center of the U.S. I Corps and occupied Keum-ko-ri, Inchang-ri (Inchangri), and the areas southeast of Euijeongbu. Its Twelfth and Sixtieth armies had reached the north bank of the Han-gang

River, sealed off highways between Seoul and Chuncheon, and begun moving toward Seoul.[109]

On the same day, the 179th Division of the Sixtieth Army reached Tobung-san Mountain, about ten miles north of Seoul. Wu Shihong (1918–2005), commander of the 179th Division, sent his 537th Regiment to attack the U.S. 25th Division, which defended Hill 92.6.[110] The U.S. 25th Division's 24th, 27th, and 35th Infantry Regiments and four FABs totaled 10,000 troops. At 2:00 AM, the 537th Regiment launched its attack on Hill 92.6 and took over the hill from the U.S. 25th Division. On the following morning, the 25th counterattacked Hill 92.6 with a regiment and several dozen tanks. The 537th Regiment suffered heavy casualties, including most of its 1st Battalion, which lost 300 men while 400 were wounded and 400 more were taken prisoner.[111] During the offensive, the CPVF's Sixtieth Army also suffered heavy casualties. The 537th Regiment lost twelve infantry platoons and four 60 mm mortar platoons. The 1st Battalion of the 536th Regiment had only four survivors out of sixteen company captains, and eight survivors out of thirty-two platoon leaders. The 2nd Battalion of the 536th lost eleven of its sixteen company captains and thirteen of its thirty-two platoon leaders. Out of 750 men, only 84 of the battalion's soldiers survived.[112]

By April 29, although the Third Army Group had reached a northern suburb of Seoul, the CPVF attacking forces had not achieved their campaign objectives of annihilating UNF divisions and brigades, or even a regiment. In fact, the U.S. Eighth Army Command had withdrawn most of its forces to safety, south of the 38th Parallel, and had established a new defensive line (known as "No Name Line" since it was never given an official name), about ten miles north of Seoul. The line started from the suburbs of Seoul in the west, extended east several miles north of the Han-gang River, then turned northeast after crossing the Pukhan-gang River and ran through the area south of Chuncheon (map 5.2).[113]

Van Fleet drew a new line of defense starting from the suburbs of Seoul in the west, extending east several miles north of the Han-gang River, turning northeast after crossing the Pukhan-gang River, and running through the area south of Chuncheon. He dispatched the U.S. 1st Cavalry Division west to Seoul in order to establish defenses and fortifications around the city. He also assembled heavy forces to defend the

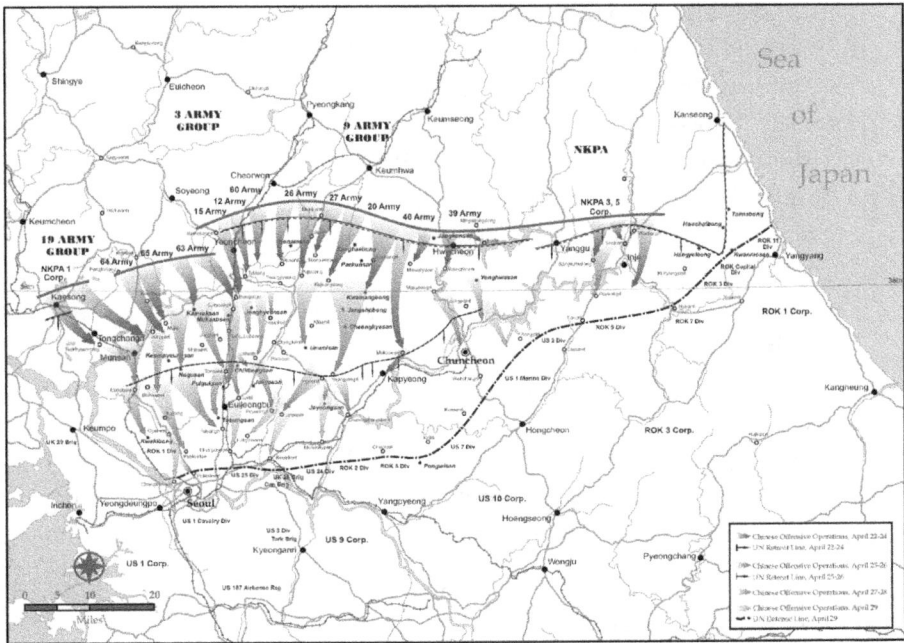

Map 5.2. Positions of the CPVF attacking forces, April 22–29

capital city, asking air and naval forces to completely block off the roads to the Kimpo peninsula to aid in the protection of Seoul. They would attempt to lure the CPVF forces into attacking the capital and would then unleash a barrage of fire from artillery, tank, air, and naval units. Van Fleet took these precautions although his intelligence informed him that supply shortages and casualties had slowed down all three Chinese army groups, especially the Nineteenth Army Group.[114]

Toward the end of April, Peng had realized that the UNF's strategy had changed to attrition warfare, which had devastated the CPVF during the first week of the Spring Offensive. Even though he had anticipated CPVF casualties of 50,000–60,000 men during the entire Spring Offensive, he had not expected such high casualties in such a short period.[115] On April 29 Peng reassessed the campaign. The UNF had established a solid defense along the Han-gang and Soyang Rivers. If the Chinese–North Korean forces tried to attack Seoul, they would merely run into the UNF trap and face a worse disaster. An advance farther south might also invite UNF amphibious landings in the Sino-Korean rear when the main strength of the CPVF lay south of the 38th Parallel.[116] Since the opportunity to encircle and annihilate several UNF divisions north of Seoul had been lost, Peng and the CPVF-NKPA Joint Command decided to stop their attacks and resupply the troops at their current locations, while awaiting further orders.[117]

When Peng issued the order on April 29 for all CPVF and NKPA forces to cease their attacks, the first stage of the Spring Offensive came to a close. Peng had previously explained to Mao and the CMC why he felt obligated to end the offensive and why the CPVF had failed to reach all of its objectives, including the annihilation of several UNF divisions and brigades. Peng's long telegram on April 26 emphasized the major problems the CPVF faced without any foreseeable solution, including inadequate preparation for attacks, lack of supplies, heavy casualties, and UNF firepower. Peng explained:

> We had originally planned to start this offensive in early May. However, for the purposes of delaying the enemy's amphibious attacks and avoiding fighting on two fronts simultaneously, we started the attack ahead of schedule, on April 22. Therefore, we were not adequately prepared, especially in terms of food and ammunition, and our transportation issues have not improved. Large numbers of new soldiers from our Nineteenth Army Group lacked essential training or rest before beginning operations. The Third Army Group started operations just seven days after it had reached the battleground. The Thirty-Ninth and Fortieth Armies have been fighting continuously for several months without rest. Furthermore, our artillery and tank units were unable to participate in the operations on time, and our air force is far from ready to take part in operations.[118]

In addition, Peng gave an objective picture of the improved UNF strategy and tactics and their impact on the battlefield. He tried to convince Mao that the traditional Chinese strategy of encirclement and annihilation no longer worked in Korea. Peng believed that "the benefits from engaging in the offense have been estimated to be so small and our efforts so futile that they were an ineffective means of thwarting the enemy's attempts to make its amphibious landings."[119]

Peng also expressed his serious concerns about a UNF landing in North Korea, which would "cut our throat." He estimated that a UNF landing force could total 100,000 troops and could take place on both coasts. He suggested pulling the Twenty-Sixth, Thirty-Eighth, Thirty-Ninth, Fortieth, and Forty-Seventh Armies back to the north and preparing an effective defense against possible landings. The main strength of the CPVF forces would remain in the "mobile areas of the 38th Parallel."[120] Mao approved Peng's plans, asking Zhou to draft a response from the CMC at once. The reply said: "We agree with your planned operational guidelines and force deployments for the end of this campaign. We trust they will be implemented accordingly."[121]

Next, the CPVF-NKPA Joint Command ordered the Chinese Nineteenth Army Group (including the NKPA I Corps) to move north of Euijeongbu, Naekal-ri, and Koyang. The army group could monitor UNF activities there. If the U.S. I Corps launched a counterattack, the Nineteenth should lure the I Corps to designated areas for possible annihilation. If the UNF abandoned Seoul, the city should be seized as soon as the opportunity presented itself. If the UNF continued to build up its defense, the Nineteenth would continue to harass the UNF with small forces around the suburbs of Seoul. The Nineteenth should also deceive the UNF forces about the CPVF-NKAP's intentions, pretending to cross the river or conducting other feigned actions to the south in order to pin down the U.S. Eighth Army's main forces on the western front. The CPVF Command ordered its Third Army Group to control the areas north of Paecheon and Yeongpyeon and to quickly resupply and supplement its forces, so as to be ready for new missions by May 5. The Ninth Army Group was pulled back to north of Pyeongkang to resupply. Its main force was stationed south of Keumhwa, Cheorwon, and Makim-ri. The NKPA III and V Corps were deployed at Inje and Yanggu and in areas along the 38th Parallel to facilitate the rapid delivery of food and ammunition to other troops.[122]

By April 29 all CPVF and NKPA forces had ceased their attacks, and the first step of the Spring Offensive had come to a close. During this stage, April 22–29, the CPVF had achieved some of its objectives, including pushing beyond the 38th Parallel to recover territory lost during the Fourth Offensive. However, although it had regained the initiative on the battlefield and forced the UNF to adopt a defensive posture, it had not been successful in annihilating UNF divisions or brigades.

The CPVF claimed a total of 23,000 UNF casualties, much fewer than it had originally planned.[123] At the same time, it had suffered unnecessarily high casualties—between 35,000 and 60,000, or about 5,000–8,000 men every day.[124] Peng continued to look for other opportunities along the Korean front to annihilate more UNF troops.

# SIX

# The Second Step:
# The Offensive in the East

PENG DEHUAI WAS DISAPPOINTED BY THE NEGLIGIBLE GAINS ON the western front in the first week of the Spring Offensive in late April 1951.[1] Given the huge CPVF casualties from April 22 to April 29, Peng was forced to look for payback by launching another offensive.[2] The Joint CPVF-NKPA Command looked for a new opportunity to strike the UNF south of the 38th Parallel. From May 16 to May 21, Chinese forces launched another large-scale attack on the UNF positions on the eastern front, in what became known as the Second Step of the Spring Offensive.[3]

In mid-May the Chinese ordered two army groups—consisting of twenty-four infantry divisions and two artillery divisions, totaling 260,000 troops—to attack the five divisions of the ROK Army as well as part of the U.S. 7th Division under the command of the U.S. Eighth Army's X Corps in the Hyeon-ri (Hyeonri) area. In the west, another Chinese army group—with eleven infantry divisions, totaling 110,000 men—would pin down the main strength of the U.S. Eighth Army's I and IX Corps north of Seoul.[4] The second step of the Spring Offensive involved 370,000 Chinese and 114,000 North Koreans, nearly half a million Communist troops. The second step's goal was to annihilate up to five ROK divisions.[5] For Peng, the strategic issue was how to annihilate more UNF divisions without unacceptable Chinese losses.

Peng faced a dilemma. Although he sought revenge and to regain the initiative, the Chinese lack of firepower and supplies made attempts to annihilate any U.S. division or British brigade futile. Any further offensive in the west or attack on Seoul would certainly bring more Chinese casualties and lead to total disaster. Thus, in early May, Peng decided to shift the offensive's focus from the west to the east. Rather than attacking the Americans, he would attack the weaker South Korean divisions, which would give him a better chance of winning the second step of the Spring Offensive and balancing the casualty sheet of the Korean War. The Chinese marshal issued operational orders to all CPVF armies in early May: "The second step of the Fifth Campaign must concentrate [our] forces to annihilate the ROK 3rd, 5th, and 9th Divisions at the Hyeon-ri area first, and then to annihilate the ROK Capital and 11th Divisions later depending on the campaign developments on the battleground."[6]

At 6:00 PM on May 16, the CPVF and NKPA began all-out attacks on the U.S. Eighth Army along the 38th Parallel. The CPVF Nineteenth Army Group feigned an attack on Seoul on the western front, while the Third Army Group struck the center of the U.S. Eighth Army to sever the connection between the eastern and western UNF forces. The Ninth Army Group, as the main attacking force, broke through ROK lines, penetrating deeply into the rear of the ROK forces.[7] Although the Ninth Army Group had destroyed the main strength of the ROK 3rd and 9th Divisions in the Hyeon-ri area by May 20, the army group was unable to annihilate three, let alone five, ROK divisions, due to the CPVF's strategic and tactical miscalculations, unfamiliar terrain, unexpected weather, and both old and new challenges.[8] Thus, the second step of the Chinese Spring Offensive, lasting from May 16 to May 21, did not achieve the campaign's goal.

Among the major reasons for failure to annihilate any ROK divisions was the fact that as soon as the Chinese attacked, the ROK divisions withdrew, using motorized transportation—making it extremely difficult for the Chinese to encircle and annihilate them. By May 20 a quick shift of reinforcements from of the U.S. Eighth Army from the west to the east stopped any further CPVF attacks. In retrospect, however, the CPVF Command had miscalculated the situation on the eastern front and made some strategic mistakes in May. First, Peng and his commanders used the same strategy of encirclement and annihilation that they had employed during the first step of the Spring Offensive. In the second step the strategy failed again, due to lack of firepower and transportation and because the Chinese joint offensive with the North Korean forces did not play out as planned. The basic agreed-on strategy was for the CPVF to attack the ROK divisions from the west while the NKPA attacked from east. Several operational mistakes, coupled with the mountainous terrain, undermined the Hyeon-ri encirclement. In addition, the CPVF Command had not yet improved its supply line. The Ninth Army Group, a seasoned Chinese force that had been in Korea since November 1950, could not achieve its campaign goal without necessary supplies.

### SHIFT TO THE EAST: PLAN AND PRESSURE

The Ninth Army Group, totaling 150,000 troops under the command of Song Shilun, was the only group that had achieved its operational goals during the first step of the Spring Offensive, April 22–29. It had opened a gap in the direction of Kapyeong, effectively separating the U.S. I from the U.S. IX Corps, posing a major threat to the right flank of the U.S. Eighth Army. The other two Chinese army groups, the Third and the Nineteenth, had been unable to penetrate deeply and encircle the U.S. I Corps on the western front. They had failed to annihilate the five UNF divisions and two brigades that the Chinese high command had expected them to destroy.[9] Even though both army groups crossed the 38th Parallel and some of their units reached the northern suburbs of Seoul, they experienced severe losses in the first week of the Spring Offensive.

When Peng was forced to call off the offensive on the western front on April 29, James Van Fleet sensed that the CPVF would attack again soon after the troops were resupplied, and that the Chinese main target would be Seoul and its surrounding areas.[10] This time, Van Fleet and Matthew Ridgway did not intend to give up Seoul to the Chinese forces, as they had during the CPVF's Third Offensive in January 1951.[11] After the U.S. I Corps had fallen back to Seoul on April 28–29, Van Fleet had established the new defensive line, No Name Line (see chapter 5).

Van Fleet assembled a large force for the defense of Seoul, including the U.S. 1st Cavalry Division; U.S. 3rd, 24th, and 25th Infantry Divisions;

British 28th and 29th Brigades; Turkish Brigade; and ROK 1st Division. Ridgway recalled that "it was Van Fleet's aim to expend fire and steel rather than flesh and blood to as great an extent as possible, and his forces made full use of our now overpowering advantage in air and in artillery of every caliber."[12] With four American infantry divisions concentrated north of Seoul, Van Fleet dispatched the U.S. 1st Cavalry west to Seoul to establish intensive fire networks and fortifications.[13] Van Fleet was determined to have a showdown with the attacking CPVF-NKPA forces at Seoul. He assigned six ROK divisions (the South Korean 3rd, 5th, 7th, 9th, 11th, and Capital Divisions) to handle the defense on the eastern front from Eun-ri (Eunri) through Hyeon-ri to the eastern coast.[14] It seemed to the Chinese commanders that the UNF defense line was imbalanced, with heavier forces in the west and lighter, mostly ROK forces in the east.

With the UNF concentrated around Seoul, in late April Peng sensed an opportunity for another large-scale Chinese attack in the east. He believed that the only effective way to stop a threatened UNF amphibious landing and regain the initiative was to launch another mass attack along the 38th Parallel.[15] On April 28 the CPVF-NKPA Joint Command planned to shift the attacking forces from the west to the east in order to strike the ROK forces on the eastern front in May.[16] The new attack could redeem the CPVF after its setback in April. The key to success was first, to pin down the American forces around Seoul and second to conceal the large shift of Chinese forces further to the east.

To keep the main strength of the U.S. Eighth Army busy at Seoul, Peng needed an effective deception campaign.[17] As Sunzi says, "warfare is the art of deceit." He continues: "Attack where he [the enemy] is not prepared; go by way of places where it would never occur to him you would go."[18] On April 29 Peng telegraphed the CPVF Nineteenth Army Group and the NKPA I Corps:

> First of all, the U.S. 1st Cavalry, 3rd, 24th, and 25th Infantry Divisions; British 28th and 29th Brigades; Turkish Brigade; and ROK 1st Division concentrated around Seoul and the southern bank [of the Han River] to lure the CPVF into a tough offensive. Therefore, to deceive the enemy, the NKPA I Corps should feign a river-crossing operation along the northern bank of the lower Han River near Seoul while attacking the enemy defense with small units. The Nineteenth Army Group should conduct similar operations along the upper Han-gang

River near Seoul to conceal the main strength of the CPVF and strike the east in early May to annihilate two to three South Korean divisions and part of the U.S. 7th Division.[19]

At the end of his telegram, Peng ordered: "Keep this top secret. Do not pass it on. Please burn this telegram after your reading."[20]

Peng believed that if the CPVF's Nineteenth Army Group and the NKPA I Corps could keep the four U.S. divisions and two British brigades outside Seoul, the CPVF might have a chance to annihilate three ROK divisions in the east. After these divisions were annihilated, the CPVF's main strength could move farther south to Wonju, on the eastern front, and then turn west to Suwon, flanking and attacking the right of the U.S. defense forces.[21] On May 1 the Political Department of the CPVF HQ issued a document called "Important Promotion Points of the Fifth Campaign," calling for Chinese forces to prepare for a new offensive.[22] Peng decided to launch the second step of the Spring Offensive because he was still obsessed with the notion that Ridgway and Van Fleet were about to make an amphibious landing in the Communist forces' rear.[23]

Peng also made a quick decision to launch the second step because he was under tremendous pressure—not only from Beijing, but also from his field generals in Korea. Mao Zedong and the CMC were not satisfied with the limited gains (such as inflicting only 23,000 UNF casualties) of the first step of the Spring Offensive. Mao instructed Peng to launch another offensive to push the UNF further south, even though Mao told Hong Xuezhi, the deputy commander in charge of CPVF logistics, on May 1 that the Chinese generals "should make good assessments and learn some lessons after each battle."[24]

At the same time, Peng felt increasing demands from his officers. Most of the CPVF commanders on the front were also dissatisfied and even upset with the results of the first step of the Spring Offensive. Shuguang Zhang points out: "Interestingly, the commanders of the Third and Nineteenth army corps [groups] did not appreciate Peng's caution. Embarrassed by the setbacks of their first battle in Korea, they demanded to carry on the offensive."[25] Some of them complained that they were "rushed to attack," "receiving unclear orders," and "missing battle opportunities" during the first step of the Spring Offensive.[26] The army group and army commanders of the Third and Nineteenth Army Groups believed that the poor performance and high casualties in their armies resulted not from their out-of-date tactics, deficient training, and poorly executed attacks but from premature attack orders. Some spoke privately of changing marshals and wanted Peng replaced with another Chinese marshal, perhaps Lin Biao.[27] As the second wave of the CPVF forces, their armies had not arrived in Korea until March or April and were not yet combat ready when they received an order to attack the U.S. I Corps.[28] All the commanders asked Peng for another chance to fight, vowing they would beat the UNF this time, since they were now ready.

Some of the commanders even saw the quick withdrawal of the U.S. I Corps as the primary reason for their failure. Their armies had not fully engaged or had a chance to show their effectiveness and strength, since the enemy had pulled out too quickly.[29] Although the Third and Nineteenth Army Groups had suffered high casualties, most of the army group commanders did not realize that their relatively meager gains in late April resulted from their underestimating the strength and technical superiority of the American forces as well as overestimating their own capabilities. The commanders still believed at the end of April that they had had the upper hand during the first stage of the campaign. During the first step of the Spring Offensive, the Third Army Group had failed to annihilate three American divisions or to capture "at least 5,000 American soldiers" as Wang Jinshan, acting commander of the Third Army Group, had boasted they would do; in fact, they had failed to wipe out any American unit larger than an infantry company.[30] The commanders all pleaded with Peng to give them permission to again clash with American forces. His generals felt ready to launch another attack, and they believed they would do what they had boasted they would before the first step as long as the Americans did not withdraw too soon.[31]

Peng sided with his field generals. Concerned with possible criticism for indecisiveness or being too conservative, no commander or senior staff member at the CPVF Command provided an objective and comprehensive assessment of the first step of the Spring Offensive.[32] Moreover, on May 8 the CPVF Political Department issued its "Instructions on the Political Tasks for the Second Step of the Fifth Campaign."

The document made it clear that the first step had been "a victory of annihilating 23,163 enemy soldiers of their main strength and gaining combat experience for the newly arrived [Chinese] armies against the U.S. armed forces."[33] Since the first step had been a "victory" in which the CPVF armies had gained experience, according to the CPVF HQ, the Chinese generals should continue the same kinds of operations in the next offensive.

## SUPPLY AND TRANSPORTATION: PROBLEM SOLVING

One of the major reasons Peng had suspended the first step of the Spring Offensive was that the Chinese were running out of ammunition and food, forcing the CPVF-NKPA Joint Command to stop the offensive and pull back forces for resupplying from April 29 to May 9. To solve the supply and transportation problems in the second step of the offensive, the CPVF Command held a Party Committee meeting on May 3 to discuss logistics. Peng pointed out two major problems at the meeting: the lack of transportation and the losses of supplies due to UNF air attacks.[34] Hong agreed with Peng and listed the reasons why transportation and supply problems remained unsolved since the last enlarged CPVF Party Committee meeting in April.[35] Besides asking for more supplies and other support from Beijing, Hong believed that the CPVF troops should take better care of their own weapons, logistics, and vehicles in order to avoid unnecessary loss and damages. For example, the CPVF had lost more than 4,000 vehicles since entering Korea.[36]

Peng showed serious concern about the heavy losses of CPVF weapons, logistics, and vehicles. He criticized the irresponsible and ignorant attitudes of "serious guerrilla-ism and selfishness among our commanders and troops. Their attitude shows a lack of responsibility toward the war and the people. We must correct it immediately and totally change their attitude."[37] After that, the meeting focused on how to solve these problems. Hong believed it important for the armies and divisions to guarantee their logistics as well as their vehicle safety and protection. Xie Fang suggested developing better plans for transportation and assisting the commanding HQs manage and distribute food and ammunition. Du Ping believed that the party committees of the CPVF units had not paid

enough attention to the logistics tasks of their forces. The CPVF committee meeting further concluded that the party committees of the army
groups, armies, and divisions should include logistics in their agendas
and strengthen the political works in their units, for example by reward-
ing people who had done a good job with logistics while punishing those
who were irresponsible.[38]

After reviewing the lessons and problems at the party committee
meeting, Hong drafted two documents: a report to Mao and the CMC in
Beijing to request the establishment of a separate CPVF logistics department, and a directive to all CPVF units in Korea.[39] On May 3 the Party
Committee of the CPVF Command issued "Directives on the Logistical Supplies Problems," including detailed instructions for improving
logistics and transportation. Fully recognizing the important role that
supply played in modern war, the directive pointed out:

> Modern war is a competition of manpower and material. In the Korean War,
> especially fighting the American army equipped with advanced technology, we
> cannot possibly expect a victory over the enemy without minimum logistical
> supplies. We must realize that our logistics task in the war is extremely difficult
> and complicated. The enemy has air control. We do not have enough transporta-
> tion vehicles. All of the war materials, including tanks, big artillery pieces, and
> engineering equipment (which a million-man army needs), must be transported
> from China to Korea. Merely depending on the efforts of our comrades in the
> logistical service, we cannot possibly accomplish this kind of arduous task. We
> need the support for the task from our entire army. Thus, logistics has the first
> priority in all of our tasks at the present time.[40]

The CPVF Command also tried to improve the situation by establishing its own logistics department in Korea before the second step
of the Spring Offensive. The CPVF submitted the report to Beijing on
May 3, and the CMC approved the CPVF's request.[41] On May 14 Peng
called for a meeting of the standing committee of the CPVF Party Committee to discuss the establishment of the CPVF Logistics Department
at the HQ at Kongsudong. Peng, Deng Hua, Hong, Han Xianchu, Xie,
and Du attended.[42] Peng began with a statement:

> The first thing we need to decide is who heads the Volunteer Force's Logistics
> Department. When the CMC decided to organize the CPVF Logistics
> Department, it required that the department should be operated under the
> command and instructions of the CPVF General HQ. The CMC now sends

another telegram to me, requiring that a CPVF deputy commander should hold a concurrent position as the chief of the CPVF Logistics Department. Now let us make a decision first: who is going to hold this concurrent post as our logistics chief?[43]

Peng was surprised when no one at the meeting volunteered to take the position. After a long silence, everyone looked at Hong, who had been in charge of logistics since the CPVF entered Korea. But Hong, who had been a commander of combat operations, was afraid of the difficult nature of the task.[44] Hong's refusal angered Peng. "You don't want to do it?" Peng asked Hong loudly, striking the table hard after he saw Hong's obstinacy. "OK, you don't have to do it." Hong asked him: "Who is going to do this job?" "I will!" Peng yelled, "You can replace me in commanding our troops!" Hong was not happy either and said, "Chief Peng, if it was an order from you, I have to obey it!" "Did I give you an order? Did I challenge you?" Peng asked angrily, "or actually are you challenging me?" Deng and the other commanders had to step in and calm them. Eventually Hong accepted the new position after Peng agreed to his condition, which was to let Hong return to his operation commanding position after the Korean War.[45]

On May 19 the CMC issued its "Decision on Strengthening the Volunteer Forces' Logistics Tasks." Beijing's high command ordered: "The Logistics Department of the CPVF should be established immediately. It will command and manage all the Chinese logistics units and facilities within Korea (including the railroads, highways, and military transportation). The CPVF Logistics Department is under the direct command of the CPVF leading commanders."[46] The CMC appointed Hong commander of the department and Zhou Chunquan its political commissar.

Hong reconfigured the system to better fit the CPVF's new positional warfare doctrine. The new system aimed at supplying front locations directly, rather than specific army units.[47] During the earlier offensives, the inadequate supplies seriously constrained CPVF operations.[48] Hong's new logistics system established area supply depots along the front lines for all troops stationed within that area. The troops moved in and out, but the area supply depot remained, and it could be used by both Chinese and North Korean troops.[49] In October 1986 Hong led a Chinese military logistics delegation that was visiting the United

States. At a dinner, Adm. James "Ace" Lyons, commander of the U.S. Navy's Pacific Fleet, talked about Hong's "unbeatable transportation line" against the U.S. Air Force in the Korean War and asked the Chinese general which university he had graduated from. "I graduated from your American university," Hong replied. Lyons was surprised and asked, "Which American military academy?" "U.S. Air Force University," Hong answered with a smile.[50]

Hong knew that his new system had improved the CPVF logistics capacity at the regiment and battalion level and increased front-line troops' combat effectiveness. These Chinese solutions to battlefield problems in Korea were effective: although the Chinese troops had a steep learning curve (about seven months), they very often achieved their battlefield objectives.[51]

## THE EASTERN COMMAND AND KOREAN COMRADES

Although Peng decided to launch the second step of the Spring Offensive in May, he needed to make difficult decisions about which army group would lead the attack and who would command the attacking forces. First he contemplated having the CPVF shift the battleground from the west to the east or, alternatively, shift the attacking forces from the Third and Nineteenth Army Groups in the west to the Ninth Army Group in the center. His first concern was not only about severe casualties among the Third and Nineteenth Army Groups, but also about their campaign performance. Peng was more level-headed than many of his aggressive field commanders. After five campaigns against the UNF, he knew the American forces were much tougher than his newly arrived field commanders believed.[52] From the operations of the CPVF's second wave during the first step of the Spring Offensive, Peng realized that this wave, although greater in number of troops, lacked the first group's tactical expertise and fighting spirit. Peng privately admitted that the first wave of the CPVF, almost all of whose troops came from the PLA Fourth Field Army, had had better training and indoctrination from their commander, Lin Biao, than did the forces from other field armies.[53]

In short, Peng lacked confidence that the second wave would prevail over the well-rested and fully equipped UNF in and around Seoul.

In consultation with his deputies Deng, Hong, Han, and Xie from the Fourth Field Army and the first group of CPVF forces, Peng decided to shift the emphasis of attacks for the second step of the Spring Offensive to the east, focusing on the ROK forces. If the CPVF forces were able to wipe out more ROK forces, it would separate and isolate the U.S. forces, making them easier to annihilate in the future.[54] For the main attacks on the eastern front, Peng decided that the Ninth Army Group would constitute the primary assault force, with support from the Third Army Group.

On May 6 Peng called a meeting at the CPVF HQ to plan the second step. Yang Dezhi, Song, and Wang attended.[55] When Peng gave the commanders their assignments in the next step of the Spring Offensive, Wang was not happy with his Third Army Group's mission of protecting the Ninth Army Group's attacks. He became upset when Peng shifted his Twelfth Army, the backbone of the Third Army Group, to the Ninth Army. And he bristled at his orders to serve in a mere supporting role in the assault; he wanted to lead the attack himself. Song refused Wang's demands and an argument broke out, becoming so fierce that Peng intervened.[56] To balance Wang's force, two divisions from the Thirty-Ninth Army, of the Ninth Army Group, were put under the command of the Third Army Group.[57] The operation planning meeting ended on a sour note.

At 10:00 PM on the evening of May 6, after the meeting, Peng issued an operational order to all the CPVF armies: "The second step of the Fifth Campaign must concentrate [our] forces to annihilate the ROK 3rd, 5th, and 9th Divisions at the Hyeon-ri area first, and then to annihilate the ROK Capital and 11th Divisions later, depending on campaign development on the battleground."[58] Thus the goal of the second step of the Spring Offensive was to annihilate three to five ROK divisions on the eastern front.

Peng's second concern was the Chinese joint operations with the NKPA corps, which had been fighting the ROK divisions along the eastern front through April. In order to achieve the goals of annihilation, the CPVF attacking forces had to join the NKPA forces in the east. The basic strategy on the eastern front would have the CPVF Ninth Army Group attack the ROK divisions from the west while the NKPA III and

V Corps attacked from the east. At the same time, the CPVF Third Army Group and NKPA forces were to attack the UNF's positions in the center. Together, they would penetrate and flank as many units as possible, preparing them for obliteration. To make sure the ROK forces did not escape, the Chinese–North Korean forces would employ three layers of pincer attacks.

To work together on this three-layer plan, the Joint Command instructed all Chinese and North Korean commanders in its operational order on May 6 "to pay special attention to keeping communications and liaisons working all the time. All the operators must know to contact the other army commands, and use the similar commanding and communication systems. All the commands must move to forward positions with simple HQ and small staff. All the commands must report their position, operation situation, and battle development in a timely fashion."[59] To carry out the Joint Command's order, the Chinese and North Korean commanders, including Song, Wang, and Gen. Kim Woong, had met on May 6 and agreed to improve communications and to establish close operational command relationships.[60]

On May 8–9 the CPVF Ninth Army Group Command and NKPA Eastern Front Advance Command held a joint operation planning meeting at the Ninth Army Group HQ.[61] The Chinese commanders were surprised at the meeting by Kim's demand that North Koreans should command the attack at Hyeon-ri, since they had been fighting the ROK divisions in the east. Kim, who spoke fluent Chinese, served as deputy commander in chief of the Joint Command.[62] He had enrolled in the CCP Political and Military University of Anti-Japanese War at Yan'an in 1937. After graduation he served as an officer in the intelligence section of the 3rd Division of the CCP New Fourth Army from 1939 to 1945, fighting the Japanese army in China. After his return to North Korea in 1947, Kim served in the North Korean People's Army, becoming a major general in February 1948.[63] After the Korean War broke out, in June 1950, he became commander of the NKPA I Corps and was promoted to lieutenant general. In late 1950 he was appointed deputy commander in chief of the CPVF-NKPA Joint Command, the highest Korean officer in the Joint Command. Kim argued that the attack on Hyeon-ri was part of an ongoing NKPA offensive in the east. After intense debate, the

Chinese and North Korean commanders eventually reached a compromise: all operations in the east would come under the joint command of Song, commander and political commissar of the Ninth Army Group; Tao Yong, his deputy commander; and Kim, commander of the NKPA's eastern front. At the meeting, Song, Wang, and Kim discussed how to improve communication and cooperation between the Chinese and the North Korean armies.[64]

The officers at the joint meeting also worked out the details of their plan for a three-layer envelopment and joint attack. The Chinese and North Korean generals agreed that after their initial attacks, the ROK divisions would probably pull out to Yangyang in the south and move closer to the U.S. forces in the west. Therefore, the key to success in annihilating the ROK 3rd, 5th, 7th, and 9th Divisions in the Hyeon-ri area lay in "whether all the CPVF and NKPA armies would be able to cut off all the retreating enemy divisions, definitively blocking their escape."[65] The blocking plan included three layers of joint CPVF-NKPA encirclement of the ROK III Corps. The Chinese Twentieth Army of the Ninth Army Group would break through the defensive line of the ROK 7th Division, then penetrate to the rear of the ROK 3rd and 9th Divisions at Hyeon-ri. Here the Twentieth Army would meet the 6th, 12th, and 32nd Divisions of the NKPA to complete the first, or inner, layer of the encirclement. The Twenty-Seventh Army would advance along the line from Puyeongri to Sangnam-ri (Sangnamri) on the west of Inje and meet the North Korean II Corps at Maesan-ri to complete the second, or the middle, layer. The Chinese Twelfth Army would break through the ROK 5th Division and move toward Changchou-ri (Changchouri), creating the third, or outer, layer together with one division of the NKPA II Corps.[66] Peng approved this plan.

To achieve the goal of annihilation, the CPVF attacking forces would have to conceal their operational intentions. Peng believed that the key to success in the second step of the Spring Offensive was the element of surprise.[67] The redeployment of 250,000 Chinese troops from the western to the eastern front must remain undetected for six to seven days. This would require precise—nearly perfect—execution. Peng and the other CPVF commanders issued a series of orders to the Third and Ninth Army Group Commands regarding communications, asking that all information on the attack be kept at as high a level as all top secret exchanges.

The Third Army Group held a commanders' meeting on May 7–9 and made operational plans after receiving its orders from the CPVF Command.[68] The army group's primary missions were to sever any connection between the U.S. forces on the western front and the ROK forces on the eastern front, in order to guarantee the Ninth Army Group's encirclement and annihilation of the South Koreans. The group had been reinforced by two divisions of the Thirty-Ninth Army, two artillery battalions from the 29th and 30th Artillery Regiments, and the 402nd Antitank Artillery Regiment.[69] After the second offensive began, the main forces of the Third Army Group would attack the ROK divisions shoulder to shoulder with the Ninth Army Group in the east, while preventing the U.S. X Corps from reinforcing the UNF troops in the east from the west.

On May 9, after ten days of rest, the main forces of the Ninth Army Groups began moving eastward. The Joint Command had required all attacking forces to be supplied with adequate ammunition and food prior to May 10.[70] This would allow the attacking troops to begin to move east during the night of May 9 or 10, reaching the staging areas before dawn on May 14, and to be ready to launch their surprise assaults by dusk of May 16. By the 15th, all the CPVF assault forces had reached their staging areas—the banks of the Pukhan-gang and Soyang-gang Rivers (between Chuncheon and Najeon-ri)—without UNF detection. The NKPA II, III, and V Corps had also reached Inje and areas east of the town. The CPVF Command ordered its Thirty-Ninth Army to cross the Soyang-gang and move to areas between Chuncheon and Hongcheon (Hongchon), where it could cover the wing of the Third and Ninth Army Groups as they covertly advanced east.[71]

## A DECEPTIVE ATTACK ON SEOUL

In early May the Nineteenth Army Group conducted its deceptive operations on the western front, commencing attacks on the U.S. I and IX Corps around Seoul. On May 6 the CPVF-NKPA Joint Command issued operational orders to the Nineteenth Army Group (east of Seoul) and the NKPA I Corps (west of Seoul) to feign attacks on the city.[72] These actions would serve to pin down the main U.S. I and IX Corps on the western front. The Nineteenth Army Group, reinforced by the 31st Artillery Regiment and the 8th, 19th, and 47th Divisions of the NKPA I Corps, decided to use its superiority in numbers and firepower to annihilate two to three enemy targets (each target was roughly the size of one battalion) located from Koyang to Kapyeong, and from Sunagsan south of Euijeongbu to Museokyeok-ri (Musokokri).[73] The army group's primary objective was to hold the main U.S. forces on the western front by carrying out offensive operations, and it was also to assist the CPVF's attacking forces on the eastern front as they made preparations to annihilate three to five ROK divisions.

The Nineteenth Army Group's deceptive activity near Seoul was one of the keys to the offensive operations' success on the eastern front. After the first step of the Spring Offensive ended on April 29, neither Van Fleet nor Ridgway could predict where or when the CPVF would next strike.[74] On May 4 Van Fleet ordered each division on the western front to assign one regiment, supported by a tank detachment, to conduct a reconnaissance mission in force, ten to twelve miles deep, in order to harass the Chinese–North Korean forces while closely monitoring their movements and deployments.[75] Ridgway agreed to let Van Fleet conduct a new large-scale offensive if the CPVF-NKPA forces did not launch another offensive themselves in May[76] (map 6.1).

After the UNF had resumed its small-scale attacks in early May, the CPVF Nineteenth Army Group Command changed its operational plans from offense to defense, a superior way to pin down the U.S. forces in the west. If the U.S. I Corps employed its main forces (four U.S. divisions) in its northern attacks, all three armies of the Nineteenth Army Group would pull back and conduct staged resistance; that is, using the defense structure known as "light front, heavy rear," it would lure the enemy into terrain favorable for counterattacks by forces the size of Chinese armies.[77] Once the attacks on the eastern front began, the Nineteenth Army Group would assemble all its main forces to launch a large-scale attack against the U.S. I Corps on the western front, facilitating the Chinese offensive in the east. Should the UNF only use a small number of troops for its northern attack, the Nineteenth Army Group would or-

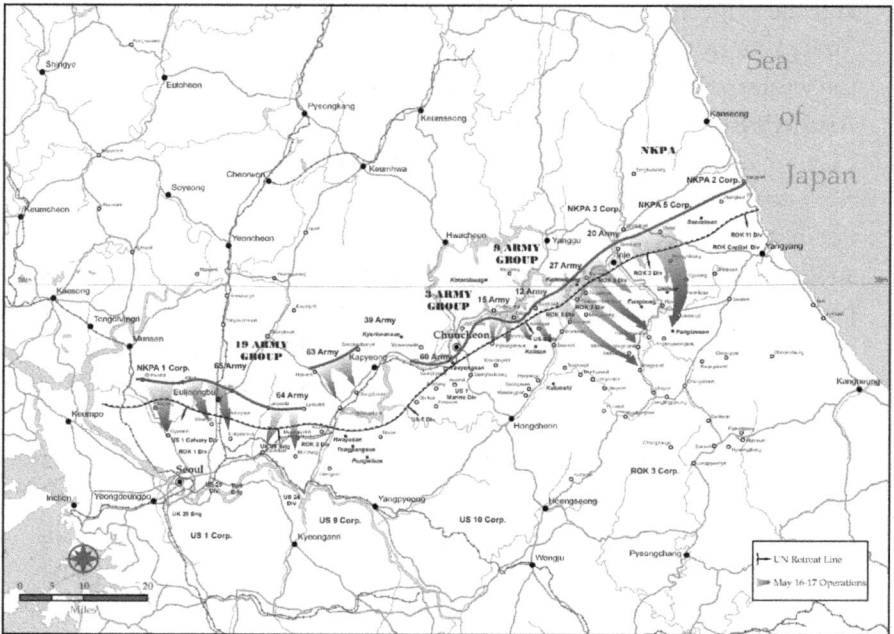

Map 6.1. Initial attacks of the second step, Spring Offensive, May 16–17

der its three armies to use favorable terrain to stop the enemy's offensive. Should the enemy not advance north at all, the Nineteenth was to maintain close contact with its forces, using small units to continually harass them.[78] In the meantime, the Nineteenth Army Group was to prepare for a large-scale crossing of the Han-gang River as a prelude to the attack on Seoul, further deceiving the UNF Command as to Chinese objectives.

Peng summoned Li Zhimin, political commissar of the Nineteenth Army Group, to give him detailed instructions in person on the deception at Seoul.[79] During their meeting, Peng told Li:

> Our success in our next actions depends on whether the Nineteenth Army Group can deceive the enemy, focusing its attention on Seoul to conceal the Third and Ninth Army Groups' attacks on the eastern front. Therefore, you must convince the enemy we are preparing to cross the Han-gang River at Cheongpyeongcheon and Museokyeok-ri. You should also send forces to Cheongpyeongcheon and Mukyeok-ri to conduct surprise attacks, capturing as many enemy soldiers as possible. To confuse and mislead the enemy, you must conduct your preparations as if they were genuine, being as systematic as possible.[80]

Along the western front on May 10, the Nineteenth Army Group began the deception operation by sending its Sixty-Fifth and Thirty-Ninth
Armies to attack the UNF defense positions at Cheonposan and on the
south bank of the Soyang-gang River. The Sixty-Fifth Army attacked
Sunagsan and Kwajaebong immediately.[81] The Thirty-Ninth Army attacked Cheongpyeongcheon on May 12. On May 13 the Sixty-Third Army
moved south to Cheongpyeongcheon and Jimok-ri. Its 188th Division
occupied the bridgehead at Cheongpyeongcheon, annihilating the UNF
defense troops in the area. The 187th Division of the Sixty-Third Army
then attacked Sangcheon-ri and overran the defense force. The Sixty-
Fourth Army moved to Kilsan-ri, northeast of Paecheon, threatening
Seoul. On May 16 its 191st Division attacked Mukyeok-ri and occupied
Osandong.[82] In the meantime, the Nineteenth Army Group and NKPA
I Corps feigned preparations to cross the Han-gang River and to attack
U.S. defensive positions east of Seoul.

After an abrupt artillery barrage at 6:00 PM on May 16, the CPVF
and NKPA assault forces started their all-out attacks on the U.S. Eighth
Army along the 38th Parallel. The Joint Command had dedicated thirteen armies to the task: nine armies of the CPVF and four army corps of
the NKPA, totaling 484,000 troops.[83] In accordance with the campaign
plans, the Sixty-Third, Sixty-Fourth, and Sixty-Fifth Armies of the Nineteenth Army Group feinted toward Seoul in order to pin U.S. forces down
on the western front. The Twelfth, Fifteenth, Thirty-Ninth, and Sixtieth
Armies of the Third Army Group attacked the center of the U.S. Eighth
Army, cutting the UNF forces in the east off from those in the west.

On the western front, the CPVF Nineteenth Army Group and NKPA
I Corps continued their offensive actions, pinning down U.S. forces and
preventing them from moving east to reinforce the beleaguered ROK
forces. On May 16 the Nineteenth Army Group Command ordered four
divisions to attack the U.S. I Corps at Koyang, Tobong-ri (Tobongri),
Tuikyewon-ri (Tuikyewonri), Keumko-ri, Museokyeok-ri, Cheongpyeongcheon, and Sangcheong-ri (Sangchongri) on the following day.[84]
Meanwhile, the Chinese Sixty-Third Army crossed the Pukhan-gang
River, occupying Tongpangsan, Nasan, Pongwisan, and Hill 508.7. Beating back UNF counterattacks, the Sixty-Third Army annihilated one
U.S. battalion and most of three ROK companies.[85]

The offensives of the Nineteenth Army Group succeeded in completely deceiving Van Fleet and Ridgway. Concluding that the CPVF and NKPA would launch a new attack "within the next 72–96 hours," Ridgway ordered Van Fleet to put off his offensive plans indefinitely and have his forces adopt a defensive disposition to protect Seoul.[86] Ridgway anticipated that the CPVF would launch new attacks from its five armies positioned at the lower valley of the Han-gang River, while three other armies (plus one NKPA corps) would conduct secondary attacks in the direction of Seoul.[87] In response, the U.S. Eighth Army rapidly redeployed its forces, shifting two more U.S. divisions to the western front. Therefore, in early May the number of U.S. infantry divisions in the west increased from four to six. After the redeployment, Van Fleet had six U.S. divisions, one British brigade, one Turkish brigade, and three ROK divisions on the western front. The UNF defense centered on Seoul, and in addition Van Fleet had the U.S. 3rd Division, British 29th Brigade, and U.S. 187th Airborne Regiment as reserve forces in Kyeongan-ri (Kyonganri), Yeongteungpo, and Kimpo on the western front.[88] The CPVF Nineteenth Army Group had successfully diverted the UNF Command's attention and strength to the western front.

In the center on May 18, the Fifteenth Army of the Third Army Group attacked the 1st and 2nd Battalions as well as headquarters of the 38th Regiment of the U.S. 2nd Infantry Division at Taesudong. Thereafter, however, the Fifteenth Army became bogged down by the U.S. 2nd Division, which quickly received reinforcements from the U.S. 1st Marine Division at Hangye-ri (Hangyeri), Yamsidae-ri (Yamsidaeri), and Tonshi-ri.[89] The 180th Division of the Sixtieth Army, Third Army Group, occupied Peopso-ri (Popsori), north of Hongcheon, and prevented the U.S. 7th Division from reinforcing troops in the east.

## STRIKE THE ROK 3RD AND 9TH DIVISIONS

On the eastern front, the CPVF and NKPA assault forces began all-out attacks on the 3rd, 5th, 7th, and 9th Divisions of the ROK III Corps on May 16.[90] The CPVF Ninth Army Group, which was the main attacking force, included the Twentieth, Twenty-seventh, and Twelfth Armies, reinforced by the 11th, 25th, 26th, and 28th Artillery Regiments; all forces were ordered to attack the ROK defense lines that evening. The official ROK history of the war states: "Contrary to the expectation of the UN forces, the CCF [Chinese Communist Forces] opened the May offensive with preparatory fire on May 16." It continues: "This type of artillery fire was atypical and appeared to be fire for registration [the prelude to an attack]."[91] The shock of the Chinese attack caused panic in ROK divisions, many of which abandoned their defensive positions and fell back. A huge gap was opened by the Ninth Army Group on the left flank of the U.S. X Corps.[92]

To ensure victory in the second step of the Spring Offensive, at 1:00 AM on May 17 Peng ordered Ninth Army Group commanders Song and Kim to take immediate and forceful action:

> After inflicting substantial losses and costs on the enemy during the first step of the campaign, we have been able to lure the U.S. forces to Chuncheon and all the way to Seoul west of Chuncheon. This has created the current excellent opportunity for us to concentrate our forces on wiping out multiple ROK units. Therefore, you must overcome all difficulties to meet your operational objectives, wiping out as many ROK forces as possible in order to isolate the U.S. forces for future annihilation. You must conduct bold flanking, penetration, and encirclement maneuvers against the enemy forces with the aim of obliterating them completely. You must seize all opportunities, attacking during the day, taking advantage of the current changes in the climate [the warmer spring weather], and capitalizing on the enemy's current confused state. You must use solid planning to direct units attached at the corps, division, and regiment level to search for fleeing enemy troops, abandoned weapons, and equipment. We wish you total victory.[93]

The Twentieth Army, the Ninth Army Group's main assault force, crossed the Soyang-gang River—approximately 50–100 yards wide and 6–15 feet deep—at 12:00 AM on May 17.[94] By 7:00 AM, the 60th Division of the Twentieth Army had rapidly penetrated sixteen miles into ROK defensive areas, occupying Heongpyeong-ri (Hongpyongri) and Omach'i on the main supply route for the ROK III Corps.[95] That evening the 178th Regiment of the 60th Division attacked the ROK 29th Regiment of the 9th Division with concentrated mortar fire along the road, killing more than five hundred ROK soldiers and capturing seventy vehicles.[96] Jongnam Na writes: "When ROK soldiers discovered the enemy in the rear, the entire force began to retreat in fear, even before the enemy's frontal attack had started. In less than two days, the ROK corps disappeared, opening a serious gap in UN defense lines."[97] The same day, the NKPA 6th Division of the V Corps occupied Kyetun-ri (Kyetunri) and advanced south in the daytime, reaching the southern mountains of Cheorntong-ri and meeting the Chinese Twentieth Army. Thus, by May 17, the CPVF-NKPA forces had completed the first, or inner layer of their encirclement of the ROK forces at Hyeon-ri, blocking retreat routes to the south, southeast, and southwest.

The Twentieth Army's 58th Division sent its 173rd Regiment to attack the heights west of the Yongpu Highway at 1:00 AM on May 18, and the 173rd Regiment seized the key height defended by the ROK 8th Regiment of the 7th Division. In this battle the ROK regiment lost two companies and "could not even resist the CPVF's penetration and encirclement"; ROK troops had many similar experiences elsewhere.[98] When the 58th Division opened an eight-mile-wide sector east of Kuman-ri, the Twentieth Army and NKPA V Corps used that gap as a breakthrough point to advance seventeen miles into the ROK rear, rapidly severing connections between the ROK 7th and 9th Divisions.[99] The Twentieth Army cut off the ROK 3rd and 9th Divisions' retreat route. On May 19 its 60th Division occupied Maesan-ri and Mangseongkok, the meeting point of the second, or middle, layer of the envelopment, even though the NKPA II Corps had not arrived.

In the meantime, the Twenty-Seventh Army of the Ninth Army Group penetrated forcefully deep into the rear of the ROK III Corps as well.[100] At 11:00 PM on May 16 the Twenty-Seventh broke through the ROK defenses at Kuman-ri and Changmodong.[101] Its 79th Division crossed the Soyang-gang River, occupying Oksandong. The division attacked several defensivee positions of the ROK 8th Regiment of the 7th Division. The Twenty-Seventh Army's reserve, the 80th Division, moved to the Eonon-ri (Eononri) area, preparing to launch attacks in the area.

To flank the ROK forces, the Twenty-Seventh sent its 81st Division to cross the Soyang-gang River near Kanmubong and penetrate into the ROK rear. The 81st Division, in tandem with the NKPA II Corps, attacked at Hajinpu-ri (Hajinpuri) and took control of Jaecheom, Pang-nae-ri, and Ihyeon. Under the command of Sun Ruifu, the division sent the 2nd Battalion of its 242nd Regiment to spearhead the penetration maneuvers by attacking the sector boundary between the ROK 7th and

5th Divisions.[102] Ridgway recalled: "Later on the second day of the drive, the ROK 5th and 7th Divisions, which held high ground to the right of Chuncheon, crumpled under heavy Chinese pressure and retreated in disorder."[103] The Chinese 2nd Battalion quickly cut into the ROK defensive line by avoiding engagement and continuing its southward advance. The battalion broke through the ROK 7th Division and infiltrated the rear on the left of the ROK 9th Division. Brig. Gen. Choi Suk, the ROK 9th Division's commander, "hurriedly ordered a withdrawal at 04:00, wary of encirclement as the battle turned fiercer with time."[104] By 5:00 AM on May 17, the Chinese 2nd Battalion had marched thirty-eight miles in nine hours, reaching and occupying the heights on both sides of Amtal-dong as well as key points at Jaecheon and Pangnae-ri (Pangnaeri). The 2nd Battalion of the 242nd Regiment had cut off the ROK's southwest retreat route forty minutes ahead of schedule on May 17, in time to catch the ROK 9th Division as it began withdrawing from its positions.[105]

At 3:00 AM on May 18 Brig. Gen. Kim, commander of the ROK 3rd Division, ordered all his forces at Hyeon-ri to withdraw via Pangda-esan to Changchon.[106] For the next two days, the CPVF Twentieth and Twenty-Seventh Armies and the NKPA V Corps attacked the retreating ROK 3rd and 9th Divisions along the roads from the hilltops south of Hyeon-ri. The ROK command lost control, and the two divisions collapsed under the attack. The official ROK war history points out:

> The ROK 9th Division suffered only very slight damage on its main line of resistance as the enemy had not pressed on its front in order to double-envelop the Hyon-ri area at the initial stage of the enemy offensive. But in its process of withdrawal, some of the battalions were blocked and, thus, were scattered.
>
> There were no commanding officers to control the situation nor was it controllable, for those who escaped enemy pursuit and assembled in total disorder in the Pangdae-san area were unable to identify their own assigned units.[107]

In the afternoon of May 18 the 242nd Regiment, 81st Division, CPVF Twenty-Seventh Army, attacked the ROK 30th Regiment of the 9th Division as it attempted to withdraw from its positions and move southwest toward the U.S. 2nd Division. The 2nd Battalion of the 242nd Regiment pelted the unprepared ROK troops with a hail of fire at a roadblock, inflicting heavy casualties and forcing the ROK regiment to pull back

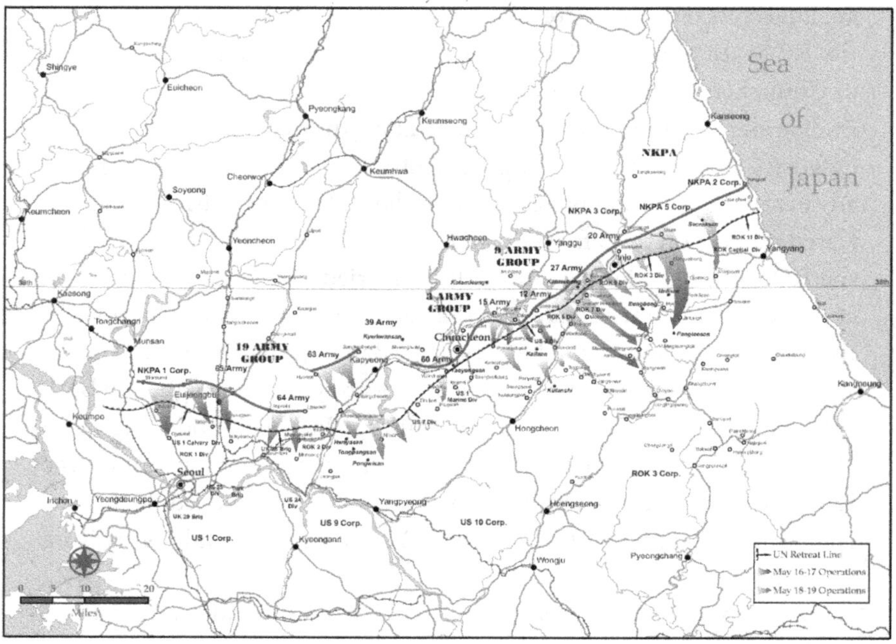

Map 6.2. Continuing attacks of the second step, Spring Offensive, May 16–19

to Hyeon-ri.[108] The CPVF 60th and 81st Divisions annihilated five ROK battalions, nearly 3,000 South Korean soldiers.[109]

Under fierce, continuous onslaughts from the CPVF Twentieth and Twenty-Seventh Armies and the NKPA V Corps, the ROK 3rd and 9th Divisions at Hyeon-ri had been slashed to pieces by May 19 and fled in all directions in total defeat. By May 20 the CPVF-NKPA forces had eliminated approximately 12,000 South Korean troops, which had been the main strength of the ROK 3rd and 9th Divisions at Hyeon-ri and in the areas south of the town. The Communist divisions also captured all of the two ROK divisions' heavy equipment and weapons, while the remaining ROK soldiers fled into the mountains.[110] Ridgway was upset by the serious losses of the ROK and recalled: "The equipment abandoned by the retreating ROK forces was nothing to be shrugged off, however. It was enough to have equipped several complete divisions."[111] The CPVF and NKPA had succeeded in achieving part of their operational goals, annihilating most of the ROK 3rd and 9th Divisions. However, they had not expected that most of the ROK forces' command posts and senior officers would flee via American airlifts and swift ground transport (map 6.2).

Because these two ROK divisions suffered heavy losses during the second step of the Spring Offensive, Ridgway decided to abolish the ROK III Corps on May 26: "As of 16:00 on the 20th, the 3rd Division had collected 3,621 soldiers (only 34.3 percent of its original strength), and the 9th Division counted 4,582 (40 percent)."[112]

Na concludes that "the ROK Army's disappointing performance at the front in April and May 1951 revealed to KMAG [Korean Military Advisory Group, the U.S. Army] analysts not only a leadership deficit at all levels of the officer corps but also serious training problems, shortage of weapons and equipment, poor logistical support, and, most seriously, a lack of confidence."[113] Ridgway recalled that after the Spring Offensive, "the ROK III Corps, badly mauled in the Chinese advance, had been deactivated and its units divided between the X Corps and the ROK I Corps."[114]

Angered by the disappointing collapse of the ROK corps in May, ROK President Syngman Rhee intended to execute some of his commanders, including even Gen. Chung Il-kwon, chief of the General Staff of the ROK Army. Eventually, Rhee dismissed Shin Sung-mo as minister of national defense as well as Chung as chief of staff in May 1951. Gen. Chung complained that "the decision on placing restrictions on the operations of the UN forces was made without any prior consultation with our government, and the fact that a new directive was given to the Commander in Chief, United Nations Command, was relayed to me only after the event. As Chief of the General Staff, I was deeply hurt by this."[115]

Na observes that "when ROK soldiers discovered the enemy in the rear, the entire force began to retreat in fear before the enemy's frontal attack had even started. In less than two days, two ROK corps disappeared, opening a serious gap in the UN defense lines."[116] He points out that "problems continued when the CPVF attacked the II and III ROK Corps at the end of May 1951. The ROK Army then suffered what one prominent Korean general later recalled as the most shameful defeat in its history. The details have not shown up in the official history of the ROK Army until recently. Veterans' memoirs revealed that ROK units dissolved under combat pressure while suffering the largest losses ever."[117]

## INCOMPLETE ENCIRCLEMENT, HEAVY CASUALTIES, AND A ONE-WEEK ATTACK—AGAIN

The CPVF-NKPA Joint Command did not reach its goal of annihilating three to five ROK divisions in the second step of the Spring Offensive, May 16–21. The joint attacking forces merely destroyed the main strength of the ROK 3rd and 9th Divisions. The failure was due to the Communists' strategic and tactical miscalculations, unfamiliar terrain, unexpected weather, and both old and new challenges. The problems that the CPVF had faced since the beginning of 1951 were the shortage of supplies, lack of artillery firepower, and heavy casualties. The new problems that the Chinese faced in May were breaks in the chain of command, the slow movement of their attacking troops, and communication difficulties with the NKPA.

Among the new challenges for the Chinese commanders was cooperation with the North Korean army corps to complete three layers of encirclement. By May 19, the CPVF Twentieth Army and the NKPA V Corps had completed only the inner, or first, layer of encirclement. The Chinese blamed the North Koreans for the failure to complete the middle and outer encirclements.[118] On May 19, the Chinese 60th Division occupied Maesan-ri and Mangseongkok, the meeting point for the middle layer of the joint envelopment, but Choi's NKPA II Corps had not arrived. After breaking through the ROK defense lines on May 17, the NKPA II Corps, consisting of the 2nd, 13th, and 27th Divisions, had been hampered by steep mountains and deep snow in the Seorak-san area. The main forces of the North Korean corps could not advance south in time to trap or annihilate the ROK troops at Hajinpu-ri (Hajinpuri) before attacking toward Kangneung.[119]

The geography of the middle and eastern parts of the Korean Peninsula also restricted the joint CPVF-NKPA forces from conducting large-scale actions. Most of the mountain ridges in the area ran north-south, which was advantageous for penetrating the area longitudinally but made any latitudinal movement challenging. Covered with a dense growth of pine trees and thick underbrush, the highest hills are about 4,500 feet, and most of the hills are at least 1,800 feet and have a steep incline, of up to 60 degrees. For all these reasons, cutting off the retreat of the fleeing ROK divisions had been made a great deal more difficult than the CPVF-NKPA command had expected.[120] Thus, the CPVF-NKPA forces on the eastern front had merely formed one-and-a-half layers of encirclement around the two ROK divisions at Hyeon-ri, and the Communist forces failed to wipe out a significant number of ROK troops.

Realizing that the NKPA II Corps had failed in its encirclement mission, Song gave new orders to the NKPA III Corps—the 1st, 15th, and 45th Divisions—to block the ROK forces' flight toward Yangyang. Song also modified his orders to the NKPA V Corps, ordering it to assist the Chinese Twentieth Army to annihilate the ROK 3rd and 9th Divisions at and around Hyeon-ri. The original plan was for the NKPA III Corps to follow the NKPA II Corps into action, but seeing that the II Corps had been held up by unexpected snow, the III Corps decided to follow the V Corps, reaching the Mantuiam-san, Yuyeobong, and Seoim-ri (Seoimri) areas.[121] Although the NKPA III Corps, one of the new and vulnerable corps of the North Korean forces, had captured Yangyang on May 21, it failed to complete its assigned encirclement and to connect with the CPVF Twenty-Seventh Army.

Another continuing problem for Chinese commanders was learning how to fight U.S. forces without suffering heavy casualties. While the CPVF Twentieth and Twenty-Seventh Armies were attacking the ROK 3rd and 9th Divisions at Hyeon-ri in the east, the Twelfth Army of the Ninth Army Group went on the offensive, attacking the ROK divisions in its center. On May 16 the Twelfth Army moved out of the Chuncheon, Napyeong-ri, and Jichon-ri areas, attacking the ROK 3rd Division at Jangsuwon, Jangpyeong-ri (Jangpongri), and Soksa-ri.[122] The Twelfth Army planned to link up with the NKPA V Corps and to cut off the ROK's southern and southeastern routes of retreat. After breaking through the ROK defense, the Twelfth Army assailed the ROK 5th Division in an attempt to destroy Jaeum-ri, reported to be defended by ROK troops. However, they found their attack halted by the U.S. 2nd Division and the French Battalion.[123]

Realizing that his 31st Division was unable to cut into the UNF rear, the Twelfth Army's commander, Zeng Shaoshan, requested permission to concentrate his 31st and 34th Divisions in an attack on the U.S. and French forces. Song denied his request.[124] No one had expected to encounter American forces. None of the precampaign intelligence or reconnaissance reports had indicated that possibility, and Song was still overwhelmed with the task of encircling all enemy forces on the eastern front.

The CPVF Command, however, ordered the Ninth Army Group to
attack the U.S. 2nd Division and French Battalion, and it reinforced the
Twelfth Army with the 181st Division of the Sixtieth Army to strengthen
the attacking forces.[125] With the 31st Division charging forward to its
planned positions, Zeng had three divisions, which struck the U.S. 2nd
Division to the left of the salient. The 34th Division staged frontal attacks on the U.S. 23rd Regiment and the French Battalion at Jaeumri, while the 35th Division established ambush and defensive positions
on the Heongyang Highway, waiting to block the retreating U.S. and
French troops and to intercept the ROK 5th Division as it attempted to
reinforce them.[126] But the U.S. 2nd Division held onto Hill 800, called
"Bunker Hill" by the American defenders. After four waves of attacks on
the Americans and French, the Twelfth Army managed to break through
UNF positions at Kali-san, but each of the three Chinese divisions suffered heavy casualties.[127] Together with the reinforced 181st Division
from the Sixtieth Army, the Twelfth Army eliminated close to 1,900
American and French troops and captured 400 POWs, including the
deputy commander of the U.S. 23rd Regiment. The Twelfth Army also
destroyed or captured more than 12 UNF tanks and 230 other vehicles.[128]
In the meantime, the Twelfth Army of the CPVF suffered more than
12,000 casualties, a loss of three regiments.

Allan Millett points out that "massive American artillery and air
firepower stopped the Chinese offensive against the U.S. X Corps," as
well as the U.S. 2nd Infantry Division, even though firepower "played
only a marginal role in saving the four ROK divisions east of the Second
Infantry Division." Millett's statistics show that the American artillery
forces fired "300,000 shells between May 17 and May 23, five times the
number of shells fired in a typical corps operation against the Germans
in 1944. One 2nd Infantry Division 105 mm howitzer battalion fired
almost 12,000 rounds in one twenty-four-hour period. The guns of 120
tanks added to the bombardment."[129] Shuang Shi describes it as the "fire
wall tactics" of the U.S. Army, which inflicted heavy casualties on the
Chinese attacking forces. The Fifteenth Army of the CPVF, for example,

suffered 10,000 casualties during the five days of the second step of the Spring Offensive.[130]

The UNF air raids in May brought additional heavy losses to the Chinese troops and their supply lines.[131] Millett states: "The CPVF Fifth Offensive, especially the second and third phases, gave the Fifth Air Force new opportunity, the best in 1951, to demonstrate its lethality against Chinese troops on the move."[132] Max Hastings concludes that "the vast majority of the 1,040,708 aerial sorties flown by UN aircraft in the course of the Korean War were close support, or fighter cover. Their importance was undisputed."[133] The UNF Command estimated that Chinese and North Koreans had lost 85,000 to 105,000 men by the time their offensive peaked on May 21. Losses for the CPVF were serious, and although the soldiers lost were easily replaced with fresh recruits, they were not veteran soldiers.

The last, but not least, ongoing problem that the Chinese had faced since early 1951 was the shortage of supplies for the Chinese forces. Although the Joint Command attempted to continue supplying its forces after May 16, it could not follow the rapid movements of those forces south of the 38th Parallel. Supplies, therefore, always lagged behind operations. By May 20 the Chinese attacking forces had again run out of ammunition across the line.[134] After fighting two almost nonstop major offensive operations within one month, all front-line forces were exceedingly battle-fatigued. Some of the front-line armies had completely run out of food, and many others were nearly in that situation. The HQ of the Twentieth Army had run out of food and for two days could cook only rice powder for its army radio section, about forty staff members and technicians who provided communications between the army group, the army, and its divisions. The other sections of the HQ resorted to sending out staff members as well as officers to dig up wild herbs.[135] Many CPVF troops were too hungry and exhausted to continue fighting. Some of the Chinese soldiers left their companies in small groups of five to ten men, looking for food on their own. Many were captured by UNF units.[136]

The UNF air raids caused severe damage to the Chinese supply and transportation lines during the second step of the Spring Offensive. On May 17, for example, the U.S. Fifth Air Force launched 717 sorties of heavy bombers with daytime attacks by B-29s and nighttime attacks by

B-26s with a new MPQ (mortar/artillery shell tracking) radar system. The next day, it conducted 880 similar sorties.[137] Chinese forces were forced to halt their attacks on May 20–21 and wait three days for supplies of food and ammunition.[138]

In late May the rainy season began, and the weather was on the side of the UNF. Several storms had destroyed some of the CPVF-NKPA's major supply routes. Lacking machinery for road repair, it took the CPVF longer than the UNF to repair mountain routes and highways. The danger loomed that a major mountain flood would quickly cut front-line forces off from their supply lines and their connections to second-line reserve forces. The CPVF also had more than 8,000 wounded soldiers on the eastern front.[139]

### THE END OF THE SECOND STEP

Although the CPVF had destroyed two ROK divisions and dealt heavy losses to another two, it had not caused serious enough damage to drive the UNF into an all-out retreat. As for materiel, the UNF logistical networks had remained essentially unaffected, delivering supplies and equipment in a timely manner throughout the campaign. The UNF commanders had learned that the Chinese–North Korean joint forces could sustain attacks for only a week at a time, and it became clear that there were severe weaknesses in CPVF's logistical support network. Thus the UNF realized that its troops could beat back CPVF attacks as long as they could hold the Chinese troops off for a week, letting shortages accomplish the rest. Although Van Fleet and Ridgway had miscalculated the CPVF's intentions in late April and early May, it took less than a week for the UNF leaders to plan and conduct a counterattack against the Chinese in the east rather than in the west. Instead of ordering all UN forces to fall back, as in previous CPVF offensives, Van Fleet ordered only those ROK and U.S. forces on the eastern front to withdraw, redeploying them near the 37th Parallel in order to establish a new defensive line running through Kuseongpo-ri (Kusongpori), Punam-ri, Changdong-ri, Hajinpu-ri, Cheorksleung, and Iku-ri (Ikuri).[140]

The movement of the U.S. and ROK forces came much earlier than the CPVF commanders had anticipated. Within ten hours, the UNF had moved more than 180 miles from west to east and south to north. By May 19 and 20, the U.S. 3rd Division had reached Punam-ri and Hajinpu-ri, filling the gap torn open in the UN forces' defensive line by the CPVF forces. In the meantime, the ROK 8th Division had reached Pyeongchang and Jecheon from Taejeon, establishing in-depth defensive positions. Once these two moves were completed, the U.S. Eighth Army had completely reestablished its lines of defense. Simultaneously, the U.S. 3rd Division shifted from the Seoul area to block further CPVF movement.[141]

In the middle section of his front, Van Fleet ordered his forces to assume an offensive posture and stage counterattacks against intruding CPVF forces. On May 20 he ordered three U.S. divisions and three brigades under the command of the U.S. I Corps to launch an immediate counterattack on CPVF forces on the western front, relieving pressure on his forces in the east. In addition, Van Fleet ordered the main forces of the U.S. X Corps to cross the Korean Peninsula along the battle line from Hongcheon and Cheonyang-ri in order to block CPVF attacks moving west and to protect U.S. and British forces on the right wing. He also deployed the U.S. 3rd Division—the reserve forces for the U.S. Eighth Army—at Kyeongan-ri, southeast of Seoul. The U.S. 3rd Division was to rapidly move east in order to fill the gaps torn open by the CPVF Ninth and Third Army Groups and various NKPA corps.[142] Finally, Van Fleet ordered the ROK 8th Division—the reserve unit for the ROK forces—to race north and reinforce ROK forces on the eastern front. Van Fleet hoped these measures would help stabilize the badly shaken UNF front.[143]

On May 20 the situation turned against the Chinese. Although the U.S. Eighth Army was severely tested, the U.S. I and IX Corps units around Seoul held fast. ROK divisions to the right of the salient and the U.S. 2nd Division to the left of the salient also held firm. In addition to the U.S. 3rd Division, the 187th Airborne regimental combat team was rushed in to block further CPVF penetration and to complete the encirclement of the incursion. The Communist forces could go no further[144] (map 6.3).

Under these circumstances, Song and Wang concluded that the offensive would only become more difficult to maintain should it go for-

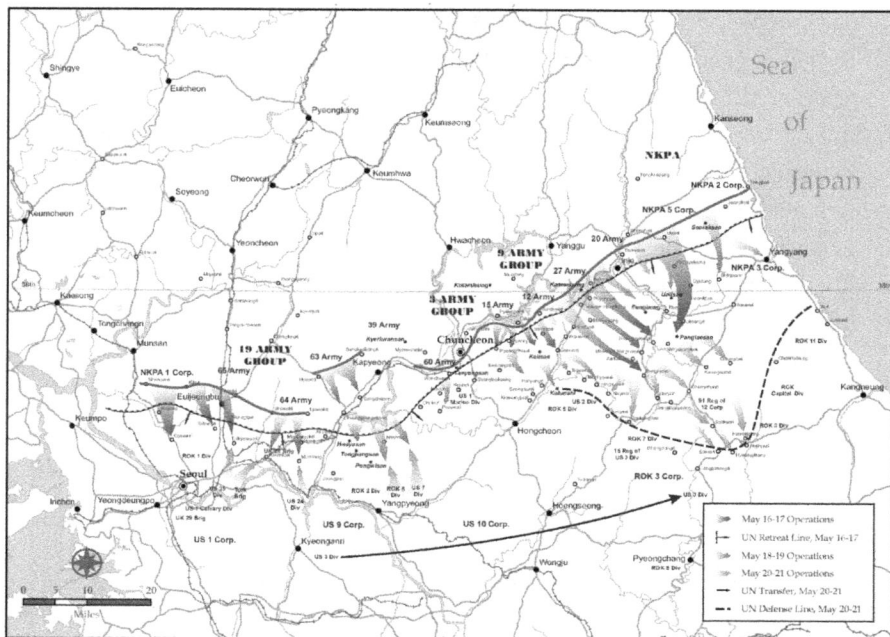

Map 6.3. CPVF attacks through the second step, Spring Offensive, May 16–21

ward, while it would fail to wipe out enough enemy units to make it cost-effective. Furthermore, the U.S. Eighth Army counterattacks seemed to have the potential for beating back the CPVF. Under such conditions, the CPVF and NKPA forces would become further dispersed and disconnected at the front. The two Chinese officers believed that the time had come for their main forces to fall back, rest, resupply, and look for opportunities to fight again in the future. They and other Chinese commanders reported their views to the CPVF Command:

> The situation at the front is clear. The American forces are moving to the east, while the ROK forces are falling back from their heavy losses. The most serious situation we now face is the shortage of food; some of our forces have been starving for quite some time now. It is our opinion that we will not be able to affect the situation at the front by continuing our attacks in the East; we would have to conduct another offensive across the entire front line. Even if we could annihilate additional enemy units, we would most likely suffer relatively large casualties and losses in the process. We believe we should stop for the moment, readjust our force deployments, restructure our forces, and prepare to fight again in the future.[145]

The CPVF command had reached the same conclusion. It believed the U.S. forces had changed their operational strategy since the previous campaigns, learning to fall back quickly as soon as they came under attack, then launching fierce counterattacks at the right moment. In addition, the UNF Command had discovered that the current offensive had not targeted the U.S. forces on the western front, as had been expected, but rather the ROK forces on the eastern front.

The American commanders and their operational staff had learned to anticipate Chinese strategies by studying the battles of Hoengseong and Chipyeong-ri from the Fourth Offensive in January–April 1951. During that campaign, the CPVF had used the same strategy, attacking the weak ROK forces on the right wing of Hoengseong before diverting the assault onto U.S. forces at Chipyeong-ri.[146]

The current attack was virtually identical. But this time the U.S. Eighth Army had not retreated or given up territory; rather, it had strengthened and reinforced the badly shaken ROK forces and commenced counterattacks from west to east, forcing CPVF forces to fall back. Apparently, Ridgway and Van Fleet had learned a great deal from the previous four campaigns. The full-scale U.S. counterattacks had begun to threaten the CPVF troops who had encircled the ROK forces and potentially could cut off and trap attacking Chinese units inside their newly established line of defense.

These conditions had led CPVF commanders on the eastern front to propose they stop offensive operations immediately and systematically withdraw.[147] Peng quickly agreed, reporting to Mao on May 21:

> During the previous campaigns, our forces were able to stretch five days' worth of rations into seven days' worth of food, using local resources to supplement their diets. The current situation does not allow this. The enemy forces at Hongcheon keep on fighting without retreating.... The U.S. 3rd Division has moved east to fill the gap between Hongcheon and Kangneung. The Fifth Campaign ... has lasted for a month. Our forces have become exhausted. They have fought twice on the western and eastern fronts, and need time to recover from their battle fatigue and summarize lessons learned from the recent offensive.
>
> Transportation to the first line has been extremely difficult ever since the campaign started.... Moreover, the rainy season is coming, and several major rivers and lakes are behind us. A large flood could cut off our supply lines completely. Since we have not been able to wipe out American forces in divisions or even regiments, and the enemy is likely overestimating our losses and casualties,

it is likely the UN forces will launch more attacks to the north. Therefore, continuing our attacks now would not create any opportunities to wipe out enemy forces, but would only result in increasing our casualties and difficulties. Instead, we should withdraw, and prepare to fight against the tiring enemy forces once our forces have rested and resupplied. This would create the right conditions to annihilate more enemy units.[148]

Mao agreed with Peng's analysis and recommendations, responding: "Given the current situation, it is absolutely the right choice to withdraw our forces, rest, resupply, and prepare to attack again."[149]

Fearful of heavy losses, Peng halted the offensive and ordered the withdrawal on May 21. On that date the Sino-Korean Joint Command issued the order to halt attacks and conclude the second step of the Spring Offensive. Overall, the CPVF and NKPA forces had annihilated 23,000 UNF troops, doing particularly well in the Hyeon-ri area, where Chinese–North Korean forces had wiped out most of the ROK 3rd and 9th Divisions and part of the U.S. 2nd and 1st Marine Divisions, and had inflicted severe casualties and losses on the ROK 5th and 7th Divisions. In large part, the goals for the second step had been achieved.[150]

But again, the numerical superiority of the Chinese attacking forces had been countered by the formidable firepower of the UNF, and the Chinese had again suffered heavy casualties. The official ROK history of the Korean War concludes: "The Chinese 'human wave' or 'sea of men' tactics was defeated by the 'sea of fire' tactics of the UN forces. The Chinese began to realize that their numerical superiority could not overcome the modern equipment of the UN forces, and also came to acknowledge that with their logistical capability, an offensive lasting more than 7–10 days could not be supported."[151] Ridgway summed the second step up this way: "The Chinese once more had to stop for breath, still far short of the goal they had boasted of. In the eastern and central sectors, they had pushed south and bought a great deal of real estate, for which they paid an exorbitant price. But the Chinese had not succeeded in trapping any of our forces."[152] The Third, Ninth, and Nineteenth Army Groups began to fall back on the night of May 22. The CPVF retreat, however, turned into a disaster.

# SEVEN

# Disastrous Withdrawal to the North

AFTER PENG DEHUAI CALLED OFF THE SECOND STEP OF THE
Chinese Spring Offensive, on May 21, 1951, the CPVF Command began
to plan an overall withdrawal of its attacking forces to positions north of
the 38th Parallel. The Chinese retreat from May 23 to June 10 became the
third step of the Spring Offensive. According to the CPVF plan, withdrawing nine armies—or including twenty-seven divisions, more than
340,000 troops—would begin the night of May 23 and would take ten
to fifteen days to complete.[1] No one in the CPVF Command anticipated
that the UNF would make a sweeping counterattack the morning of
May 23, twelve hours before the Chinese withdrawal was scheduled to
begin. This surprise attack turned the third step of the Spring Offensive
into the most disastrous operation in the CPVF's history, as Chinese
forces suffered 45,000–60,000 casualties, "the most severe loss since our
forces had entered Korea."[2]

Several factors contributed to the Chinese military disaster.[3] First,
the UNF's rapid advance and its overwhelming firepower, both on the
ground and from the air, certainly caught the Chinese by surprise and
inflicted heavy casualties. However, it was the CPVF Command's failure
to develop a contingency plan that led to the disastrous conclusion of
the Chinese Spring Offensive. Confronted with an unexpected all-out
UNF counteroffensive on May 23, the unprepared and confused Chinese
forces panicked, causing their defensive lines to collapse.

Second, by May 24, the second day of the UNF attacks, communication broke down among the Chinese general headquarters, army groups,
and army commands. Two of the three army group commands—the

Nineteenth and the Third—were paralyzed. The Nineteenth Army Group Command did not have accurate information about its two armies. The Third Army Group's communication network was devastated by a UNF air raid on May 24. Unable to communicate by radio or telephone for three days, the group's command had no way to organize an orderly withdrawal or conduct any effective defense. The group lost 15,000 men in four days.[4]

And third, because the CPVF's chain of command collapsed at such an early stage of the withdrawal, it brought disorder and chaos to Chinese forces from May 24 to May 27. The army commands, which depended on the CPVF command hierarchy, had to manage a chaotic withdrawal to save their troops. Incapable of overcoming the UNF infiltration attacks, two armies became isolated. Many divisional commands were forced to make their own decisions and attempted to fight their way out of the UNF encirclement without supplies. Several divisions were unable to coordinate an effective defense, suffering heavy casualties or even a total loss. The 180th Division of the Sixtieth Army collapsed and suffered 7,644 casualties, including 5,000 men who were captured by the U.S. 24th Division.[5]

On May 27 Peng organized a primary defense line by deploying the CPVF Fifteenth, Twentieth, Twenty-Sixth, Sixty-Third, and Sixty-Fourth Armies along the 38th Parallel.[6] After fierce fighting from May 30 to June 10, the CPVF finally stabilized the front line, halting the UNF advance. The third step became a disastrous withdrawal, with severe casualties and territorial losses. The Chinese Spring Offensive from April 22 to June 10 had failed. Instead of driving the UNF southward, the CPVF had actually lost ground by the end of the third step, as its front line was pushed north of the 38th Parallel.

## AN UNEXPECTED UNF COUNTERATTACK AND THE UNPREPARED CPVF COMMAND

While the joint CPVF-NKPA forces attacked the ROK divisions in the east on May 16–17, Matthew Ridgway became deeply concerned that the Chinese–North Korean attacks would cut the U.S. Eighth Army line of defense into several pieces.[7] On May 18 he telegraphed James Van Fleet, asking him to launch an attack immediately "to relieve the pressure on the forces in the east by attacking in the west to threaten enemy lines of communication in the Iron Triangle (map 2.4).[8] On May 19 Ridgway flew from Tokyo to the Korean front, convening an operational conference with Van Fleet, Maj. Gen. Edward M. "Ned" Almond, commander of the U.S. X Corps, and Maj. Gen. William Hoge, commander of the U.S. IX Corps. Believing that the CPVF and NKPA forces were overstretched, Ridgway determined that the counterattack would no longer be limited to the Iron Triangle, but would be an all-out offensive. He ordered the U.S. Eighth Army to stage large-scale attacks on May 20 by employing its I, IX, and X Corps: "The Eighth Army will attack on May 20. The corps missions are as the followings: (a) X Corps will check and stop the penetration on its east flank and will attack in coordination with east flank of IX Corps and will protect IX Corps flank; (b) IX Corps will attack and seize high ground west of the Chunchon basin; and (c) I Corps will attack on the axis Seoul-Cheorwon and protect the left (west) flank of IX Corps."[9]

Van Fleet agreed with Ridgway that the CPVF and NKPA faced tremendous logistical difficulties, which would not only eventually force them to stop their attacks but also provide UNF an opportunity for a rapid advance, cutting the Communists' lines of supply and retreat. Van Fleet immediately ordered his U.S. I and IX Corps and U.S. 1st Marine Division to launch attacks on May 20, moving along Line Topeka from Munsan-ri to Chuncheon.[10] He assembled fourteen divisions, one brigade, and two regiments to launch frontal attacks on the CPVF line of defense. He left three divisions and three brigades in reserve. After they advanced to Line Topeka, the U.S. I and IX Corps would continue their assaults on the Iron Triangle in two columns—one moving through Euijeongbu to the Keumhwa Highway, and the other moving from the Chuncheon Highway north, to control a long railway axis west of Hwacheon Lake.[11]

The UNF counterattacks, which began on May 20 on the western front, spread out from the west to the middle front on May 23 and to the eastern front on May 24. Most of the UNF divisions launched their full-scale attacks during daytime on the twenty-third, exactly seven days after the CPVF and NKPA forces had initiated their attacks at Hyeon-ri.

This was the UNF strategy—to attack the Chinese–North Korean forces on the day their hand-carried supplies would be running out. Since the CPVF troops could carry only enough food and ammunition for a week, the UNF officers called the Chinese operations "one-week attacks." And in fact on May 23, the seventh day after the CPVF launched its second attack, 90 percent of the CPVF-NKPA forces had nearly exhausted their supplies of food and materiel and were preparing to withdraw north to resupply.[12]

On May 21, when Peng ended the second step of the Spring Offensive on the eastern front, the Chinese–North Korean Joint Command had decided to withdraw their main forces across the front line to the north for rest and resupply on the night of May 23. The Joint Command did not plan any large-scale defense between May 21 and May 26. At 4:00 PM on the twenty-first, Peng and Deng Hua issued an order to all the CPVF army group commands:

> To allow our main forces to rest and create more favorable conditions for annihilating enemy forces later, we have decided to withdraw the main forces of all our armies to the line of Wicheon-ri (Wichonri), Soyeong, Munhyeo-ri, Sanyang-ri, Yanggu, Wontong-ri (Wontongri), and north of Wontong-ri.... Each CPVF army group shall assign one division or one army to conduct mobile defensive maneuvers from their current positions to protect [the withdrawing troops] and deplete the enemy forces step by step in order to buy more time.[13]

Neither Peng nor his deputies was expecting a major UNF counterattack on May 23.

At 11:00 PM on May 21, Peng cabled Mao Zedong and explained the CPVF's withdrawal plan;[14] Mao agreed with the plan.[15] To avoid congestion along the retreat routes, the plan was to pull the 340,000 Chinese attacking forces back in an orderly fashion in three groups, and it would take ten to fifteen days to complete the withdrawal. The lack of a contingency plan or an organized defense made the CPVF retreating forces vulnerable.

The CPVF's failure to prepare its forces against an all-out UNF counterattack resulted from the following factors. First, the CPVF Command had not expected an immediate UNF counterattack and did not have a contingency plan. Its order specified that all forces should begin to pull back to designated northern areas on the night of May 23.[16] None of the Chinese leaders had anticipated that the UNF Command would be launching its counterattacks on such a large scale.[17] Based on its experience in the Third and Fourth Offensives, January–April 1951, the CPVF Command expected the earliest UNF counterattack would be at least ten days after the CPVF-NKPA forces stopped the second step of the Spring Offensive.[18] On the morning of May 23, when the UNF Command launched its all-out counteroffensive, the CPVF Command was unable to respond effectively.

Second, the CPVF Command had not committed any forces to protect the Chinese withdrawal as a whole. Instead, the command made piecemeal plans, leaving decisions to group commands at tactical levels. As noted above, each army group was asked to cover its own withdrawal, employing "one division or one army to conduct mobile defensive maneuvers." In this standard type of mobile defense, a small unit might be able to cover a broad front line or a large area by moving from one place to another against possible UNF attacks without constructing defensive positions in depth. But once these forces were committed in such small numbers, they could have little impact on the strategic level. Even though they might be able to respond to a small pursuit and cover a Chinese unit retreat, they would not be able to protect the front line against a general attack. According to the CPVF's May 21 order, the main strength of the Nineteenth Army Group was to pull back north of Wicheon-ri and Yeoncheon (Yonchon) in order to rest and resupply. The army group would employ one army (or four divisions) to cover its withdrawal from Euijeongbu in the west to Cheongpyeongcheon in the east. The army's defensive line was in the favorable terrain at Tongtucheon, Paecheon, and Kilsan-ri between Euijeongbu and Cheongpyeongcheon.[19] The Third Army Group was to withdraw north to Cheorwon and Keumhwa, in the Iron Triangle area, for rest and resupplying. That army group was to assign one army to protect its retreating troops at Kapyeong in the west and Chuncheon in the east, conducting phased resistance by taking advantage of the mountainous areas north of Hwacheon.[20] The main forces of the Ninth Army Group were to withdraw east of Hwacheon, Sanyang-ri, and Keumhwa to rest and resupply. That group was to have assigned one division to conduct a phased defense, exploiting the Soyang-gang River and Hwacheon Lake for its operations.[21]

Apparently, one Chinese division was not enough to cover a withdrawal of 110,000 troops against a large-scale UNF counterattack. The CPVF Ninth Army Group was attacked by five UNF divisions: the U.S. 3rd, 7th, and 24th Divisions and the ROK 2nd and 6th Divisions, from the U.S. I and IX Corps.[22]

Third, the Chinese command did not have a clear plan for its next operation after the cross-front withdrawal. The CPVF Command intended to wait for the UNF's next move, and then plan accordingly. When the Nineteenth Army Group asked the CPVF Command where the last defense line would be, the command replied:

> When our main forces withdraw to the north to rest and resupply, the enemy will surely follow us to attack. Its speed in intercepting us will depend on its size, as well as the effectiveness of our mobile defense. As for the distance of our withdrawal, this will be determined gradually as time goes on. We remain unclear exactly how many casualties we inflicted on the enemy during this recent campaign, and are unaware to what degree it has supplemented its forces.[23]

The army group commands planned to return to the staging positions from which they had launched the first step of the Spring Offensive, in late April. On May 22, however, the CPVF Command issued a tactical instruction to all the army group commands about how to deal with a possible UNF counterattack.[24] The CPVF Command also ordered its strategic reserve to occupy positions near the 38th Parallel, building up last lines of defense from which no unit would be permitted to retreat.[25]

After May 22 each army group command made its own plan. Their withdrawals were poorly planned and deeply flawed. Most planned to withdraw at a slow pace, since they thought they would be returning from a major victory over the UNF. In fact, the UNF had lost only one British battalion and two ROK divisions during the entire Spring Offensive. In contrast, the damaged CPVF armies "were extremely exhausted and had no supplies at all."[26] They were desperate for rest and supplies. When the UNF launched its rapid and effective counterattacks on May 23, the Chinese forces simply sped up their northward retreat and gave up their first-line defense (map 7.1).

Once the UNF had initiated its full-scale counterattacks, the CPVF Command informed all army groups of the situation, sending the fol-

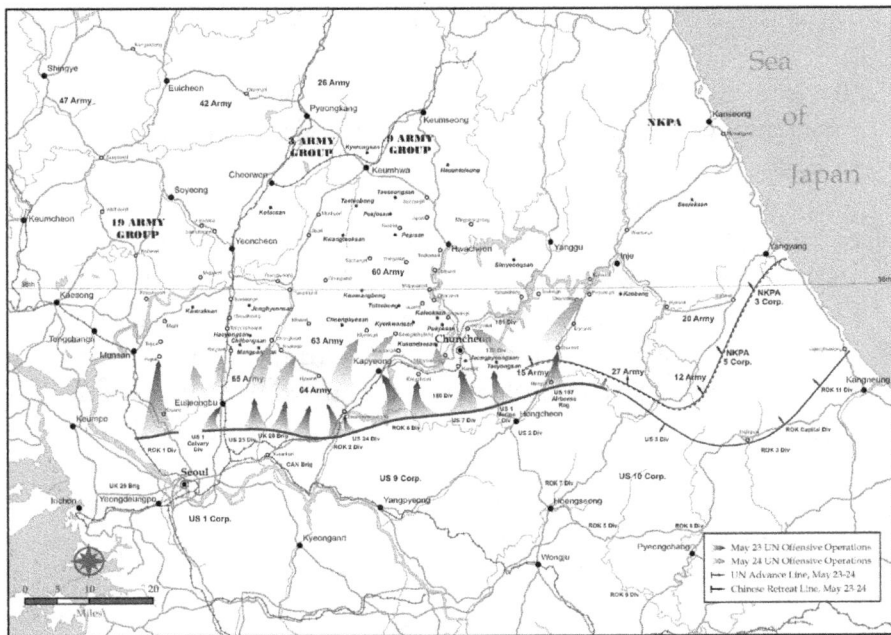

Map 7.1. UNF attacks, May 23–24

lowing instructions on May 24: "All armies must overcome all difficulties to create good coverage of occupied positions, laying effective plans and selecting advantageous terrain to annihilate enemy units with ambush and counterattack maneuvers. Otherwise, we will not only be unable to safely transport wounded soldiers and give our main forces the opportunity to rest, but will also likely suffer unnecessary casualties and losses."[27] By the night of May 24, under ferocious UNF attacks, the CPVF and NKPA found themselves unable to conduct the mobile defense they had originally planned. What the UNF task forces or mobile forces had punched two major holes in the Chinese line on the western front. The CPVF's main line of defense collapsed like a line of dominos across the entire front: first in the west on May 24, next in the middle on May 25, and then in the east on May 26. The CPVF's retreat was out of the control of the CPVF Command and its army group commands from May 23 to May 29.

## COLLAPSE IN THE WEST

The third step of the Chinese Spring Offensive was clearly a botched withdrawal operation. Its failure was rooted both in plan and execution. The CPVF neglected to anticipate a UNF counterattack and to plan a general defense, and its army group commands failed to adapt to a changing situation and to execute a protected withdrawal. After the information flow stopped and each army was on its own, the chain of command was broken between the Nineteenth Army Group and its armies in the west on May 24. The Nineteenth Army Group—consisting of the Sixty-Third, Sixty-Fourth, and Sixty-Fifth Armies, with more than 100,000 troops—had faced the U.S. I Corps in the west throughout the Spring Offensive.[28]

Before the offensive, the CPVF chain of command had not included the army group command. The CPVF Command could issue its orders directly to the armies. Hong Xuezhi recalled:

> During the withdrawal of the Fourth Offensive Campaign [in April 1951], the CPVF HQ commanded our armies directly and organized the retreat of one army after another. Since we had the army group commands this time [in the Fifth Offensive Campaign], the CPVF Command did not issue its orders to the armies. The command only issued its orders to the army groups, and then each army group organized its own armies' withdrawal.[29]

After receiving the CPVF Command's withdrawal instruction on May 21, the Nineteenth Army Group ordered its main strength to pull back north of Wicheon-ri and Yeoncheon for rest and resupply on May 22. On the same day, the group command assigned its Sixty-Fifth Army to cover the withdrawal of its 110,000 troops for fifteen to twenty days by conducting a mobile defense at the Tongtucheon and Kilsan-ri area. Unprepared for quick and forceful UNF counterattacks, the Nineteenth Army Group Command did not give its Sixty-Fifth Army any contingency plan or emergency instructions. The command lost control of the Sixty-Third and Sixty-Fifth Armies May 24–26. The command did not know that the Sixty-Fifth, which was supposed to cover the army group's withdrawal for up to twenty days, had given up after a one-day defense on May 23 and kept retreating north for three days.[30] The Chinese western front line collapsed on the second day of the UNF counterattacks.

Nevertheless, the Nineteenth Army Group Command blamed the failure on the western front on the North Korean I Corps.[31] In the west, the U.S. I Corps commanded the U.S. 1st Cavalry and 25th Infantry Divisions, ROK 1st Division, and Commonwealth 1st Division (formerly the British 28th and 29th Brigades) to attack the CPVF-NKPA forces along the Euijeongbu–Cheorwon axis, using the Turkish and Canadian Brigades as reserve forces.[32] On May 23 the ROK 1st Division, supported by massive U.S. air, artillery, and tank firepower, quickly smashed the defensive line of the NKPA I Corps at Kwansan-ri.[33] A Chinese military history describes the NKPA I Corps as "not prepared at all for the UN forces' fast and fierce attacks."[34] The NKPA defense on the western front collapsed on May 23, the first day of the UNF counterattack. The North Korean army fell back all the way to Maji-ri and Tupu-ri and crossed the Imjin River to the north. The NKPA's faster-than-expected fallback quickly exposed the western wing of the Chinese Sixty-Fifth Army, assigned by the Nineteenth Army Group to protect its withdrawal in the west. The army did not even receive updated information about the North Korean withdrawal from the Nineteenth Command after the NKPA I Corps had fled its defensive positions on May 23.[35]

The Sixty-Fifth Army—consisting of the 193rd, 194th, and 195th Divisions, totaling 29,000 men—had planned a mobile defense to cover a front fifty miles wide, from Euijeongbu and Cheongpyeongcheon to Yeoncheon and Munan-ri. Its mission was to protect the army group's retreat, step by step.[36] In fact, the army could hold its defenses for only one day after the NKPA I Corps retreated. The unexpected flight of the North Koreans left no time for the Sixty-Fifth Army Command to organize an effective defense. Its three divisions had barely had time to reach their positions before the mechanized UNF forces overran them on May 23. According to Senior Col. Yang Di (b. 1921), who was deputy chief of the Operational Department in the CPVF General HQ in 1951, most of the defense forces on the western front had just arrived at their positions and were cooking their breakfasts when the fast-moving UNF attacking forces crashed into them.[37]

The Nineteenth Army Group Command did not "control their forces closely and firmly, strengthening wireless radio communications and personally directing their units' withdrawal efforts," as the CPVF Command had instructed on May 22.[38] In fact, the chain of command broke when the Nineteenth Army Group Command neither received any battleground updates from the Sixty-Fifth Army for days nor gave any new orders to the army. Without close communication and effective control, the Sixty-Fifth's defensive line quickly collapsed.

On May 23 under the command of the U.S. I Corps, the U.S. 1st Cavalry, U.S. 24th and 25th infantry Divisions, and Commonwealth 1st Division launched attacks on the defensive positions of the Sixty-Fifth Army across the western front.[39] Later that day the ROK 1st Division joined the offensive, attacking the Sixty-Fifth from the west and threatening to cut off the Chinese retreat northward at the Imjin-gang River.[40] The Chinese troops, who had just marched for miles, rushed to defend their positions, faced with one of the worst combat situations in the Sixty-Fifth's history. Attacked from two directions, the Sixty-Fifth's troops suffered heavy casualties and did not hold out long. For example, the Ninth Company of the 3rd Battalion, 577th Regiment, 193rd Division, lost its position when only 9 out of 145 men were left in the company.[41] The 2nd Battalion of the 579th Regiment started the defense in the morning with 299 troops in its battalion combat team; it withdrew from its position with only 37 men that evening.[42] The 580th Regiment of the 194th Division barely held its positions under strong attacks for six hours by the U.S. 24th Division.[43]

On the first day of the attacks, many of the Sixty-Fifth's troops were also running out of ammunition. The army had replaced its light arms with Russian-made weapons before it entered Korea in February and March. Even though the Russian infantry weapons were new and automatic, China could not supply ammunition to those troops armed with Russian weapons. Moreover, because the Russian weapons' firing rate was so rapid, they required large supplies of ammunition. When Russians sold the weapons to China, they agreed to provide eight to twenty units of ammunition for the arms.[44] Due to lack of transportation, each Chinese infantryman usually had to carry two to three units of ammunition for his weapon, which was not enough for even one day of intensive fighting. During its defensive battle, the Sixty-Fifth Army lost 12 percent of its automatic rifles, 16 percent of its light machine guns, 12 percent of its heavy machine guns, and 15 percent of its 60 mm mortars.[45] The troops also ran out of ammunition.

With his three divisions were seriously damaged and nearly cut off by fast-moving American tank forces, Xiao Yingtang (1914–80), commander of the Sixty-Fifth Army, ordered his troops to make a short tactical retreat during the night of May 23, moving back about two to four miles, to allow the men to have a quick break and to regroup.[46] Xiao did not realize that this brief retreat would turn into a rout. None of the defense troops of the 193rd, 194th, and 195th Divisions could stop their withdrawal in the night, and their forces retreated north for fifteen to twenty miles during the next day. The Sixty-Fifth Army had fallen back from the line at Euijeongbu and Cheongpyeongcheon all the way to Yongam-ri and Mangpangsan by May 25.[47] The army continued its nonstop withdrawal until it reached the Yeoncheon area, about forty-five to sixty miles north of its assigned defensive line, on May 26.[48] Surprisingly, the Nineteenth Army Group did not know about its defending army's rapid retreat for three days and certainly had no control of it.

The Nineteenth Army Group Command was not in charge of its Sixty-Fifth Army's defense or withdrawal operations. Yang Dezhi recalled that it was not until May 27 when "*Four days after* the Sixty-Fifth Army began its defense against the enemy, the army command *suddenly* reported to the army group command" that the army "had suffered heavy casualties, and had lost some of its defensive positions." The army also reported that it "had retreated north about twenty to thirty miles" (in fact, about twice that distance) from its assigned defensive line.[49] The Chinese defense in the west collapsed on May 24, when the Sixty-Fifth gave up its defense in a single day.

In turn, the Sixty-Fifth Army's quick retreat left a huge gap between the Nineteenth and Third Army Groups, putting the Sixty-Third Army, the next Chinese force in line on the western front, in an extremely precarious position. The Sixty-Third also fell back without an order from the Nineteenth Army Group Command. This domino effect began to spread throughout the entire line of defense from west to east, since the command, once again, had no control of the defense of one of its armies.

The Sixty-Third Army—the Nineteenth Army Group's elite force— had advanced much further south than the other two armies in the group during the second step of the Spring Offensive. The sudden and total withdrawal of the Sixty-Fifth Army to the north had fully exposed the

Sixty-Third Army's western wing, putting the Sixty-Third in danger of being encircled by U.S. and ROK forces. Fu Chongbi, the thirty-five-year-old commander of the Sixty-Third, realized that he must act quickly to avoid losing his army. After one month of nonstop offensive operations since April, the Sixty-Third Army retained only 20,000 out of its original 30,000 men, along with 6,998 rifles, 2,408 automatic rifles, 546 light machine guns, 148 heavy machine guns, and 240 artillery pieces, including 60 mm mortars.[50] The army consisted of the 187th, 188th, and 189th Divisions; it now faced the U.S. 1st Cavalry and 25th Divisions and the Commonwealth 1st Division. The three UNF divisions totaled 50,000 soldiers, 1,300 artillery pieces, and 180 tanks. Fu knew that his army needed to withdraw immediately. However, he had not received any new orders from the Nineteenth Army Group Command.[51] Shuguang Zhang seems correct when he points out that since the Chinese Civil War it "had been the rule, not the exception, for field commanders to disregard higher authorities."[52]

Risking possible court-martial, on May 24 Fu independently decided to immediately withdraw his three divisions to the north bank of the Han-gang River.[53] When his last division, the 187th, crossed the Han-gang at midnight, the ROK 2nd Division had just arrived at the river to cut off the Sixty-Third Army's retreat, missing the Chinese withdrawing forces by just several hundred yards.[54] Fortunately, in the darkness, the South Korean forces did not discover that 20,000 Chinese troops were crossing the river in front of them. Fu did not even inform Xu Xin, commander of 187th Division, of the arrival of the ROK division. Fu feared that if word got out, the Chinese soldiers might panic or open fire on the South Koreans, thus alerting the enemy of their presence.[55] Three days after the Sixty-Third crossed the Han-gang River, Yang ordered the army to withdraw north toward Cheorwon. Again, the army group command had failed to provide any effective orders. Fu was lucky and faced no court-martial.

In fact, Peng realized that the army group had serious problems with command, control, and communication that had broken the chain of command and paralyzed the CPVF's command capability. Although Peng dominated the strategic planning and tactical decisions and took seriously his role as commander in chief, the Chinese forces had not adopted an effective command-and-control doctrine. Zhang states that the Chinese forces "had at no point adopted a command control system that would meet the requirements of modern warfare.... Although they engaged in large-scale battles with the Nationalists during the Civil War, field commanders continued to enjoy a great deal of autonomy, making their own decisions at campaign, battle, and combat levels."[56] To solve the CPVF's command, control, and communication problems, Peng proposed to Mao on May 27 to promote the army group commanders to CPVF deputy commanders for "closer communications with various army groups."[57] To keep the army group commanders with Peng at the CPVF HQ should maintain the chain of command, reduce communication layers and information processing, and increase effectiveness.

By May 27 the vanguard of the UNF had advanced fifty to eighty miles after they had broken through the Nineteenth Army Group's defensive lines in the west on May 24. It had become clear that the UNF would not ease up on their offensive and sought to expand attacks in territory still held by the Chinese–North Korean forces north of the 38th Parallel.

### DISORDER IN THE MIDDLE

The collapse of the Nineteenth Army Group's defense fully exposed the western flank of the Third Army Group on the middle front with no warning. The Third Army Group commanded the Twelfth, Fifteenth, and Sixtieth Armies, with a total of 100,000 troops. A day after receiving the CPVF Command's instruction to withdraw on May 21, the Third Army Group followed the order and pulled back north to the Iron Triangle area, for rest and resupplying. The army group command assigned the Sixtieth Army to cover the withdrawal of its 100,000 troops by conducting a mobile resistance.[58] Its defensive area would stretch from Jail-ri (Jailri) and Paejiesan, bordering the Ninth Army Group on the east, to Kapyeong and Chuncheon, bordering the Nineteenth Army Group on the west.[59] The May 22 order made it clear that "the Sixtieth Army shall undertake the defensive tasks for this army group.... It shall conduct a phased defense against the advancing enemy forces, relying on the mountains southwest of Hwacheon.... It must begin moving to these designated areas tonight."[60]

Nevertheless, Wang Jinshan, acting commander of the Third Army Group, was concerned about his defense since he did not have adequate forces. The Sixtieth Army was the only one under his command during the second step of the Spring Offensive. Between May 16 and May 22, CPVF Command removed two of his three armies, the Twelfth and Fifteenth, and placed them under the command of the Ninth Army Group in an attempt to strengthen offensive operations against the ROK divisions at Hyeon-ri. On May 22 the Third Army Group Command reestablished its command of the Twelfth and Fifteenth Armies. But the command learned that the main strength of the Twelfth Army was still in the east. It was therefore too far away to defend the middle front. The Fifteenth Army had suffered severe losses and needed immediate rest and resupplying. On May 22 Wang ordered the Fifteenth to withdraw north immediately, one day earlier than the other armies, to avoid the traffic congestion on the narrow mountain roads that the Chinese had experienced during the first step of the Spring Offensive, in late April.[61] However, Wang neglected to report this order to the CPVF Command for approval. The CPVF Command did not learn of the order until several days later, when the advancing UNF troops cut off the retreat of several CPVF divisions through the gap created by the Fifteenth Army's early withdrawal.[62]

On May 23 the U.S. IX Corps commanded the U.S. 24th and 7th Divisions and ROK 6th and 2nd Divisions to attack Chuncheon and Hwacheon on the middle front. In the meantime, the U.S. 1st Marine and 2nd and 3rd Infantry Divisions, ROK 7th and 8th Divisions, U.S. 187th Airborne Regiment, and ROK 1st Marine Regiment were ordered to attack toward Inje and Yanggu. The British 28th Brigade and ROK 5th and 9th Divisions were held in reserve.[63] The UNF main attacks on the middle front began at the same time the Third Army Group HQ was beginning to withdraw. Moving along the highways, with tank units spearheading the advance, the mechanized UNF troops were a good deal faster in their northward advance than the Chinese commanders had expected.[64] The Third Army Group was badly handicapped by the UNF attacks, especially because fear of aerial assault made the Chinese unable to move in daylight. The Sixtieth Army had found itself right in the center of the hole punched by the UNF on the middle front. Under the UNF counterattacks, the Third Army Group failed to reorganize its retreating armies for three days after the army group communication network was demolished by a UNF air raid on May 24.[65]

Wei Jie (1914–87), the thirty-five-year-old commander of the Sixtieth Army, was concerned about his defensive mission; he was aware that it would not be easy for his army to defend the middle front.[66] He had no intact army, only one division. Two of his three divisions, the 179th and 181st Divisions, had been reassigned to the Twelfth Army to support attacks on the ROK's flank at Hyeon-ri from May 16 to May 22. They were on their way back to the Sixtieth Army; however, they required two to three days to reach their new defensive positions in the center. Some of their regiments would not be ready until May 27, four days after the UNF attacks. Other forces reached their designated areas but were unable to control key heights and highways to block the movements of the UNF task forces. The Sixtieth Army did not have time to assemble its divisions before the rapidly approaching UNF task forces encircled them.[67]

During the UNF counterattacks on May 23–29, the American commanders emphasized speed rather than space as the measurement of their success. Hoge, for example, "directed pursuit tactics and authorized them to bypass enemy groups up to company in size."[68] Hoge and Almond organized quite a number of task forces, such as Task Force Hazel, Task Force Yoke, and Task Force Newman. Each of these task forces included one or two tank companies or platoons, an engineering company or platoon, and reconnaissance platoons or squads, with trucks to carry an extra supply of rations, gasoline, and ammunition. When Maj. Charles Newman halted the tanks in his task force and tried to correct faulty radio communication with the reconnaissance squad, Almond was not happy and "ordered Newman to forget communications, to move his tanks at twenty miles an hour, and to 'keep going until you hit a mine.'"[69] According to Allan Millett, "the pattern of the pursuit became fixed by June 1. Corps and division commanders would form tank-infantry task forces that would press ahead along the roads in every corridor; they usually headed for a lateral road junction that would allow follow-on forces to envelop the Chinese and Koreans to the right or left."[70] The army group commanders of the CPVF, such as Yang, Wang, and Song, did not have a contingency plan to stop the UNF counterat-

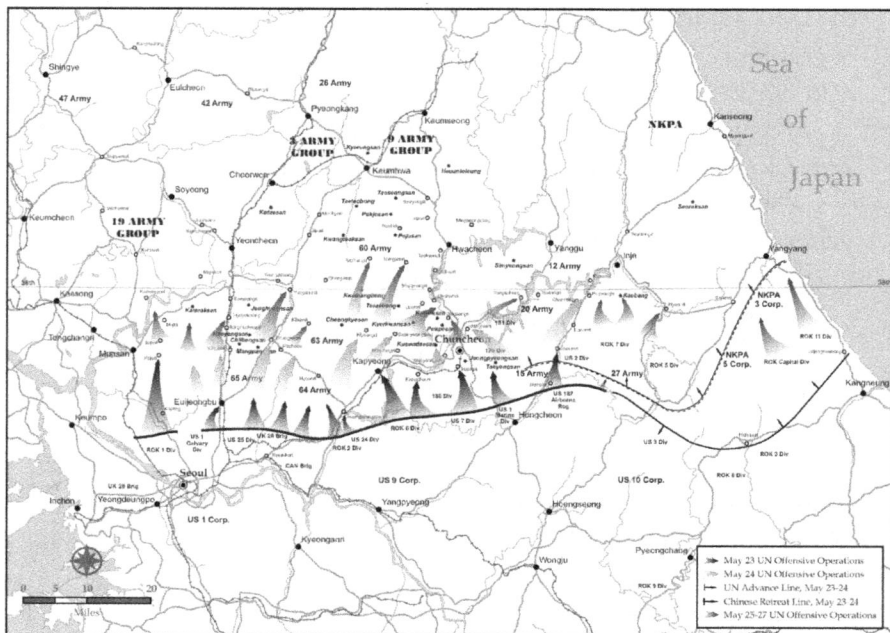

Map 7.2. UNF attacks, May 23–27

tacks. The army and division commanders began a race with the UNF advancing troops, which resulted in the collapse of the CPVF defense along the 38th Parallel (map 7.2).

The fast-moving U.S. task forces actually threatened the safety of the CPVF General HQ. According to Hong, Peng was so involved in directing CPVF army groups to plug the holes in the front line that he overlooked an American task force headed rapidly in the direction of Cheorwon, less than thirty miles from CPVF HQ at Kongseokdong.[71] There were no CPVF troops between the CPVF HQ and the Americans. Hong learned of this mishap and immediately ordered the Forty-Second Army—which was resting at Yangteok, approximately sixty miles behind Kongseokdong—to rush to Cheorwon to protect the CPVF HQ. The following day the Forty-Second Army deployed two of its divisions at Cheorwon, in hastily built field defenses, just as the American task force reached their position.[72]

U.S. task forces effectively interrupted the Third Army Group's withdrawal and quickly cut the Sixtieth Army into several pieces. The May 22 defense orders from the Third Army Group to the Sixtieth became unrealistic and probably dangerous, given the U.S. task forces' rapid advance and successful encirclement. The rapidly changing battlefield situation and the impotent command of the Third Army Group put tremendous pressure on Wei. Moreover, his political loyalty to and trust in his superior officers had a fatal impact on his divisions. The Sixtieth Army was determined to carry out the Third Army Group Command's May 22 orders to "establish two lines of defense. The first line runs from Kateoksan to Myeongjisan and Hill 625.1, while the second line runs from Hills 722 and 1286.5 to Seokyeongsan, Kwamangbong, and Kwaneumsan."[73]

The only problem was that Wei did not have enough men. At that moment, his 179th Division was still on the south bank of the Pukhangang River, and his 181st Division was still about eighty to a hundred miles away. However, Wei never complained about the army group's orders, though they were far from realistic or feasible. The army command sent new orders to its two divisions on May 23: "The 179th Division, with its attachment of the 46th Artillery Regiment, should ... move to Kapyeong, Kwaneumsan, and Hyuteoksan, establishing defensive positions via Jiuam-ri and Tuidong-ri in two columns on the night of May 25. . . . The 181st Division shall transport wounded soldiers from its present location. After completing this mission, it is to move to the Shinri, Kwamangbong, Kwaneumsan, and Sanghaebong areas on May 26 ... to build up defensive positions at Kwamangbong and Kwaneumsan."[74] Apparently both divisions were to be deployed at the second defensive line of the Sixtieth Army, since they were unable to reach the first line on time.

On the same day Wei received an urgent telegram from the Third Army Group:

> Due to the lack of transportation, our wounded soldiers have not been moved from the battleground to the safety in the north. None of the Twelfth Army's 5,000 wounded men have been transported. The Fifteenth Army still has about 2,000 wounded soldiers at Susadong, who cannot walk unaided. And the Sixtieth Army has about 1,000 wounded stranded. Therefore, the army group

command has decided that all forces temporarily halt their withdrawal, to build up strong defense on the front. The withdrawal shall be resumed after all wounded soldiers have been transported out. All the armies are expected to operate in accordance with this order and inform us of the result.[75]

It was clear that all three armies of the Third Army Group must conduct defensive operations at their locations at a time when wounded soldiers of each army were being transported from the front to the rear areas in the north. However, the commanders of the Sixtieth Army incorrectly interpreted this order as making the Sixtieth Army responsible for covering all three armies as they transported their wounded soldiers. Based on this misunderstanding, Wei immediately ordered the 180th Division, which had already begun its withdrawal by crossing the Pukhan-gang River, to establish defensive positions south of Chuncheon, Kapyeong, and the Pukhan-gang.[76] Eventually, according to the CPVF Command's campaign assessment report in July 1951, the Third Army Group left 8,000 wounded soldiers behind during the third step of the Spring Offensive, in late May.[77]

To make matters even worse, in the afternoon of May 24 the Sixtieth Army Command received a report from its 180th Division that the Sixty-Third Army of the Nineteenth Army Group in the west was retreating to the north. This unexpected retreat, after the Sixty-Fifth Army's early withdrawal, left the Sixtieth Army's western flank completely open. Deng Shijun, chief of staff of the Sixtieth, was extremely upset: "Damned, running away? They [the Sixty-Third's troops] can run, but they should let the 180th Division know first!"[78] The withdrawal of these two armies before May 24 left only one CPVF force south of the Pukhan: the 180th Division of the Sixtieth Army.

The Sixtieth Army Command had been trying everything possible to save its division between May 24 and May 26. Under precarious circumstances, Wei proposed two options to the Third Army Group Command on May 24. The first option was to order the 180th Division to conduct small-scale counterattacks along the south bank of the Pukhan-gang River, while trying to maintain its position for two days, from May 24 to May 25. During the night of May 25, the division could withdraw its main force north of the Pukhan-gang, while the 179th Division moved its forces from the south to the north bank of the Soyang-gang River.

The second option was to order the 180th Division to conduct large-scale counterattacks, covered by the 179th Division in the east, doing everything it could to annihilate part of the UNF attacking forces. This might win the division more time to cover the main army's northward retreat, giving it the opportunity to transport more wounded soldiers out of the area.[79]

The worst scenario came into play when vehicles carrying the Third Army Group's radio equipment were destroyed in a series of American air raids on May 24. The group commanders lost communications with their three armies from May 24 to May 26.[80] This paralyzed the CPVF Command on the middle front, and the Third Army Group Command was unable to respond to the Sixtieth Army's request for advice until the evening of May 26. The Sixtieth Army Command had to send out its staff members and reconnaissance team to look for the superior HQ. For three days, the army and division commands did not receive any updates on the UNF attacks, no information from the CPVF Command, and no new orders from the Third Army Group Command. Finally, the Third Command resumed its radio communication on May 26 and approved the Sixtieth Army's first option, ordering it to send one division to rescue the 180th by controlling the mountain passes stretching from north of Kapyeong to Shinyeon-gang.[81] Unfortunately, neither the 179th nor the 181st Divisions could stop the UNF attacking forces, and they failed in their rescue missions. This miscue cost the Sixtieth Army and its 180th Division two very valuable days, sealing the division's fate.

### THE LOST DIVISION

Wei's only hope for his first-line defense was his 180th Division, which consisted of the 538th, 539th, and 540th Regiments and totaled 11,000 men armed with Russian weapons. The 180th had been the only division under his command during the second step of the Spring Offensive. However, the division was still engaged at the south bank of the Pukhan-gang River, due to the lack of communication when the CPVF Command called off the second step on May 20. The 3rd Battalion of the 538th Regiment had suffered heavy casualties in the fight at Hill 336.8 against the U.S. 1st Marine Division.[82] After Zheng Qigui (1913–90), commander of the 180th Division, received the May 21 order from the Sixtieth Army, he informed Wei that the 180th would not be able to reach the defensive area for two days. Zheng was a seasoned PLA commander who had survived the Long March, served as regimental commander and commissar in Anti-Japanese War, and become deputy commander and commander of the 180th Division in the Chinese Civil War.[83] His political loyalty and total confidence in his superior officers handicapped his own decision making. Zheng believed it was his first priority to carry out the Sixtieth Army Command's orders, rather than trying to do what was best for his own division. When the Third Army Group Command lost communication with its troops for three days and the Sixtieth Army failed to help, Zheng was lost. He did not know until he was punished by a court-martial that the first charge against him was "political disloyalty."[84]

The broken chain of command between the Third Army Group and the Sixtieth Army delayed the withdrawal of the 180th Division. On May 23 Wei insisted that his forces—especially the 180th Division—should come to designated areas for defensive maneuvers because he was following orders from the Third Army Group Command. He issued an order that day:

> The 180th Division, attached to two companies of the 2nd Artillery Division, should send one infantry regiment north to build up checking positions north of Han-gang River. The division's main forces are to be deployed south of the Pukhan River, covering the [Third] Army Group's main forces and wounded soldiers as they move north. The division's defense areas are from Kateoksan to Myeongjisan, and also including Paekjiesan and Sanghaebong. It must make sure that it maintains contact with the Sixty-Third Army on its western flank at all times.[85]

Wei did not know that the Sixty-Third Army would retreat the next day. This was the first army command order that delayed the 180th Division's withdrawal.

The second order from the Sixtieth Army that diminished the 180th's chance of survival on May 23, when the army command received the confusing order from the Third Army Group to cover evacuation of the wounded soldiers.[86] Based on the misunderstanding mentioned above, Wei immediately ordered the 180th Division, which had already begun its withdrawal by crossing the Pukhan River, to establish defensive positions south of Chuncheon, Kapyeong, and the Pukhan-gang River.[87]

Sensing the danger of the situation, Duan Longzhang and Wang Zhen-bang—deputy commander and chief of staff of the 180th, respectively—proposed that Zheng withdraw the division's main force north of the river and keep only a small force to defend the south bank on May 23, so the entire division would not be in danger of being trapped with its back against the river. However, Zheng disagreed with their proposal, and they were obliged to report their dispute to the Sixtieth Army Command, where the army commanders also disagreed among themselves.[88] Zha Yusheng, deputy commander of the Sixtieth, agreed with the proposal, but Wei rejected it, believing that the army group's order was to not withdraw and that "the army group's order must be faithfully implemented."[89] On May 24 the Sixtieth Army Command gave up its last chance to save the 180th Division. The division ordered troops that had already crossed the river to return and establish a defensive position on the south bank of the Pukhan-gang River.

On May 23–24, the 180th Division began to move into its positions to protect the Sixtieth Army and the entire Third Army Group on the middle front. When the Fifteenth Army of the Third Army Group unexpectedly withdrew on May 22, it left the 180th Division's eastern flank entirely exposed, putting the division in grave jeopardy. On May 23, knowing the Sixty-Third Army was ready to retreat to the north and leave his western side completely open, Zheng became troubled. He immediately ordered his main forces to prepare to cross the Pukhan-gang, move to the northwest of Chuncheon, and establish a new and defensible line.[90]

May 24 was an extremely tough day for the 180th, and without having consolidated its defenses, the division lost many troops in bloody combat against UNF. That day a task force from the U.S. 24th Division penetrated into the 180th's western flank and rear, occupying Kpayeong, Kiyeong-ri, and Seonghwangdang. The ROK 6th Division attacked the 180th's front, occupying Kangchon and the Kangchon Ferry on the Pukhan-gang River. The U.S. 7th Division's task forces attacked and occupied Chuncheon on the 180th's eastern flank and rear.[91] Thus the 180th was besieged on three sides by U.S. and ROK forces and had its back against the Pukhan-gang River. Its 540th Regiment reported the heavy casualties and loss of Seonghwangdang, the division's retreat route. The

Third Company of the 1st Battalion, 540th Regiment, had only 10 soldiers left out of 170 men by the end of May 24. When the troops of its 3rd Battalion ran out of ammunition, the battalion commanders used their last grenade to meet their death, together with the UNF attacking soldiers.[92] After May 24 the 180th Division, having lost most of its combat troops, began to retreat.

The Chinese division still had one last chance to escape the UNF encirclement on May 25. By that time the 180th Division Command knew it had been surrounded on three sides by the U.S. 24th Division and ROK 6th Division, and that its northern retreat route was being threatened by the U.S. 7th Infantry and 1st Marine Divisions that were quickly approaching Chuncheon and Shinyeon-gang, south of Chuncheon. The 180th deputy commander and chief of staff proposed that the division recross the Pukhan-gang River.[93] When Zheng stubbornly refused once again, the dispute was reported to the Sixtieth Army Command. Receiving the disputed request from the 180th Division, Wei agreed that if Seonghwangtang was lost to UNF attacking forces, the 180th should immediately withdraw north of the Pukhan-gang. "The 180th Division is to cross Pukhan-gang River," he ordered, "establishing defensive positions along the riverbank to check the advancing enemy troops. The 179th Division shall defend Salibong and Sapyeon-ri to hold back the enemy advance, and the 181st Division is to quickly beat back any enemy units in pursuit of our forces before relocating to Hwacheon to act as the corps's reserve force."[94] In the meantime, the Sixtieth Army Command reported its decision to the Third Army Group Command. But, as noted above, the Third Army Group was unable to respond to the Sixtieth Army's request until May 26.

The 180th Division did not recross the Pukhan-gang River until dawn on May 25. During the crossing, the division lost 600 officers and soldiers due to the rapid current and UNF air raids.[95] That morning the 180th continued to retreat north and reached Kyerkwansan, Pukpesan, Sangpangdong, and Myeongwol-ri (Myongwolri). However, it was unable to establish a main line of resistance against the U.S. 24th and ROK 6th Divisions. The 180th was caught in a terrible situation, with command and control disrupted due to the disarray of the withdrawal. The division command narrowly escaped being besieged by conducting a desperate hide-and-seek type battle with the UNF, suffering continued heavy casualties.[96]

Lt. Col. Guan Zhichao—political commissar of the 2nd Battalion of the 539th Regiment—recalls that his Fifth Company had only 20 soldiers left out of 160 men by the end of May 25.[97] His regiment had only about 1,000 men left that day out of 3,000 soldiers. The Eighth Company, 1st Battalion, 540th Regiment, had 30 men alive, including wounded, out of 180 soldiers.[98] The 538th Regiment lost its Fifth and Seventh Companies: all of the officers and soldiers, including their captains, were killed in their defensive battles on May 26.[99] The ROK 6th Division seized its positions at Kyerkwansan, while the U.S. 24th Division occupied Kangchon at the rear of its right flank. The U.S. 7th Division attacked from Chuncheon, occupying the 179th Division's positions at Soseong-ri (Sosongri) and Tuidong-ri.[100] The 180th Division had become isolated in the Pukpesan, Kateoksan, and Owol-ri (Owolri) areas.

On May 26 the U.S. 7th Division broke through the CPVF 179th Division's defensive positions. As a result, the U.S. troops soon occupied Okonam-ri, Mapyeong-ri, and Pangha Bridge and completely severed the connections between the 179th and 180th Divisions, as well as blocking the 180th Division's retreat.[101] The 180th had been encircled. At 6:00 PM on May 26, the division attempted to break out to the northwest. Taking advantage of the terrain and the light of the moon, the division was able to move farther north. By 9:00 AM on May 27, the remnants of the division reached Eunbong, which had been occupied by the UNF. Following five days of continuous fighting and marching, the 180th Division was left with 2,000–3,000 out of 11,000 soldiers and almost no ammunition; its men had gone without food for days.[102] For nearly a week, soldiers had been collapsing on the ground, dying of starvation. Some died from eating poisonous wild plants and snakes. Dozens of soldiers, fearing capture by the UN forces, committed suicide by blowing themselves up with hand grenades and other explosives.[103] Others, overcome by extreme exhaustion and hunger following their five-day defense and retreat, chose to remain behind to become POWs rather than to retreat further.[104]

The morale of the 180th Division was low by May 27. Some of the commanders lost control of their troops: some of the men refused to fol-

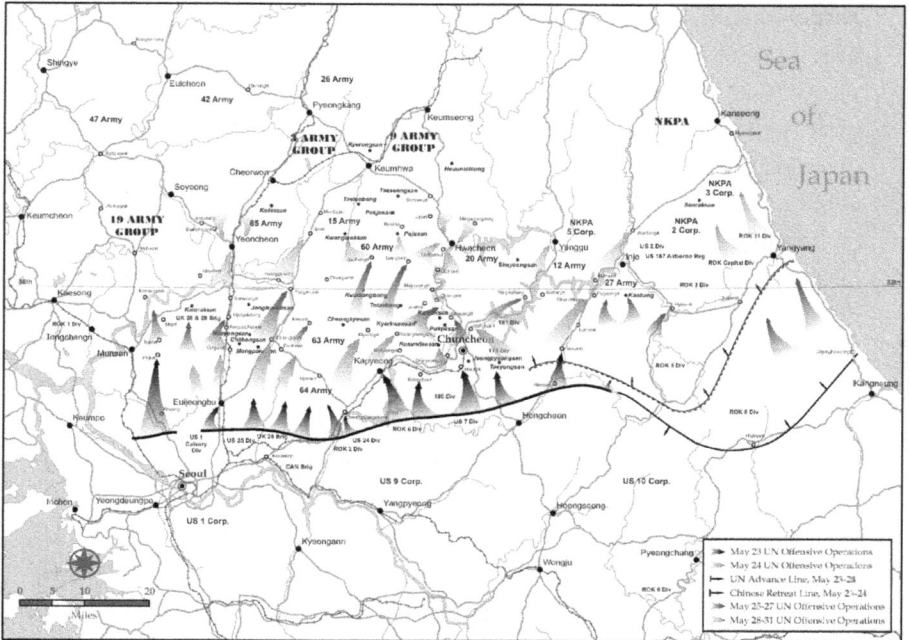

Map 7.3. UNF attacks and CPVF withdrawal, May 23–31

low orders, and some deserted in groups with their weapons. Liu Yaohu
(1917–51), commander of the 540th Regiment, who tried to stop the collapse and re-organize a defense, was shot to death from behind by his
own men.[105] One of his captains let the remnants of his company, about
two platoons, surrender to the attacking UNF troops.

The 180th Division's chain of command collapsed in the afternoon
of May 27. Peng pointed out the failure of the 180th Division Command, stating: "The division did not have a carefully designed operational plan."[106] At 4:00 PM on May 27, the 180th Division Command
destroyed its radio equipment and burned the radio code manuals, ter-
minating its only means of communication with the Sixtieth Army and
outside support. Its remaining troops, approximately 600 men, were
regrouped into three companies to make a final attempt to break out,
toward Sachang-ri.[107] By May 28, however, they were still unable to escape the fortified UNF defense. Filled with despair, Zheng encouraged

his troops to attempt one last-ditch breakout effort on their own, thus relinquishing his duties, and the 180th Division dissolved as a result of his instructions.[108] One later charge against Zheng was that he had given up the command and dismantled his division (map 7.3).

Mao and the other CMC leaders in Beijing were extremely concerned about the fate of the 180th Division. Mao telegraphed Peng at 2:00 AM on May 31: "How about the situation of the 180th Division of the Sixtieth Army? [We are] having serious concerns."[109] By that time, only a small number of the 180th's troops had managed to break free and return to CPVF-occupied positions. Zeng, Deputy Commander Duan Longzhang, and several staff members returned to the CPVF on May 30. According to the divisional command's report titled "The Combat Casualties of the 180th Division's Breakout," the division had lost 7,644 troops and 654 officers, including 9 regimental commanders, 49 battalion officers, and 201 captains and political instructors at the company level.[110] Nevertheless, some of the returning officers faced court-martials and severe punishment.

The military prosecutors used some successful cases of CPVF troop breakouts in the east against the 180th commanders for their inability to command and control. In contrast to the total destruction of the 180th Division, several CPVF units provided examples of well-executed retreats in the face of a superior UNF encircling force. Among other cases on the eastern front, the CPVF Twenty-Seventh Army and the 91st Regiment of the Twelfth Army had also been encircled, but these two Chinese forces had broken out of the UNF encirclement and returned to their units during the third step of the Spring Offensive.[111] In the east, the U.S. X Corps had launched the all-out counterattacks against the CPVF Ninth Army Group on May 23. The U.S. 1st Marine, 2nd, 3rd, and 7th Infantry Divisions; U.S. 187th Airborne Regiment; and ROK 5th, 6th, and 7th Divisions attacked the Twelfth, Twentieth, and Twenty-Seventh Armies of the Ninth Army Group.[112]

Without organizing an effective defense, the Ninth Army Group Command had decided to employ only one division from the Twenty-Seventh Army to conduct a one-month "mobile defense operation" against the UNF attacking forces.[113] However, the division had no way of defending an eighty-mile-long front line between Jaeum-ri, Kali-san,

Pyeongchon-ri, the Hwacheon Lake, and Taetong-ri to cover the army group's withdrawal, an evacuation of 150,000 troops, which was scheduled for May 23.[114] Moreover, the Thirty-Ninth Army of the Ninth Army Group withdrew during the night of May 22, a day ahead of other armies. Almond took advantage of this act and quickly enlarged the attacks, cutting off the retreat of the CPVF Twenty-Seventh Army on May 24.[115] Making matters even worse, the U.S. 187th Airborne Regiment made parachute landings at Eonon-ri and in the Pupyeong-ri (Pupyongri) area on May 25–26.[116]

For three days the Twenty-Seventh Army held its defensive positions against UNF attacks from both sides, in order to protect its army group's withdrawal. The Twenty-Seventh Army Command was flexible with its defense. For example, the command sent its 79th Division to stop the U.S. 187th Regiment and to defend the crossing of the Soyang-gang River. When the 79th Division could not hold its position, the army command ordered all its forces south of the Soyang-gang to cross the river on May 27, before the U.S. 187th Regiment could trap them.[117] After the army was cut off, Peng Deqing (1910–99), commander of the Twenty-Seventh Army, and Liu Haotian (1912–84), the army's political commissar, remained calm.[118] They carefully analyzed the situation and maintained firm control of all their divisions. They constantly changed retreat routes to avoid strong UNF tank forces. The army command always maintained close and constant radio communications with the Ninth Army Group and CPVF Commands, securing intelligence on the UNF and receiving new instructions on next moves. They also fought for nearly a week with no proper food, living on tree bark and grass.[119]

### STABILIZING THE LINE

From May 27 onward, the CPVF Command began organizing a defense across the entire front. Peng Dehuai decided to postpone several armies' rest and resupplying in the north and to redeploy them on May 27 in order to defend the Euicheon, Kocheon, Sapyeon-ri, Shinkye, Nam-cheonjeon, and Sonan areas along the 38th Parallel. Peng reported his new defense plan to Mao at 11:00 PM on the twenty-seventh.[120] Peng candidly informed Mao of the serious situation on the front and re-

quested an earlier entry of the third wave of the CPVF as reinforcements to prevent the situation from deteriorating even further.[121] The
UNF continued its northward attacks toward Cheorwon, Keumhwa,
and Yanggu. Its objective was to occupy the Iron Triangle of Keumhwa,
Cheorwon, and Pyeongkang, destroying the logistical support base and
transportation network of the CPVF and NKPA. The UNF's continued
attacks thwarted Peng's original plans to use a phased defense in order
to "gradually abandon Keumhwa, Yanggu, Inje, Keumseong, and Cheorwon, in exchange for maintaining the areas of Hoeyang, Pyeongkang,
Seopo-ri, and Anpyeon" once the CPVF and NKPA main forces had
withdrawn to the north.[122]

After Mao approved his new plan, Peng began to deploy from west
to east the CPVF Sixty-Fifth, Sixty-Third, Sixty-Fourth, Fifteenth,
Twenty-Sixth, and Twentieth Armies and the NKPA II, III, and V Corps
at Jipo-ri, Hwacheon, Yanggu, and Kanseong, north of the Imjin-gang
and Hantancheon Rivers.[123] He also ordered the Chinese Forty-Second
and Forty-Seventh Armies to move from their positions in the north to
establish new defensive positions in Shinmok-ri and east of Euicheon
and Namcheonjeon.[124] On May 28 Peng sent a strongly worded telegram
to his generals:

> During our current withdrawal, the enemy has exploited our forces' fatigue
> and transportation difficulties, chasing our forces in hot pursuit with aircraft
> and mechanized troops. We have not yet managed to do anything to hold this
> pursuit in check. Although our forces are tired and short of supplies, this is
> no excuse. Operational command has left much to be desired. We have not
> employed adequate forces or firepower to control highways; senior command
> post personnel have left front forces too early when their troops were under
> attack; and operational forces have not been used in any kind of systematic,
> effective way.
> Where our forces are solidly in control of positions, they must do everything
> in their power to hold the enemy invasion in check. Commanders of all armies
> must personally inspect the connection between two armies on both sides, set
> up telephone lines, and organize transportation of food supplies and wounded
> soldiers. Should any force allow the enemy into our positions, its commanders
> will be severely disciplined.[125]

One day later, at 10:00 PM on May 29, the CPVF Command issued
"Instructions on Block Enemy Pursuit and Attacks," providing detailed
defensive tactics to its three army groups and all the armies:

> All forces must maintain their present force posture, doing everything they can
> to block the enemy's rapid advance, maintain dividing lines, and keep control of
> all positions—including those held by second- and third-line forces in prepara-
> tion for battle. Commanders at the corps and even army level must personally
> inspect and adjust their units' established positions, especially on both sides
> of all connections between two units. Telephone line connections must be
> installed between regiments and between divisions. Support firepower networks
> and coordination between various infantry units must be well established at
> all connection points. Highways must be obstructed by any means available,
> including destruction of roads, emplacement of mines, and use of antitank guns.
> Troops at the rear must be organized to transport food to the front and move
> wounded soldiers from the front to the rear. Overall, if the enemy attacks are not
> held in check, we will face a much graver situation in the future.[126]

Mao generally agreed with Peng's defense arrangement and replied:
"All of the orders you have issued to our armies are necessary and correct. The armies should continue to do whatever they can to stop the
enemy forces at Keumhwa, Cheorwon, and Soyeong, as well as the areas south of these towns. The Forty-Second Army should move east of
Euicheon, and the Forty-Seventh Army will do better if relocated to
Nancheon and Shinmok-ri."[127]

To stop the continued offensive of the U.S. I and IX Corps in the
west, the CPVF Command attempted to establish a new defensive line
along the 38th Parallel to protect the Iron Triangle, a key point for CPVF
transportation and supply. On the western front, at 9:00 PM on May 27,
the Sixty-Fifth Army received its new orders: to defend Cheorwon along
Hantancheon and not to withdraw further.[128] By May 28, however, the
U.S. I and IX Corps had concentrated its attacks on four divisions and
had overrun the defensive positions of the Sixty-Fifth Army, occupying Keumko-ri (Kimkori), Yeongpyeon, and Hantancheon, south of
Yeoncheon. The UNF corps immediately began putting pressure on
Cheorwon, threatening the CPVF's logistical support base north of
Cheorwon.[129] The CPVF Command reinforced the Sixty-Third Army
at its most crucial positions on the western front, a fifteen-mile front
running in an east-west direction south of Cheorwon and Yeoncheon.
The Sixty-Third Army faced the U.S. 1st Cavalry and 25th Divisions, as
well as the British 28th and 29th Brigades.

The CPVF Command ordered the Sixty-Third Army to hold its positions for fifteen to twenty days. Yang and Li Zhimin, his political com-

missar, were not confident that the Sixty-Third would be able to hold out for that long. They telegraphed Peng that "although the Sixty-Third Army has been ordered to quickly make its operational plans, it might be unable to accomplish the task assigned by the CPVF Command." Peng gave clear instructions to Yang: "Even if the entire Sixty-Third Army loses all of its troops in the defense, Cheorwon must be held for fifteen to twenty days."[130]

By June 1 the U.S. I and IX Corps had assembled their main forces to attack positions held by the Sixty-Third Army. The fiercest battles occurred on the Sixty-Third's right wing at the mountain pass of Yeoncheon, held by its 187th Division. The UNF assembled five infantry battalions, supported by four artillery battalions, to attack the 3rd Battalion, 561st Regiment, and 187th Division. The 3rd Battalion stopped the waves of attacks and held its position for four days and three nights. During the last few days of the defense, Fu had to fall back on his last reserves to help the right wing of the 187th Division continue its defensive operations. He ordered all artillery units to provide fire support to the 187th Division's positions, and Xu managed to stop the attacks by the U.S. 1st Cavalry Division.[131] Peng was so concerned about the Sixty-Third Army's situation that he made three direct calls to Fu and asked for complete assessments of the battle situation, while repeatedly stressing the importance of resisting the UNF attacks[132] (map 7.4).

On its left, the 189th Division of the Sixty-Third Army also managed to withstand repeated attacks by the U.S. 25th Division. To save its forces from being depleted by American carpet bombing and artillery attacks, the CPVF Command instructed its Sixty-Third Army to change from static defensive to mobile defensive maneuvers.[133] On June 4, the U.S. attacking forces conducted another ferocious assault, sending wave after wave of attacks against the Sixty-Third. The U.S. artillery continued shelling CPVF positions, not withholding its fire even after soldiers from both sides had begun engaging in hand-to-hand combat. To hold the 189th Division's defensive positions, the Sixty-Third Army was obliged to throw its reserve force, the 188th Division, into action.[134] On June 5, the CPVF Command ordered the Sixty-Third to fall back to the second line of defense, where it was to continue conducting mobile defensive operations and also continue to check the enemy's advance. At one particularly

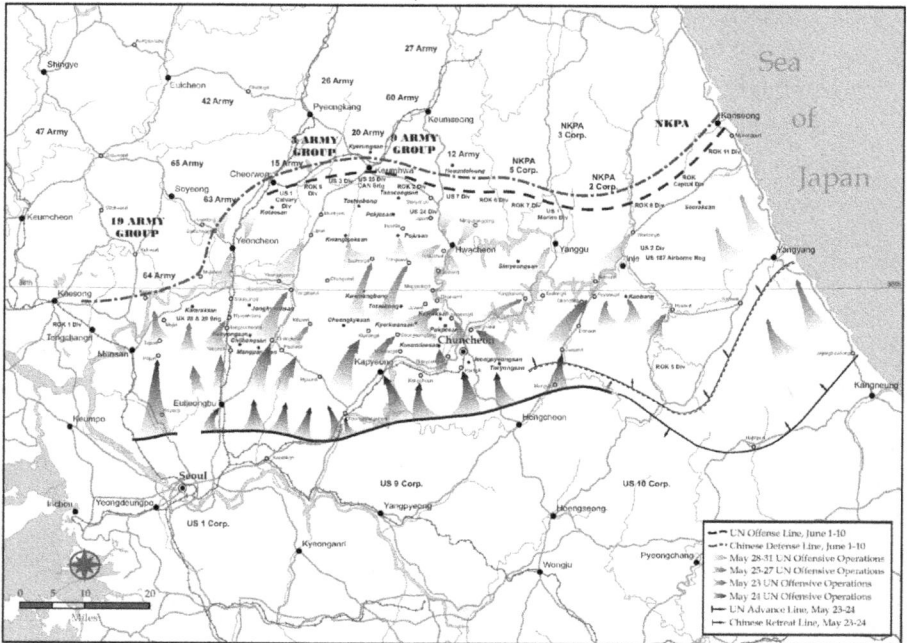

Map 7.4. UNF offensive and CPVF defensive lines, May 23–June 10

fierce moment in the fighting, the 188th Division blasted open a reservoir
northeast of Cheorwon, holding back the UNF's tanks and advancing
artillery for a few days.

By June 10 the CPVF had withdrawn from the Cheorwon and
Keumhwa areas after a solid, stable line of defense had been established
by the Twenty-Sixth, Twenty-Seventh, Forty-Second, and Forty-Seventh Armies. The Sixty-Third Army had successfully completed its mission, staving off the U.S. forces for twelve days. It suffered more than
10,000 casualties, but its sacrifice bought time for the CPVF main forces
to establish the next lines of defense.[135]

On the middle front, the Fifteenth Army faced an emergency. Peng
called Qin Jiwei (1914–97), commander of the Fifteenth Army, on May
29 when the defense army was only halfway to its destination.[136] Peng is
said to have yelled at Qin: "An unidentified enemy force has advanced to
Kilsan-ri and Yangmun-ri [Yangmunri], southeast of Yeongpyeon. You

must stop this force from advancing for seven to ten days."[137] Although his army had been reduced to one-third of its original strength and had no food and ammunition, Qin replied to Peng that he would hold the UNF attacking force back for at least ten days.[138] He knew it must be an emergency since Peng had personally issued the order to him, bypassing the Third Army Group Command, Qin's direct superior. On May 29 the Fifteenth Army deployed three lines of defense against a strong UNF attacking force, including the U.S. 3rd and 25th Divisions, Canadian 25th Brigade, and ROK 9th Division.[139] On May 29 the Canadian 25th Brigade spearheaded the attacks, but the Fifteenth Army held its positions for several days. Over the following week, the U.S. 3rd and 25th Divisions took turns attacking the Fifteenth Army, with positions changing hands multiple times and both sides suffering heavy casualties.[140] By June 7 the Fifteenth Army had successfully held the line for ten days with 1,286 casualties, giving the CPVF some critical time to establish the second line of defense.

On the eastern front, the CPVF ordered the Ninth Army Group to deploy the Twentieth, Twenty-Sixth, and Twenty-Seventh Armies to defend the Hwacheon, Sehyeong-ri, and Keumseong areas in the east, "holding back the enemy for twenty days to one month and striving to wipe out two to three American battalions by annihilating from two companies to one battalion at a time."[141] It was thought that the eastern defense would facilitate the CPVF's force adjustments and redeployment, food and ammunition resupply, and a counterattack on UNF forces. After a quick resupply, the CPVF forces were immediately deployed to their designated areas, building up defensive works and facilities and conducting blocking maneuvers against the rapidly approaching UNF forces. The first-line defense supported the Twentieth Army, reinforced by the Twenty-Sixth Army and several artillery regiments.[142]

In the east, the Twentieth Army ordered its 58th Division to seize the key tactical points of Chilseong-ri, Taekamail, Seongsan, Eulkidong, Cheomjeongdong, and Taeldong ahead of the UNF attacking forces. The army also had its 59th Division assemble on both sides of the highway running from Sanyang-ri to Jumpa-ri. On May 28 the U.S. 7th and 24th Divisions, followed by the ROK 3rd Division, used a tank group vanguard to attack the positions held by the 58th Division at Hwacheon. Under continuing attacks, the 58th Division lost its positions to the U.S. 7th Division on May 28. The next day the 58th Division threw in its reserve force, the 172nd Regiment, to join the 174th Regiment's counter-attacks. Together the two regiments defeated one reinforced company of the U.S. 7th Division and part of the ROK 3rd Division, taking back their defensive positions.[143] With food and ammunition running low, the 58th Division combined tactics of defensive maneuvers and coun-terattacks, slowing down the UNF advance on the eastern front to only several miles over a seven-day period.[144] Eventually, the UNF halted its advance on June 10.

Throughout the third step of the Spring Offensive, the CPVF learned valuable lessons on how to conduct defensive actions against the UNF despite its technical superiority. This knowledge came at a high cost, however, as Chinese forces suffered 50,000 casualties during its defense, including 20,000 POWs.[145] Peng was candid about the difficulties in the early summer of 1951, giving the following assessment: "Under un-contested enemy artillery, tank, and air bombardment, there is no such thing as holding static defensive positions. However, it is possible to inflict casualties on the enemy by conducting active mobile defensive operations. Korea is long, narrow country. The enemy forces are ad-vancing in an even, tight formation, without any bulging part and gaps. The enemy's firepower is so strong that our forces cannot move at all during the daytime."[146] In Peng's view at that time, the CPVF had suf-fered many more casualties than the UNF in conducting a positional defense against the UNF attacking forces without air cover or superior equipment.

The Chinese Spring Offensive, from April 22 through June 10, 1951, was the largest and longest Communist military operation of the war, as well as the largest battle since WWII. The CPVF-NKPA Joint Command deployed more than 700,000 men, including 600,000 CPVF troops. Yet the offensive failed. The UNF put up a strong defense and an effective counterattack, driving the Communists back north of the 38th Parallel and inflicting 90,000 casualties. After the Chinese forces lost the Spring Offensive, the Communists never again came close to Seoul or mounted another major southward incursion of such magnitude. Their defeat forced Mao to reconsider both his political and military aims. Realizing the huge gap between Chinese capabilities and the ambitious aim of driving the UNF from the peninsula, the Chinese leaders began to look for alternative such as a negotiated settlement rather than a victory.

# EIGHT

# From Battleground to Negotiating Table

WHEN THE CHINESE LOST THEIR SPRING OFFENSIVE ON JUNE 10, 1951, the war in Korea between China and the United States reached a stalemate. Chinese leaders realized the limit of China's military power as well as the capabilities of the UNF, not only in defending their positions, but also in inflicting heavy casualties on the CPVF. Beijing conceded that the CPVF could not reunify Korea by force of arms, nor could it continue the war for any purpose that would justify the sacrifice of additional Chinese lives.[1] The CPVF commanders accepted the fact that it was nearly impossible for them to win the war in Korea while they faced more formidable UN and U.S. forces on a limited battleground, and that the war would be protracted, with no end in sight. By the summer of 1951, the CPVF was no longer expected to recapture Seoul and drive into South Korea. Although the armies could achieve temporary success in limited sectors, any success came at a high cost. Peng Dehuai redefined the CPVF's mission as "fighting a protracted war, and defending ourselves actively."[2] The failed Spring Offensive led Chinese leaders to replace its ambitious goal of driving the UNF out of Korea with the aim of merely defending China's security and ending the war through negotiations. Beijing was willing to accept a settlement without total victory. The offensive was the turning point that not only reshaped the rest of the war but also led to the truce negotiations that began on July 10, 1951.

During the truce negotiations in 1951–53, the fighting continued. The Chinese high command accepted the fact that despite their numerical superiority, Chinese forces did not possess the capabilities and resources to win.[3] In fact, there was the danger that the CPVF might not be able to hold their defense positions along the 38th Parallel and could possibly be pushed farther north under continuous UNF attacks after the Spring Offensive. The CPVF Command made some important strategic and tactical changes to defend their frontal positions in 1951–53, and it became the longest positional warfare in the PLA's history. The scale, intensity, and destructiveness of the trench warfare between the CPVF and UNF were probably matched only by those of WWI in Europe. By the summer of 1951 the nature of the Korean War had changed, evolving from a mobile warfare to a stalemate, or a war of trenches. Chinese commanders shifted their focus from annihilating UNF divisions and brigades in mobile warfare to securing their front lines in positional defense, except for two minor offensives that took place in the fall of 1952 and in July 1953. The CPVF continued fighting the war, while negotiating for peace, off and on for two more years. The Korean Truce Agreement was finally signed on July 27, 1953.

After the conclusion of the Spring Offensive, the CPVF maintained a relatively stable front line, increasing its air force, artillery, and tank units and beefing up logistical support to limit casualties and negate the UNF firepower that it had suffered from in the spring of 1951. The Korean War was the beginning of China's military modernization and professionalism in terms of command, organization, and training. The PRC's first foreign war experience rapidly changed some of its military culture, largely influenced by Soviet technology and American military practices. In this respect, the United States turned out to be a "useful adversary" for China in the Korean War.[4] Indeed, the CPVF increasingly became a mirror image of its American counterpart in its prosecution of the war. In the meantime, the fighting continued. Since the end of 1951, when the two sides agreed on the demarcation line, the nature of the war had changed. Even though the Chinese soldiers did not know it, the goal no longer was to win the war.[5] Much bloody fighting lay ahead, but the front lines remained essentially unchanged. Both sides simply dug in and prepared to stay.

STALEMATE: TRENCH WARFARE AND TUNNEL DEFENSE

During the Spring Offensive, from April 22 to June 10, 1951, the CPVF based its operations on a conventional approach: it aimed to annihilate complete UNF units, such as an entire division or brigade. But before the end of the campaign, Chinese leaders realized that this practice had proved ineffective in Korea, where they faced a technically superior force. In a telegram of May 26, Mao agreed with Peng that "all the past campaigns have proved it difficult for our forces to accomplish their tasks of annihilating several U.S. divisions, or one division, or even one regiment, after they were encircled by our forces through strategic and tactical flanking operations."[6] Clearly, the battered CPVF troops lacked the firepower to break through the UNF lines through either surprise attacks or force of numbers. Mao came up with a new tactic—"eating sticky candy bit by bit"—or attrition tactics to eliminate UNF troops bit by bit.[7] Under this guideline, the CPVF adopted a different fighting system that focused on more cautious defensive strategies and tactics. Their planning transformed their system from large-scale operations into piecemeal warfare.

After the Spring Offensive, the CCP Central Committee held a meeting in Beijing to discuss the CPVF's next step. Most committee members considered it proper that the CPVF should stop at the 38th Parallel and conduct limited offensive operations. The Chinese leaders agreed that China should begin truce talks while continuing to fight a defensive war so as to work toward a negotiated settlement. Nie Rongzhen concurred with this view. The acting chief of the PLA's General Staff believed that "we had already achieved our political goal, i.e., that the enemy should be driven out of northern Korea. Our pausing at the 38th Parallel, in fact, was a return to the pre-war status quo. This would be easily accepted by all the parties in the war."[8] The military forces on the battleground had reached a new balance: stalemate.

In contrast to the situations the Chinese had faced in both WWII and the Chinese Civil War, in Korea it was difficult for either side to overpower its opponent completely. On the UNF side, even if the firepower and troops to drive the Chinese back to the Yalu were available, the will to do so was lacking. Although Matthew Ridgway believed that the U.S.

Eighth Army, if it had been ordered to do so, "could have pushed right on to the Yalu in the spring of 1951," he also believed the "price for such a drive would have been far too high."[9] In June James Van Fleet ordered limited operations to consolidate UNF positions, but nothing more. Unless one side or the other was willing to pay the cost in casualties and for the equipment required to carry out a major offensive, which would have been enormous, the war was effectively at a draw.[10] On the Chinese side, heavy casualties in the spring, continuous shortages of supplies, and lack of firepower had made any new CPVF offensive almost impossible. After the summer of 1951, both sides began to dig in and trench warfare began. The front lines changed very little for the remainder of the war.

On June 25–27, 1951, Peng chaired the Enlarged Party Committee Meeting of the CPVF to discuss Mao's piecemeal strategy and the Central Committee's new policy of limited war. The CPVF commanders agreed with Peng's plan for the next stage of war: always having established positions behind the front lines; fighting seesaw warfare to wear down the UNF's effective strength; taking offensive actions only after being fully prepared; and coordinating offensive and defensive operations closely.[11] The CPVF should be able to defend the areas between the 38th and 38.5th Parallels unless the UNF increased its forces on the front or made amphibious landings in the CPVF's rear. The CPVF Command basically abandoned mobile campaigns with large-scale movement back and forth, the way it had been operating since Chinese forces entered Korea. Shuguang Zhang points out that "what Peng envisioned, in essence, was an overall defensive action with small-scale assaults."[12] In August Peng had to delay his planned Sixth Offensive after Mao questioned his preparedness.[13] Eventually, Peng gave up any plan for another large-scale offensive campaign. He telegraphed all army commanders that the CPVF Command had "decided not to plan for any major offensives from November to the end of the year [of 1951] unless unexpected circumstances require [us] to do so."[14] The summer of 1951 marked the turning point of the war, when the CPVF changed its operational strategy from offense to defense.

In the fall of 1951, the CPVF concentrated on strengthening its defensive lines. The Chinese forces built up three lines with permanent defense works and facilities. The first line was from Cheorwon, Keumhwa, to Munteung-ri and was manned by eight CPVF armies and three NKPA corps. The second line was from Keumcheon and Anhap to Koseong and was defended by nine CPVF armies and four NKPA corps. The third line from Haecheon and Euicheon to Tongcheon and employed two CPVF armies.[15] The CPVF-NKPA defense lines were tested when the UNF launched attacks against the CPVF-NKPA front lines from August 18 to September 18. The U.S. X Corps ordered the U.S. 2nd and ROK 5th Divisions to attack Hills 983.1, 940, and 773.1, held mostly by the NKPA troops. The U.S. and ROK forces used 126 howitzers, 72 large and medium cannons, and 40 tanks to shell the defense positions, with over 360,000 rounds of artillery fire spent during a four-day period. The UNF then employed thirteen battalions to attack the defense positions for seven days. By the end of August, after several rounds of seesaw battles, the UNF attacking forces had taken three hills. Having seen the difficulties in the NKPA's defense, Peng telegraphed Kim Un and suggested that "we'd better not [sic] to recover the lost positions if they are difficult to take back to avoid excessive casualties."[16] Kim agreed and ordered his defense troops to pull out of the Taeuan area. The U.S. X Corps continued its attacks until September 18 and occupied about seventy square miles of CPVF-NKPA territory.

To avoid losing additional territory, the CPVF held another enlarged Party Committee meeting on September 4–10, 1951, including all high-ranking commanders at or above army levels. To limit defense casualties and negate UNF firepower, the Party Committee decided an underground tunnel system should be constructed along the 38th Parallel in the fall of 1951.[17] Strengthening the defensive capacity of the CPVF would certainly improve the Chinese negotiating position in any future settlement. The "underground great wall," as the tunnel system became known, was built along the front line.[18] Statistics released at the exhibition on the WRUSAK, in Dandong, Liaoning Province, in 2010 showed that in 1952–53, the CPVF dug more than 780 miles of underground tunnels, and the various kinds of surface entrenchment and communication lines along the front amounted to a total length of approximately 3,900 miles, roughly comparable to the length of the Great Wall.[19] Between April 26 and May 1, 1952, the CPVF Command held an army chiefs of staff meeting to standardize the construction of defensive tunnels: every underground tunnel should be at least 100 feet deep from the top of the main cavity, must have more than two exits, should be four feet wide and six feet high, and should be connected to trenches and other fieldworks.[20]

The CPVF also constructed defensive works and a tunnel system along the western and eastern coasts against a possible UNF landing in North Korea. The antilanding defense system was completed by early 1953, with 1,950 miles of trenches, 450 miles of tunnels, and 605 permanent concrete bunkers.[21] Mao praised the trench defense works in a speech in August 1952: "Whether we can defend our positions is a question that was resolved last year. The solution was to hide in grottos. We dug out a two-level fortification. We hid in the tunnels when the enemy came over. It operated like this: the enemy occupied the surface positions, but the underground level remained ours. Once the enemy entered the surface positions, we started counterattacks and inflicted heavy casualties on them."[22] Peng recalled: "Our surface defense warfare had transformed itself into an underground, tenacious defense warfare. The actual operations included constructing step by step more underground tunnel fortifications in depth along the 38th Parallel."[23] Peng believed that the CPVF tunnel defense had successfully stopped the UNF attacks like those at Pork Chop Hill (map 8.1).

In mid-October 1952 the Chinese defense tunnels were tested by the sudden onset of the UNF Keumhwa Offensive. The U.S. 7th and ROK 2nd Divisions began intensive shelling of the Chinese positions defended by the CPVF Twelfth and Fifteenth Armies in the Osong Mountain region on October 14. At that time the UNF attacking forces occupied Hills 597.9 and 537.7, two small geographic features known as Triangle Hill in the West and as Shangganling in China.[24] By October 16 the UNF attack had forced Chinese troops off the ridge and into their tunnels. For more than a month, the 29th and 45th Divisions of the Fifteenth Army and the 31st Division of the Twelfth Army, totaling 43,000 troops, fought a seesaw action in a specific pattern. During the day, UNF troops would force the Chinese troops into the tunnels, but at night, the Chinese would counterattack and recover their surface positions, only to lose them again when daylight came. The CPVF Command reinforced the Chinese defense with 2nd and 7th Artillery Divisions,

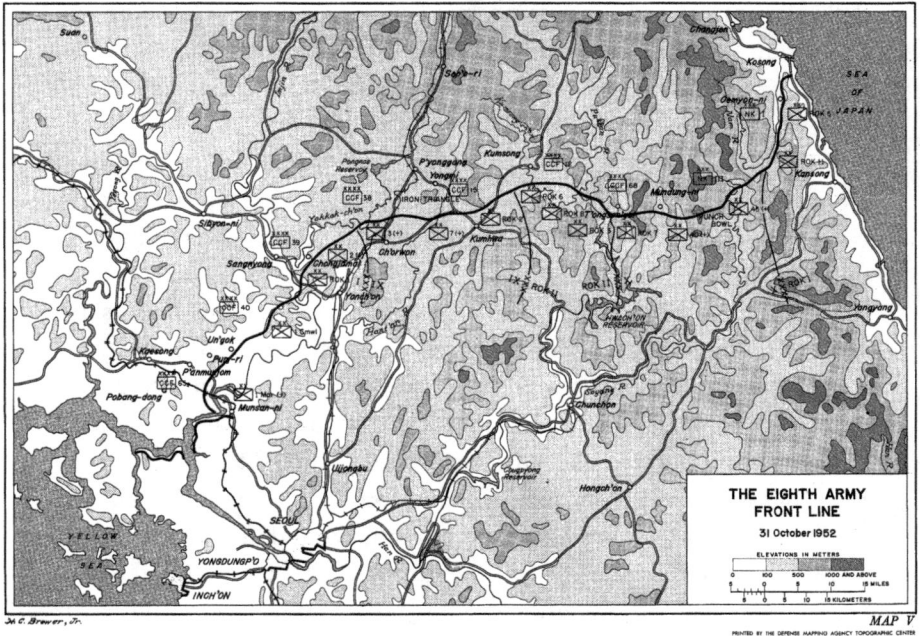

Map 8.1. The Eighth Army Front Line, October 31, 1952

bombing the UNF with 350,000 rounds of shells during the battle.[25] The Battle of Triangle Hill soon turned into one of the bloodiest of the war.

The 45th Division of the CPVF Fifteenth Army was part of the defensive force on the hills. Capt. Zheng Yanman, Eighth Company, 134th Regiment, 45th Division, recalled during an interview that his company was sent to the hill as reinforcements to the tunnel defense on October 18. When his company went underground, Zheng faced major tactical problems. The three tunnels were cut off from each other, and the underground network had suffered severe damage from the attacks. Bodies, shells, and garbage were everywhere, and the soldiers were suffering from severe shortages of supplies, food, and more important, water. Zheng recalled that there were about a hundred soldiers inside the tunnels, remnants from six different companies. About fifty of the men were wounded and had received no medicine or medical assistance. In one of the shelter holes, Zheng found more than twenty corpses. "Nor did anybody care about safety," he said, "and there were seven accidental rifle and two grenade discharges in the tunnels during the first morning after we moved in. I was really mad when I learned that several of my men were wounded by these accidental discharges."[26]

During the night of October 29, the Eighth Company pulled out of the tunnels and moved down the hill. Zheng found it hard to believe that only six men were able to walk down the hill with him: "When we moved up the hill just twelve days ago, I remembered, two hundred young men were running and jumping, full of energy and dreams. Now there were only six of them."[27] At the 134th Regiment HQ, Zheng learned that his regiment had lost most of its leaders. The 45th Division lost many commanders, including 65 percent of its captains, 90 percent of its lieutenants, and 100 percent of its sergeants. The division also lost 8,752 soldiers out of 10,000 men. The Fifteenth Army suffered a total of 15,792 casualties out of 30,000 men from late October to early November, when the Battle of Triangle Hill finally came to an end.[28] The CPVF lost about 180 square miles to the UNF.

Nevertheless, by the end of 1952 Chinese defense forces managed to control the hills without giving up any land. Peng believed that the key to the successful defense was the tunnels, which had played a vital role in defending the positions and preserving the Chinese forces. The success of the Battle of Triangle Hill greatly boosted the Chinese confidence, morale, and determination to defend and maintain the demilitarized zone in the truce negotiations. The CPVF tunnel defense had not only protected Chinese front lines, but it also aided in the Chinese attacks on selected UNF targets. Peng recalled: "With the consolidating and stabilizing of our trench warfare by summer and fall 1951, we began to carry out the chairman's tactic of 'biting sticky candy,' that is, concentrating available manpower and firepower, constructing covert offense launching positions, and then attacking and eliminating one small unit of the enemy forces [each time]."[29] By the end of the war, Peng believed that the CPVF had "developed a whole new set of tactics for active defense in trench warfare. Even with inferior equipment and technology, we could defend our positions when the enemy was attacking. Having been able to conduct both offensive and defensive operations we had the initiative in our hands on the battleground."[30]

## MORE FORCES AND IMPROVED SUPPLY
## AND TRANSPORTATION SYSTEMS

To achieve the dual goals of active defense and limited offensives, Peng demanded more troops from China. In June 1951 the Twentieth Army Group, under the command of Yang Chengwu and consisting of the Sixty-Seventh and Sixty-Eighth Armies, entered Korea. In addition, the Fiftieth Army, which had returned to China in the winter, returned to Korea. Given that the imminent truce talks might restrict future entry of troops, Beijing decided to send more forces into Korea. In September the Twenty-Third Army Group, under the command of Dong Qiwu (1899–1989) and consisting of the Thirty-Sixth and Thirty-Seventh Armies, entered Korea.[31] By October 1951 the number of Chinese troops in Korea had reached its highest point since China had entered the Korean War a year earlier. The CPVF Command had five army groups, consisting of nineteen armies with fifty-six infantry divisions, twelve artillery divisions, and four tank regiments, for a total of 920,000 men. The logistics, transportation, and technical support forces included four railroad engineering divisions, one public security division, fourteen combat engineering regiments, and six supply headquarters, totaling another 220,000 men.

Thus, by the fall of 1951, there were 1.14 million men in the Chinese forces in Korea. Moreover, since September 1951, five divisions of the Chinese Air Force had been put under the CPVF Command. They numbered more than 20,000 men, including ground service personnel. These air force divisions kept their bases inside China, and the pilots flew into Korea only when carrying out missions. By December 1952 Chinese forces in Korea had once again reached a record high: 1.45 million men in fifty-nine infantry divisions, ten artillery divisions, five anti-aircraft divisions, and seven tank regiments.[32] At the same time, the CPVF also commanded some troops within Chinese territory, including the Fifty-Fourth Army, with 50,000 troops, and nine air force divisions, totaling another 40,000 men. Some Chinese naval forces were also engaged in the war. From 1951 to 1953, the PLA Navy had one torpedo-boat brigade and two coast artillery units participating in the war, even though their naval bases were in China. The CPVF numbers remained stable until the armistice agreement was signed in July 1953. Mao had committed nearly one-quarter of China's military strength to North Korea's defense. After the 1951 Spring Offensive, the NKPA also reached its highest number of troops. By 1952 it had six army corps and some local troops, totaling 450,000 men.

Starting in 1952 the PLA began rotating Chinese troops into Korea so they could gain experience in modern warfare. Through this rotation, not only could PLA troops gain experience fighting U.S. forces, but the CPVF troops already in Korea could be relieved for needed rest. The PLA had previously fought against the Japanese Army and Chinese Nationalist Army, but it knew little about the U.S, British, Canadian, and other technologically well-equipped Western forces. Korea became a combat laboratory that offered Chinese officers and soldiers essential combat training. By the end of the war, about 73 percent of the Chinese infantry troops had been rotated into Korea (25 of 34 armies, or 79 of 109 infantry divisions). More than 52 percent of the Chinese air force divisions, 55 percent of tank units, 67 percent of artillery divisions, and all railroad engineering divisions had been sent to Korea. As a result of this process, additional Chinese troops were sent to Korea, including five Chinese air force divisions under the CPVF Command.[33]

The CPVF urgently needed large numbers of weapons and ammunition with the number of Chinese forces in Korea increasing and with the rapid development of trench warfare, especially after the second wave of CPVF forces entered Korea in large numbers. On May 25, 1951, during the third step of the Spring Offensive, Mao sent Xu Xiangqian, chief of the PLA General Staff, and a delegation to Moscow the Soviet Union to purchase weapons and equipment for sixty Chinese divisions (see chapter 3).[34] Xu also intended "to get Soviet assistance for our construction of ordnance factories, the standardization of our infantry's weaponry system, the transfer of technology, and blueprints to produce various artillery pieces below 152 mm in barrel size."[35]

Eventually, the Chinese delegation reached an agreement with the Soviets to borrow $1.34 billion from the Soviet Union, "most of which was spent on the war," as Nie recalled. According to him, "to replace our equipment and weapons completely, we bought enough Soviet-made weapons to arm 100 Chinese divisions. The first part of our purchase provided the weapons and equipment for 37 Chinese divisions.... After that, we gradually replaced our old weapons with Soviet-made weapons in Korea and set up a series of new military industries in China" that were capable of manufacturing Soviet-type weapons and munitions.[36] The Soviet government agreed to deliver the arms for sixty Chinese divisions in 1951–52. Stalin also agreed to provide the CPVF in 1951 with 120 85 mm AAA guns and 2.3 million rounds of AAA shells to protect the CPVF against what was called Operation Air Strangler, a series of increasing U.S. air raids.[37]

Since the Soviet Union did not have sufficient transportation to deliver the arms at once, it shipped the CPVF arms for only sixteen infantry divisions in 1951. By the end of the year, the CPVF had received from the Soviet Union 64,000 rifles, 30,030 automatic rifles, 4,400 light machine guns, 1,900 heavy machine guns, 3,100 mortars, and 2,900 rocket launchers. The arms for the remaining forty-four divisions were delivered in annual installments until 1954.[38]

In early 1952 China shipped more weapons to the CPVF forces in Korea: 24,686 rifles, 104,002 automatic rifles, 33,148 hand guns, 1,833 light and heavy machine guns, 846 mortars, 1,315 rocket launchers, and 1,266 artillery pieces. During that year, the CPVF Logistics Command and the PLA defense industry, working together, repaired more than 75,984 rifles and 14,180 artillery pieces.[39] These repaired weapons were returned to the front-line troops. From June 1952 to June 1953, China sent more weapons to the CPVF forces in Korea, including 20,130 rifles, 95,652 automatic rifles, 58,135 hand guns, 5,732 light machine guns, 465 heavy machine guns, 1,392 60 mm mortars, 1,539 85 mm mortars, 1,276 rocket launchers, and 2,237 artillery pieces. By the end of the war, China had sent the CPVF in Korea 480,000 rifles and 13,000 artillery guns.[40]

With the arrival of Russian-made artillery pieces, the CPVF Command emphasized the role of firepower. By the end of 1951, CPVF combat troops had a total of 6,486 mortars (60–120 mm), 3,122 rocket launchers (90 mm), 1,770 field guns (57–75 mm), 520 howitzers (105–155 mm), 72 Katusha rocket guns, 3,338 anti-aircraft machine guns, 1,136 AAA guns (37–85 mm), and 154 T34 tanks.[41] The Chinese respected their opponents' superior technology, and to narrow the gap, China purchased more modern weapons and equipment from the Soviet Union from 1951 to 1953.[42] Thereafter, Chinese weaponry became standardized. The Soviets also transferred technology for the production of rifles, machine guns, and artillery pieces. In 1952 the CMC made its first "Five-Year Plan for National Defense," focusing on air force, artillery, and tank force development.[43] By that year the CPVF had twelve artillery divisions at the front: four howitzer divisions (the 1st, 2nd, 7th, and 8th Artillery Divisions), four AAA divisions (the 61st, 62nd, 63rd, and 64th Artillery Divisions), two antitank divisions (the 31st and 32nd Artillery Divisions), and two multirocket launcher divisions (the 21st and 22nd Artillery Divisions).

At the end of the Spring Offensive, the front line gradually stabilized. The CPVF improved its logistics and transportation by establishing its own logistics department in Korea in the spring of 1951.[44] The new system improved CPVF logistics capacity at regiment and battalion levels and increased the front-line troops' combat effectiveness.[45] The CPVF had strengthened its organizational work on the logistics supply and transportations. Hong concluded that "after we turned to positional warfare, the front line became relatively stable, our supply headquarters were strengthened a great deal, we improved our transportation and communication methods, and the storage of supplies increased with each passing day."[46]

Starting in the summer of 1951, the CPVF Logistics Department focused on solutions for wartime transportation in Korea. It established the CPVF Railway Command, with He Jinnian as its commander. He commanded four railway engineering divisions, totaling more than 50,000 railroad engineering troops. In 1951 the CPVF Engineering Command was established, with Chen Zhengfeng as its commander. Chen had eleven highway engineering regiments, totaling 48,000 troops.[47] Both railway and highway engineering commands operated under the CPVF Logistics Department and improved the CPVF transportation and communication in Korea. Nie concluded that "the glorious achievement of the CPVF transportation services is one of the major reasons that we won the Korean War."[48] During the second half of 1951, 6,000 Russian trucks arrived in Korea for the CPVF.

By the end of the war, the CPVF Logistics Command had ten railroad engineering divisions, fifteen combat engineering regiments, and five AAA divisions. From 1950 to 1953 the CPVF engineering forces had constructed more than 1,500 miles of new roads and highways and 400 miles of new railways in North Korea. The engineering forces rebuilt and repaired 5,000 miles of roads and highways and 490 miles of railways. They repaired and rebuilt 2,294 bridges. In 1951–53 they also constructed 15,337 buildings, including warehouses, storages, shelters, air defense positions, and train stations.[49] Nie pointed out that "as a result, we consumed an unprecedented amount of war materials. During the first two years, we transported from China to Korea a total of 2.6 million tons of more than 9,000 different kinds of war supplies. Every single campaign consumed enormous quantities of war materials. In the summer offensive of 1953, for instance, a twenty-minute artillery barrage consumed more than 1,900 tons of shells."[50]

In 1952, with improved transportation, the CPVF had increased its ammunition supply to its combat troops and met their needs for their trench warfare. During the Battle of Triangle Hill in October 1952, for instance, the CPVF Fifteenth Army consumed a huge amount of ammunition in defending their trench positions and underground tunnels. On October 14, the first day of their defense, the troops of the Fifteenth Army on Hills 597.9 and 537.7 used nearly 400,000 rounds of bullets. In a one-day defense on October 30, they fired 19,000 rounds of mortar shells. During the forty-three-day Battle of Triangle Hill, the Fifteenth Army used a total of 16,000 tons of supplies. They consumed 5,113.4 tons of ammunition, or approximately 120 tons of ammunition daily. In 1952 China shipped to its forces in Korea a total of 90 million rounds of bullets: 33.4 million rounds of rifle bullets, 48.8 million rounds of automatic rifle bullets, and 7.8 million rounds of machine gun bullets. In 1952 China also sent to the CPVF 3.5 million rounds of artillery shells: 1.11 million rounds of mortar shells, 1.1 million rounds of AAA shells, 732,704 rounds of field artillery shells, 571,214 rounds of howitzer shells, and 35,856 rounds of tank gun shells. During the same year, about 1.67 million grenades, 2,140 tons of explosives, and 2,461 land mines were supplied to Chinese forces in Korea.[51]

In 1953 the CPVF Logistic Department further improved its transportation and was able to supply more ammunition to Chinese combat forces. During the CPVF's Summer Counteroffensive of 1953, the Sixtieth Army consumed 1,398 tons of ammunition during its attacks on June 10–15, more than 279.5 tons of ammunition per day and about 2.5 times more ammunition than that used in the Battle of Triangle Hill the year before. During the Battle of Keumseong—the CPVF's last operation, between July 13 and July 27, 1953—the Chinese logistics department successfully transported 15,000 tons of war materials to the front within one week, including 7,000 tons of artillery shells and 700,000 bullets.[52] On July 13 the CPVF Command assembled more than 1,110 artillery pieces for its pre-attack barrage against the UNF front positions at Keumseong. During the offensive, the CPVF Logistics Department successfully supplied the attacking forces with 30,000 tons of war materials, including 19,000 tons of ammunition and 700,000 artillery shells.[53]

With efficient resupplying, by June 27, 1953, the CPVF forces had stored sufficient ammunition along the first and second defensive lines, including 1.87 million rounds of 82 mm mortar shells, 38,458 rounds of other mortar shells (107–120 mm), 543,845 rounds of field artillery shells, and 61,027 rounds of U.S. 105 mm howitzer shells. At the same time, the CPVF Logistic Department had stored more ammunition in the rear areas in North Korea, including 487,499 rounds of mortar shells (82–120 mm), 409,699 rounds of field artillery shells, and 148,606 rounds of U.S. 105 mm howitzer shells. The CPVF also stored a large amount of ammunition in Manchuria, across the Yalu River from North Korea, including 700,000 rounds of mortar shells (82–120 mm), 257,000 rounds of field artillery shells, 20,000 rounds of Japanese 105 mm howitzer shells, 120,000 rounds of U.S. 105 mm howitzer shells, 90,000 rounds of Russian 122 mm howitzer shells, and 10,000 rounds of U.S. 155 mm howitzer shells.[54]

## ENGAGED CHINESE AND RUSSIAN AIR FORCES

In the fall of 1951 the CPVF began committing its new air force, created on November 11, 1949, to the war in Korea.[55] The development of the Chinese Air Force sped up after the Korean War broke out. Its first division, the Air Force 4th Division, was formed in Nanjing in June 1950, the 3rd in Shenyang in October, and the 2nd in Shanghai in November.[56] By mid-June 1951 the PLA had twenty air force divisions: sixteen fighter divisions, two bomber divisions, and two fighter or bomber divisions. In

March 1951 the CPVF–North Korean Joint Air Force Command was established to conduct air operations in Korea with Liu Zhen (1915–92) as the commander and Chang Qiankun (1904–73) and Wang Lian (NKPA Air Force) as deputy commanders.[57] In September 1951 the 4th Division (MiG-15 fighter division) became the first Chinese air force division deployed at the front under the Joint Air Force Command.[58] By October 1951 the CPVF-NKPA Joint Air Force Command had a total of 450 fighters and bombers for air operations and engagement in Korea.[59]

The 2nd, 3rd, 8th, and 10th Divisions joined the 4th after October, and seven more air force divisions participated in the war through 1953, with 60,000 pilots, ground personnel, and security troops. These air force divisions kept their bases in China proper while their Soviet-trained pilots flew into Korea to carry out their missions. Soviet Air Force officers also coordinated the Chinese and North Korean air operations. By the end of 1953, the PLA had 3,000 fighters and bombers, making China's Air Force the third largest in the world.[60]

Wang Hai (b. 1925) served as the wing (battalion) commander of the PLA Air Force 3rd Division. Born in 1925 to a Christian family in the Fuyin Village, Yantai, Shandong Province, Wang became a Christian when he was six. He participated in the village underground anti-Japanese movement led by the CCP in 1944 and became a CCP member in 1945. Wang enrolled in the Mudanjiang Aviation School, Heilongjiang Province, in June 1946, studying aviation mechanics from Japanese Air Force engineers who had not returned to Japan after WWII. In 1947 Wang began to learn flying with fifteen other student pilots. They had several out-of-date Japanese aircraft and a dozen Japanese veteran instructors. By 1949 their training facilities had been tremendously improved, and in July of that year the CMC delegation traveled to Moscow to sign a deal with the Soviet Union, which agreed to sell 434 military aircraft to the PLA. The Soviets also sent 878 aviation experts to China, helping to establish the PLA Air Force in November, 1949.[61]

On October 20, 1951, fifty MiG-15 jet fighters of the 3rd Division, including six MiG-15s in Wang's wing, moved into the front airport along the Yalu. On the twenty-third, the 3rd Division began engaging U.S. F-80, F-84, and F-86 fighters in North Korea. On November 4 twenty-two MiG-15 fighters of the 7th Regiment ambushed twenty F-80 and

F-84 fighters or bombers over Kaechon. The MiG-15s attacked the F-84s from a high altitude to 12,000 feet and shot down two F-84s—the first time they had defeated an F-84.[62] Wang had his first victory on November 18 when his 9th Regiment attacked twenty F-84s over Sukchon with the support of eighty-eight Soviet fighters. Before pulling out of the front on January 14, 1952, the 3rd Division engaged in twenty-one air-to-air battles and conducted 2,318 sorties.[63] In its second tour, from May 1, 1952, to January 26, 1953, the division had a record thirty-one battles and 1,147 takeoffs. During the two tours, the 3rd Division had forty-four fighters shot down and nineteen damaged. The division lost eighteen pilots, including one regiment commander and six wing commanders.[64]

Wang was shot down once in 1953 but was rescued by peasants after he parachuted into Manchuria. In June 1984 Wang visited the United States and met the joint chiefs of the U.S. armed forces in Washington. He was surprised at the meeting when Gen. Charles A. Gabriel, chief of the U.S. Air Force, told Wang that he had served as an F-86 Sabre pilot in the Korean War from December 1951 to December 1952. They had actually met over the Yalu in an air battle on August 29, 1952.[65] Gabriel visited Beijing and met Wang again in October 1985. In a letter dated June 10, 1992, Gabriel wrote Wang that "my favorite quote is still your Chinese expression: 'From exchanges of blows come good friends.'"[66]

Chinese forces began learning how to combine their air force and their ground operations, although this cooperation was not fully established until the last phase of the Korean War. The first joint effort took place on November 29–30, 1951, when Chinese forces launched an amphibious attack, supported by aircraft, on Dahoo Island, off North Korea's coast. On November 29 the 28th Regiment of the 10th Air Force Division sent ten Tu (Tupolev)–2 bombers to attack the UNF naval warships in the Dahoo harbors. On November 30 the 24th Regiment of the 8th Air Force Division sent nine Tu-2 bombers to Dahoo, bombing the UNF defensive positions on the island. Though the CPVF lost five out of nine bombers during the joint attack, the landing succeeded.[67]

During its participation in the Korean War from September 1951 to July 1953, the Chinese Air Force launched 26,491 sorties, engaged in 366 battles, and shot down 330 UNF planes.[68] The Chinese Air Force lost 339 planes, including 224 MiG-15 and MiG-15bis fighters, and 151 planes were damaged. The Chinese also lost 116 pilots during the air war over Korea.[69] The NKPA had 240 planes in several air force divisions that participated in air battles from 1951 to 1953. North Korea lost about 150 planes.

From November 1950 to July 1953, twelve Soviet Air Force divisions were engaged in the air war, including 72,000 Russian pilots, technicians, ground service members, and anti-air defense troops. In 1952, at the peak of Soviet involvement in the war, 26,000 Russian air force personnel were sent to North Korea under the command of the Soviet Sixty-Fourth Air Force Army. According to official Russian statistics, the Sixty-Fourth Air Force Army launched 63,000 sorties, including 818 large-scale sorties (at or above the regimental scale). More than 2,820 Russian fighter pilots engaged in air battles. The Soviet Air Force Army Command organized 1,400 battles, and Soviet fighters shot down 1,106 UNF planes and damaged 335. Thirty of the UNF planes were shot down in nighttime air combat. And the AAA forces of the Soviet Sixty-Fourth Air Force Army also shot down 212 UNF planes and damaged 10.[70] Thus, the Soviet Air Force shot down 1,318 UNF planes, including 650 F-86 Sabre, F-80 Shooting Star, and F-9F jet fighters. The Soviet Sixty-Fourth Air Force Army lost 345 fighters and more than 200 pilots, with a total of 299 deaths in the Korean War.[71]

To avoid international conflict, the Soviet command transported most of the dead Soviets to China and buried them in the Soviet Red Army Cemetery in Lushun (Port Arthur). Among the 2,030 Soviet graves were those of 142 Russian pilots. Nie concluded: "The Soviets played an important role in the air defense struggle in cooperation with Chinese and Korean troops. In retrospect, the Soviet Union under the leadership of Stalin supported our War to Resist America and Aid Korea both morally and materially."[72]

### NEGOTIATING WHILE FIGHTING

With the war effectively stalemated in Korea, the Soviets were ready for peace talks that would secure North Korea's regime and strengthen the Soviet Union's position in Asia. On June 23, 1951, the Soviet ambassador to the United Nations, Jacob Malik, unexpectedly called the U.S. government's Soviet Union expert, George Kennan, proposing discussions leading to a cease-fire and armistice that would end the Korean conflict. In Beijing the CCP Central Committee discussed the Soviet proposal as well as China's next step in Korea. Most committee members considered it proper that the Chinese forces should stop at the 38th Parallel but continue to fight while China worked toward a negotiated settlement. Chinese leaders believed that they had already achieved their political goal, driving the enemy out of North Korea. Stopping at the 38th Parallel, in fact, was a return to the prewar status quo that was acceptable to the parties in the war. At a meeting presided over by Mao on July 2, the CMC committed to this "dual strategy" for the rest of the war.[73] The Chinese convinced the North Koreans of this new strategy in the summer of 1951.[74] When the Beijing *People's Daily* endorsed the Soviet proposal, it appeared that all the key warring powers except South Korea were willing to negotiate.[75] But ROK President Syngman Rhee adamantly opposed any settlement that would leave Korea divided.[76]

The Truman administration was eager for peace talks. At the MacArthur hearings in early June, Secretary of State Dean Acheson had implied that the United States was willing to accept an armistice based on the 38th Parallel, provided certain conditions were met. Given the green light by Washington, Ridgway followed up with some timely peace feelers. In a radio message on June 30, Ridgway indicated his willingness to name a representative to begin discussions for a cease-fire and armistice. He suggested the meeting take place on a Danish hospital ship in Wonsan Harbor. The Communist reply, signed by Kim Il-sung for North Korea and Peng for the CPVF, came two days later, suggesting that talks begin on July 10 at Kaesong, a neutral city between the two sides' front lines. After Ridgway agreed to the changes, the Korean truce negotiations began.[77]

When the UNF delegation under Vice Adm. Turner C. Joy met the Chinese–North Korean delegation for the first time at Kaesong on July 10, hopes were high for an early end to the fighting. The UNF delegation quickly discovered, however, that the Chinese–North Korean delegation was less interested in achieving peace than they were in using the talks for propaganda purposes and making it seem that the UNF had lost the war. The Communists began by surrounding, and thus bringing under their control, the previously neutral city of Kaesong. When the UNF delegation arrived under a white flag, as previously agreed, the Communists presented this to the world as a token of surrender. When the delegates took their seats, the Communists sat in high chairs, while the UNF delegation sat in low ones. At some meetings, the two delegations sat for hours in silence, glaring at one another across the table. It was an ominous beginning for the peace talks, which were to drag on for more than two years.[78]

During the early weeks of the meetings, the major disagreement on the agenda was about the demarcation line. The Chinese and North Koreans insisted the cease-fire line should be along the 38th Parallel, which the Truman administration had seemed to endorse in January 1951 when first suggesting the peace talks. During the Chinese Spring Offensive in May–June, however, the UNF had moved into areas north of the 38th Parallel, areas that provided a more natural defensive position, and Ridgway insisted the line must be in keeping with the military realities. He did not object to surrendering some areas south of the parallel that could not be easily defended, but he wished to retain a buffer zone established along the general line of battle, much of which was north of the 38th Parallel.[79] In August the negotiations were suspended.

After the UNF took Heartbreak Ridge and Bloody Ridge in bitter fighting, the talks resumed on October 25, 1951. This time, at Ridgway's insistence, they took place at the village of Panmunjom, about midway between the two front lines. Ridgway favored a tough, hard-line position in dealing with the Communists, and he opposed a cease-fire until agreement on the demarcation line had been reached. Washington, however, backed a softer stand to create more favorable conditions for peace. On November 14, after rejecting Ridgway's appeals, the Joint Chiefs of Staff ordered him to "press for an early settlement" of the fighting. Accordingly, Ridgway ordered Van Fleet to cease all major offensive operations and seize only the terrain needed for defense, such as outposts. In this way, the UNF negotiators hoped that the existing main line of resistance could be frozen into the final demarcation line as of the effective date of the armistice. On November 27 the Communists accepted the proposal, but no agreement on a cease-fire was reached. The Chinese instead used the time to strengthen their defensive positions, well aware that the

Western powers were growing increasingly weary of the war, and confident that time was on their side. When the war finally ended nineteen months later, the final demarcation line differed only slightly from the main line of resistance as of the end of 1951.[80]

From late 1951 to early 1953, POW issues were the source of deadlock in the truce negotiations. The UN delegation proposed a voluntary repatriation of POWs, while the Chinese–North Korean delegation insisted on a return of all their prisoners. The issue was made more contentious by the exchange of POW lists, which the Communists had reluctantly agreed to on December 18, 1951. During the early months of the war, the Communists had reported through radio broadcasts and news releases the capture of over 65,000 UNF prisoners. When the UNF delegation received the list, however, they were shocked to learn the Communists held only 7,142 ROK soldiers and 4,417 UNF personnel, for a total of 11,559 prisoners.[81]

On May 7, 1952, in a public statement, President Harry Truman stated bluntly that there would be no "forced repatriation of prisoners of war," despite the insistence of Communists. "We will not buy an armistice by turning over human beings for slaughter or slavery," Truman continued.[82] He could not have made his position more clear. Unfortunately, the Communists were equally adamant on this issue. If a massive number of Communist prisoners declined repatriation and the glories of their system in favor of freedom, this would constitute a major propaganda setback. This is precisely what happened. In April, after screening, the UNF Command reported that only 70,000 of the 132,000 prisoners held in UNF custody were willing to go home. The Communists, of course, found these figures humiliating and totally unacceptable.[83]

The POW issue not only deadlocked the peace negotiations, but it also had other tragic consequences. It played a major role in sparking riots in a number of the UN prison camps in South Korea. One of the worst—and the best known—took place at Koje-do, an isolated, hilly island a few miles from Pusan. The problems at Koje-do began as early as the summer of 1951, when several prisoners were killed inside the compounds. In February 1952 the UNF Command began screening the prisoners one by one to determine who wished to be repatriated to China and North Korea and who did not.[84] This had the effect of increasing the disorder, and riots and murders inside the compounds continued. On May 7, 1952, U.S. Brig. Gen. Francis T. Dodd, commander of the Koje-do POW camps, met with representatives of Compound 76, who abducted him and dragged him into the camp. Brig. Gen. Charles F. Colson took command and, after negotiating with the Communist prisoners, managed to secure the release of Dodd on May 10, but only after Dodd had signed a humiliating confession. The entire affair received intense media coverage and amounted to a major propaganda victory for the Communists. Order gradually returned to the camps, in part because many of the American and ROK guards were replaced with other UNF troops.[85]

Despite the continuing fighting, by the spring of 1953 there were some positive signs in favor of an armistice. The new U.S. president, former Gen. Dwight D. Eisenhower, publicly stated his determination to do everything possible to bring the war to an end. Accordingly, the U.S. government dropped hints that if the deadlock in the peace negotiations was not broken quickly, the Chinese Nationalists could be unleashed to invade the mainland, and the United States might use atomic bombs to end the war. Eisenhower wrote in his memoirs that after this, the "prospects for armistice negotiations seemed to improve."[86] Stalin's death on March 5, however, probably had more to do with improving the prospects for peace than Eisenhower's threats did. Only ten days after the death of Stalin, the new Soviet leader, Georgy M. Malenkov, seemed to extend an olive branch when he declared there was no existing dispute between Moscow and Washington that could not be peacefully solved. Eisenhower replied in a cautiously worded speech, challenging Malenkov to match his words with deeds, including "an honorable peace" in Korea.[87]

From March 7 to 24, Prime Minister and Foreign Minister Zhou Enlai led a delegation of Chinese government officials and CCP leaders to Moscow to attend Stalin's funeral. According to Chen Jian, Zhou held extensive discussions with the new Soviet leaders, including Malenkov, Nikita Khrushchev, Lavrenty Beria, Vyacheslav Molotov, and Nikolay Bulganin, and talked about how to end the Korean War. Chen points out that "the result of these discussions was a consensus that 'the Chinese and North Korean side was now in a position to conclude the war on the basis of reasonable compromises with the enemy.' Recently released Russian sources also confirm that, while Zhou was in Moscow for Stalin's funeral, the Chinese and the Soviets worked out a common stand to 'speed up the negotiations and the conclusion of an armistice' in Korea."[88]

For all these reasons, an armistice became more likely. The big break came on March 28, 1953, when Chinese and North Korean negotiators unexpectedly agreed to an earlier International Red Cross proposal for an exchange of sick and wounded POWs. Two days later, Zhou issued a statement that promised a breakthrough on the POW issue, suggesting that all POWs who did not wish to be repatriated should be turned over to a neutral state.[89] On April 20 the UNF Command delivered 6,670 sick and wounded North Korean and Chinese prisoners, receiving 684 UNF prisoners in exchange.[90] Maj. Gen. Chai Chengwen, secretary general of the CPVF at the Panmunjom talks, describes the resumption of the truce negotiations: "On April 26, more than 100 reporters from all over the world gathered outside the negotiating tent at Panmunjom. At 11:00 AM the representatives from both delegations walked into the tent again. The negotiating talks restarted after a break of six months and eighteen days."[91] This was clearly a sign that the Chinese were ready for peace.

The negotiators at Panmunjom were now able to carry on discussions with the serious intent of breaking the deadlock on the POWs. There were still many problems, however, such as determining which of the neutral nations would assume the responsibility for those POWs who did not wish to return home. Finally, on June 7, the negotiators came to an agreement on this difficult issue. Based on a proposal made earlier by India, prisoners who did not wish to be repatriated would be turned over to a five-member Neutral Nations Repatriation Commission. The commission would assume responsibility for these prisoners for a maximum of 120 days and, if necessary, attempt to relocate them. The road was now clear for an armistice.[92]

Not surprisingly, as the two sides drew closer together in trying to work out the last details, Syngman Rhee became a major obstacle to a settlement. Rhee was opposed to any armistice that did not provide for a united Korea, with him in control. In April he had even threatened to withdraw the ROK forces from UNF Command and continue the war alone. He made radio broadcasts, staged mass rallies, and issued press releases—all aimed at undermining the talks. More seriously, on June 18 he directed ROK prison guards to release approximately 25,000 North Korean prisoners who had refused repatriation. Not surprisingly, the prisoners quickly disappeared into the hills of South Korea. Although infuriated, Communist negotiators did not allow Rhee's action to sabotage the peace negotiations. But on June 20 Peng suggested to Mao that the date for signing the truce be postponed in order to have time to inflict 15,000 more casualties on Rhee's troops. Mao agreed that signing the truce must be postponed.[93] A few days later Rhee promised that although he would not sign the armistice, he would not obstruct it either.[94]

On July 23, 1953, staff officers reached agreement on the final demarcation line, and the stage was set for the signing of the Korean Armistice. At 9:57 AM on a windy July 27, the delegates entered the building at Panmunjom from opposite sides and took their places behind the tables in an atmosphere that has been described as "marked by cold courtesy on both sides."[95] Gen. William K. Harrison for the UNF and Gen. Nam Il for North Korea sat down without a word of greeting and began to sign the first of nine copies of the armistice. By 10:12 AM the signing was completed, and the two men departed through their separate exits as silently as they had entered. In the distance the sound of artillery could still be heard; both sides continued heavy shelling until 10:00 PM that night, when the armistice went into effect. At that moment the sky suddenly lit up with dozens of multicolored flares, signifying the end of the war. It was two years and seventeen days since the talks had begun.[96]

On July 27 the Chinese–North Korean delegation issued a statement: "Both sides in the truce negotiations have completely reached the Korean Armistice Agreement. Both sides also agreed that the Truce Agreement will be signed first by our delegation's chief representative General Nam Il and the other delegation's chief representative Lieutenant General Harrison at ten o'clock (local time) in the morning of July 27 at Panmunjom, Korea. Then, they will send the Truce Agreement respectively to Marshal Kim Il-sung, NKPA supreme commander, General Peng Dehuai, CPVF commander, and General Clark, UN commander, for their signatures."[97] The same day, Nam went to Pyongyang (P'yŏngyang) with the original document of the armistice. At 10:00 PM

Kim Il-sung signed the armistice at the premier's mansion. At 9:30 AM on July 28, Peng signed it at the CPVF delegation's meeting room in Kaesong.[98] Later, he wrote about his feelings at that moment: "When I signed the armistice, I was thinking that we had already created a precedent for many others that would exist for years to come. This [cease-fire] sounded laudable to the peoples [of the world]. I, however, felt a bit disappointed because we had just become so well organized for combat. We had not fully used our might to deliver bigger blows to the enemy."[99]

On August 5, in accordance with agreements reached during the negotiations, the prisoner exchange, known as Operation Bid Switch, began at Panmunjom. The Communists had returned 3,597 Americans by the time the exchange ended on September 6.[100] Twenty-one Americans refused repatriation and went to China.[101] Among the 21,300 Chinese POWs, 7,110 were repatriated to China in three different groups in September and October.[102] Roughly another 14,200 Chinese prisoners went to the ROC.[103]

After the Korean Armistice Agreement was signed on July 27, 1953, the CPVF Command began to schedule its troops' withdrawal from North Korea. The first CPVF withdrawal took place in 1954–55: seven divisions returned to China between September 16 and October 3, 1954; six between March 31 and April 20, 1955; and six more divisions between October 10 and 26, 1955. The bulk of the CPVF withdrawal completed in 1958: six divisions returned to China between March 16 and April 25, and six more divisions between July 11 and August 14. Finally, the CPVF General HQ and the last three divisions, totaling 70,000 troops, returned to China by October 25, 1958, the eighth anniversary of China's War to Resist the United States and Aid Korea.[104]

# Conclusion: What China Learned

BETWEEN 1950 AND 1953, MORE THAN 2.4 MILLION CHINESE troops participated in the Korean War. In addition, twelve air force divisions participated in the war, including 672 pilots and 59,000 ground service personnel. China also sent 600,000 civilian laborers to Korea. They entered Korea and worked in logistical supply, support services, and railroad and highway construction. Thus, a total of 3.1 million Chinese "volunteers" eventually participated in the Korean War.[1] The course of the war was never the same after China intervened. Allan Millett, Bin Yu, and I conclude that "observers had every reason to believe that, although the PRC government did not declare war on any foreign country and the Chinese forces entered Korea in the name of the Volunteers, this war, in fact, was the largest foreign war in Chinese military history."[2] It appears that Mao Zedong felt he had few political alternatives to sending Chinese troops to Korea, if he wanted the full acceptance of the Communist world in the early 1950s. His alliance with the Soviet Union and North Korea pulled China into a war in Korea that changed the Chinese military forever. China's intervention in the Korean War was a by-product of the Cold War between two superpowers. With that intervention, China became the leader of the Communist camp in Asia.

After the Chinese-American confrontation in Korea, China and East Asia became a focal point of the global Cold War. Although that war was dominated by the confrontation between the United States and the Soviet Union, China's position in the Cold War after Korea was not peripheral but, in many key senses, central.[3] In retrospect, China's early Cold War experience—as exemplified in China's participation in the

Korean War—not only contributed significantly to shaping the specific course of the Cold War in Asia but also, and more importantly, helped create conditions for the Cold War to remain "cold" by being positioned between the two superpowers. The active role that China played in East Asia turned this main Cold War battlefield into a sort of buffer between Moscow and Washington. With China and East Asia in the middle, it was less likely that the Soviet Union and the United States would become involved in a direct military confrontation.[4] Some Western historians agree that the alliance between Beijing and Moscow was the cornerstone of the international Communist alliance system in the 1950s.[5]

For China, the Cold War was not a cold war; it was a hot war. China's Cold War was primarily military. The PLA's fighting in the Korean War reshaped China's relations with the Soviet Union and the United States, giving the PRC a belligerent outlook. China's intervention in the Korean War transformed the Cold War from a bipolar standoff in the 1950s to multiple-front confrontations in the 1960s and made the competition between the two superpowers less significant.

From October 19, 1950, to July 27, 1953, confronted by U.S. air and naval superiority, the CPVF suffered heavy casualties, including Mao's son, Mao Anying (1922–50), a Russian translator at the CPVF General HQ who died in an air raid.[6] According to Chinese military records, Chinese casualties in the Korean War break down as follows: 183,108 dead, 383,218 wounded, 455,199 hospitalized, 21,400 POWs, and 4,221 missing in action, totaling 1,047,146 casualties.[7] The Chinese soldiers who served in the Korean War faced a greater chance of being killed or wounded than those who served in either WWII or the Chinese Civil War. But China did not withdraw its forces from Korea until 1958. At that point, the CPVF had been in Korea for eight years since its first entry in October 1950—two years and nine months of actual combat, and five years and three months after the Korean Armistice was signed on July 27, 1953. The Korean War was the first time Chinese armed forces engaged in large-scale military operations outside of China. Thinly disguised by the title of "volunteers," the Chinese military went all-out in engaging one of the best militaries in the world. The Korean War was the only meaningful reference point for sustained PLA contingency operations beyond China's border. The Chinese generals recalled their fighting in the Korean War as a heroic rescue and an extension of their own struggle against world imperialism. Chinese history books portray China as a "beneficent victor" of the Korean War. Peter Gries observes that "to many Chinese, Korea marks the end of the 'Century of Humiliation' and the birth of 'New China.'"[8]

The PRC spent about 10 billion yuan (equal to $3.3 billion according to the exchange rate at that time) on the war. The Chinese government transported into Korea 5.6 million tons of goods and supplies during the intervention and lost 399 airplanes, 12,916 tanks and other vehicles, 4,371 artillery pieces, and 87,559 guns.[9] In the years 1950 through 1953, China's military spending represented 41 percent, 43 percent, 33 percent, and 34 percent, respectively, of the government's total budget.[10] Neverthe-less, Mao judged China's intervention a victory because it saved North Korea's Communist regime, shaped China's relations with the Soviet Union, and secured China's northeastern border by preventing North Korea from being conquered or controlled by the United States or an-other Western power. The military intervention in Korea gave China a permanent influence in East Asia. It had improved the CCP's interna-tional status and projected a powerful image of China leading Commu-nist countries against the United States.[11] China's increasing political ambition and rising international position demanded a strong, modern military to enhance "China's prestige and influence in the international arena."[12]

Peng Dehuai stated that the Korean War began the transformation of the Chinese military into a modern force.[13] Peng made important stra-tegic and tactical changes to the CPVF after the 1951 Spring Offensive as the CPVF adjusted to changing conditions and continually reassessed its own performance. The Spring Offensive was the most important battle in the Korean War. It was the most decisive battle between Chi-nese and U.S. forces because the UNF employed its superior technology while the Chinese used the full power of their human resources. The battle resulted in 105,000 Chinese casualties and took away any further chance for the Chinese to initiate a major new offensive to cross the 38th Parallel. The Spring Offensive was thus a tragic defeat for the Chinese.

The lessons learned from the Spring Offensive had an impact on subsequent developments in China, including Mao's strategy and tactics of revolutionary war, China's decisions during the rest of the Korean War, the PLA modernization, civil-military relations, and China's decision to make its own atomic bombs. The first lesson of the Spring Offensive taught Mao to change his goal from driving the UNF out of Korea to a more modest one of defending the security of China and ending the war with a negotiated settlement. From the conclusion of the Spring Offensive until the end of the war, the CPVF adopted more cautious and realistic strategies, such as replacing mobile warfare with trench warfare; scaling down its objective from targeting multiple UNF divisions to attacking one battalion during each campaign; and maintaining a relatively stable front line. After the Korean War, the Chinese generals were convinced that Chinese armed forces were still a regional and not a global force, and that China would fight limited wars in terms of both theaters of war and geopolitical objectives. This would force the PLA to confront the continued relevance of China's traditional approach, even though China had moved into the central stage of the international Cold War.

Because the failure of the PLA in the Spring Offensive demonstrated the limits of Chinese military power, from then on Chinese leaders used the PLA only for border security operations. Because China had not won a decisive victory in Korea, it learned not to use its newfound strength to rush headlong into new conflicts. In the sixty years since the Korean War ended, China has never waged a total war or made such a major commitment to an intervention. Rather, it has limited its conflicts to small-scale ones, such as artillery bombardments of the GMD-held offshore islands in 1954–55 and 1958, a four-week surgical attack on India in 1962, supporting operations north of the 20th Parallel in North Vietnam in 1965–68, limited border conflicts with the Soviet Union in 1969–71, and a four-week invasion of Vietnam in 1979.[14] The limited objectives saved the overconfident and unprepared PLA again and again from a humiliating defeat like its 1951 Spring Offensive, when it took on a foe in challenging terrain.

Mao died in 1976, and Deng Xiaoping (1904–97) came to power in 1978 as a member of the second generation of CCP leadership. Deng became the chairman of the CMC and reinstalled himself as the chief of the PLA General Staff in 1982. The high command faithfully supported

Deng's leadership. He carried on the strategy of limited war and told the Chinese military that the PLA needed to contemplate a new and different international environment and must participate in China's ongoing reforms.[15] In 1985 Deng explained his strategic thoughts to the high-ranking commanders. First, the Chinese armed forces should expect a "local war" or a "limited war" rather than a "total war" or a "nuclear war" in the future. Second, the next "local war" or "limited war" needed a professional army with modern technology. This was another strategic transition, from Mao's "people's war" doctrine to a new "people's war under modern conditions" doctrine.[16]

After the events in Tiananmen Square in the summer of 1989, Jiang Zemin (b. 1926) came to the power as a member of the third generation of CCP leadership. In November of the same year, he became chairman of the CMC at the Fifth Plenary Session of the CCP Thirteenth Central Committee.[17] As the PLA's first civilian commander in chief, Jiang used the authority of that position to assume the top post as chairman of the CCP and CMC and president of the country. In the 1990s Jiang launched another round of military reforms known as the "two transformations." First, the PLA would be changed from an army prepared for "local wars under ordinary conditions" to an army prepared to fight and win "local wars under modern high-tech conditions." Second, the PLA would be transformed from an army based on quantity to one based on quality.[18] Jiang's doctrine of fighting "local wars under modern high-tech conditions" became the guideline for the PLA's institutional reforms under the third generation of the high command.[19] Thus, the limited war strategy developed after the 1951 Spring Offensive continued through the generations of the Chinese military leadership.

The second lesson of the Spring Offensive was that the technology gap between the adversaries and poor logistics had contributed to China's failure. Thereafter, the CPVF emphasized the role of technology and firepower, increasing its air force, artillery, and tank units and beefing up its logistical operations. To narrow the technology gap, China purchased enough weapons and equipment from the Soviet Union to arm sixty infantry divisions in 1951–54.[20] As the result, Chinese weaponry was standardized. The Soviets also shared technology for the production of rifles, machine guns, and artillery pieces. By the end of 1955, the PLA had armed 106 infantry divisions, 9 cavalry and security divisions, 17 artillery divisions, 17 AAA divisions, and 4 tank and armored divisions with Soviet weapons. These included 800,000 automatic rifles, 11,000 artillery pieces, and 3,000 tanks and armored vehicles. By 1957 the Army had completed its standardization program.

The PLA Navy also armed nine gunboat brigades with 200 Soviet-made vessels. With Soviet technology and training, the Navy established a submarine force in June 1954. By the end of 1955, the Navy had 500 gunboats, 300 support vessels, and 300 heavy coastal artillery pieces.[21] The PLA Air Force armed thirty-three divisions with Soviet equipment and technology and relied almost exclusively on Soviet-designed aircraft. From 1951 to 1955, China purchased 5,000 Russian aircraft.[22] Nonetheless, Jeanne Wilson points out that the Soviet Union sought to keep China's armed forces dependent on the Soviets to prevent China from developing connections with the West.[23] For example, the Soviet leaders offered fighter and bombers to the PLA Air Force, but they did not allow schematics or any type of production information to be passed to the Chinese. This forced the Chinese military leaders to keep turning to their northern neighbors for military supplies. Throughout the 1950s, China spent about $2 billion on arms purchases. For Peng, who became China's first defense minister in 1954, there was no other way to supply the navy and air force.[24]

Technology took an increasingly large part of China's military budget through the 1950s. While the Army's infantry troops decreased from 61.1 percent of its total in 1950 to 42.3 percent in 1958, its artillery units increased from 20.4 percent in 1950 to 31.9 percent in 1958; tank units increased from less than 1 percent to 4.8 percent in 1958; and engineering units increased from 1.6 percent in 1950 to 4.4 percent in 1958. The Air Force had increased to 12.2 percent of the PLA's total forces and the Navy to 5.8 percent by 1958.[25]

The possibility of an American nuclear attack on China during the Korean War posed new challenges to the Chinese military. Gen. Douglas MacArthur's threat of using atomic weapons against Chinese troops in North Korea and Northeast China in 1951 and President Dwight Eisenhower's new policy of "rolling back" and "massive retaliation"[26] with nuclear bombs were of immediate concern to Beijing in 1952–53.

With no strategic weapons, China had to depend on nuclear protection from the Soviet Union, which had developed atomic weapons in the late 1940s. After Stalin's death, Soviet Cold War policy changed, and Moscow called for a relaxation of international tensions and peaceful coexistence between the Communist camp and the free world. The Soviet Union complained about the aggressive Chinese actions in 1954 and expressed its unwillingness to use its atomic weapons in case of U.S. retaliation against the PLA's amphibious operations in the Taiwan Strait in 1955. Beijing felt nuclear pressures from both superpowers: an increasing nuclear threat from the United States and decreasing protection from the Soviet Union's nuclear umbrella. It became apparent that China could not ensure its own national defense or avoid international humiliations without its own nuclear weapons.[27] Furthermore, a great country like China needed its own nuclear weapons to demonstrate its abilities, achievements, and prosperity and to improve its status on the world stage. In January 1955 China began its first nuclear weapons program, known as Project 02. In 1960 the first Chinese-made missile was launched in China's northwestern desert, with China's first nuclear bomb test following on October 16, 1964, and its first hydrogen bomb on June 17, 1967. Less than fifteen years after the Korean War, China had become a nuclear power.[28]

The new generations of the Chinese military leadership continue to emphasize the importance of military science and technology. Jiang stated clearly at the beginning of the twenty-first century that "we should energetically push forward a Revolution of Military Affairs with Chinese characteristics, so as to ensure that our armed forces keep up with the current rapid developments in science, technology, and Revolution of Military Affairs." Jiang made the PLA's information-based capability the key for China's military modernization. He also said that promoting "a Revolution of Military Affairs" would bring about profound changes to every aspect of the Chinese army-building program.[29] In November 2002, when Jiang retired, Hu Jintao (b. 1942) became chairman of the CCP at the Sixteenth CCP National Congress. In March 2003, at the Sixth National People's Congress, Hu was elected president of the PRC. In September 2004 Jiang gave up command of the Chinese military at the Fourth Plenary Session of the Sixteenth CCP National Congress.

Hu then became the new civilian commander in chief of the PLA, as a member of the fourth generation of the Chinese leadership. He nurtured a relationship with the PLA by supporting the growing military professionalism with an emphasis on improvements in technology. Hu stated that the PLA should use different methods of warfare in future conflicts, including a high-tech approach to circumvent the enemy's strength and to confront the enemy in ways it would not be able to match. Thus China would "not be intimidated by a military superpower," and China's foreign policy would "not be constrained by its military weakness."[30] According to Hu and his new high command, the PLA should make a "leap-over" transition from an army with mechanical and semimechanical equipment to an army equipped with digital facilities.

The third lesson of the Spring Offensive was that to apply new technology and weaponry, the PLA needed to professionalize itself. Thus it launched a reform movement in the 1950s. Following the Soviet model, the Chinese reform included major institutional changes, a centralized command system, advanced training and educational programs, the establishment of a ranking system, and the reorganization of the country's defense industries. Soviet support in military affairs was critical for the PLA's modernization and professionalism. If it was the Soviet model that had shaped the revolutionary and Communist nature of the new China, it was Russian aid and military technology that helped the Chinese military transform itself in the early 1950s from a peasant rebellion army into a professional, regular force. The military reform eventually transformed the PLA, as Ellis Joffe writes, "from a guerrilla army with antiquated equipment and outdated tactics into a fairly modern and professional army" in the 1950s.[31]

Throughout the last half of the twentieth century, the armed forces of the CCP consisted of rural conscripts and volunteers who collectively had little formal education. The PLA had been a peasant army: as many as 67.4 percent of its officers in 1951 were illiterate. Only 16.4 percent of all the ranks and files could pass the third-grade literature test in that year.[32] In other words, the majority of the PLA generals, commanders, and officers could not read or write.[33] After 1951 the PLA established an officer training system from a primary to an advanced level. This curriculum and training trend moved the PLA away from traditional peasant army and guerrilla warfare tactics toward large-scale operations.[34] Secondary or higher education and professional training are critical for the officer corps in a professional army. The PLA also opened new military academies and colleges across the country. By 1959 it had 129 military academies, including 26 war colleges, 72 technology institutes, and 16 cadet schools, with a total enrollment of 253,000 officer students.[35]

When Peng became defense minister, he created a highly centralized command structure by reorganizing the PLA's field armies into regional military commands—in other words, turning mobile armies or "nomadic troops," into regional armies or "residential troops."[36] In the 1950s the Chinese military had six grand regional commands, for the eastern, northern, northeastern, northwestern, southwestern, and south central regions of the country. Each region was further subdivided into several provincial commands.[37]

As part of his reforms, Peng also established a Soviet-style system of military ranks in 1955. Some of the CCP leaders opposed the new ranking system since it changed the PLA tradition of equality among soldiers and commanders. However, Mao approved the system and awarded the rank of marshal to ten top PLA commanders: Peng Dehuai, Zhu De, Nie Rongzhen, Lin Biao, Chen Yi, Xu Xiangqian, Liu Bocheng, Ye Jianying, He Long, and Luo Ronghuan. No one else ever received that rank. In May 1992 Nie, the last surviving marshal, died, and currently the highest military rank in China is general. On September 27, 1955, Premier Zhou Enlai appointed 10 grand generals and 57 generals. Then the military regional commands appointed 175 lieutenant generals, 800 major generals, and 32,000 colonels and majors. Between 1955 and 1966, an additional 5 generals, 2 lieutenant generals, and 560 major generals were promoted from within the services.[38] Marshal Lin criticized Peng's reform and the PLA ranking system as part of the "Soviet revisionist military structure."[39] After he succeeded Peng as defense minister, Lin abolished the ranking system in 1966.

Ironically, while the PLA was becoming more institutionalized as the result of the reforms in the 1950s, the CCP and Chinese society was becoming more radicalized and ideological. The gap between the army and the party caused a series of political problems, which eventually terminated the reform programs in the early 1960s. Chinese military reform took place only within the greater context of a newly founded republic and within the constraints of how far the Communist Party was willing to go and what Chinese society at large could support. The revolutionary society emphasized ideological factors, the human spirit, and independence, and was characterized by irrational decisions and extremist programs. In contrast, the military favored technological improvements, institutional control, rational decisions, regular programs, and more dependence on Russian aid. The political gap divided the military leaders and resulted in their having different opinions about Chinese military modernization. Peng was among the first of the top Chinese leaders to be purged by Mao in 1959 because of his opposition to the latter's unrealistic domestic economic program.

Thus, some of the elements in Chinese military culture and Communist ideology survived the Korean War and have remained unchanged since 1951. The new leadership in Beijing will not abandon the deliberate approach to military reform that previous generations employed with success. One of the surviving elements is the party's control of the PLA. To keep the military under control, a continuing coalition between the PLA and the CCP is necessary. At the National People's Congress in 2005, Hu's vision for "harmony and innovation"[40] became government policy for China's further development. To achieve harmony in China in the modern era, it is important to build on the country's long and rich traditions and preserve them in innovative ways. The PLA needs to follow the fundamental principle of absolute Communist Party leadership over the armed forces. In other words, the PLA should support the Hu administration by showing its loyalty to the Party Center. The army's ranks and files should value social harmony, share Communist views, and live with them as social norms. The high command needs to contribute in various ways to promote social harmony. In this socioeconomic climate, the concept of harmony is becoming increasingly important to Chinese society as well as the rest of the world.

The PLA still belongs to the Communist Party since the latter controls the resources for the military's budget and individual promotions for professional careers in the military. Since the state has adapted well to economic and social changes and effectively responded to the rising demands and expectations of the PLA, its political institutions may be able to manage some of the discontent or different opinions within the PLA in the near future.[41] In the past two decades, growing disparities in wealth and increasing social and political tensions within China, as well as international conflicts, have caused a new set of challenges for China's sustained development.

Another surviving element is the importance of the human factor in warfare, and the tactic of the massed attack continues to play a critical role in Chinese military strategy. On February 17, 1979, for example, the PLA sent 220,000 troops to invade Vietnam. Many of the PLA's commanding officers were shocked by the high casualties in their offensive campaigns. During nineteen days of attacks, the PLA suffered 26,000 casualties, about 1,350 men per day.[42] Gerald Segal points out that "in contrast to Korea, Chinese troops performed poorly. In Korea, they adequately defended North Korea, but in 1979 they failed to punish Vietnam."[43] During the 1979 Sino-Vietnamese War, 37,300 Vietnamese troops were killed, and 2,300 were captured.[44]

Very few Chinese became POWs in 1979. Before the Chinese invaded Vietnam, all PLA infantrymen received a little metal box, like a tiny candy can, with a ring. First Lt. Xu Xiangyao recalled that it was their "personal glory bomb." "Keep it in your left pocket," he told the author that the men were instructed. "If you are wounded, disabled, or about to be captured by the Vietnamese, you can use it. Just pull the ring: it will explode for an immediate, heroic death. You will be remembered as a revolutionary martyr."[45] The men knew that they would commit suicide rather than surrender in shame. The "glory bomb" brought back the fear of danger and death to the men. The haughty tank men seemed to treat the "glory bomb" as a joke, laughing at it as if this suicide device was just for infantrymen.[46] This is one of the lessons that the PLA learned incorrectly from the Korean War. It was no surprise when Chen Fuliang's wife told the author that her husband was lucky to have become one of the Korean War POWs.

Our historical overview shows the changing characteristics of the PLA in recent years. The analysis includes three elements of the process by which the Chinese military transformed itself from a peasant army to a professional one. The first element is the human resources available for military reforms. The stories about peasant soldiers help us understand how their values, duties, and concerns affected the military as an institution. The PLA is firmly entrenched in the PRC and is one of the few organizations whose past is still praised. The second element is the pressure for reform in spite of Chinese society's backward technology, poor living standards, lack of education and professional training, and authoritarian government. The third is the military's ability to compromise with the country while shaping both Chinese and international views of the PLA. The objective of this analysis has been to present the national interests, security concerns, perceived threats, and international conditions that made up the context of Chinese military reform.

The analysis provides an interpretation of changing military culture that defines the unique characteristics of the PLA. These characteristics unique to the Chinese military through history have evolving features that transformed the PLA from a traditional Chinese army to a modern world-class force. The Chinese army survived the Cold War in 1946–91 and succeeded in China's economic reform in the 1980s through the 2000s. Whether or not the military leaders of the new generation are eventually accepted by the Communist Party and government as leading actors, they will help shape China's domestic and foreign policies in the future.

In November 2012 Xi Jinping (b. 1953) became the chairman of the CCP at the Party's Eighteenth National Congress, as a member of the fifth generation of leaders. As the new commander in chief of the PLA, Xi faces more opportunities and challenges, and more hopes and difficulties, in 2012–22. The new leaders will seek a growing role on the global political stage while assuring the international community that China is not pursuing a policy of military and political hegemony in any conventional sense. However, while China is repositioning itself as a new center of gravity in the Asia-Pacific region, its new demands may create problems. A possible source of crisis is the highly sensitive and increasingly disputed islands in the South China Sea and the Pacific, where Japan, the Philippines, and Vietnam may make bolder moves leading toward an armed clash. The PLA needs to develop new strategies and tactics to deal with a possible crisis.

# Notes

### INTRODUCTION

1. I was the academic consultant on the Australian documentary film *Kapyong*. I traveled with Dennis K. Smith, the director, and his crew to, interview Chinese veterans in Beijing, Shanghai, Nanjing, Suzhou, Shenyang, Changchun, and Dandong in March–April 2008. The documentary was released in 2011 and is available online.

2. Pvt. Chen Fuliang's family members, interview by the author in Shangzhuang, Lishui County, Jiangsu, March 13–14, 2008. Chen served as an army private in the Third Company, 176th Regiment, 59th Division, Twentieth Army, Ninth Army Group of the Chinese People's Volunteers Force (CPVF) in the Korean War. He was captured by the United Nations Force (UNF) during the Chinese Spring Offensive Campaign in May 1951.

3. Chen Xiuying, daughter of Chen Fuliang, interview by the author in Shangzhuang, Lishui County, Jiangsu, March 13–14, 2008.

4. He Ming, *Zhongcheng: zhiyuanjun zhanfu guilai renyuan de kanke jingli* [Loyalty: the hard time for the CPVF POWs after their repatriation] (Beijing: Zhongguo wenshi chubanshe, 1998), 1–2. Maj. Gen. He (PLA, ret.) served as the political commissar of the 193rd Division, Sixty-Fifth Army, Nineteenth Army Group of the CPVF during the Korean War. See also Zhang Zeshi, "Wo cengshi zhiyuanjun zhanfu daibiao [I served as the CPVF POWs' representative]," in *Jimidang* [Classified files], ed. *Fenghuang zhoukan* [Phoenix weekly] (Beijing: Zhongguo fazhan chubanshe, 2011), 2:338–39. Staff Sergeant Zhang (PLA ret.) served in the 180th Division, Sixtieth Army, Third Army Group of the CPVF during the Korean War. He was captured by the UNF during the Chinese Spring Offensive Campaign in May 1951.

5. Da Ying, *Zhiyuanjun zhanfu jishi: xuji* [Voices from the CPVF POWs: concluding volume] (Beijing: Zhongguo qingnian chubanshe, 1993), 92.

6. Quoted in Xu Yan, *Mao Zedong yu kangmei yuanchao zhanzheng* [Mao Zedong and the WRUSAK], 2nd ed. (Beijing: Jiefangjun chubanshe, 2006), 3; Chu Yun, *Chaoxian zhanzheng neimu quangongkai* [Declassifying the Korean War] (Beijing: Shishi chubanshe, 2005), 161; Shen Zhihua, "China Sends Troops to Korea: Beijing's Policy-Making Process," in *China and the United States: A New Cold War History*, ed. Xiaobing Li and Hongshan Li (Lanham, MD: University Press of America, 1998), 13.

7. Chen Hui, "18 wan kangmei yuanchao lieshi xunzong [Tracing the 180,000 martyrs of the WRUSAK]," in *Kangmei yuanchao: 60 nianhou de huimou* [The WRUSAK:

a retrospective look after 60 years], ed. Zhang Xingxing (Beijing: Dangdai zhongguo chubanshe, 2011), 127; Li Qingshan, *Zhiyuanjun yuanchao jishi* [The CPVF records of aiding Korea] (Beijing: Zhonggong dangshi chubanshe, 2008), 13; Shuang Shi, *Kaiguo diyi zhan: kangmei yuanchao zhanzheng quanjing jishi* [The first war since the founding of the state: the complete story of the WRUSAK] (Beijing: Zhonggong dangshi chuban-she, 2004), 2:836–37.

8. Xi Jinping, "Zai jinin zhongguo renmin zhiyuanjun kangmei yuanchao chuguo zuozhan 60 zhounian zuotanhui shangde jianghua [Speech at the sixtieth anniversary celebration of the CPVF's participation in the WRUSAK]," *Renmin ribao* [People's daily], October 26, 2010, http://paper.people.com.cn/rmrb/html/2010–10/26.

9. In a telegram to Zhou Enlai, who was in Moscow, Mao agreed on October 14, 1950, to send 260,000 Chinese troops to Korea at once. And Mao's telegram to Stalin on November 13, 1950, informed the Soviet leaders that China was sending eight more divisions to Korea. See Mao Zedong, "Zhiyuanjun ruchao zuozhan de fangzhen he bushu [The strategy and plan for the CPVF's warfighting in Korea]" and "Chaoxian zhanju shi keyi gaibian de [The war situation in Korea can be turned around]," in Mao Zedong, *Jianguo yilai Mao Zedong junshi wengao* [Mao Zedong's military manuscripts since the founding of the PRC] (Beijing: Junshi kexue chubanshe and Zhongyang wenxian chu-banshe, 2010), 1:258–59 and 349.

10. Xu Yan, "Chinese Forces and Their Casualties in the Korean War," trans. Xiao-bing Li, *Chinese Historians* 6, no. 2 (1993): 50.

11. Originally, in order to maintain its tradition of equality among the soldiers and commanders during and after the Chinese Civil War of 1946–49, the PLA did not have ranks. After the Korean War ended in 1953, the PLA reorganized its services into a Soviet-style structure. As part of his effort to reform the PLA, Peng Dehuai, the first defense minister of the PRC, established a Soviet-style system of military ranks in 1955, when 10 marshals, 10 grand generals, 57 generals, 175 lieutenant generals, and 800 major generals were created by the PLA. The ranks mentioned in this work were awarded in 1955 unless an endnote provides further information on the officer. For more details, see Xiaobing Li, "Military Ranks, People's Liberation Army," in *China at War: An Encyclope-dia*, ed. Xiaobing Li (Santa Barbara, CA: ABC-CLIO, 2012), 274–76.

12. Peng Dehuai, *Peng Dehuai junshi wenxuan* [Selected military papers of Peng Dehuai] (Beijing: Zhongyang wenxian chubanshe, 1988), 379. Hereafter cited as *Peng's Military Papers*.

13. Burton I. Kaufman, *The Korean Conflict* (Westport, CT: Greenwood, 1999); William W. Stueck, *The Korean War: An International History* (Princeton: Princeton University Press, 1995); Chen Jian, *China's Road to the Korean War: The Making of the Sino-American Confrontation* (New York: Columbia University Press, 1994); Sergei N. Goncharov, John W. Lewis, and Xue Litai, *Uncertain Partners: Stalin, Mao, and the Ko-rean War* (Stanford: Stanford University Press, 1993).

14. David Halberstam, *The Coldest Winter: America and the Korean War* (New York: Hyperion, 2007); Allan R. Millett, *The War for Korea, 1950–1951: They Came from the North* (Lawrence: University Press of Kansas, 2010); William Bowers, ed., *Striking Back: Combat in Korea, March–April 1951* (Lexington: University Press of Kentucky, 2010), and *The Line: Combat in Korea, January–February 1951* (Lexington: University Press of Kentucky, 2008); Brian Catchpole, *The Korean War, 1950–53* (New York: Carroll and Graf, 2000); Stanley Sandler, *The Korean War: No Victors, No Vanquished* (Lexington:

University Press of Kentucky, 1999); Billy Mossman, *U.S. Army in the Korean War: Ebb and Flow, November 1950–July 1951* (Washington: Army Center of Military History and Government Printing Office, 1990).

15. Bowers, *Striking Back,* 409.

16. Chen Jian, *Mao's China and the Cold War* (Chapel Hill: University of North Carolina Press, 2001), 2–4.

17. Shuguang Zhang, *Mao's Military Romanticism: China and the Korean War, 1950–53* (Lawrence: University Press of Kansas, 1995).

18. Qi Dexue, *Ni buliaojie de chaoxian zhanzheng* [The Korean War you don't know] (Shenyang, China: Liaoning renmin chubanshe, 2011); Jiang Tingyu, *Jiedu kangmei yuanchao zhanzheng* [Understanding the WRUSAK] (Beijing: Jiefangjun chubanshe, 2011); Zhang Xingxing, ed., *Kangmei yuanchao: 60 nianhou de huimou* [The WRUSAK: a retrospective look after 60 years], (Beijing: Dangdai zhongguo chubanshe, 2011); Deng Feng, "Kangmei yuanchao yanjiu zongshu, 1996–2006 [Korean War history research in China, 1996–2006]," paper presented at the International Cold War Conference, Changchun, Jilin, China, July 14–17, 2006; Chen Zhonglong, ed., *Kangmei yuanchao zhanzheng lun* [On the WRUSAK] (Beijing: Junshi wenyi chubanshe, 2001).

19. Bin Yu, "What China Learned from Its 'Forgotten War' in Korea," in *Mao's Generals Remember Korea,* trans. and ed. Xiaobing Li, Allan R. Millett, and Bin Yu (Lawrence: University Press of Kansas, 2000), 9.

20. Shen, "China Sends Troops to Korea," 13; Chu, *Chaoxian zhanzheng neimu quangongkai* [Declassifying the Korean War], 161.

21. Gen. Yang Dezhi was the commander of the Nineteenth Army Group in 1951–53 and deputy commander of the CPVF in 1952–53; for more biographical information about him, see note 22 in chapter 3. Gen. Song Shilun was the commander of the Ninth Army Group in 1950–53, and deputy commander of the CPVF in 1951–53; for more biographical information about him, see note 64 in chapter 2. Lt. Gen. Wang Jinshan was the acting commander of the Third Army Group in 1951–53; for more biographical information about him, see note 55 in chapter 6. Lt. Gen. Zeng Shaoshan was the commander of the Twelfth Army in 1951–53 and deputy commander of the Third Army Group in 1952–53; for more biographical information about him, see note 71 in chapter 5. Lt. Gen. Wei Jie was the commander of the Sixtieth Army in 1951–53; for more biographical information about him, see note 66 in chapter 7. Maj. Gen. Fu Chongbi was the commander of the Sixty-Third Army in 1951–53; for more biographical information about him, see note 88 in chapter 5.

22. Gen. You Taizhong was the commander of the 34th Division in 1951–53. Gen. Xu Xin was the commander of the 187th Division. Maj. Gen. Chen Xinzhong was the commander of the 190th Division. Senior Col. Zheng Qigui was the commander of the 180th Division. Col. Zhao Zuorui was the political commissar of the 358th Regiment.

23. Lt. Col. Guan Zhichao was the political commissar of the 2nd Battalion and commander of the 1st Battalion, 359th Regiment, in 1951–53. Maj. Huo Zhenlu was the deputy commander of the 3rd Battalion, 101st Regiment. Capt. Wang Xuedong was the commander of the First Company, 172nd Regiment. Capt. Zheng Yanman was the commander of the Eighth Company, 134th Regiment. Capt. Zhou Baoshan was the commander of the Fourth Company, 374th Regiment.

24. Among the recent publications, see Ralph D. Sawyer, ed., *The Seven Military Classics of Ancient China* (New York: Basic, 2007); Jeremy Black, *Rethinking Military History*

(New York: Routledge, 2004); John Keegan, *A History of Warfare* (New York: Knopf, 1993).

25. Mao highly praised *The Art of Warfare* and considered it a scientific truth, quoting Sunzi: "Know the enemy and know yourself, and you can fight a hundred battles with no danger of defeat" ("Problems of Strategy in China's Revolutionary War," in Mao Zedong, *Selected Works of Mao Tse-tung* [Beijing: Foreign Languages Press, 1977], 1:190; hereafter cited as *Selected Works of Mao*).

26. For recent and major works, see Geoffrey Parker, ed., *The Cambridge History of Warfare* (New York: Cambridge University Press, 2008); John A. Lynn, *Battle: A History of Combat and Culture* (New York: Basic, 2008); Victor Hanson, *Carnage and Culture: Landmark Battles in the Rise of Western Power* (New York: Anchor, 2002); John K. Fairbank and Frank A. Kierman Jr., eds., *Chinese Ways in Warfare* (Cambridge: Harvard University Press, 1974).

27. For more details on the Western way of war, see Hanson, *Carnage and Culture*; Geoffrey Parker, introduction to *The Cambridge History of Warfare*, 2–9; Keegan, *A History of Warfare*.

28. Keegan, *A History of Warfare*, 214; see also 221, 332–33.

29. Robin Higham and David A. Graff, introduction to *A Military History of China*, updated ed., eds. David A. Graff and Robin Higham (Lexington: University Press of Kentucky, 2012), 13.

30. Alastair Iain Johnston, *Cultural Realism: Strategic Culture and Grand Strategy in Chinese History* (Princeton: Princeton University Press, 1995), 6–11; John K. Fairbank, "Introduction: The Varieties of the Chinese Military Experience," in *Chinese Ways in Warfare*, eds. Fairbank and Kierman, 1–26; and Edward L. Dreyer, "Continuity and Change," in *A Military History of China*, eds. Higham and Graff, 19–38.

31. Fairbank, "Introduction," 6–7.

32. William R. Thompson, "The Military Superiority Thesis and the Ascendancy of Western Eurasia," *Journal of World History* 10, no. 1 (1999): 178. See also Hans Van de Ven, introduction to *Warfare in Chinese History*, ed. Hans Van de Ven (Boston: Brill Academic, 2000), 1–22; Kenneth Swope, lecture notes for "Non-Western Military History" class at Norwich University, 2010, 1–2; Harold Tanner, interviews by the author at the Southwest Conference on Asian Studies, Dallas, TX, October 6, 2012.

33. Higham and Graff, introduction, 14.

34. He, *Zhongcheng* [Loyalty], 411–14; Da, *Zhiyuanjun zhanfu jishi* [Voices from the CPVF POWs], 20, 84–88; Compilation Committee, "Chaoxian zhanzheng zhong zai meifang de zhongguo zhanfu jizhongying qingkuang zongshu [The overview of the CPVF POWs' condition in the UNF camps during the Korean War]," in *Meijun jizhongying qinliji* [Personal stories of the CPVF POWs in UN/U.S. camps], ed. Zhang Zeshi, (Beijing: Zhongguo wenshi chubanshe, 1996), 1–3.

35. Xiaobing Li, *A History of the Modern Chinese Army* (Lexington: University Press of Kentucky, 2007), 87–90, 115–19.

36. Sunzi, *The Art of War*, in Ralph D. Sawyer, trans. and ed., *The Seven Military Classics of Ancient China* (New York: Basic, 2007), 159.

37. Mao Zedong, "On Protracted War," in *Selected Works of Mao*, 2:143–44.

38. Sunzi, *The Art of War*, in Sawyer, *The Seven Military Classics of Ancient China*, 156.

39. For understandable reasons, some of the officials and scholars asked that their names not be mentioned in the book.

40. The Chinese party documents include CCP Central Archives, comps., *Zhonggong zhongyang wenjian xuanji, 1921–49* [Selected documents of the CCP Central Committee, 1921–49] (Beijing: Zhonggong zhongyang dangxiao chubanshe, 1989–92); CCP Central Archives, Central Archival and Manuscript Research Division, and CCP Organization Department, comps., *Zhongguo gongchandang zuzhishi ziliao, 1921–97* [Documents of the CCP organization's history, 1921–97] (Beijing: Zhonggong dangshi chubanshe, 2000); *Nanfangjiu dangshi ziliao* [Party history records of the CCP Southern Bureau] (Chongqing, China: Chongqing renmin chubanshe, 1986); *Zhonggong zhongyang Nanjingjiu: zhonggong lishi ziliao* [The Nanjing Bureau of the CCP Central Committee: CCP historical documents] (Beijing: Zhonggong zhongyang dangshi chubanshe, 1990); and Xinhuashe, *Xinhuashe wenjian ziliao huibian* [A collection of documentary materials of the New China News Agency] (Beijing: Xinhuashe, n.d.).

41. The Archives of the PRC Ministry of Foreign Affairs, formerly the Archives Section of the General Office of the Foreign Ministry, contain 330,000 volumes of documents, which are mainly in paper form, with some microfilms, photos, audiotapes, videotapes, and compact discs. They record China's foreign policy and diplomatic activities since the founding of the PRC in 1949. The archives declassified about 10,000 volumes of the documents in 2004 and about 60,000 in 2009.

42. Chinese leaders' papers and manuscripts include Mao Zedong, *Mao Zedong junshi wenji* [Collected military works of Mao Zedong] (Beijing: Junshi kexue chubanshe, 1993), and *Mao Zedong junshi wenxuan: neibuben* [Selected military papers of Mao Zedong: internal edition] (Beijing: Jiefangjun zhanshi chubanshe, 1981); Zhu De, *Zhu De junshi wenxuan* [Selected military papers of Zhu De] (Beijing: Jiefangjun chubanshe, 1986); Peng, *Peng's Military Papers*; Liu Bocheng, *Liu Bocheng junshi wenxuan* [Selected military papers of Liu Bocheng] (Beijing: Jiefangjun chubanshe, 1992); Nie Rongzhen, *Nie Rongzhen junshi wenxuan* [Selected military papers of Nie Rongzhen] (Beijing: Jiefangjun chubanshe, 1992); Xu Xiangqian, *Xu Xiangqian junshi wenxuan* [Selected military papers of Xu Xiangqian] (Beijing: Jiefangjun chubanshe, 1992); He Long, *He Long junshi wenxuan* [Selected military papers of He Long] (Beijing: Jiefangjun chubanshe, 1989); Chen Yi, *Chen Yi junshi wenxuan* [Selected military papers of Chen Yi] (Beijing: Jiefangjun chubanshe, 1996).

43. Mao, *Jianguo yilai Mao Zedong junshi wengao*, and *Jianguo yilai Mao Zedong wengao, 1949–76* [Mao Zedong's manuscripts since the founding of the state, 1949–76) (Beijing: Zhongyang wenxian chubanshe, 1989–93); Liu Shaoqi, *Jianguo yilai Liu Shaoqi wengao, 1949–52* [Liu Shaoqi's manuscripts since the founding of the state, 1949–52] (Beijing: Zhongyang wenxian chubanshe, 2005). See also Deng Xiaoping, *Selected Works of Deng Xiaoping* (Beijing: Foreign Languages Press, 1994).

44. Part of this research resulted in Xiaobing Li, Allan R. Millett, and Bin Yu, trans. and eds., *Mao's Generals Remember Korea* (Lawrence: University Press of Kansas, 2000).

45. Some of the generals agreed to use their names; other, interviewees' names are not be mentioned in this book, for understandable reasons.

46. Some of their stories about the Korean War are included in Richard Peters and Xiaobing Li, eds., *Voices from the Korean War: Personal Stories of American, Korean, and Chinese Soldiers* (Lexington: University Press of Kentucky, 2004).

47. Among the Chinese border conflicts are the First Taiwan Strait Crisis, September 1954–January 1955; Second Taiwan Strait Crisis, August–October 1958; Sino-Indian War, October–November 1962; and Sino-Soviet border conflicts, March–August 1969.

For more details of these conflicts, see Li, *A History of the Modern Chinese Army,* chapters 6–8; Mark A. Ryan, David M. Finkelstein, and Michael A. McDevitt, eds., *Chinese Warfighting: The PLA Experience since 1949* (New York: M. E. Sharpe, 2003).

## 1. BEIJING'S DECISION

1. Among the major works by leading Chinese military historians are Xu Yan, *Mao Zedong yu kangmei yuanchao zhanzheng* [Mao Zedong and the WRUSAK], 2nd ed. (Beijing: Jiefangjun chubanshe, 2006); Feng Xianzhi and Li Jie, *Mao Zedong yu kangmei yuanchao* [Mao Zedong: resisting the U.S. and aiding Korea] (Beijing: Zhongyang wenxian chubanshe, 2000); Yang Fengan and Wang Tiancheng, *Beiwei 38 duxian: Peng Dehuai yu chaoxian zhanzheng* [The north latitude 38th Parallel: Peng Dehuai and the Korean War] (Beijing: Zhongyang wenxian chubanshe, 2009); Chai Chengwen, *Banmendian tanpan jishi* (The true story of the Panmunjom negotiations] (Beijing: Shishi chubanshe, 2000). Senior Col. Yang (PLA, ret.) was Peng's military assistant and deputy director of Peng's executive office at CPVF general headquarters in 1950–53. Maj. Gen. Chai (PLA, ret.) served as chargé d'affaires of the PRC to the DPRK from July 10 to August 12, 1950, when China opened its embassy in Pyongyang. Chai was then head of the PRC military mission to North Korea from August 1950 to January 1955. Between July 1951 and July 1953, he served in the Chinese-North Korean delegation to the Korean truce talks at Panmunjom as the secretary general and liaison officer of the CPVF, holding a rank equivalent to colonel. He became a senior colonel in 1955 and a major general in 1961. See Tan Zheng, *Zhongguo renmin zhiyuanjun renwulu* [Veterans' profile of the CPVF] (Beijing: Zhonggong dangshi chubanshe, 1992), 529–30; *Xinghuo liaoyuan* Composition Department, *Zhongguo renmin jiefangjun jiangshuai minglu* [Marshals and generals of the PLA] (Beijing: Jiefangjun chubanshe, 1987–92), 3:368.

2. Andrew B. Kennedy, "Military Audacity: Mao Zedong, Liu Shaoqi, and China's Adventure in Korea," in *History and Neorealism,* eds. Ernest May, Richard Rosecrance, and Zara Steiner (Cambridge: Cambridge University Press, 2010), 201–202. See also Yuan Xi, "Zhenxiang [The truth]," *Suibi* [Daily records], no. 6, 1999: 12–15.

3. Shen Zhihua, *Mao Zedong, Stalin he chaoxian zhanzheng* [Mao Zedong, Stalin, and the Korean War] (Guangzhou: Guangdong renmin chubanshe, 2004); William W. Stueck, *The Korean War: An International History* (Princeton: Princeton University Press, 1995); Chen Jian, *China's Road to the Korean War: The Making of the Sino-American Confrontation* (New York: Columbia University Press, 1994).

4. Xu, *Mao Zedong yu kangmei yuanchao zhanzheng* [Mao Zedong and the WRUSAK], 64–65.

5. Mao Zedong telegram to Lin Biao, October 31, 1949, in Mao Zedong, *Jianguo yilai Mao Zedong wengao, 1949–76* [Mao Zedong's manuscripts since the founding of the state, 1949–76] (Beijing: Zhongyang wenxian chubanshe, 1989), 1:107. Hereafter cited as *Mao's Manuscripts since 1949.*

6. ROC Ministry of Defense, *Guojun houqin shi* [Logistics history of the GMD armed forces] (Taipei: Guofangbu shizheng bianyiju, 1992), 6:199–200.

7. Mao Zedong telegram to Lin Biao, October 31, 1949, in Mao, *Mao's Manuscripts since 1949,* 1:106–107. Lin Biao was one of the most brilliant military leaders of the CCP and the defense minister of the PRC in 1959–71. He participated in the CCP-led Nanchang Uprising against Jiang Jieshi's government in August 1927. Lin served as a battalion, regiment, and division commander in the CCP Red Army in 1927–31. He rose

quickly through the ranks because of his success in combat and loyalty to Mao. At the age of twenty-five, Lin became commander of the Red Fourth Army and then the president of the Red Army University. During WWII, Lin commanded the Eighth Route Army's 115th Division. Then he was appointed president of the CCP's Anti-Japanese Military and Political University at Yanan. At the beginning of the Chinese Civil War, Lin was appointed commander and political commissar of all the CCP forces in the northeast to fight against Jiang's arriving armies. In November 1948 the CCP reorganized its troops into the Chinese People's Liberation Army (PLA) and established four field armies. Lin became the commander of the Fourth Field Army, totaling 800,000 troops. His successful campaigns against GMD forces brought about an early victory for the CCP in the Civil War and made him one of the top CCP leaders. During the Cultural Revolution, Lin became the second most powerful leader in the country, after Mao—who made Lin his successor in 1969. Two years later, however, Lin was accused of leading a military coup against Mao, and Lin and his family members were killed in a plane crash in Mongolia on September 13, 1971. It remains unclear whether Lin was trying to flee the country and whether the crash was truly an accident. See *Xinghuo liaoyuan* Composition Department, *Zhongguo renmin jiefangjun jiangshuai minglu* [Marshals and generals of the PLA] (Beijing: Jiefangjun chubanshe, 1992), 1:10–11.

8. Mao telegram to Lin, in Mao, *Mao's Manuscripts since 1949*, 1:107.

9. He Di, "The Last Campaign to Unify China: The CCP's Unrealized Plan to Liberate Taiwan, 1949–50," in *Chinese Warfighting: The PLA Experience since 1949*, ed. Mark A. Ryan, David M. Finkelstein, and Michael A. McDevitt (New York: M. E. Sharpe, 2003), 82–84; Xiaobing Li, *A History of the Modern Chinese Army* (Lexington: University Press of Kentucky, 2007), 76.

10. Wu Ruilin, *Kangmei yuanchao zhong de 42 jun* [The Forty-Second Army in the WRUSAK] (Beijing: Jincheng chubanshe, 1995), 6–7. Lt. Gen. Wu (PLA, ret.) was the commander of the Forty-Second Army of the CPVF in the Korean War in 1950–53. See *Xinghuo liaoyuan* Composition Department, *Zhongguo renmin jiefangjun jiangshuai minglu* [Marshals and generals of the PLA], 1:296–97; Tan, *Zhongguo renmin zhiyuanjun renwulu* [Veterans' profile of the CPVF], 297–98. See also Yang and Wang, *Beiwei 38 duxian* [The north latitude 38th Parallel], 45.

11. Xiaobing Li, "PLA Attacks and Amphibious Operations during the Taiwan Strait Crises of 1954–55 and 1958," in *Chinese Warfighting*, eds. Ryan, Finkelstein, and McDevitt, 148.

12. CMC document, drafted by Mao Zedong, "Junwei guanyu gongji Jinmen shili de jiaoxun de tongbao [CMC circular on the lesson of the failed Jinmen attack, October 29, 1949]," in Mao, *Mao's Manuscripts since 1949*, 1:101.

13. Quoted in Ye Fei, *Ye Fei huiyilu* [Memoirs of Ye Fei] (Beijing: Jiefangjun chubanshe, 1988), 608. See also staff member of the Tenth Army Group headquarters, interview by the author in Hangzhou, Zhejiang, July 6, 2006. Gen. Ye (PLA) was the commander of the Tenth Army Group in 1949–55. See *Xinghuo liaoyuan* Composition Department, *Zhongguo renmin jiefangjun jiangshuai minglu* [Marshals and generals of the PLA], 1:58–59.

14. Gen. Su Yu (PLA) participated in the CCP-led Nanchang Uprising and joined the Red Army in 1927. During the Anti-Japanese War of 1937–45, his division established the CCP military base in the southern provinces. In the Chinese Civil War of 1946–49, Su became deputy commander of the East China Command in 1947 and then

commander of the Third Field Army in 1948–49. After the founding of the PRC in 1949, he served in numerous positions. See *Xinghuo liaoyuan* Composition Department, *Zhongguo renmin jiefangjun jiangshuai minglu* [Marshals and generals of the PLA], 1:38–39.

15. Yang Guoyu, *Dangdai Zhongguo haijun* [Contemporary Chinese navy] (Beijing: Zhongguo shehui kexue chubanshe, 1987), 17.

16. The first group of 89 PLA Air Force pilots graduated from training schools in May 1950. The PLA Air Force organized its first division in Nanjing with fifty Soviet-made fighters and bombers. The GMD Air Force on Taiwan had about two hundred fighters and bombers at that time. Meanwhile, the PLA Navy expanded to fifty-one medium warships, fifty-two landing boats, and thirty support vessels, totaling 43,000 tons. The GMD Navy had a total tonnage of 100,000 at that time. See ROC Ministry of Defense, *Guojun houqin shi* [Logistics history of the GMD armed forces], 6:262 and 277.

17. For Mao's "anger" and "fury" over the "ill-treatments" and his feeling like a "half prisoner," see Alexander V. Pantsov with Steven I. Levine, *Mao: The Real Story* (New York: Simon and Schuster, 2012), 369–71; Lorenz M. Luthi, *The Sino-Soviet Split: Cold War in the Communist World* (Princeton: Princeton University Press, 2008), 31–33; Jung Chang and Jon Halliday, *Mao: The Unknown Story* (New York: Knopf, 2005), 351–53; Philip Short, *Mao: A Life* (New York: Henry Holt, 1999), 424.

18. During their second meeting on December 24, for example, "Stalin did not mention the treaty at all," but instead mainly discussed with Mao "the activities of the Communist Parties in Asian countries" (Pei Jianzhang, *Zhonghua renmin gongheguo waijiaoshi, 1949–56* [Diplomatic history of the PRC, 1949–56] [Beijing: Shijie zhishi chubanshe, 1994], 18). The purpose of Mao's trip to Moscow was to sign a Sino-Soviet alliance treaty and get military and economic aid from the Soviet Union.

19. Quoted in Shuguang Zhang, *Mao's Military Romanticism: China and the Korean War, 1950–53* (Lawrence: University Press of Kansas, 1995), 23–24.

20. Shi Zhe, *Zai lishi juren shenbian* [At the side of historical giants] (Beijing: Zhongyang wenxian chubanshe, 1991), 412. Shi was Mao's Russian translator during his trip to Moscow.

21. Chen, *China's Road to the Korean War,* 3.

22. Zhou Enlai Military Record Compilation Team, *Zhou Enlai junshi huodong jishi* [Zhou Enlai military affairs record] (Beijing: Zhongyang wenxian chubanshe, 2000), 2:117–18.

23. CCP Central Archival and Manuscript Research Division, *Zhou Enlai nianpu, 1949–76* [A chronological record of Zhou Enlai, 1949–76] (Beijing: Zhongyang wenxian chubanshe, 1997), 1:23–5.

24. For a more detailed discussion, see Chen, *China's Road to the Korean War,* 63–69; Niu Jun, "The Origins of the Sino-Soviet Alliance," in *Brothers in Arms: The Rise and Fall of the Sino-Soviet Alliance, 1945–63,* ed. Odd Arne Westad (Washington: Woodrow Wilson Center Press, 1998), 47–89.

25. See, for example, Mao Zedong, "Report to the Second Plenary Session of the CCP Seventh Central Committee," *Selected Works of Mao Tse-tung* (Beijing: Foreign Languages Press, 1977), 4:362–3 and 365.

26. Chen, *China's Road to the Korean War,* 8.

27. For more on the Sino-Soviet alliance, see Odd Arne Westad, ed., *Brothers in Arms;* Michael M. Sheng, *Battling Western Imperialism: Mao, Stalin, and the United*

*States* (Princeton: Princeton University Press, 1997); Vladislav Zubok and Constantine Pleshakov, *Inside the Kremlin's Cold War: From Stalin to Khrushchev* (Cambridge: Harvard University Press, 1996); Gordon H. Chang, *Friends and Enemies: The United States, China, and the Soviet Union* (Stanford: Stanford University Press, 1990).

28. Shuguang Zhang, *Deterrence and Strategic Culture: Chinese-American Confrontations, 1949–58* (Ithaca: Cornell University Press, 1992), 32; Li, *A History of the Modern Chinese Army*, 120.

29. Mao Zedong, telegrams to Liu Shaoqi, "Guanyu tongyi diao sigeshi yanxi haizhan deng wenti [Approval of disposing four divisions for landing campaign exercise]," February 10, 1950, and "Mao guanyu queding xianda Dinghai zaida Jinmen de fangzhen de piyu [Mao's comments on the proposal of attacking Dinghai first, Jinmen second]," March 28, 1950, and telegram to Su Yu, "Guanyu sanbing xunlian wenti de dianbao [Instructions on paratroops training]," in Mao, *Mao's Manuscripts since 1949*, 1:256–57 and 282.

30. Marshal Nie Rongzheng became a Chinese student activist when he was studying in Paris in 1919, and he joined the CCP in 1922. He went to the Soviet Union for further education in the military and defense industry in 1924–25. After returning to China, Nie served as secretary and instructor in Huangpu (Whampoa) Military Academy's Political Department, where Zhou Enlai was the director. During the Nanchang Uprising, he was the CCP's representative to the Eleventh Army. With his organizational skills and Soviet military training, Nie became a deputy director of the Political Department in the Chinese Red Army HQ in the late 1920s and political commissar of the Red Army's First Army Group in the Long March of 1934–35. During the Anti-Japanese War of 1937–45, he was the political commissar of the 115th Division of the Eighth Route Army and commander and political commissar of the North China Military Region. During the Chinese Civil War, Nie served as the second secretary of the CCP's Northern China Bureau and commanded the PLA's Northern Military Region. In 1948–49 he worked closely with Mao on a daily basis after the Communist leadership moved from Yanan, the remote Communist capital in the northwest, to North China, closer to the Civil War battlegrounds. Nie successfully protected the CCP HQ and PLA high command by defeating GMD attacks and personally saved Mao's life once in an air raid, when Mao refused to leave his bedroom for a shelter. Nie's efforts enabled Mao to achieve military and political success throughout the war, and Nie became one of Mao's closest colleagues and most trusted generals. See *Xinghuo liaoyuan* Composition Department, *Zhongguo renmin jiefangjun jiangshuai minglu* [Marshals and generals of the PLA], 1:18–9; Nie Rongzhen Biography Compilation Team, *Nie Rongzhen zhuan* [Biography of Nie Rongzhen] (Beijing: Dangdai zhongguo chubanshe, 2006), 423–37.

31. Xiao Jinguang, *Xiao Jinguang huiyilu* [Memoirs of Xiao Jinguang] (Beijing: Jiefangjun chubanshe, 1988), 2:8, 26.

32. He, "The Last Campaign to Unify China," 82–83.

33. Gen. Jiang Weiguo (Chiang Wei-kuo, GMD Army), interview by the author at the Rongzong Hospital in Taipei, May 23, 1994. Jiang recalled that his father, Jiang Jieshi, and the GMD intelligence had information about the PLA landing preparations in the spring of 1950.

34. CCP History Research Division, *Zhongguo gongchandang lishi dashiji, 1919–87* [Major events in the history of the CCP, 1919–87] (Beijing: Renmin chubanshe, 1989), 191–92.

35. Gen. Ye Fei (PLA), interview by the author in Hangzhou, Zhejiang, July 1996. Gen. Ye served as the commander of the Tenth Army Group, Third Field Army of the PLA in 1949–51.

36. Xu, *Mao Zedong yu kangmei yuanchao zhanzheng* [Mao Zedong and the WRUSAK], 53–54.

37. Col. Lee Jong Kan (NKPA, ret.), interview by the author in Harbin, Heilongjiang, July 2002. Also see Lee Jong Kan, "A North Korean Officer's Story," in *Voices from the Korean War: Personal Stories of American, Korean, and Chinese Soldiers*, ed. Richard Peters and Xiaobing Li (Lexington: University Press of Kentucky, 2004): 76–84.

38. Xu Longnan, "Chaoxian zhanzheng zhong zhuanru chaoxian renminjun de zhongguo chaoxianzhu canzhan junren caifanglu [Interviews with ethnic Korean soldiers in China who joined the NKPA during the Korean War]," *Lengzhan guojishi yanjiu* [Cold War international history studies] 11 (2011): 117–46.

39. CMC telegram to Lin Biao and others, "Junwei tongyi disi yezhanjun zhong chaoxian guanbing hui chaoxian de dianbao [Agree to return the Korean officers and soldiers of the Fourth Field Army to Korea]," January 11, 1950, drafted by Liu Shaoqi, in Liu Shaoqi, *Jianguo yilai Liu Shaoqi wengao, 1949–52* [Liu Shaoqi's manuscripts since the founding of the state, *1949–52*] (Beijing: Zhongyang wenxian chubanshe, 2005), 1:319. Hereafter cited as *Liu's Manuscripts since 1949*.

40. Lee Jong Kan, interview; Lee, "A North Korean Officer's Story"; Nie Rongzhen, "Beijing's Decision to Intervene," in *Mao's Generals Remember Korea*, trans. and ed. Xiaobing Li, Allan R. Millett, and Bin Yu (Lawrence: University Press of Kansas, 2001), 47–48.

41. The PLA Korean soldiers returned to North Korea with 12,000 rifles, 620 machine guns, and 240 artillery pieces. See Liu Shaoqi, telegram to Mao Zedong, January 22, 1950, in Liu, *Liu's Manuscripts since 1949*, 1:320–21.

42. Maj. Gen. Chai Junwu (Chai Chengwen, PLA), "Zhongguo zhu chaoxian canzan Chai Junwu de baogao [Report by Chai Junwu, chargé of Chinese embassy to North Korea, July 17, 1950]," File# 106-00001-04 (1), Archives Department, PRC Ministry of Foreign Affairs, Beijing. Hereafter cited as PRC Foreign Ministry Archives.

43. Zhou Enlai, "Zhou Enlai yu bei chaoxian dashi guanyu jianli zhongchao youxian dianhua xianlu de beiwanglu [Memorandum, Zhou Enlai to North Korean Ambassador Lee; establishing new wired telephone lines between China and North Korea]," July 29, 1950, File# 106-00023-02 (1), PRC Foreign Ministry Archives.

44. Maj. Gen. Chai Chengwen (PLA), interview by the author in Beijing, July 2000.

45. Nikita Khrushchev, *Memoirs of Khrushchev*, ed. Sergei Khrushchev (University Park: Pennsylvania State University Press, 2006), 2:91.

46. Ibid.

47. Ibid., 2:92.

48. Xu, *Mao Zedong yu kangmei yuanchao zhanzheng* [Mao Zedong and the WRUSAK], 53–54.

49. Mao was very dissatisfied about this and later commented: "They [the North Koreans] are our next door neighbor, but they did not consult with us about the outbreak of the war" (quoted in Shen Zhihua, "China Sends Troops to Korea: Beijing's Policy-Making Process," in *China and the United States: A New Cold War History*, ed. Xiaobing Li and Hongshan Li [Lanham, MD: University Press of America, 1998], 20).

50. Zhongnanhai (which literally means "middle and southern seas") was an imperial palace in the Forbidden City in the center of Beijing which became the home of

Mao, Zhu, Zhou, and several other top CCP leaders after 1949. Most of the important CCP, PRC, and PLA meetings, such as those of the Politburo, are still held there.

51. Shi Zhe, "Mao Zedong Comments on the Outbreak of the Korean War, June 25–28, 1950," in *Chinese Communist Foreign Policy and the Cold War in Asia: New Documentary Evidence, 1944–50*, trans. and ed. Shuguang Zhang and Jian Chen (Chicago: Imprint, 1996), 153. See also Shi, *Zai lishi juren shenbian* [At the side of historical giants], 492.

52. Shi, *Zai lishi juren shenbian* [At the side of historical giants], 153.

53. Xiaobing Li, "Truman and Taiwan: A U.S. Policy Change from Face to Faith," in *Northeast Asia and the Legacy of Harry S. Truman: Japan, China, and the Two Koreas*, ed. James I. Matray (Kirksville, MO: Truman State University Press, 2012), 127–28.

54. David M. Finkelstein, *Washington's Taiwan Dilemma, 1949–50: From Abandonment to Salvation* (Fairfax, VA: George Mason University Press, 1993), 332–33.

55. Chief Gen. Hao Bocun (Hau Pei-stun, GMD Army, ret.), interview by the author in Taipei, May 23–24, 1994. Chief Gen. Hao served as the commander of the GMD front artillery force on Jinmen Island in 1950.

56. Li Changjiu and Shi Lujia, eds., *Zhongmei guanxi erbainian* [History of Sino-American relations] (Beijing: Xinhua chubanshe, 1984), 170. See also CCP Central Archival and Manuscript Research Division, *Zhou Enlai nianpu* [A chronological record of Zhou Enlai], 1:51; Zhou Enlai, "Guanyu meiguo wuzhuang qinlue zhongguo lingtu Taiwan de shengming [The statement of protesting against American armed invasion of Chinese territory Taiwan]," in Zhou Enlai, *Zhou Enlai junshi wenxun* [Selected military papers of Zhou Enlai] (Beijing: Renmin chubanshe, 1997), 4:29–31 (hereafter cited as *Zhou's Military Papers*).

57. Mao Zedong, "Tuanjie qilai dabai mei diguo zhuyi de renhe tiaoxun [Unite and defeat any provocation of U.S. imperialism]," June 28, 1950, in Mao Zedong, *Jianguo yilai Mao Zedong junshi wengao* [Mao Zedong's military manuscripts since the founding of the PRC] (Beijing: Junshi kexue chubanshe and Zhongyang wenxian chubanshe, 2010), 1:154–55 (hereafter cited as *Mao's Military Manuscripts since 1949*). See also *Mao Zedong on Diplomacy* (Beijing: Foreign Languages Press, 1998), 106.

58. Xiao, *Xiao Jinguang huiyilu* [Memoirs of Xiao Jinguang], 2:26; Zhou Enlai Military Record Compilation Team, *Zhou Enlai junshi huodong jishi* [Zhou Enlai military affairs record], 2:128–19.

59. Mao Zedong, "Sanda yundong de weida shengli [The great achievements of the three glorious movements]," October 23, 1951, in Mao, *Mao's Manuscripts since 1949*, 2:481. See also *Mao Zedong xuanji* [Selected works of Mao Zedong] (Beijing: Renmin chubanshe, 1978), 5:50–52.

60. Chief Gen. Hao Bocun (Hau Pei-tsun, GMD Army, ret.), interviews by the author in Taipei, May 23–24, 1994. As the commander of the front artillery force on Jinmen Island, Hao felt relieved when he was informed of the U.S. Seventh Fleet's patrol in the Taiwan Strait in June 1950. See also Xiao, *Xiao Jinguang huiyilu* [Memoirs of Xiao Jinguang], 2:26.

61. Liu Shufa, *Chen Yi nianpu, 1901–72* [A chronological record of Chen Yi, 1901–72] (Beijing: Renmin chubanshe, 1995), 2:632–33; Xinghuo liaoyuan Composition Department, *Zhongguo renmin jiefangjun jiangshuai minglu* [Marshals and generals of the PLA], 1:8–9.

62. Mao Zedong, instruction on Nie Rongzhen's report, "Zhanshi fangqi gongda Jinmen de baogao [Temporarily postpone the attacking campaign on Jinmen]," November

11, 1950, in Mao, *Mao's Military Manuscripts since 1949,* 1:344; Ye, *Ye Fei huiyilu* [Memoirs of Ye Fei], 613–14.

63. Li, "Truman and Taiwan," 119–20.

64. Quoted in Military History Research Division, CAMS, *Zhongguo renmin zhiyuanjun kangmei yuanchao zhanshi* [Combat experience of the CPVF in the WRUSAK] (Beijing: Junshi kexue chubanshe, 1990), 60. Mao Zedong made the same point in his directive to the East Military Region Command on August 11, 1950, in Mao, *Mao's Military Manuscripts since 1949,* 1:181–82.

65. Xu, *Mao Zedong yu kangmei yuanchao zhanzheng* [Mao Zedong and the WRUSAK], 59.

66. Quoted in Matthew B. Ridgway, *The Korean War* (Garden City, NY: Doubleday, 1967), 37.

67. Maj. Gen. William C. Chase (U.S. Army) arrived in Taiwan on May 1, 1951, to establish this group. For more details, see Finkelstein, *Washington's Taiwan Dilemma,* 336.

68. U.S. Department of State, *Foreign Relations of the United States: China, Korea, Vietnam, and Indochina, 1945–72* (Washington: Government Printing Office, 1982–89), 6:414.

69. Quoted in Ridgway, *The Korean War,* 37–38.

70. William Wei, "Political Power Grows out of the Barrel of a Gun: Mao and the Red Army," in *A Military History of China,* updated ed., ed. David A. Graff and Robin Higham (Lexington: University Press of Kentucky, 2012), 234.

71. CCP Central Archival and Manuscript Research Division, *Zhu De nianpu, 1886–1976* [A chronological record of Zhu De, 1886–1976] (Beijing: Renmin chubanshe, 1986), 392; *Xinghuo liaoyuan* Composition Department, *Zhongguo renmin jiefangjun jiangshuai minglu* [Marshals and generals of the PLA], 1:4–5.

72. After receiving Roshchin's telegram to Moscow, Stalin confirmed the Chinese leaders' concerns about a possible UNF invasion of North Korea. In a telegram to Zhou Enlai on July 5, 1950, Stalin agreed that "we consider it correct to concentrate immediately 9 Chinese divisions on the Chinese-Korean border for volunteer actions in North Korea in case the enemy crosses the 38th parallel. We will try to provide air cover for these units" (quoted in Kathryn Weathersby, trans. and ed., "New Russian Documents on the Korean War," *Bulletin: Cold War International History Project,* nos. 6–7 [Winter 1995–96]: 43).

73. "Junwei guanyu baowei guofang wenti jueyi shixiang gei Mao Zedong de baogao [The CMC national defense report to Mao from Nie Rongzhen]," July 7, 1950, in Mao, *Mao's Manuscripts since 1949,* 1:428; ibid., 1:159, note 1; Mao Zedong, "Memorandum, Mao Zedong to Nie Rongzhen, July 7, 1950," in *Chinese Communist Foreign Policy and the Cold War in Asia,* trans. and ed. Zhang and Chen, 156; Nie, "Beijing's Decision to Intervene," 39–40.

74. Mao Zedong, "Guanyu baowei dongbei bianfang de piyu [Approval of the CMC national defense report]," July 8, 1950, in Mao, *Mao's Military Manuscripts since 1949,* 1:158–59. See also Xu, *Mao Zedong yu kangmei yuanchao zhanzheng* [Mao Zedong and the WRUSAK], 65.

75. Lei Yingfu, "The Establishment of the Northeast Border Defense Army, July 1950," trans. and ed. Xiaobing Li, Don Duffy, and Zujian Zhang, *Chinese Historians* 7, nos. 1–2 (1994): 127–29. Maj. Gen. Lei (PLA, ret.) was director of the Operation Depart-

ment of the PLA general staff and Premier Zhou's military secretary. See also Feng and Li, *Mao Zedong yu kangmei yuanchao* [Mao Zedong: resisting the U.S. and aiding Korea], 4; Xu Yan, *Diyici jiaoliang: kangmei yuanchao zhanzheng de lishi huigu yu fansi* [The first encounter: a historical retrospective of the WRUSAK] (Beijing: Zhongguo guangbo dianshi chubanshe, 1990), 16–18.

76. According to the CMC order, the main task of the NEBDA was to defend the borders of the Northeast. For more details, see CCP Central Military Commission, "The CMC Orders to Defend the Northeast Borders, July 13 July, 1950," in *Chinese Communist Foreign Policy and the Cold War in Asia,* trans. and ed. Zhang and Chen, 156 note 16; Chen, *China's Road to the Korean War,* 135–37.

77. For the PLA organizational structure and field army system, see Fang Zhu, *Gun Barrel Politics: Party-Army Relations in Mao's China* (Boulder, CO: Westview, 1998), 16, 31, 48–49; Li, *A History of the Modern Chinese Army,* 76; Xiaoxiao Li, "Fourth Field Army," in *China at War: An Encyclopedia,* ed. Xiaobing Li, (Santa Barbara, CA: ABC-CLIO, 2012), 126–28.

78. Lei, "The Establishment of the Northeast Border Defense Army," 127–9; Xu, *Diyici jiaoliang* [The first encounter], 16–18; Feng and Li, *Mao Zedong yu kangmei yuanchao* [Mao Zedong: resisting the U.S. and aiding Korea], 4.

79. CMC, telegram to Gao Gang, August 5, 1950, "Dongbei bianfangjun yingzai yuenei wancheng yiqie zuozhan zhunbei [The NEBDA must complete all the combat preparation in August]," drafted by Mao Zedong, in Mao, *Mao's Military Manuscripts since 1949,* 1:179–80.

80. This last-minute trade-off of leading commanders before the war took place because, first of all, Deng was one of the best commanders in the Fourth Field Army and had just led the successful landing on Hainan Island. In addition Huang, known as a playboy among the commanders, had just made a secret trip to Hong Kong for fun. See Yang Di, *Zai zhiyuanjun silingbu de suiyueli: xianwei renzhi de zhenshi qingkuang* [My years at the CPVF General HQ: untold true stories] (Beijing: Jiefangjun chubanshe, 1998), 7–8. Senior Col. Yang served as the deputy chief of the Operation Section of the CPVF command in 1950–53.

81. Hong Xuezhi, "The CPVF's Combat and Logistics," in *Mao's Generals Remember Korea,* 107–109.

82. Yang, *Zai zhiyuanjun silingbu de suiyueli* [My years at the CPVF General HQ], 47.

83. Mao Zedong, opening speech at the Third Plenary of the First CPPCC, October 23, 1951, in Mao Zedong, *Mao Zedong wenji* [Collected works of Mao Zedong] (Beijing: Renmin chubanshe, 1993–99), 6:184 (hereafter cited as *Collected Works of Mao*). Mao's speech was also published in *Renmin ribao* [People's daily], October 24, 1951.

84. Zhang, *Mao's Military Romanticism,* 1.

85. Ellis Joffe, *Party and Army: Professionalism and Political Control in the Chinese Officer Corps, 1948–64* (Cambridge: Harvard University Press, 1967), ix.

86. The quoted text was omitted when the telegram was published in Mao Zedong, *Mao Zedong junshi wenji* [Collected military works of Mao Zedong] (Beijing: Junshi kexue chubanshe, 1993), 6:122–23 (hereafter cited as *Collected Military Works of Mao*). The omitted sentences were published for the first time in CCP Central Archives, Central Archival and Manuscript Research Division, "Guanyu zhongguo renmin zhiyuanjun chudong chaoxian zuozhan de yizu dianwen [CCP telegrams for the CPVF to fight the war in Korea]," *Dang de wenxian* [Party archives and documents] 5 (2000): 8.

87. This account is based on Wang Yuqing, "Mao Zedong yu Wang Jifan he Zhou Shizhao de tanhua [Mao's conversations with Wang Jifan and Zhou Shizhao on October 27, 1950]," *Junshi lishi* [Military history], 11 (2001): 88–93; Wang Yuqing, "Mao Zedong he wo yeye Wang Jifan de tanhua [Mao Zedong's conversation with my grandfather Wang Jifan]," *Guandong zhuojia* [Authors from northeast China] 9 (2003): 12–14. See also Xu, *Mao Zedong yu kangmei yuanchao zhanzheng* [Mao Zedong and the WRUSAK], 146.

88. Zhou Enlai, speech at the CPVF commanders meeting, February 17, 1958, in *Zhou's Military Papers*, 4:394–96.

89. Xu, *Mao Zedong yu kangmei yuanchao zhanzheng* [Mao Zedong and the WRUSAK], 59. See also Du Ping, *Zai zhiyuanjun zongbu: Du Ping huiyilu* [At the CPVF General HQ: memoirs of Du Ping]) (Beijing: Jiefangjun chubanshe, 1989), 15, 17–18. Lt. Gen. Du joined the CCP and the Chinese Red Army in 1930. During the Chinese Civil War, he served as director of the organization departments of the Northeast Field Army and then the Fourth Field Army. After the founding of the PRC, he was director of the political department in the Thirteenth Army Group. After the Korean War, Du became director of the political departments and deputy political commissar of the Shenyang and then the Nanjing Regional Commands. He served as the director of the Political Department of the CPVF General HQ in 1950–53 and was given the rank of lieutenant general in 1955 (see *Xinghuo liaoyuan* Composition Department, *Zhongguo renmin jiefangjun jiangshuai minglu* [Marshals and generals of the PLA], 1:254–55; Tan, *Zhongguo renmin zhiyuanjun renwulu* [Veterans' profile of the CPVF], 185–86).

90. Bo Yibo, *Ruogan zhongda juece yu shijian de huigu* [Recollections of certain important decisions and events] (Beijing: Zhonggong zhongyang dangxiao chubanshe, 1991), 1:43.

91. Mao Zedong, "Mao's Dispatch of Chinese Troops to Korea: Forty-Six Telegrams, July-October 1950," trans. and ed. Xiaobing Li, Xi Wang, and Chen Jian, *Chinese Historians* 5, no. 1 (992): 64. See also CCP Central Military Commission, "Telegram, CCP Central Military Commission to Gao Gang, August 5, 1950," in *Chinese Communist Foreign Policy and the Cold War in Asia,* trans. and ed. Zhang and Chen, 157.

92. Quoted in Du Ping, "Political Mobilization and Control," in *Mao's Generals Remember Korea,* 62; and Zhang, *Mao's Military Romanticism,* 81.

93. Military History Research Division, CAMS, *Zhongguo renmin zhiyuanjun kangmei yuanchao zhanshi* [Combat experience of the CPVF in the WRUSAK], 6.

94. Mao Zedong, *Collected Works of Mao,* 6:93–94. See also Mao Zedong, "Chaoxian zhanju he women de fangzhen [Korean War situation and our policy]," speech at the Ninth Plenary of the Central Government of the PRC, September 5, 1950, in Mao, *Mao's Military Manuscripts since 1949,* 1:201–203.

95. Maj. Gen. Xu Changyou (PLA, ret.), interviews by the author in Shanghai, April 26–27, 2000. Maj. Gen. Xu served as the deputy secretary general of the CCP Central Military Commission.

96. Chen Jiakang, "Guanyu bangzhu Jieke yunsong zuozhan wuzi dao chaoxian gei Zhou Enlai de baogao [Report, Chen Jiakang to Zhou Enlai; Korea's request for aiming equipment and transporting Czechoslovakia's war materials to North Korea]," September 3, 1950, File# 106-00022-04 (1), 1, PRC Foreign Ministry Archives.

97. Quoted in Shen, "China Sends Troops to Korea," 28, and *Mao Zedong, Stalin he chaoxian zhanzheng* [Mao Zedong, Stalin, and the Korean War], 221.

98. Chai, interview.

99. Nie, "Beijing's Decision to Intervene," 41; Wang Shuzeng, *Zhongguo renmin zhiyu-anjun zhengzhan jishi* [The true story of the CPVF's war experience] (Beijing: Jiefangjun wenyi, 2000), 85; Shen, *Mao Zedong, Stalin he chaoxian zhanzheng* [Mao Zedong, Stalin, and the Korean War], 228–29.

100. Quoted in Shen, "China Sends Troops to Korea," 29. See also Chen, *China's Road to the Korean War*, 281, note 78.

101. Mao talked about this difficult decision a couple of times during and after the Korean War. See Nie Rongzhen, *Nie Rongzhen huiyilu* [Memoirs of Nie Rongzhen] (Beijing: Jiefangjun chubanshe, 1984), 2:935; Xu, *Mao Zedong yu kangmei yuanchao zhan-zheng* [Mao Zedong and the WRUSAK], 4.

102. For more detailed discussions on the Soviet factor, see Tao Wenzhao, *Zhongmei guanxishi, 1949–72* [PRC-U.S. Relations, 1949–72] (Shanghai: Shanghai renmin chu-banshe, 1999), 24–25; Qi Dexue, "Guanyu kangmei yuanchao zhanzheng de jige wenti [Several issues on the WRUSAK]," *Zhonggong dangshi yanjiu* [Studies on CCP history] 1 (1998): 75–76; Andrew Scobell, *China's Use of Military Force: Beyond the Great Wall and the Long March* (Cambridge: Cambridge University Press, 2003), 82–89.

103. The Sino-Soviet Treaty of Friendship, Alliance, and Mutual Assistance stated that if one side was attacked by a third country, the other side "must go all out to provide military and other assistance." Mao Zedong, telegram to Liu Shaoqi, January 25, 1950, in Mao, *Mao's Manuscripts since 1949*, 1:251–2. See also Mao Zedong, "Telegram to Liu Shaoqi, 5:00 AM January 25, 1950," in *Chinese Communist Foreign Policy and the Cold War in Asia*, trans. and ed. Zhang and Chen, 140–41.

104. Quoted in Peng Dehuai, "My Story of the Korean War," in *Mao's Generals Remember Korea*, trans. and ed. Xiaobing Li, Allan R. Millett, and Bin Yu (Lawrence: University Press of Kansas, 2001), 32.

105. Yang and Wang, *Beiwei 38 duxian* [The north latitude 38th Parallel], 90. After the Korean War, Peng was appointed defense minister of the PRC and became one of the ten marshals of the PLA in 1955. But in 1959 Mao dismissed Peng from all posts, accusing him of leading an "anti-Party clique" or a "military club" against Mao's policy of the Great Leap Forward (Peng Dehuai Biography Compilation Team, *Yige zhenzheng de ren: Peng Dehuai* [A real man: Peng Dehuai] [Beijing: Renmin chubanshe, 1994], 237, 313). In 1967, at the beginning of the Cultural Revolution, Peng was arrested and imprisoned. He died on November 29, 1974. See Allan R. Millett, *Their War for Korea: American, Asian, and European Combatants and Civilians, 1945–53* (Washington: Brassy's, 2002), 106–11.

106. Wang Yan et al., *Peng Dehuai zhuan* [Biography of Peng Dehuai] (Beijing: Dang-dai zhongguo chubanshe, 1993), 402.

107. Peng, "My Story of the Korean War," 33. See also Peng Dehuai Biography Compilation Team, *Yige zhenzheng de ren* [A real man], 166–67.

108. Nie, "Beijing's Decision to Intervene," 42; Wang et al., *Peng Dehuai zhuan* [Biography of Peng Dehuai], 402–403; Bruce A. Elleman, *Modern Chinese Warfare, 1795–1989* (London: Routledge, 2001), 246–47.

109. Nie, "Beijing's Decision to Intervene," 42; and Feng and Li, *Mao Zedong yu kang-mei yuanchao* [Mao Zedong: resisting the U.S. and aiding Korea], 18–22.

110. Mao Zedong, "Zuchen zhongguo renmin zhiyuanjun de mingling [CMC order to establish the Chinese People's Volunteer Force]," in *Collected Military Works of Mao*, 6:109–10 and CCP Central Military Commission, "Order on the Formation of the Chi-

nese People's Volunteer Force," in *Chinese Communist Foreign Policy and the Cold War in Asia,* trans. and ed. Zhang and Chen, 164–65.

111. Quoted in CCP Central Archives, Central Archival and Manuscript Research Division,"Mao Zedong tan zhongguo guanyu kangmei yuanchao baojia weiguo de jueding [Mao's conversation on China's decision on the WRUSAK]," *Dang de wenxian* [Party archives and documents] 5 (2000): 113.

112. Quoted in Yang and Wang, *Beiwei 38 duxian* [The north latitude 38th Parallel], 106. See also Xu Yan, "Chinese Forces and Their Casualties in the Korean War," trans. Xiaobing Li, *Chinese Historians* 6, no. 2 (1993): 48.

113. CCP Central Archival and Manuscript Research Division, *Zhou Enlai nianpu* [A chronological record of Zhou Enlai], 1:85–87; and Hong Xuezhi, *Hong Xuezhi huiyilu* [Memoirs of Hong Xuezhi] (Beijing: Jiefangjun chubanshe, 2007), 373–74.

114. Mao Zedong, telegrams to Chen Yi, "Qingling dijiu bingtuan tiqian beishang [Order the Ninth Army Group to move north ahead of schedule]," October 12 and 14, and to Zhou Enlai, "Women renwei yingdang canzhan bixu canzhan [We believe that we should and must enter the war]," October 13, and Mao Zedong, "Chaoxian qingkuang he dui wojun ruchao canzhan de yijian [The guidelines and deployment for the CPVF to enter Korea and participate in the war]," October 14, 1950, in Mao, *Mao's Military Manuscripts since 1949,* 1:246, 248, 252–53, 256–59; Mao Zedong, "Telegram to Chen Yi, October 12, 1950," "Telegram to Zhou Enlai, October 13, 1950," "Telegram to Chen Yi, October 14, 1950," and "Telegram to Zhou Enlai, October 14, 1950," in *Chinese Communist Foreign Policy and the Cold War in Asia,* trans. and ed. Zhang and Chen, 168–71.

115. For a more detailed discussion of the 1950 PLA demobilization, see Han Huaizhi, *Dangdai zhongguo jundui de junshi gongzuo* [Contemporary Chinese military affairs] (Beijing: Zhongguo shehui kexue chubanshe, 1989), vol. 1, chapters 1–2, 5.

116. Tan Jingjiao, *Kangmei yuanchao zhanzheng* [The WRUSAK] (Beijing: Zhongguo shehui kexue chubanshe, 1990), 24–25; Wang Shuzeng, *Yuandong chaoxian zhanzheng* [The Korean War in the Far East] (Beijing: Jiefangjun wenyi chubanshe, 2000), 1:79–80.

117. Col. Yang Shaojun (PLA, ret.), interview by the author at the PLA Logistics College, in Beijing, July 1994. Col. Yang served as a PLA recruiting officer in the early 1950s.

118. Among the recent Chinese books that credit the Korean War mobilization to the victory in the Civil War are Wang, *Yuandong chaoxian zhanzheng* [The Korean War in the Far East], 1:138–9; Tan, *Kangmei yuanchao zhanzheng* [The WRUSAK], 24–25; Xu, *Diyici jiaoliang* [The first encounter], 28–29.

119. Yang Shaojun, interview. Also see Li Hongjie, *Zhenyi de zhanzheng, weida de jingshen* [The just war and great spirit] (Guangzhou: Guangdong renmin chubanshe, 2001), 20–22; Zhao Shaoquan, *Xinbian zhongguo xiandaishi* [New history of modern China] (Nanchang, China: Jiangxi renmin chubanshe, 1987) 3:41–42, 46–47.

120. Capt. Zhou Baoshan (CPVF), interview by the author in Harbin, Heilongjiang, April 2000. Also see Lee, "A North Korean Officer's Story," 76–80.

121. Du, "Political Mobilization and Control," 66; Jiang Yonghui, *38 jun zai chaoxian* [The Thirty-Eighth Army in Korea], 2nd ed. (Shenyang, China: Liaoning renmin chubanshe, 2009), 20. Maj. Gen. Jiang (PLA) was the deputy commander of the Thirty-Eighth Army of the CPVF in 1950–52.

122. Du, "Political Mobilization and Control," 67.

123. Zhou Enlai, "Kangmei yuanchao yundong zhong cunzai de sixiang wenti [The psychological problems in the movement to resist the U.S. and aid Korea]," in *Zhou's*

*Military Papers*, 4:111–17. See also Capt. Zhou Baoshan (CPVF), interview by the author, Harbin, Heilongjiang, April 2000.

124. Maj. Gen. Wang Yang joined the CCP and the Eighth Route Army in 1937. He served as a commander of the squad, platoon, company, battalion, and regiment through the Anti-Japanese War. During the Chinese Civil War he became chief of staff, deputy commander, and commander of the 116th Division of the Thirty-Ninth Army of the PLA. After the Korean War, Wang became deputy commander and commander of the Thirty-Ninth Army; chief of staff and deputy commander of the Shenyang Regional Command and deputy commander of the Beijing Regional Command; and minister of the PRC's Seventh Ministry of Machine-Building Industry (the Space and Navigation Ministry, or China's equivalent of the U.S. National Aeronautics and Space Administration). Wang was made senior colonel in 1955 and major general in 1964. See Tan, *Zhongguo renmin zhiyuanjun renwulu* [Veterans' profile of the CPVF], 319.

125. Capt. Zhou Baoshan (CPVF), interview by the author, in Harbin, Heilongjiang, April 2000. See also Zhou Baoshan, "China's Crouching Dragon," in *Voices from the Korean War: Personal Stories of American, Korean, and Chinese Soldiers*, ed. Richard Peters and Xiaobing Li (Lexington: University Press of Kentucky, 2004), 87.

126. Mao approved the Zhou Enlai and Nie Rongzhen's July 22 report on July 23 (see Mao, Zedong, "Guanyu dongbei bianfangjun you dongbei junqu zhihui yu gongying de piyu [Instruction on the report of the Northeast Military Region commands and supplies all of the NEBDA forces]," in *Mao's Military Manuscripts since 1949*, 1:171). For the July 22 report, see Zhou and Nie, "Guanyu dongbei bianfangjun you dongbei junqu zhihui yu gongying de baogao [The Northeast Military Region commands and supplies all of the NEBDA forces]," July 22, 1950, in *Zhou's Military Papers*, 4:38–40.

127. CCP Heilongjiang Provincial Committee, "Guanyu dongbei bianfangjun houqin gongying yu zuozhan zhunbei de baogao [Report on the logistics supplies and war preparation for the NEBDA troops]," September 30, 1950, in Heilongjiang Provincial Archives, Harbin, China; Zhou Zhong, *Kangmei yuanchao zhanzheng houqinshi jianbianben* [A concise history of the logistics in the WRUSAK] (Beijing: Jindun chubanshe, 1993), 18–19.

128. Li Ying et al., *40 jun zai chaoxian* [The Fortieth Army in Korea] (Shenyang, China: Liaoning renmin chubanshe, 2010), 3; Jiang, *38 jun zai chaoxian* [The Thirty-eighth Army in Korea), 20–21.

129. Chu Yun, *Chaoxian zhanzheng neimu quangongkai* [Declassifying the Korean War] (Beijing: Shishi chubanshe, 2005), 161; Shen, "China Sends Troops to Korea," 13.

130. China's military spending represented 41 percent of its total government annual budget in 1950, 43 percent in 1951, 33 percent in 1952, and 34 percent in 1953. For more details, see Military History Research Division, CAMS, *Zhongguo renmin zhiyuanjun kangmei yuanchao zhanshi* [Combat experience of the CPVF in the WRUSAK], 233–34.

## 2. FROM THE YALU TO SEOUL

1. Han Huaizhi, *Dangdai zhongguo jundui de junshi gongzuo* [Contemporary Chinese military affairs] (Beijing: Zhongguo shehui kexue chubanshe, 1989), 1:452; Wu Ruilin, *Kangmei yuanchao zhong de 42 jun* [The Forty-Second Army in the WRUSAK] (Beijing: Jincheng chubanshe, 1995), 44. In fact, the PLA sent the first Chinese troops into Korea in August 1950, after Mao approved Nie's request to deploy the Chinese anti-aircraft artillery units south of the Yalu River to protect the bridges on August 4. For more details,

see Nie Rongzhen, "Beijing's Decision to Intervene," in *Mao's Generals Remember Korea,* trans. and ed. Xiaobing Li, Allan R. Millett, and Bin Yu (Lawrence: University Press of Kansas, 2001), 48; Nie Rongzhen Biography Compilation Team, *Nie Rongzhen zhuan* [Biography of Nie Rongzhen] (Beijing: Dangdai zhongguo chubanshe, 2006), 293.

2. Wu, *Kangmei yuanchao zhong de 42 jun* [The Forty-Second Army in the WRUSAK], 44.

3. Hong Xuezhi, *Hong Xuezhi huiyilu* [Memoirs of Hong Xuezhi] (Beijing: Jiefangjun chubanshe, 2007), 376; and Du Ping, *Zai zhiyuanjun zongbu: Du Ping huiyilu* [At the CPVF General HQ: memoirs of Du Ping] (Beijing: Jiefangjun chubanshe, 1989), 38.

4. Peng concentrated his forces to outnumber the enemy wherever the situation permitted in order to eliminate entire enemy battalions, regiments, or divisions, rather than to simply repel the enemy from the peninsula. Peng Dehuai Biography Compilation Team, *Yige zhenzheng de ren: Peng Dehuai* [A real man: Peng Dehuai] (Beijing: Renmin chubanshe, 1994), 178; Peng Dehuai, "My Story of the Korean War," in *Mao's Generals Remember Korea,* trans. and ed. Xiaobing Li, Allan R. Millett, and Bin Yu (Lawrence: University Press of Kansas, 2001), 32–33; Military History Research Division, CAMS, *Zhongguo renmin zhiyuanjun kangmei yuanchao zhanshi* [Combat experience of the CPVF in the WRUSAK] (Beijing: Junshi kexue chubanshe, 1990), 11; Feng Xianzhi and Li Jie, *Mao Zedong yu kangmei yuanchao* [Mao Zedong: resisting the U.S. and aiding Korea] (Beijing: Zhongyang wenxian chubanshe, 2000), 30.

5. Peng Dehuai, "Zai zhongguo renmin zhiyuanjun shi yishang ganbu dongyuan dahui shang de jianghua [Speech at the CPVF Army and Division Commanders meeting]," October 14, 1950, in Peng Dehuai, *Peng Dehuai junshi wenxuan* [Selected military papers of Peng Dehuai] (Beijing: Zhongyang wenxian chubanshe, 1988), 324. Hereafter cited as *Peng's Military Papers.* Although the date in the book is "October 14," the leading scholars in China believe that it should be October 16. See Xu Yan, *Mao Zedong yu kangmei yuanchao zhanzheng* [Mao Zedong and the WRUSAK], 2nd ed. (Beijing: Jiefangjun chubanshe, 2006), 132.

6. Quoted in William W. Stueck, *The Road to Confrontation: American Policy toward China and Korea, 1947–1950* (Chapel Hill: University of North Carolina Press, 1981), 3.

7. Xiaobing Li, "China's Intervention and the CPVF Experience in the Korean War," in *The Korean War at Fifty: International Perspectives,* ed. Mark F. Wilkinson (Lexington: Virginia Military Institute Press, 2004), 144–45.

8. Luan Kechao, *Xue yu huo de jiaoliang: kangmei yuanchao jishi* [The contest: blood vs. fire; the record of resisting America and aiding Korea] (Beijing: Huayi chubanshe, 2008), 203; Xu Yan, "Chinese Forces and Their Casualties in the Korean War," trans. Xiaobing Li, *Chinese Historians* 6, no. 2 (1993): 50.

9. Mao Zedong, telegram to Zhou Enlai, October 14, 1950, in Mao Zedong, *Mao Zedong junshi wenxuan: neibuben* [Selected military papers of Mao Zedong: internal edition] (Beijing: Jiefangjun zhanshi chubanshe, 1981; hereafter cited as *Selected Military Papers of Mao*), 2:649–50. (To convince Stalin to give China military aid, Mao told Zhou, then in Moscow, that he had asked Peng to defend North Korea.) See also Mao Zedong, "Mao's Telegrams during the Korean War, October–December 1950," trans. and ed. Xiaobing Li and Glenn Tracy, *Chinese Historians* 5, no. 2 (1992): 73–74.

10. Peng Dehuai, "Zai zhongguo renmin zhiyuanjun shi yishang ganbu dongyuan dahui shang de jianghua [Speech at the CPVF Army and Division Commanders meeting]," October 14, 1950, in Peng, *Peng's Military Papers,* 325.

11. Ibid., 325–26.

12. Hong, *Hong Xuezhi huiyilu* [Memoirs of Hong Xuezhi], 374–75; Du, *Zai zhiyuan-jun zongbu* [At the CPVF General HQ], 34–37.

13. Mao, telegram to Deng Hua and other CPVF commanders, October 18, 1950, in Mao Zedong, *Jianguo yilai Mao Zedong wengao, 1949–76* [Mao Zedong's manuscripts since the founding of the state, 1949–76] (Beijing: Zhongyang wenxian chubanshe, 1989), 1: 568–69 (hereafter cited as *Mao's Manuscripts since 1949*). See also Mao Zedong, "Telegram to Deng Hua and Others, 9:00 PM, October 18, 1950," in *Chinese Communist Foreign Policy and the Cold War in Asia: New Documentary Evidence, 1944–50*, trans. and ed. Shuguang Zhang and Jian Chen (Chicago: Imprint, 1996), 178–79.

14. Quoted in Wu Xinquan, *Chaoxian zhanchang 1,000 tian: 39 jun zai chaoxian* [One thousand days on the Korean battleground: the Thirty-Ninth Army in Korea] (Shenyang, China: Liaoning renmin chubanshe, 1996), 20–21. Lt. Gen. Wu was the commander of the Thirty-Ninth Army of the CPVF in 1950–53. See also Wang Yan et al., *Peng Dehuai zhuan* [Biography of Peng Dehuai] (Beijing: Dangdai zhongguo chubanshe, 1993), 409–10.

15. Hong, *Hong Xuezhi huiyilu* [Memoirs of Hong Xuezhi], 376; Li Ying, *Jiekai zhan-zheng xumu de xianfeng: 40 jun zai chaoxian* [Vanguard of the early actions in the war: the Fortieth Army in Korea] (Shenyang, China: Liaoning renmin chubanshe, 1996), 5–6.

16. Mark A. Ryan, David M. Finkelstein, and Michael A. McDevitt, "Introduction: Patterns of PLA Fighting," in *Chinese Warfighting: The PLA Experience since 1949*, ed. Mark A. Ryan, David M. Finkelstein, and Michael A. McDevitt (New York: M. E. Sharpe, 2003), 7.

17. Nie Rongzhen Biography Compilation Team, *Nie Rongzhen zhuan* [Biography of Nie Rongzhen], 294–95.

18. Ryan, Finkelstein, and McDevitt, "Introduction," 7.

19. Shuguang Zhang, "Command, Control, and the PLA's Offensive Campaigns in Korea, 1950–1951," in *Chinese Warfighting*, 112.

20. Allan R. Millett, *The War for Korea, 1950–1951: They Came from the North* (Lawrence: University Press of Kansas, 2010), 300–301.

21. Marshal Chen Yi was one of the most brilliant military leaders of the CCP. He participated in the Nanchang Uprising, and joined forces with Zhu De in April 1928. He served as party representative of the 1st Division and then commander of the 12th Division of the Fourth Red Army. During the Anti-Japanese War, Chen was vice commissar in 1939, then deputy commander and chief staff in 1940, and acting commander of the New Fourth Army in 1941. Under his command, the New Fourth Army increased from four divisions to seven in 1945. In 1947, during the Chinese Civil War, Chen was appointed commander of the East China Field Army. A year later he became commander and political commissar of the Third Field Army, which contained a million troops and took over Nanjing, Shanghai, and many cities in southeast China. After the founding of the PRC, Chen was appointed mayor of Shanghai and commander and political commissar of the East China Regional Command. In 1954 he was appointed vice premier of the PRC and vice chairman of the CMC. In 1955 he became one of the ten marshals of the PLA. In 1958 Chen was appointed minister of foreign affairs. He was purged by Mao in 1966 and died in 1972, during the Chinese Cultural Revolution. See *Xinghuo liaoyuan* Composition Department, *Zhongguo renmin jiefangjun jiangshuai minglu* [Marshals and generals of the PLA], (Beijing: Jiefangjun chubanshe, 1992), 1:8–9; Liu Shufa, *Chen Yi*

*nianpu, 1901–72* [A chronological record of Chen Yi, 1901–72] (Beijing: Renmin chuban-she, 1995), 2:1224–26.

22. Quoted in Hong Xuezhi, *Kangmei yuanchao zhanzheng huiyi* [Recollections of the WRUSAK] (Beijing: Jiefangjun wenyi chubanshe, 1990), 47. See also Xu, *Mao Ze-dong yu kangmei yuanchao zhanzheng* [Mao Zedong and the WRUSAK], 152.

23. Hong, *Kangmei yuanchao zhanzheng huiyi* [Recollections of the WRUSAK], 37–38; Wang Shuzeng, *Yuandong chaoxian zhanzheng* [The Korean War in the Far East] (Beijing: Jiefangjun wenyi chubanshe, 2000), 1:152–55.

24. Shuang Shi, *Kaiguo diyi zhan: kangmei yuanchao zhanzheng quanjing jishi* [The first war since the founding of the state: the complete story of the WRUSAK] (Beijing: Zhonggong dangshi chubanshe, 2004), 1:93; Wang et al., *Peng Dehuai zhuan* [Biography of Peng Dehuai], 411–15.

25. Du, *Zai zhiyuanjun zongbu* [At the CPVF General HQ], 50; Yang Di, *Zai zhiyu-anjun silingbu de suiyueli: xianwei renzhi de zhenshi qingkuang* [My years at the CPVF General HQ: untold true stories] (Beijing: Jiefangjun chubanshe, 1998), 47; Yang Fengan and Wang Tiancheng, *Beiwei 38 duxian: Peng Dehuai yu chaoxian zhanzheng* [The north latitude 38th Parallel: Peng Dehuai and the Korean War] (Beijing: Zhongyang wenxian chubanshe, 2009), 146.

26. CCP Central Committee, telegram to the Thirteenth Army Group, October 25, 1950, drafted by Mao, in Mao, *Mao's Manuscripts since 1949*, 1:291; Mao Zedong, "Tele-gram to Peng Dehuai and Deng Hua, 6:00 A M, October 25, 1950," in *Chinese Communist Foreign Policy and the Cold War in Asia,* trans. and ed. Zhang and Chen, 191.

27. Deng also served as the first deputy commander of the Northeast Regional Com-mand, commander of the Shenyang Regional Command, and lieutenant governor of Sichuan Province. See *Xinghuo liaoyuan* Composition Department, *Zhongguo renmin jiefangjun jiangshuai minglu* [Marshals and generals of the PLA], 1:56–57; Tan Zheng, *Zhongguo renmin zhiyuanjun renwulu* [Veterans' profile of the CPVF] (Beijing: Zhong-gong dangshi chubanshe, 1992), 72–74; Hu Haipo and Yu Hongjun, *Genzhe Mao Zedong da tianxia* [Follow Mao Zedong to seize state power] (Changsha, China: Hunan renmin chubanshe, 2009), 74.

28. Gen. Han Xianchu joined the CCP and the Red Army in 1930. He served as a squad, platoon, company, battalion, and regiment commander in the early 1930s. Dur-ing the Anti-Japanese War, Han became a regiment and brigade commander of the 115th Division of the Eighth Route Army. During the Chinese Civil War, he served as com-mander of the Fortieth Army and deputy commander of the Twelfth and Thirteenth Army Groups. After his return from the Korean War, Han was appointed commander of the Fuzhou and later the Lanzhou Regional Commands, deputy chief staff of the PLA, and governor of Fujian Province. He was made general in 1955. See *Xinghuo liaoyuan* Composition Department, *Zhongguo renmin jiefangjun jiangshuai minglu* [Marshals and generals of the PLA], 1:146–47; Tan, *Zhongguo renmin zhiyuanjun renwulu* [Veterans' profile of the CPVF], 604–605.

29. Hong, *Hong Xuezhi huiyilu* [Memoirs of Hong Xuezhi], 376; Du Ping, "Political Mobilization and Control," in *Mao's Generals Remember Korea,* trans. and ed. Xiaobing Li, Allan R. Millett, and Bin Yu (Lawrence: University Press of Kansas, 2000), 73–74; Yang, *Zai zhiyuanjun silingbu de suiyueli* [My years at the CPVF General HQ], 51.

30. Hong, *Kangmei yuanchao zhanzheng huiyi* [Recollections of the WRUSAK]), 48–49; Yang, *Zai zhiyuanjun silingbu de suiyueli* [My years at the CPVF General HQ], 52.

31. Du, *Zai zhiyuanjun zongbu* [At the CPVF General HQ], 71–72.

32. Capt. Zhou Baoshan (CPVF), interview by the author in Harbin, Heilongjiang, April 2000. Also see Zhou Baoshan, "China's Crouching Dragon," in *Voices from the Korean War: Personal Stories of American, Korean, and Chinese Soldiers*, ed. Richard Peters and Xiaobing Li (Lexington: University Press of Kentucky, 2004), 88.

33. Sunzi, *The Art of War*, trans. Roger Ames (New York: Ballantine, 1993), 123.

34. Matthew B. Ridgway, *The Korean War* (Garden City, NY: Doubleday, 1967), 52.

35. Yang, *Zai zhiyuanjun silingbu de suiyueli* [My years at the CPVF General HQ], 51; Xu, *Mao Zedong yu kangmei yuanchao zhanzheng* [Mao Zedong and the WRUSAK], 131–32.

36. Yang and Wang, *Beiwei 38 duxian* [The north latitude 38th Parallel], 147–48; Wang et al., *Peng Dehuai zhuan* [Biography of Peng Dehuai], 414–15.

37. Ridgway, *The Korean War*, 52–53; Millett, *The War for Korea, 1950–1951*, 298–303; David Halberstam, *The Coldest Winter: America and the Korean War* (New York: Hyperion, 2007), 379–82.

38. Quoted in Yang and Wang, *Beiwei 38 duxian* [The north latitude 38th Parallel], 147–48. See also Wang et al., *Peng Dehuai zhuan* [Biography of Peng Dehuai], 414, 446.

39. CMC, "Junwei guanyu nanchaoxian jundui zhandou tedian de tongbao [The Central Military Commission's circular on the combat characteristics of South Korean troops]," October 30, 1950, drafted by Mao, in Mao, *Mao's Manuscripts since 1949*, 1:630–31; Mao, "Mao's Telegrams during the Korean War," 66–67.

40. Mao Zedong, telegram to Peng, "Guanyu dahao zhiyuanjun chuguo diyizhang gei Peng Dehuai deng de dianbao [The CPVF should win the first battle after they left the country]," 2:30 AM, October 21, 1950, in Mao, *Mao's Manuscripts since 1949*, 1:575–76. See also Mao, *Mao's Manuscripts since 1949*, 1:268–69.

41. Mao Zedong, telegram to Peng, "Zhengqu zhanji xunsu wancheng zhanyi bushu [Capture the battle opportunity; finalize the operation plan immediately]," 3:30 AM, October 21, 1950, in Mao Zedong, *Mao Zedong junshi wenji* [Collected military works of Mao Zedong] (Beijing: Junshi kexue chubanshe, 1993), 6:130–31 (hereafter cited as *Collected Military Works of Mao*). See also Mao, *Mao's Military Manuscripts since 1949*, 1:270.

42. Mao Zedong, telegram to Peng, 4:00 AM, October 21, 1950, in Mao, *Mao's Manuscripts since 1949*, 1:578; Mao, *Mao's Military Manuscripts since 1949*, 1:271.

43. Peng Dehuai, telegram to Deng Hua and the CMC, 4:00 PM, October 21, 1950, in Peng, *Peng's Military Papers*, 328–29. See also Mao, *Mao's Military Manuscripts since 1949*, 1:274, note 2.

44. Peng's telegram of 7:00 PM, October 22, 1950, is included as a footnote in Mao Zedong, telegram to Peng, October 23, 1950, in Mao, *Mao's Manuscripts since 1949*, 1:588–90. See also Mao Zedong, "Telegram to Peng Dehuai, October 23, 1950," in *Chinese Communist Foreign Policy and the Cold War in Asia*, trans. and ed. Zhang and Chen, 183–84.

45. Mao Zedong, telegram to Peng and Gao Gang, "Guanyu chaoxian zhanju [On the war situation in Korea]," October 23, 1950, in Mao, *Mao's Manuscripts since 1949*, 1:589. See also Mao, *Mao's Military Manuscripts since 1949*, 1:279.

46. Wang et al., *Peng Dehuai zhuan* [Biography of Peng Dehuai], 416; Tan Jingjiao, *Kangmei yuanchao zhanzheng* [The WRUSAK] (Beijing: Zhongguo shehui kexue chubanshe, 1990), 32–33.

47. Hong, *Hong Xuezhi huiyilu* [Memoirs of Hong Xuezhi], 390–91; Du, "Political Mobilization and Control," 73–74; Yang, *Zai zhiyuanjun silingbu de suiyueli* [My years at the CPVF General HQ], 51–52.

48. Quoted in Yang and Wang, *Beiwei 38 duxian* [The north latitude 38th Parallel], 149. See also Wang et al., *Peng Dehuai zhuan* [Biography of Peng Dehuai], 418.

49. Wen Yucheng joined the Red Army in 1929 and the CCP in 1932. He served as a battalion propaganda officer, political department director, and regiment political commissar in the Red Army. During the Anti-Japanese War he became chief of the political organization office of the Political Department in the New Fourth Army; political commissar of the 18th Brigade, 6th Division, New Fourth Army; and political commissar and commander of the 34th Division of the Northeast Region. During the Chinese Civil War Wen was appointed commander of the 145th Division, deputy commander of the Forty-First Army, and commander of the Fortieth Army. After the Korean War he became chief of staff of the Guangzhou Regional Command, deputy chief staff of the PLA, and commander of the Beijing Regional Command. He was made lieutenant general in 1955. See *Xinghuo liaoyuan* Composition Department, *Zhongguo renmin jiefangjun jiangshuai minglu* [Marshals and generals of the PLA], 1:474–75; Tan, *Zhongguo renmin zhiyuanjun renwulu* [Veterans' profile of the CPVF], 631–32.

50. Li, *Jiekai zhanzheng xumu de xianfeng* [Vanguard of the early actions in the war], 27; Military History Research Division, *Zhongguo renmin zhiyuanjun kangmei yuanchao zhanshi* [Combat experience of the CPVF in the WRUSAK], 19–20; Roy E. Appleman, *South to the Naktong, North to the Yalu (June–November 1950), U.S. Army in the Korean War* (Washington: Office of the Chief of Military History and Government Printing Office, 1961), 673.

51. Composition Committee, ed., *38 xian shang de jiaofeng: kangmei yuanchao zhanzheng jishi* [Fighting over the 38th Parallel: the recorded truth of the WRUSAK] (Beijing: Jiefangjun wenyi chubanshe, 2010), 68–69; Li Ying et al., *40 jun zai chaoxian* [The Fortieth Army in Korea] (Shenyang, China: Liaoning renmin chubanshe, 2010), 19–27; Li, *Jiekai zhanzheng xumu de xianfeng* [Vanguard of the early actions in the war], 28–40; Appleman, *South to the Naktong*, 675–77.

52. Tan, *Zhongguo renmin zhiyuanjun renwulu* [Veterans' profile of the CPVF], 74; *Xinghuo liaoyuan* Composition Department, *Zhongguo renmin jiefangjun jiangshuai minglu* [Marshals and generals of the PLA], 2:139.

53. Hong, *Hong Xuezhi huiyilu* [Memoirs of Hong Xuezhi], 396–97; Jiang Yonghui, *38 jun zai chaoxian* [The Thirty-Eighth Army in Korea], 2nd ed. (Shenyang, China: Liaoning renmin chubanshe, 2009), 33–34; Shuguang Zhang, *Mao's Military Romanticism: China and the Korean War, 1950–53* (Lawrence: University Press of Kansas, 1995), 103.

54. Li et al., *40 jun zai chaoxian* [The Fortieth Army in Korea], 42–44; Military History Research Division, *Zhongguo renmin zhiyuanjun kangmei yuanchao zhanshi* [Combat experience of the CPVF in the WRUSAK], 21–22.

55. CMC, "The Central Military Commission's Circular on the Combat Characteristics of South Korean Troops, October 30, 1950," drafted by Mao, in Mao, *Mao's Manuscripts since 1949*, 1:630–31; Mao, "Mao's Telegrams during the Korean War," 66–67.

56. Zhou, interview by the author. Also see Zhou, "China's Crouching Dragon," 86.

57. Military History Research Division, *Zhongguo renmin zhiyuanjun kangmei yuanchao zhanshi* [Combat experience of the CPVF in the WRUSAK], 24; Appleman, *South to the Naktong*, 689–708.

58. This statement explains the CPVF commanders' perception of the U.S. forces. The Chinese believed, for example, that the U.S. mechanized units had tremendous firepower and mobility but depended heavily on roads and bridges. Therefore the U.S. troops tended to stay near the roads and were not flexible enough to occupy advantageous terrain, thus providing the CPVF with opportunities to cut them into pieces. See Li Qingshan, *Zhiyuanjun yuanchao jishi* [The CPVF records of aiding Korea] (Beijing: Zhonggong dangshi chubanshe, 2008), 142.

59. For more details, see Military History Research Division, *Zhongguo renmin zhiyuanjun kangmei yuanchao zhanshi* [Combat experience of the CPVF in the WRUSAK], 27; Xu Yan, *Diyici jiaoliang: kangmei yuanchao zhanzheng de lishi huigu yu fansi* [The first encounter: a historical retrospective of the WRUSAK] (Beijing: Zhongguo guangbo dianshi chubanshe, 1990), 47.

60. Tan, *Kangmei yuanchao zhanzheng* [The WRUSAK], 46-47; Li, *Zhiyuanjun yuanchao jishi* [The CPVF records of aiding Korea], 141.

61. Peng Dehuai, "Ruchao zuozhan diyici zhanyi de jiben zongjie ji dierbu zuozhan fangzhen [The general report on the first campaign after entering Korea and operational plan for the next step]," November 13, 1950, speech at the First Enlarged Meeting of the CPVF Party Committee, in Peng, *Peng's Military Papers*, 335; Hong, *Hong Xuezhi huiyilu* [Memoirs of Hong Xuezhi], 401; Du, *Zai zhiyuanjun zongbu* [At the CPVF General HQ], 72.

62. Peng, "My Story of the Korean War," 33. The small American unit Peng mentioned consisted of three battalions of the U.S. 1st Cavalry Division. See also Military History Research Division, *Zhongguo renmin zhiyuanjun kangmei yuanchao zhanshi* [Combat experience of the CPVF in the WRUSAK], 27.

63. Zhang, *Mao's Military Romanticism*, 106.

64. Song Shilun joined the CCP in 1927 and the Red Army in 1929. He served as commander and political commissar of CCP guerrilla teams in Hunan and as division and army chief staff in the Red Army. During the Anti-Japanese War, Song became regiment and division commander in the Eighth Route Army. During the Chinese Civil War, he was appointed commander and political commissar of the Ninth Army Group. Song was made a general in 1955. See *Xinghuo liaoyuan* Composition Department, *Zhongguo renmin jiefangjun jiangshuai minglu* [Marshals and generals of the PLA], 1:100-101; Tan, *Zhongguo renmin zhiyuanjun renwulu* [Veterans' profile of the CPVF], 326-27; Hu and Yu, *Genzhe Mao Zedong da tianxia* [Follow Mao Zedong to seize state power], 57.

65. Hong, *Kangmei yuanchao zhanzheng huiyi* [Recollections of the WRUSAK], 90-91; Wang et al., *Peng Dehuai zhuan* [Biography of Peng Dehuai], 423.

66. For more details on the UN peace initiatives and the Chinese delegation's reactions in November–December 1950, see Yafeng Xia, *Negotiating with the Enemy: U.S.-China Talks during the Cold War, 1949-72* (Bloomington: Indiana University Press, 2006), 46; William W. Stueck, *The Korean War: An International History* (Princeton: Princeton University Press, 1995), 139-41.

67. Walter Bedell Smith, "Memorandum by the Director of the Central Intelligence Agency to the President, November 1, 1950," in U.S. Department of State, *Foreign Relations of the United States: China, Korea, Vietnam, and Indochina, 1945-72* (Washington: Government Printing Office, 1982-89), 7:1025. Hereafter cited as *FRUS*.

68. Mao Zedong, telegram to Peng and Deng Hua, November 5, 1950, *Collected Military Works of Mao*, 6:197.

69. Mao Zedong, telegram to Peng, "Zhengqu zai Wonsan-Sunchon tieluxian yibei chuangzao zhanchang [Must open a front north of the Wonsan-Sunchon railroad]," 1:00 A M on November 5, 1950, in Mao, *Mao's Manuscripts since 1949*, 1:647. See also Mao, *Mao's Military Manuscripts since 1949*, 1:335–36.

70. Quoted in Mao, "Telegram to Peng Dehuai and Deng Hua," in *Chinese Communist Foreign Policy and the Cold War in Asia*, trans. and ed. Zhang and Chen, 191.

71. Mao Zedong, telegram to Peng, Deng, and Pak Il-yu, "Tongyi zhiyuanjun xiayibu de zuozhan fangzhen he bushu [Approval of the CPVF's plan and deployment for the next campaign]," November 9, 1950, in Mao, *Collected Military Works of Mao*, 6:198. See also Mao, *Mao's Military Manuscripts since 1949*, 1:342–43.

72. Hong, *Hong Xuezhi huiyilu* [Memoirs of Hong Xuezhi], 408–10; Du, "Political Mobilization and Control," 73–74.

73. Peng Dehuai, "Zai zhiyuanjun diyici dangwei kuoda huiyi shang de baogao [Speech at the first expanded meeting of the CPVF Party Committee]," November 14, 1950, in Peng, *Peng's Military Papers*, 337; Du, "Political Mobilization and Control," 74–75.

74. Mao approved the CPVF Command's request to release the UNF POWs before the Second Offensive Campaign. See Mao Zedong, "Telegram to Peng Dehuai, Deng Hua, and Pak Il-yu, November 18, 1950," in *Chinese Communist Foreign Policy and the Cold War in Asia*, trans. and ed. Zhang and Chen, 205. See also Du, "Political Mobilization and Control," 79–83.

75. Peng, "My Story of the Korean War," 33; Military History Research Division, *Zhongguo renmin zhiyuanjun kangmei yuanchao zhanshi* [Combat experience of the CPVF in the WRUSAK], 36.

76. Quoted in Halberstam, *The Coldest Winter*, 389.

77. Jiang, *38 jun zai chaoxian* [The Thirty-Eighth Army in Korea], 153–54; Du, *Zai zhiyuanjun zongbu* [At the CPVF General HQ], 103–104.

78. Guo Baoheng and Hu Zhiyuan, *Chipin hanjiang nanbei: 42 jun zai chaoxian* [Fighting over the Han River: the Forty-Second Army in Korea] (Shenyang, China: Liaoning renmin chubanshe, 1996), 110–11; Jiang, *38 jun zai chaoxian* [The Thirty-Eighth Army in Korea], 118–21.

79. Hong, *Hong Xuezhi huiyilu* [Memoirs of Hong Xuezhi], 421–23; Yang, *Zai zhiyuanjun silingbu de suiyueli* [My years at the CPVF General HQ], 51–52; Jiang, *38 jun zai chaoxian* [The Thirty-Eighth Army in Korea], 166–71, 194–95, 218–19.

80. Wu, *Chaoxian zhanchang 1,000 tian* [One thousand days on the Korean battleground], 164–74; Du, *Zai zhiyuanjun zongbu* [At the CPVF General HQ], 120.

81. Capt. Wang Xuedong (CPVF), interview by the author in Harbin, Heilongjiang, April 2000. For more details, see Wang Xuedong, "The Chosin Reservoir: A Chinese Captain's Story," in *Voices from the Korean War: Personal Stories of American, Korean, and Chinese Soldiers*, 119.

82. Cui Xianghua and Chen Dapeng, *Tao Yong jiangjun zhuan* [Biography of General Tao Yong] (Beijing: Jiefangjun chubanshe, 1989), 393.

83. Zhao Yihong, *27 jun chuanqi* [The legacy of the Twenty-Seventh Army] (Jilin, China: Jilin renmin chubanshe, 1995), 415; Hong, *Hong Xuezhi huiyilu* [Memoirs of Hong Xuezhi], 427; Xu, *Diyici jiaoliang* [The first encounter], 58–59.

84. Wang, interview by the author.

85. Corp. Harold L. Mulhausen (U.S. Marine Corps, ret.), interviews by the author in Edmond, Oklahoma, September 2005 and March 2006. Corp. Mulhausen served in

A Company, 7th Regiment, U.S. 1st Marine Division in 1950–52. See also Harold L. Mulhausen, "The Chosin Reservoir: A Marine's Story," in *Voices from the Korean War: Personal Stories of American, Korean, and Chinese Soldiers*, 98–116; Russell A. Gugeler, *Combat Actions in Korea* (Washington: Center of Military History, U.S. Army, 1987), 54–79; Robert Leckie, *Conflict: The History of the Korean War* (New York: Da Capo, 1996), 209–11, 219–20; Burton I. Kaufman, *The Korean Conflict* (Westport, CT: Greenwood, 1999), 48–49.

86. Wang, interview by the author and "The Chosin Reservoir," 121–22. See also Du, *Zai zhiyuanjun zongbu* [At the CPVF General HQ], 122; Yang, *Zai zhiyuanjun silingbu de suiyueli* [My years at the CPVF General HQ], 74.

87. Peng, "My Story of the Korean War," 33; Hong, *Hong Xuezhi huiyilu* [Memoirs of Hong Xuezhi], 427; Billy C. Mossman, *U.S. Army in the Korean War: Ebb and Flow, November 1950–July 1951* (Washington: Army Center of Military History and Government Printing Office, 1990), 132–37.

88. Wang, interview by the author.

89. Peng, "My Story of the Korean War," 34–35; Hong, *Kangmei yuanchao zhanzheng huiyi* [Recollections of the WRUSAK], 92–93; Yang, *Zai zhiyuanjun silingbu de suiyueli* [My years at the CPVF General HQ], 72–74.

90. Among the CPVF casualties in the Second Offensive Campaign were 50,000 noncombat dead. See Military History Research Division, *Zhongguo renmin zhiyuanjun kangmei yuanchao zhanshi* [Combat experience of the CPVF in the WRUSAK], 48; Xu, *Diyici jiaoliang* [The first encounter], 60.

91. Mulhausen, interviews by the author. See also Max Hastings, *The Korean War* (New York: Simon and Schuster, 1987), 152–62; Patrick C. Roe, *The Dragon Strikes: China and the Korean War, June–December 1950* (Novato, CA: Presidio, 2000), 333–43.

92. Bin Yu, "What China Learned from Its 'Forgotten War' in Korea," in *Mao's Generals Remember Korea*, trans. and ed. Xiaobing Li, Allan R. Millett, and Bin Yu (Lawrence: University Press of Kansas, 2000), 17.

93. The CPVF claimed that the UNF had total casualties of 36,000 men, including 24,000 American troops. See Hong, *Hong Xuezhi huiyilu* [Memoirs of Hong Xuezhi], 429; Du, *Zai zhiyuanjun zongbu* [At the CPVF General HQ], 125; Military History Research Division, *Zhongguo renmin zhiyuanjun kangmei yuanchao zhanshi* [Combat experience of the CPVF in the WRUSAK], 48. The Chinese figures, however, do not coincide with the UNF Command's own casualty accounting. The U.S. Eighth Army had more than 10,000 casualties by December 3, 1950 (Millett, *The War for Korea, 1950–1951*, 347). U.S. X Corps had 8,735 battle casualties between November 27 and December 10 (Mossman, *U.S. Army in the Korean War*, 147). And the Marines had suffered 4,418 battle and 7,313 nonbattle casualties (Hastings, *The Korean War*, 164).

94. Mao Anying was Peng's Russian interpreter and secretary at the CPVF General HQ. For more on his death, see Hong Xuezhi, "The CPVF's Combat and Logistics," in *Mao's Generals Remember Korea*, 118–21; Du, *Zai zhiyuanjun zongbu* [At the CPVF General HQ], 94–98; Yang, *Zai zhiyuanjun silingbu de suiyueli* [My years at the CPVF General HQ], 292–95; Li, *Zhiyuanjun yuanchao jishi* [The CPVF records of aiding Korea], 149–53.

95. CMC, "Gei Peng Dehuai, Song Shilun, Tao Yong, Chen Yi de dianbao [Telegram to Song Shilun, Tao Yong, Chen Yi, Peng Dehuai, and others]," December 17, 1950, drafted by Mao, in Mao, *Selected Military Papers of Mao*, 2:682–83.

96. Bin Yu discusses some of the PLA tactics such as outnumbering the enemy whenever the situation permitted in order to wipe out entire enemy units; engaging the

enemy in mobile operations; and achieving surprise whenever possible in order to avoid the usually superior enemy firepower ("What China Learned from Its 'Forgotten War' in Korea," 14).

97. Wang, interview by the author. Also see Wang, "The Chosin Reservoir," 117, 123; Zhao, *27 jun chuanqi* [The legacy of the Twenty-Seventh Army], 418, 420.

98. Quoted in Ye Yumeng, *Chubing chaoxian: kangmei yuanchao lishi jishi* [A true history of China's entry into the Korean War] (Beijing: Shiyue wenxue chubanshe, 1989), 244.

99. Quoted in Military History Research Division, *Zhongguo renmin zhiyuanjun kangmei yuanchao zhanshi* [Combat experience of the CPVF in the WRUSAK], 162. For more details on Kim's visit, see Li, *Zhiyuanjun yuanchao jishi* [The CPVF records of aiding Korea], 156–60.

100. Quoted in Xu, *Mao Zedong yu kangmei yuanchao zhanzheng* [Mao Zedong and the WRUSAK], 189. In a telegram to Russian Ambassador Roshchin on December 5, Gromyko reiterated this point that China would win the war and should not negotiate with the United States at that time (Kathryn Weathersby, trans. and ed., "New Russian Documents on the Korean War," *Bulletin: Cold War International History Project*, nos. 6–7 [Winter 1995–96]: 51–52.)

101. Mao Zedong, telegram to Peng, "Wo zhiyuanjun bixu yueguo 38 xian zuozhan [The CPVF must cross the 38th Parallel for engagements]," December 13, 1950, in Mao, *Collected Military Works of Mao*, 6:239. See also Mao, *Mao's Military Manuscripts since 1949*, 1:408–409.

102. The peace proposal suggested that the Chinese stop their offensive at the 38th Parallel and then, on the basis of a ceasefire, convene a meeting between the major powers with interests in Korea to discuss a solution of the Korean crisis. For more details on the proposal, see Stueck, *The Korean War*, 145–48; Xia, *Negotiating with the Enemy*, 46.

103. Mao Zedong, telegram to Peng, December 21, 1950, in Mao, *Collected Military Works of Mao*, 6:245. See also Mao Zedong, "Telegram to Peng Dehuai, December 21, 1950," in *Chinese Communist Foreign Policy and the Cold War in Asia*, trans. and ed. Zhang and Chen, 216–18.

104. Mao Zedong, telegram to Peng and Pak Il-yu, December 26, 1950, in Mao, *Mao's Manuscripts since 1949*, 1:734–36. See also Mao, *Mao's Military Manuscripts since 1949*, 1:420–22.

105. Mao Zedong, telegram to Peng and Pak Il-yu, December 26, 1950, in Mao, *Mao's Manuscripts since 1949*, 1:734–36. Mao used the slogan to boost the CPVF's morale: "After finishing this campaign, all main armies should . . . strengthen political mobilization of the troops (not to go back to the motherland until the enemy forces in Korea have been eliminated)" (Mao Zedong, "Telegram to Peng Dehuai and Pak Il-yu, December 26, 1950," in *Chinese Communist Foreign Policy and the Cold War in Asia*, trans. and ed. Zhang and Chen, 219).

106. Mossman, *U.S. Army in the Korean War*, 160–2; Millett, *The War for Korea, 1950–1951*, 386–87; Stanley Weintraub, *MacArthur's War: Korea and the Undoing of an American Hero* (New York: Free Press, 2000), 285.

107. Peng, "My Story of the Korean War," 34; Hong, *Hong Xuezhi huiyilu* [Memoirs of Hong Xuezhi], 435–37.

108. Millett, *The War for Korea, 1950–1951*, 384–87; Mossman, *U.S. Army in the Korean War*, 192–98; Weintraub, *MacArthur's War*, 300.

109. Hong, *Kangmei yuanchao zhanzheng huiyi* [Recollections of the WRUSAK], 107; Du, *Zai zhiyuanjun zongbu* [At the CPVF General HQ], 159.

110. Ridgway, *The Korean War*, 94–95; Millett, *The War for Korea, 1950–1951*, 384–85; Mossman, *U.S. Army in the Korean War*, 198–200.

111. Peng Dehuai, telegram to all the CPVF armies and CMC, January 4, 1951, in Peng, *Peng's Military Papers*, 360–63.

112. Brian Catchpole, *The Korean War, 1950–53* (New York: Carroll and Graf, 2000), 101–102; Millett, *The War for Korea, 1950–1951*, 384–87; Mossman, *U.S. Army in the Korean War*, 201–202.

113. Li, "China's Intervention and the CPVF Experience in the Korean War," 144–45.

114. The 8,500 casualties of the Third Offensive Campaign consisted of 5,800 CPVF casualties and 2,700 NKPA casualties. The Communist forces claimed to have annihilated 19,000 enemy troops during the campaign, most of whom were ROK troops. For detailed Chinese figures, see Military History Research Division, *Zhongguo renmin zhiyuanjun kangmei yuanchao zhanshi* [Combat experience of the CPVF in the WRUSAK], 48; Xu, *Diyici jiaoliang* [The first encounter], 67.

115. "Zhu hancheng guangfu [Celebrate the liberation of Seoul],"*Renmin ribao* [People's daily], January 5, 1951.

116. Xiaobing Li, "Chinese Army in the Korean War, 1950–53," *New England Journal of History* 60, nos. 1–3 (2003–4): 282.

117. Hong, *Kangmei yuanchao zhanzheng huiyi* [Recollections of the WRUSAK], 90–91.

118. Peng and Kim held the first, and the only, joint CPVF-NKPA army commanders' meeting at the CPVF HQ to review the Third Offensive Campaign on January 25–29, 1951, as the UNF launched large-scale assaults along the Han River on the 25th. Caught by surprise, Peng and Kim changed the meeting's agenda from assessing the Third Campaign to preparing the Fourth Campaign. See Hong, *Hong Xuezhi huiyilu* [Memoirs of Hong Xuezhi], 448; Yang, *Zai zhiyuanjun silingbu de suiyueli* [My years at the CPVF General HQ], 98–99.

119. Yang, *Zai zhiyuanjun silingbu de suiyueli* [My years at the CPVF General HQ], 103–104; Jiang, *38 jun zai chaoxian* [The Thirty-Eighth Army in Korea], 301, 363; Mossman, *U.S. Army in the Korean War*, 253–54.

120. Jiang, *38 jun zai chaoxian* [The Thirty-Eighth Army in Korea], 301, 327–32, 405–408; Mossman, *U.S. Army in the Korean War*, 254–56.

121. Yang, *Zai zhiyuanjun silingbu de suiyueli* [My years at the CPVF General HQ], 102–106; Li, *Jiekai zhanzheng xumu de xianfeng* [Vanguard of the early actions in the war], 224–40; Wu, *Kangmei yuanchao zhong de 42 jun* [The Forty-Second Army in the WRUSAK], 105–106; Guo and Hu, *Chipin hanjiang nanbei* [Fighting over the Han River), 212–21; Mossman, *U.S. Army in the Korean War*, 266–69.

122. Peng Dehuai, telegram to all the CPVF armies and CMC, 12:00 AM, February 17, 1951, in Peng, *Peng's Military Papers*, 373–74; Yang, *Zai zhiyuanjun silingbu de suiyueli* [My years at the CPVF General HQ], 106.

123. Yang, *Zai zhiyuanjun silingbu de suiyueli* [My years at the CPVF General HQ], 106–109, 111–13; Li, *Jiekai zhanzheng xumu de xianfeng* [Vanguard of the early actions in the war], 240–50; Guo and Hu, *Chipin hanjiang nanbei* [Fighting over the Han River], 223–31.

124. For more information on the battle of Chipyong-ni, see Gugeler, *Combat Actions in Korea*, 100–125; Halberstam, *The Coldest Winter*, 535–66, 569–88; Stanley Sandler, *The Korean War: No Victors, No Vanquished* (Lexington: University Press of Kentucky,

278 NOTES TO PAGES 60–63

1999), 136, 161; William T. Bowers, "Korea and the Cold War," in Bowers ed., *Striking Back: Combat in Korea, March–April 1951* (Lexington: University Press of Kentucky, 2010): 10–11; Millett, *The War for Korea, 1950–1951*, 401–403, 406–10.

125. U.S. State Department, "Memorandum for the Record of a Department of State-Joint Chiefs of Staff Meeting, February 13, 1953," *FRUS* 7: 177.

126. Wang et al., *Peng Dehuai zhuan* [Biography of Peng Dehuai], 449; Yang, *Zai zhiyuanjun silingbu de suiyueli* [My years at the CPVF General HQ], 109.

127. Peng, "My Story of the Korean War," 35. See also Wang et al., *Peng Dehuai zhuan* [Biography of Peng Dehuai], 452–54; Yang and Wang, *Beiwei 38 duxian* [The north latitude 38th Parallel], 287.

128. Quoted in Peng, "My Story of the Korean War," 35.

129. Xu, *Mao Zedong yu kangmei yuanchao zhanzheng* [Mao Zedong and the WRUSAK], 202–203; Zhang, *Mao's Military Romanticism*, 143.

130. Mao Zedong, telegram to Stalin, "Chaoxian zhanju he caiqu lunfan zuozhan de fangzhen [On the war situation in Korea and the rotation plan of the CPVF]," March 1, 1951, in Mao, *Mao's Manuscripts since 1949*, 2:153.

131. Quoted in Peng, "My Story of the Korean War," 35. See also Xu, *Mao Zedong yu kangmei yuanchao zhanzheng* [Mao Zedong and the WRUSAK], 208.

132. Ridgway, *The Korean War*, 116.

133. The Iron Triangle is an area about twenty miles north of the 38th Parallel, between Keumhwa in the east, Cheorwon in the west, and Pyonggang in the north. It was strategically important for the CPVF to control the Iron Triangle as the base both for its defense of the north and for its Spring Offensive into the South. In 1951–53 the area became one of the major battlegrounds between the CPVF and UNF. After the armistice was signed on July 27, 1953, Keumhwa remained in North Korea, but Cheorwon and Pyonggang belonged to South Korea.

134. The CPVF announced they had annihilated 78,000 UNF troops in the fourth campaign. See Military History Research Division, *Zhongguo renmin zhiyuanjun kangmei yuanchao zhanshi* [Combat experience of the CPVF in the WRUSAK], 85; Xu, *Diyici jiaoliang* [The first encounter], 80.

135. Liaoning Provincial Government, work reports and meeting minutes, January–May 1951, in Liaoning Provincial Archives, Shenyang, Liaoning; Xu, "Chinese Forces and Their Casualties in the Korean War," 49, 51.

136. Xiaoming Zhang, *Red Wings over the Yalu: China, the Soviet Union, and the Air War in Korea* (College Station: Texas A & M University Press, 2002), 145–46.

### 3. THE LAST BATTLE FOR VICTORY

1. Mao Zedong, telegram to Stalin, "Chaoxian zhanju he caiqu lunfan zuozhan de fangzhen [On the war situation in Korea and the rotation plan of the CPVF]," March 1, 1951, in Mao Zedong, *Jianguo yilai Mao Zedong wengao, 1949–76* [Mao Zedong's manuscripts since the founding of the state, 1949–76] (Beijing: Zhongyang wenxian chubanshe, 1989; hereafter cited as *Mao's Manuscripts since 1949*), 2:153.

2. Hong Xuezhi, *Hong Xuezhi huiyilu* [Memoirs of Hong Xuezhi] (Beijing: Jiefangjun chubanshe, 2007), 461; Du Ping, *Zai zhiyuanjun zongbu: Du Ping huiyilu* [At the CPVF General HQ: memoirs of Du Ping] (Beijing: Jiefangjun chubanshe, 1989), 209, 219–20; Xu Yan, "Chinese Forces and Their Casualties in the Korean War," trans. Xiaobing Li, *Chinese Historians* 6, no. 2 (1993): 50.

3. The first wave of the CPVF, which entered Korea in late October and November, had nine armies—the Twentieth, Twenty-Sixth, Twenty-Seventh, Thirty-Eighth, Thirty-Ninth, Fortieth, Forty-Second, Fiftieth, and Sixty-Sixth—totaling twenty-seven infantry divisions and three artillery divisions. All told, there were 450,000 troops. See Xu, "Chinese Forces and Their Casualties in the Korean War," 48–49; Li Qingshan, *Zhiyuanjun yuanchao jishi* [The CPVF records of aiding Korea] (Beijing: Zhonggong dangshi chubanshe, 2008), 143; Luan Kechao, *Xue yu huo de jiaoliang: kangmei yuanchao jishi* [The contest: blood vs. fire; the record of resisting America and aiding Korea] (Beijing: Huayi chubanshe, 2008), 108; Yao Youzhi and Li Qingshan, *Zhiyuanjun yongcuo qiangdi de 10 da zhanyi* [The CPVF's ten major battles against a strong enemy] (Shenyang, China: Baishan chubanshe, 2009), 51, 55–56; Roy E. Appleman, *South to the Naktong, North to the Yalu (June–November 1950), U.S. Army in the Korean War* (Washington: Office of the Chief of Military History and Government Printing Office, 1961), 768–69.

4. CMC, telegram to Peng Dehuai, Song Shilun, Tao Yong, and PLA regional commands, "Zhiyuanjun fuchao lunfan zuozhan bushu de ruogan gaibian [Some changes in the rotation plan of the CPVF armies in Korea]," February 18, 1951, in Zhou Enlai, *Zhou Enlai junshi wenxun* [Selected military papers of Zhou Enlai] (Beijing: Renmin chubanshe, 1997): 4:158–61 (hereafter cited as *Zhou's Military Papers*).

5. CMC, telegram to Peng Dehuai, "Duidi fanji de bushu yu 19 bingtuan de kaijin [The counterattack plan and advance of the Nineteenth Army Group]," February 11, 1951], ibid., 4:154–56.

6. Hong, *Hong Xuezhi huiyilu* [Memoirs of Hong Xuezhi], 464–65; Xu, "Chinese Forces and Their Casualties in the Korean War," 50; Yao and Li, *Zhiyuanjun yongcuo qiangdi de 10 da zhanyi* [The CPVF's ten major battles against a strong enemy], 151, 155–56; Allan R. Millett, *The War for Korea, 1950–1951: They Came from the North* (Lawrence: University Press of Kansas, 2010), 426.

7. Billy C. Mossman, *U.S. Army in the Korean War: Ebb and Flow, November 1950–July 1951* (Washington: Army Center of Military History and Government Printing Office, 1990), 437; Peng Dehuai, "Zai zhongguo renmin zhiyuanjun diwuci dangwei kuodahui shang de jianghua [Speech at the CPVF Enlarged Fifth Party Committee conference]," April 6, 1951, in Peng Dehuai, *Peng Dehuai junshi wenxuan* [Selected military papers of Peng Dehuai] (Beijing: Zhongyang wenxian chubanshe, 1988), 385–86 (hereafter cited as *Peng's Military Papers*); Composition Committee, ed., *38 xian shang de jiaofeng: kangmei yuanchao zhanzheng jishi* [Fighting over the 38th Parallel: the recorded truth of the WRUSAK] (Beijing: Jiefangjun wenyi chubanshe, 2010), 286.

8. Peng Dehuai, telegram to all CPVF army commanders and the CMC, at 5:00 PM, March 14, 1951, in Peng, *Peng's Military Papers*, 379.

9. Sunzi, *The Art of War*, trans. John Minford (New York: Viking, 2002), 75.

10. Chinese official statistics reported that the CPVF had lost more than 85,000 men. See Wang Yan et al., *Peng Dehuai zhuan* [Biography of Peng Dehuai] (Beijing: Dangdai zhongguo chubanshe, 1993), 472; Military History Research Division, CAMS, *Zhongguo renmin zhiyuanjun kangmei yuanchao zhanshi* [Combat experience of the CPVF in the WRUSAK] (Beijing: Junshi kexue chubanshe, 1990), 109; Xu Yan, *Mao Zedong yu kangmei yuanchao zhanzheng* [Mao Zedong and the WRUSAK], 2nd ed. (Beijing: Jiefangjun chubanshe, 2006), 21. But the UNF Command statistics showed that the total did not include the CPVF's 20,000 troops missing in action, of whom 12,000 were POWs of the

UNF. Thus, the total Chinese casualties were about 105,000 men. See Millett, *The War for Korea, 1950–1951,* 452.

11. Xu Yan, *Diyici jiaoliang: kangmei yuanchao zhanzheng de lishi huigu yu fansi* [The first encounter: a historical retrospective of the WRUSAK] (Beijing: Zhongguo guangbo dianshi chubanshe, 1990), 340–43; Shuguang Zhang, *Mao's Military Romanticism: China and the Korean War, 1950–53* (Lawrence: University Press of Kansas, 1995), 255; and Shuguang Zhang, "China's Strategic Culture and the Cold War Confrontations," in *Reviewing the Cold War: Approaches, Interpretations, Theory,* ed. Odd Arne Westad (London: Frank Cass, 2000), 262.

12. Mao, telegram to Stalin, "Chaoxian zhanju he caiqu lunfan zuozhan de fangzhen [On the war situation in Korea and the rotation plan of the CPVF]," March 1, 1951, 2:153.

13. Military History Research Division, *Zhongguo renmin zhiyuanjun kangmei yuanchao zhanshi* [Combat experience of the CPVF in the WRUSAK], 125–26.

14. Mao's order to Peng was added by Mao to the CMC telegram to the CPVF Command, April 28, 1951. See Mao Zedong, *Mao Zedong junshi wenji* [Collected military works of Mao Zedong] (Beijing: Junshi kexue chubanshe, 1993), 6:275 (hereafter cited as *Collected Military Works of Mao*). The UNF forces in this campaign were the U.S. 3rd, 25th, and 24th Divisions; Turkish Brigade; British 28th Brigade; and ROK 1st Division. The U.S. 3rd Division, which arrived in Korea in September 1950, consisted of the 7th, 15th, and 30th Infantry Regiments and four field artillery battalions (FABs), totaling 10,000 troops. The U.S. 25th Division, which arrived in July, consisted of the 24th, 27th, and 35th Infantry Regiments and four FABs, totaling another 10,000 troops. The U.S. 24th Division, which also arrived in July, consisted of the 19th, 21st, and 34th Infantry Regiments and four FABs, again totaling 10,000 troops. The Turkish 1st Brigade, which arrived in Korea on October 17, consisted of three infantry battalions, totaling 5,000 men. The British 28th Brigade, which replaced the 27th Brigade in April 1951, consisted of four infantry battalions, totaling 5,000 troops. And the ROK 1st Division consisted of the 11th, 12th, and 13th Regiments, totaling 8,000 troops.

15. Zhang, *Mao's Military Romanticism,* 24.

16. Mao Zedong, "Problems of Strategy in China's Revolutionary War," in Mao Zedong, *Selected Works of Mao Tse-tung* (Beijing: Foreign Languages Press, 1977), 1:248. See also Mao, *Collected Military Works of Mao,* 1:758.

17. Mao Zedong, "Concentrate a Superior Force to Destroy the Enemy Forces One by One," in Mao, *Selected Works of Mao,* 4:104; Mao, *Collected Military Works of Mao,* 3:484–85.

18. Mao, telegram to Stalin, "Chaoxian zhanju he caiqu lunfan zuozhan de fangzhen [On the war situation in Korea and the rotation plan of the CPVF]," March 1, 1951, 2:153.

19. Sunzi, *The Art of War,* trans. Minford, 19.

20. Xu, *Mao Zedong yu kangmei yuanchao zhanzheng* [Mao Zedong and the WRUSAK], 219–20.

21. Mao, telegram to Stalin, "Chaoxian zhanju he caiqu lunfan zuozhan de fangzhen [On the war situation in Korea and the rotation plan of the CPVF]," March 1, 1951, 2:153.

22. Yang Dezhi, *Yang Dezhi huiyilu* [Memoirs of Yang Dezhi] (Beijing: Jiefangjun chubanshe, 1992), 519–20; Yang Dezhi, "Combat Experience in Korea," in *Mao's Generals Remember Korea,* trans. and ed. Xiaobing Li, Allan R. Millett, and Bin Yu (Lawrence: University Press of Kansas, 2000), 147–48. Gen. Yang joined the CCP and the Red

Army in 1928. Promoted from a squad, platoon, company, and regiment commander to a division commander, he participated in the Long March in 1934–35. During the Anti-Japanese War Yang became the commander of the 344th Brigade of the 115th Division and the 2nd Column of the Eighth Route Army. In the Chinese Civil War he served as a commander of the PLA's Second and Nineteenth Army Groups in the Northern Regional Command. During the Korean War, Yang was commander of the Nineteenth Army Group of the CPVF in 1951–52; deputy commander of the CPVF in 1952–53; and commander of the CPVF in 1953–55. He was given the rank of general in 1955. After his return to China, Yang became commander of the Jinan, Wuhan, and later Kunming Regional Commands. He also served as chief of the PLA General Staff, vice minister of defense for the PRC, and deputy secretary general of the CMC. See *Xinghuo liaoyuan* Composition Department, *Zhongguo renmin jiefangjun jiangshuai minglu* [Marshals and generals of the PLA] (Beijing: Jiefangjun chubanshe, 1992), 1:92–93; Tan Zheng, *Zhongguo renmin zhiyuanjun renwulu* [Veterans' profile of the CPVF] (Beijing: Zhonggong dangshi chubanshe, 1992), 210–11; Hu Haipo and Yu Hongjun, *Genzhe Mao Zedong da tianxia* [Follow Mao Zedong to seize state power] (Changsha, China: Hunan renmin chubanshe, 2009), 134.

23. The Sixty-Fourth Army of the Nineteenth Army Group consisted of the 190th, 191st, and 192nd Divisions, totaling 28,000 men. See CMC telegram to Peng Dehuai, Gao Gang, Yang Dezhi, and Li Zhimin, "Duidi fanji de bushu yu 19 bingtuan de kaijin [Counterattack plan and the Nineteenth Army Group's advance]," February 11, 1951, in Zhou, *Zhou's Military Papers*, 4:154–56.

24. The Sixty-Third Army of the Nineteenth Army Group consisted of the 187th, 188th, and 189th Divisions, totaling 29,000 troops.

25. The Sixty-Fifth Army of the Nineteenth Army Group consisted of the 193rd, 194th, and 195th Divisions, totaling 29,000 men. See Mao Zedong, letter to Zhou, "Guanyu zai chaoxian zhanchang lunfan zuozhan wenti [About the troop rotation on the Korean battleground]," February 7, 1951, in Mao, *Mao's Manuscripts since 1949*, 2:104–105.

26. CMC telegram to Peng Dehuai, Song Shilun, Tao Yong, and PLA regional commands, "Zhiyuanjun fuchao lunfan zuozhan bushu de ruogan gaibian [Some changes in the rotation plan of the CPVF armies in Korea]," February 18, 1951, in Zhou, *Zhou's Military Papers*, 4:158.

27. Zhou Enlai, telegram to Peng Dehuai and Gao Gang, "Dierfan budui ruchao canzhao zhuwenti [Issues on the second wave's entering Korea and participating in the war]," March 3, 1951, in ibid., 4:166–70. Grand Gen. Chen Geng was appointed commander of the Third Army Group of the CPVF in March 1951. See Chen Geng Zhuan Compilation Team, *Chen Geng zhuan* [Biography of Chen Geng] (Beijing: Dangdai zhongguo chubanshe, 2007), 396; Shuang Shi, *Kaiguo diyi zhan: kangmei yuanchao zhanzheng quanjing jishi* [The first war since the founding of the state: the complete story of the WRUSAK] (Beijing: Zhonggong dangshi chubanshe, 2004), 1:360.

28. The Twelfth Army of the Third Army Group consisted of the 31st, 34th, and 35th Divisions, totaling 30,000 troops.

29. The Fifteenth Army of the Third Army Group consisted of the 29th, 44th, and 45th Divisions, totaling 32,000 men.

30. The Sixtieth Army consisted of the 179th, 180th, and 181st Divisions, totaling 31,000 troops. Its men left Sichuan in January, walking for a week from Sichuan to

Shaanxi, and then traveled by train to Cang County, Hebei, where they replaced their WWII weapons with new Russian-made arms, including artillery guns (Lt. Col. Guan Zhichao, interview by the author, in Nanjing, Jiangsu, March 13–14, 2008). Guan was battalion commander and political commissar of the 1st and 2nd Battalions, 539th Regiment, 180th Division, Sixtieth Army, Third Army Group of the CPVF in 1951–53.

31. CMC telegram to Peng Dehuai, Song Shilun, Tao Yong, and PLA regional commands, "Zhiyuanjun fuchao lunfan zuozhan bushu de ruogan gaibian [Some changes in the rotation plan of the CPVF armies in Korea]," February 18, 1951, in Zhou, *Zhou's Military Papers,* 4:159.

32. Ibid.; Mao Zedong, letter to Zhou and Nie, February 2, 1951, in Mao, *Mao's Manuscripts since 1949,* 2:104–105.

33. Zhou Enlai, telegram to Kim Il-sung, "Qiangxiu zugou de jichang shi kongjun zaori canzhan de zhongxin keti [Urgent construction of enough airports is the key issue for the air force's early participation in the war]," March 15, 1951, in Zhou, *Zhou's Military Papers,* 4:171–73; Zhou, telegram to Peng Dehuai and Gao Gang, "Kongjun canzhan ji xiujian jichang fangan [Plans for the Air Force participating in the war and airport construction]," March 22, 1951, in ibid., 4:175–80.

34. Xu, "Chinese Forces and Their Casualties in the Korean War," 50. However, on April 14, 1951, the UNF Far East Command's intelligence summary indicated that the CPVF had 478,556 soldiers in fifty-one divisions. See Millett, *The War for Korea, 1950–1951,* 426.

35. Military History Research Division, *Zhongguo renmin zhiyuanjun kangmei yuanchao zhanshi* [Combat experience of the CPVF in the WRUSAK], 92; Shuang, *Kaiguo diyi zhan* [The first war since the founding of the state], 1:359; Xu, "Chinese Forces and Their Casualties in the Korean War," 50–51.

36. Quoted in Wang et al., *Peng Dehuai zhuan* [Biography of Peng Dehuai], 456. See also Peng Dehuai, telegram to the CMC, March 14, 1951, in Peng, *Peng's Military Papers,* 378–81.

37. This section is omitted from Mao, telegram to Stalin, "Chaoxian zhanju he caiqu lunfan zuozhan de fangzhen [On the war situation in Korea and the rotation plan of the CPVF]," March 1, 1951, 2:153. The section is in Mao Zedong, telegram to Stalin, March 1, 1951, in Zhou, *Zhou's Military Papers,* 4: 162.

38. Shen Zhihua, *Mao Zedong, Stalin he chaoxian zhanzheng* [Mao Zedong, Stalin, and the Korean War] (Guangzhou: Guangdong renmin chubanshe, 2004), 334–35; Zhao Jianli and Liang Yuhong, *Fenghuo 38 xian: diwuci zhanyi zhanshi baogao* [The flames of battle raging across the 38th Parallel: combat report on the fifth campaign] (Beijing: Junshi kexue chubanshe, 2007), 316.

39. Kathryn Weathersby, trans. and ed., "New Russian Documents on the Korean War," *Bulletin: Cold War International History Project,* nos. 6–7 [Winter 1995–96]: 43. See also Shen Zhihua, "Kangmei yuanchao zhanzheng zhong de sulian kongjun [The Soviet Air Force in the WRUSAK]," *Zhonggong dangshi yanjiu* [Studies on CCP history] 2 (2000): 27–29; Composition Committee, ed., *38 xian shang de jiaofeng* [Fighting over the 38th Parallel], 408.

40. Wang Dinglie and Lin Hu, *Dangdai Zhongguo kongjun* [Contemporary Chinese Air Force] (Beijing: Shehui kexue chubanshe, 1989), 78–79, 109–10; Chu Feng, "50 niandai zhongsu junshi guanxi yanjiu [Sino-Soviet military relations during the 1950s]," PhD diss., Party Academy of the CCP Central Committee, 2006, 25–26.

41. The two Soviet AAA divisions had 155 AAA guns of 85 mm and 140 of 37 mm. See Shuang, *Kaiguo diyi zhan* [The first war since the founding of the state], 2:516–17.

42. Shi Zhe, *Zai lishi juren shenbian* [At the side of historical giants] (Beijing: Zhongyang wenxian chubanshe, 1991), 497–98, 500; Wang and Lin, *Dangdai Zhongguo kongjun* [Contemporary Chinese Air Force], 129.

43. Weathersby, "New Russian Documents on the Korean War," 48; Shen, *Mao Zedong, Stalin he chaoxian zhanzheng* [Mao Zedong, Stalin, and the Korean War], 330.

44. Mao telegraphed Stalin on November 15, 1950, to confirm Stalin's "proposal to reinforce Belov's aviation force by an additional delivery of MiG-15 planes to China in two lots, numbering 120 pieces and to create a command apparatus for the air corps" (Weathersby, "New Russian Documents on the Korean War," 49).

45. Mao included Peng's request in his telegram to Stalin on March 1, 1951. See Shen Zhihua, trans. and ed., *Chaoxian zhanzheng: eguo danganguan de jiemi wenjian* [The Korean War: declassified documents from Russian archives] (Taipei: Zhongyang yanjiuyuan, 2003), 2:708; Wang Yan et al., *Peng Dehuai nianpu, 1898–1974* [A chronological record of Peng Dehuai, 1898–1974] (Beijing: Renmin chubanshe, 1998), 480.

46. Weathersby, "New Russian Documents on the Korean War," 59. See also Shen, *Mao Zedong, Stalin he chaoxian zhanzheng* [Mao Zedong, Stalin, and the Korean War], 334–35; Zhao and Liang, *Fenghuo 38 xian* [The flames of battle raging across the 38th Parallel], 316.

47. For more information on MiG Alley, see Conrad C. Crane, *American Airpower Strategy in Korea, 1950–53* (Lawrence: University Press of Kansas, 2000), 50, 65, 68–69, 85; William W. Stueck, *The Korean War in World History* (Lexington: University Press of Kentucky, 2004), 78; Allan R. Millett, *Their War for Korea: American, Asian, and European Combatants and Civilians, 1945–53* (Washington: Brassy's, 2002), 57, 60–62, 225, 234.

48. Shen, "Kangmei yuanchao zhanzheng zhong de sulian kongjun [The Soviet Air Force in the WRUSAK]"; Chu, "50 niandai zhongsu junshi guanxi yanjiu [Sino-Soviet military relations during the 1950s]," 39, 43; Xiaoming Zhang, *Red Wings over the Yalu: China, the Soviet Union, and the Air War in Korea* (College Station: Texas A & M University Press, 2002), 219–21.

49. Chen Jian, *Mao's China and the Cold War* (Chapel Hill: University of North Carolina Press, 2001), 3–4, 90–91.

50. Shen, "The Soviet Air Force in the WRUSAK," 24–26. See also Jon Halliday, "Air Operation in Korea: The Soviet Side of the Story," in *A Revolutionary War: Korea and the Transformation of the Postwar World,* ed. William J. Williams (Chicago: Imprint, 1993), 154.

51. In 1951, there were 442 Soviet advisers in Beijing: 310 chief military advisers, 72 economic and technology advisers, 47 government and foreign policy advisers, and 13 intelligence and national security chief advisers. See Shen, *Mao Zedong, Stalin he chaoxian zhanzheng* [Mao Zedong, Stalin, and the Korean War], 371. Shen found this information in the archives of the Second Division, ROC Defense Ministry, Defense Intelligence Agency, in Taiwan. He believes that the numbers collected by the intelligence agents in the 1950s were incomplete. For more on the Soviets' sending military advisers, see also Weathersby, "New Russian Documents on the Korean War," 45.

52. Chu, "50 niandai zhongsu junshi guanxi yanjiu [Sino-Soviet military relations during the 1950s]," 45–47; Yang Guoyu, *Dangdai Zhongguo haijun* [Contemporary Chinese navy] (Beijing: Zhongguo shehui kexue chubanshe, 1987), 48–49.

53. The Russian military advisers did not participate in the CPVF planning or operations on the Korean front until the fall of 1951. Mao telegraphed Stalin on August 27 and September 8, requesting eighty-three Soviet military advisers for the Chinese forces in Korea: ten for the CPVF Command, ten for the five army group commands, and sixty-three for the twenty-one infantry armies. Stalin approved Mao's request on September 10, and Russian military advisers arrived at the CPVF Command at Kongsudong, northwest of Ichon, in October 1951. See Shen, *Mao Zedong, Stalin he chaoxian zhanzheng* [Mao Zedong, Stalin, and the Korean War], 372; Yang Di, *Zai zhiyuanjun silingbu de suiyueli: xianwei renzhi de zhenshi qingkuang* [My years at the CPVF General HQ: untold true stories] (Beijing: Jiefangjun chubanshe, 1998), 193–95.

54. Peng Dehuai Biography Compilation Team, *Yige zhanzheng de ren: Peng Dehuai* [A real man: Peng Dehuai] (Beijing: Renmin chubanshe, 1994), 164–67; Zhao and Liang, *Fenghuo 38 xian* [The flames of battle raging across the 38th Parallel], 89, 92–94; Peng Dehuai, "My Story of the Korean War," in *Mao's Generals Remember Korea*, trans. and ed. Xiaobing Li, Allan R. Millett, and Bin Yu (Lawrence: University Press of Kansas, 2001), 30–37; Millett, *Their War for Korea*, 106–11.

55. Wang et al., *Peng Dehuai nianpu* [A chronological record of Peng Dehuai], 265–79; Tan, *Zhongguo renmin zhiyuanjun renwulu* [Veterans' profile of the CPVF], 614–15; Xinghuo liaoyuan Composition Department, *Zhongguo renmin jiefangjun jiangshuai minglu* [Marshals and generals of the PLA], 1:20–21.

56. Wang et al., *Peng Dehuai zhuan* [Biography of Peng Dehuai], 142–44, 294–98, 400–405; Zhao and Liang, *Fenghuo 38 xian* [The flames of battle raging across the 38th Parallel], 291–92.

57. Hong, *Hong Xuezhi huiyilu* [Memoirs of Hong Xuezhi], 461; Du, *Zai zhiyuanjun zongbu* [At the CPVF General HQ], 218–19; Yang, *Zai zhiyuanjun silingbu de suiyueli* [My years at the CPVF General HQ], 124–26; Tan Jingjiao, *Kangmei yuanchao zhanzheng* [The WRUSAK] (Beijing: Zhongguo shehui kexue chubanshe, 1990), 133.

58. Maj. Gen. Xie Fang was appointed deputy director of the Training Department of the CMC, vice president of the PLA Logistics College, and vice president of the Academy of Military Science after his return to China. He was promoted to major general in 1955. See Tan, *Zhongguo renmin zhiyuanjun renwulu* [Veterans' profile of the CPVF], 658–59; Xinghuo liaoyuan Composition Department, *Zhongguo renmin jiefangjun jiangshuai minglu* [Marshals and generals of the PLA], 3:619.

59. Hong, *Hong Xuezhi huiyilu* [Memoirs of Hong Xuezhi], 461–62; Yang, *Zai zhiyuanjun silingbu de suiyueli* [My years at the CPVF General HQ, 126–27.

60. Du, *Zai zhiyuanjun zongbu* [At the CPVF General HQ], 218; Tan, *Kangmei yuanchao zhanzheng* [The WRUSAK], 133.

61. CMC, telegram to Peng, "Tongyi diwuci zhanyi de zuozhan fangzhen yu zhanyi hou de bingli bushu [Agree the operation plan of the Fifth Campaign and deployment after the campaign]," April 28, 1951, in Zhou, *Zhou's Military Papers*, 4:193.

62. Ibid.

63. U.S. Department of State, *Foreign Relations of the United States: China, Korea, Vietnam, and Indochina, 1945–72* (Washington: Government Printing Office, 1982–89), 7:396.

64. Mike Gonzales, curator of the U.S. 45th Infantry Division Museum, interview by the author, in Oklahoma City, OK, July 14, 2004. See also "Actions in the Korean

Conflict," U.S. Army, 45th Division Archives, "The Korean War Files: Records of 1951," 45th Division Museum, Oklahoma City, OK; William R. O'Connell, *The Thunderbird: A History of the U.S. 45th Infantry Division in Korea, 1951–53* (Tokyo: Toppan, 1954), 11.

65. Sunzi, *The Art of War*, in Ralph D. Sawyer, trans. and ed., *The Seven Military Classics of Ancient China* (New York: Basic, 2007), 179.

66. For more details on the CPVF Command meeting on March 11, 1951, see Hong Xuezhi, *Kangmei yuanchao zhanzheng huiyi* [Recollections of the WRUSAK] (Beijing: Jiefangjun wenyi chubanshe, 1990), 136–38; Du, *Zai zhiyuanjun zongbu* [At the CPVF General HQ], 218–19; Zhao and Liang, *Fenghuo 38 xian* [The flames of battle raging across the 38th Parallel], 291–93.

67. Gen. Hong Xuezhi became deputy chief and later chief and political commissar of the GLD of the PLA after his return from Korea. He also served as director of the National Defense Industry of the PRC State Council and deputy secretary general of the CMC. See Tan, *Zhongguo renmin zhiyuanjun renwulu* [Veterans' profile of the CPVF], 492–93; Xinghuo liaoyuan Composition Department, *Zhongguo renmin jiefangjun jiangshuai minglu* [Marshals and generals of the PLA], 1:126–27.

68. For the UNF air raid on November 25, 1950, which killed Mao Anying, Mao Zedong's oldest son, see Hong Xuezhi, "The CPVF's Combat and Logistics," in *Mao's Generals Remember Korea*, trans. and ed. Xiaobing Li, Allan R. Millett, and Bin Yu (Lawrence: University Press of Kansas, 2000) 118–21; Du, *Zai zhiyuanjun zongbu* [At the CPVF General HQ], 94–97; Li, *Zhiyuanjun yuanchao jishi* [The CPVF records of aiding Korea], 149–53; Composition Committee, ed., *38 xian shang de jiaofeng* [Fighting over the 38th Parallel], 104–109.

69. Hong, *Kangmei yuanchao zhanzheng huiyi* [Recollections of the WRUSAK], 136. See also Zhang, *Mao's Military Romanticism*, 145–46.

70. Quoted in Yang Fengan and Wang Tiancheng, *Beiwei 38 duxian: Peng Dehuai yu chaoxian zhanzheng* [The north latitude 38th Parallel: Peng Dehuai and the Korean War] (Beijing: Zhongyang wenxian chubanshe, 2009), 292–93. Yang was Peng's military assistant and deputy director of Peng's office at the CPVF HQ. See also Hong, *Kangmei yuanchao zhanzheng huiyi* [Recollections of the WRUSAK], 136.

71. For more details, see Luo Yinwen, *Deng Hua jiangjun zhuan* [Biography of Gen. Deng Hua] (Beijing: Zhongyang dangxiao chubanshe, 1995).

72. Quoted in Yang and Wang, *Beiwei 38 duxian* [The north latitude 38th Parallel], 292–93. See also Hong, *Hong Xuezhi huiyilu* [Memoirs of Hong Xuezhi], 462.

73. Du, *Zai zhiyuanjun zongbu* [At the CPVF General HQ], 219; Xu, *Mao Zedong yu kangmei yuanchao zhanzheng* [Mao Zedong and the WRUSAK], 211.

74. Quoted in Yang and Wang, *Beiwei 38 duxian* [The north latitude 38th Parallel], 292–93. See also Hong, *Kangmei yuanchao zhanzheng huiyi* [Recollections of the WRUSAK], 137. Several years after the failure of the Spring Offensive, Peng admitted privately: "We can say now that Hong Xuezhi's thinking was right" (quoted in Zhu Shiliang, *Peng Dehuai zai chaoxian zhanchang* [Peng Dehuai in the battleground of Korea] [Shenyang, China: Liaoning renmin chubanshe, 1996], 278). See also Li, *Zhiyuanjun yuanchao jishi* [The CPVF records of aiding Korea], 284; Wang Shuzeng, *Juezhan chaoxian: chaoxian zhanchang shi wojun tong meijun jiaoliang de lianbingchang* [The showdown in Korea: the battleground for a competition between the Chinese army and American army] (Beijing: Jiefangjun wenyi chubanshe, 2007), 298.

75. Bin Yu, "What China Learned from Its 'Forgotten War' in Korea," in *Mao's Generals Remember Korea*, trans. and ed. Xiaobing Li, Allan R. Millett, and Bin Yu (Lawrence: University Press of Kansas, 2000), 22.

76. Millett, *Their War for Korea*, 110.

77. Mossman, *U.S. Army in the Korean War*, 344–45; Millett, *The War for Korea, 1950–1951*, 411–12, 415–16.

78. Matthew B. Ridgway, *The Korean War* (Garden City, NY: Doubleday, 1967), 116; Mossman, *U.S. Army in the Korean War*, 347–50.

79. Ridgway, *The Korean War*, 117; Millett, *The War for Korea, 1950–1951*, 417–18.

80. Peng, "Zai zhongguo renmin zhiyuanjun diwuci dangwei kuodahui shang de jianghua [Speech at the CPVF Enlarged Fifth Party Committee conference]," 386.

81. Ibid. See also Yang and Wang, *Beiwei 38 duxian* [The north latitude 38th Parallel], 296.

82. Sunzi, *The Art of War*, in Sawyer, *The Seven Military Classics of Ancient China*, 161.

83. Peng, "Zai zhongguo renmin zhiyuanjun diwuci dangwei kuodahui shang de jianghua [Speech at the CPVF Enlarged Fifth Party Committee conference]," 386.

84. Ibid., 386–87.

85. For example, Senior Col. Yang Di, deputy director of the Operation Division of the CPVF Command, had serious doubts about the campaign objective of eliminating several UNF divisions. See Yang, *Zai zhiyuanjun silingbu de suiyueli* [My years at the CPVF General HQ], 128–29.

86. Peng, "Zai zhongguo renmin zhiyuanjun diwuci dangwei kuodahui shang de jianghua [Speech at the CPVF Enlarged Fifth Party Committee conference]," 386–87.

87. Quoted in Hong, *Hong Xuezhi huiyilu* [Memoirs of Hong Xuezhi], 465. See also Du, *Zai zhiyuanjun zongbu* [At the CPVF General HQ], 221; Yang and Wang, *Beiwei 38 duxian* [The north latitude 38th Parallel], 295–97.

88. Quoted in Wang et al., *Peng Dehuai zhuan* [Biography of Peng Dehuai], 463.

89. Yang and Wang, *Beiwei 38 duxian* [The north latitude 38th Parallel], 296; Military History Research Division, *Zhongguo renmin zhiyuanjun kangmei yuanchao zhanshi* [Combat experience of the CPVF in the WRUSAK], 127–28.

90. Peng Dehuai, telegram to Mao, April 10, 1951, in Mao, *Mao's Manuscripts since 1949*, 2:239, note 2.

91. Mao Zedong, telegram to Peng, April 13, 1951, ibid., 2:239.

92. Hong, *Kangmei yuanchao zhanzheng huiyi* [Recollections of the WRUSAK)] 140–41. See also Du, *Zai zhiyuanjun zongbu* [At the CPVF General HQ], 227–28; Yang, *Zai zhiyuanjun silingbu de suiyueli* [My years at the CPVF General HQ], 131; Military History Research Division, *Zhongguo renmin zhiyuanjun kangmei yuanchao zhanshi* [Combat experience of the CPVF in the WRUSAK], 128; Li, *Zhiyuanjun yuanchao jishi* [The CPVF records of aiding Korea], 287; Yao and Li, *Zhiyuanjun yongcuo qiangdi de 10 da zhanyi* [The CPVF's ten major battles against a strong enemy], 155; Zhu, *Peng Dehuai zai chaoxian zhanchang* [Peng Dehuai in the battleground of Korea], 227.

93. Peng Dehuai, telegram to all CPVF army commands and copied to CMC and PLA Northeast Military Region Command at 11:00 P.M. on April 12, 1951, quoted in China Academy of Military Science, "The Unforgotten Korean War: Chinese Perspective and Appraisals," unpublished manuscript, 2006, 396.

94. Peng Dehuai, telegram to all CPVF commanders, April 18, 1951, in Peng, *Peng's Military Papers*, 390–92.

95. Sunzi, *The Art of War*, trans. Roger Ames (New York: Ballantine, 1993), 157.

96. The British 27th Brigade was made up of one British infantry battalion, a New Zealand artillery regiment, and one Canadian and one Australian infantry battalion. Lt. Maurie Pears, interviews by the author at the Australian War Memorial, Canberra, Australia, October 6–7, 2011. Lt. Pears served in the Australian infantry battalion of the British 27th Brigade. See also Brian Catchpole, *The Korean War, 1950–53* (New York: Carroll and Graf, 2000), 129–34.

97. Du, *Zai zhiyuanjun zongbu* [At the CPVF General HQ], 221, 226; Tan, *Kangmei yuanchao zhanzheng* [The WRUSAK], 137; Luan, *Xue yu huo de jiaoliang* [The contest], 204.

98. Hong, *Hong Xuezhi huiyilu* [Memoirs of Hong Xuezhi], 465; Yang, *Zai zhiyuanjun silingbu de suiyueli* [My years at the CPVF General HQ], 125–26; Chu Yun, *Chaoxian zhanzheng neimu quangongkai* [Declassifying the Korean War] (Beijing: Shishi chubanshe, 2005), 289.

99. Yang, *Yang Dezhi huiyilu* [Memoirs of Yang Dezhi], 540–41; Military History Research Division, *Zhongguo renmin zhiyuanjun kangmei yuanchao zhanshi* [Combat experience of the CPVF in the WRUSAK], 92; Li, *Zhiyuanjun yuanchao jishi* [The CPVF records of aiding Korea], 290–93.

100. Peng, "Zai zhongguo renmin zhiyuanjun diwuci dangwei kuodahui shang de jianghua [Speech at the CPVF Enlarged Fifth Party Committee conference]," 387.

101. Jiang Yonghui, *38 jun zai chaoxian* [The Thirty-Eighth Army in Korea], 2nd ed. (Shenyang, China: Liaoning renmin chubanshe, 2009), 302; Military History Research Division, *Zhongguo renmin zhiyuanjun kangmei yuanchao zhanshi* [Combat experience of the CPVF in the WRUSAK], 92–93.

102. Mao Zedong, telegram to Stalin, March 1, 1951, in Mao, *Mao's Manuscripts since 1949*, 2:152.

103. Starting in the fall of 1952, the PLA began to rotate Chinese troops into Korea to gain experience with modern warfare. By the end of the war, about 73 percent of the Chinese infantry troops had been rotated (25 of 34 armies, or 79 of 109 infantry divisions). More than 52 percent of the Chinese air force divisions, 55 percent of the tank units, 67 percent of the artillery divisions, and 100 percent of the railroad engineering divisions had been sent to Korea. The PLA did the same thing during the Vietnam War. See Nie Rongzhen, "Beijing's Decision to Intervene," in *Mao's Generals Remember Korea*, trans. and ed. Xiaobing Li, Allan R. Millett, and Bin Yu (Lawrence: University Press of Kansas, 2000), 49; Xu, "Chinese Forces and Their Casualties in the Korean War," 52; Xiaobing Li, *A History of the Modern Chinese Army* (Lexington: University Press of Kentucky, 2007), 106, 218–19.

104. Lt. Col. Guan Zhichao (PLA, ret.), interviews by the author in Nanjing, Jiangsu, March 13–14, 2008.

105. Capt. Zhao Baoshan (CPVF), interview by the author in Harbin, Heilongjiang, April 2000; also see Zhou Baoshan, "China's Crouching Dragon," in *Voices from the Korean War: Personal Stories of American, Korean, and Chinese Soldiers*, ed. Richard Peters and Xiaobing Li (Lexington: University Press of Kentucky, 2004), 85–96.

106. CMC telegram to Peng Dehuai, Song Shilun, Tao Yong, and PLA regional commands, "Zhiyuanjun fuchao lunfan zuozhan bushu de ruogan gaibian [Some changes in the rotation plan of the CPVF armies in Korea]," February 18, 1951, in Zhou, *Zhou's Military Papers*, 4:158.

107. CCP Central Committee, telegrams to Chen Geng on his mission in Vietnam, June 18 and 30, 1950, in Liu Shaoqi, *Jianguo yilai Liu Shaoqi wengao, 1949–52* [Liu Shaoqi's manuscripts since the founding of the state, 1949–52] (Beijing: Zhongyang wenxian chubanshe), 2:256–57. Chen became acting commander in chief of the CPVF in 1952 and deputy chief of the PLA General Staff in 1955. He was promoted to grand general in 1955. For more information on Chen, see chapter 2. See also Tan, *Zhongguo renmin zhiyuanjun renwulu* [Veterans' profile of the CPVF], 388–90; *Xinghuo liaoyuan* Composition Department, *Zhongguo renmin jiefangjun jiangshuai minglu* [Marshals and generals of the PLA], 1:26–27.

108. Chen Geng Zhuan Compilation Team, *Chen Geng zhuan* [Biography of Chen Geng], 397–99; Wang, *Juezhan chaoxian* [The showdown in Korea], 299; Shuang, *Kaiguo diyi zhan* [The first war since the founding of the state], 1:360.

109. Lt. Gen. Du Yide joined the Red Army in 1929 and the CCP in 1930. He served as commander of a squad, platoon, and company and then as political commissar of a battalion, regiment, and division in the Red Army. During the Anti-Japanese War he became deputy commander of the 4th Brigade, 129th Division, Eighth Route Army, and commander of the Hebei Regional Command. In the Chinese Civil War he was commander of the Tenth Army and deputy commander and later political commissar of the Third Army Group. After his return to China, Du became vice political commissar and deputy commander of the PLA Navy and commander of the Lanzhou Regional Command. He was ranked lieutenant general in 1955 and lieutenant general of the PLAN in 1963. See Tan, *Zhongguo renmin zhiyuanjun renwulu* [Veterans' profile of the CPVF], 186–87; *Xinghuo liaoyuan* Composition Department, *Zhongguo renmin jiefangjun jiangshuai minglu* [Marshals and generals of the PLA], 1:256–57. Maj. Gen. Wang Yunrui joined the Red Army in 1931 and the CCP in 1932. He served as regiment commander and divisional chief of staff in the Red Army. During the Anti-Japanese War he became a staff member of the 129th Division Command of the Eighth Route Army and chief staff of the Central China Command. In the Chinese Civil War he was appointed chief of staff of the Second Column and later chief of staff of the Third Army Group. After his return to China, Wang became the chief of staff of the Nanjing Regional Command and vice president of the China Academy of Military Science. He became a major general in 1955. See Tan, *Zhongguo renmin zhiyuanjun renwulu* [Veterans' profile of the CPVF], 61–62; *Xinghuo liaoyuan* Composition Department, *Zhongguo renmin jiefangjun jiangshuai minglu* [Marshals and generals of the PLA], 2:111.

110. For more information, see Wang Jinshan, *Wang Jinshan wenji* [Collected papers of Wang Jinshan] (Beijing: Junshi kexue chubanshe, 1992), introduction; Tan, *Zhongguo renmin zhiyuanjun renwulu* [Veterans' profile of the CPVF], 40–41.

111. The Huaihai Campaign was one of the major offensive campaigns fought by the PLA that guaranteed the final victory of the CCP over the GMD during the Chinese Civil War. The campaign took place between the Huai River in the west and Huang Hai (Yellow Sea) in the east (which explains its name) from November 1948 to January 1949. The troops of the PLA who fought the campaign were under the command of Deng Xiaoping, Liu Bocheng, Chen Yi, and Su Yu. See Odd Arne Westad, *Decisive Encounters: The Chinese Civil War, 1946–50* (Stanford: Stanford University Press, 2003), 205–11.

112. Quoted in Yang, *Zai zhiyuanjun silingbu de suiyueli* [My years at the CPVF General HQ], 128. See also Zhao and Liang, *Fenghuo 38 xian* [The flames of battle raging across the 38th Parallel], 28.

113. Luo, *Deng Hua jiangjun zhuan* [Biography of Gen. Deng Hua], 173; Xu Yipeng, *Zhihu: chaoxian tingzhan gaocheng juedoulu* [A straight curve: the leaders' struggle over the Korean armistice] (Nanjing, China: Jiangsu renmin chubanshe, 1997), 7–9.

114. Chen Geng Zhuan Compilation Team, *Chen Geng zhuan* [Biography of Chen Geng], 580.

115. Yang Dezhi, "Command Experience in Korea," in *Mao's Generals Remember Korea*, trans. and ed. Xiaobing Li, Allan R. Millett, and Bin Yu (Lawrence: University Press of Kansas, 2001): 147–49; Yang, *Yang Dezhi huiyilu* [Memoirs of Yang Dezhi], 614–15.

116. For biographical information on Yang, see note 22 in this chapter. See also Tan, *Zhongguo renmin zhiyuanjun renwulu* [Veterans' profile of the CPVF], 210–11; *Xinghuo liaoyuan* Composition Department, *Zhongguo renmin jiefangjun jiangshuai minglu* [Marshals and generals of the PLA], 1:92–93.

117. Composition Committee, ed., *38 xian shang de jiaofeng* [Fighting over the 38th Parallel], 299–300; Chu, *Chaoxian zhanzheng neimu quangongkai* [Declassifying the Korean War], 291, 292–93; Yang, "Command Experience in Korea," 147–48.

118. Quoted in Yang, *Zai zhiyuanjun silingbu de suiyueli* [My years at the CPVF General HQ], 128.

119. Zhao and Liang, *Fenghuo 38 xian* [The flames of battle raging across the 38th Parallel], 28; Yang, *Zai zhiyuanjun silingbu de suiyueli* [My years at the CPVF General HQ], 130.

120. Yang, *Yang Dezhi huiyilu* [Memoirs of Yang Dezhi], 545.

121. Ibid., 547.

122. Lt. Gen. Tao Yong joined the Red Army in 1929 and the CCP in 1931. He served as a commander at the squad, platoon, company, battalion, regiment, and division levels in the Red Army. During the Anti-Japanese War he became a regiment commander and divisional commander and political commissar of the New Fourth Army. In the Chinese Civil War he was appointed a divisional commander and political commissar, commander of the Twenty-third Army, and later deputy commander of the Ninth Army Group. After his return to China, Tao became commander of the East Sea Fleet of the PLA Navy, deputy commander of the PLA Navy, and deputy commander of the Nanjing Regional Command. He was ranked lieutenant general of the PLAN in 1955. Tao committed suicide during the Cultural Revolution. See Tan, *Zhongguo renmin zhiyuanjun renwulu* [Veterans' profile of the CPVF], 563; *Xinghuo liaoyuan* Composition Department, *Zhongguo renmin jiefangjun jiangshuai minglu* [Marshals and generals of the PLA], 1:432–33. Lt. Gen. Qin Jian joined the Red Army in 1929 and the CCP in 1931. He served as a commander at the squad, platoon, company, and battalion levels in the Red Army. During the Anti-Japanese War he became a regimental commander in the 115th Division of the Eighth Route Army and regiment and divisional commander in the New Fourth Army. In the Chinese Civil War he was appointed commander of a division and deputy commander of an army in the East China Regional Command, and chief of staff of the Fourth and later the Ninth Army Group. After his return to China, Qin became deputy chief of staff of the Nanjing Regional Command. He became a lieutenant general in 1955. See Tan, *Zhongguo renmin zhiyuanjun renwulu* [Veterans' profile of the CPVF], 623–24; *Xinghuo liaoyuan* Composition Department, *Zhongguo renmin jiefangjun jiangshuai minglu* [Marshals and generals of the PLA], 1:468–69.

123. For biographical information about Song Shilun, see note 64 in chapter 2.

124. Capt. Wang Xuedong (CPVF), interview by the author in Harbin, Heilongjiang, April 2000. For more details, see Wang Xuedong, "The Chosin Reservoir: A Chinese

Captain's Story," in *Voices from the Korean War: Personal Stories of American, Korean, and Chinese Soldiers,* ed. Richard Peters and Xiaobing Li (Lexington: University Press of Kentucky, 2004), 119. See also Corp. Harold L. Mulhausen (U.S. Marine Corps, ret.), interviews by the author in Edmond, OK, September 2005 and March 2006; Harold L. Mulhausen, "The Chosin Reservoir: A Marine's Story," in *Voices from the Korean War: Personal Stories of American, Korean, and Chinese Soldiers,* 98–116; Cui Xianghua and Chen Dapeng, *Tao Yong jiangjun zhuan* [Biography of General Tao Yong] (Beijing: Jiefangjun chubanshe, 1989), 393.

125. CMC, "Gei Peng Dehuai, Song Shilun, Tao Yong, Chen Yi de dianbao [Telegram to Song Shilun, Tao Yong, Chen Yi, Peng Dehuai, and others]," December 17, 1950, drafted by Mao, in Mao, *Selected Military Papers of Mao,* 2:682–83.

126. Yang, *Zai zhiyuanjun silingbu de suiyueli* [My years at the CPVF General HQ], 128.

127. Peng Dehuai, telegram to Mao, April 10, 1951, in Mao, *Mao's Manuscripts since 1949,* 2:239, note 2.

128. Mao Zedong, telegram to Peng, April 13, 1951, ibid., 2:239.

129. Peng, "Zai zhongguo renmin zhiyuanjun diwuci dangwei kuodahui shang de jianghua [Speech at the CPVF Enlarged Fifth Party Committee conference]," 386.

130. Hong, *Kangmei yuanchao zhanzheng huiyi* [Recollections of the WRUSAK], 137; Military History Research Division, *Zhongguo renmin zhiyuanjun kangmei yuanchao zhanshi* [Combat experience of the CPVF in the WRUSAK], 129. See note 44 in chapter 7 for additional basic units.

131. Quoted in Hong, "The CPVF's Combat and Logistics," 132.

132. For more details on Hong's meeting with Zhou in Beijing in April 1951, see Hong, *Hong Xuezhi huiyilu* [Memoirs of Hong Xuezhi], 488–92; Hong, "The CPVF's Combat and Logistics," 122–29; Li, *Zhiyuanjun yuanchao jishi* [The CPVF records of aiding Korea], 303–304.

133. Quoted in Hong, "The CPVF's Combat and Logistics," 129.

134. Quoted in ibid., 128–29. See also Hong, *Hong Xuezhi huiyilu* [Memoirs of Hong Xuezhi], 493.

135. For the details of the CPVF Command meeting on May 14, 1951, see Hong, *Kangmei yuanchao zhanzheng huiyi* [Recollections of the WRUSAK], 181–83; Hong, "The CPVF's Combat and Logistics," 132–36; Luan, *Xue yu huo de jiaoliang* [The contest], 230.

136. Quoted in Zhou Zhong, *Kangmei yuanchao zhanzheng houqinshi jianbianben* [A concise history of the logistics in the WRUSAK] (Beijing: Jindun chubanshe, 1993), 87–88. See also Hong, "The CPVF's Combat and Logistics," 135.

137. Gen. Zhou Chunquan joined the CCP in 1926 and the Red Army in 1928. He became a division commander and political commissar, army political commissar, and deputy director of the Political Department of the Red Army HQ. During the Anti-Japanese War Zhou served as commander of the Logistics Department of the Northeast Coalition Army and chief of the Logistics Department of the Northeast Regional Command. During the Chinese Civil War he was appointed chief of the Logistics Department of the PLA Fourth Field Army. After his return to China, he became deputy chief of the GLD of the PLA. He was made a general in 1955. See Tan, *Zhongguo renmin zhiyuanjun renwulu* [Veterans' profile of the CPVF], 441–42; *Xinghuo liaoyuan* Composition Department, *Zhongguo renmin jiefangjun jiangshuai minglu* [Marshals and generals of the PLA], 1:122–23. Maj. Gen. Zhang Mingyuan joined the CCP and the Red Army in 1931.

He became a commander at the platoon, company, battalion, and regiment levels in the Red Army. During the Anti-Japanese War Zhang served as chief of the Transportation Bureau of the Eighth Route Army. During the Chinese Civil War he was appointed deputy chief of the Logistics Department of the PLA Fourth Field Army. After his return to China, he became deputy chief of the GLD of the PLA. He became a major general in 1955. See Tan, *Zhongguo renmin zhiyuanjun renwulu* [Veterans' profile of the CPVF], 346; *Xinghuo liaoyuan* Composition Department, *Zhongguo renmin jiefangjun jiangshuai minglu* [Marshals and generals of the PLA], 3:67. Gov. Du Zheheng joined the CCP in 1936 and the Eighth Route Army in 1938, during the Anti-Japanese War. In the Chinese Civil War he was appointed vice political commissar of the Logistics Department of the Northeast Regional Command. After his return to China, he became governor of Liaoning Province. See Tan, *Zhongguo renmin zhiyuanjun renwulu* [Veterans' profile of the CPVF], 190.

138. Nie, "Beijing's Decision to Intervene," 53.

139. Col. Wang Po (PLA, ret.), PLA Logistics Academy, interview by the author in Beijing, July 1994. See also Zhou, *Kangmei yuanchao zhanzheng houqinshi jianbianben* [A concise history of the logistics in the WRUSAK], 25–29.

140. Ministry of Foreign Affairs to Foreign Affairs Office, Northeast China Executive Committee, "Guanyu bangzhu chaoxian xiujian yiyao canku de baogao [Helping North Korea construct more medicine warehouses]," April 8, 1953, in "Zhou Enlai zongli youguan chaoxian dianwen de pishi" [Premier Zhou Enlai's approvals and instructions on North Korean telegrams and documents]," 1953, File# 106-00034-01 (1), 2–3, Archives Department, PRC Foreign Affairs Ministry, Beijing; Teng Daiyuan to Li Kenong, "Guanyu chaoxian renminjun zai dongbei zhanyong wo chepi de baogao [About the rail cars in Northeast China halted by the North Korean People's Army]," June 29, 1951, File# 106-00026-02 (1), ibid.; Col. Wang Po, PLA Logistics College, interview by the author in Beijing, July 1994.

141. Shuguang Zhang, "Command, Control, and the PLA's Offensive Campaigns in Korea, 1950–1951," in *Chinese Warfighting: The PLA Experience since 1949*, ed. Mark A. Ryan, David M. Finkelstein, and Michael A. McDevitt (New York: M. E. Sharpe, 2003), 110–11, 113.

142. Yang and Wang, *Beiwei 38 duxian* [The north latitude 38th Parallel], 296–97; Military History Research Division, *Zhongguo renmin zhiyuanjun kangmei yuanchao zhanshi* [Combat experience of the CPVF in the WRUSAK], 128; Zhao and Liang, *Fenghuo 38 xian* [The flames of battle raging across the 38th Parallel], 28.

143. Weathersby, "New Russian Documents on the Korean War," 48; Shen, *Chaoxian zhanzheng* [The Korean War], 617.

144. Nie Rongzhen, *Nie Rongzhen huiyilu* [Memoirs of Nie Rongzhen] (Beijing: Jiefangjun chubanshe, 1984), 2:757.

145. Quoted in Shen, *Mao Zedong, Stalin he chaoxian zhanzheng* [Mao Zedong, Stalin, and the Korean War], 334–35.

146. Zhang, *Red Wings over the Yalu*, 146–48.

147. Xu Xiangqian, *Lishi de huigu* [History in retrospect] (Beijing: Jiefangjun chubanshe, 1988), 805–806; *Xinghuo liaoyuan* Composition Department, *Zhongguo renmin jiefangjun jiangshuai minglu* [Marshals and generals of the PLA], 1:16–17.

148. Xu Xiangqian, "The Purchase of Arms from Moscow," in *Mao's Generals Remember Korea*, 139–48; Xu, *Lishi de huigu* [History in retrospect], 797–805.

149. Mao Zedong, telegram to Xu Xiangqian, "Guanyu tong sulian tanpan dinggou junshi zhuangbei he binggong jianshe wenti [Purchase military equipment and arms and build our defense industry through negotiations with the Soviet Union]," July 12, 1951, in Mao, *Mao's Military Manuscripts since 1949*, 1:533–34. Mao said: "Regarding the weaponry manufacturing, [we] agree to follow the current Soviet standard for weapons, ammunition, and equipment to standardize [our] models and makes." Zhou Enlai added three points to Mao's telegram: "(1) The Soviets have agreed to establish four new manufacturing factories [in China] to produce seven weapons and their accessories. [We] may invite their designing and planning teams to come first. (2) The new ammunition manufacturing factories should combine with our current factories. [With the Soviet Union we] should make our final decisions after their designing and planning teams have visited China. (3) [We] should sign two contracts first for weapons' blueprints and designs for the weaponry and ammunition productions. Sign the other contracts after the designing and planning" (ibid. 1:534). See CCP Central Archival and Manuscript Research Division, *Zhou Enlai nianpu, 1949–76* [A chronological record of Zhou Enlai, 1949–76] (Beijing: Zhongyang wenxian chubanshe, 1997), 1:157–58; Nie, *Nie Rongzhen huiyilu* [Memoirs of Nie Rongzhen], 2:-758.

150. Ministry of Foreign Affairs, "Youguan polan diyi he dierpi yuanchao wuzi tong-guo zhongguo zhuanyun de wenjian [Documents of transporting Poland's first and second shipments of aiding North Korea materials through China]," April 20–October 25, 1951, File# 109-00161-02 (1), Archives Department, PRC Foreign Affairs Ministry; "Youguan zhongguo zhengfu bangzhu luomania he jiekesiluofake zhengfu jiesong cha-oxian ertong he zhuanyun yuanchao wuzi de wenjian [Documents of Chinese government assisting the governments of Romania and Czechoslovakia to transport Korean children [to Europe] and aiding Korea materials]," April 1–30, 1952, File# 109-00232-01 (1), ibid.

151. Ministry of Railroad Transportation, "Guanyu bangzhu luomania yunsong yu-anchao wuzi de baogao [Reports and documents on assisting Romania transport aiding North Korea materials]," April 9–May 4, 1951, File# 109-00144-02 (1), ibid.

152. Mao Zedong, letter to Zhou Enlai, "Zai chaoxian zhanchang lunfan zuozhan de bingli biancheng [The force rotation of the CPVF armies on the Korean battleground]," February 7, 1951, in Mao, *Mao's Military Manuscripts since 1949*, 1:462–63; Hong, *Kangmei yuanchao zhanzheng huiyi* [Recollections of the WRUSAK], 184; Hong, "The CPVF's Combat and Logistics," 136.

153. Military History Research Division, *Zhongguo renmin zhiyuanjun kangmei yu-anchao zhanshi* [Combat experience of the CPVF in the WRUSAK], 121, 127.

154. Shen, *Mao Zedong, Stalin he chaoxian zhanzheng* [Mao Zedong, Stalin, and the Korean War], 273.

## 4. THE FIRST STEP

1. When the second wave arrived, the CPVF forces in Korea had doubled, from 450,000 troops in January to 950,000 men by mid-April, including 770,000 combat troops in forty-two infantry divisions, eight artillery divisions, and four AAA divisions. See Hong Xuezhi, *Hong Xuezhi huiyilu* [Memoirs of Hong Xuezhi] (Beijing: Jiefangjun chubanshe, 2007), 464–65; Luan Kechao, *Xue yu huo de jiaoliang: kangmei yuanchao jishi* [The contest: blood vs. fire; the record of resisting America and aiding Korea] (Beijing: Huayi chubanshe, 2008), 202–203; Xu Yan, "Chinese Forces and Their Casualties in the

Korean War," trans. Xiaobing Li, *Chinese Historians* 6, no. 2 (1993): 50; Allan R. Millett, *The War for Korea,1950–1951: They Came from the North* (Lawrence: University Press of Kansas, 2010), 426.

2. Peng Dehuai, telegram to all CPVF army commanders and the CMC, at 5:00 PM, March 14, 1951, in Peng Dehuai, *Peng Dehuai junshi wenxuan* [Selected military papers of Peng Dehuai] (Beijing: Zhongyang wenxian chubanshe, 1988), 378. Hereafter cited as *Peng's Military Papers*.

3. The total number of CPVF artillery pieces had increased to 6,000. See Shuang Shi, *Kaiguo diyi zhan: kangmei yuanchao zhanzheng quanjing jishi* [The first war since the founding of the state: the complete story of the WRUSAK] (Beijing: Zhonggong dangshi chubanshe, 2004), 1:359–60; PLA History Archives Compilation Committee, ed., *Paobing* [The artillery force] (Beijing: Jiefangjun chubanshe, 1999), 249, 254; Military History Research Division, CAMS, *Zhongguo renmin zhiyuanjun kangmei yuanchao zhanshi* [Combat experience of the CPVF in the WRUSAK] (Beijing: Junshi kexue chubanshe, 1990), 95.

4. Hong, *Hong Xuezhi huiyilu* [Memoirs of Hong Xuezhi], 464–65; Xu, "Chinese Forces and Their Casualties in the Korean War," 48–50; Billy C. Mossman, *U.S. Army in the Korean War: Ebb and Flow, November 1950–July 1951* (Washington: Army Center of Military History and Government Printing Office, 1990), 437; Millett, *The War for Korea, 1950–1951*, 426.

5. Peng Dehuai, "Zai zhongguo renmin zhiyuanjun diwuci dangwei kuodahui shang de jianghua [Speech at the CPVF Enlarged Fifth Party Committee conference]," April 6, 1951, Peng, *Peng's Military Papers*, 386.

6. Mao Zedong, telegram to Peng, "Zhuyi zai diwuci zhanyi zhong geidiyi jinkenengdade daji [Strike as hard as possible on the enemy forces in the Fifth Campaign]," April 28, 1951, in Mao Zedong, *Jianguo yilai Mao Zedong junshi wengao* [Mao Zedong's military manuscripts since the founding of the PRC] (Beijing: Junshi kexue chubanshe and Zhongyang wenxian chubanshe, 2010; hereafter cited as *Mao's Military Manuscripts since 1949*), 1:477.

7. Quoted in Peng Dehuai, "My Story of the Korean War," in *Mao's Generals Remember Korea*, trans. and ed. Xiaobing Li, Allan R. Millett, and Bin Yu (Lawrence: University Press of Kansas, 2001), 32–35; Wang Yan et al., *Peng Dehuai zhuan* [Biography of Peng Dehuai] (Beijing: Dangdai zhongguo chubanshe, 1993), 453; Xu Yan, *Mao Zedong yu kangmei yuanchao zhanzheng* [Mao Zedong and the WRUSAK], 2nd ed. (Beijing: Jiefangjun chubanshe, 2006), 201–202.

8. Du Ping, *Zai zhiyuanjun zongbu: Du Ping huiyilu* [At the CPVF General HQ: memoirs of Du Ping] (Beijing: Jiefangjun chubanshe, 1989), 237–38; Yang Fengan and Wang Tiancheng, *Beiwei 38 duxian: Peng Dehuai yu chaoxian zhanzheng* [The north latitude 38th Parallel: Peng Dehuai and the Korean War], (Beijing: Zhongyang wenxian chubanshe, 2009), 312–13. Col. Yang was Peng's military assistant and deputy director of the Peng's office at the CPVF General HQ.

9. Yang Di, *Zai zhiyuanjun silingbu de suiyueli: xianwei renzhi de zhenshi qingkuang* [My years at the CPVF General HQ: untold true stories] (Beijing: Jiefangjun chubanshe, 1998), 125; Li Ying et al., *40 jun zai chaoxian* [The Fortieth Army in Korea] (Shenyang, China: Liaoning renmin chubanshe, 2010), 188–94; Tan Jingjiao, *Kangmei yuanchao zhanzheng* [The WRUSAK] (Beijing: Zhongguo shehui kexue chubanshe, 1990), 138–39.

10. CMC, telegram to Peng, "Tongyi diwuci zhanyi de zuozhan fangzhen yu zhanyi hou de bingli bushu [Agree the operation plan of the Fifth Campaign and deployment after the campaign]," April 28, 1951, in Zhou Enlai, *Zhou Enlai junshi wenxun* [Selected military papers of Zhou Enlai] (Beijing: Renmin chubanshe, 1997; hereafter cited as *Zhou's Military Papers*): 4:193–95, including Peng's telegram to Mao and CMC on April 26, 1951. See also Shuang, *Kaiguo diyi zhan* [The first war since the founding of the state], 1:372–73.

11. Yang, *Zai zhiyuanjun silingbu de suiyueli* [My years at the CPVF General HQ], 125, 130; Chu Yun, *Chaoxian zhanzheng neimu quangongkai* [Declassifying the Korean War] (Beijing: Shishi chubanshe, 2005), 294–95.

12. The first wave of the CPVF, which entered Korea in late October and November, consisted of two army groups, the Ninth and Thirteenth, and had nine armies—the Twentieth, Twenty-Sixth, Twenty-Seventh, Thirty-Eighth, Thirty-Ninth, Fortieth, Forty-Second, Fiftieth, and Sixty-Sixth—totaling twenty-seven infantry divisions and three artillery divisions. The first group of the CPVF totaled 450,000 troops. See Xu, "Chinese Forces and Their Casualties in the Korean War," 48–49; Roy E. Appleman, *South to the Naktong, North to the Yalu (June–November 1950), U.S. Army in the Korean War* (Washington: Office of the Chief of Military History and Government Printing Office, 1961), 768–69.

13. Peng, "My Story of the Korean War," 32–35; Zhao Yihong, *27 jun chuanqi* [The legacy of the Twenty-Seventh Army] (Jilin, China: Jilin renmin chubanshe, 1995), 440–44.

14. From January 25 to April 21, the CPVF engaged in the Fourth Campaign, which was a series of mobile battles. See Wu Xinquan, *Chaoxian zhanchang 1,000 tian: 39 jun zai chaoxian* [One thousand days on the Korean battleground: the Thirty-Ninth Army in Korea] (Shenyang, China: Liaoning renmin chubanshe, 1996), 304–90 (Wu was the commander of the Thirty-Ninth Army in the Korean War; see note 99 for more biographical information about him); Li et al., *40 Jun zai chaoxian* [The Fortieth Army in Korea], 144–47.

15. NCO Han Shunzhou (PLA, ret.), interview by the author in Beijing, August 2010. Han served as a noncommissioned officer in the 3rd Battalion, 241st Regiment, 81st Division, Twenty-Seventh Army, Ninth Army Group of the CPVF during the Spring Offensive in 1951.

16. During the Second Offensive, the Ninth Army Group's Twentieth and Twenty-Seventh Armies launched the attacks against the U.S. 1st Marine and 7th Infantry Divisions at the Chosin Reservoir in North Korea on November 27. For more details on the Second Offensive, see the previous chapter and Xiaobing Li, *A History of the Modern Chinese Army* (Lexington: University Press of Kentucky, 2007), 97–101; Capt. Wang Xuedong (CPVF), interview by the author, in Harbin, Heilongjiang, April 2000 (Capt. Wang served in First Company, 172nd Regiment, 58th Division, Twentieth Army, CPVF Ninth Army Group in 1950–53); Wang Xuedong, "The Chosin Reservoir: A Chinese Captain's Story," in *Voices from the Korean War: Personal Stories of American, Korean, and Chinese Soldiers*, ed. Richard Peters and Xiaobing Li (Lexington: University Press of Kentucky, 2004), 117–24.

17. CMC telegram to Peng Dehuai, Song Shilun, Tao Yong, and PLA regional commands, "Zhiyuanjun fuchao lunfan zuozhan bushu de ruogan gaibian [Some changes in the rotation plan of the CPVF armies in Korea]," February 18, 1951, in Zhou Enlai, *Zhou's Military Papers*, 4:158–61.

18. Hong, *Hong Xuezhi huiyilu* [Memoirs of Hong Xuezhi], 473.

19. The Twentieth Army was reinforced the 11th and 26th Regiments from the 1st Artillery Division. See Military History Research Division, *Zhongguo renmin zhiyuanjun kangmei yuanchao zhanshi* [Combat experience of the CPVF in the WRUSAK], 95. The Twenty-Sixth Army was reinforced with the 27th Artillery Regiment and three companies of the 401st Antitank Regiment. See Tan, *Kangmei yuanchao zhanzheng* [The WRUSAK], 137. The Twenty-Seventh Army was reinforced with the 25th and 30th Artillery Regiments and three companies of the 401st Antitank Regiment. See Zhao, *27 Jun chuanqi* [The legacy of the Twenty-Seventh Army], 440–41.

20. Zhou Zhong, *Kangmei yuanchao zhanzheng houqinshi jianbianben* [A concise history of the logistics in the WRUSAK] (Beijing: Jindun chubanshe, 1993), 74.

21. Peng Dehuai, "Zai zhongguo renmin zhiyuanjun diwuci dangwei kuodahui shang de jianghua [Speech at the CPVF Enlarged Fifth Party Committee conference]," April 6, 1951, in Peng, *Peng's Military Papers*, 388–89; Hong, *Hong Xuezhi huiyilu* [Memoirs of Hong Xuezhi], 465–66; Du, *Zai zhiyuanjun zongbu* [At the CPVF General HQ], 221.

22. Wu, *Chaoxian zhanchang 1,000 tian* [One thousand days on the Korean battleground], 405–408. See also Du, *Zai zhiyuanjun zongbu* [At the CPVF General HQ], 238–39.

23. CMC telegram to Peng Dehuai, Song Shilun, Tao Yong, and PLA regional commands, "Zhiyuanjun fuchao lunfan zuozhan bushu de ruogan gaibian [Some changes in the rotation plan of the CPVF armies in Korea]," February 18, 1951, in Zhou, *Zhou's Military Papers*: 4:158–61.

24. Zhou Enlai, telegram to Peng and Gao, March 3, 1951, "Dierfan budui ruchao canzhan zhuwenti" [Issues on the second wave's entering Korea and participating in the war]," in Zhou, *Zhou's Military Papers*, 4:166–70; Chen Geng Zhuan Compilation Team, *Chen Geng zhuan* [Biography of Chen Geng] (Beijing: Dangdai zhongguo chubanshe, 2007), 396.

25. Lt. Col. Guan Zhichao (PLA, ret.), interviews by the author, in Nanjing, Jiangsu, March 13–14, 2008. Lt. Col. Guan was the battalion commander and political commissar of the 1st and 2nd Battalions, 539th Regiment, 180th Division, Sixtieth Army, Third Army Group in 1951–53. See also Chen Zhonglong, *60 jun rencai: rencai shi zheyang zhujiu de* [The elite of the Sixtieth Army: their successful stories] (Beijing: Zhongguo youyi chubanshe, 2005), 95–96.

26. Yang, *Zai zhiyuanjun silingbu de suiyueli* [My years at the CPVF General HQ], 130; Xu Yipeng, *Cuojue: 180 shi chaoxian shoucuoji* [Miscalculation: the setback of the 180th Division in Korea] (Nanjing, China: Jiangsu renmin chubanshe, 1997), 7–10.

27. As late as April 6, 1951, Peng still had the campaign starting in early or mid-May, if "the enemy forces advanced [northward] slowly" (Peng Dehuai, "Zai zhongguo renmin zhiyuanjun diwuci dangwei kuodahui shang de jianghua [Speech at the CPVF Enlarged Fifth Party Committee conference]," 386).

28. Peng Dehuai, telegram to all CPVF armies and copied to the CMC, 9:00 PM, April 18, 1951, in Peng, *Peng's Military Papers*, 390–92; Du, *Zai zhiyuanjun zongbu* [At the CPVF General HQ], 226.

29. Quoted in Wang et al., *Peng Dehuai zhuan* [Biography of Peng Dehuai], 466. For more information on the U.S. 40th and 45th Divisions, see chapter 3.

30. Quoted in Military History Research Division, CAMS, *Kangmei yuanchao zhanzhengshi* [History of the WRUSAK] (Beijing: Junshi kexue chubanshe, 2000), 2:321.

31. The unverified information about a UNF landing came from the Soviet intelligence that two American divisions that had arrived in Japan would be soon used for an amphibious landing on the east or west coast. The 45th Division was responsible for the security of Hokkaido, northernmost island of Japan, through the rest of 1951. Mike Gonzales, curator of the U.S. 45th Infantry Division Museum, interview by the author, in Oklahoma City, OK, July 14, 2004; U.S. Army, 45th Division Archives, "The Korean War Files: Records of 1951," 45th Division Museum, Oklahoma City, OK. See William R. O'Connell, *The Thunderbird: A History of the U.S. 45th Infantry Division in Korea, 1951–53* (Tokyo: Toppan, 1954), 11–12.

32. CMC, telegram to Peng, "Tongyi diwuci zhanyi de zuozhan fangzhen yu zhanyi hou de bingli bushu [Agree the operation plan of the Fifth Campaign and deployment after the campaign]," April 28, 1951, 4:195 note 2. See also Military History Research Division, *Kangmei yuanchao zhanzhengshi* [History of the WRUSAK], 2:322.

33. Brian Catchpole, *The Korean War, 1950–53* (New York: Carroll and Graf, 2000), 120.

34. Qi Dexue, *Ni buliaojie de chaoxian zhanzheng* [The Korean War you don't know] (Shenyang, China: Liaoning renmin chubanshe, 2011), 90–91; Xu Yan, *Diyici jiaoliang: kangmei yuanchao zhanzheng de lishi huigu yu fansi* [The first encounter: a historical retrospective of the WRUSAK] (Beijing: Zhongguo guangbo dianshi chubanshe, 1990), 41. See also Shuang, *Kaiguo diyi zhan* [The first war since the founding of the state], 1:80–81.

35. David Halberstam, *The Coldest Winter: America and the Korean War* (New York: Hyperion, 2007), 605–606; David McCullough, "Truman Fires MacArthur," in *The Cold War: A Military History,* ed. Robert Cowley (New York: Random House, 2005), 96–97.

36. Hong, *Hong Xuezhi huiyilu* [Memoirs of Hong Xuezhi], 469; Yang, *Zai zhiyuanjun silingbu de suiyueli* [My years at the CPVF General HQ], 122; Military History Research Division, *Zhongguo renmin zhiyuanjun kangmei yuanchao zhanshi* [Combat experience of the CPVF in the WRUSAK], 95.

37. Matthew B. Ridgway, *The Korean War* (Garden City, NY: Doubleday, 1967), 163, 166–67; Mossman, *U.S. Army in the Korean War,* 371, 374.

38. Hong, *Hong Xuezhi huiyilu* [Memoirs of Hong Xuezhi], 466; Military History Research Division, *Zhongguo renmin zhiyuanjun kangmei yuanchao zhanshi* [Combat experience of the CPVF in the WRUSAK], 131.

39. Quoted in Peng, "My Story of the Korean War," 35. See also Wang et al., *Peng Dehuai zhuan* [Biography of Peng Dehuai], 453; Xu, *Mao Zedong yu kangmei yuanchao zhanzheng* [Mao Zedong and the WRUSAK], 201–202.

40. Mao Zedong, telegrams to Peng, April 13, 17, and 28, 1951, in Mao, *Mao's Military Manuscripts since 1949,* 1: 473–74, 477; Mao Zedong, *Jianguo yilai Mao Zedong wengao, 1949–76* [Mao Zedong's manuscripts since the founding of the state, 1949–76] (Beijing: Zhongyang wenxian chubanshe, 1989), 2:239, 248, 265.

41. Du, *Zai zhiyuanjun zongbu* [At the CPVF General HQ], 238; Yang and Wang, *Beiwei 38 duxian* [The north latitude 38th Parallel], 313.

42. Yang Dezhi, *Yang Dezhi huiyilu* [Memoirs of Yang Dezhi] (Beijing: Jiefangjun chubanshe, 1992), 549; Yang, *Zai zhiyuanjun silingbu de suiyueli* [My years at the CPVF General HQ], 129.

43. Tan Zheng, *Zhongguo renmin zhiyuanjun renwulu* [Veterans' profile of the CPVF] (Beijing: Zhonggong dangshi chubanshe, 1992), 640–41. Lt. Gen. Zeng Siyu joined the Red Army in 1928 and the CCP in 1931. Promoted from a squad, platoon, and company

commander to a regiment political commissar, he participated in the Long March in 1934–35. During the Anti-Japanese War, Zeng became the political commissar of the 686th and 689th Regiments of the 115th Division, and of the 3rd Brigade of the Eighth Route Army. In the Chinese Civil War he served as commander of the PLA's Sixty-Fourth Army. During the Korean War, Zeng became deputy commander of the Nineteenth Army Group. He was given the rank of lieutenant general in 1955. After his return to China, Zeng became deputy commander and commander of the Shenyang, Wuhan, and later Ji'nan Regional Commands. He also served as the governor of Hubei Province. See *Xinghuo liaoyuan* Composition Department, *Zhongguo renmin jiefangjun jiangshuai minglu* [Marshals and generals of the PLA], (Beijing: Jiefangjun chubanshe, 1992), 1:482–83.

44. Yang, *Zai zhiyuanjun silingbu de suiyueli* [My years at the CPVF General HQ], 129–30. In 1986 Zeng asked Senior Col. Yang Di, deputy chief of the Operational Department in the CPVF General HQ, why Yang Dezhi had refused his request for one more day to get his army combat ready on April 22, 1951.

45. Yang, *Yang Dezhi huiyilu* [Memoirs of Yang Dezhi], 519–20; Yang Dezhi, "Combat Experience in Korea," in *Mao's Generals Remember Korea*, trans. and ed. Xiaobing Li, Allan R. Millett, and Bin Yu (Lawrence: University Press of Kansas, 2000), 147–48.

46. Yang Dezhi, *Weile heping* [For the sake of peace] (Beijing: Changzheng chubanshe, 1987), 52–56.

47. Hong, *Hong Xuezhi huiyilu* [Memoirs of Hong Xuezhi], 473; Chu, *Chaoxian zhanzheng neimu quangongkai* [Declassifying the Korean War], 295.

48. Yang, *Yang Dezhi huiyilu* [Memoirs of Yang Dezhi], 551; Zhao Jianli and Liang Yuhong, *Fenghuo 38 xian: diwuci zhanyi zhanshi baogao* [The flames of battle raging across the 38th Parallel: combat report on the fifth campaign] (Beijing: Junshi kexue chubanshe, 2007), 104.

49. Yang, *Zai zhiyuanjun silingbu de suiyueli* [My years at the CPVF General HQ], 129–30; Composition Committee, ed., *38 xian shang de jiaofeng: kangmei yuanchao zhanzheng jishi* [Fighting over the 38th Parallel: the recorded truth of the WRUSAK] (Beijing: Jiefangjun wenyi chubanshe, 2010), 306.

50. Du, *Zai zhiyuanjun zongbu* [At the CPVF General HQ], 239; Li Qingshan, *Zhiyuanjun yuanchao jishi* [The CPVF records of aiding Korea] (Beijing: Zhonggong dangshi chubanshe, 2008), 294.

51. Catchpole, *The Korean War,* 121.

52. Peng admitted three other strategic mistakes: the 1932 attack on GMD forces in Ganzhou City, Jiangxi Province; the 1940 "Hundred-Regiment Battle" against the Japanese; and the 1948 Xifu campaign against the GMD. See Du, *Zai zhiyuanjun zongbu* [At the CPVF General HQ], 101–104, 207–209, 218–22, 355–63; Xie Lifu, *Chaoxian zhanzheng shilu* [Field records of the Korean War] (Beijing: Shijie zhishi chubanshe, 1993), 2:456–58.

53. Song Shilun, commander of the Ninth Army Group, later passed Mao's words on the Spring Offensive to the CPVF commanders. See Du, *Zai zhiyuanjun zongbu* [At the CPVF General HQ], 250; Military History Research Division, *Zhongguo renmin zhiyuanjun kangmei yuanchao zhanshi* [Combat experience of the CPVF in the WRUSAK], 110–11.

54. Mao Zedong, "Present Situation and Our Tasks," in Mao Zedong, *Selected Works of Mao Tse-tung* (Beijing: Foreign Languages Press, 1977), 4:161; Peng Dehuai, "Di bingli

fenbu ji wojun zhanshu wenti [Enemy force deployment and our army's tactical issues]," November 12, 1948, in Peng, *Peng's Military Papers*, 294.

55. Sunzi, *The Art of War*, trans. Roger Ames (New York: Ballantine, 1993), 127.

56. For more details on the U.S. 32nd Regiment, see Capt. Wang Xuedong (CPVF), interview by the author; Wang, "The Chosin Reservoir," 122–23; Mossman, *U.S. Army in the Korean War*, 132–37.

57. Thomas Fleming, "The Man Who Saved Korea," in *The Cold War*, 114.

58. Jongnam Na, "Making Cold War Soldiers: The Americanization of the South Korean Army, 1945–55," PhD diss. (Chapel Hill: University of North Carolina, 2006), 93.

59. William T. Bowers conclusion to *Striking Back: Combat in Korea, March–April 1951*, ed. William T. Bowers (Lexington: University Press of Kentucky, 2010):408–409.

60. The U.S. Eighth Army G-2 reported to Van Fleet on April 18, 1951, about a major Chinese attack between April 20 and May 1. See Mossman, *U.S. Army in the Korean War*, 437; Millett, *The War for Korea, 1950–1951*, 426.

61. Corp. Harold L. Mulhausen (U.S. Marine Corps, ret.), interviews by the author in Edmond, OK, March 22–24, 2007. See also Harold L. Mulhausen, "The Chosin Reservoir: A Marine's Story," in *Voices from the Korean War: Personal Stories of American, Korean, and Chinese Soldiers*, 97–116.

62. Bowers, conclusion to *Striking Back*, 409–10.

63. Millett, *The War for Korea, 1950–1951*, 426.

64. Sunzi, *The Art of War*, trans. Ames, 151.

65. Capt. Wang Xuedong (CPVF), interview by the author in Harbin, Heilongjiang, April 2000. Also see Wang, "The Chosin Reservoir," 124.

66. Mao Zedong, "Chaoxian zhanju he women de fangzhen [The Korean War's situation and our policy]," speech at the PRC Ninth Central Government Plenary Conference on September 5, 1950, in Mao Zedong, *Mao Zedong wenji* [Collected works of Mao Zedong] (Beijing: Renmin chubanshe, 1993–99), 6: 93–4.

67. Shuguang Zhang, *Mao's Military Romanticism: China and the Korean War, 1950–53* (Lawrence: University Press of Kansas, 1995), 153.

68. Ibid.

69. Yang, *Zai zhiyuanjun silingbu de suiyueli* [My years at the CPVF General HQ], 131. Some Chinese officers remember that the first directive was issued on April 13. See Du, *Zai zhiyuanjun zongbu* [At the CPVF General HQ], 227.

70. Hong Xuezhi, *Kangmei yuanchao zhanzheng huiyi* [Recollections of the WRUSAK] (Beijing: Jiefangjun wenyi chubanshe, 1990), 151–52; Yang and Wang, *Beiwei 38 duxian* [The north latitude 38th Parallel], 297. See also Shuang, *Kaiguo diyi zhan* [The first war since the founding of the state], 1:367–68.

71. Quoted in Du, *Zai zhiyuanjun zongbu* [At the CPVF General HQ], 228–29. See also Xu, *Mao Zedong yu kangmei yuanchao zhanzheng* [Mao Zedong and the WRUSAK], 210.

72. Peng, telegram to all CPVF armies and the CMC, April 18, 1951, 391.

73. Hong, *Kangmei yuanchao zhanzheng huiyi* [Recollections of the WRUSAK], 152, 154; Military History Research Division, *Zhongguo renmin zhiyuanjun kangmei yuanchao zhanshi* [Combat experience of the CPVF in the WRUSAK], 131.

74. Du, *Zai zhiyuanjun zongbu* [At the CPVF General HQ], 238–39; Cui Xianghua and Chen Dapeng, *Tao Yong jiangjun zhuan* [Biography of General Tao Yong] (Beijing: Jiefangjun chubanshe, 1989), 396; Tan, *Kangmei yuanchao zhanzheng* [The WRUSAK], 137.

75. Li et al., *40 Jun zai chaoxian* [The Fortieth Army in Korea], 188; Yang and Wang, *Beiwei 38 duxian* [The north latitude 38th Parallel], 313; Military History Research Division, *Zhongguo renmin zhiyuanjun kangmei yuanchao zhanshi* [Combat experience of the CPVF in the WRUSAK], 131; Li, *Zhiyuanjun yuanchao jishi* [The CPVF records of aiding Korea], 293; Wang Shuzeng, *Juezhan chaoxian: chaoxian zhanchang shi wojun tong meijun jiaoliang de lianbingchang* [The showdown in Korea: the battleground for a competition between the Chinese army and American army] (Beijing: Jiefangjun wenyi chubanshe, 2007), 301; Chu, *Chaoxian zhanzheng neimu quangongkai* [Declassifying the Korean War], 289.

76. Peng, telegram to all CPVF armies and the CMC, April 18, 1951, 391.

77. Yang, *Yang Dezhi huiyilu* [Memoirs of Yang Dezhi], 549; Tan, *Kangmei yuanchao zhanzheng* [The WRUSAK], 137.

78. Hong, *Kangmei yuanchao zhanzheng huiyi* [Recollections of the WRUSAK], 152; Yang and Wang, *Beiwei 38 duxian* [The north latitude 38th Parallel], 313; Military History Research Division, *Zhongguo renmin zhiyuanjun kangmei yuanchao zhanshi* [Combat experience of the CPVF in the WRUSAK], 132; Composition Committee, ed., *38 xian shang de jiaofeng* [Fighting over the 38th Parallel], 306; Li, *Zhiyuanjun yuanchao jishi* [The CPVF records of aiding Korea], 294; Wang, *Juezhan chaoxian* [The showdown in Korea], 301; Chu, *Chaoxian zhanzheng neimu quangongkai* [Declassifying the Korean War], 289.

79. Peng, telegram to all CPVF armies and the CMC, April 18, 1951, 391.

80. Hong, *Hong Xuezhi huiyilu* [Memoirs of Hong Xuezhi], 466; Tan, *Kangmei yuanchao zhanzheng* [The WRUSAK], 137.

81. Yang and Wang, *Beiwei 38 duxian* [The north latitude 38th Parallel], 313; Military History Research Division, *Zhongguo renmin zhiyuanjun kangmei yuanchao zhanshi* [Combat experience of the CPVF in the WRUSAK], 131–32.

82. Yang and Wang, *Beiwei 38 duxian* [The north latitude 38th Parallel], 313; Li, *Zhiyuanjun yuanchao jishi* [The CPVF records of aiding Korea], 294; Zhao and Liang, *Fenghuo 38 xian* [The flames of battle raging across the 38th Parallel], 35–36; Wang, *Juezhan chaoxian* [The showdown in Korea], 301; Chu, *Chaoxian zhanzheng neimu quangongkai* [Declassifying the Korean War], 289.

83. Peng, "My Story of the Korean War," 36.

84. Yang, *Yang Dezhi huiyilu* [Memoirs of Yang Dezhi], 551; Du, *Zai zhiyuanjun zongbu* [At the CPVF General HQ], 240–41; Millett, *The War for Korea, 1950–1951*, 433, 570 note 136; Stanley Sandler, *The Korean War: No Victors, No Vanquished* (Lexington: University Press of Kentucky, 1999), 141.

85. Peng Dehuai, telegram to Mao and the CMC, April 26, 1951, in Zhou, *Zhou's Military Papers*, 4:195 note 2.

86. Mao met Wu Ruilin first and other CPVF army commanders the next day. For more details, see Wu Ruilin, *Kangmei yuanchao zhong de 42 jun* [The Forty-Second Army in the WRUSAK] (Beijing: Jincheng chubanshe, 1995), 128–57; Wu Ruilin, "Da Mao zhuxi wen [Answering Mao's questions]," in Political Department of the PLA 75200 Unit, ed., *Yuxue chaoxian: 42 jun laozhanshi kangmei yuanchao qinliji* [Bleeding Korea: personal experiences of Fortieth Army veterans in the WRUSAK], (Beijing: Jiefangjun chubanshe, 2001), 582–87. Wu was the commander of the Forty-Second Army of the CPVF in 1950–53.

87. Wu, *Kangmei yuanchao zhong de 42 jun* [The Forty-Second Army in the WRUSAK], 135–40; Hong, *Kangmei yuanchao zhanzheng huiyi* [Recollections of the WRUSAK],

153; Xu, *Mao Zedong yu kangmei yuanchao zhanzheng* [Mao Zedong and the WRUSAK], 219–20.

88. Quoted in Peng, "My Story of the Korean War," 36. See also Hong, *Kangmei yuanchao zhanzheng huiyi* [Recollections of the WRUSAK], 192; Cui and Chen, *Tao Yong jiangjun zhuan* [Biography of General Tao Yong], 398; Li, *Zhiyuanjun yuanchao jishi* [The CPVF records of aiding Korea], 337, 340.

89. Mao Zedong, telegram to Peng, June 11, 1951, in Mao, *Mao's Military Manuscripts since 1949*, 1:502.

90. For more details on Hong's meeting with Zhou in Beijing in April 1951, see Hong, *Hong Xuezhi Huiyilu* [Memoirs of Hong Xuezhi], 488–92; Hong, *Kangmei yuanchao zhanzheng huiyi* [Recollections of the WRUSAK], 122–9; Li, *Zhiyuanjun yuanchao jishi* [The CPVF records of aiding Korea], 303–304.

91. Wang et al., *Peng Dehuai zhuan* [Biography of Peng Dehuai], 463; Military History Research Division, *Zhongguo renmin zhiyuanjun kangmei yuanchao zhanshi* [Combat experience of the CPVF in the WRUSAK], 135.

92. UNF planes attacked the CPVF supply depot at the Samdung train station on April 8, 1951. For more details, see Du, *Zai zhiyuanjun zongbu* [At the CPVF General HQ], 229–31; Zhou, *Kangmei yuanchao zhanzheng huoqinshi jianbianben* [A concise history of the logistics in the WRUSAK], 59–60; Li, *Zhiyuanjun yuanchao jishi* [The CPVF records of aiding Korea], 289–90.

93. Hong Xuezhi, "The CPVF's Combat and Logistics," in *Mao's Generals Remember Korea*, 126; Hong, *Hong Xuezhi huiyilu* [Memoirs of Hong Xuezhi], 488–92; Hong, *Kangmei yuanchao zhanzheng huiyi* [Recollections of the WRUSAK], 122–29; Li, *Zhiyuanjun yuanchao jishi* [The CPVF records of aiding Korea], 303–304.

94. Hong, *Kangmei yuanchao zhanzheng huiyi* [Recollections of the WRUSAK], 137; Military History Research Division, *Zhongguo renmin zhiyuanjun kangmei yuanchao zhanshi* [Combat experience of the CPVF in the WRUSAK], 129.

95. Wu Ruilin, *Wu Ruilin huiyilu* [Memoirs of Wu Ruilin] (Beijing: Zhongguo dangan chubanshe, 1995), 3:143–45; Yang, *Zai zhiyuanjun silingbu de suiyueli* [My years at the CPVF General HQ], 132.

96. Wu, *Chaoxian zhanchang 1,000 tian* [One thousand days on the Korean battleground], 603–606; Li et al., *40 Jun zai chaoxian* [The Fortieth Army in Korea], 200; Catchpole, *The Korean War*, 120. Lt. Gen. Wu Xinquan joined the Red Army and the CCP in 1930. Promoted from a squad and company commander to a battalion and regiment political commissar in the Red Army, he participated in the Long March in 1934–35. During the Anti-Japanese War Wu became the political commissar of the 687th and 688th Regiments of the 115th Division and political commissar of the 2nd Brigade of the Eighth Route Army. In the Chinese Civil War he served as commander and political commissar of the 6th Division of the Northeastern Command and deputy commander and commander of the PLA's Thirty-Ninth Army. After his return to China, Wu became deputy chief of staff and then chief of staff of the Shenyang Regional Command and deputy commander of the PLA Artillery Force. He was made a lieutenant general in 1955. See *Xinghuo liaoyuan* Composition Department, *Zhongguo renmin jiefangjun jiangshuai minglu* [Marshals and generals of the PLA], 1:292–93; Tan, *Zhongguo renmin zhiyuanjun renwulu* [Veterans' profile of the CPVF], 291–92.

97. Li et al., *40 Jun zai chaoxian* [The Fortieth Army in Korea], 188–89; Military History Research Division, *Zhongguo renmin zhiyuanjun kangmei yuanchao zhanshi* [Com-

bat experience of the CPVF in the WRUSAK], 138–39; Shuang, *Kaiguo diyi zhan* [The first war since the founding of the state], 1:369–70.

98. Zhao and Liang, *Fenghuo 38 xian* [The flames of battle raging across the 38th Parallel], 53; Luan, *Xue yu huo de jiaoliang* [The contest], 205.

99. Li et al., *40 Jun zai chaoxian* [The Fortieth Army in Korea], 194–202; Wang Shuzeng, *Yuandong chaoxian zhanzheng* [The Korean War in the Far East] (Beijing: Jiefangjun wenyi chubanshe, 2000), 2:705–707.

100. Wang Hechuan, *Zhongguo dadi shang de jufeng: 40 jun zhengzhan jingli* [The hurricane over China: war experiences of the Fortieth Army] (Beijing: Jiefangjun wenyi chubanshe, 2004), 331–34.

101. Wu, *Chaoxian zhanchang 1,000 tian* [One thousand days on the Korean battleground], 414–15; Tan, *Kangmei yuanchao zhanzheng* [The WRUSAK], 139; Li et al., *40 Jun zai chaoxian* [The Fortieth Army in Korea], 203.

102. Lt. Gen. Zhang Yixiang joined the Red Army in 1929 and the CCP in 1932. He served as commander of a squad, platoon, company, battalion, and regiment in the Red Army and participated in the Long March in 1934–35. During the Anti-Japanese War Zhang became deputy commander and commander of the 14th and 16th Regiments and deputy commander of the 5th Brigade of the New Fourth Army. In the Chinese Civil War he served as deputy commander, commander, and political commissar of the PLA's Twentieth Army. After his return to China, Zhang became deputy chief of staff and chief of staff of the Fuzhou Regional Command and commander of the PLA Second Artillery (Strategic Missile) Force. He was made a lieutenant general in 1955. See *Xinghuo liaoyuan* Composition Department, *Zhongguo renmin jiefangjun jiangshuai minglu* [Marshals and generals of the PLA], 1:334–35; Tan, *Zhongguo renmin zhiyuanjun renwulu* [Veterans' profile of the CPVF], 385–86.

103. Du, *Zai zhiyuanjun zongbu* [At the CPVF General HQ], 238–39; Luan, *Xue yu huo de jiaoliang* [The contest], 205–206.

104. Military History Research Division, *Zhongguo renmin zhiyuanjun kangmei yuanchao zhanshi* [Combat experience of the CPVF in the WRUSAK], 131; Millett, *The War for Korea, 1950–1951*, 431.

105. Col. Wang Po (PLA, ret.), interview by the author at the PLA Logistics College, Beijing, July 1994; Zhou, *Kangmei yuanchao zhanzheng huoqinshi jianbianben* [A concise history of the logistics in the WRUSAK], 75.

106. Du, *Zai zhiyuanjun zongbu* [At the CPVF General HQ], 229–31; Zhao and Liang, *Fenghuo 38 xian* [The flames of battle raging across the 38th Parallel], 53.

107. Lt. Gen. Zhang Renchu joined the Red Army in 1927 and the CCP in 1928. He served as commander of a squad, platoon, company, battalion, and regiment in the Red Army and participated in the Long March in 1934–35. During the Anti-Japanese War Zhang became deputy commander and commander of the 686th Regiment of the 115th Division and commander of the 10th Brigade of the Shandong Command. In the Chinese Civil War he served as commander of the PLA's Twenty-Sixth Army. After his return to China, Zhang became deputy commander of the Jinan Regional Command. He was made a lieutenant general in 1955. See *Xinghuo liaoyuan* Composition Department, *Zhongguo renmin jiefangjun jiangshuai minglu* [Marshals and generals of the PLA], 1:316–17; Tan, *Zhongguo renmin zhiyuanjun renwulu* [Veterans' profile of the CPVF], 342.

108. NCO Han Shunzhou (PLA, ret.), interview by the author in Beijing, July 2010. Noncommissioned officer Han served in the 3rd Battalion, 241st Regiment, 81st Divi-

sion, Twenty-Seventh Army of the CPVF Ninth Army Group. See also Tan, *Kangmei yuanchao zhanzheng* [The WRUSAK], 137; Zhao, *27 Jun chuanqi* [The legacy of the Twenty-Seventh Army], 443.

109. Quoted in China Academy of Military Science, "The Unforgotten Korean War: Chinese Perspective and Appraisals," unpublished manuscript, 2006, 411. "The Unforgotten Korean War" is an unpublished manuscript written by retired PLA officers and officer historians and sponsored by the Office of Net Assessment, Office of the U.S. Secretary of Defense, in 2006. I received a copy of the entire manuscript from Allan Millett and the chapters in it on the Spring Offensive from Steven Levine. Millett believes that this manuscript is "an invaluable source on the war from the PLA's perspective for 1950–51 and covers the five major Chinese offensives of that period, complete with maps" (*The War for Korea, 1950–1951*, 589).

110. Han Shunzhou, interview by the author; Zhao, *27 Jun chuanqi* [The legacy of the Twenty-Seventh Army], 443–44.

111. Ridgway, *The Korean War*, 171–72; Mossman, *U.S. Army in the Korean War*, 389; and Donald Knox, *The Korean War: An Oral History* (San Diego, CA: Harcourt Brace Jovanovich, 1985–88), 2:170–71.

112. Xu, *Mao Zedong yu kangmei yuanchao zhanzheng* [Mao Zedong and the WRUSAK], 212; Wang Yongping, "Diwuci zhanyi jingyan jiaoxun dui women de qishi [Our understanding of the lessons and experience of the Fifth Offensive Campaign]," in *Kangmei yuanchao zhanzhenglun* [On the WRUSAK], ed. Chen Zonglong (Beijing: Junshi wenyi chubanshe, 2001), 258.

113. Yang and Wang, *Beiwei 38 duxian* [The north latitude 38th Parallel], 314–15; Zhao and Liang, *Fenghuo 38 xian* [The flames of battle raging across the 38th Parallel], 57.

114. Capt. Wang Xuedong (CPVF), interview by the author, in Harbin, Heilongjiang, April 2000. Capt. Wang served in First Company, 172nd Regiment, 58th Division, Twentieth Army, CPVF Ninth Army Group in 1950–53.

115. Li et al., *40 Jun zai chaoxian* [The Fortieth Army in Korea], 202–203; Military History Research Division, *Zhongguo renmin zhiyuanjun kangmei yuanchao zhanshi* [Combat experience of the CPVF in the WRUSAK], 95, 97.

116. Marc D. Bernstein, "Red Eclipse: Massive Attack; Korean War Killing Zone," *Military Heritage*, October 2011, 37.

117. Richard P. Hallion, "The Air War in Korea: Coalition Air Power in the Context of Limited War," paper presented at Korea: In from the Cold, Canberra, Australia, October 5–7, 2011.

118. Han Shunzhou, interview by the author; Tan, *Kangmei yuanchao zhanzheng* [The WRUSAK], 133.

119. Nie Rongzhen, "Beijing's Decision to Intervene," in *Mao's Generals Remember Korea*, trans. and ed. Xiaobing Li, Allan R. Millett, and Bin Yu (Lawrence: University Press of Kansas, 2000), 52–53.

120. Maurie Pears (Australian Royal Regiment, ret.), interviews by the author at the Australian War Museum at Canberra, Australia, October 6–7, 2011. Pears served in the Third Royal Australian Regiment in the Korean War. Also see Ben Evans, *Out in the Cold: Australia's Involvement in the Korean War, 1950–53* (Canberra, Australia: Department of Australians' Veterans' Affairs, 2010), 45–50; Mossman, *U.S. Army in the Korean War*, 398–409; Michael Hickey, *The Korean War: The West Confronts Communism* (New York: Overlook, 1999), 214–18.

121. Millett, *The War for Korea, 1950–1951*, 431.

122. China Academy of Military Science, "The Unforgotten Korean War," 422–23; Zhao and Liang, *Fenghuo 38 xian* [The flames of battle raging across the 38th Parallel], 59; Mossman, *U.S. Army in the Korean War*, 383–85.

123. Theodore White, "The Killing Ground," in *No Bugles, No Drums: An Oral History of the Korean War*, ed. Rudy Tomedi (New York: Wiley and Son, 1994), 123–24, 128–29; Millett, *The War for Korea, 1950–1951*, 432.

124. Nie, "Beijing's Decision to Intervene," 52–53; Yang Qinghua,"Zhongguo renmin zhiyuanjun houqin sixiang de xiangcheng yu fazhan [Establish and develop the CPVF's logistics conception]," in *Kangmei yuanchao zhanzhenglun* [On the WRUSAK], ed. Chen, 347.

125. Yang, *Zai zhiyuanjun silingbu de suiyueli* [My years at the CPVF General HQ], 133; Military History Research Division, *Zhongguo renmin zhiyuanjun kangmei yuanchao zhanshi* [Combat experience of the CPVF in the WRUSAK], 98.

126. Li et al., *40 Jun zai chaoxian* [The Fortieth Army in Korea], 203–204, 212; China Academy of Military Science, "The Unforgotten Korean War," 422–23.

127. Quoted in Wang et al., *Peng Dehuai zhuan* [Biography of Peng Dehuai], 466.

128. CMC, telegram to Peng, "Tongyi diwuci zhanyi de zuozhan fangzhen yu zhanyi hou de bingli bushu [Agree the operation plan of the Fifth Campaign and deployment after the campaign]," April 28, 1951.

### 5. THE COSTLY OFFENSIVE IN THE WEST

1. Allan R. Millett, *The War for Korea, 1950–1951: They Came from the North* (Lawrence: University Press of Kansas, 2010), 429.

2. Chinese official statistics show a total of 65,000–105,000 casualties in the Spring Offensive from April 22 to June 10, 1951. An estimated half of the total, between 35,000 and 60,000, took place during the first step of the offensive on the western front, April 22–29. See Military History Research Division, CAMS, *Zhongguo renmin zhiyuanjun kangmei yuanchao zhanshi* [Combat experience of the CPVF in the WRU-SAK] (Beijing: Junshi kexue chubanshe, 1990), 152; Tan Jingjiao, *Kangmei yuanchao zhanzheng* [The WRUSAK] (Beijing: Zhongguo shehui kexue chubanshe, 1990), 159; Composition Committee, ed., *38 xian shang de jiaofeng: kangmei yuanchao zhanzheng jishi* [Fighting over the 38th Parallel: the recorded truth of the WRUSAK] (Beijing: Jiefangjun wenyi chubanshe, 2010), 330. For the UNF statistics, the U.S. Army's official history estimated that from April 22 to April 30 "enemy forces suffered between 75,000 and 80,000 killed and wounded. 50,000 of these in the Seoul sector" (quoted in Billy C. Mossman, *U.S. Army in the Korean War: Ebb and Flow, November 1950–July 1951* [Washington: Army Center of Military History and Government Printing Office, 1990], 437). See also Gu Cheng et al., trans. and eds., *Chaoxian zhanzheng: dijun shiliao* [ROK Army Archives: the Korean War] (Harbin, China: Heilongjiang chaoxian minzu chubanshe, 1988–90), 2:5; Stanley Sandler, *The Korean War: No Victors, No Vanquished* (Lexington: University Press of Kentucky, 1999), 142; Marc D. Bernstein, "Red Eclipse: Massive Attack; Korean War Killing Zone," *Military Heritage*, October 2011, 39.

3. Peng expected the Spring Offensive to annihilate 60,000 UNF troops, with estimated casualties of 50,000–60,000 CPVF troops. See Peng Dehuai, telegram to

all CPVF armies and copied to the CMC, 9:00 PM, April 18, 1951, in Peng Dehuai, *Peng Dehuai junshi wenxuan* [Selected military papers of Peng Dehuai] (Beijing: Zhongyang wenxian chubanshe, 1988), 390–92 (hereafter cited as *Peng's Military Papers*); Du Ping, *Zai zhiyuanjun zongbu: Du Ping huiyilu* [At the CPVF General HQ: memoirs of Du Ping] (Beijing: Jiefangjun chubanshe, 1989), 221.

4. Yang Dezhi, *Yang Dezhi huiyilu* [Memoirs of Yang Dezhi] (Beijing: Jiefangjun chubanshe, 1992), 553. Also see Gu et al., trans. and eds., *Chaoxian zhanzheng* [ROK Army Archives], 2:5–6.

5. Mao Zedong, telegram to Peng, "Zhuyi zai diwuci zhanyi zhong geidiyi jinkenengdade daji [Strike as hard as possible on the enemy forces in the Fifth Campaign]," April 28, 1951, in Mao Zedong, *Jianguo yilai Mao Zedong junshi wengao* [Mao Zedong's military manuscripts since the founding of the PRC] (Beijing: Junshi kexue chubanshe and Zhongyang wenxian chubanshe, 2010), 1:477.

6. Korean Institute of Military History, ROK Ministry of Defense, *The Korean War* (Seoul: Korean Institute of Military History, 1998), 2:607. The official U.S. Army history states that "the total strength of Chinese forces in Korea as of that date [April 22] was believed to be about 542,000 and that of North Korean forces to be over 197,000" (quoted in Mossman, *U.S. Army in the Korean War*, 437).

7. Du, *Zai zhiyuanjun zongbu* [At the CPVF General HQ], 208–209; Yan Xinning, *Wei Jie zhongjiang* [Lt. Gen. Wei Jie] (Beijing: Jiefangjun wenyi chubanshe, 2005), 33.

8. Mao Zedong, "On Protracted War," in Mao Zedong, *Selected Works of Mao Tse-tung* (Beijing: Foreign Languages Press, 1977), 2:156.

9. Ibid.

10. Ibid., 158–59.

11. Yang Di, *Zai zhiyuanjun silingbu de suiyueli: xianwei renzhi de zhenshi qingkuang* [My years at the CPVF General HQ: untold true stories] (Beijing: Jiefangjun chubanshe, 1998), 131. Some Chinese officers remember that the first directive was issued on April 13. See Du, *Zai zhiyuanjun zongbu* [At the CPVF General HQ], 227; Military History Research Division, *Zhongguo renmin zhiyuanjun kangmei yuanchao zhanshi* [Combat experience of the CPVF in the WRUSAK], 128; Tan, *Kangmei yuanchao zhanzheng* [The WRUSAK], 134.

12. Peng, telegram to all CPVF armies and the CMC, April 18, 1951, 392; Wang Yan et al., *Peng Dehuai zhuan* [Biography of Peng Dehuai] (Beijing: Dangdai zhongguo chubanshe, 1993), 463.

13. Hong Xuezhi, *Hong Xuezhi huiyilu* [Memoirs of Hong Xuezhi] (Beijing: Jiefangjun chubanshe, 2007), 466; Du, *Zai zhiyuanjun zongbu* [At the CPVF General HQ], 227–29.

14. For example, see Nineteenth Army Group Command, "Dahao chuguo diyizhang de zhanduo dongyuanling [Campaign mobilization directive: win the first battle in Korea]," April 1951, quoted in Yang, *Yang Dezhi huiyilu* [Memoirs of Yang Dezhi], 546–47.

15. Sandler, *The Korean War*, 142. See also William T. Bowers, conclusion to *Striking Back: Combat in Korea, March–April 1951*, ed. William T. Bowers (Lexington: University Press of Kentucky, 2010), 409–10.

16. Matthew B. Ridgway, *The Korean War* (Garden City, NY: Doubleday, 1967), 171–72; Mossman, *U.S. Army in the Korean War*, 389; Donald Knox, *The Korean War: An Oral History* (San Diego, CA: Harcourt Brace Jovanovich, 1985–88), 2:170–71; Korean Institute of Military History, *The Korean War*, 2:609.

17. Richard Peters and Xiaobing Li, "The Chosin Reservoir Retreat and Advance to the North," in *Voices from the Korean War: Personal Stories of American, Korean, and Chinese Soldiers*, ed. Richard Peters and Xiaobing Li (Lexington: University Press of Kentucky, 2004), 33–34; Bowers, conclusion to *Striking Back*, 409.

18. See Yang, *Yang Dezhi huiyilu* [Memoirs of Yang Dezhi], 549; Yang, *Zai zhiyuanjun silingbu de suiyueli* [My years at the CPVF General HQ], 129–30.

19. Du, *Zai zhiyuanjun zongbu* [At the CPVF General HQ], 239; Korean Institute of Military History, *The Korean War*, 2:612–15.

20. Yang, *Yang Dezhi huiyilu* [Memoirs of Yang Dezhi], 555–56; Zhao Jianli and Liang Yuhong, *Fenghuo 38 xian: diwuci zhanyi zhanshi baogao* [The flames of battle raging across the 38th Parallel: combat report on the Fifth Campaign] (Beijing: Junshi kexue chubanshe, 2007), 113.

21. Wang Shuzeng, *Yuandong chaoxian zhanzheng* [The Korean War in the Far East] (Beijing: Jiefangjun wenyi chubanshe, 2000), 2:703–704.

22. Yang, *Yang Dezhi huiyilu* [Memoirs of Yang Dezhi], 552. See also Wang Shuzeng, *Juezhan chaoxian: chaoxian zhanchang shi wojun tong meijun jiaoliang de lianbingchang* [The showdown in Korea: the battleground for a competition between the Chinese army and American army] (Beijing: Jiefangjun wenyi chubanshe, 2007), 308.

23. Yang, *Yang Dezhi huiyilu* [Memoirs of Yang Dezhi], 552.

24. Quoted in Zhao and Liang, *Fenghuo 38 xian* [The flames of battle raging across the 38th Parallel], 106–107.

25. Maj. Gen. Chen Xinzhong joined the Red Army in 1928 and the CCP in 1932. He participated in the Long March. He served as commander of a squad, platoon, and company in the Red Army. During the Anti-Japanese War Chen became a commander at the battalion, regiment, and brigade levels in the Eighth Route Army. During the Chinese Civil War he became commander of the 190th Division, Sixty-Fourth Army of the PLA. After his return to China, Chen was appointed deputy commander and commander of the Sixty-Fourth Army. In 1955 he was granted the rank of major general. See *Xinghuo liaoyuan* Composition Department, *Zhongguo renmin jiefangjun jiangshuai minglu* [Marshals and generals of the PLA], (Beijing: Jiefangjun chubanshe, 1992), 3:142; Tan Zheng, *Zhongguo renmin zhiyuanjun renwulu* [Veterans' profile of the CPVF] (Beijing: Zhonggong dangshi chubanshe, 1992), 402; Tan, *Kangmei yuanchao zhanzheng* [The WRUSAK], 137.

26. Korean Institute of Military History, *The Korean War*, 2:614–16.

27. Quoted in Zhao and Liang, *Fenghuo 38 xian* [The flames of battle raging across the 38th Parallel], 107.

28. Mao, "On Protracted War," in Mao, *Selected Works of Mao Tse-tung*, 2:156.

29. The Ninth Company had about 210 men; the Seventh Company had 180 men; and the Eighth Company had 200 men. See Zhao and Liang, *Fenghuo 38 xian* [The flames of battle raging across the 38th Parallel], 107.

30. Quoted in Gu et al., trans. and eds., *Chaoxian zhanzheng* [ROK Army Archives], 2:58.

31. Jeff Kinard, "Human Wave Attacks," in *The Encyclopedia of the Korean War*, ed. Spencer C. Tucker, 2nd ed. (Santa Barbara, CA: ABC-CLIO, 2010), 1:343–44. For more details on the "human waves," see Sandler, *The Korean War*, 142–43; Max Hastings, *The Korean War* (New York: Simon and Schuster, 1987), 81, 96, 335.

32. Edward C. O'Dowd, *Chinese Military Strategy in the Third Indochina War: The Last Maoist War* (London: Routledge, 2007), 144.

33. Brian Steed, *Armed Conflict: The Lessons of Modern Warfare* (New York: Ballantine, 2003), 59.

34. Ibid., 59–60.

35. Bruce A. Elleman, *Modern Chinese Warfare, 1795–1989* (London: Routledge, 2001), 247.

36. Capt. Wang Xuedong (CPVF), interview by the author, in Harbin, Heilongjiang, April 2000. For more details of the early Chinese attacks, also see Wang Xuedong, "The Chosin Reservoir: A Chinese Captain's Story," in *Voices from the Korean War: Personal Stories of American, Korean, and Chinese Soldiers*, ed. Richard Peters and Xiaobing Li (Lexington: University Press of Kentucky, 2004), 117–24; Bin Yu, "What China Learned from Its 'Forgotten War' in Korea," in *Mao's Generals Remember Korea*, trans. and ed. Xiaobing Li, Allan R. Millett, and Bin Yu (Lawrence: University Press of Kansas, 2001), 14, 15–17.

37. Brian R. Cornell, "The Origins of the Human Wave Phenomenon in Chinese Military History and the Korean War (1950–53)," paper written for "Non-Western Military History" class at Norwich University, 2011, 9.

38. O'Dowd, *Chinese Military Strategy in the Third Indochina War*, 145.

39. Richard Peters and Xiaobing Li, "Perspectives on the War," in *Voices from the Korean War: Personal Stories of American, Korean, and Chinese Soldiers*, 263.

40. Jongnam Na, "Making Cold War Soldiers: The Americanization of the South Korean Army, 1945–55," PhD diss. (Chapel Hill: University of North Carolina, 2006), 94.

41. Bernstein, "Red Eclipse," 37.

42. Theodore White, "The Killing Ground," in *No Bugles, No Drums: An Oral History of the Korean War*, ed. Rudy Tomedi (New York: Wiley and Son, 1994), 123. White was sent to Korea and joined the all-black U.S. 24th Infantry Regiment in the middle of April 1951, just in time to take part in the Ridgway's defense against the Chinese Spring Offensive.

43. Ibid., 127.

44. Zhao and Liang, *Fenghuo 38 xian* [The flames of battle raging across the 38th Parallel], 107.

45. Korean Institute of Military History, *The Korean War*, 2:615; Gu et al., trans. and eds., *Chaoxian zhanzheng* [ROK Army Archives], 2:63–65.

46. Du, *Zai zhiyuanjun zongbu* [At the CPVF General HQ], 241–42; Composition Committee, ed., *38 xian shang de jiaofeng* [Fighting over the 38th Parallel], 308–309; Wang, *Juezhan chaoxian* [The showdown in Korea], 308.

47. Yang, *Yang Dezhi huiyilu* [Memoirs of Yang Dezhi], 552; Military History Research Division, *Zhongguo renmin zhiyuanjun kangmei yuanchao zhanshi* [Combat experience of the CPVF in the WRUSAK], 135.

48. Luo Xuanyou, *Chaoxian zhanzheng: zhengzhan jishi* [The Korean War: the battle records] (Beijing: Jiefangjun wenyi chubanshe, 2007), 328–29.

49. See note 25 above for biographical information on Chen. See also Tan, *Zhongguo renmin zhiyuanjun renwulu* [Veterans' profile of the CPVF], 402; *Xinghuo liaoyuan* Composition Department, *Zhongguo renmin jiefangjun jiangshuai minglu* [Marshals and generals of the PLA], 3:142.

50. O'Dowd, *Chinese Military Strategy in the Third Indochina War*, 144.

51. Shuang Shi, *Kaiguo diyi zhan: kangmei yuanchao zhanzheng quanjing jishi* [The first war since the founding of the state: the complete story of the WRUSAK] (Beijing: Zhonggong dangshi chubanshe, 2004), 1:373.

52. Quoted in CMC, telegram to Peng, "Tongyi diwuci zhanyi de zuozhan fangzhen yu zhanyi hou de bingli bushu [Agree the operation plan of the Fifth Campaign and deployment after the campaign]," April 28, 1951, in Zhou Enlai, *Zhou Enlai junshi wenxun* [Selected military papers of Zhou Enlai] (Beijing: Renmin chubanshe, 1997): 4:193.

53. Ridgway, *The Korean War*, 173.

54. George F. Futrell, *The United States Air Force in the Korean War* (Washington: Office of Air Force History, 1983), 336–37.

55. Sandler, *The Korean War*, 142.

56. Du, *Zai zhiyuanjun zongbu* [At the CPVF General HQ[, 92. See also Du Ping, "Political Mobilization and Control," in *Mao's Generals Remember Korea*, 86.

57. Hong, *Hong Xuezhi huiyilu* [Memoirs of Hong Xuezhi], 473; Tan, *Kangmei yuanchao zhanzheng* [The WRUSAK], 141–42.

58. Yang, *Yang Dezhi huiyilu* [Memoirs of Yang Dezhi], 552; Military History Research Division, *Zhongguo renmin zhiyuanjun kangmei yuanchao zhanshi* [Combat experience of the CPVF in the WRUSAK], 153–55.

59. Yang, *Zai zhiyuanjun silingbu de suiyueli* [My years at the CPVF General HQ], 130; Luan Kechao, *Xue yu huo de jiaoliang: kangmei yuanchao jishi* [The contest: blood vs. fire; the record of resisting America and aiding Korea] (Beijing: Huayi chubanshe, 2008), 208; Wang, *Yuandong chaoxian zhanzheng* [The Korean War in the Far East], 2:704.

60. Du, *Zai zhiyuanjun zongbu* [At the CPVF General HQ], 241–42; Composition Committee, ed., *38 xian shang de jiaofeng* [Fighting over the 38th Parallel], 308–309; Wang, *Juezhan chaoxian* [The showdown in Korea], 308; Xu Yan, *Mao Zedong yu kangmei yuanchao zhanzheng* [Mao Zedong and the WRUSAK], 2nd ed. (Beijing: Jiefangjun chubanshe, 2006), 212; Shuang, *Kaiguo diyi zhan* [The first war since the founding of the state], 1:373.

61. Zhao and Liang, *Fenghuo 38 xian* [The flames of battle raging across the 38th Parallel], 113; Military History Research Division, *Zhongguo renmin zhiyuanjun kangmei yuanchao zhanshi* [Combat experience of the CPVF in the WRUSAK], 133; Luan, *Xue yu huo de jiaoliang* [The contest], 208.

62. Xu, *Mao Zedong yu kangmei yuanchao zhanzheng* [Mao Zedong and the WRUSAK], 212.

63. Yang, *Zai zhiyuanjun silingbu de suiyueli* [My years at the CPVF General HQ], 130; Yan, *Wei Jie zhongjiang* [Lt. Gen. Wei Jie], 33.

64. Yang, *Yang Dezhi huiyilu* [Memoirs of Yang Dezhi], 551–53; Yang, *Zai zhiyuanjun silingbu de suiyueli* [My years at the CPVF General HQ], 130; Li Qingshan, *Zhiyuanjun yuanchao jishi* [The CPVF records of aiding Korea] (Beijing: Zhonggong dangshi chubanshe, 2008), 302; Wang, *Yuandong chaoxian zhanzheng* [The Korean War in the Far East], 2:713–14; Gu et al., trans. and eds., *Chaoxian zhanzheng* [ROK Army Archives], 2:90, 91, 95–97.

65. Military History Research Division, *Zhongguo renmin zhiyuanjun kangmei yuanchao zhanshi* [Combat experience of the CPVF in the WRUSAK], 131–32; Zhao and Liang, *Fenghuo 38 xian* [The flames of battle raging across the 38th Parallel], 78.

66. Tan, *Kangmei yuanchao zhanzheng* [The WRUSAK], 139–40.

67. Mossman, *U.S. Army in the Korean War*, 394.

68. Zhao and Liang, *Fenghuo 38 xian* [The flames of battle raging across the 38th Parallel], 80.

69. Ibid., 80; Military History Research Division, *Zhongguo renmin zhiyuanjun kangmei yuanchao zhanshi* [Combat experience of the CPVF in the WRUSAK], 133, 135.

70. China Academy of Military Science, "The Unforgotten Korean War: Chinese Perspective and Appraisals," unpublished manuscript, 2006, 417; Tan, *Kangmei yuanchao zhanzheng* [The WRUSAK], 139–40; Military History Research Division, *Zhongguo renmin zhiyuanjun kangmei yuanchao zhanshi* [Combat experience of the CPVF in the WRUSAK], 133.

71. Lt. Gen. Zeng Shaoshan joined the Red Army in 1929 and the CCP in 1933 and participated in the Long March. Zeng served as commander of a platoon and company, and as staff member in the division and army HQs in the Red Army. During the Anti-Japanese War he became chief of the operation section of the 385th Brigade Command, chief staff of the 13th Regiment, and later brigade chief staff of the Eighth Route Army. During the Chinese Civil War Zeng became commander of the 3rd and 13th Columns and commander of the Eleventh and Twelfth Armies of the PLA. He was commander of the Twelfth Army of the CPVF Third Army Group during the Spring Offensive and was deputy commander of the Third Army Group in 1952–53. After his return to China, Zeng was appointed deputy commander, political commissar, and chief of staff of the Third Army Group and later of the Shenyang Regional Command. He was made a lieutenant general in 1955. Zeng also served as governor of Liaoning Province. See *Xinghuo liaoyuan* Composition Department, *Zhongguo renmin jiefangjun jiangshuai minglu* [Marshals and generals of the PLA], 1:476; Tan, *Zhongguo renmin zhiyuanjun renwulu* [Veterans' profile of the CPVF] 637–38.

72. Hong, *Hong Xuezhi huiyilu* [Memoirs of Hong Xuezhi], 466; Tan, *Kangmei yuanchao zhanzheng* [The WRUSAK], 137; Zhao and Liang, *Fenghuo 38 xian* [The flames of battle raging across the 38th Parallel], 70–74.

73. Xu, *Mao Zedong yu kangmei yuanchao zhanzheng* [Mao Zedong and the WRUSAK], 212.

74. Gen. You Taizhong joined the Red Army in 1931 and the CCP in 1934 and participated in the Long March. He served as a commander at the squad, platoon, company, and battalion levels in the Red Army. During the Anti-Japanese War he commanded a battalion, a regiment, and the 16th Brigade of the Eighth Route Army. During the Chinese Civil War You became commander of the 34th Division of the Twelfth Army of the PLA. He was commander of the Twelfth Army of the CPVF Third Army Group during the Spring Offensive and was deputy commander of the Third Army Group in 1952–53. After his return to China, You was appointed deputy commander of the Twelfth Army in 1953, commander of the Twenty-Seventh Army in 1960, and later commander of the Chengdu and Guangzhou Regional Commands. He was promoted to major general in 1955 and to general in 1988. See Tan, *Zhongguo renmin zhiyuanjun renwulu* [Veterans' profile of the CPVF], 64; *Xinghuo liaoyuan* Composition Department, *Zhongguo renmin jiefangjun jiangshuai minglu* [Marshals and generals of the PLA], 2:118.

75. Quoted in Zhao and Liang, *Fenghuo 38 xian* [The flames of battle raging across the 38th Parallel], 78.

76. Yan, *Wei Jie zhongjiang* [Lt. Gen. Wei Jie], 32–33; Tan, *Kangmei yuanchao zhanzheng* [The WRUSAK], 139–40; Xu Yipeng, *Cuojue: 180 shi chaoxian shoucuoji* [Miscalculation: the setback of the 180th Division in Korea] (Nanjing, China: Jiangsu renmin chubanshe, 1997), 40–41.

77. Gen. Wang Chenghan joined the Red Army in 1930 and the CCP in 1933, and participated in the Long March. He served as a commander at the squad, platoon, company, and battalion levels in the Red Army. During the Anti-Japanese War he became a battalion and regiment commander in the Eighth Route Army. During the Chinese Civil War Wang was appointed brigade commander and later commander of the 181st Division of the Sixty-First Army of the PLA. During the Spring Offensive, Wang was commander of the 181st Division, Sixtieth Army, Third Army Group of the CPVF. He was deputy commander of the Sixtieth Army in 1952–53. After his return to China, Wang was appointed commander of the Sixtieth Army, deputy commander of the Tibet Regional Command, and commander of the Chengdu Regional Command. He was promoted to major general in 1955 and general in 1988. See *Xinghuo liaoyuan* Composition Department, *Zhongguo renmin jiefangjun jiangshuai minglu* [Marshals and generals of the PLA], 2:87; Tan, *Zhongguo renmin zhiyuanjun renwulu* [Veterans' profile of the CPVF], 47–48.

78. Wang Zibo joined the CCP in 1938 and became a company political instructor and then regimental political commissar of the 129th Division of the Eighth Route Army in the Anti-Japanese War. During the Chinese Civil War Wang was appointed political commissar, deputy commander, and commander of a regiment of the PLA. After his return to China, Wang became an army commander and deputy commander of the Nanjing Regional Command. See Tan, *Zhongguo renmin zhiyuanjun renwulu* [Veterans' profile of the CPVF], 32.

79. Zhao and Liang, *Fenghuo 38 xian* [The flames of battle raging across the 38th Parallel], 61–62.

80. Luan, *Xue yu huo de jiaoliang* [The contest], 206; Li, *Zhiyuanjun yuanchao jishi* [The CPVF records of aiding Korea], 294.

81. Sandler, *The Korean War,* 142.

82. Wu Yansheng joined the Eighth Route Army and the CCP in 1937. He became a commander at the squad, platoon, company, and battalion levels in the Eighth Route Army during the Anti-Japanese War. During the Chinese Civil War Wu was appointed as chief of staff, deputy commander, and commander of a regiment of the PLA. See Zhao and Liang, *Fenghuo 38 xian* [The flames of battle raging across the 38th Parallel], 78; Shuang, *Kaiguo diyi zhan* [The first war since the founding of the state], 1:372; Tan, *Zhongguo renmin zhiyuanjun renwulu* [Veterans' profile of the CPVF], 294.

83. Li Ying et al., *40 jun zai chaoxian* [The Fortieth Army in Korea] (Shenyang, China: Liaoning renmin chubanshe, 2010), 194–96; Ridgway, *The Korean War,* 172; Mossman, *U.S. Army in the Korean War,* 383,390; Millett, *The War for Korea, 1950–1951,* 432; Sandler, *The Korean War,* 139–40.

84. Maurie Pears (Australian Royal Army, ret.), interviews by the author at the Australian War Museum at Canberra, Australia, October 6–7, 2011. Also see Ben Evans, *Out in the Cold: Australia's Involvement in the Korean War, 1950–53* (Canberra, Australia: Department of Australians' Veterans' Affairs, 2010), 45–50; Mossman, *U.S. Army in the Korean War,* 398–409.

85. Michael Hickey, *The Korean War: The West Confronts Communism* (New York: Overlook, 1999), 216.

86. Sandler, *The Korean War,* 142.

87. Luo, *Chaoxian zhanzheng* [The Korean War], 327; Brian Catchpole, *The Korean War, 1950–53* (New York: Carroll and Graf, 2000), 128; Hastings, *The Korean War,* 226.

88. Maj. Gen. Fu Chongbi joined the Red Army in 1932 and the CCP in 1933 and participated in the Long March. He served as a party branch secretary, company political instructor, and battalion and regimental political commissar in the Red Army. During the Anti-Japanese War he was a political commissar at the battalion, regiment, and brigade levels. During the Chinese Civil War Fu was a brigade commander and political commissar, deputy political commissar of the Sixty-Fourth Army, and deputy political commissar and commander of the Sixty-Third Army of the PLA. During the Spring Offensive, he commanded the Sixty-Fourth Army, Nineteenth Army Group of the CPVF. After his return to China, Fu was appointed commander of the Sixty-Third Army and deputy commander of the Beijing and Shenyang Regional Commands. He became a major general in 1955. See *Xinghuo liaoyuan* Composition Department, *Zhongguo renmin jiefangjun jiangshuai minglu* [Marshals and generals of the PLA], 3:553; Tan, *Zhongguo renmin zhiyuanjun renwulu* [Veterans' profile of the CPVF], 653.

89. Tan, *Kangmei yuanchao zhanzheng* [The WRUSAK], 140–41; *Xinghuo liaoyuan* Composition Department, *Zhongguo renmin jiefangjun jiangshuai minglu* [Marshals and generals of the PLA], 3:553; Tan, *Zhongguo renmin zhiyuanjun renwulu* [Veterans' profile of the CPVF], 653.

90. Gen. Xu Xin joined the Eighth Route Army and the CCP in 1937. He became a commander at the squad, platoon, company, and battalion levels in the Eighth Route Army during the Anti-Japanese War. During the Chinese Civil War Xu was appointed chief of staff, deputy commander, and commander of a regiment of the PLA. He was later promoted to chief of staff of the 188th Division and deputy commander and chief of staff of the 187th Division. After his return to China, Xu served as deputy commander of the Sixty-Third Army, commander of the Sixty-Sixth Army, and first deputy chief of the PLA General Staff. He was granted the rank of senior colonel in 1955 and promoted to major general in 1964 and general in 1988. See Shuang, *Kaiguo diyi zhan* [The first war since the founding of the state], 1:112–14; *Xinghuo liaoyuan* Composition Department, *Zhongguo renmin jiefangjun jiangshuai minglu* [Marshals and generals of the PLA] 3:376; Tan, *Zhongguo renmin zhiyuanjun renwulu* [Veterans' profile of the CPVF], 531–32.

91. Du, *Zai zhiyuanjun zongbu* [At the CPVF General HQ], 239–40; Zhao and Liang, *Fenghuo 38 xian* [The flames of battle raging across the 38th Parallel], 97; Composition Committee, ed., *38 xian shang de jiaofeng* [Fighting over the 38th Parallel], 308.

92. Yang, *Yang Dezhi huiyilu* [Memoirs of Yang Dezhi], 551; Military History Research Division, *Zhongguo renmin zhiyuanjun kangmei yuanchao zhanshi* [Combat experience of the CPVF in the WRUSAK], 133–34; Shuang, *Kaiguo diyi zhan* [The first war since the founding of the state], 1:375–78.

93. Senior Col. Wang Zhongchun (PLA), interview by the author in Changchun, Jilin, July 14–17, 2006. Senior Col. Wang is deputy director of the Division of Training and Research, College of Defense Studies, NDU. See also Yang Fengan and Wang Tiancheng, *Beiwei 38 duxian: Peng Dehuai yu chaoxian zhanzheng* [The north latitude 38th Parallel: Peng Dehuai and the Korean War], (Beijing: Zhongyang wenxian chubanshe, 2009), 321–22; Millett, *The War for Korea, 1950–1951*, 433; Hastings, *The Korean War*, 216–18, 226.

94. Ridgway, *The Korean War*, 172–73; Mossman, *U.S. Army in the Korean War*, 413; Composition Committee, ed., *38 xian shang de jiaofeng* [Fighting over the 38th Parallel], 307.

95. John C. McManus, *The 7th Infantry Regiment: Combat in an Age of Terror; The Korean War through the Present* (New York: Tom Doherty, 2008), 59–61; Millett, *The War for Korea, 1950–1951*, 434; Catchpole, *The Korean War*, 122–28.

96. Dr. Liu Zhiqing (a professor at CAMS), interviews by the author in Changchun, Jilin, July 14–17, 2006. See also Zhao and Liang, *Fenghuo 38 xian* [The flames of battle raging across the 38th Parallel], 99–100; Chu Yun, *Chaoxian zhanzheng neimu quangongkai* [Declassifying the Korean War] (Beijing: Shishi chubanshe, 2005), 295; Li, *Zhiyuanjun yuanchao jishi* [The CPVF records of aiding Korea], 295–96.

97. Yang, *Yang Dezhi huiyilu* [Memoirs of Yang Dezhi], 551; Mossman, *U.S. Army in the Korean War*, 421–2; Millett, *The War for Korea, 1950–1951*, 433; Hickey, *The Korean War*, 227–28.

98. Zhao and Liang, *Fenghuo 38 xian* [The flames of battle raging across the 38th Parallel], 98–101; Shuang, *Kaiguo diyi zhan* [The first war since the founding of the state], 1:374–77; Sandler, *The Korean War*, 141.

99. Mossman, *U.S. Army in the Korean War*, 424.

100. Ibid., 393–96; Du, *Zai zhiyuanjun zongbu* [At the CPVF General HQ], 229–31; Composition Committee, ed., *38 xian shang de jiaofeng* [Fighting over the 38th Parallel], 307–308.

101. The Chinese figures do not coincide with the UNF Command's statistics, which confirmed British losses of 708: 63 killed, 75 wounded, and 570 captured. For more details, see Hickey, *The Korean War*, 230–32.

102. One of the 570 captured Glosters was Capt. Anthony Farrar-Hockley, who spent two years as a prisoner in North Korea and later became General Sir Farrar-Hockley, commander of NATO. Farrar-Hockley published a book on his experience in the Korean War, *The Edge of the Sword* (London: Frederick Muller, 1954). See also Sandler, *The Korean War*, 141.

103. Ridgway, *The Korean War*, 172–73.

104. Quoted in Mossman, *U.S. Army in the Korean War*, 429.

105. Quoted in ibid., 428.

106. The regiment belonged to the U.S. 3rd Division. See Yang, *Yang Dezhi huiyilu* [Memoirs of Yang Dezhi], 553; China Academy of Military Science, "The Unforgotten Korean War," 421–22; Mossman, *U.S. Army in the Korean War*, 397.

107. Xu, *Mao Zedong yu kangmei yuanchao zhanzheng* [Mao Zedong and the WRUSAK], 212; Li, *Zhiyuanjun yuanchao jishi* [The CPVF records of aiding Korea], 295–96.

108. Yang, *Yang Dezhi huiyilu* [Memoirs of Yang Dezhi], 553; Military History Research Division, *Zhongguo renmin zhiyuanjun kangmei yuanchao zhanshi* [Combat experience of the CPVF in the WRUSAK], 135.

109. Hong, *Hong Xuezhi huiyilu* [Memoirs of Hong Xuezhi], 475; Tan, *Kangmei yuanchao zhanzheng* [The WRUSAK], 140; Shuang, *Kaiguo diyi zhan* [The first war since the founding of the state], 1:379.

110. Maj. Gen. Wu Shihong joined the Red Army in 1933 and the CCP in 1934 and participated in the Long March. He served as a commander at the squad and platoon levels in the Red Army. During the Anti-Japanese War he became a commander at the company, battalion, and regiment levels and chief of staff of a brigade of the 129th Division, Eighth Route Army. During the Chinese Civil War Wu was appointed brigade commander and deputy commander of the 179th Division of the Sixtieth Army of the PLA. During the Spring Offensive he commanded the 179th Division of the Sixtieth

Army, Third Army Group of the CPVF. After his return to China, Wu became chief of staff, deputy commander, and commander of the Sixtieth Army. He was promoted to senior colonel in 1955 and major general in 1964. Wu served as deputy commander of the Nanjing Regional Command before his retirement from the PLA. See Tan, *Zhongguo renmin zhiyuanjun renwulu* [Veterans' profile of the CPVF], 287–88; *Xinghuo liaoyuan* Composition Department, *Zhongguo renmin jiefangjun jiangshuai minglu* [Marshals and generals of the PLA], 2:563.

111. Zhao and Liang, *Fenghuo 38 xian* [The flames of battle raging across the 38th Parallel], 142–43; Sandler, *The Korean War*, 143.

112. Yan, *Wei Jie zhongjiang* [Lt. Gen. Wei Jie], 265; Chen Zhonglong, *60 jun rencai: rencai shi zheyang zhujiu de* [The elite of the Sixtieth Army: their successful stories] (Beijing: Zhongguo youyi chubanshe, 2005), 45–46, 125–26, 205–207.

113. Millett, *The War for Korea, 1950–1951*, 434; McManus, *The 7th Infantry Regiment*, 69.

114. White, "The Killing Ground," 136–37; Mossman, *U.S. Army in the Korean War*, 435; Millett, *The War for Korea, 1950–1951*, 434.

115. Peng, telegram to all CPVF armies and the CMC, April 18, 1951, 390–92. See also Du, *Zai zhiyuanjun zongbu* [At the CPVF General HQ], 221; Yang and Wang, *Beiwei 38 duxian* [The north latitude 38th Parallel], 322–23.

116. Wang et al., *Peng Dehuai zhuan* [Biography of Peng Dehuai], 466–67.

117. Liu Zhiqing, interviews by the author. See also Du, *Zai zhiyuanjun zongbu* [At the CPVF General HQ], 241.

118. Quoted in Military History Research Division, CAMS, *Kangmei yuanchao zhanzhengshi* [History of the WRUSAK] (Beijing: Junshi kexue chubanshe, 2000), 2:321–22.

119. Quoted in Wang et al., *Peng Dehuai zhuan* [Biography of Peng Dehuai], 466.

120. Quoted in China Academy of Military Science, "The Unforgotten Korean War," 418.

121. Quoted in CMC, telegram to Peng, "Tongyi diwuci zhanyi de zuozhan fangzhen yu zhanyi hou de bingli bushu [Agree the operation plan of the Fifth Campaign and deployment after the campaign]," April 28, 1951, 4:193.

122. China Academy of Military Science, "The Unforgotten Korean War," 422–23.

123. The official statistics show that the CPVF eliminated 23,163 UNF troops in April 22–30. See Du, *Zai zhiyuanjun zongbu* [At the CPVF General HQ], 242; Military History Research Division, *Zhongguo renmin zhiyuanjun kangmei yuanchao zhanshi* [Combat experience of the CPVF in the WRUSAK], 137; Luo, *Chaoxian zhanzheng* [The Korean War], 328–29.

124. Peng, telegram to all CPVF armies and the CMC, April 18, 1951, 390–92; Du, *Zai zhiyuanjun zongbu* [At the CPVF General HQ], 221; Military History Research Division, *Zhongguo renmin zhiyuanjun kangmei yuanchao zhanshi* [Combat experience of the CPVF in the WRUSAK], 137, 157.

### 6. THE SECOND STEP

1. Peng pointed out the "limited results" of the first step of the Spring Offensive Campaign in his telegram to Mao and the CMC, April 26, 1951. The telegram was quoted in CMC, telegram to Peng, "Tongyi diwuci zhanyi de zuozhan fangzhen yu zhanyi hou de bingli bushu [Agree the operation plan of the Fifth Campaign and deployment after the campaign]," April 28, 1951, in Zhou Enlai, *Zhou Enlai junshi wenxun* [Selected military papers of Zhou Enlai] (Beijing: Renmin chubanshe, 1997), 4:195.

2. The Chinese statistics show a total of 80,000–85,000 casualties in the Spring Offensive from April 22 to June 10, 1951. An estimated half of those casualties took place during the first step of the offensive on the western front, April 22–29. See Military History Research Division, CAMS, *Zhongguo renmin zhiyuanjun kangmei yuanchao zhanshi* [Combat experience of the CPVF in the WRUSAK] (Beijing: Junshi kexue chubanshe, 1990), 152; Tan Jingjiao, *Kangmei yuanchao zhanzheng* [The WRUSAK] (Beijing: Zhongguo shehui kexue chubanshe, 1990), 159. For other statistics, see Korean Institute of Military History (ROK), *The Korean War* (Seoul: Korean Institute of Military History, 1998), 2:5; Stanley Sandler, *The Korean War: No Victors, No Vanquished* (Lexington: University Press of Kentucky, 1999), 142.

3. Because of the second offensive in May 1951, the April offensive was thereafter called the first phase of the Spring Offensive, or "First Step, Fifth Offensive Campaign." See Peng Dehuai, "My Story of the Korean War," in *Mao's Generals Remember Korea,* trans. and ed. Xiaobing Li, Allan R. Millett, and Bin Yu (Lawrence: University Press of Kansas, 2001), 35–36; Qi Dexue, *Ni buliaojie de chaoxian zhanzheng* [The Korean War you don't know] (Shenyang, China: Liaoning renmin chubanshe, 2011), 137–39.

4. The two CPVF army groups in the east and center were the Ninth Army Group, containing the Twelfth, Twentieth, and Twenty-Seventh Armies; and the Third Army Group, containing the Fifteenth, Thirty-Ninth, and Sixtieth Armies. See Tan, *Kangmei yuanchao zhanzheng* [The WRUSAK], 146–47.

5. Peng Dehuai and Deng Hua, telegram to the CMC, all CPVF army groups, and Northeast Military Region at 10:00 PM, May 6, 1951, in Peng Dehuai, *Peng Dehuai junshi wenxuan* [Selected military papers of Peng Dehuai] (Beijing: Zhongyang wenxian chubanshe, 1988), 392–93 (hereafter cited as *Peng's Military Papers*); Peng Dehuai, *Peng Dehuai zishu* [Autobiography of Peng Dehuai] (Beijing: Renmin chubanshe, 1981), 262; Yang Fengan and Wang Tiancheng, *Beiwei 38 duxian: Peng Dehuai yu chaoxian zhanzheng* [The north latitude 38th Parallel: Peng Dehuai and the Korean War] (Beijing: Zhongyang wenxian chubanshe, 2009), 322–23; Wang Yan et al., *Peng Dehuai zhuan* [Biography of Peng Dehuai] (Beijing: Dangdai zhongguo chubanshe, 1993), 367–68.

6. Peng and Deng telegram to the CMC et al., May 6, 1951, 392–93.

7. Hong Xuezhi, *Hong Xuezhi huiyilu* [Memoirs of Hong Xuezhi] (Beijing: Jiefangjun chubanshe, 2007), 476; Luan Kechao, *Xue yu huo de jiaoliang: kangmei yuanchao jishi* [The contest: blood vs. fire; the record of resisting America and aiding Korea] (Beijing: Huayi chubanshe, 2008), 209–10; War History Division, NDU, *Zhongguo renmin zhiyuanjun zhanshi jianbian* [A concise history of the CPVF war-fighting] (Beijing: Jiefangjun chubanshe, 1992), 80.

8. Du Ping, *Zai zhiyuanjun zongbu: Du Ping huiyilu* [At the CPVF General HQ: memoirs of Du Ping] (Beijing: Jiefangjun chubanshe, 1989), 242; Luo Xuanyou, *Chaoxian zhanzheng: zhengzhan jishi* [The Korean War: the battle records] (Beijing: Jiefangjun wenyi chubanshe, 2007), 331.

9. As noted in chapter 4, Mao asked Peng on April 28 to "concentrate on striking hard the puppet [ROK] 1st Division, U.S. 3rd, 24th, and 25th Divisions, Turkish Brigade, and British 28th Brigade, and annihilate [them] as much as possible in the current campaign" (Mao Zedong, telegram to Peng, "Zhuyi zai diwuci zhanyi zhong geidiyi jinkenengdade daji [Strike as hard as possible on the enemy forces in the Fifth Campaign]," April 28, 1951, in Mao Zedong, *Jianguo yilai Mao Zedong junshi wengao* [Mao

Zedong's military manuscripts since the founding of the PRC] [Beijing: Junshi kexue chubanshe and Zhongyang wenxian chubanshe, 2010], 1:477).

10. Billy C. Mossman, *U.S. Army in the Korean War: Ebb and Flow, November 1950–July 1951* (Washington: Army Center of Military History and Government Printing Office, 1990), 438; Allan R. Millett, *The War for Korea, 1950–1951: They Came from the North* (Lawrence: University Press of Kansas, 2010), 444–45; Max Hastings, *The Korean War* (New York: Simon and Schuster, 1987), 228–29; Sandler, *The Korean War,* 142.

11. Donald Knox, *The Korean War: An Oral History* (San Diego, CA: Harcourt Brace Jovanovich, 1985–88), 2:194–95, 197; Michael Hickey, *The Korean War: The West Confronts Communism* (New York: Overlook, 1999), 235; Sandler, *The Korean War,* 131.

12. Matthew B. Ridgway, *The Korean War* (Garden City, NY: Doubleday, 1967), 173.

13. Knox, *The Korean War,* 2:195–97, 200–201; Millett, *The War for Korea, 1950–1951,* 434.

14. Mossman, *U.S. Army in the Korean War,* 439; Brian Catchpole, *The Korean War, 1950–53* (New York: Carroll and Graf, 2000), 136; John C. McManus, *The 7th Infantry Regiment: Combat in an Age of Terror; The Korean War through the Present* (New York: Tom Doherty, 2008), 70.

15. Peng, *Peng Dehuai zishu* [Autobiography of Peng Dehuai], 262; Yang Di, *Zai zhiyuanjun silingbu de suiyueli: xianwei renzhi de zhenshi qingkuang* [My years at the CPVF General HQ: untold true stories] (Beijing: Jiefangjun chubanshe, 1998), 133–34; Yang and Wang, *Beiwei 38 duxian* [The north latitude 38th Parallel], 322–23; Wang et al., *Peng Dehuai zhuan* [Biography of Peng Dehuai], 467.

16. Military History Research Division, *Zhongguo renmin zhiyuanjun kangmei yuanchao zhanshi* [Combat experience of the CPVF in the WRUSAK] 138; Zhao Jianli and Liang Yuhong, *Fenghuo 38 xian: diwuci zhanyi zhanshi baogao* [The flames of battle raging across the 38th Parallel: combat report on the Fifth Campaign] (Beijing: Junshi kexue chubanshe, 2007), 148.

17. Yang Dezhi, *Yang Dezhi huiyilu* [Memoirs of Yang Dezhi] (Beijing: Jiefangjun chubanshe, 1992), 557; Yang and Wang, *Beiwei 38 duxian* [The north latitude 38th Parallel], 323; Li Qingshan, *Zhiyuanjun yuanchao jishi* [The CPVF records of aiding Korea] (Beijing: Zhonggong dangshi chubanshe, 2008), 310.

18. Sunzi, *The Art of War,* trans. Roger Ames (New York: Ballantine, 1993), 104, 105.

19. Quoted in Wang et al., *Peng Dehuai zhuan* [Biography of Peng Dehuai], 467.

20. Ibid.

21. Peng and Deng telegram to the CMC et al., May 6, 1951, 394–95.

22. Du, *Zai zhiyuanjun zongbu* [At the CPVF General HQ], 242.

23. Hong, *Hong Xuezhi huiyilu* [Memoirs of Hong Xuezhi], 485; Yang, *Zai zhiyuanjun silingbu de suiyueli* [My years at the CPVF General HQ], 133–34; Yang and Wang, *Beiwei 38 duxian* [The north latitude 38th Parallel], 323; Wang et al., *Peng Dehuai zhuan* [Biography of Peng Dehuai], 467.

24. Shuguang Zhang points out that Mao even "rejected Peng's suggestion to suspend the advance of the CPV main forces" in late April (*Mao's Military Romanticism: China and the Korean War, 1950–53* [Lawrence: University Press of Kansas, 1995]), 150). See also Yan Xinning, *Wei Jie zhongjiang* [Lt. Gen. Wei Jie] (Beijing: Jiefangjun wenyi chubanshe), 2005), 37. For more details on Hong's meeting with Mao on May 1, 1951, in Beijing, as well as his meeting with Zhou Enlai in April, see Hong Xuezhi, "The CPVF's Combat and Logistics," in *Mao's Generals Remember Korea,* trans. and ed. Xiaobing Li,

Allan R. Millett, and Bin Yu (Lawrence: University Press of Kansas, 2000), 122–29; Li, *Zhiyuanjun yuanchao jishi* [The CPVF records of aiding Korea], 303–304.

25. Zhang, *Mao's Military Romanticism*, 150.

26. Yang, *Yang Dezhi huiyilu* [Memoirs of Yang Dezhi], 554–56; Zhao and Liang, *Fenghuo 38 xian* [The flames of battle raging across the 38th Parallel], 35–36.

27. Among the CPVF army commanders who complained were Zeng Shaoshan, commander of the Twelfth Army, and Qin Jiwei, commander of the Fifteenth Army, who talked about "changing the commander in chief" on May 6–7, 1951 (Yan, *Wei Jie zhongjiang* [Lt. Gen. Wei Jie], 38–39).

28. Yang, *Zai zhiyuanjun silingbu de suiyueli* [My years at the CPVF General HQ], 132–33; Composition Committee, ed., *38 xian shang de jiaofeng: kangmei yuanchao zhanzheng jishi* [Fighting over the 38th Parallel: the recorded truth of the WRUSAK] (Beijing: Jiefangjun wenyi chubanshe, 2010), 302–303; Yan, *Wei Jie zhongjiang* [Lt. Gen. Wei Jie], 25, 33–34.

29. Shuang Shi, *Kaiguo diyi zhan: kangmei yuanchao zhanzheng quanjing jishi* [The first war since the founding of the state: the complete story of the WRUSAK] (Beijing: Zhonggong dangshi chubanshe, 2004), 1:380–81; Luo, *Chaoxian zhanzheng* [The Korean War], 329; Li, *Zhiyuanjun yuanchao jishi* [The CPVF records of aiding Korea], 295–96.

30. Quoted in Yang, *Zai zhiyuanjun silingbu de suiyueli* [My years at the CPVF General HQ], 128. See also Zhao and Liang, *Fenghuo 38 xian* [The flames of battle raging across the 38th Parallel], 28.

31. Hong Xuezhi, *Kangmei yuanchao zhanzheng huiyi* [Recollections of the WRUSAK] (Beijing: Jiefangjun wenyi chubanshe, 1990), 156; Wang Shuzeng, *Juezhan chaoxian: chaoxian zhanchang shi wojun tong meijun jiaoliang de lianbingchang* [The showdown in Korea: the battleground for a competition between the Chinese army and American army] (Beijing: Jiefangjun wenyi chubanshe, 2007), 309.

32. Yang, *Zai zhiyuanjun silingbu de suiyueli* [My years at the CPVF General HQ], 134; Shuang, *Kaiguo diyi zhan* [The first war since the founding of the state], 1:384.

33. Quoted in Du, *Zai zhiyuanjun zongbu* [At the CPVF General HQ], 243. See also Zhao and Liang, *Fenghuo 38 xian* [The flames of battle raging across the 38th Parallel], 148.

34. For more details on the CPVF Party Committee meeting on May 3, 1951, see Hong, *Kangmei yuanchao zhanzheng huiyi* [Recollections of the WRUSAK], 181; Zhou Zhong, *Kangmei yuanchao zhanzheng houqinshi jianbianben* [A concise history of the logistics in the WRUSAK] (Beijing: Jindun chubanshe, 1993), 83–84. See also Zhao and Liang, *Fenghuo 38 xian* [The flames of battle raging across the 38th Parallel], 160; Luan, *Xue yu huo de jiaoliang* [The contest], 209.

35. Hong, *Hong Xuezhi huiyilu* [Memoirs of Hong Xuezhi], 495–96.

36. Hong reported the loss of vehicles to the CPVF Party Committee meeting on May 3, 1951 (*Kangmei yuanchao zhanzheng huiyi* [Recollections of the WRUSAK], 181). See also Du, *Zai zhiyuanjun zongbu* [At the CPVF General HQ], 232.

37. Quoted in Zhao and Liang, *Fenghuo 38 xian* [The flames of battle raging across the 38th Parallel], 150. See also Peng, *Peng Dehuai zishu* [Autobiography of Peng Dehuai], 262–63.

38. Col. Wang Po (PLA, ret.), interview by the author at the PLA Logistics College, Beijing, July 1994. Also see Du, *Zai zhiyuanjun zongbu* [At the CPVF General HQ], 250.

39. Hong, "The CPVF's Combat and Logistics," 132; Jiang Tingyu, *Jiedu kangmei yuanchao zhanzheng* [Understanding the WRUSAK] (Beijing: Jiefangjun chubanshe, 2011), 54.

40. Quoted in Hong, *Kangmei yuanchao zhanzheng huiyi* [Recollections of the WRUSAK], 181.

41. Nie Rongzhen, *Nie Rongzhen huiyilu* [Memoirs of Nie Rongzhen] (Beijing: Jiefangjun chubanshe, 1984), 2:751; Zhou, *Kangmei yuanchao zhanzheng huoqinshi jianbianben* [A concise history of the logistics in the WRUSAK], 83.

42. Du, *Zai zhiyuanjun zongbu* [At the CPVF General HQ], 243; Hong, "The CPVF's Combat and Logistics," 133.

43. Quoted in Hong, *Hong Xuezhi huiyilu* [Memoirs of Hong Xuezhi], 496.

44. Hong, *Kangmei yuanchao zhanzheng huiyi* [Recollections of the WRUSAK], 181–82; Wang, *Juezhan chaoxian* [The showdown in Korea], 311–12; Luan, *Xue ye huo de jiaoliang* [The contest], 230.

45. Hong, "The CPVF's Combat and Logistics," 133–35; Composition Committee, ed., *38 xian shang de jiaofeng* [Fighting over the 38th Parallel], 320–22; Li, *Zhiyuanjun yuanchao jishi* [The CPVF records of aiding Korea], 305–307.

46. Quoted in Nie Rongzhen Biography Compilation Team, *Nie Rongzhen zhuan* [Biography of Nie Rongzhen] (Beijing: Dangdai zhongguo chubanshe, 2006), 297. See also Zhou, *Kangmei yuanchao zhanzheng huoqinshi jianbianben* [A concise history of the logistics in the WRUSAK], 87–88.

47. Nie Rongzhen, "Beijing's Decision to Intervene," in *Mao's Generals Remember Korea*, trans. and ed. Xiaobing Li, Allan R. Millett, and Bin Yu (Lawrence: University Press of Kansas, 2000), 53.

48. Col. Wang Po (PLA, ret.), interview by the author at the PLA Logistics College, Beijing, July 1994; Du, *Zai zhiyuanjun zongbu* [At the CPVF General HQ], 231–33; China Academy of Military Science, "The Unforgotten Korean War: Chinese Perspective and Appraisals," unpublished manuscript, 2006, 486–88; Li, *Zhiyuanjun yuanchao jishi* [The CPVF records of aiding Korea], 289.

49. Ministry of Foreign Affairs to Foreign Affairs Office, Northeast China Executive Committee, "Helping North Korea Construct More Medicine Warehouses, April 8, 1953," in "Premier Zhou Enlai's Approvals and Instructions on North Korean Telegrams and Documents, 1953," File# 106-00034-01 (1), 2–3 (31 pages); and Teng Daiyuan to Li Kenong, "Guanyu chaoxian renminjun zai dongbei zhanyong shepi de baogao [About the rail cars in Northeast China halted by the NKPA]," June 29, 1951, File# 106-00026-02 (1), Archives Department, PRC Foreign Affairs Ministry, Beijing. See also Nie, *Nie Rongzhen huiyilu* [Memoirs of Nie Rongzhen], 2:752.

50. Quoted in Luo, *Chaoxian zhanzheng* [The Korean War], 399.

51. Shuguang Zhang, "Command, Control, and the PLA's Offensive Campaigns in Korea, 1950–1951," in *Chinese Warfighting: The PLA Experience since 1949*, ed. Mark A. Ryan, David M. Finkelstein, and Michael A. McDevitt (New York: M. E. Sharpe, 2003), 110–11, 113.

52. Peng Dehuai, "Guanyu chijiu zuozhan fangzhen he jinhou zuozhan de zhidao yuanze [The guiding principles and operation directives for the prolonged war in the future]," in Peng, *Peng's Military Papers*, 403–404.

53. China Academy of Military Science, "The Unforgotten Korean War," 427. For more details on the Fourth Field Army of the PLA, see War History Division, NDU,

*Zhongguo renmin jiefangjun zhanshi jianbian* [A concise history of the PLA revolutionary war] (Beijing: Jiefangjun chubanshe, 2001), 324–28; Xiaobing Li, *A History of the Modern Chinese Army* (Lexington: University Press of Kentucky, 2007), 76, 89, 107, 130–33; Odd Arne Westad, *Decisive Encounters: The Chinese Civil War, 1946–50* (Stanford: Stanford University Press, 2003), 241.

54. Wang et al., *Peng Dehuai zhuan* [Biography of Peng Dehuai], 467.

55. Lt. Gen. Wang Jinshan joined the Red Army in 1930 and the CCP in 1932 and participated in the Long March. He served as commander of a squad, platoon, company, battalion, regiment, and division in the Red Army. During the Anti-Japanese War Wang became the commander of the 769th Regiment and deputy commander of the 385th Brigade, 129th Division, Eighth Route Army. During the Chinese Civil War he was appointed commander of the 6th Division, deputy commander and later commander and political commissar of the Twelfth Army, and deputy commander of the Twentieth Army Group of the PLA. After his return to China, Wang became deputy commander of the Shandong and Beijing Regional Commands and vice minister of the PRC Ministry of Public Security. In 1955 he was granted the rank of lieutenant general. See *Xinghuo liaoyuan* Composition Department, *Zhongguo renmin jiefangjun jiangshuai minglu* [Marshals and generals of the PLA], (Beijing: Jiefangjun chubanshe, 1992), 1:164–65; Tan Zheng, *Zhongguo renmin zhiyuanjun renwulu* [Veterans' profile of the CPVF] (Beijing: Zhonggong dangshi chubanshe, 1992), 40–41.

56. Zhao and Liang, *Fenghuo 38 xian* [The flames of battle raging across the 38th Parallel], 150–51; Shuang, *Kaiguo diyi zhan* [The first war since the founding of the state], 1:833–35; Yan, *Wei Jie zhongjiang* [Lt. Gen. Wei Jie], 37.

57. The two divisions transferred from the Thirty-Ninth Army to the Third Army Group in May 1951 were the 115th and 116th Divisions. See Tan, *Kangmei yuanchao zhanzheng* [The WRUSAK], 146–47; Luan, *Xue yu huo de jiaoliang* [The contest], 209, 211.

58. Peng and Deng telegram to the CMC et al., May 6, 1951, 392–93.

59. Ibid.

60. Du, *Zai zhiyuanjun zongbu* [At the CPVF General HQ], 242–43; China Academy of Military Science, "The Unforgotten Korean War," 427–28; Li, *Zhiyuanjun yuanchao jishi* [The CPVF records of aiding Korea], 308.

61. Shuang, *Kaiguo diyi zhan* [The first war since the founding of the state], 1:383–84; Military History Research Division, *Zhongguo renmin zhiyuanjun kangmei yuanchao zhanshi* [Combat experience of the CPVF in the WRUSAK], 139–40.

62. The CPVF Command and NKPA Command had met in early December 1950 and agreed to establish the CPVF-NKPA Joint Command, with Peng as commander in chief and political commissar and Kim as deputy commander in chief. See Jiang, *Jiedu kangmei yuanchao zhanzheng* [Understanding the WRUSAK], 35.

63. For more information about Kim, see Zhao and Liang, *Fenghuo 38 xian* [The flames of battle raging across the 38th Parallel], 157.

64. Tan, *Kangmei yuanchao zhanzheng* [The WRUSAK], 146–47; Cui Xianghua and Chen Dapeng, *Tao Yong jiangjun zhuan* [Biography of General Tao Yong] (Beijing: Jiefangjun chubanshe, 1989), 396.

65. Quoted in Luan, *Xue yu huo de jiaoliang* [The contest], 211. After intensive discussion, the Chinese and North Korean commanders at the joint conference reached the conclusion that "after attacks by the CPVF and NKPA forces, the ROK divisions on the east front might possibly withdraw to Yangyang or move closer to American forces.

Therefore, the key to the objective of annihilating of the ROK divisions at Hyeon-ri was to cut off all enemy retreat and block them solidly from getting out" (China Academy of Military Science, "The Unforgotten Korean War," 429).

66. Yang and Wang, *Beiwei 38 duxian* [The north latitude 38th Parallel], 323; Zhao and Liang, *Fenghuo 38 xian* [The flames of battle raging across the 38th Parallel], 176; Luan, *Xue yu huo de jiaoliang* [The contest], 209–11.

67. Yang, *Zai zhiyuanjun silingbu de suiyueli* [My years at the CPVF General HQ], 134; Wang et al., *Peng Dehuai zhuan* [Biography of Peng Dehuai], 467; Li, *Zhiyuanjun yuanchao jishi* [The CPVF records of aiding Korea], 308.

68. Yan, *Wei Jie zhongjiang* [Lt. Gen. Wei Jie], 39–40; Shuang, *Kaiguo diyi zhan* [The first war since the founding of the state], 1:384–85.

69. Tan, *Kangmei yuanchao zhanzheng* [The WRUSAK], 146–47; Luan, *Xue yu huo de jiaoliang* [The contest], 209, 211; Military History Research Division, *Zhongguo renmin zhiyuanjun kangmei yuanchao zhanshi* [Combat experience of the CPVF in the WRUSAK], 102.

70. Peng and Deng telegram to the CMC et al., May 6, 1951, 392–95.

71. Du, *Zai zhiyuanjun zongbu* [At the CPVF General HQ], 244; Tan, *Kangmei yuanchao zhanzheng* [The WRUSAK], 147; Wang Shuzeng, *Yuandong chaoxian zhanzheng* [The Korean War in the Far East] (Beijing: Jiefangjun wenyi chubanshe, 2000), 2:722–23.

72. Peng and Deng telegram to the CMC et al., May 6, 1951, 392–95.

73. Yang, *Yang Dezhi huiyilu* [Memoirs of Yang Dezhi], 557; Yang and Wang, *Beiwei 38 duxian* [The north latitude 38th Parallel], 323; Li, *Zhiyuanjun yuanchao jishi* [The CPVF records of aiding Korea], 309–10; Luan, *Xue yu huo de jiaoliang* [The contest], 209–11.

74. Mossman, *U.S. Army in the Korean War*, 438–40; Hickey, *The Korean War*, 234–35.

75. Millett, *The War for Korea, 1950–1951*, 434–35, 442–43.

76. Ridgway, *The Korean War*, 173–74.

77. China Academy of Military Science, "The Unforgotten Korean War," 432; Zhao and Liang, *Fenghuo 38 xian* [The flames of battle raging across the 38th Parallel], 166.

78. Peng and Deng telegram to the CMC et al., May 6, 1951, 394.

79. Gen. Li Zhimin was made director of the Political Department of the CPVF General HQ in 1952, deputy commissar of the CPVF in 1954, and commissar in 1955. He was granted the rank of general in 1955. For more information, see Tan, *Zhongguo renmin zhiyuanjun renwulu* [Veterans' profile of the CPVF], 249–50; *Xinghuo liaoyuan* Composition Department, *Zhongguo renmin jiefangjun jiangshuai minglu* [Marshals and generals of the PLA], 1:80–81.

80. Quoted in China Academy of Military Science, "The Unforgotten Korean War," 432.

81. Tan, *Kangmei yuanchao zhanzheng* [The WRUSAK], 146–47; Zhao and Liang, *Fenghuo 38 xian* [The flames of battle raging across the 38th Parallel], 168.

82. China Academy of Military Science, "The Unforgotten Korean War," 433; Luan, *Xue yu huo de jiaoliang* [The contest], 211; Li, *Zhiyuanjun yuanchao jishi* [The CPVF records of aiding Korea], 310.

83. The Chinese forces totaled 370,000 troops: 110,000 men in the Nineteenth Army Group, 110,000 men in the Third, and 150,000 men in the Ninth. The North Korean forces totaled 114,000 troops. See Xu Yan, *Mao Zedong yu kangmei yuanchao zhanzheng* [Mao Zedong and the WRUSAK], 2nd ed. (Beijing: Jiefangjun chubanshe, 2006), 209; Ridgway, *The Korean War*, 174–75; Millett, *The War for Korea, 1950–1951*, 426.

84. Yang, *Yang Dezhi huiyilu* [Memoirs of Yang Dezhi], 557; Shuang, *Kaiguo diyi zhan* [The first war since the founding of the state], 1:385; Mossman, *U.S. Army in the Korean War*, 440.

85. Military History Research Division, *Zhongguo renmin zhiyuanjun kangmei yuanchao zhanshi* [Combat experience of the CPVF in the WRUSAK], 104; Tan, *Kangmei yuanchao zhanzheng* [The WRUSAK], 151; Millett, *The War for Korea, 1950–1951*, 444–45.

86. Ridgway, *The Korean War*, 174.

87. Millett, *The War for Korea, 1950–1951*, 442–43; Korean Institute of Military History, *The Korean War*, 2:661.

88. Mossman, *U.S. Army in the Korean War*, 438–39; Hastings, *The Korean War*, 229; McManus, *The 7th Infantry Regiment*, 68–70.

89. Tan, *Kangmei yuanchao zhanzheng* [The WRUSAK], 150–51; Clark C. Munroe, *The Second U.S. Infantry Division in Korea, 1950–51* (Tokyo: Toppan, 1954), 133; Hastings, *The Korean War*, 228.

90. Yang, *Zai zhiyuanjun silingbu de suiyueli* [My years at the CPVF General HQ], 134; He Zongguang, *Wo zai chaoxian zhanchang: 1950–53* [I was there: the Korean battleground, 1950–53] (Beijing: Changzheng chubanshe, 2011), 253–54; China National Military Museum, ed., *Kangmei yuanchao zhanzheng fengyunlu* [The operational files of the WRUSAK] (Beijing: Huacheng chubanshe, 1999), 195–96.

91. Korean Institute of Military History, *The Korean War*, 2:663, 665.

92. Ridgway, *The Korean War*, 175; Millett, *The War for Korea, 1950–1951*, 443.

93. Quoted in China Academy of Military Science, "The Unforgotten Korean War," 437–38.

94. China National Military Museum, ed., *Kangmei yuanchao zhanzheng fengyunlu* [The operational files of the WRUSAK], 196; Tan, *Kangmei yuanchao zhanzheng* [The WRUSAK], 147; Military History Research Division, *Zhongguo renmin zhiyuanjun kangmei yuanchao zhanshi* [Combat experience of the CPVF in the WRUSAK], 103.

95. China Academy of Military Science, "The Unforgotten Korean War," 434 note 786.

96. Composition Committee, ed., *38 xian shang de jiaofeng* [Fighting over the 38th Parallel], 325–27; Zhao and Liang, *Fenghuo 38 xian* [The flames of battle raging across the 38th Parallel], 171.

97. Jongnam Na, "Making Cold War Soldiers: The Americanization of the South Korean Army, 1945–55," PhD diss. (Chapel Hill: University of North Carolina, 2006), 97.

98. Gu Cheng et al., trans. and eds., *Chaoxian zhanzheng: dijun shiliao* [ROK Army Archives: the Korean War] (Harbin, China: Heilongjiang chaoxian minzu chubanshe, 1988–90), 2:125–26. The ROK 8th Regiment of the 7th Division lost the Sixth and Tenth Companies in the battle. See also Na, "Making Cold War Soldiers," 92.

99. Shuang, *Kaiguo diyi zhang* [The first war since the founding of the state], 1:385; Military History Research Division, *Zhongguo renmin zhiyuanjun kangmei yuanchao zhanshi* [Combat experience of the CPVF in the WRUSAK], 103–104.

100. NCO Han Shunzhou (PLA, ret.), interview by the author in Beijing in July 2010. Noncommissioned officer Han served in the 3rd Battalion, 241st Regiment, 81st Division, Twenty-Seventh Army, of the CPVF Ninth Army Group in May 1951, during the Spring Offensive.

101. Zhao Yihong, *27 jun chuanqi* [The legacy of the Twenty-Seventh Army] (Jilin, China: Jilin renmin chubanshe, 1995), 446; Tan, *Kangmei yuanchao zhanzheng* [The WRUSAK], 148–49; Luan, *Xue yu huo de jiaoliang* [The contest], 212.

102. Military History Research Division, *Zhongguo renmin zhiyuanjun kangmei yuanchao zhanshi* [Combat experience of the CPVF in the WRUSAK], 103–104; Composition Committee, ed., *38 xian shang de jiaofeng* [Fighting over the 38th Parallel], 327–28; Li, *Zhiyuanjun yuanchao jishi* [The CPVF records of aiding Korea], 310–11.

103. Ridgway, *The Korean War*, 175.

104. Korean Institute of Military History, *The Korean War*, 2:675.

105. China Academy of Military Science, "The Unforgotten Korean War," 435.

106. Gu et al., trans. and eds., *Chaoxian zhanzheng* [ROK Army Archives], 2:128; Composition Committee, ed., *38 xian shang de jiaofeng* [Fighting over the 38th Parallel], 327.

107. Korean Institute of Military History, *The Korean War*, 2:675; see also 681.

108. China Academy of Military Science, "The Unforgotten Korean War," 435.

109. Zhao and Liang, *Fenghuo 38 xian* [The flames of battle raging across the 38th Parallel], 179; Shuang, *Kaiguo diyi zhan* [The first war since the founding of the state], 1:385–86.

110. Military History Research Division, *Zhongguo renmin zhiyuanjun kangmei yuanchao zhanshi* [Combat experience of the CPVF in the WRUSAK], 103–105; Tan, *Kangmei yuanchao zhanzheng* [The WRUSAK], 148–49; Mossman, *U.S. Army in the Korean War*, 468.

111. Ridgway, *The Korean War*, 176.

112. Korean Institute of Military History, *The Korean War*, 2:691.

113. Na, "Making Cold War Soldiers," 104.

114. Ridgway, *The Korean War*, 179.

115. Quoted in Korean Institute of Military History, *The Korean War*, 2:713.

116. Na, "Making Cold War Soldiers," 97.

117. Ibid. The prominent South Korean general was Paik Sun-yup, commander of the ROK 1st Infantry Division in June 1950 when the Korean War broke out. He was promoted to commander of the ROK I Corps in April 1951. Made a lieutenant general in 1952, he served as commander of the ROK II Corps. He was appointed chief of staff of the ROK Army in July 1952. Promoted to the rank of general in January 1953, he became the first four-star general in the ROK Armed Forces. See Paik Sun-yup, *From Pusan to Panmunjom: Wartime Memoirs of the Republic of Korea's First Four-Star General* (Dulles, VA: Brassey's, 1992), chapters 5–7.

118. Tan, *Kangmei yuanchao zhanzheng* [The WRUSAK], 149; Military History Research Division, *Zhongguo renmin zhiyuanjun kangmei yuanchao zhanshi* [Combat experience of the CPVF in the WRUSAK], 103; Shuang, *Kaiguo diyi zhan* [The first war since the founding of the state], 1:385–86.

119. Yang, *Zai zhiyuanjun silingbu de suiyueli* [My years at the CPVF General HQ], 134; Li, *Zhiyuanjun yuanchao jishi* [The CPVF records of aiding Korea], 312; Shuang, *Kaiguo diyi zhan* [The first war since the founding of the state], 1:386.

120. Hong, *Kangmei yuanchao zhanzheng huiyi* [Recollections of the WRUSAK], 47; Yang, *Zai zhiyuanjun silingbu de suiyueli* [My years at the CPVF General HQ], 31–34.

121. Military History Research Division, *Zhongguo renmin zhiyuanjun kangmei yuanchao zhanshi* [Combat experience of the CPVF in the WRUSAK], 103; Shuang, *Kaiguo diyi zhan* [The first war since the founding of the state], 1:386.

122. Hong, *Hong Xuezhi huiyilu* [Memoirs of Hong Xuezhi], 476–77; Tan, *Kangmei yuanchao zhanzheng* [The WRUSAK], 149; Xu Yaguang, "Jianku de beiche xingcheng [The difficult withdrawal to the north]," in *Laozhanshi yishi* [Personal stories of the veterans], ed. Ge Chumin (Beijing: Zhongguo duiwai fanyi chuban gongsi, 2000), 86–87. NCO Xu served as a company officer in the 101st Regiment, 34th Division, Twelfth Army of the CPVF Third Army Group during the Spring Offensive, April–June 1951.

123. Du, *Zai zhiyuanjun zongbu* [At the CPVF General HQ], 244–45; Luan, *Xue yu huo de jiaoliang* [The contest], 212; Mossman, *U.S. Army in the Korean War,* 448–50; Munroe, *The Second U.S. Infantry Division in Korea,* 131–35.

124. The Twelfth Army had been under the command of the Third Army Group since it entered Korea in March 1951. The army was reassigned to the command of the Ninth Army Group only for the second step of the Spring Offensive, at the CPVF commanders meeting on May 6, 1951. See Yan, *Wei Jie zhongjiang* [Lt. Gen. Wei Jie], 37–38.

125. Du, *Zai zhiyuanjun zongbu* [At the CPVF General HQ], 244–45; Zhao and Liang, *Fenghuo 38 xian* [The flames of battle raging across the 38th Parallel], 178–79.

126. For more details on the Battle of Bunker Hill, see Russell A. Gugeler, *Combat Actions in Korea* (Washington: Center of Military History, U.S. Army, 1987), 166–82; Munroe, *The Second U.S. Infantry Division in Korea,* 132–36; Catchpole, *The Korean War,* 136. See also Military History Research Division, *Zhongguo renmin zhiyuanjun kangmei yuanchao zhanshi* [Combat experience of the CPVF in the WRUSAK], 104.

127. Hong, *Hong Xuezhi huiyilu* [Memoirs of Hong Xuezhi], 476; Tan, *Kangmei yuanchao zhanzheng* [The WRUSAK], 150.

128. Zhao and Liang, *Fenghuo 38 xian* [The flames of battle raging across the 38th Parallel], 179; Composition Committee, ed., *38 xian shang de jiaofeng* [Fighting over the 38th Parallel], 327; Munroe, *The Second U.S. Infantry Division in Korea,* 132–35; Millett, *The War for Korea, 1950–1951,* 445.

129. Millett, *The War for Korea, 1950–1951.*

130. Shuang, *Kaiguo diyi zhan* [The first war since the founding of the state], 1:390; see also 395.

131. Yang Wanfu (POW), interviews by the author in the Rongjia Zhongxin (Glorious Retirement Center for Veterans) in Taipei, June 8–10, 2010. As a Chinese POW, Yang went to Taiwan after the Korean Armistice. He said during the interview: "The American airplanes dropped a lot of napalm bombs. They burned lots of trees and hills. But not just the fire, they were poisoning. Many Chinese soldiers were burned to death or seriously burned."

132. Millett, *The War for Korea, 1950–1951,* 447.

133. Hastings, *The Korean War,* 266.

134. Du, *Zai zhiyuanjun zongbu* [At the CPVF General HQ], 246; Xu, "Jianku de beiche xingcheng [The difficult withdrawal to the north]," 87–89; Tan, *Kangmei yuanchao zhanzheng* [The WRUSAK], 152; Military History Research Division, CAMS, *Junqi piaopiao: xinzhongguo 50 nian junshi dashi shushi, 1949–99* [PLA flag fluttering: The facts about China's major military events in the past fifty years, 1949–99] (Beijing: Jiefangjun chubanshe, 1999), 1:135–36.

135. Zhao and Liang, *Fenghuo 38 xian* [The flames of battle raging across the 38th Parallel], 188–89; Shuang, *Kaiguo diyi zhang* [The first war since the founding of the state], 1:395.

136. Chang Buting, interviews by the author in the Rongjia Zhongxin (Glorious Retirement Center for Veterans) in Taipei, June 8–10, 2010. Chang was captured by the

UNF in May 1951, during the Spring Offensive. He did not go back to China, moving to Taiwan after the Korean Armistice in 1953.

137. Gu et al., trans. and eds., *Chaoxian zhanzheng* [ROK Army Archives], 2:112–13.

138. Yang, *Zai zhiyuanjun silingbu de suiyueli* [My years at the CPVF General HQ], 137; Peng Dehuai Biography Compilation Team, *Yige zhanzheng de ren: Peng Dehuai* [A real man: Peng Dehuai] (Beijing: Renmin chubanshe, 1994), 189; Xu, *Mao Zedong yu kangmei yuanchao zhanzheng* [Mao Zedong and the WRUSAK], 215; War History Division, *Zhongguo renmin zhiyuanjun zhanshi jianbian* [A concise history of the CPVF war-fighting], 82–83.

139. Peng's telegram to Mao at 11:00 PM, May 21, 1951, quoted in the endnotes of Mao's telegram to Peng, May 22, 1951, Mao, "Shoubing xiuzheng zhunbei zaizhan shi zhengque de [It is correct for the CPVF to stop offensive and rest for the next campaign]," May 22, 1951, in Mao Zedong, *Jianguo yilai Mao Zedong junshi wengao* [Mao Zedong's military manuscripts since the founding of the PRC] (Beijing: Junshi kexue chubanshe and Zhongyang wenxian chubanshe, 2010; hereafter cited as *Mao's Military Manuscripts since 1949*), 1:485, note 3. In his reply to Peng, Mao agreed to stop the Spring Offensive (ibid.). See also Hong, *Hong Xuezhi huiyilu* [Memoirs of Hong Xuezhi], 477; Li, *Zhiyuanjun yuanchao jishi* [The CPVF records of aiding Korea], 312; Xu, *Mao Zedong yu kangmei yuanchao zhanzheng* [Mao Zedong and the WRUSAK], 216; Composition Committee, ed., *38 xian shang de jiaofeng* [Fighting over the 38th Parallel], 330–31.

140. Mossman, *U.S. Army in the Korean War*, 467; Millett, *The War for Korea, 1950–1951*, 443; John Toland, *In Mortal Combat: Korea, 1950–1953* (New York: William Morrow, 1991), 460–61.

141. Knox, *The Korean War*, 2:197–99; Sandler, *The Korean War*, 143–44; Allan R. Millett, *Their War for Korea: American, Asian, and European Combatants and Civilians, 1945–53* (Washington: Brassey's, 2002), 86–87, 93.

142. Millett, *The War for Korea, 1950–1951*, 445.

143. Thomas Fleming, "The Man Who Saved Korea," in *The Cold War: A Military History*, ed. Robert Cowley (New York: Random House, 2005), 117; Toland, *In Mortal Combat*, 461–63.

144. Catchpole, *The Korean War*, 136; Toland, *In Mortal Combat*, 461.

145. Quoted in China Academy of Military Science, "The Unforgotten Korean War," 443–44.

146. For more details on the battle of Jipyeong-ri, see Gugeler, *Combat Actions in Korea*, 100–125; William T. Bowers, "Operation Swing—The Push to the East," in *Striking Back: Combat in Korea, March–April 1951*, ed. William T. Bowers (Lexington: University Press of Kentucky, 2010), 221–30.

147. Hong, *Kangmei yuanchao zhanzheng huiyi* [Recollections of the WRUSAK], 47; Yang, *Zai zhiyuanjun silingbu de suiyueli* [My years at the CPVF General HQ], 31–4; Wang et al., *Peng Dehuai zhuan* [Biography of Peng Dehuai], 369–70; China National Military Museum, ed., *Kangmei yuanchao zhanzheng fengyunlu* [The operational files of the WRUSAK], 196.

148. Quoted in China Academy of Military Science, "The Unforgotten Korean War," 448–49.

149. Mao, "Shoubing xiuzheng zhunbei zaizhan shi zhengque de [It is correct for the CPVF to stop offensive and rest for the next campaign]," Mao, *Mao's Military Manuscripts since 1949*, 1:485.

150. CAMS, *Kangmei yuanchao zhanzhengshi* (History of the WRUSAK), 2:276–8.

151. Korean Institute of Military History, *The Korean War,* 2:715.

152. Ridgway, *The Korean War,* 176.

### 7. DISASTROUS WITHDRAWAL TO THE NORTH

1. Peng Dehuai and Deng Hua, telegram to all CPVF army groups, copied to the CMC at 4:00 PM, May 21, 1951, in Peng Dehuai, *Peng Dehuai junshi wenxuan* [Selected military papers of Peng Dehuai] (Beijing: Zhongyang wenxian chubanshe, 1988; hereafter cited as *Peng's Military Papers),* 396.

2. Hong Xuezhi, *Hong Xuezhi huiyilu* [Memoirs of Hong Xuezhi] (Beijing: Jiefangjun chubanshe, 2007), 483.

3. Peng admitted the severe losses during the third step of the Spring Offensive in Peng Dehuai, "My Story of the Korean War," in *Mao's Generals Remember Korea,* trans. and ed. Xiaobing Li, Allan R. Millett, and Bin Yu (Lawrence: University Press of Kansas, 2001), 35–36. See also Wang Yan et al., *Peng Dehuai zhuan* [Biography of Peng Dehuai] (Beijing: Dangdai zhongguo chubanshe, 1993), 471–72. Other CPVF commanders had a similar view of the disastrous withdrawal to the north from May 23 to June 10, 1951. See Military History Research Division, CAMS, *Zhongguo renmin zhiyuanjun kangmei yuanchao zhanshi* [Combat experience of the CPVF in the WRUSAK] (Beijing: Junshi kexue chubanshe, 1990), 108, 109; China National Military Museum, ed., *Kangmei yuanchao zhanzheng jishi* [A chronological record of the WRUSAK] (Beijing: Jiefangjun chubanshe 2008), 122–23.

4. Yang Dezhi, *Yang Dezhi huiyilu* [Memoirs of Yang Dezhi] (Beijing: Jiefangjun chubanshe, 1992), 559; War History Division, NDU, *Zhongguo renmin zhiyuanjun zhanshi jianbian* [A concise history of the CPVF war-fighting] (Beijing: Jiefangjun chubanshe, 1992), 84; Chu Yun, *Chaoxian zhanzheng neimu quangongkai* [Declassifying the Korean War] (Beijing: Shishi chubanshe, 2005), 299–302; Li Qingshan, *Zhiyuanjun yuanchao jishi* [The CPVF records of aiding Korea] (Beijing: Zhonggong dangshi chubanshe, 2008), 316–17.

5. Shuang Shi, *Kaiguo diyi zhan: kangmei yuanchao zhanzheng quanjing jishi* [The first war since the founding of the state: the complete story of the WRUSAK] (Beijing: Zhonggong dangshi chubanshe, 2004), 1:423; Composition Committee, ed., *38 xian shang de jiaofeng: kangmei yuanchao zhanzheng jishi* [Fighting over the 38th Parallel: the recorded truth of the WRUSAK] (Beijing: Jiefangjun wenyi chubanshe, 2010), 347–48. For more details on the 180th Division, see also Hong, *Hong Xuezhi huiyilu* [Memoirs of Hong Xuezhi], 477–78, 482–83; Peng Dehuai Biography Compilation Team, *Yige zhanzheng de ren: Peng Dehuai* [A real man: Peng Dehuai] (Beijing: Renmin chubanshe, 1994), 190–92; Military History Research Division, CAMS, *Junqi piaopiao: xinzhongguo 50 nian junshi dashi shushi, 1949–99* [PLA flag fluttering: The facts about China's major military events in the past fifty years, 1949–99] (Beijing: Jiefangjun chubanshe, 1999), 1:135; Hu Haipo and Yu Hongjun, *Genzhe Mao Zedong da tianxia* [Follow Mao Zedong to seize state power] (Changsha, China: Hunan renmin chubanshe, 2009), 98–99.

6. Mao Zedong, telegram to Peng, "Jianjue zudi yu Kimhwa-Chorwn yixian [Stop the enemy definitely along the Kimhwa-Chorwen line]," 2:00 AM, May 31, 1951, in Mao Zedong, *Jianguo yilai Mao Zedong junshi wengao* [Mao Zedong's military manuscripts

since the founding of the PRC] (Beijing: Junshi kexue chubanshe and Zhongyang wenxian chubanshe, 2010; hereafter cited as *Mao's Military Manuscripts since 1949*), 1:494–95.

7. Matthew B. Ridgway, *The Korean War* (Garden City, NY: Doubleday, 1967), 175; John Toland, *In Mortal Combat: Korea, 1950–1953* (New York: William Morrow, 1991), 460–61; Donald Knox, *The Korean War: An Oral History* (San Diego, CA: Harcourt Brace Jovanovich, 1985–88), 2:199.

8. Quoted in Billy C. Mossman, *U.S. Army in the Korean War: Ebb and Flow, November 1950–July 1951* (Washington: Army Center of Military History and Government Printing Office, 1990), 465. See also Allan R. Millett, *The War for Korea, 1950–1951: They Came from the North* (Lawrence: University Press of Kansas, 2010), 448.

9. Ridgway, *The Korean War*, 178. See also Mossman, *U.S. Army in the Korean War*, 464; Michael Hickey, *The Korean War: The West Confronts Communism* (New York: Overlook, 1999), 236; Brian Catchpole, *The Korean War, 1950–53* (New York: Carroll and Graf, 2000), 136–37; Millett, *The War for Korea, 1950–1951*, 448–50; Toland, *In Mortal Combat*, 461–62.

10. Ridgway, *The Korean War*, 178; Catchpole, *The Korean War*, 137; Robert Leckie, *Conflict: The History of the Korean War* (New York: Da Capo, 1996), 290.

11. For Van Fleet's plan, see Mossman, *U.S. Army in the Korean War*, 464; Theodore White, "The Killing Ground," in *No Bugles, No Drums: An Oral History of the Korean War*, ed. Rudy Tomedi (New York: Wiley and Son, 1994), 124; Toland, *In Mortal Combat*, 462; Max Hastings, *The Korean War* (New York: Simon and Schuster, 1987), 228–29.

12. Hong, *Hong Xuezhi huiyilu* [Memoirs of Hong Xuezhi], 477; Yang Fengan and Wang Tiancheng, *Beiwei 38 duxian: Peng Dehuai yu chaoxian zhanzheng* [The north latitude 38th Parallel: Peng Dehuai and the Korean War] (Beijing: Zhongyang wenxian chubanshe, 2009), 331; Luan Kechao, *Xue yu huo de jiaoliang: kangmei yuanchao jishi* [The contest: blood vs. fire; the record of resisting America and aiding Korea] (Beijing: Huayi chubanshe, 2008), 213; China National Military Museum, ed., *Kangmei yuanchao zhanzheng fengyunlu* [The operational files of the WRUSAK] (Beijing: Huacheng chubanshe, 1999), 196.

13. Peng and Deng, telegram to all CPVF army groups, copied to the CMC, May 21, 1951, in Peng, *Peng's Military Papers*, 396.

14. Peng's telegram to Mao at 11:00 PM, May 21, 1951, quoted in the endnotes of Mao's telegram to Peng, May 22, 1951, Mao, "Shoubing xiuzheng zhunbei zaizhan shi zhengque de [It is correct for the CPVF to stop offensive and rest for the next campaign]," May 22, 1951, in Mao, *Mao's Military Manuscripts since 1949*, 1:485 note 3.

15. Ibid., 1:485.

16. Du Ping, *Zai zhiyuanjun zongbu: Du Ping huiyilu* [At the CPVF General HQ: memoirs of Du Ping] (Beijing: Jiefangjun chubanshe, 1989), 221; Military History Research Division, *Zhongguo renmin zhiyuanjun kangmei yuanchao zhanshi* [Combat experience of the CPVF in the WRUSAK], 106; Li, *Zhiyuanjun yuanchao jishi* [The CPVF records of aiding Korea], 313.

17. Du, *Zai zhiyuanjun zongbu* [At the CPVF General HQ], 247; Luan, *Xue yu huo de jiaoliang* [The contest], 213; Composition Committee, ed., *38 xian shang de jiaofeng* [Fighting over the 38th Parallel], 335.

18. For the UNF counterattacks after the CPVF Third and Fourth Offensives, see chapter 2. See also China Academy of Military Science, "The Unforgotten Korean War: Chinese Perspective and Appraisals," unpublished manuscript, 2006, 447; Hu and Yu,

*Genzhe Mao Zedong da tianxia* [Follow Mao Zedong to seize state power], 98–99; Shuang, *Kaiguo diyi zhan* [The first war since the founding of the state], 1:397.

19. Yang, *Yang Dezhi huiyilu* [Memoirs of Yang Dezhi], 559; Li, *Zhiyuanjun yuanchao jishi* [The CPVF records of aiding Korea], 313.

20. Lt. Col. Guan Zhichao (PLA, ret.), interviews by the author in Nanjing, March 13–14, 2008. Guan joined the Eighth Route Army and the CCP in 1941. He served as a commander of squad and a platoon and as political instructor of a company in the Anti-Japanese War. During the Chinese Civil War he became deputy political commissar of a battalion in the PLA. He was the political commissar of the 2nd Battalion, 539th Regiment, 180th Division, Sixtieth Army, Third Army Group of the CPVF during the Spring Offensive. After his return to China, Guan was appointed commander of the 540th Regiment in 1953, deputy commander and commander of the 181st Division in 1970, and vice president of the PLA Nanjing Political Academy in 1978. He was ranked a major in 1955 and promoted to lieutenant colonel in 1962. He retired from the PLA in 1985. See Chen Zhonglong, *60 jun rencai: rencai shi zheyang zhujiu de* [The elite of the Sixtieth Army: their successful stories] (Beijing: Zhongguo youyi chubanshe, 2005), 106–107. See also Yan Xinning, *Wei Jie zhongjiang* [Lt. Gen. Wei Jie] (Beijing: Jiefangjun wenyi chubanshe], 2005), 48; Shuang, *Kaiguo diyi zhan* [The first war since the founding of the state], 1:398.

21. Peng and Deng, telegram to all CPVF army groups, copied to the CMC, May 21, 1951, in Peng, *Peng's Military Papers*, 396–97.

22. Mossman, *U.S. Army in the Korean War*, 470–73; Millett, *The War for Korea, 1950–1951*, 448–50.

23. Quoted in Yang, *Yang Dezhi huiyilu* [Memoirs of Yang Dezhi], 559. See also Shuang, *Kaiguo diyi zhan* [The first war since the founding of the state], 1:398.

24. Tan Jingjiao, *Kangmei yuanchao zhanzheng* [The WRUSAK] (Beijing: Zhongguo shehui kexue chubanshe, 1990), 153–54.

25. Yang Di, *Zai zhiyuanjun silingbu de suiyueli: xianwei renzhi de zhenshi qingkuang* [My years at the CPVF General HQ: untold true stories] (Beijing: Jiefangjun chubanshe, 1998), 138; Yang and Wang, *Beiwei 38 duxian* [The north latitude 38th Parallel], 332–33; Li, *Zhiyuanjun yuanchao jishi* [The CPVF records of aiding Korea], 313.

26. Hong, *Hong Xuezhi huiyilu* [Memoirs of Hong Xuezhi], 477.

27. Quoted in China Academy of Military Science, "The Unforgotten Korean War," 455.

28. Yang, *Yang Dezhi huiyilu* [Memoirs of Yang Dezhi], 559; Composition Committee, ed., *38 xian shang de jiaofeng* [Fighting over the 38th Parallel], 335–36; Chu, *Chaoxian zhanzheng neimu quangongkai* [Declassifying the Korean War], 299–305.

29. Hong, *Hong Xuezhi huiyilu* [Memoirs of Hong Xuezhi], 477–78. The quote from Hong is also in Yan, *Wei Jie zhongjiang* [Lt. Gen. Wei Jie], 46.

30. Senior Col. Wang Zhongchun (PLA), interviews by the author in Changchun, Jilin, July 14–17, 2006. Senior Col. Wang is deputy director of the College of Defense Strategy, NDU, in Beijing. See also Yang, *Yang Dezhi huiyilu* [Memoirs of Yang Dezhi], 559; Shuang, *Kaiguo diyi zhan* [The first war since the founding of the state], 1:411; Luan, *Xue yu huo de jiaoliang* [The contest], 213–14; Millett, *The War for Korea, 1950–1951*, 451–52.

31. Military History Research Division, *Zhongguo renmin zhiyuanjun kangmei yuanchao zhanshi* [Combat experience of the CPVF in the WRUSAK], 107; Shuang, *Kaiguo diyi zhan* [The first war since the founding of the state], 1:400.

32. Gu Cheng et al., trans. and eds., *Chaoxian zhanzheng: dijun shiliao* [ROK Army Archives: the Korean War] (Harbin, China: Heilongjiang chaoxian minzu chubanshe, 1988–90), 2:240–48; Composition Committee, ed., *38 xian shang de jiaofeng* [Fighting over the 38th Parallel], 335–36; Mossman, *U.S. Army in the Korean War*, 470–72.

33. Korean Institute of Military History (ROK), *The Korean War* (Seoul: Korean Institute of Military History, 1998), 2:724–25.

34. China Academy of Military Science, "The Unforgotten Korean War," 450.

35. Composition Committee, ed., *38 xian shang de jiaofeng* [Fighting over the 38th Parallel], 335–36; Li, *Zhiyuanjun yuanchao jishi* [The CPVF records of aiding Korea], 314.

36. Yang, *Yang Dezhi huiyilu* [Memoirs of Yang Dezhi], 559; Shuang, *Kaiguo diyi zhan* [The first war since the founding of the state], 1:397–98, 399.

37. Yang, *Zai zhiyuanjun silingbu de suiyueli* [My years at the CPVF General HQ], 137–38. Senior Col. Yang Di (PLA, ret.) joined the Eighth Route Army and the CCP in 1938. He served as a commander at the squad, platoon, and company levels in the Eighth Route Army, and later as a staff member in the Eighth Route Army HQ in the Anti-Japanese War. During the Chinese Civil War he became a regiment commander and chief of staff in the Northeast Regional Command; later he was chief of the operation section of the Thirteenth Army Group Command in the PLA. Yang was the deputy chief and later chief of the Operation Department of the CPVF General Command during the Korean War. After his return to China, he was appointed chief of the Operation Department of the Shenyang Regional Command, then the chief of staff and deputy commander of the Fortieth Army, and chief of staff of the Shenyang Regional Command of the PLA. He was made a colonel in 1955 and a senior colonel in 1960. For more details, see Tan Zheng, *Zhongguo renmin zhiyuanjun renwulu* [Veterans' profile of the CPVF] (Beijing: Zhonggong dangshi chubanshe, 1992), 193.

38. Quoted in Tan, *Kangmei yuanchao zhanzheng* [The WRUSAK], 153–54.

39. Ridgway, *The Korean War*, 178; Li, *Zhiyuanjun yuanchao jishi* [The CPVF records of aiding Korea], 313.

40. Korean Institute of Military History, *The Korean War*, 2:725–26; Shuang, *Kaiguo diyi zhan* [The first war since the founding of the state], 1:399.

41. Zhao Jianli and Liang Yuhong, *Fenghuo 38 xian: diwuci zhanyi zhanshi baogao* [The flames of battle raging across the 38th Parallel: combat report on the Fifth Campaign] (Beijing: Junshi kexue chubanshe, 2007), 211; Chu, *Chaoxian zhanzheng neimu quangongkai* [Declassifying the Korean War], 299–300.

42. Yang, *Yang Dezhi huiyilu* [Memoirs of Yang Dezhi], 559; Yang and Wang, *Beiwei 38 duxian* [The north latitude 38th Parallel], 333.

43. Dr. Dong Zhenying (PLA, ret.), interviews by the author in Beijing, March 16–17, 2008. Dong was a CPVF medic nurse in the 193rd Division of the Sixty-Fifth Army in 1951–53. See also Zhao and Liang, *Fenghuo 38 xian* [The flames of battle raging across the 38th Parallel], 211.

44. One unit of ammunition for a hand gun was 24 bullets; for a rifle, 80; an automatic rifle, 140; a light machine gun, 800; a heavy machine gun, 1,600; and an anti-aircraft machine gun, 1,000. One unit for a 37 mm anti-aircraft gun was 120 shells; for a 60 mm mortar, 30; a 76.2 mm anti-aircraft gun, 80; an 82 mm mortar, 40; a 107 mm mortar, 30; a 120 mm mortar, 30; a 122 mm howitzer, 50; a 152 mm howitzer, 50; and a 155 mm howitzer, 30. One unit for a man was four hand grenades. For more details, see Zhou

Zhong, *Kangmei yuanchao zhanzheng houqinshi jianbianben* [A concise history of the logistics in the WRUSAK] (Beijing: Jindun chubanshe, 1993), 74, 78.

45. Senior Col. Yang Shaojun (PLA, ret.), interviews by the author in Beijing, August 2008. A senior faculty member at the PLA General Academy of Logistics, Yang published several books and a dozen articles on the PLA's logistics and supplies.

46. Maj. Gen. Xiao Yingtang joined the Red Army in 1929 and the CCP in 1932; he participated in the Long March. Xiao served as a commander of a platoon, company, and battalion and as division staff member in the Red Army. During the Anti-Japanese War he was a commander of a battalion, regiment, and brigade of the Eighth Route Army. During the Chinese Civil War Xiao was division commander, deputy commander, chief of staff, and then commander of the Sixty-Fifth Army of the PLA. He commanded the Sixty-Fifth Army, Nineteenth Army Group, CPVF, during the Spring Offensive and was deputy chief of staff of the CPVF General Command in 1952–53. After his return to China, Xiao was appointed deputy commander of the Inner Mongolia Regional Command of the PLA. He was made a major general in 1955. For more details, see Tan, *Zhongguo renmin zhiyuanjun renwulu* [Veterans' profile of the CPVF], 278; *Xinghuo liaoyuan* Composition Department, *Zhongguo renmin jiefangjun jiangshuai minglu* [Marshals and generals of the PLA], (Beijing: Jiefangjun chubanshe, 1992), 2:541.

47. Yang, *Yang Dezhi huiyilu* [Memoirs of Yang Dezhi], 560; China Academy of Military Science, "The Unforgotten Korean War," 450; Shuang, *Kaiguo diyi zhan* [The first war since the founding of the state], 1:400.

48. Military History Research Division, *Zhongguo renmin zhiyuanjun kangmei yuanchao zhanshi* [Combat experience of the CPVF in the WRUSAK], 109; Composition Committee, ed., *38 xian shang de jiaofeng* [Fighting over the 38th Parallel], 335; Li, *Zhiyuanjun yuanchao jishi* [The CPVF records of aiding Korea], 314.

49. Yang, *Yang Dezhi huiyilu* [Memoirs of Yang Dezhi], 560. When Yang asked about the last defensive line on May 22, the CPVF General Command replied: "Although we have struck the UNF forces [on May 16–22], we have not yet wiped out their units. According to previous experiences, the enemy force would conduct so-called 'magnetic operations' by using its highly modernized transportation in an attempt to deplete and expend our forces." The telegram continued: "The line of our next counterattacks would be ... counterattack staging positions of the Fifth Offensive Campaign and also the last defense line"(quoted in China Academy of Military Science, "The Unforgotten Korean War," 445).

50. Zhao and Liang, *Fenghuo 38 xian* [The flames of battle raging across the 38th Parallel], 285.

51. When Fu withdrew the Sixty-Third Army without an order from the army group command, the party committee of the army made a decision to protect their commander. For more details, see Shuang, *Kaiguo diyi zhan* [The first war since the founding of the state], 1:401.

52. Shuguang Zhang, "Command, Control, and the PLA's Offensive Campaigns in Korea, 1950–1951," in *Chinese Warfighting: The PLA Experience since 1949*, ed. Mark A. Ryan, David M. Finkelstein, and Michael A. McDevitt (New York: M. E. Sharpe, 2003), 113.

53. China Academy of Military Science, "The Unforgotten Korean War," 450; Shuang, *Kaiguo diyi zhan* [The first war since the founding of the state], 1:401.

54. Korean Institute of Military History, *The Korean War*, 2:731–33.

55. China Academy of Military Science, "The Unforgotten Korean War," 450; Shuang, *Kaiguo diyi zhan* [The first war since the founding of the state], 1:402–403.

56. Zhang, "Command, Control, and the PLA's Offensive Campaigns in Korea," 113.

57. Quoted in China Academy of Military Science, "The Unforgotten Korean War," 459 note 828. Among other commanders, Chen Geng, commander of the Third Army Group, was promoted to second deputy commander of the CPVF on June 1, 1951; Song Shilun, commander of the Ninth Army Group, was promoted to third deputy commander of the CPVF the same day; and Yang Dezhi, commander of the Nineteenth Army Group, was promoted to second deputy commander of the CPVF after Chen returned to China in 1952.

58. Military History Research Division, *Zhongguo renmin zhiyuanjun kangmei yuanchao zhanshi* [Combat experience of the CPVF in the WRUSAK], 105; Chen, *60 jun rencai* [The elite of the Sixtieth Army], 46, 106–107, 126, 150–51; Yan, *Wei Jie zhongjiang* [Lt. Gen. Wei Jie], 48–49.

59. Tan, *Kangmei yuanchao zhanzheng* [The WRUSAK], 153.

60. Quoted in China Academy of Military Science, "The Unforgotten Korean War," 451.

61. Tan, *Kangmei yuanchao zhanzheng* [The WRUSAK], 154; Shuang, *Kaiguo diyi zhan* [The first war since the founding of the state], 1:405; Yan, *Wei Jie zhongjiang* [Lt. Gen. Wei Jie], 47; Li, *Zhiyuanjun yuanchao jishi* [The CPVF records of aiding Korea], 313.

62. Xu Yipeng, *Cuojue: 180 shi chaoxian shoucuoji* [Miscalculation: the setback of the 180th Division in Korea] (Nanjing, China: Jiangsu renmin chubanshe, 1997), 105; China Academy of Military Science, "The Unforgotten Korean War," 451.

63. Yan, *Wei Jie zhongjiang* [Lt. Gen, Wei Jie], 46–47; Xu, ibid., 51; Millett, *The War for Korea, 1950–1951*, 448–50.

64. Yang and Wang, *Beiwei 38 duxian* [The north latitude 38th Parallel], 332–33; Yan, *Wei Jie zhongjiang* [Lt. Gen. Wei Jie], 56; Xu, *Cuojue* [Miscalculation], 107–109; Li, *Zhiyuanjun yuanchao jishi* [The CPVF records of aiding Korea], 313.

65. Luan, *Xue yu huo de jiaoliang* [The contest], 214; Shuang, *Kaiguo diyi zhan* [The first war since the founding of the state], 1:405, 408, 416; Composition Committee, ed., *38 xian shang de jiaofeng* [Fighting over the 38th Parallel], 337–38; Millett, *The War for Korea, 1950–1951*, 451–52.

66. Lt. Gen. Wei Jie joined the Red Army in 1927 and the CCP in 1933. He participated in the Long March of 1934–35. Wei served as commander of a squad, platoon, company, battalion, and regiment and as a division chief of staff in the Red Army. During the Anti-Japanese War he was a commander of a regiment, brigade, and division of the Eighth Route Army. During the Chinese Civil War Wei was brigade and division commander, and later commander of the Sixty-First and Sixtieth Armies of the PLA. He commanded the Sixtieth Army, Third Army Group of the CPVF, during the Spring Offensive in 1951. After his return to China, Wei was appointed deputy commander of the Chengdu Regional Command of the PLA. He was granted the rank of lieutenant general in 1955. For more details, see Tan, *Zhongguo renmin zhiyuanjun renwulu* [Veterans' profile of the CPVF], 62; *Xinghuo liaoyuan* Composition Department, *Zhongguo renmin jiefangjun jiangshuai minglu* [Marshals and generals of the PLA], 1:180–81.

67. Chen, *60 jun rencai* [The elite of the Sixtieth Army], 150–51, 206–207; Li, *Zhiyuan-jun yuanchao jishi* [The CPVF records of aiding Korea], 317.

68. Mossman, *U.S. Army in the Korean War*, 472.

69. Ibid., 481.

70. Millett, *The War for Korea, 1950–1951*, 448.

71. Hong, *Hong Xuezhi huiyilu* [Memoirs of Hong Xuezhi], 481–82; Shuang, *Kaiguo diyi zhan* [The first war since the founding of the state], 1:410.

72. Wu Ruilin, *Kangmei yuanchao zhong de 42 jun* [The Forty-Second Army in the WRUSAK] (Beijing: Jincheng chubanshe, 1995), 160–62; Yang and Wang, *Beiwei 38 duxian* [The north latitude 38th Parallel], 335–36; Wang Shuzeng, *Juezhan chaoxian: chaoxian zhanchang shi wojun tong meijun jiaoliang de lianbingchang* [The showdown in Korea: the battleground for a competition between the Chinese army and American army] (Beijing: Jiefangjun wenyi chubanshe, 2007), 317–18.

73. Yan, *Wei Jie zhongjiang* [Lt. Gen. Wei Jie], 52; Composition Committee, ed., *38 xian shang de jiaofeng* [Fighting over the 38th Parallel], 337; Wang Shuzeng, *Zhongguo renmin zhiyuanjun zhengzhan jishi* [The true story of the CPVF's war experience] (Beijing: Jiefangjun wenyi chubanshe, 2000), 535; Xu, *Cuojue* [Miscalculation], 91.

74. Quoted in Li, *Zhiyuanjun yuanchao jishi* [The CPVF records of aiding Korea], 318. See also Chen Zhonglong, *Guangrong de linfenlu* [The glorious brigade of Linfen] (Beijing: Zhonggong dangshi chubanshe, 2007), 322–23.

75. Quoted in China Academy of Military Science, "The Unforgotten Korean War," 451. See also Wang, *Zhongguo renmin zhiyuanjun zhengzhan jishi* [The true story of the CPVF's war experience], 535; Shuang, *Kaiguo diyi zhan* [The first war since the founding of the state], 1:406; Li, *Zhiyuanjun yuanchao jishi* [The CPVF records of aiding Korea], 318.

76. Lt. Col. Guan Zhichao (PLA, ret.), interviews by the author in Nanjing, March 13–14, 2008. Guan was the political commissar of the 2nd Battalion, 539th Regiment, 180th Division, Sixtieth Army, Third Army Group of the CPVF during the Spring Offensive. See also Yan, *Wei Jie zhongjiang* [Lt. Gen. Wei Jie], 52; Xu, *Cuojue* [Miscalculation], 95.

77. Shuang, *Kaiguo diyi zhan* [The first war since the founding of the state], 1:423; Xu, *Cuojue* [Miscalculation], 183.

78. Quoted in Yan, *Wei Jie zhongjiang* [Lt. Gen. Wei Jie], 53. See also Li, *Zhiyuanjun yuanchao jishi* [The CPVF records of aiding Korea], 318.

79. China Academy of Military Science, "The Unforgotten Korean War," 453–54.

80. Guan Zhichao, interviews by the author. See also Xu, *Cuojue* [Miscalculation], 103, 107, 109.

81. China Academy of Military Science, "The Unforgotten Korean War," 454.

82. Yan, *Wei Jie zhongjiang* [Lt. Gen. Wei Jie], 46–47; Xu, *Cuojue* [Miscalculation], 77–78.

83. Since Zheng had served as a political commissar at the regimental and divisional levels for many years before 1951, Peng concluded after the Spring Offensive that "the commanding officers of the division did not have much experience of independent combat commanding" (quoted in Li, *Zhiyuanjun yuanchao jishi* [The CPVF records of aiding Korea], 318–19). For more details on Zheng, see Tan, *Zhongguo renmin zhiyuanjun renwulu* [Veterans' profile of the CPVF], 449–50; Composition Committee, ed., *38 xian shang de jiaofeng* [Fighting over the 38th Parallel], 348.

84. Quoted in Yang and Wang, *Beiwei 38 duxian* [The north latitude 38th Parallel], 344 In July 1951. Zheng was dismissed from his position as the commander of the 180th Division and assigned to work in logistics at the Third Army Group HQ. After his return to China, Zheng served at a deputy commander at the divisional level. He was promoted to colonel in 1955 and senior colonel in 1963. For his dismissal, see Du, *Zai zhiyuanjun zongbu* [At the CPVF General HQ], 251.

85. Quoted in Li, *Zhiyuanjun yuanchao jishi* [The CPVF records of aiding Korea], 318. See also Chen, *Guangrong de linfenlu* [The glorious brigade of Linfen], 322–3; Xu, *Cuojue* [Miscalculation], 91.

86. China Academy of Military Science, "The Unforgotten Korean War," 451; Wang, *Zhongguo renmin zhiyuanjun zhengzhan jishi* [The true story of the CPVF's war experience], 535; Shuang, *Kaiguo diyi zhan* [The first war since the founding of the state], 1:406; Li, *Zhiyuanjun yuanchao jishi* [The CPVF records of aiding Korea], 318.

87. Yan, *Wei Jie zhongjiang* [Lt. Gen. Wei Jie], 52; Xu, *Cuojue* [Miscalculation], 95; Luan, *Xue yu huo de jiaoliang* [The contest], 214.

88. Guan Zhichao, interviews by the author. See also Li, *Zhiyuanjun yuanchao jishi* [The CPVF records of aiding Korea], 318; Xu, *Cuojue* [Miscalculation], 95–96.

89. Quoted in Yan, *Wei Jie zhongjiang* [Lt. Gen. Wei Jie], 53. See also Shuang, *Kaiguo diyi zhan* [The first war since the founding of the state], 1:406–407; Zhao and Liang, *Fenghuo 38 xian* [The flames of battle raging across the 38th Parallel], 228–29.

90. Composition Committee, ed., *38 xian shang de jiaofeng* [Fighting over the 38th Parallel], 339; Li, *Zhiyuanjun yuanchao jishi* [The CPVF records of aiding Korea], 318–19.

91. Korean Institute of Military History, *The Korean War*, 2:727; Xu Yan, *Diyici jiaoliang: kangmei yuanchao zhanzheng de lishi huigu yu fansi* [The first encounter: a historical retrospective of the WRUSAK] (Beijing: Zhongguo guangbo dianshi chubanshe, 1990), 92–93; Shuang, *Kaiguo diyi zhan* [The first war since the founding of the state], 1:416; Millett, *The War for Korea, 1950–1951*, 450–52.

92. Xu, *Cuojue* [Miscalculation], 101–102; Composition Committee, ed., *38 xian shang de jiaofeng* [Fighting over the 38th Parallel], 338; Li, *Zhiyuanjun yuanchao jishi* [The CPVF records of aiding Korea], 319.

93. Shuang Shi, *Kaiguo diyi zhan: kangmei yuanchao zhanzheng quanjing jishi* [The first war since the founding of the state], 1:416; Xu, *Cuojue* [Miscalculation], 106, 110; Wang Shuzeng, *Yuandong chaoxian zhanzheng* [The Korean War in the Far East] (Beijing: Jiefangjun wenyi chubanshe, 2000), 2:762–63; Millett, *The War for Korea, 1950–1951*, 451.

94. Quoted in Yan, *Wei Jie zhongjiang* [Lt. Gen. Wei Jie], 58–59. See also Chen, *Guangrong de linfenlu* [The glorious brigade of Linfen], 329–30; Li, *Zhiyuanjun yuanchao jishi* [The CPVF records of aiding Korea], 321; Luan, *Xue yu huo de jiaoliang* [The contest], 214; Gu et al., trans. and eds., *Chaoxian zhanzheng* [ROK Army Archives], 2:25–26.

95. Guan Zhichao, interviews by the author. See also Composition Committee, ed., *38 xian shang de jiaofeng* [Fighting over the 38th Parallel], 338; Li, *Zhiyuanjun yuanchao jishi* [The CPVF records of aiding Korea], 320.

96. Chang Pu-ting (POW), interviews by the author in the Rongjia Zhongxin (Glorious Retirement Center for Veterans) in Taipei, July 2008. Chang served in the 180th Division, Sixtieth Army, Third Army Group of the CPVF. He and his unit entered Korea

in March 1951 and participated in the Spring Offensive. See also Korean Institute of Military History, *The Korean War,* 2:728–30; Shuang, *Kaiguo diyi zhan* [The first war since the founding of the state], 1:418.

97. Guan Zhichao, interviews by the author. See also Xu, *Cuojue* [Miscalculation], 112–13.

98. Guo Rengao (POW), interviews by the author in the Rongjia Zhongxin (Glorious Retirement Center for Veterans) in Taipei, July 2008. Guo served in the 540th Regiment, 180th Division, Sixtieth Army, Third Army Group of the CPVF during the Spring Offensive. See also Hsiu-huan Chou, ed., *Zhanhou waijiao shiliao huibian: hanzhan yu fangong yishi pian* [Documentary collection: foreign affairs of postwar Taiwan; the Korean War and Chinese Communist defectors] (Taipei: Academia Historica, 2005), 3:200–201; Composition Committee, ed., *38 xian shang de jiaofeng* [Fighting over the 38th Parallel], 342.

99. Shuang, *Kaiguo diyi zhan* [The first war since the founding of the state], 1:418; Xu, *Cuojue* [Miscalculation], 113–14.

100. Mossman, *U.S. Army in the Korean War,* 478–79; Composition Committee, ed., *38 xian shang de jiaofeng* [Fighting over the 38th Parallel], 340.

101. Chen, *Guangrong de linfenlu* [The glorious brigade of Linfen], 334–37; Li, *Zhiyuanjun yuanchao jishi* [The CPVF records of aiding Korea], 320.

102. Peng Dehuai recalled: "The soldiers had a big problem with food and became extremely exhausted" ("My Story of the Korean War," 35). See also Xu, *Cuojue* [Miscalculation], 144; Shuang, *Kaiguo diyi zhan* [The first war since the founding of the state], 1:419.

103. Yan, *Wei Jie zhongjiang* [Lt. Gen. Wei Jie], 68; Shuang, *Kaiguo diyi zhan* [The first war since the founding of the state], 1:421. See also Bureau of Intelligence Service, ROC Ministry of Foreign Affairs, "Chiang zongtong zhi fangong yishi shu [President Chiang's message to anti-Communist compatriots]," Content No. 172–73, File No. 5975, "Anti-Communist POW Files, July 1953," ROC Ministry of Foreign Affairs Archives, Taipei.

104. Shiun Shui-de (POW), interviews by the author in the Rongjia Zhongxin (Glorious Retirement Center for Veterans) in Taipei, July 2008. Shiun served in the 180th Division during the Spring Offensive. See also Shen Xingyi, "Yiwan siqian ge zhengren: hanzhan shiqi 'fangong yishi' zhi yanjiu [14,000 witnesses: studies of the "anti-Communist heroes" from the Korean War]," master's thesis, National Taiwan Normal University, 1996), 206–207.

105. Liu Yaohu joined the Eighth Route Army and the CCP in 1938. He served as commander of a squad, platoon, and company in the Anti-Japanese War. During the Chinese Civil War Liu became a deputy commander and later a commander of a battalion in the PLA. He was appointed acting commander and deputy commander of the 540th Regiment, 180th Division, Sixtieth Army, Third Army Group of the CPVF in the Spring Offensive and was killed in May 1951. See Shuang, *Kaiguo diyi zhan* [The first war since the founding of the state], 1:418; Military History Research Division, *Zhongguo renmin zhiyuanjun kangmei yuanchao zhanshi* [Combat experience of the CPVF in the WRUSAK], "Fulu: zhongguo renmin zhiyuanjun tuan yishang ganbu xisheng mingdan [Appendix: CPVF commanders (at regimental level and above) KIA list]," 15–16.

106. Peng, "My Story of the Korean War," 35. POWs Chen Ling-yun and Chang Han-cheng recalled the collapse of the chain of command in late May 1951 before they were captured by the UNF. Chen served in the Third Company, 1st Battalion, 541st Regiment, 180th Division; Chang was in the Second Company, 1st Battalion, 540th Regiment, 180th Division. See ROC Embassy in Bangkok, Thailand, telegram to the Ministry of Foreign Affairs, Taiwan, May 17, 1954, "Fangong yishi zai fangwen taiguo shi zuode jianzheng [The testimonies of the anti-Communist compatriots during their visits in Thailand]," April 9–May 8, 1954, Content No. 43, File No. 4044, "Anti-Communist POW Files," ROC Ministry of Foreign Affairs Archives, Taipei.

107. Luan, *Xue yu huo de jiaoliang* [The contest], 215; Xu, *Cuojue* [Miscalculation], 150.

108. Hong, *Kangmei yuanchao zhanzheng huiyi* (Recollections of the WRUSAK), 167–8; Du, *Zai zhiyuanjun zongbu* [At the CPVF General HQ], 221; Yan, *Wei Jie zhongjiang* [Lt. Gen. Wei Jie], 69; Li, *Zhiyuanjun yuanchao jishi* [The CPVF records of aiding Korea], 321; Shuang, *Kaiguo diyi zhan* [The first war since the founding of the state], 1:420–22.

109. Mao Zedong, telegram to Peng, "Jianjue zudi yu Kimhwa-Chorwn yixian [Stop the enemy definitely along the Keumhwa-Cheorwon line],"in Mao, *Mao's Military Manuscripts since 1949*, 1:494–95.

110. Shuang, *Kaiguo diyi zhan* [The first war since the founding of the state], 1:423. See also Xu, *Diyici jiaoliang* [The first encounter], 92–93; Xu, *Cuojue* [Miscalculation], 184.

111. Hong, *Hong Xuezhi huiyilu* [Memoirs of Hong Xuezhi], 479; Du, *Zai zhiyuanjun zongbu* [At the CPVF General HQ], 251; Li, *Zhiyuanjun yuanchao jishi* [The CPVF records of aiding Korea], 323–26.

112. Military History Research Division, *Zhongguo renmin zhiyuanjun kangmei yuanchao zhanshi* [Combat experience of the CPVF in the WRUSAK], 106–107; Mossman, *U.S. Army in the Korean War*, 472–73; Clark C. Munroe, *The Second U.S. Infantry Division in Korea, 1950–51* (Tokyo: Toppan, 1954), 136–38.

113. Peng and Deng, telegram to all CPVF army groups, copied to the CMC, May 21, 1951, in Peng, *Peng's Military Papers*, 396–97.

114. Zhao Yihong, *27 jun chuanqi* [The legacy of the Twenty-Seventh Army] (Jilin, China: Jilin renmin chubanshe, 1995), 448. POW Chen Wan-shiu recalled the failed defense of the Twenty-Seventh Army in late May 1951. Chen served in the Twenty-Seventh before its men were captured by the UNF. See ROC Embassy in Bangkok, Thailand, telegram to the Ministry of Foreign Affairs, Taiwan, May 17, 1954, "Fangong yishi zai fangwen taiguo shi zuode jianzheng [The testimonies of the anti-Communist compatriots during their visits in Thailand]."

115. Mossman, *U.S. Army in the Korean War*, 472–73; Catchpole, *The Korean War*, 136–37.

116. Mossman, *U.S. Army in the Korean War*, 474–75; Millett, *The War for Korea, 1950–1951*, 451.

117. Zhao and Liang, *Fenghuo 38 xian* [The flames of battle raging across the 38th Parallel], 246; Li, *Zhiyuanjun yuanchao jishi* [The CPVF records of aiding Korea], 326, 331.

118. Maj. Gen. Peng Deqing joined the Red Army in 1926 and the CCP in 1930. He served as a guerrilla company commander and later a battalion political commissar in the Red Army. During the Anti-Japanese War Peng became a company political instructor, battalion political commissar, and chief of the political section of a regiment and

brigade in the New Fourth Army. During the Chinese Civil War he was a brigade and division political commissar, chief of staff, and commander. Later he became deputy commander of the Twenty-Second and Twenty-Third Armies and commander of the Twenty-Seventh Army of the PLA. After his return to China, Peng became deputy commander of the East China Sea Fleet of the PLA Navy. He was made a major general in 1955 and served as vice minister and minister of the Transportation Ministry of the PRC in the 1960s and 1970s. See Tan, *Zhongguo renmin zhiyuanjun renwulu* [Veterans' profile of the CPVF], 615–16; *Xinghuo liaoyuan* Composition Department, *Zhongguo renmin jiefangjun jiangshuai minglu* [Marshals and generals of the PLA], 3:525. Lt. Gen. Liu Haotian joined the CCP in 1931 and Red Army in 1932; he participated in the Long March. Liu served as commander of a squad, platoon, and company and as a political commissar of battalion in the Red Army. During the Anti-Japanese War he became deputy director of the political section of the 2nd Brigade, 115th Division, Eighth Route Army. During the Chinese Civil War he was a brigade and division political commissar, and later political commissar of the Twenty-Seventh Army of the PLA. After his return to China, Liu became the commander of the East China Sea Fleet of the PLA Navy in the 1960s. He was made a lieutenant general in 1955. See Tan, *Zhongguo renmin zhiyuanjun renwulu* [Veterans' profile of the CPVF], 153; *Xinghuo liaoyuan* Composition Department, *Zhongguo renmin jiefangjun jiangshuai minglu* [Marshals and generals of the PLA], 1:242–43; Zhao, *27 jun chuanqi* [The legacy of the Twenty-Seventh Army], 448–49; Tan, *Kangmei yuanchao zhanzheng* [The WRUSAK], 154–55.

119. Yang, *Zai zhiyuanjun silingbu de suiyueli* [My years at the CPVF General HQ], 147; Military History Research Division, *Zhongguo renmin zhiyuanjun kangmei yuanchao zhanshi* [Combat experience of the CPVF in the WRUSAK], 106, 108, 113.

120. China Academy of Military Science, "The Unforgotten Korean War," 459.

121. The first wave of the CPVF, which entered Korea in late October and November, were two army groups, the Ninth and Thirteenth, with nine armies—the Twentieth, Twenty-Sixth, Twenty-Seventh, Thirty-Eighth, Thirty-Ninth, Fortieth, Forty-Second, Fiftieth, and Sixty-Sixth, totaling twenty-seven infantry divisions and three artillery divisions, or 450,000 troops. With the arrival of the second wave, the CPVF forces in Korea had doubled from 450,000 troops in January to 950,000 men in mid-April, including 770,000 combat troops in forty-two infantry divisions, eight artillery divisions, and four AAA divisions. See Xu Yan, "Chinese Forces and Their Casualties in the Korean War," trans. Xiaobing Li, *Chinese Historians* 6, no. 2 (1993): 48–50; Roy E. Appleman, *South to the Naktong, North to the Yalu (June–November 1950), U.S. Army in the Korean War* (Washington: Office of the Chief of Military History and Government Printing Office, 1961), 768–69.

122. China Academy of Military Science, "The Unforgotten Korean War," 459.

123. Zhao and Liang, *Fenghuo 38 xian* [The flames of battle raging across the 38th Parallel], 255.

124. Mao agreed with Peng's plan. See Mao, telegram to Peng, "Jianjue zudi yu Kimhwa-Chorwn yixian [Stop the enemy definitely along the Keumhwa-Cheorwon line]," 1:494–95. See also Political Department of the PLA 75200 Unit, ed., *Yuxue chaoxian: 42 jun laozhanshi kangmei yuanchao qinliji* [Bleeding Korea: personal experiences of Fortieth Army veterans in the WRUSAK], (Beijing: Jiefangjun chubanshe, 2001), 231 and 564; Yang and Wang, *Beiwei 38 duxian* [The north latitude 38th Parallel], 336; Wang, *Juezhan chaoxian* [The showdown in Korea], 317–18.

125. Quoted in China Academy of Military Science, "The Unforgotten Korean War," 460.

126. Quoted in ibid., 460–61.

127. Mao, telegram to Peng, "Jianjue zudi yu Kimhwa-Chorwn yixian [Stop the enemy definitely along the Keumhwa-Cheorwon line]," 1:494–95.

128. Yang, *Yang Dezhi huiyilu* [Memoirs of Yang Dezhi], 560; Wang et al., *Peng Dehuai zhuan* [Biography of Peng Dehuai], 471; Tan, *Kangmei yuanchao zhanzheng* [The WRUSAK], 155; Composition Committee, ed., *38 xian shang de jiaofeng* [Fighting over the 38th Parallel], 355; Chu, *Chaoxian zhanzheng neimu quangongkai* [Declassifying the Korean War], 300; Wang, *Juezhan chaoxian* [The showdown in Korea], 319–20; Luo Xuanyou, *Chaoxian zhanzheng: zhengzhan jishi* [The Korean War: the battle records] (Beijing: Jiefangjun wenyi chubanshe, 2007), 332–33.

129. Mossman, *U.S. Army in the Korean War,* 485–86.

130. Quoted in China Academy of Military Science, "The Unforgotten Korean War," 462.

131. Zhao and Liang, *Fenghuo 38 xian* [The flames of battle raging across the 38th Parallel], 260–65; Luan, *Xue yu huo de jiaoliang* [The contest], 220; Chu, *Chaoxian zhanzheng neimu quangongkai* [Declassifying the Korean War], 300–301; Luo, *Chaoxian zhanzheng* [The Korean War], 333–35.

132. China Academy of Military Science, "The Unforgotten Korean War," 463–64; Shuang, *Kaiguo diyi zhan* [The first war since the founding of the state], 1:432–34.

133. China Academy of Military Science, "The Unforgotten Korean War," 463.

134. Zhao and Liang, *Fenghuo 38 xian* [The flames of battle raging across the 38th Parallel], 290–91; Composition Committee, ed., *38 xian shang de jiaofeng* [Fighting over the 38th Parallel], 355–38; Luo, *Chaoxian zhanzheng* [The Korean War], 335–37; Chu, *Chaoxian zhanzheng neimu quangongkai* [Declassifying the Korean War], 301–305.

135. Yang, *Yang Dezhi huiyilu* [Memoirs of Yang Dezhi], 566, 568; Shuang, *Kaiguo diyi zhan* [The first war since the founding of the state], 1:437.

136. Gen. Qin Jiwei joined Red Army in 1927 and the CCP in 1930; he participated in the Long March. Qin served as commander of a squad, platoon, company, and battalion in the Red Army. During the Anti-Japanese War he was deputy commander of a battalion, regiment, and brigade in the 129th Division, Eighth Route Army. During the Chinese Civil War Qin was a division commander and political commissar, and later commander of the Fifteenth Army of the PLA. After his return to China, he was appointed deputy commander of the Yunnan Provincial Command and made a lieutenant general in 1955. He was made deputy commander and commander of the Kunming Regional Command in 1956–57, commander of the Chengdu Regional Command in 1957, and commander of the Beijing Regional Command in 1975. In 1988 Qin became the defense minister of the PRC and was made a general. For more details, see *Xinghuo liaoyuan* Composition Department, *Zhongguo renmin jiefangjun jiangshuai minglu* [Marshals and generals of the PLA], 1:398–99; Tan, *Zhongguo renmin zhiyuanjun renwulu* [Veterans' profile of the CPVF], 509–10.

137. Quoted in Zhao and Liang, *Fenghuo 38 xian* [The flames of battle raging across the 38th Parallel], 270.

138. Tan, *Kangmei yuanchao zhanzheng* [The WRUSAK], 157; *Xinghuo liaoyuan* Composition Department, *Zhongguo renmin jiefangjun jiangshuai minglu* [Marshals and gen-

erals of the PLA], 1:398–99; Tan, *Zhongguo renmin zhiyuanjun renwulu* [Veterans' profile of the CPVF], 509–10.

139. Mossman, *U.S. Army in the Korean War*, 478–79.

140. Military History Research Division, *Zhongguo renmin zhiyuanjun kangmei yuanchao zhanshi* [Combat experience of the CPVF in the WRUSAK], 107; Luan, *Xue yu huo de jiaoliang* [The contest], 218–19; Shuang, *Kaiguo diyi zhan* [The first war since the founding of the state], 1:428–32; Wang, *Juezhan chaoxian* [The showdown in Korea], 319–21.

141. Quoted in China Academy of Military Science, "The Unforgotten Korean War," 459.

142. Military History Research Division, *Zhongguo renmin zhiyuanjun kangmei yuanchao zhanshi* [Combat experience of the CPVF in the WRUSAK], 108; Li, *Zhiyuanjun yuanchao jishi* [The CPVF records of aiding Korea], 315.

143. Tan, *Kangmei yuanchao zhanzheng* [The WRUSAK], 158; Composition Committee, ed., *38 xian shang de jiaofeng* [Fighting over the 38th Parallel], 348–55.

144. Mossman, *U.S. Army in the Korean War*, 480; Zhao and Liang, *Fenghuo 38 xian* [The flames of battle raging across the 38th Parallel], 270.

145. Military History Research Division, *Zhongguo renmin zhiyuanjun kangmei yuanchao zhanshi* [Combat experience of the CPVF in the WRUSAK], 122–24; Shuang, *Kaiguo diyi zhan* [The first war since the founding of the state], 1:423; Li, *Zhiyuanjun yuanchao jishi* [The CPVF records of aiding Korea], 316, 331–32.

146. Peng Dehuai, telegram to Mao, June 1, 1951, in Mao, *Mao's Military Manuscripts since 1949*, 1:498 note 1.

### 8. FROM BATTLEGROUND TO NEGOTIATING TABLE

1. The Central Committee of the CCP held a meeting in Beijing after the Spring Offensive and discussed strategic changes for the CPVF in Korea from large-scale offensive campaign to active defensive operation. See Nie Rongzhen, "Beijing's Decision to Intervene," in *Mao's Generals Remember Korea*, trans. and ed. Xiaobing Li, Allan R. Millett, and Bin Yu (Lawrence: University Press of Kansas, 2001), 46; Hong Xuezhi, *Kangmei yuanchao zhanzheng huiyi* [Recollections of the WRUSAK] (Beijing: Jiefangjun wenyi chubanshe, 1990), 188; Feng Xianzhi and Li Jie, *Mao Zedong yu kangmei yuanchao* [Mao Zedong: resisting the U.S. and aiding Korea] (Beijing: Zhongyang wenxian chubanshe, 2000), 74–75; Xu Yan, *Mao Zedong yu kangmei yuanchao zhanzheng* [Mao Zedong and the WRUSAK], 2nd ed. (Beijing: Jiefangjun chubanshe, 2006), 233–34.

2. Quoted in Yang Dezhi, "Command Experience in Korea," in *Mao's Generals Remember Korea*, 151. See also Wang Yan et al., *Peng Dehuai zhuan* [Biography of Peng Dehuai] (Beijing: Dangdai zhongguo chubanshe, 1993), 472–73.

3. For the Chinese leaders' view, see Zhou Enlai, "Kangmei yuanchao jushi de fanzhan qiantu [The situation and future development of the WRUSAK]," in Zhou Enlai, *Zhou Enlai junshi wenxun* [Selected military papers of Zhou Enlai] (Beijing: Renmin chubanshe, 1997), 4:108–109 (hereafter cited as *Zhou's Military Papers*); Nie Rongzhen Biography Compilation Team, *Nie Rongzhen zhuan* [Biography of Nie Rongzhen] (Beijing: Dangdai zhongguo chubanshe, 2006), 296; Xu, *Mao Zedong yu kangmei yuanchao zhanzheng* [Mao Zedong and the WRUSAK], 233.

4. I borrow this term from Thomas J. Christensen's work on grand strategy and Sino-American relations. But "useful adversary" refers here to the learning curve of

the CPVF in Korea through its engagements with the UNF. See Christensen, *Useful Adversaries: Grand Strategy, Domestic Mobilization, and Sino-American Conflict, 1947–58* (Princeton: Princeton University Press, 1996), 1–2.

5. The Chinese leaders informed the North Koreans of this strategic change. See the PRC Ministry of Foreign Affairs to Gan Yetao, Chinese chargé d'affairs in Pyongyang, "Lee Xiangchao fangwen Beijing [Lee Xiangchao's visit to Beijing]," February 17, 1953, File# 106-00034-01 (1), Archives Department, PRC Foreign Affairs Ministry, Beijing.

6. Mao Zedong, telegram to Peng, "Dui meiyingjun zai jige yuenei zhida xiao jian-miezhan [Attack the American and British troops in small scale only for next several months]," May 26, 1951], in Mao Zedong, *Jianguo yilai Mao Zedong junshi wengao* [Mao Zedong's military manuscripts since the founding of the PRC] (Beijing: Junshi kexue chubanshe and Zhongyang wenxian chubanshe, 2010; hereafter cited as *Mao's Military Manuscripts since 1949*), 1:490–91.

7. Mao discussed his piecemeal strategy with the CPVF commanders on May 27 and June 4, 1951, in Beijing. See Wu Ruilin, *Kangmei yuanchao zhong de 42 jun* [The Forty-Second Army in the WRUSAK] (Beijing: Jincheng chubanshe, 1995), 128–50; Peng Dehuai, "My Story of the Korean War," in *Mao's Generals Remember Korea*, trans. and ed. Xiaobing Li, Allan R. Millett, and Bin Yu (Lawrence: University Press of Kansas, 2001), 36; Du Ping, *Zai zhiyuanjun zongbu: Du Ping huiyilu* [At the CPVF General HQ: memoirs of Du Ping] (Beijing: Jiefangjun chubanshe, 1989), 262–64.

8. Nie, "Beijing's Decision to Intervene," 46.

9. Matthew B. Ridgway, *The Korean War* (Garden City, NY: Doubleday, 1967), 150–51. Ridgway estimated the cost for such a drive at 100,000 UNF casualties.

10. Wang et al., *Peng Dehuai zhuan* [Biography of Peng Dehuai], 472; Xu, *Mao Zedong yu kangmei yuanchao zhanzheng* [Mao Zedong and the WRUSAK], 233; Hastings, *The Korean War*, 228–30; Sandler, *The Korean War*, 146.

11. Peng Dehuai, "Guanyu chijiu zuozhan fangzhen he jinhou zuozhan de zhidao yuanze [The guiding principles and operation directives for the prolonged war in the future]," in Peng Dehuai, *Peng Dehuai junshi wenxuan* [Selected military papers of Peng Dehuai] (Beijing: Zhongyang wenxian chubanshe, 1988), 403–10 (hereafter cited as *Peng's Military Papers*).

12. Shuguang Zhang, *Mao's Military Romanticism: China and the Korean War, 1950–53* (Lawrence: University Press of Kansas, 1995), 156.

13. Mao telegraphed Peng twice to convey his reluctance about Peng's planned Sixth Offensive. See Mao Zedong, telegrams to Peng, August 19 and 21, 1951, in Mao, *Mao's Military Manuscripts since 1949*, 1:546.

14. Quoted in Luan Kechao, *Xue yu huo de jiaoliang: kangmei yuanchao jishi* [The contest: blood vs. fire; the record of resisting America and aiding Korea] (Beijing: Huayi chubanshe, 2008), 226. See also Shuang Shi, *Kaiguo diyi zhan: kangmei yuanchao zhan-zheng quanjing jishi* [The first war since the founding of the state: the complete story of the WRUSAK] (Beijing: Zhonggong dangshi chubanshe, 2004), 2:498–99.

15. Du, *Zai zhiyuanjun zongbu* [At the CPVF General HQ], 264; Tan Jingjiao, *Kangmei yuanchao zhanzheng* [The WRUSAK] (Beijing: Zhongguo shehui kexue chubanshe, 1990), 175; Li Qingshan, *Zhiyuanjun yuanchao jishi* [The CPVF records of aiding Korea] (Beijing: Zhonggong dangshi chubanshe, 2008), 340, 351–52.

16. Quoted in China Academy of Military Science, "The Unforgotten Korean War: Chinese Perspective and Appraisals," unpublished manuscript, 2006, 549.

17. After the enlarged Party Committee meeting of the CPVF Command, the Joint Command issued a new order to all CPVF and NKPA troops on September 16, 1951. See Hong Xuezhi, *Hong Xuezhi huiyilu* [Memoirs of Hong Xuezhi] (Beijing: Jiefangjun chubanshe, 2007), 539–40; Yang, "Combat Experience in Korea," 153–54; Military History Research Division, CAMS, *Zhongguo renmin zhiyuanjun kangmei yuanchao zhanshi* [Combat experience of the CPVF in the WRUSAK] (Beijing: Junshi kexue chubanshe, 1990), 126–27; Wang et al., *Peng Dehuai zhuan* [Biography of Peng Dehuai], 474–75; Tan, *Kangmei yuanchao zhanzheng* [The WRUSAK], 227–28; Xu Yan, *Diyici jiaoliang: kangmei yuanchao zhanzheng de lishi huigu yu fansi* [The first encounter: a historical retrospective of the WRUSAK] (Beijing: Zhongguo guangbo dianshi chubanshe, 1990), 123; Luan, *Xue yu huo de jiaoliang* [The contest], 287.

18. For more details on the trench warfare and underground tunnels in Korea, see Yang, "Command Experience in Korea," 154; Yang Dezhi, *Yang Dezhi huiyilu* [Memoirs of Yang Dezhi] (Beijing: Jiefangjun chubanshe, 1992), 597–601; Du, *Zai zhiyuanjun zongbu* [At the CPVF General HQ], 542–57;Xu, *Diyici jiaoliang* [The first encounter], 122–25; Capt. Zheng Yanman (CPVF), interview by the author in Harbin, Heilongjiang, August 2002. Zheng was captain of the Eighth Company, 134th Regiment, 45th Division, Fifteenth Army, Third Army Group of the CPVF in 1951–53. Also see Zheng Yanman, "The Chinese Go Underground," in *Voices from the Korean War: Personal Stories of American, Korean, and Chinese Soldiers*, ed. Richard Peters and Xiaobing Li (Lexington: University Press of Kentucky, 2004), 173–84.

19. The statistics are from the Memorial Museum of the WRUSAK, Dandong, China. See also Wang et al., *Peng Dehuai zhuan* [Biography of Peng Dehuai], 483; Composition Committee, ed., *38 xian shang de jiaofeng: kangmei yuanchao zhanzheng jishi* [Fighting over the 38th Parallel: the recorded truth of the WRUSAK] (Beijing: Jiefangjun wenyi chubanshe, 2010), 491–93; Xu, *Diyici jiaoliang* [The first encounter], 123–24; Wang Shuzeng, *Juezhan chaoxian: chaoxian zhanchang shi wojun tong meijun jiaoliang de lianbingchang* [The showdown in Korea: the battleground for a competition between the Chinese army and American army] (Beijing: Jiefangjun wenyi chubanshe, 2007), 387–88.

20. Tan, *Kangmei yuanchao zhanzheng* [The WRUSAK], 229; Shuang, *Kaiguo diyi zhan* [The first war since the founding of the state], 2:487, 560; Luan, *Xue yu huo de jiaoliang* [The contest], 288–89.

21. Zhang Aiping, *Zhongguo renmin jiefangjun* [The Chinese People's Liberation Army] (Beijing: Dangdai zhongguo chubanshe, 1994), 1:132–34; Military History Research Division, *Zhongguo renmin zhiyuanjun kangmei yuanchao zhanshi* [Combat experience of the CPVF in the WRUSAK], 188; Luan, *Xue yu huo de jiaoliang* [The contest], 288.

22. Mao Zedong, "Bianda biantan bianwen [Fighting while negotiating and stabilizing]," speech at the 38th meeting of the First National Plenary of the Chinese People's Political Consultative Conference, August 4, 1952, in Mao, *Mao's Military Manuscripts since 1949*, 2:50–52.

23. Peng, "My Story of the Korean War," 36. See also Wang et al., *Peng Dehuai zhuan* [Biography of Peng Dehuai], 474.

24. For more on the Battle of Triangle Hill, see Brian Catchpole, *The Korean War, 1950–53* (New York: Carroll and Graf, 2000), 171–72; Stanley Sandler, *The Korean War: No Victors, No Vanquished* (Lexington: University Press of Kentucky, 1999), 255. For

more on the Battle of Shangganling, see Hong, *Hong Xuezhi huiyilu* [Memoirs of Hong Xuezhi], 551–58; Yang, "Command Experience in Korea," 170–82; Du, *Zai zhiyuanjun zongbu* [At the CPVF General HQ], 542–57; Luan, *Xue yu huo de jiaoliang* [The contest], 303–308; Composition Committee, ed., *38 xian shang de jiaofeng* [Fighting over the 38th Parallel], 459–65; China National Military Museum, ed., *Kangmei yuanchao zhanzheng fengyunlu* [The operational files of the WRUSAK] (Beijing: Huacheng chubanshe, 1999), 223–28; Chen Zhonglong, ed., *Kangmei yuanchao zhanzheng lun* [On the WRUSAK] (Beijing: Junshi wenyi chubanshe, 2001), 435–41; Zhang Songshan, *Tanpai: zhengduo Shangganling jishi* [The showdown: the true story of the Battle of Shangganling] (Nanjing, China: Jiangsu renmin chubanshe, 1998).

25. Du, *Zai zhiyuanjun zongbu* [At the CPVF General HQ], 544, 552,556; Shuang, *Kaiguo diyi zhan* [The first war since the founding of the state], 2:647, 656.

26. Zheng Yanman, interview by the author.

27. Ibid.

28. China Academy of Military Science, "The Unforgotten Korean War," 626–27; Zheng, "The Chinese Go Underground," 184.

29. Peng, "My Story of the Korean War," 36.

30. Ibid., 37.

31. For some details on the Twenty-Third Army Group's entry into Korea, see Du, *Zai zhiyuanjun zongbu* [At the CPVF General HQ], 279; China National Military Museum, ed., *Kangmei yuanchao zhanzheng jishi* [A chronological record of the WRUSAK] (Beijing: Jiefangjun chubanshe 2008), 167; Tan, *Kangmei yuanchao zhanzheng* [The WRUSAK], 227–28; Luan, *Xue yu huo de jiaoliang* [The contest], 224. Gen. Dong Qiwu had been a GMD army commander during WWII; he was made a lieutenant general in 1940. During the Chinese Civil War, he served as the provincial governor and deputy commander of the GMD Northwest Frontier Military Region, fighting against the CCP forces. In September 1949 he and his forces came over to the CCP side. In December 1949 his forces were reorganized as the PLA's Twenty-Third Army Group, and he was appointed the group's commander. Dong commanded his army group in the Korean War from September to December 1951. After his return to China, he was made a in 1955 and elected vice chairman of the CPPCC in 1978. He became a CCP member in 1980. See Tan Zheng, *Zhongguo renmin zhiyuanjun renwulu* [Veterans' profile of the CPVF] (Beijing: Zhonggong dangshi chubanshe, 1992), 619; *Xinghuo liaoyuan* Composition Department, *Zhongguo renmin jiefangjun jiangshuai minglu* [Marshals and generals of the PLA], (Beijing: Jiefangjun chubanshe, 1992), 1:148–49.

32. Xu Yan, "Chinese Forces and Their Casualties in the Korean War," trans. Xiaobing Li, *Chinese Historians* 6, no. 2 (1993): 50–51. In 1952–53, the Chinese Army had a total of 6.5 million troops, 5.1 million in China and 1.4 million in Korea (Composition Committee, ed., *38 xian shang de jiaofeng* [Fighting over the 38th Parallel], 489–90).

33. Nie Rongzhen, *Nie Rongzhen huiyilu* [Memoirs of Nie Rongzhen] (Beijing: Jiefangjun chubanshe, 1984), 2:745–46; Xu, "Chinese Forces and Their Casualties in the Korean War," 54; Xiaobing Li, "China's Intervention and the CPVF Experience in the Korean War," in *The Korean War at Fifty: International Perspectives*, ed. Mark F. Wilkinson (Lexington: Virginia Military Institute Press, 2004), 136–37.

34. Mao telegraphed Stalin on April 28, 1951, proposing to send a Chinese military delegation to Moscow to buy arms. Stalin replied on May 2, agreeing to negotiate terms for providing China with Russian-made weapons and ammunition. See Shen Zhihua,

trans. and ed., *Chaoxian zhanzheng: eguo danganguan de jiemi wenjian* [The Korean War: declassified documents from Russian archives] (Taipei: Zhongyang yanjiuyuan, 2003), 2:751.

35. Xu Xiangqian, "The Purchase of Arms from Moscow," in *Mao's Generals Remember Korea*, 141–42. See also *Xinghuo liaoyuan* Composition Department, *Zhongguo renmin jiefangjun jiangshuai minglu* [Marshals and generals of the PLA], 1:16–17; *Contemporary China* Editorial Department, *Xu Xiangqian zhuan* [Biography of Xu Xiangqian] (Beijing: Dangdai zhongguo chubanshe, 1991).

36. Nie, "Beijing's Decision to Intervene," 58.

37. China Academy of Military Science, "The Unforgotten Korean War," 508; *Contemporary China* Editorial Department, *Xu Xiangqian zhuan* [Biography of Xu Xiangqian], 505–507.

38. Xu Xiangqian, *Lishi de huigu* [History in retrospect] (Beijing: Jiefangjun chubanshe, 1988), 801–802; Zhang, *Zhongguo renmin jiefangjun* [The Chinese People's Liberation Army], 1:135–36.

39. Zhou Zhong, *Kangmei yuanchao zhanzheng houqinshi jianbianben* [A concise history of the logistics in the WRUSAK] (Beijing: Jindun chubanshe, 1993), 174.

40. Senior Col. Yang Shaojun (PLA, ret.), interviews by the author in Beijing, August 2008.

41. Zhang, *Zhongguo renmin jiefangjun* [The Chinese People's Liberation Army], 1:143–44; Military History Research Division, *Zhongguo renmin zhiyuanjun kangmei yuanchao zhanshi* [Combat experience of the CPVF in the WRUSAK], 159.

42. Xu, "The Purchase of Arms from Moscow," 145.

43. Peng Dehuai, "Sinian lai de junshi gongzuo zongjie he jinhou junshi jianshe shang de jige jiben wenti [China's military experience in the past four years and the fundamental issues for our future military development]," in Peng, *Peng's Military Papers*, 474–76.

44. Ministry of Foreign Affairs to Foreign Affairs Office, Northeast China Executive Committee, "Guanyu bangzhu chaoxian xiujian yiyao canku de baogao [Helping North Korea construct more medicine warehouses]," April 8, 1953, in "Zhou Enlai zongli youguan chaoxian dianwen de pishi" [Premier Zhou Enlai's approvals and instructions on North Korean telegrams and documents]," 1953, File# 106-00034-01 (1), 2–3, Archives Department, PRC Foreign Affairs Ministry, Beijing; Teng Daiyuan to Li Kenong, "Guanyu chaoxian renminjun zai dongbei zhanyong wo chepi de baogao [About the rail cars in Northeast China halted by the North Korean People's Army]," June 29, 1951, File# 106-00026-02 (1), ibid.; Col. Wang Po (PLA, ret.), interview by the author at the PLA Logistics Academy in Beijing, July 1994.

45. Shuguang Zhang, "Command, Control, and the PLA's Offensive Campaigns in Korea, 1950–1951," in *Chinese Warfighting: The PLA Experience since 1949*, ed. Mark A. Ryan, David M. Finkelstein, and Michael A. McDevitt (New York: M. E. Sharpe, 2003), 110–11, 113.

46. Hong Xuezhi, "The CPVF's Combat and Logistics," in *Mao's Generals Remember Korea*, 137.

47. Zhang, *Zhongguo renmin jiefangjun* [The Chinese People's Liberation Army], 2:312; Tan, *Zhongguo renmin zhiyuanjun renwulu* [Veterans' profile of the CPVF], 392–93. Chen Zhengfeng was made a senior colonel in 1955.

48. Nie, "Beijing's Decision to Intervene," 57.

49. Tan, *Kangmei yuanchao zhanzheng* [The WRUSAK], 211–12; Military History Research Division, *Zhongguo renmin zhiyuanjun kangmei yuanchao zhanshi* [Combat experience of the CPVF in the WRUSAK], 230; Li, *Zhiyuanjun yuanchao jishi* [The CPVF records of aiding Korea], 495–96; Jiang Tingyu, *Jiedu kangmei yuanchao zhanzheng* [Understanding the WRUSAK] (Beijing: Jiefangjun chubanshe, 2011), 225; see also Qi Dexue, *Ni buliaojie de chaoxian zhanzheng* [The Korean War you don't know] (Shenyang, China: Liaoning renmin chubanshe, 2011), 171, 179.

50. Nie, "Beijing's Decision to Intervene," 50.

51. Zhou, *Kangmei yuanchao zhanzheng houqinshi jianbianben* [A concise history of the logistics in the WRUSAK], 140, 156–57.

52. Hong, *Hong Xuezhi huiyilu* [Memoirs of Hong Xuezhi], 566–67. For more details on the Battle of Keumseong, see Du, *Zai zhiyuanjun zongbu* [At the CPVF General HQ], 597–602; Yao Youzhi and Li Qingshan, *Zhiyuanjun yongcuo qiangdi de 10 da zhanyi* [The CPVF's ten major battles against a strong enemy] (Shenyang, China: Baishan chubanshe, 2009), 305–27; War History Division, NDU, *Zhongguo renmin zhiyuanjun zhanshi jianbian* [A concise history of the CPVF war-fighting] (Beijing: Jiefangjun chubanshe, 1992), 167–70; Chen, ed., *Kangmei yuanchao zhanzheng lun* [On the WRUSAK], 275–78; Li Hongjie, *Zhengyi de zhanzheng, weida de jingshen* [The just war and great inspiration] (Guangzhou: Guangdong renmin chubanshe, 2001), 121–22.

53. Yang, *Yang Dezhi huiyilu* [Memoirs of Yang Dezhi], 742–43; Luan, *Xue yu huo de jiaoliang* [The contest], 345; Composition Committee, ed., *38 xian shang de jiaofeng* [Fighting over the 38th Parallel], 525, 527.

54. Military History Research Division, *Zhongguo renmin zhiyuanjun kangmei yuanchao zhanshi* [Combat experience of the CPVF in the WRUSAK], 212, 188; PLA History Archives Compilation Committee, ed., *Paobing* [The artillery force] (Beijing: Jiefangjun chubanshe, 1999), 272–77.

55. Wang Dinglie and Lin Hu, *Dangdai Zhongguo kongjun* [Contemporary Chinese Air Force] (Beijing: Shehui kexue chubanshe, 1989), 17–25; China National Military Museum, ed., *Kangmei yuanchao zhanzheng fengyunlu* [The operational files of the WRUSAK], 345–50; Xiaobing Li, *A History of the Modern Chinese Army* (Lexington: University Press of Kentucky, 2007), 106, 108–10.

56. Zhang, *Zhongguo renmin jiefangjun* [The Chinese People's Liberation Army], 2:65, 67–68; Han Huaizhi, *Dangdai zhongguo jundui de junshi gongzuo* [Contemporary Chinese military affairs] (Beijing: Zhongguo shehui kexue chubanshe, 1989), 2:72–73; Wang Suhong and Wang Yubin, *Kongzhan zai chaoxian* [The air war in Korea] (Beijing: Jiefangjun wenyi chubanshe, 1992), 98, 104; Xiaoming Zhang, *Red Wings over the Yalu: China, the Soviet Union, and the Air War in Korea* (College Station: Texas A & M University Press, 2002), 224–26; Dennis D. Showalter, "The First Jet War," in *The Cold War: A Military History*, ed. Robert Cowley (New York: Random House, 2005), 128.

57. Gen. Liu Zhen joined the Red Army in 1928 and the CCP in 1932. He participated in the Long March. Liu served as commander of a squad, platoon, company, and battalion and as political commissar of a regiment and division in the Red Army. During the Anti-Japanese War he was a commander of a regiment and brigade of the 115th Division, Eighth Route Army; and of a brigade and division in the New Fourth Army. During the Chinese Civil War Liu was division commander, army deputy commander, and later commander and political commissar of the Thirty-Ninth Army, and deputy commander of the Thirteenth Army Group of the PLA. In 1950–53, Liu became commander of the

Northeast Air Force and commander of the CPVF Air Force. After his return to China, he was appointed commander of the Northeast and Shenyang Air Force Commands, deputy commander of the PLA Air Force, and commander of the Xinjiang Regional Command. He was made an air force general in 1955. For more details, see Tan, *Zhongguo renmin zhiyuanjun renwulu* [Veterans' profile of the CPVF], 134–35; *Xinghuo liaoyuan* Composition Department, *Zhongguo renmin jiefangjun jiangshuai minglu* [Marshals and generals of the PLA], 1:66–67. Lt. Gen. Chang Qiankun joined the CCP in 1925. He studied aviation technology in the Soviet Union and served in the Soviet Air Force in the 1930s. After his return to China in 1938, Chang became a staff member in the Eighth Route Army HQ during the Anti-Japanese War. During the Chinese Civil War he became superintendent of the PLA Northeast Aviation Academy and chief of the Aviation Bureau of the CMC. In 1950–53, he was deputy commander of the CPVF Air Force. After his return to China, Chang was appointed deputy commander of the PLA Air Force. He became a lieutenant general in the PLA Air Force in 1955. For more details, see Tan, *Zhongguo renmin zhiyuanjun renwulu* [Veterans' profile of the CPVF], 586–87; *Xinghuo liaoyuan* Composition Department, *Zhongguo renmin jiefangjun jiangshuai minglu* [Marshals and generals of the PLA], 1:442–43.

58. Yang Fengan and Wang Tiancheng, *Beiwei 38 duxian: Peng Dehuai yu chaoxian zhanzheng* [The north latitude 38th Parallel: Peng Dehuai and the Korean War] (Beijing: Zhongyang wenxian chubanshe, 2009), 386; Wang and Lin, *Dangdai Zhongguo kongjun* [Contemporary Chinese Air Force], 130–31; Li, *Zhiyuanjun yuanchao jishi* [The CPVF records of aiding Korea], 477.

59. Since December 1950, the Soviet Union had provided the Chinese Air Force with 582 MiG-15 jet fighters in three groups. These fighters went to the 2nd, 3rd, 4th, 6th, 7th, 9th, 12th, and 14th Air Force Divisions in 1951. See Military History Research Division, *Zhongguo renmin zhiyuanjun kangmei yuanchao zhanshi* [Combat experience of the CPVF in the WRUSAK], 159; Shuang, *Kaiguo diyi zhan* [The first war since the founding of the state], 2:517.

60. Xu, *Mao Zedong yu kangmei yuanchao zhanzheng* [Mao Zedong and the WRUSAK], 397; and Xiaoming Zhang, "Air Combat for the People's Republic," in *Chinese Warfighting: The PLA Experience since 1949*, ed. Mark A. Ryan, David M. Finkelstein, and Michael A. McDevitt (New York: M. E. Sharpe, 2003), 278.

61. Gen. Wang became deputy commander and commander of the 9th Regiment, 3rd Air Force Division in 1952, and deputy commander of the 3rd Division in 1953. After his return to China, he was given the rank of lieutenant colonel of the PLA Air Force in 1955. Wang was promoted to division commander in 1956, air force colonel in 1959, and deputy commander of the 2nd Air Force Army in 1965. He served as the chief of the Training Department in the PLA Air Force HQ in 1969. Wang was appointed air force commander of the Guangzhou Regional Command in 1975. He became deputy commander of the PLA Air Force in November 1982 and was commander in 1985–92. Wang was made an air force general in 1988. See Tan, *Zhongguo renmin zhiyuanjun renwulu* [Veterans' profile of the CPVF], 27–28.

62. Wang Hai, *Wode zhandou shengya* [My military career] (Beijing: Zhongyang wenxian chubanshe, 2000), 11–18, 78–79; and Chen, ed., *Kangmei yuanchao zhanzheng lun* [On the WRUSAK], 296.

63. Wang, *Wode zhandou shengya* [My military career], 112–13; Wang and Wang, *Kongzhan zai chaoxian* [The air war in Korea], 137–41; Li, *Zhiyuanjun yuanchao jishi*

[The CPVF records of aiding Korea], 483–84; Composition Committee, ed., *38 xian shang de jiaofeng* [Fighting over the 38th Parallel], 410–11; China National Military Museum, ed., *Kangmei yuanchao zhanzheng fengyunlu* [The operational files of the WRUSAK], 359–60.

64. The Chinese air force divisions began their rotation in Korea in early 1952. See Wang, *Wode zhandou shengya* [My military career], 132, 144; Tan, *Kangmei yuanchao zhanzheng* [The WRUSAK], 198, 208; Wang and Lin, *Dangdai Zhongguo kongjun* [Contemporary Chinese Air Force], 130–31.

65. Both Gen. Wang and Gen. Gabriel were told by their own interpreters that "you shot down your counterpart during that battle." Obviously, the two interpreters translated it in opposite ways (Bernard E. Trainor, "Washington Talk: Joint Chiefs of Staff; Inside the 'Tank': Bowls of Candy and Big Brass," *New York Times,* January 11, 1988). See also Li, *Zhiyuanjun yuanchao jishi* [The CPVF records of aiding Korea], 487–88.

66. A photocopy of the letter was included in Wang, *Wode zhandou shengya* [My military career], 310–11. See also Composition Committee, ed., *38 xian shang de jiaofeng* [Fighting over the 38th Parallel], 412.

67. Hong, *Hong Xuezhi huiyilu* [Memoirs of Hong Xuezhi], 511; Chen, ed., *Kangmei yuanchao zhanzheng lun* [On the WRUSAK], 301; Xiaobing Li, "Chinese Army in the Korean War, 1950–53," *New England Journal of History* 60, nos. 1–3 (2003): 286.

68. For the Chinese statistics on UNF plane losses, see Wang and Wang, *Kongzhan zai chaoxian* [The air war in Korea], 249–50; Composition Committee, ed., *38 xian shang de jiaofeng* [Fighting over the 38th Parallel], 415, 416. UNF statistics shows that U.S. Air Force, Navy, and Marine Corps lost a total of 2,998 planes during the Korean War, 1,644 of which were lost in operations and 1,354 in combat. See Richard P. Hallion, "The Air War in Korea: Coalition Air Power in the Context of Limited War," paper presented at Korea: In from the Cold, Canberra, Australia, October 5–7, 2011, 82–83. Also see Wang, *Wode zhandou shengya* [My military career], 149–50; Zhang, *Zhongguo renmin jiefangjun* [The Chinese People's Liberation Army], 2:101–103. For more on the UNF statistics, see George F. Futrell, *The United States Air Force in the Korean War* (Washington: Office of Air Force History, 1983), 216–18.

69. Wang, *Wode zhandou shengya* [My military career], 149–50; Zhang, *Zhongguo renmin jiefangjun* [The Chinese People's Liberation Army], 2:101–103; Shuang, *Kaiguo diyi zhan* [The first war since the founding of the state], 2:819.

70. These statistics differ from those in Boris Yeltsin's letter to the U.S. Senate Committee on Searching for American MIAs in the Korean War, in June 1992. In thei letter, Russian President Yeltsin wrote: "There were 1,309 U.S. airplanes were shot down in North Korea, and 262 American pilots were rescued" (quoted in Composition Committee, ed., *38 xian shang de jiaofeng* [Fighting over the 38th Parallel], 416). See also Zhang, *Red Wings over the Yalu,* 202–203; Shen Zhihua, *Mao Zedong, Stalin he chaoxian zhanzheng* [Mao Zedong, Stalin, and the Korean War] (Guangzhou: Guangdong renmin chubanshe, 2004), 338.

71. Shen Zhihua, "Kangmei yuanchao zhanzheng zhong de sulian kongjun [The Soviet Air Force in the WRUSAK]," *Zhonggong dangshi yanjiu* [Studies on CCP history] 2 (2000): 27–29; Zhang, *Red Wings over the Yalu,* 219–21; Shuang, *Kaiguo diyi zhan* [The first war since the founding of the state], 2:820.

72. Nie, "Beijing's Decision to Intervene," 58.

73. Mao Zedong, telegram to Peng, July 2, 1951, in Mao Zedong, *Jianguo yilai Mao Zedong wengao, 1949–76* [Mao Zedong's manuscripts since the founding of the state, 1949–76] (Beijing: Zhongyang wenxian chubanshe, 1989), 2:379–80.

74. PRC Ministry of Foreign Affairs to Gan Yetao, "Lee Xiangchao fangwen Beijing [Lee Xiangchao's visit to Beijing]," 15; PRC Ministry of Foreign Affairs to Northeastern Executive Committee, "Guanyu anpai beichaoxian daibiao zai Andong he qita diqu gongzuo de shiyi [Arrange North Korean representatives working in Andong and other areas]," April 3, 1953, 1; Zhou Enlai, speech (draft) on the third anniversary of the Korean War, June 24, 1953, 24–25, in "Zhou Enlai zongli youguan beichaoxian dianbao he wenjian de piwen yu zhishi [Premier Zhou Enlai's approvals and instructions on North Korean telegrams and documents]," 1953, File# 106-00034-01 (1), Archives Department, PRC Foreign Affairs Ministry, Beijing.

75. PRC Ministry of Foreign Affairs to Gan Yetao, "Lee Xiangchao fangwen Beijing [Lee Xiangchao's visit to Beijing]," 25.

76. Dean Acheson, *Present at the Creation: My Years in the State Department* (New York: Norton, 1969), 523–33; Max Hastings, *The Korean War* (New York: Simon and Schuster, 1987), 230.

77. Nie, *Nie Rongzhen huiyilu* [Memoirs of Nie Rongzhen], 2:741–42; Hong, *Hong Xuezhi huiyilu* [Memoirs of Hong Xuezhi], 539–40; Yang, *Yang Dezhi huiyilu* [Memoirs of Yang Dezhi], 571–73; Du, *Zai zhiyuanjun zongbu* [At the CPVF General HQ], 266–71, 337–41; Wang et al., *Peng Dehuai zhuan* [Biography of Peng Dehuai], 472–73; Feng and Li, *Mao Zedong yu kangmei yuanchao* [Mao Zedong: resisting the U.S. and aiding Korea], 72–84; Chai Chengwen, Huang Zhengji, and Zhang Changjin, *Sanda tupuo: xin zhongguo zouxiang shijie de baogao* [The three breakthroughs: a report on how new China entered the world] (Beijing: Jiefangjun chubanshe, 1994), 112–15; Alexander V. Pantsov with Steven I. Levine, *Mao: The Real Story* (New York: Simon and Schuster, 2012), 386.

78. Yang Di, *Zai zhiyuanjun silingbu de suiyueli: xianwei renzhi de zhenshi qingkuang* [My years at the CPVF General HQ: untold true stories] (Beijing: Jiefangjun chubanshe, 1998), 168–69; Luan, *Xue yu huo de jiaoliang* [The contest], 245–46; James L. Stokesbury, *A Short History of the Korean War* (New York: William Morrow, 1988), 144–46; Hastings, *The Korean War*, 231–32.

79. Ridgway, *The Korean War*, 202–203; Acheson, *Present at the Creation*, 535–36; Yafeng Xia, *Negotiating with the Enemy: U.S.-China Talks during the Cold War, 1949–72* (Bloomington: Indiana University Press, 2006), 58–62.

80. Hastings, *The Korean War*, 232–33; Clay Blair, *The Forgotten War: America in Korea, 1950–53* (New York: Times, 1987), 955–61.

81. Chai Chengwen and Zhao Yongtian, *Banmendian tanpan* [The Panmunjom negotiations], 2nd ed. (Beijing: Jiefangjun chubanshe, 1992), 200–203, 210; Blair, *The Forgotten War*, 961–64; and Lewis H. Carlson, *Remembered Prisoners of a Forgotten War: An Oral History of Korean War POWs* (New York: St. Martin's, 2002), 2–3, 214.

82. Quoted in Sergei N. Goncharov, John W. Lewis, and Xue Litai, *Uncertain Partners: Stalin, Mao, and the Korean War* (Stanford: Stanford University Press, 1993), 77–79. For more information on Truman's policy toward the POW issues, see Charles S. Young, "Voluntary Repatriation and Involuntary Tattooing of Korean War POWs," in *Northeast Asia and the Legacy of Harry S. Truman: Japan, China, and the Two Koreas*, ed. James I. Matray (Kirksville, MO: Truman State University Press, 2012), 149–51.

83. Chai Chengwen, "The Korean Truce Negotiations," in *Mao's Generals Remember Korea*, 223–24. Between July 1951 and July 1953, Maj. Gen. Chai (PLA, ret.) served in the Chinese–North Korean delegation to the truce talks at Panmunjom as the secretary general and liaison officer of the CPVF Command. After his return to China, Chai served as envoy extraordinary and minister plenipotentiary of the PRC to Denmark from 1955 to 1956. He was appointed deputy chief of the Second Department (Military Intelligence Service) of the PLA General Staff in the 1950s. Chai was made a senior colonel in 1955 and a major general in 1961. He became chief of the Foreign Affairs Bureau of the Ministry of Defense of the PRC in the 1960s, retiring in 1982. For more information on Chai, see Tan, *Zhongguo renmin zhiyuanjun renwulu* [Veterans' profile of the CPVF], 529–30; *Xinghuo liaoyuan* Composition Department, *Zhongguo renmin jiefangjun jiangshuai minglu* [Marshals and generals of the PLA], 3:368.

84. Col. Zhao Zuorui (POW), interview by the author in Benxi, Liaoning, July 1998. Col. Zhao was political commissar of the 538th Regiment, 180th Division, Sixtieth Army, Third Army Group of the CPVF when he was captured by the UNF during the Spring Offensive in May 1951. By 1952 there were 132,000 Chinese and North Korean Communist prisoners in the UNF camps. About 70,000 of them were held at Koje-do. See also Zhao Zuorui, "Organizing the Riots on Koje," in *Voices from the Korean War: Personal Stories of American, Korean, and Chinese Soldiers*, 212–15; Pendleton Woods, "An American Officer Observes the Koje Island Uprising," in *Voices from the Korean War: Personal Stories of American, Korean, and Chinese Soldiers*, and 242–44. First Lt. Woods (U.S. Army, ret.) served as the public information officer, U.S. 45th Infantry Division HQ, during the riots in the UNF's Koje-do POW camp.

85. PRC Ministry of Foreign Affairs, "Guanyu chaoxian zhanfu qianfan de badian [Eight points on the issue of repatriating Korean War POWs]," November 4, 1952, File# 105-00235-09 (1); "Zhongguo waijiaobu yazhousi sizhang Chen Jiakang yu Indu zhuhua daibiao guanyu chaoxian tingzhan xieding ji qita youguan wenti de huiyi jilu [The meeting minutes of Chen Jiakang, chief of the Bureau of Asian Affairs, Ministry of Foreign Affairs of the PRC, with the head of Indian Mission to China on the Korean Armistice and other related issues]," November 12, 1952, File# 105-00027-08, Archives Department, PRC Foreign Affairs Ministry, Beijing. See also Shen Xingyi, "Yiwan siqian ge zhengren: hanzhan shiqi 'fangong yishi' zhi yanjiu" [14,000 witnesses: studies of the "anti-Communist heroes" from the Korean War], master's thesis, National Taiwan Normal University, 1996), 82–84; Sandler, *The Korean War*, 214–15; Catchpole, *The Korean War*, 208–10.

86. Dwight D. Eisenhower, *Mandate for Change, 1953–56: The White House Years* (Garden City, NY: Doubleday, 1963), 180–81. Leading Democrats in the United States and prominent newspapers in Great Britain and India expressed concern that such steps could lead to an extension of the war. See Walter G. Hermes, *Truce Tent and Fighting Front, U.S. Army in the Korean War* (Washington: Government Printing Office, 1988), 408–409

87. Quoted in Blair, *The Forgotten War*, 971. See also Hermes, *Truce Tent and Fighting Front*, 412; Xia, *Negotiating with the Enemy*, 71–72.

88. Chen Jian, *Mao's China and the Cold War* (Chapel Hill: University of North Carolina Press, 2001), 112. See also Staff of the Foreign Ministry of the Soviet Union, "Background Report on the Korean War, August 9, 1966," trans. Kathryn Weathersby, *Journal of American–East Asian Relations* 2 (Winter 1993): 445.

89. Zhou Enlai, "Guanyu chaoxian tingzhan tanpan wenti de shengming [The statement on the issues of the Korean truce negotiations]," March 30, 1950, in *Zhou's Military*

*Papers,* 4:314–18; Du, *Zai zhiyuanjun zongbu* [At the CPVF General HQ], 588–89; Xu, *Mao Zedong yu kangmei yuanchao zhanzheng* [Mao Zedong and the WRUSAK], 330–31; Hu Haipo and Yu Hongjun, *Genzhe Mao Zedong da tianxia* [Follow Mao Zedong to seize state power] (Changsha, China: Hunan renmin chubanshe, 2009), 161.

90. Yang and Wang, *Beiwei 38 duxian* [The north latitude 38th Parallel], 423; Tan, *Kangmei yuanchao zhanzheng* [The WRUSAK], 287; Wang, *Juezhan chaoxian* [The showdown in Korea]; 461; Carlson, *Remembered Prisoners of a Forgotten War,* 214; Hermes, *Truce Tent and Fighting Front,* 417–19; Xia, *Negotiating with the Enemy,* 72.

91. Chai, "The Korean Truce Negotiations," 228.

92. Du, *Zai zhiyuanjun zongbu* [At the CPVF General HQ], 502–503; Xia, *Negotiating with the Enemy,* 73; Burton I. Kaufman, *The Korean Conflict* (Westport, CT: Greenwood, 1999), 66–67; Hermes, *Truce Tent and Fighting Front,* 431–32; Carlson, *Remembered Prisoners of a Forgotten War,* 214.

93. Peng Dehuai, telegram to Mao, June 20, 1953, in Mao, *Mao's Military Manuscripts since 1949,* 2:148, note 2; Mao Zedong, telegram to Peng, "Tingzhan qianzi bixu tuichi [The signing of the truce must be postponed]," June 21, 1953, ibid., 2:148.

94. For the Battle of Keumseong on July 13–25, 1953, see Du, *Zai zhiyuanjun zongbu* [At the CPVF General HQ], 597–602; Yao and Li, *Zhiyuanjun yongcuo qiangdi de 10 da zhanyi* [The CPVF's ten major battles against a strong enemy], 305–27; War History Division, *Zhongguo renmin zhiyuanjun zhanshi jianbian* [A concise history of the CPVF war-fighting], 167–70; Chen, ed., *Kangmei yuanchao zhanzheng lun* [On the WRUSAK], 275–78; Li, *Zhengyi de zhanzheng, weida de jingshen* [The just war and great spirit], 121–22. See also Xu, *Mao Zedong yu kangmei yuanchao zhanzheng* [Mao Zedong and the WRUSAK], 330–31; Stokesbury, *A Short History of the Korean War,* 247–48; Hermes, *Truce Tent and Fighting Front,* 450–51.

95. Richard Peters and Xiaobing Li, "Trench Warfare and Peace" in *Voices from the Korean War: Personal Stories of American, Korean, and Chinese Soldiers,* ed. Richard Peters and Xiaobing Li (Lexington: University Press of Kentucky, 2004), 47.

96. Hong, *Hong Xuezhi huiyilu* [Memoirs of Hong Xuezhi], 571; Yang, *Yang Dezhi huiyilu* [Memoirs of Yang Dezhi], 749–50; Du, *Zai zhiyuanjun zongbu* [At the CPVF General HQ], 604–608; Yang, *Zai zhiyuanjun silingbu de suiyueli* [My years at the CPVF General HQ], 280–81; Joseph C. Goulden, *Korea: The Untold Story of the War* (New York: Times, 1982), 644–6. For the text of the Korean Armistice, see Hermes, *Truce Tent and Fighting Front,* Appendix C.

97. Quoted in Chai, "The Korean Truce Negotiations," 232.

98. Hong, *Hong Xuezhi huiyilu* [Memoirs of Hong Xuezhi], 571; Du, *Zai zhiyuanjun zongbu* [At the CPVF General HQ], 604–605; Wang et al., *Peng Dehuai zhuan* [Biography of Peng Dehuai], 487; Yang and Wang, *Beiwei 38 duxian* [The north latitude 38th Parallel], 452; Shuang, *Kaiguo diyi zhan* [The first war since the founding of the state], 2:835.

99. Peng, "My Story of the Korean War," 37.

100. For a complete list of the UNF prisoners exchanged, see Hermes, *Truce Tent and Fighting Front,* Appendix C.

101. For more information on these UNF POWs, see Carlson, *Remembered Prisoners of a Forgotten War,* 202–12; Shuang, *Kaiguo diyi zhan* [The first war since the founding of the state], 2:850–51; and Guo Weijing, *Diyideng zhanfuying: lianheguojun zhanfu zai chaoxian* [The first-class POW camps: the UN POWs in Korea] (Beijing: Shijie zhishi chubanshe, 1999), 269–306. As a CPVF officer, Guo served in the CPVF delegation to

the Panmunjom truce negotiations and the POW Administration of the Political Department at the CPVF General HQ in 1951–54. He retired from the PLA in 1956.

102. The Chinese official number was 26,000 POWs held by the UNF. See PRC Ministry of Foreign Affairs to Gan Yetao, "Lee Xiangchao fangwen Beijing [Lee Xiangchao's visit to Beijing]"; Zhou, speech (draft) on the third anniversary of the Korean War, June 24, 1953.

103. Ye Gongchao, Foreign Minister of the ROC, to the GMD Central Committee on August 11, 1953, Content No. 172–73, File No. 5975, Anti-Communist POW Files," ROC Ministry of Foreign Affairs Archives, Taipei; Yang Wanfu (POW), interviews by the author in the Rongjia Zhongxin (Glorious Retirement Center for Veterans) in Taipei, July 2008. See also Shen, "Yiwan siqian ge zhengren" [14,000 witnesses], 168–73; Xu, *Diyici jiaoliang* [The first encounter], 308–10; Shuang, *Kaiguo diyi zhan* [The first war since the founding of the state], 2:847.

104. Yang, *Yang Dezhi huiyilu* [Memoirs of Yang Dezhi], 766; Li, *Zhiyuanjun yuanchao jishi* [The CPVF records of aiding Korea], 527.

### CONCLUSION

1. Xu Yan, "Chinese Forces and Their Casualties in the Korean War," trans. Xiaobing Li, *Chinese Historians* 6, no. 2 (1993): 49, 51; War History Division, NDU, *Zhongguo renmin zhiyuanjun zhanshi jianbian* [A concise history of the CPVF war-fighting] (Beijing: Jiefangjun chubanshe, 1992), 176; Li Song, "Dandong: zhiyuanjun yinghun de zhuixun [Dandong: search for the spirit of the CPVF martyrs]," in *Kangmei yuanchao: 60 nianhou de huimou* [The WRUSAK: a retrospective look after 60 years], ed. Zhang Xingxing (Beijing: Dangdai zhongguo chubanshe, 2011), 139.

2. Xiaobing Li, Allan Millett, and Bin Yu, introduction to *Mao's Generals Remember Korea,* translated and edited by Xiaobing Li, Allan R. Millett, and Bin Yu (Lawrence: University Press of Kansas, 2001), 6.

3. Chen Jian and Xiaobing Li, "China and the End of the Global Cold War," in *The Cold War: From Détente to the Soviet Collapse,* ed. Malcolm Muir Jr. (Lexington: Virginia Military Institute Press, 2006), 120.

4. Ibid.

5. For the importance of the Sino-Soviet alliance, see John Lewis Gaddis, *The Cold War: A New History* (New York: Penguin, 2005); Odd Arne Westad, ed., *Brothers in Arms: The Rise and Fall of the Sino-Soviet Alliance, 1945–63* (Washington: Woodrow Wilson Center Press, 1998) and Westad, *The Global Cold War: Third World Interventions and the Making of Our Times* (New York: Cambridge University Press, 2005); Robert S. Ross and Jiang Changbin, eds., *Re-Examining the Cold War: U.S.-China Diplomacy, 1954–1973* (Cambridge: Harvard University Press, 2001); Thomas J. Christensen, *Useful Adversaries: Grand Strategy, Domestic Mobilization, and Sino-American Conflict, 1947–58* (Princeton: Princeton University Press, 1996); Michael M. Sheng, *Battling Western Imperialism: Mao, Stalin, and the United States* (Princeton: Princeton University Press, 1997); Vladislav Zubok and Constantine Pleshakov, *Inside the Kremlin's Cold War: From Stalin to Khrushchev* (Cambridge: Harvard University Press, 1996); Michael H. Hunt, *The Genesis of Chinese Communist Foreign Policy* (New York: Columbia University Press, 1996).

6. Mao Anying was killed on November 25, 1950. For more details, see Hong Xuezhi, "The CPVF's Combat and Logistics," in *Mao's Generals Remember Korea,* 118–21; Du

Ping, *Zai zhiyuanjun zongbu: Du Ping huiyilu* [At the CPVF General HQ: memoirs of Du Ping] (Beijing: Jiefangjun chubanshe, 1989), 92–98; Yang Di, *Zai zhiyuanjun silingbu de suiyueli: xianwei renzhi de zhenshi qingkuang* [My years at the CPVF General HQ: untold true stories] (Beijing: Jiefangjun chubanshe, 1998), 293–95.

7. Chen Hui, "18 wan kangmei yuanchao lishi xunzong [Tracing the 180,000 martyrs of the WRUSAK]," in *Kangmei yuanchao: 60 nianhou de huimou* [The WRUSAK: a retrospective look after 60 years], ed. Zhang Xingxing (Beijing: Dangdai zhongguo chubanshe, 2011), 127; Xu, "Chinese Forces and Their Casualties in the Korean War," 56–57; Li Qingshan, *Zhiyuanjun yuanchao jishi* [The CPVF records of aiding Korea] (Beijing: Zhonggong dangshi chubanshe, 2008), 13; Shuang Shi, *Kaiguo diyi zhan: kangmei yuanchao zhanzheng quanjing jishi* [The first war since the founding of the state: the complete story of the WRUSAK] (Beijing: Zhonggong dangshi chubanshe, 2004), 2:836–37. The UNF intelligence statisticians put Chinese losses far higher: 1.5 million casualties, including killed in action, died of wounds or disease, missing in action, and wounded in action. For example, see Walter G. Hermes, *Truce Tent and Fighting Front, U.S. Army in the Korean War* (Washington: Government Printing Office, 1988), 477–78.

8. Peter Hays Gries, *China's New Nationalism: Pride, Politics, and Diplomacy* (Berkeley: University of California Press, 2004), 56.

9. Nie Rongzhen, "Beijing's Decision to Intervene," in *Mao's Generals Remember Korea*, trans. and ed. Xiaobing Li, Allan R. Millett, and Bin Yu (Lawrence: University Press of Kansas, 2000), 50; Zhou Zhong, *Kangmei yuanchao zhanzheng houqinshi jianbianben* [A concise history of the logistics in the WRUSAK] (Beijing: Jindun chubanshe, 1993), 1; Tan Jingjiao, *Kangmei yuanchao zhanzheng* [The WRUSAK] (Beijing: Zhongguo shehui kexue chubanshe, 1990), 357; Shuang, *Kaiguo diyi zhan* [The first war since the founding of the state], 2:837–38.

10. Military History Research Division, CAMS, *Zhongguo renmin zhiyuanjun kangmei yuanchao zhanshi* [Combat experience of the CPVF in the WRUSAK] (Beijing: Junshi kexue chubanshe, 1990), 233–34.

11. See, for example, Mao Zedong, concluding remarks at the Second Plenary Session of the CCP Seventh Central Committee, March 13, 1949, in Mao Zedong, *Selected Works of Mao Tse-tung* (Beijing: Foreign Languages Press, 1977), 4:1464; Mao Zedong, "Address to the Preparatory Meeting of the New Political Consultative Conference," in ibid., 1470.

12. Ellis Joffe, *The Chinese Army after Mao* (Cambridge: Harvard University Press, 1987), 1.

13. Peng Dehuai, "Sinian lai de junshi gongzuo zongjie he jinhou junshi jianshe shang de jige wenti [China's military experience in the past four years and the fundamental issues for our future military development]," December 1953, in Peng Dehuai, *Peng Dehuai junshi wenxuan* [Selected military papers of Peng Dehuai] (Beijing: Zhongyang wenxian chubanshe, 1988), 468–69.

14. For more details of these border conflicts, see Xiaobing Li, *A History of the Modern Chinese Army* (Lexington: University Press of Kentucky, 2007), chapters 6–8; Mark A. Ryan, David M. Finkelstein, and Michael A. McDevitt, eds., *Chinese Warfighting: The PLA Experience since 1949* (New York: M. E. Sharpe, 2003).

15. Deng Xiaoping, "Speech at an Enlarged Meeting of the CMC, June 4, 1985," in Deng Xiaoping, *Selected Works of Deng Xiaoping* (Beijing: Foreign Languages Press, 1994), 3:131–33.

16. Deng Xiaoping, "Streamline the Army and Raise Its Combat Effectiveness," in ibid., 2:284–87.

17. *Selected Documents of the Fifteenth CCP National Congress* (Beijing: New Star Publishing House, 1997), 104–106.

18. Quoted in PRC Ministry of Defense, *White Papers of China's National Defense, 1998–2010* (Beijing: Foreign Languages Press, 2000–2012), 2:645.

19. Wang Wenrong, "Daixu: xuexi guanche Jiang zhuxi zhongda zhanlue cixiang [Introduction: studying and carrying out President Jiang's important strategic thoughts]," in Sun Kejia, *Zhongguo tese de junshi biange* [A revolution in military affairs with Chinese characteristics] (Beijing: Changzheng chubanshe, 2003), 1.

20. The Soviet Union delivered weapons to China for sixteen infantry divisions in 1951, and for forty-four divisions in 1952–54. See Xu Xiangqian, "The Purchase of Arms from Moscow," in *Mao's Generals Remember Korea*, 145; Nie Rongzhen, *Nie Rongzhen huiyilu* [Memoirs of Nie Rongzhen] (Beijing: Jiefangjun chubanshe, 1984), 2:758.

21. Yang Guoyu, *Dangdai Zhongguo haijun* [Contemporary Chinese navy] (Beijing: Zhongguo shehui kexue chubanshe, 1987), 233, 239–40; Military History Research Division, CAMS, *Zhongguo renmin jiefangjun de qishinian, 1927–97* [Seventy years of the PLA, 1927–97] (Beijing: Junshi kexue chubanshe, 1997), 455, 461.

22. Wang Dinglie and Lin Hu, *Dangdai Zhongguo kongjun* [Contemporary Chinese Air Force] (Beijing: Shehui kexue chubanshe, 1989), 68, 82; Military History Research Division, *Zhongguo renmin jiefangjun de qishinian* [Seventy years of the PLA], 461.

23. Jeanne L. Wilson, *Strategic Partners: Russian-Chinese Relations in the Post-Soviet Era* (Armonk, NY: M. E. Sharpe, 2004), 70.

24. Ming-Yen Tsai, *From Adversaries to Partners: Chinese and Russian Military Cooperation after the Cold War* (Westport, CT: Praeger, 2003), 25–27.

25. Military History Research Division, *Zhongguo renmin jiefangjun de qishinian* [Seventy years of the PLA], 457–58.

26. John Foster Dulles, memorandum on meeting with President Dwight Eisenhower, March 6, 1955, White House Memoranda, Box 3, "Meeting with the President 1955 (4)," John Foster Dulles Papers, Dwight Eisenhower Library, Abilene, KS.

27. Nie Rongzhen, "Jianxi qibu de woguo wodan shiye [A rough start for China's nuclear and missile programs]," in *Liangdan yixing: zhongguo hewuqi daodan weixing yu feichuan quanjishi* [Two bombs and one star: a complete record of China's nuclear weapons, missiles, satellites, and spaceships], ed. PLA General Armaments Department, (Beijing: Jiuzhou chubanshe, 2001), 5.

28. Xiaobing Li, "Nuclear Program," in *China at War: An Encyclopedia*, Xiaobing Li ed. (Santa Barbara, CA: ABC-CLIO, 2012), 331–32.

29. Jiang Zemin, speech to the PLA delegation to the Tenth National People's Congress on March 9, 2003, in Beijing, *Jiefangjun bao* [PLA daily], March 10, 2003.

30. Hu Jintao, speech at the "Four General Departments" (*sizongbu*) meeting, August 2000, *Taiyangbao* [Sun daily], September 5, 2000.

31. Joffe, *The Chinese Army after Mao*, 2.

32. Military History Research Division, *Zhongguo renmin jiefangjun de qishinian* [Seventy years of the PLA], 395–96.

33. Ibid.

34. Ibid., 458; Han Huaizhi, *Dangdai zhongguo jundui de junshi gongzuo* [Contemporary Chinese military affairs] (Beijing: Zhongguo shehui kexue chubanshe, 1989), 2:86.

35. Han, *Dangdai zhongguo jundui de junshi gongzuo* [Contemporary Chinese military affairs], 2:86.

36. Each PLA army was reorganized from a mobile field force into a local force, stationed at one place. For more details, see Li, *A History of the Modern Chinese Army*, 126.

37. For example, the Third Field Army became the East China Command. Its four army groups, including fifteen armies, were reorganized into six provincial and metropolitan commands, including Zhejiang, Fujian, Jiangsu, Shanghai, and coastal areas along the Taiwan Strait. See Military History Research Division, *Zhongguo renmin jiefangjun de qishinian* [Seventy years of the PLA], 454–55; Fang Zhu, *Gun Barrel Politics: Party-Army Relations in Mao's China* (Boulder, CO: Westview, 1998), 47–52.

38. Military History Research Division, *Zhongguo renmin jiefangjun de qishinian* [Seventy years of the PLA], 459–60; *Xinghuo liaoyuan* Composition Department, *Zhongguo renmin jiefangjun jiangshuai minglu* [Marshals and generals of the PLA] (Beijing: Jiefangjun chubanshe, 1987–92), 1:1–10.

39. Quoted in Zhang Aiping, *Zhongguo renmin jiefangjun* [The Chinese People's Liberation Army] (Beijing: Dangdai zhongguo chubanshe, 1994), 1:170–71.

40. Quoted in Xiaobing Li, *Civil Liberties in China* (Santa Barbara, CA: ABC-CLIO, 2010), xvi.

41. For example, Maj. Gen. Zhu Chenghu, the dean at NDU, told a group of foreign journalists in July 2005 that China would attack over a hundred American cities with nuclear weapons if the United States interfered in a war between China and Taiwan. Members of the U.S. Congress called for Zhu to be fired. But the Chinese government did not reject Zhu's statement, and a spokesperson for the Ministry of Foreign Affairs said that Zhu's comment was his own personal opinion. This spokesperson declined to comment on whether or not the speech represented the Chinese government's view. Jonathan D. Pollack has pointed out that as China becomes more involved in "sub- and pan-regional security affairs," it is "acquiring military capabilities that it believes will ultimately enable a short-warning, high-intensity attack against Taiwan. These include a growing inventory of short-range ballistic missiles, advanced conventionally powered submarines and other naval platforms, longer-range aircraft, and a host of related capabilities" ("The Transformation of the Asian Security Order: Assessing China's Impact," in *Power Shift: China and Asia's New Dynamics,* ed. by David Shambaugh [Berkeley: University of California Press, 2005], 339). See also Wang Zheng, "U.S. Congress Calls for Sacking of Chinese General," *Epoch Times,* July 25, 2005, http://www.theepochtimes.com/news/5-7-25/30545.html; David Shambaugh, "The Rise of China and Asia's New Dynamics," in *Power Shift,* 11.

42. Tian Fuzi, *Zhongyeu zhanzheng jishilu* [Factual records of the Sino-Vietnam War] (Beijing: Jiefangjun wenyi chubanshe, 2004), 92, 328.

43. Gerald Segal, "Foreign Policy," in *China in the Nineties: Crisis Management and Beyond,* ed. David S. G. Goodman and Gerald Segal (Oxford: Oxford University Press, 1991), 173.

44. Xiaobing Li, *A History of the Modern Chinese Army,* 258.

45. First Lt. Xu Xiangyao (PLA, ret.), interviews by the author in Oklahoma City, OK, February 24–25, 2005. Xu served in the PLA and participated in the Sino-Vietnamese War in the spring of 1979.

46. According to Xu, the "glory bomb" was not just for infantry troops. All of the Chinese who went to Vietnam during the 1979 war and other military actions in the 1980s carried this suicide device, including nurses, doctors, and officers (Xu, interviews by the author).

# Bibliography

CHINESE-LANGUAGE SOURCES

*Archives, Manuscripts, and Collected Military Papers*

Archives Department, PRC Foreign Affairs Ministry, Beijing.

CCP Central Archives, comps. *Zhonggong zhongyang wenjian xuanji, 1921–49* [Selected documents of the CCP Central Committee, 1921–49]. 18 vols. Beijing: Zhonggong zhongyang dangxiao chubanshe, 1989–92.

CCP Central Archives, Central Archival and Manuscript Research Division. "Guanyu zhongguo renmin zhiyuanjun chudong chaoxian zuozhan de yizu dianwen [CCP telegrams for the CPVF to fight the war in Korea]." *Dang de wenxian* [Party archives and documents] 5 (2000): 1–11.

———. "Mao Zedong tan zhongguo guanyu kangmei yuanchao baojia weiguo de jueding [Mao's conversation on China's decision on the WRUSAK]." *Dang de wenxian* [Party archives and documents]. 5 (2000): 113–30.

CCP Central Archives, Central Archival and Manuscript Research Division, and CCP Organization Department, comps. *Zhongguo gongchandang zuzhishi ziliao, 1921–97* [Documents of the CCP organization's history, 1921–97]. 14 vols. Beijing: Zhonggong dangshi chubanshe, 2000.

Chen Yi. *Chen Yi junshi wenxuan* [Selected military papers of Chen Yi]. Beijing: Jiefangjun chubanshe, 1996.

Chou, Hsiu-huan, ed. *Zhanhou waijiao shiliao huibian: hanzhan yu fangong yishi pian* [Documentary collection: foreign affairs of postwar Taiwan; the Korean War and Chinese Communist defectors]. 3 vols. Taipei: Academia Historica, 2005.

He Long. *He Long junshi wenxuan* [Selected military papers of He Long]. Beijing: Jiefangjun chubanshe, 1989.

Heilongjiang Provincial Archives, Harbin, Heilongjiang, China.

Liaoning Provincial Archives, Shenyang, Liaoning, China.

Liu Bocheng. *Liu Bocheng junshi wenxuan* [Selected military papers of Liu Bocheng]. Beijing: Jiefangjun chubanshe, 1992.

Liu Shaoqi. *Jianguo yilai Liu Shaoqi wengao, 1949–52* [Liu Shaoqi's manuscripts since the founding of the state, 1949–52]. 4 vols. Beijing: Zhongyang wenxian chubanshe, 2005.

Mao Zedong. *Jianguo yilai Mao Zedong junshi wengao* [Mao Zedong's military manuscripts since the founding of the PRC]. 3 vols. Beijing: Junshi kexue chubanshe and Zhongyang wenxian chubanshe, 2010.

———. *Jianguo yilai Mao Zedong wengao, 1949–76* [Mao Zedong's manuscripts since the founding of the state, 1949–76]. 13 vols. Beijing: Zhongyang wenxian chubanshe, 1989–93.

———. *Mao Zedong junshi wenji* [Collected military works of Mao Zedong]. 6 vols. Beijing: Junshi kexue chubanshe, 1993.

———. *Mao Zedong junshi wenxuan: neibuben* [Selected military papers of Mao Zedong: internal edition]. 2 vols. Beijing: Jiefangjun zhanshi chubanshe, 1981.

———. *Mao Zedong wenji* [Collected works of Mao Zedong). 8 vols. Beijing: Renmin chubanshe, 1993–99.

———. *Mao Zedong xuanji* [Selected works of Mao Zedong]. 5 vols. Beijing: Renmin chubanshe, 1977–78.

*Nanfangjiu dangshi ziliao* [Party history records of the CCP Southern Bureau]. Chongqing, China: Chongqing renmin chubanshe, 1986.

Nie Rongzhen. *Nie Rongzhen junshi wenxuan* [Selected military papers of Nie Rongzhen]. Beijing: Jiefangjun chubanshe, 1992.

Peng Dehuai. *Peng Dehuai junshi wenxuan* [Selected military papers of Peng Dehuai]. Beijing: Zhongyang wenxian chubanshe, 1988.

ROC Ministry of Foreign Affairs Archives. "Anti-Communist POW Files." Taipei.

Shen Zhihua, trans. and ed. *Chaoxian zhanzheng: eguo danganguan de jiemi wenjian* [The Korean War: declassified documents from Russian archives]. 3 vols. Taipei: Zhongyang yanjiuyuan, 2003.

Wang Jinshan. *Wang Jinshan wenji* [Collected papers of Wang Jinshan]. Beijing: Junshi kexue chubanshe, 1992.

Xinhuashe. *Xinhuashe wenjian ziliao huibian* [A collection of documentary materials of the New China News Agency]. Beijing: Xinhuashe, n.d.

Xu Xiangqian. *Xu Xiangqian junshi wenxuan* [Selected military ppers of Xu Xiangqian]. Beijing: Jiefangjun chubanshe, 1992.

*Zhonggong zhongyang Nanjingjiu: zhonggong lishi ziliao* [The Nanjing Bureau of the CCP Central Committee: CCP historical documents]. Beijing: Zhonggong zhongyang dangshi chubanshe, 1990.

Zhou Enlai. *Zhou Enlai junshi wenxun* [Selected military papers of Zhou Enlai]. 4 vols. Beijing: Renmin chubanshe, 1997.

Zhu De. *Zhu De junshi wenxuan* [Selected military papers of Zhu De]. Beijing: Jiefangjun chubanshe, 1986.

### Official Chronicles, Recollections, and Memoirs

Bo Yibo. *Ruogan zhongda juece yu shijian de huigu* [Recollections of certain important decisions and events]. 2 vols. Beijing: Zhonggong zhongyang dangxiao chubanshe, 1991.

CCP Central Archival and Manuscript Research Division. *Mao Zedong nianpu, 1893–1949* [A chronological record of Mao Zedong, 1893–1949]. Three vols. Beijing: Zhongyang wenxian chubanshe, 1993.

———. *Mao Zedong zhuan, 1893–1976* [Biography of Mao Zedong, 1893–1976]. Two vols. Beijing. Zhongyang wenxian chubanshe, 1996.

———. *Zhou Enlai nianpu, 1949–76* [A chronological record of Zhou Enlai, 1949–76]. Three vols. Beijing: Zhongyang wenxian chubanshe, 1997.

————. *Zhu De nianpu, 1886–1976* [A chronological record of Zhu De, 1886–1976]. Beijing: Renmin chubanshe, 1986.

Chai Chengwen. *Banmendian tanpan jishi* [The true Story of the Panmunjom negotiations]. Beijing: Shishi chubanshe, 2000.

Chai Chengwen and Zhao Yongtian. *Banmendian tanpan* [The Panmunjom negotiations]. 2nd ed. Beijing: Jiefangjun chubanshe, 1992.

China National Military Museum, ed. *Kangmei yuanchao zhanzheng jishi* [A chronological record of the WRUSAK]. Beijing: Jiefangjun chubanshe, 2008.

Du Ping. *Zai zhiyuanjun zongbu: Du Ping huiyilu* [At the CPVF General HQ: memoirs of Du Ping]. Beijing: Jiefangjun chubanshe, 1989.

He Zongguang. *Wo zai chaoxian zhanchang: 1950–53* [I was there: the Korean battleground, 1950–53]. Beijing: Changzheng chubanshe, 2011.

Hong Xuezhi. *Hong Xuezhi huiyilu* [Memoirs of Hong Xuezhi]. Beijing: Jiefangjun chubanshe, 2007.

————. *Kangmei yuanchao zhanzheng huiyi* [Recollections of the WRUSAK]. Beijing: Jiefangjun wenyi chubanshe, 1990.

Jiang Yonghui. *38 jun zai chaoxian* [The Thirty-Eighth Army in Korea]. 2nd ed. Shenyang, China: Liaoning renmin chubanshe, 2009.

Liu Shufa. *Chen Yi nianpu, 1901–72* [A chronological record of Chen Yi, 1901–72]. 2 vols. Beijing: Renmin chubanshe, 1995.

Nie Rongzhen. *Nie Rongzhen huiyilu* [Memoirs of Nie Rongzhen]. 2 vols. Beijing: Jiefangjun chubanshe, 1984.

Peng Dehuai. *Peng Dehuai zishu* [Autobiography of Peng Dehuai]. Beijing: Renmin chubanshe, 1981.

Political Department of the PLA 75200 Unit, ed. *Yuxue chaoxian: 42 jun laozhanshi kangmei yuanchao qinliji* [Bleeding Korea: personal experiences of Fortieth Army veterans in the WRUSAK). Beijing: Jiefangjun chubanshe, 2001.

ROC Ministry of Defense. *Guojun houqin shi* [Logistics history of the GMD armed forces). 8 vols. Taipei: Guofangbu shizheng bianyiju, 1992.

Shi Zhe. *Zai lishi juren shenbian* [At the side of historical giants]. Beijing: Zhongyang wenxian chubanshe, 1991.

Wang Hai. *Wode zhandou shengya* [My military career]. Beijing: Zhongyang wenxian chubanshe, 2000.

Wang Yan et al. *Peng Dehuai nianpu, 1898–1974* [A chronological record of Peng Dehuai, 1898–1974]. Beijing: Renmin chubanshe, 1998.

Wu Ruilin. *Kangmei yuanchao zhong de 42 jun* [The Forty-Second Army in the WRUSAK]. Beijing: Jincheng chubanshe, 1995.

————. *Wu Ruilin huiyilu* [Memoirs of Wu Ruilin. 3 vols. Beijing: Zhongguo dangan chubanshe, 1995.

Wu Xinquan. *Chaoxian zhanchang 1,000 tian: 39 jun zai chaoxian* [One thousand days on the Korean battleground: the Thirty-Ninth Army in Korea]. Shenyang, China: Liaoning renmin chubanshe, 1996.

Xiao Jinguang. *Xiao Jinguang huiyilu* [Memoirs of Xiao Jinguang]. 2 vols. Beijing: Jiefangjun chubanshe, 1988.

Xu Xiangqian. *Lishi de huigu* [History in retrospect]. Beijing: Jiefangjun chubanshe, 1988.

Yang Dezhi. *Weile heping* [For the sake of peace]. Beijing: Changzheng chubanshe, 1987.

————. *Yang Dezhi huiyilu* [Memoirs of Yang Dezhi]. Beijing: Jiefangjun chubanshe, 1992.

Yang Di. *Zai zhiyuanjun silingbu de suiyueli: xianwei renzhi de zhenshi qingkuang* [My years at the CPVF General HQ: untold true stories]. Beijing: Jiefangjun chubanshe, 1998.

Zhang Zeshi."Wo cengshi zhiyuanjun zhanfu daibiao [I served as the CPVF POWs' representative]." In *Jimidang* [Classified files], edited by *Fenghuang zhoukan* [Phoenix weekly], 2:335–39. Beijing: Zhongguo fazhan chubanshe, 2011.

Zhou Enlai Military Record Compilation Team. *Zhou Enlai junshi huodong jishi* [Zhou Enlai military affairs record]. 2 vols. Beijing: Zhongyang wenxian chubanshe, 2000.

### Books, Articles, and Other Materials

CCP History Research Division. *Zhongguo gongchandang lishi dashiji, 1919–87* [Major events in the history of the CCP, 1919–87]. Beijing: Renmin chubanshe, 1989.

Chai Chengwen, Huang Zhengji, and Zhang Changjin. *Sanda tupuo: xin zhongguo zouxiang shijie de baogao* [The three breakthroughs: a report on how new China entered the world]. Beijing: Jiefangjun chubanshe, 1994.

Chen Geng Zhuan Compilation Team. *Chen Geng zhuan* [Biography of Chen Geng]. Beijing: Dangdai zhongguo chubanshe, 2007.

Chen Hui. "18 wan kangmei yuanchao lishi xunzong [Tracing the 180,000 martyrs of the WRUSAK]." In *Kangmei yuanchao: 60 nianhou de huimou* [The WRUSAK: a retrospective look after 60 years], edited by Zhang Xingxing, 127–38. Beijing: Dangdai zhongguo chubanshe, 2011.

Chen Zhonglong, ed. *60 jun rencai: rencai shi zheyang zhujiu de* [The elite of the Sixtieth Army: their successful stories]. Beijing: Zhongguo youyi chubanshe, 2005.

————. *Guangrong de linfenlu* [The glorious brigade of Linfen]. Beijing: Zhonggong dangshi chubanshe, 2007.

————, ed. *Kangmei yuanchao zhanzheng lun* [On the WRUSAK]. Beijing: Junshi wenyi chubanshe, 2001.

China National Military Museum, ed. *Kangmei yuanchao zhanzheng fengyunlu* [The operational files of the WRUSAK]. Beijing: Huacheng chubanshe, 1999.

Chu Feng. "50 niandai zhongsu junshi guanxi yanjiu [Sino-Soviet military relations during the 1950s]." PhD diss., Party Academy of the CCP Central Committee, 2006.

Chu Yun. *Chaoxian zhanzheng neimu quangongkai* [Declassifying the Korean War]. Beijing: Shishi chubanshe, 2005.

Compilation Committee. "Chaoxian zhanzheng zhong zai meifang de zhongguo zhanfu jizhongying qingkuang zongshu [The overview of the CPVF POWs' condition in the UNF camps during the Korean War]." In *Meijun jizhongying qinliji* [Personal stories of the CPVF POWs in UN/U.S. camps], edited by Zhang Zeshi, 1–14. Beijing: Zhongguo wenshi chubanshe, 1996.

Composition Committee, ed. *38 xian shang de jiaofeng: kangmei yuanchao zhanzheng jishi* [Fighting over the 38th Parallel: the recorded truth of the WRUSAK]. Beijing: Jiefangjun wenyi chubanshe, 2010.

*Contemporary China* Editorial Department. *Xu Xiangqian zhuan* [Biography of Xu Xiangqian]. Beijing: Dangdai zhongguo chubanshe, 1991.

Cui Xianghua and Chen Dapeng. *Tao Yong jiangjun zhuan* [Biography of General Tao Yong]. Beijing: Jiefangjun chubanshe, 1989.

Da Ying. *Zhiyuanjun zhanfu jishi: xuji* [Voices from the CPVF POWs: concluding volume]. Beijing: Zhongguo qingnian chubanshe, 1993.

Deng Feng. "Kangmei yuanchao yanjiu zongshu, 1996–2006 [Korean War history research in China, 1996–2006]." Paper presented at the International Cold War Conference, Changchun, Jilin, China, July 14–17, 2006.

Feng Xianzhi and Li Jie. *Mao Zedong yu kangmei yuanchao* [Mao Zedong: resisting the U.S. and aiding Korea]. Beijing: Zhongyang wenxian chubanshe, 2000.

*Fenghuang zhoukan* [Phoenix Weekly], ed. *Jimidang* [Classified files]. 3 vols. Beijing: Zhongguo fazhan chubanshe, 2011.

Ge Chumin, ed. *Laozhanshi yishi* [Personal stories of the veterans]. Beijing: Zhongguo duiwai fanyi chuban gongsi, 2000.

Gu Cheng et al., trans. and eds. *Kangmei yuanchao zhanzheng: dijun shiliao* [ROK Army Archives: the Korean War]. 5 vols. Harbin, China: Heilongjiang chaoxian minzu chubanshe, 1988–90.

Guo Baoheng and Hu Zhiyuan. *Chipin hanjiang nanbei: 42 jun zai chaoxian* [Fighting over the Han River: the Forty-Second Army in Korea]. Shenyang, China: Liaoning renmin chubanshe, 1996.

Guo Weijing. *Diyideng zhanfuying: lianheguojun zhanfu zai chaoxian* [The first-class POW camps: the UN POWs in Korea]. Beijing: Shijie zhishi chubanshe, 1999.

Han Huaizhi. *Dandai zhongguo jundui de junshi gongzuo* [Contemporary Chinese military affairs]. 2 vols. Beijing: Zhongguo shehui kexue chubanshe, 1989.

He Ming. *Zhongcheng: zhiyuanjun zhanfu guilai renyuan de kanke jingli* [Loyalty: the hard time for the CPVF POWs after their repatriation]. Beijing: Zhongguo wenshi chubanshe, 1998.

Hu Haipo and Yu Hongjun. *Genzhe Mao Zedong da tianxia* [Follow Mao Zedong to seize state power]. Changsha, China: Hunan renmin chubanshe, 2009.

Jiang Tingyu. *Jiedu kangmei yuanchao zhanzheng* [Understanding the WRUSAK]). Beijing: Jiefangjun chubanshe, 2011.

Li Changjiu and Shi Lujia, eds. *Zhongmei guanxi erbainian* [History of Sino-American relations]. Beijing: Xinhua chubanshe, 1984.

Li Feng. *Juezhan chaoxian* [The showdown in Korea]. Wuhan, China: Changjiang wenyi chubanshe, 2010.

Li Hongjie. *Zhengyi de zhanzheng, weida de jingshen* [The just war and great inspiration]. Guangzhou: Guangdong renmin chubanshe, 2001.

Li Qingshan. *Zhiyuanjun yuanchao jishi* [The CPVF records of aiding Korea]. Beijing: Zhonggong dangshi chubanshe, 2008.

Li Song. "Dandong: zhiyuanjun yinghun de zhuixun [Dandong: search for the spirit of the CPVF martyrs]." In *Kangmei yuanchao: 60 nianhou de huimou* [The WRUSAK: a retrospective look after 60 years], edited by Zhang Xingxing, 139–45. Beijing: Dangdai zhongguo chubanshe, 2011.

Li Ying. *Jiekai zhanzheng xumu de xianfeng: 40 jun zai chaoxian* [Vanguard of the early actions in the war: the Fortieth Army in Korea]. Shenyang, China: Liaoning renmin chubanshe, 1996.

Li Ying et al. *40 jun zai chaoxian* [The Fortieth Army in Korea]. Shenyang, China: Liaoning renmin chubanshe, 2010.

Liu Zheng. *Chaoxian: 1950* [Korea: 1950]. Beijing: Renmin chubanshe, 2010.

Luan Kechao. *Xue yu huo de jiaoliang: kangmei yuanchao jishi* [The contest: blood vs. fire; the record of resisting America and aiding Korea]. Beijing: Huayi chubanshe, 2008.

Luo Xuanyou. *Chaoxian zhanzheng: zhengzhan jishi* [The Korean War: the battle records]. Beijing: Jiefangjun wenyi chubanshe, 2007.

Luo Yinwen. *Deng Hua jiangjun zhuan* [Biography of Gen. Deng Hua]. Beijing: Zhongyang dangxiao chubanshe, 1995.

Military History Research Division, CAMS. *Junqi piaopiao: xinzhongguo 50 nian junshi dashi shushi, 1949–99* [PLA flag fluttering: the facts about China's major military events in the past fifty Years, 1949–99]. 2 vols. Beijing: Jiefangjun chubanshe, 1999.

———. *Kangmei yuanchao zhanzhengshi* [History of the WRUSAK]. 3 vols. Beijing: Junshi kexue chubanshe, 2000.

———. *Zhongguo renmin jiefangjun de qishinian, 1927–97* [Seventy years of the PLA, 1927–97). Beijing: Junshi kexue chubanshe, 1997.

———. *Zhongguo renmin zhiyuanjun kangmei yuanchao zhanshi* [Combat experience of the CPVF in the WRUSAK]. Beijing: Junshi kexue chubanshe, 1990.

Nie Rongzhen."Jianxin qibu de woguo wodan shiye" [A rough start for China's nuclear and missile programs." In *Liangdan yixing: zhongguo hewuqi daodan weixing yu feichuan quanjishi* [Two bombs and one star: a complete record of China's nuclear weapons, missiles, satellites, and spaceships], ed. PLA General Armaments Department, 2–21. Beijing: Jiuzhou chubanshe, 2001.

Nie Rongzhen Biography Compilation Team. *Nie Rongzhen zhuan* [Biography of Nie Rongzhen]. Beijing: Dangdai zhongguo chubanshe, 2006.

Pei Jianzhang. *Zhonghua renmin gongheguo waijiaoshi, 1949–56* [Diplomatic history of the People's Republic of China, 1949–56]. Beijing: Shijie zhishi chubanshe, 1994.

Peng Dehuai Biography Compilation Team. *Yige zhenzheng de ren: Peng Dehuai* [A real man: Peng Dehuai]. Beijing: Renmin chubanshe, 1994.

PLA General Armaments Department, ed. *Liangdan yixing: zhongguo hewuqi daodan weixing yu feichuan quanjishi* [Two bombs and one star: a complete record of China's nuclear weapons, missiles, satellites, and spaceships]. Beijing: Jiuzhou chubanshe, 2001.

PLA History Archives Compilation Committee, ed. *Paobing* [The artillery force]. Beijing: Jiefangjun chubanshe, 1999.

Political Department of the PLA 75200 Unit, ed. *Yuxue chaoxian: 42 jun laozhanshi kangmei yuanchao qinliji* [Bleeding Korea: the personal experiences of the Fortieth Army Veterans in the WRUSAK]. Beijing: Jiefangjun chubanshe, 2001.

Political Tasks Research Division, CAMS. *Zhongguo gongchandang zhengzhi gongzuo qishinian* [Seventy years of the CCP's political work in the Chinese military]. 6 vols. Beijing: Jiefangjun chubanshe, 1992.

Qi Dexue. "Guanyu kangmei yuanchao zhanzheng de jige wenti [Several issues on the WRUSAK]." *Zhonggong dangshi yanjiu* [Studies on CCP history] 1 (1998): 65–82.

———. *Ni buliaojie de chaoxian zhanzheng* [The Korean War you don't know].
Shenyang, China: Liaoning renmin chubanshe, 2011.

Shen Xingyi. "Yiwan siqian ge zhengren: hanzhan shiqi 'fangong yishi' zhi yanjiu [14,000 witnesses: studies of the "anti-Communist heroes" from the Korean War]." Master's thesis, National Taiwan Normal University, 1996.

Shen Zhihua. "Kangmei yuanchao zhanzheng zhong de sulian kongjun [The Soviet Air Force in the WRUSAK]." *Zhonggong dangshi yanjiu* [Studies on CCP history] 2 (2000): 19–32.

———. *Mao Zedong, Stalin, he chaoxian zhanzheng* [Mao Zedong, Stalin, and the Korean War]. Guangzhou: Guangdong renmin chubanshe, 2004.

Shuang Shi. *Kaiguo diyi zhan: kangmei yuanchao zhanzheng quanjing jishi* [The first war since the founding of the state: the complete story of the WRUSAK]. 2 vols. Beijing: Zhonggong dangshi chubanshe, 2004.

Tan Jingjiao. *Kangmei yuanchao zhanzheng* [The WRUSAK]. Beijing: Zhongguo shehui kexue chubanshe, 1990.

Tan Zheng. *Zhongguo renmin zhiyuanjun renwulu* [Veterans' profile of the CPVF]. Beijing: Zhonggong dangshi chubanshe, 1992.

Tao Wenzhao. *Zhongmei guanxishi; 1949–72* [PRC-U.S. Relations, 1949–72]. Shanghai: Shanghai renmin chubanshe, 1999.

Tian Fuzi. *Zhongyeu zhanzheng jishilu* [Factual records of the Sino-Vietnam War]. Beijing: Jiefangjun wenyi chubanshe, 2004.

Tian Yi, ed. *Chaoxian zhanchang qinliji* [Personal accounts of the Korean battleground]. Wuhan, China: Changjiang wenyi chubanshe, 2011.

Wang Dinglie and Lin Hu. *Dangdai Zhongguo kongjun* [Contemporary Chinese Air Force]. Beijing: Shehui kexue chubanshe, 1989.

Wang Hechuan. *Zhongguo dadi shang de jufeng: 40 jun zhengzhan jingli* [The hurricane over China: war experiences of the Fortieth Army]. Beijing: Jiefangjun wenyi chubanshe, 2004.

Wang Shuzeng. *Juezhan chaoxian: chaoxian zhanchang shi wojun tong meijun jiaoliang de lianbingchang* [The showdown in Korea: the battleground for a competition between the Chinese army and American army]. Beijing: Jiefangjun wenyi chubanshe, 2007.

———. *Yuandong chaoxian zhanzheng* [The Korean War in the Far East]. 2 vols. Beijing: Jiefangjun wenyi chubanshe, 2000.

———. *Zhongguo renmin zhiyuanjun zhengzhan jishi* [The true story of the CPVF's war experience]. Beijing: Jiefangjun wenyi, 2001.

Wang Suhong and Wang Yubin. *Kongzhan zai chaoxian* [The air war in Korea]. Beijing: Jiefangjun wenyi chubanshe, 1992.

Wang Wenrong. "Daixu: xuexi guanche Jiang zhuxi zhongda zhanlue cixiang [Introduction: studying and carrying out President Jiang's important strategic thoughts]." In Sun Kejia, *Zhongguo tese de junshi biange* [A revolution of military affairs with Chinese characteristics], 1–10. Beijing: Changzheng chubanshe, 2003.

Wang Yan et al. *Peng Dehuai zhuan* [Biography of Peng Dehuai]. Beijing: Dangdai zhongguo chubanshe, 1993.

Wang Yongping. "Diwuci zhanyi jingyan jiaoxun dui women de qishi [Our understanding of the lessons and experience of the Fifth Offensive Campaign]." In *Kangmei yuanchao zhanzhenglun* [On the WRUSAK], edited by Chen Zhonglong, 257–64. Beijing: Junshi wenyi chubanshe, 2001.

Wang Yuqing. "Mao Zedong he wo yeye Wang Jifan de tanhua [Mao Zedong's conversation with my grandfather Wang Jifan]." *Guandong zhuojia* [Authors from northeast China] 9 (2003): 1–21.

———. "Mao Zedong yu Wang Jifan he Zhou Shizhao de tanhua [Mao's conversations with Wang Jifan and Zhou Shizhao on October 27, 1950]." *Junshi lishi* [Military history] 11 (2001): 73–124.

War History Division, NDU. *Zhongguo renmin jiefangjun zhanshi jianbian* [A concise history of the PLA revolutionary war]. Beijing: Jiefangjun chubanshe, 2001.

———. *Zhongguo renmin zhiyuanjun zhanshi jianbian* [A concise history of the CPVF war-fighting]. Beijing: Jiefangjun chubanshe, 1992.

Xie Lifu. *Chaoxian zhanzheng shilu* [Field records of the Korean War]. 2 vols. Beijing: Shijie zhishi chubanshe, 1993.

*Xinghuo liaoyuan* Composition Department. *Zhongguo renmin jiefangjun jiangshuai minglu* [Marshals and generals of the PLA]. 3 vols. Beijing: Jiefangjun chubanshe, 1987–92

Xiong Guangkai. *Guoji zhanlue yu xin junshi biange* [International strategy and revolution in military affairs]. Beijing: Qinghua daxue chubanshe, 2003.

Xu Longnan. "Chaoxian zhanzheng zhong zhuanru chaoxian renminjun de zhongguo chaoxianzu canzhan junren caifanglu [Interviews with ethnic Korean soldiers in China who joined the NKPA during the Korean War]." *Lengzhan guojishi yanjiu* [Cold War international history studies] 11 (2011): 117–46.

Xu Yaguang. "Jianku de beiche xingcheng [The difficult withdrawal to the north]." In *Laozhanshi yishi* [Personal stories of the veterans], edited by Ge Chumin, 86–91. Beijing: Zhongguo duiwai fanyi chuban gongsi, 2000.

Xu Yan. *Diyici jiaoliang: kangmei yuanchao zhanzheng de lishi huigu yu fansi* [The first encounter: a historical retrospective of the WRUSAK]. Beijing: Zhongguo guangbo dianshi chubanshe, 1990.

———. *Junshijia Mao Zedong* [Mao Zedong as a Military Leader]. Beijing: Zhongyang wenxian chubanshe, 1995.

———. *Mao Zedong yu kangmei yuanchao zhanzheng* [Mao Zedong and the WRUSAK]. 2nd ed. Beijing: Jiefangjun chubanshe, 2006.

Xu Yipeng. *Cuojue: 180 shi chaoxian shoucuoji* [Miscalculation: the setback of the 180th Division in Korea]. Nanjing, China: Jiangsu renmin chubanshe, 1997.

———. *Zhihu: chaoxian tingzhan gaocheng juedoulu* [A straight curve: the leaders' struggle over the Korean armistice]. Nanjing, China: Jiangsu renmin chubanshe, 1997.

Yan Xinning. *Wei Jie zhongjiang* [Lt. Gen. Wei Jie]. Beijing: Jiefangjun wenyi chubanshe, 2005.

Yang Fengan and Wang Tiancheng. *Beiwei 38 duxian: Peng Dehuai yu chaoxian zhanzheng* [The north latitude 38th Parallel: Peng Dehuai and the Korean War]. Beijing: Zhongyang wenxian chubanshe, 2009.

Yang Guoyu. *Dangdai Zhongguo haijun* [Contemporary Chinese navy]. Beijing: Zhongguo shehui kexue chubanshe, 1987.

Yang Qinghua. "Zhongguo renmin zhiyuanjun houqin sixiang de xiangcheng yu fazhan [Establish and develop the CPVF's logistics conception]." In *Kangmei yuanchao zhanzhenglun* [On the WRUSAK], edited by Chen Zhonglong, 345–51. Beijing: Junshi wenyi chubanshe, 2001.

Yao Youzhi and Li Qingshan. *Zhiyuanjun yongcuo qiangdi de 10 da zhanyi* [The CPVF's ten major battles against a strong enemy]. Shenyang, China: Baishan chubanshe, 2009.

Ye Yumeng. *Chubing chaoxian: kangmei yuanchao lishi jishi* [A true history of China's entry into the Korean War]. Beijing: Shiyue wenxue chubanshe, 1989.

Yu Wei and Wu Zhifei. *Women kuaguo yalujiang* [We cross the Yalu River]. Beijing: Zhonggong dangshi chubanshe, 2010.

Yuan Xi. "Zhenxiang [The truth]." *Suibi* [Daily records], no. 6 (1999): 1–24.

Zhang Aiping. *Zhongguo renmin jiefangjun* [The Chinese People's Liberation Army]. 2 vols. Beijing: Dangdai zhongguo chubanshe, 1994.

Zhang Baijia and Niu Jun, eds. *Lengzhan yu zhongguo* [The Cold War and China]. Beijing: Shijie zhishi chubanshe, 2002.

Zhang Songshan. *Tanpai: zhengduo Shangganling jishi* [The showdown: the true story of the Battle of Shangganling]. Nanjing, China: Jiangsu renmin chubanshe, 1998.

Zhang Xingxing, ed. *Kangmei yuanchao: 60 nianhou de huimou* [The WRUSAK: a retrospective look after 60 years]. Beijing: Dangdai zhongguo chubanshe, 2011.

Zhang Xiuping, Mao Yuanyou, and Huang Pumin. *Yingxiang zhongguo de yibaici zhanzheng* [The hundred battles that shaped China]. Nanning, China: Guangxi renmin chubanshe, 2003.

Zhang Zeshi. "Wo cengshi zhiyuanjun zhanfu daibiao" [I served as the CPVF POWs' representative]. In *Jimidang* [Classified files], ed. *Fenghuang zhoukan* [Phoenix weekly], 2:338–39. Beijing: Zhongguo fazhan chubanshe, 2011.

Zhao Jianli and Liang Yuhong. *Fenghuo 38 xian: diwuci zhanyi zhanshi baogao* [The flames of battle raging across the 38th Parallel: combat report on the fifth campaign]. Beijing: Junshi kexue chubanshe, 2007.

Zhao Shaoquan. *Xinbian zhongguo xiandaishi* [New history of modern China]. 3 vols. Nanchang, China: Jiangxi renmin chubanshe, 1987.

Zhao Yihong. *27 jun chuanqi* [The legacy of the Twenty-Seventh Army). Jilin, China: Jilin renmin chubanshe, 1995.

Zhou Zhong. *Kangmei yuanchao zhanzheng huoqinshi jianbianben* [A concise history of the logistics in the WRUSAK]. Beijing: Jindun chubanshe, 1993.

Zhu Shiliang. *Peng Dehuai zai chaoxian zhanchang* [Peng Dehuai in the battleground of Korea]. Shenyang, China: Liaoning renmin chubanshe, 1996.

## ENGLISH-LANGUAGE SOURCES

### Archives, Documents, Memoirs, and Papers

Acheson, Dean. *Present at the Creation: My Years in the State Department*. New York: Norton, 1969.

CCP Central Military Commission. "The CMC Orders to Defend the Northeast Borders, July 13 July, 1950." In *Chinese Communist Foreign Policy and the Cold War in Asia: New Documentary Evidence, 1944–50*, translated and edited by Shuguang Zhang and Jian Chen, 156. Chicago: Imprint, 1996.

———. "Order on the Formation of the Chinese People's Volunteer Force, October 8, 1950." In *Chinese Communist Foreign Policy and the Cold War in Asia: New Documentary Evidence, 1944–50*, translated and edited by Shuguang Zhang and Jian Chen, 164–65. Chicago: Imprint, 1996.

———. "Telegram, CCP Central Military Commission to Gao Gang, August 5, 1950." In *Chinese Communist Foreign Policy and the Cold War in Asia: New Documentary Evidence, 1944–50*, translated and edited by Shuguang Zhang and Jian Chen, 157. Chicago: Imprint, 1996.

Deng Xiaoping. *Selected Works of Deng Xiaoping*. 3 vols. Beijing: Foreign Languages Press, 1994.

Eisenhower, Dwight D. *Mandate for Change, 1953–56: The White House Years*. Garden City, NY: Doubleday, 1963.

Eisenhower Papers; John Foster Dulles Papers. Dwight Eisenhower Library. Abilene, KS.

Farrar-Hockley, Anthony. *The Edge of the Sword*. London: Frederick Muller, 1954.

Hurley Papers. University of Oklahoma Library, Norman.

Khrushchev, Nikita. *Memoirs of Khrushchev*. Edited by Sergei Khrushchev. 2 vols. University Park: Pennsylvania State University Press, 2006.

Lei Yingfu. "The Establishment of the Northeast Border Defense Army, July 1950." Translated and edited by Xiaobing Li, Don Duffy, and Zujian Zhang. *Chinese Historians* 7, nos. 1–2 (1994): 124–29.

Mao Zedong. *Mao Zedong on Diplomacy*. Beijing: Foreign Languages Press, 1998.

———. "Mao's Dispatch of Chinese Troops to Korea: Forty-Six Telegrams, July–October 1950." Translated and edited by Xiaobing Li, Xi Wang, and Chen Jian. *Chinese Historians* 5, no. 1 (992): 63–87.

———. "Mao's Telegrams during the Korean War, October–December 1950." Translated and edited by Xiaobing Li and Glenn Tracy. *Chinese Historians* 5, no. 2 (1992): 65–85.

———. "Memorandum, Mao Zedong to Nie Rongzhen, July 7, 1950." In *Chinese Communist Foreign Policy and the Cold War in Asia: New Documentary Evidence, 1944–50*, translated and edited by Shuguang Zhang and Jian Chen, 156. Chicago: Imprint, 1996.

———. *Selected Works of Mao Tse-tung*. 4 vols. Beijing: Foreign Languages Press, 1977.

———. "Telegram to Chen Yi, October 12, 1950." In *Chinese Communist Foreign Policy and the Cold War in Asia: New Documentary Evidence, 1944–50*, translated and edited by Shuguang Zhang and Jian Chen, 168. Chicago: Imprint, 1996.

———. "Telegram to Chen Yi, October 14, 1950." In *Chinese Communist Foreign Policy and the Cold War in Asia: New Documentary Evidence, 1944–50*, translated and edited by Shuguang Zhang and Jian Chen, 169. Chicago: Imprint, 1996.

———. "Telegram to Deng Hua and Others, 9:00 PM, October 18, 1950." In *Chinese Communist Foreign Policy and the Cold War in Asia: New Documentary Evidence, 1944–50*, translated and edited by Shuguang Zhang and Jian Chen, 178–79. Chicago: Imprint, 1996.

———. "Telegram to Liu Shaoqi, 5:00 AM January 25, 1950." In *Chinese Communist Foreign Policy and the Cold War in Asia: New Documentary Evidence, 1944–50*, translated and edited by Shuguang Zhang and Jian Chen, 140–41. Chicago: Imprint, 1996.

———. "Telegram to Peng Dehuai and Deng Hua, 6:00 AM, October 25, 1950." In *Chinese Communist Foreign Policy and the Cold War in Asia: New Documentary Evidence, 1944–50*, translated and edited by Shuguang Zhang and Jian Chen, 191–92. Chicago: Imprint, 1996.

———. "Telegram to Peng Dehuai and Pak Il-yu, December 26, 1950." In *Chinese Communist Foreign Policy and the Cold War in Asia: New Documentary Evidence, 1944–50*, translated and edited by Shuguang Zhang and Jian Chen, 218–19. Chicago: Imprint.

———. "Telegram to Peng Dehuai, December 21, 1950." In *Chinese Communist Foreign Policy and the Cold War in Asia: New Documentary Evidence, 1944–50*, translated and edited by Shuguang Zhang and Jian Chen, 216–18. Chicago: Imprint, 1996.

———. "Telegram to Peng Dehuai, Deng Hua, and Pak Il-yu, November 18, 1950." In *Chinese Communist Foreign Policy and the Cold War in Asia: New Documentary Evidence, 1944–50*, translated and edited by Shuguang Zhang and Jian Chen, 205. Chicago: Imprint, 1996.

———. "Telegram to Peng Dehuai, October 23, 1950." In *Chinese Communist Foreign Policy and the Cold War in Asia: New Documentary Evidence, 1944–50*, translated and edited by Shuguang Zhang and Jian Chen, 183–84. Chicago: Imprint, 1996.

———. "Telegram to Zhou Enlai, October 13, 1950." In *Chinese Communist Foreign Policy and the Cold War in Asia: New Documentary Evidence, 1944–50,* translated and edited by Shuguang Zhang and Jian Chen, 168–69. Chicago: Imprint, 1996.

———. "Telegram to Zhou Enlai, October 14, 1950." In *Chinese Communist Foreign Policy and the Cold War in Asia: New Documentary Evidence, 1944–50,* translated and edited by Shuguang Zhang and Jian Chen, 169–71. Chicago: Imprint, 1996.

———. *The Writings of Mao Zedong, 1949–76,* edited by Michael Y. M. Kau and John K. Leung. 3 vols. New York: M. E. Sharpe, 1986–92.

Paik Sun-yup. *From Pusan to Panmunjom: Wartime Memoirs of the Republic of Korea's First Four-Star General.* Dulles, VA: Brassey's, 1992.

PRC Ministry of Defense. *White Papers of China's National Defense, 1998–2010.* 12 vols. Beijing: Foreign Languages Press, 2000–2012.

Ridgway, Matthew B. *The Korean War.* Garden City, NY: Doubleday, 1967.

*Selected Documents of the Fifteenth CCP National Congress.* Beijing: New Star Publishing House, 1997.

Shi Zhe. "Mao Zedong Comments on the Outbreak of the Korean War, June 25–28, 1950." In *Chinese Communist Foreign Policy and the Cold War in Asia: New Documentary Evidence, 1944–50,* translated and edited by Shuguang Zhang and Jian Chen, 153. Chicago: Imprint, 1996.

Staff of the Foreign Ministry of the Soviet Union. "Background Report on the Korean War, August 9, 1966." Translated by Kathryn Weathersby. *Journal of American–East Asian Relations* 2 (Winter 1993): 438–65.

U.S. Army. 45th Division Archives. "The Korean War Files: Records of 1951." 45th Division Museum, Oklahoma City, OK.

U.S. Central Intelligence Agency. *Foreign Relations of the United States: China, Korea, Vietnam, and Indochina, 1945–72.* 8 vols. Washington: Government Printing Office, 1982–89.

Weathersby, Kathryn, trans. and ed. "New Russian Documents on the Korean War." *Bulletin: Cold War International History Project,* nos. 6–7 (Winter 1995–96): 30–125.

Zhang, Shuguang, and Jian Chen, trans. and eds. *Chinese Communist Foreign Policy and the Cold War in Asia: New Documentary Evidence, 1944–50.* Chicago: Imprint, 1996.

### Books, Articles, and Other Materials

Appleman, Roy E. *Disaster in Korea: The Chinese Confront MacArthur.* College Station: Texas A & M University Press, 1989.

———. *South to the Naktong, North to the Yalu (June–November 1950), U.S. Army in the Korean War.* Washington: Office of the Chief of Military History and Government Printing Office, 1961.

Bernstein, Marc D. "Red Eclipse: Massive Attack; Korean War Killing Zone." *Military Heritage,* October 2011, 32–39.

Blair, Clay. *The Forgotten War: America in Korea, 1950–53.* New York: Times, 1987.

Black, Jeremy. *Rethinking Military History.* New York: Routledge, 2004.

Bowers, William T. Conclusion to *Striking Back: Combat in Korea, March–April 1951,* edited by William T. Bowers, 408–11. Lexington: University Press of Kentucky, 2010: 408–11.

———. "Korea and the Cold War." In *Striking Back: Combat in Korea, March–April 1951,* edited by William T. Bowers, 1–20. Lexington: University Press of Kentucky, 2010.

————. *The Line: Combat in Korea, January–February 1951.* Lexington: University Press of Kentucky, 2008.

————. "Operation Swing—The Push to the East." In *Striking Back: Combat in Korea, March–April 1951,* edited by William T. Bowers, 220–311. Lexington: University Press of Kentucky, 2010.

————, ed. *Striking Back: Combat in Korea, March–April 1951.* Lexington: University Press of Kentucky, 2010.

Breslin, Shaun. *Mao: Profiles in Power.* New York: Longman, 1998.

Carey, Charles W. *Living through the Korean War.* Detroit: Greenhaven, 2006.

Carlson, Lewis H. *Remembered Prisoners of a Forgotten War: An Oral History of Korean War POWs.* New York: St. Martin's, 2002.

Catchpole, Brian. *The Korean War, 1950–53.* New York: Carroll and Graf, 2000.

Chai Chengwen. "The Korean Truce Negotiations." In *Mao's Generals Remember Korea,* translated and edited by Xiaobing Li, Allan R. Millett, and Bin Yu, 184–232. Lawrence: University Press of Kansas, 2001.

Chang, Gordon H. *Friends and Enemies: The United States, China, and the Soviet Union.* Stanford: Stanford University Press, 1990.

Chang, Jung, and Jon Halliday. *Mao: The Unknown Story.* New York: Knopf, 2005.

Chen Jian. *China's Road to the Korean War: The Making of the Sino-American Confrontation.* New York: Columbia University Press, 1994.

————. *Mao's China and the Cold War.* Chapel Hill: University of North Carolina Press, 2001.

Chen Jian and Xiaobing Li. "China and the End of the Global Cold War." In *The Cold War: From Détente to the Soviet Collapse,* edited by Malcolm Muir Jr., 120–31. Lexington: Virginia Military Institute Press, 2006.

China Academy of Military Science. "The Unforgotten Korean War: Chinese Perspective and Appraisals." Unpublished manuscript, 2006.

Christensen, Thomas J. *Useful Adversaries; Grand Strategy, Domestic Mobilization, and Sino-American Conflict, 1947–58.* Princeton: Princeton University Press, 1996.

Cowley, Robert, ed. *The Cold War: A Military History.* New York: Random House, 2005.

Cornell, Brian R. "The Origins of the Human Wave Phenomenon in Chinese Military History and the Korean War (1950–53)." Paper written for "Non-Western Military History" class at Norwich University, 2011.

Crane, Conrad C. *American Airpower Strategy in Korea, 1950–53.* Lawrence: University Press of Kansas, 2000.

Cummings, Bruce. *The Origins of the Korean War.* 2 vols. Lawrence: University Press of Kansas, 1981 and 1990.

Domes, Jurgen. *Peng Te-huai: The Man and the Image.* London: C. Hurst, 1985.

Dreyer, Edward L. "Continuity and Change." In *A Military History of China,* updated ed., edited by David A. Graff and Robin Higham, 19–38. Lexington: University Press of Kentucky, 2012.

Du Ping. "Political Mobilization and Control." In *Mao's Generals Remember Korea,* translated and edited by Xiaobing Li, Allan R. Millett, and Bin Yu, 61–105. Lawrence: University Press of Kansas, 2001.

Ecker, Richard E. *Korean Battle Chronology: Unit-by-Unit United States Casualty Figures and Medal of Honor Citations.* Jefferson, NC: McFarland, 2005.

Elleman, Bruce A. *Modern Chinese Warfare, 1795–1989.* London: Routledge, 2001.

Evans, Ben. *Out in the Cold: Australia's Involvement in the Korean War, 1950–53.* Canberra, Australia: Department of Australians' Veterans' Affairs, 2010.

Fairbank, John K. "Introduction: The Varieties of the Chinese Military Experience," in *Chinese Ways in Warfare,* edited by John K. Fairbank and Frank A. Kierman Jr., 1–26. Cambridge: Harvard University Press, 1974.

Fairbank, John K., and Frank A. Kierman, Jr., eds. *Chinese Ways in Warfare.* Cambridge: Harvard University Press, 1974.

Farrar-Hockley, Anthony. *The British Part in the Korean War.* 2 vols. London: Her Majesty's Stationery Office, 1995.

Fehrenbach, T. R. *This Kind of War.* Dulles, VA: Potomac, 2008.

Finkelstein, David M. *Washington's Taiwan Dilemma, 1949–50: From Abandonment to Salvation.* Fairfax, VA: George Mason University Press, 1993.

Fleming, Thomas. "The Man Who Saved Korea." In *The Cold War: A Military History,* edited by Robert Cowley, 104–19. New York: Random House, 2005.

Foot, Rosemary. *The Practice of Power: U.S. Relations with China since 1949.* Oxford: Oxford University Press, 1997.

Futrell, George F. *The United States Air Force in the Korean War.* Washington: Office of Air Force History, 1983.

Gaddis, John Lewis. *The Cold War: A New History.* New York: Penguin, 2005.

Goncharov, Sergei N., John W. Lewis, and Xue Litai. *Uncertain Partners: Stalin, Mao, and the Korean War.* Stanford: Stanford University Press, 1993.

Goulden, Joseph C. *Korea: The Untold Story of the War.* New York: Times, 1982.

Graff, David A., and Robin Higham eds. *A Military History of China.* Updated ed. Lexington: University Press of Kentucky, 2012.

Gries, Peter Hays. *China's New Nationalism: Pride, Politics, and Diplomacy.* Berkeley: University of California Press, 2004.

Gugeler, Russell A. *Combat Actions in Korea.* Washington: Center of Military History, U.S. Army, 1987.

Halberstam, David. *The Coldest Winter: America and the Korean War.* New York: Hyperion, 2007.

Halliday, Jon. "Air Operation in Korea: The Soviet Side of the Story." In *A Revolutionary War: Korea and the Transformation of the Postwar World,* edited by William J. Williams, 141–63. Chicago: Imprint, 1993.

Hallion, Richard P. "The Air War in Korea: Coalition Air Power in the Context of Limited War." Paper presented at Korea: In from the Cold, Canberra, Australia, October 5–7, 2011.

Hanson, Thomas E. *Combat Ready? The Eighth U.S. Army on the Eve of the Korean War.* College Station: Texas A & M University Press, 2010.

Hanson, Victor. *Carnage and Culture: Landmark Battles in the Rise of Western Power.* New York: Anchor, 2002.

Hastings, Max. *The Korean War.* New York: Simon and Schuster, 1987.

He Di. "The Last Campaign to Unify China: The CCP's Unrealized Plan to Liberate Taiwan, 1949–50." In *Chinese Warfighting: The PLA Experience since 1949,* edited by Mark A. Ryan, David M. Finkelstein, and Michael A. McDevitt, 73–90. New York: M. E. Sharpe, 2003.

Hermes, Walter G. *Truce Tent and Fighting Front, U.S. Army in the Korean War.* Washington: Government Printing Office, 1988.

Hickey, Michael. *The Korean War: The West Confronts Communism*. New York: Overlook, 1999.

Higham, Robin, and David A. Graff. Introduction to *A Military History of China*, updated ed., edited by David A. Graff and Robin Higham, 1–18. Lexington: University Press of Kentucky, 2012.

Hong Xuezhi. "The CPVF's Combat and Logistics." In *Mao's Generals Remember Korea*, translated and edited by Xiaobing Li, Allan R. Millett, and Bin Yu, 106–138. Lawrence: University Press of Kansas, 2001.

Hunt, Michael H. *The Genesis of Chinese Communist Foreign Policy*. New York: Columbia University Press, 1996.

Huo, Hwei-ling."A Study of the Chinese Decision to Intervene in the Korean War." PhD diss., Columbia University, 1989.

Jencks, Harlan W. *From Muskets to Missiles: Politics and Professionalism in the Chinese Army, 1945–81*. Boulder, CO: Westview, 1982.

Joffe, Ellis. *The Chinese Army after Mao*. Cambridge: Harvard University Press, 1987.

———. *Party and Army: Professionalism and Political Control in the Chinese Officer Corps, 1948– 64*. Cambridge: Harvard University Press, 1967.

Johnston, Alastair Iain. *Cultural Realism: Strategic Culture and Grand Strategy in Chinese History*. Princeton: Princeton University Press, 1995.

Karmel, Solomon. *China and the People's Liberation Army*. New York: St. Martin's, 2000.

Kaufman, Burton I. *The Korean Conflict*. Westport, CT: Greenwood, 1999.

———. *The Korean War: Challenges in Crisis, Credibility, and Command*. 2nd ed. New York: McGraw-Hill, 1997.

Keegan, John. *A History of Warfare*. New York: Knopf, 1993.

Kennedy, Andrew B. "Military Audacity: Mao Zedong, Liu Shaoqi, and China's Adventure in Korea." In *History and Neorealism*, edited by Ernest May, Richard Rosecrance, and Zara Steiner, 201–27. Cambridge: Cambridge University Press, 2010.

Kinard, Jeff. "Human Wave Attacks." In *The Encyclopedia of the Korean War*, edited by Spencer C. Tucker, 1:343–44. 2nd ed. Santa Barbara, CA: ABC-CLIO, 2010.

Knox, Donald. *The Korean War: An Oral History*. 2 vols. San Diego, CA: Harcourt Brace Jovanovich, 1985–88.

Korean Institute of Military History, ROK Ministry of Defense. *The Korean War*. 3 vols. Seoul: Korean Institute of Military History, 1998.

Leckie, Robert. *Conflict: The History of the Korean War*. New York: Da Capo, 1996.

Lee Jong Kan. "A North Korean Officer's Story." In *Voices from the Korean War: Personal Stories of American, Korean, and Chinese Soldiers*, edited by Richard Peters and Xiaobing Li, 76–84. Lexington: University Press of Kentucky, 2004.

Lee, Jongsoo. *The Partition of Korea after World War II: A Global History*. New York: Palgrave Macmillan, 2006.

Li, Xiaobing. "China's Intervention and the CPVF Experience in the Korean War." In *The Korean War at Fifty: International Perspectives*, edited by Mark F. Wilkinson, 130–40. Lexington: Virginia Military Institute Press, 2004.

———. "Chinese Army in the Korean War, 1950–53." *New England Journal of History* 60, nos. 1–3 (2003–4): 276–92.

———. *Civil Liberties in China*. Santa Barbara, CA: ABC-CLIO, 2010.

———. *A History of the Modern Chinese Army*. Lexington: University Press of Kentucky, 2007.

———. "Military Ranks, People's Liberation Army." In *China at War: An Encyclopedia,* edited Xiaobing Li, 274–76. Santa Barbara, CA: ABC-CLIO, 2012.

———. "Nuclear Program." In *China at War: An Encyclopedia,* edited by Xiaobing Li, 328–32. Santa Barbara, CA: ABC-CLIO, 2012.

———. "PLA Attacks and Amphibious Operations during the Taiwan Strait Crises of 1954–55 and 1958." In *Chinese Warfighting: The PLA Experience since 1949,* edited by Mark A. Ryan, David M. Finkelstein, and Michael A. McDevitt, 143–72. New York: M. E. Sharpe, 2003.

———. "Truman and Taiwan: A U.S. Policy Change from Face to Faith." In *Northeast Asia and the Legacy of Harry S. Truman: Japan, China, and the Two Koreas,* edited by James I. Matray, 119–44. Kirksville, MO: Truman State University Press, 2012.

———. *Voices from the Vietnam War: Stories from American, Asian, and Russian Veterans.* Lexington: University Press of Kentucky, 2010.

Li, Xiaobing, and Hongshan Li, eds. *China and the United States: A New Cold War History.* Lanham, MD: University Press of America, 1998.

Li, Xiaobing, Allan R. Millett, and Bin Yu. Introduction to *Mao's Generals Remember Korea,* translated and edited by Xiaobing Li, Allan R. Millett, and Bin Yu, 1–8. Lawrence: University Press of Kansas, 2001.

———, trans. and eds. *Mao's Generals Remember Korea.* Lawrence: University Press of Kansas, 2001.

Li, Xiaoxiao. "Fourth Field Army." In *China at War: An Encyclopedia,* edited by Xiaobing Li, 126–28. Santa Barbara, CA: ABC-CLIO, 2012.

Lilley, James R., and David Shambaugh, eds. *China's Military Faces the Future.* New York: M. E. Sharpe, 1999.

Lovejoy, Charles, and Bruce Watson, eds. *China's Military Reforms.* Boulder, CO: Westview, 1986.

Luthi, Lorenz M. *The Sino-Soviet Split: Cold War in the Communist World.* Princeton: Princeton University Press, 2008.

Lynn, John A. *Battle: A History of Combat and Culture.* New York: Basic, 2008.

MacDonald, C. A. *Korea, the War before Vietnam.* New York: Free Press, 1987.

Mahoney, Kevin. *Formidable Enemies: The North Korean and Chinese Soldier in the Korean War.* Novato, CA: Presidio, 2001.

Malkasian, Carter. "Toward a Better Understanding of Attrition: The Korean and Vietnam Wars." *Journal of Military History* 68 (2004): 911–42.

Mansourov, Alexandre Yourievich. "Communist War Coalition Formation and the Origins of the Korean War." PhD diss., Columbia University, 1997.

McCullough, David. "Truman Fires MacArthur." In *The Cold War: A Military History,* edited by Robert Cowley, 71–103. New York: Random House, 2005.

McManus, John C. *The 7th Infantry Regiment: Combat in an Age of Terror; The Korean War through the Present.* New York: Tom Doherty, 2008.

Millett, Allan R. *The Korean War.* Washington: Potomac, 2007.

———. *The War for Korea, 1945–1950: A House Burning.* Lawrence: University Press of Kansas, 2005.

———. *The War for Korea, 1950–1951: They Came from the North.* Lawrence: University Press of Kansas, 2010.

———. *Their War for Korea: American, Asian, and European Combatants and Civilians, 1945–53.* Washington: Brassey's, 2002.

Mossman, Billy C. *U.S. Army in the Korean War: Ebb and Flow, November 1950–July 1951.* Washington: Army Center of Military History and Government Printing Office, 1990.

Mulhausen, Harold L. "The Chosin Reservoir: A Marine's Story." In *Voices from the Korean War: Personal Stories of American, Korean, and Chinese Soldiers,* edited by Richard Peters and Xiaobing Li, 97–116. Lexington: University Press of Kentucky, 2004.

Munroe, Clark C. *The Second U.S. Infantry Division in Korea, 1950–51.* Tokyo: Toppan, 1954.

Na, Jongnam. "Making Cold War Soldiers: The Americanization of the South Korean Army, 1945–55." PhD diss., University of North Carolina, Chapel Hill, 2006.

Nie Rongzhen. "Beijing's Decision to Intervene." In *Mao's Generals Remember Korea,* translated and edited by Xiaobing Li, Allan R. Millett, and Bin Yu, 38–60. Lawrence: University Press of Kansas, 2001.

Niu Jun."The Origins of the Sino-Soviet Alliance." In *Brothers in Arms: The Rise and Fall of the Sino-Soviet Alliance, 1945–63,* edited by Odd Arne Westad, 47–89. Washington: Woodrow Wilson Center Press, 1998.

O'Connell, William R. *The Thunderbird: A History of the U.S. 45th Infantry Division in Korea, 1951–53.* Tokyo: Toppan, 1954.

O'Dowd, Edward C. *Chinese Military Strategy in the Third Indochina War: The Last Maoist War.* London: Routledge, 2007.

Ohn, Chang-il. "The Joint Chiefs of Staff and U.S. Policy and Strategy Regarding Korea, 1945–53." PhD diss., University of Kansas, 1983.

Pantsov, Alexander V., with Steven I. Levine. *Mao: The Real Story.* New York: Simon and Schuster, 2012.

Park, Il-Song. "The Dragon from the Stream: The ROK Army in Transition and the Korean War, 1950–53." PhD diss., Ohio State University, 2007.

Parker, Geoffrey, ed. *The Cambridge History of Warfare.* New York: Cambridge University Press, 2008.

———. Introduction to *The Cambridge History of Warfare,* edited by Geoffrey Parker, 1–15. New York: Cambridge University Press, 2008.

Peng Dehuai. "My Story of the Korean War," in *Mao's Generals Remember Korea,* translated and edited by Xiaobing Li, Allan R. Millett, and Bin Yu, 30–37. Lawrence: University Press of Kansas, 2001.

Peters, Richard, and Xiaobing Li. "The Chosin Reservoir Retreat and Advance to the North." In *Voices from the Korean War: Personal Stories of American, Korean, and Chinese Soldiers,* edited by Richard Peters and Xiaobing Li, 25–34. Lexington: University Press of Kentucky, 2004.

———. "Perspectives on the War." In *Voices from the Korean War: Personal Stories of American, Korean, and Chinese Soldiers,* edited by Richard Peters and Xiaobing Li, 259–64. Lexington: University Press of Kentucky, 2004.

———. "Trench Warfare and Peace." In *Voices from the Korean War: Personal Stories of American, Korean, and Chinese Soldiers,* edited by Richard Peters and Xiaobing Li, 40–48. Lexington: University Press of Kentucky, 2004.

———, eds. *Voices from the Korean War: Personal Stories of American, Korean, and Chinese Soldiers.* Lexington: University Press of Kentucky, 2004.

Pollack, Jonathan D. "The Transformation of the Asian Security Order: Assessing China's Impact." In *Power Shift: China and Asia's New Dynamics,* edited by David Shambaugh, 335–64. Berkeley: University of California Press, 2005.

Rice, Edward E. *Mao's War*. Berkeley: University of California Press, 1974.

Roe, Patrick C. *The Dragon Strikes: China and the Korean War, June–December 1950*. Novato, CA: Presidio, 2000.

Ross, Robert S., and Jiang Changbin, eds. *Re-Examining the Cold War: U.S.-China Diplomacy, 1954–1973*. Cambridge: Harvard University Press, 2001.

Ryan, Mark A., David M. Finkelstein, and Michael A. McDevitt. "Introduction: Patterns of PLA Fighting." In *Chinese Warfighting: The PLA Experience since 1949*, edited by Mark A. Ryan, David M. Finkelstein, and Michael A. McDevitt, 3–22. New York: M. E. Sharpe, 2003.

———, eds. *Chinese Warfighting: The PLA Experience since 1949*. New York: M. E. Sharpe, 2003.

Sandler, Stanley. *The Korean War: No Victors, No Vanquished*. Lexington: University Press of Kentucky, 1999.

Sawyer, Ralph D., ed. *The Seven Military Classics of Ancient China*. New York: Basic, 2007.

Scobell, Andrew. *China's Use of Military Force: Beyond the Great Wall and the Long March*. Cambridge: Cambridge University Press, 2003.

Segal, Gerald. "Foreign Policy." In *China in the Nineties: Crisis Management and Beyond*, edited by David S. G. Goodman and Gerald Segal, 154–81. Oxford: Oxford University Press, 1991.

Shambaugh, David. *Modernizing China's Military: Progress, Problems, and Prospects*. Berkeley: University of California Press, 2002.

———. "The Rise of China and Asia's New Dynamics." In *Power Shift: China and Asia's New Dynamics*, edited by David Shambaugh, 1–19. Berkeley: University of California Press, 2005.

Shen Zhihua. "China Sends Troops to Korea: Beijing's Policy-Making Process." In *China and the United States: A New Cold War History*, edited by Xiaobing Li and Hongshan Li, 13–47. Lanham, MD: University Press of America, 1998.

Sheng, Michael M. *Battling Western Imperialism: Mao, Stalin, and the United States*. Princeton: Princeton University Press, 1997.

Short, Philip. *Mao: A Life*. New York: Henry Holt, 1999.

Showalter, Dennis D. "The First Jet War." In *The Cold War: A Military History*, edited by Robert Cowley, 120–37. New York: Random House, 2005.

Smith, Charles R. *U.S. Marines in the Korean War*. Washington: History Division, U.S. Marine Corps, 2007.

———, ed. *China's Military in Transition*. Oxford: Clarendon Press of Oxford University Press, 1997.

Steed, Brian. *Armed Conflict: The Lessons of Modern Warfare*. New York: Ballantine, 2003.

Stokesbury, James L. *A Short History of the Korean War*. New York: William Morrow, 1988.

Stueck, William W. *The Korean War: An International History*. Princeton: Princeton University Press, 1995.

———, ed. *The Korean War in World History*. Lexington: University Press of Kentucky, 2004.

———. *Rethinking the Korean War: A New Diplomatic and Strategic History*. Princeton: Princeton University Press, 2004.

———. *The Road to Confrontation: American Policy toward China and Korea, 1947–1950*. Chapel Hill: University of North Carolina Press, 1981.

Sunzi. *The Art of War*. In Ralph D. Sawyer, trans. and ed., *The Seven Military Classics of Ancient China*, 145–86. New York: Basic, 2007.

———. *The Art of War*. Translated with an introduction by Roger Ames. New York: Ballantine, 1993.

———. *The Art of War*. Translated and with an introduction by John Minford. New York: Viking, 2002.

Swope, Kenneth. Lecture notes for "Non-Western Military History" class at Norwich University, 2010.

Thompson, William R. "The Military Superiority Thesis and the Ascendancy of Western Eurasia." *Journal of World History* 10, no. 1 (1999): 143–78.

Tien, Chen-Ya. *Chinese Military Theory*. Oakville, ON: Mosaic, 1992.

Toland, John. *In Mortal Combat: Korea, 1950–1953*. New York: William Morrow, 1991.

Tomedi, Rudy, ed. *No Bugles, No Drums: An Oral History of the Korean War*. New York: Wiley and Son, 1994.

Tsai, Ming-Yen. *From Adversaries to Partners: Chinese and Russian Military Cooperation after the Cold War*. Westport, CT: Praeger, 2003.

Van de Ven, Hans. Introduction to *Warfare in Chinese History*, edited by Hans Van de Ven, 1–22. Boston: Brill Academic, 2000.

———, ed. *Warfare in Chinese History*. Boston: Brill Academic, 2000.

Wang Xuedong. "The Chosin Reservoir: A Chinese Captain's Story." In *Voices from the Korean War: Personal Stories of American, Korean, and Chinese Soldiers*, edited by Richard Peters and Xiaobing Li, 117–26. Lexington: University Press of Kentucky, 2004.

Wei, William. "Political Power Grows out of the Barrel of a Gun: Mao and the Red Army." In *A Military History of China*, edited by David A. Graff and Robin Higham, 229–48. Updated ed. Lexington: University Press of Kentucky, 2012.

Weintraub, Stanley. *MacArthur's War: Korea and the Undoing of an American Hero*. New York: Free Press, 2000.

Westad, Odd Arne, ed. *Brothers in Arms: The Rise and Fall of the Sino-Soviet Alliance, 1945–63*. Washington: Woodrow Wilson Center Press, 1998.

———. *Decisive Encounters: The Chinese Civil War, 1946–50*. Stanford: Stanford University Press, 2003.

———. *The Global Cold War: Third World Interventions and the Making of Our Times*. New York: Cambridge University Press, 2005.

White, Theodore. "The Killing Ground." In *No Bugles, No Drums: An Oral History of the Korean War*, edited by Rudy Tomedi, 123–30. New York: Wiley and Son, 1994.

Whiting, Allen S. *China Crosses the Yalu: The Decision to Enter the Korean War*. Stanford: Stanford University Press, 1960.

Whitson, William W., and Chen-Hsia Huang. *The Chinese High Command: A History of Communist Military Politics, 1927–71*. New York: Praeger, 1973.

Wilkinson, Mark F., ed. *The Korean War at Fifty: International Perspectives*. Lexington: Virginia Military Institute Press, 2004.

Wilson, Jeanne L. *Strategic Partners: Russian-Chinese Relations in the Post-Soviet Era*. Armonk, NY: M. E. Sharpe, 2004.

Woods, Pendleton. "An American Officer Observes the Koje Island Uprising." In *Voices from the Korean War: Personal Stories of American, Korean, and Chinese Soldiers*, edited by Richard Peters and Xiaobing Li, 242–44. Lexington: University Press of Kentucky, 2004.

Worthing, Peter M. *A Military History of Modern China: From the Manchu Conquest to Tiananmen Square.* Westport, CT: Praeger, 2007.

Xia, Yafeng. *Negotiating with the Enemy: U.S.-China Talks during the Cold War, 1949–72.* Bloomington: Indiana University Press, 2006.

Xu Xiangqian. "The Purchase of Arms from Moscow." In *Mao's Generals Remember Korea,* translated and edited by Xiaobing Li, Allan R. Millett, and Bin Yu, 139–46. Lawrence: University Press of Kansas, 2001.

Xu Yan. "Chinese Forces and Their Casualties in the Korean War." Translated by Xiaobing Li. *Chinese Historians* 6, no. 2 (1993): 45–64.

Yang Dezhi. "Command Experience in Korea." In *Mao's Generals Remember Korea,* translated and edited by Xiaobing Li, Allan R. Millett, and Bin Yu, 147–83. Lawrence: University Press of Kansas, 2001.

You, Ji. *The Armed Forces of China.* New York: Tauris, 1999.

Young, Charles S. "Voluntary Repatriation and Involuntary Tattooing of Korean War POWs." In *Northeast Asia and the Legacy of Harry S. Truman: Japan, China, and the Two Koreas,* edited by James I. Matray, 145–70. Kirksville, MO: Truman State University Press, 2012.

Yu, Bin. "What China Learned from Its 'Forgotten War' in Korea." In *Mao's Generals Remember Korea,* translated and edited by Xiaobing Li, Allan R. Millett, and Bin Yu, 9–29. Lawrence: University Press of Kansas, 2001.

Zhang, Shuguang. "China's Strategic Culture and the Cold War Confrontations." In *Reviewing the Cold War: Approaches, Interpretations, Theory,* ed. Odd Arne Westad, 250–73. London: Frank Cass, 2000.

———. "Command, Control, and the PLA's Offensive Campaigns in Korea, 1950–1951." In *Chinese Warfighting: The PLA Experience since 1949,* edited by Mark A. Ryan, David M. Finkelstein, and Michael A. McDevitt, 91–122. New York: M. E. Sharpe, 2003.

———. *Deterrence and Strategic Culture: Chinese-American Confrontations, 1949–58.* Ithaca: Cornell University Press, 1992.

———. *Mao's Military Romanticism: China and the Korean War, 1950–53.* Lawrence: University Press of Kansas, 1995.

Zhang, Xiaoming. "Air Combat for the People's Republic." In *Chinese Warfighting: The PLA Experience since 1949,* edited by Mark A. Ryan, David M. Finkelstein, and Michael A. McDevitt, 270–300. New York: M. E. Sharpe, 2003.

———. *Red Wings over the Yalu: China, the Soviet Union, and the Air War in Korea.* College Station: Texas A & M University Press, 2002.

Zhao Zuorui. "Organizing the Riots on Koje." In *Voices from the Korean War: Personal Stories of American, Korean, and Chinese Soldiers,* edited by Richard Peters and Xiaobing Li, 242–58. Lexington: University Press of Kentucky, 2004.

Zheng Yanman. "The Chinese Go Underground." In *Voices from the Korean War: Personal Stories of American, Korean, and Chinese Soldiers,* edited by Richard Peters and Xiaobing Li, 173–84. Lexington: University Press of Kentucky, 2004.

Zhou Baoshan. "China's Crouching Dragon." In *Voices from the Korean War: Personal Stories of American, Korean, and Chinese Soldiers,* edited by Richard Peters and Xiaobing Li, 85–96. Lexington: University Press of Kentucky, 2004.

Zhu, Fang. *Gun Barrel Politics: Party-Army Relations in Mao's China.* Boulder, CO: Westview, 1998.

Zubok, Vladislav, and Constantine Pleshakov. *Inside the Kremlin's Cold War: From Stalin to Khrushchev.* Cambridge: Harvard University Press, 1996.

# Index

XIAOBING LI is Professor and Chair of the Department of History and Geography and Director of the Western Pacific Institute at the University of Central Oklahoma. His works include *A History of the Modern Chinese Army; Voices from the Korean War: Personal Stories of American, Korean, and Chinese Soldiers* (with Richard Peters); *Mao's Generals Remember Korea* (with Allan R. Millett); and other books and articles on the Korean War. He served in the People's Liberation Army in China.